Dan Gookin's

Naked Office

Dan Gookin

SYBEX® San Francisco · London

Associate Publisher: Joel Fugazzotto

Acquisitions Editor: Bonnie Bills

Developmental Editor: Colleen Wheeler Strand

Production Editor: Kylie Johnston

Technical Editor: Acey Bunch

Copyeditor: Linda Recktenwald

Book Designer and Compositor: Owen Wolfson

Proofreaders: Emily Hsuan, Laurie O'Connell, Nancy Riddiough, Monique van den Berg

Indexer: Lynnzee Elze

Cover Designer/Illustrator: Richard Miller, Calyx Design

Library of Congress Card Number: 2003103566

ISBN: 0-7821-4223-0

Manufactured in the United States of America

10 9 8 7 6 5 4 3 2 1

Acknowledgments

I would like to acknowledge Julia Kelly for her help with the Outlook part of the book, and my sister, Dr. Jody Gookin, for her assistance with the PowerPoint section.

CONTENTS

PART 2

15 Excel Templates, Samples, and Web Mischief 370

PART 3

PART 4
PowerPoint 503

INTRODUCTION

To be Naked is to be Exposed, Vulnerable.

To be nude is to be without clothes.

Ever wonder why they have nudist colonies and not naked colonies? That's because some folks enjoy walking around without any clothes on. Why aren't there naked colonies? There are! They are full of *computer users*. Computer users walk around cold, alone, and unprotected, navigating the narrow back alleys of programs such as those in Microsoft® Office, weary from frustration and thirsting for more knowledge. How sad.

Well, pity the poor naked user no more!

This book isn't about rendering you naked but rather stripping the fancy trappings from the programs you know well in Microsoft Office. The pages that follow expose you to the finer points of Office, revealing what happens when you scratch the surface and discover how you can do more with Office and how to make your stuff look great. The end result is that you become a more efficient, productive, and clever Office user. Instead of your feeling old, exposed, unsupported, it's Microsoft Office itself that's rendered naked.

About This Book

This book is not my personal love poem to Microsoft Office. You see, when it comes to using a computer, I'm on *your* side. I get frustrated just like you do. For example, have you ever done something sweet in Excel only to forget what it was or how it worked just a few hours later? Or perhaps you think you have all of PowerPoint down pat, and then someone you know shows you a presentation that makes your jaw drop. Well, this book contains the solutions to those puzzles, the answers to those questions, and the remedies to the ills that plague anyone using Microsoft Office.

Above all, this book has *attitude*. I'm not out to try and teach you how to worship Microsoft Office. I don't want to justify some of the mysterious ways it does things. No way! So rather than bore you with what you already know or can figure out on your own, I'm here to show you the best and most useful parts of Microsoft Office. It's what I call the nifty stuff, the handy and useful things, the shortcuts, the tips, and the special features that will give your creations that extra-added *wow* factor.

Oh, and I don't need to mention that by reading this book you'll become smarter, lose weight, and actually appear younger than you were just hours ago!

What's Covered Here

Like every other book on Microsoft Office, this book covers the basic three Office programs—Microsoft Word, the word processor; Microsoft Excel, the spreadsheet; and Microsoft Outlook, the e-mail and contact program—plus one bonus program, Microsoft PowerPoint, the presentation tool.

Unlike any other book on Microsoft Office, however, this one covers an amazing *three editions* of the Office suite: Office 2000, Office XP (also called Office 2002), and Office 2003. So you're getting one dozen programs covered in this single book. Such a deal!

Even though the editors and I didn't officially test the material, we're pretty certain that most of it works for Office 97 as well. So, in a way, this book is also valuable to Office 97 users.

And don't think that my approach leads to clutter! The silent truth is that these different versions of Office are all truly similar to one another, similar enough that there are only scattered places in this book where separate steps or figures are required. The information in this book is crafted and presented so that it doesn't really matter which version of Office you have; all the tricks, tips, and solutions work without anyone feeling left out.

This book covers such intermediate Office topics as:

- Precisely formatting a paragraph in Word
- Using drawings and pictures inside a document
- Using tabs to set up a "cast list"
- Knowing when to use a table in Word and when to just insert an Excel worksheet
- Formatting a worksheet so that only certain pages print
- Redoing Excel charts on-the-fly
- Automatically organizing your e-mail
- Knowing the difference between repeating and recurring tasks in Outlook
- Properly manipulating your audience when using PowerPoint
- And many, many more!

What You Won't Find in This Book

Basics? This book skips 'em. I assume that you can use the mouse and that you've probably been in Word or Excel or even Outlook once or thrice and have gone through the basic motions. Thanks to the Windows interface and the basic, solid designs of the programs, that stuff is easy.

Specifically, you won't find the following information in this book:

- Basic or getting-started anything
- Upgrading or installing Office
- Understanding the friendly Office Assistant
- Mowing your lawn with that golf course crisscross effect
- Healing with herbs and roots
- Anything technical that they do on CSI

Seriously, this book assumes that you know the basics of computer operation and do know your way around a computer and Microsoft Office specifically.

This book covers only Word, Excel, Outlook, and PowerPoint. It does not cover OneNote, Publisher, Access, FrontPage, PhotoDraw, or any other programs included with various editions of Microsoft Office.

Macros are covered briefly here. I show how to record a macro, but I just don't have enough room to get into the meaty information on programming. Alas!

Outlook is covered as far as a single user is concerned. Information on setting meetings or using Outlook with the Exchange Server is not covered here. If your computer is connected to an Exchange Server, then your network administrator will be more help to you than any information anyone could ever put into a book.

There is no information here on conducting online meetings or using the Internet to collaborate on documents. My studies have shown that few people use such features. Based on that, taking up space to cover them here would be wasteful.

This book doesn't cover how to use Windows, any version. I assume that you can use Windows in at least a basic manner. That's all this book cares about.

Conventions

This book refers to the Microsoft Office as "Office." The applications are referred to by their common names: Word, Excel, Outlook, and PowerPoint. Though the official names all include the words "Microsoft" and "Office" and probably some ™ or ® thing there somewhere, they're not used here.

If there are any differences between the various versions of Office, these will be indicated in the text. For example, if Word 2000 does something differently from Word XP or Word 2003, then it will be noted. Fortunately, such instances are rare; I would say that over 95 percent of Office is generic enough that there was no need to continually include separate steps. (This book could even cover Office 97, though there are a few more differences.)

Do note that the figures are mostly of Office 2003, though some specific figures for Office 2000 are also included. (Office 2003 and Office XP are visually similar.)

This is an active book with many steps and tutorials that show you how things get done. The steps are numbered, often with comments (or even substeps) between them:

1. Pick up the phone handset.
2. Dial **1234**.

   Press the numbers 1, then 2, then 3, then 4 on the telephone.
3. Wait for someone to answer.

The stuff you type (Step 2) appears in **bold text**.

Key combinations are specified using the + character. Ctrl+D means to press the Ctrl (control) key and type a D, just as you would press Shift+D to get a capital letter D when typing.

The Windows key on your keyboard is labeled "Win" in this book. So if I tell you to press Win+D, it means to press the Windows key, tap the D key, and then release both keys.

There are three icons used in the book:

Note icons flag information that needs to be, well, noted. They're asides or supplemental information to what's already written in the text.

While I like to say that everything *in the book is a tip, some tips are more important than others. You'll find them flagged with this icon.*

The warning is for something not to do or something to avoid, such as "Don't drink iced tea with the spoon in the glass."

Various sidebars highlight specific information. Two types of sidebars appear most often:

The "Nerd's Corner" sidebars contain trivial or aside information that computer nerds might find interesting. (I just can't help myself sometimes and must lapse into computer trivia or by-the-way information that only the nerdiest readers will find appealing.)

The "Keyboard Master" sidebars contain keyboard "accelerators" or methods of accomplishing common tasks in Windows by using the keyboard alone. You'll find that using these Keyboard Master techniques is faster than using the mouse. And anyone watching you perform a keyboard accelerator will be very impressed—useful stuff!

About You!

Greetings, gentle reader! To get the most out of this book I am assuming the following things about you. Let me put on my Computer Book Author Psychic Turban and describe you:

-  You're very attractive, underpaid at work, and underappreciated by your family.
-  You have a computer with Microsoft Office installed, edition 2003, XP (or 2002), or 2000.
-  You're well versed with your version of Windows.
-  You understand enough about Microsoft Office to consider yourself an *intermediate* user.

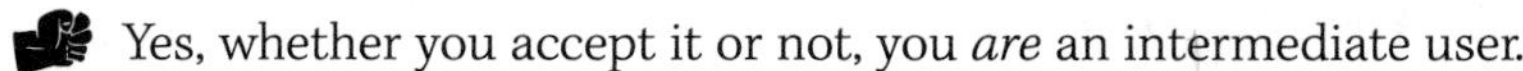

- Yes, whether you accept it or not, you *are* an intermediate user.
- You're willing to learn more about Office so that you can become a more efficient and impressive computer user, at least better than the doofs you work with.
- You have some secret talent, such as rolling your tongue or wiggling your ears.
- When you show up at the Post Office, invariably there will be a line.
- I can see by the Ten of Swords that your former lover is trying to win you back but the county jail stationery just isn't tugging at your heart.

Okay! Okay! Time to remove the Psychic Turban!

What Now?

Now you're ready to start reading the book!

Where to Start Reading

You do not need to read this book from front to back. It's designed so that you can start anywhere. For example, you don't have to complete a tutorial in Chapter 1 to do the exercises in Chapter 3. Feel free to dive in and start reading anywhere.

This book is divided into four parts, each of which covers a specific program in Microsoft Office:

- From Word to Paragraph to Document
- Excel
- Outlook
- PowerPoint

Each part has various chapters that present specific issues based on the part's subject.

You can start reading in any chapter in any order. The book is cross-referenced so if something is covered in an earlier chapter you'll know where to look.

Where You Can Get More Information

As a computer book author, it's my duty to provide you with as complete and accurate information as possible. If anything appears confusing or you require additional information, then I feel I owe it to you to give you that information. Therefore I'm offering my e-mail address should you have any questions regarding this book or its subject:

`dgookin@wambooli.com`

I promise to reply to all e-mail sent to me. However, I cannot troubleshoot your PC, nor can I provide answers to questions on topics not directly covered by this book.

I also offer a free weekly newsletter that contains tips, how-tos, bonus lessons, and Q&A for this and all my books. You can read more information about my free "Weekly Wambooli Salad" newsletter at:

`http://www.wambooli.com/newsletter/weekly/`

In addition to the newsletter, supplemental information specific to this book can be found on my website at:

`http://www.wambooli.com/help/office/`

Any errors, omissions, or additional information—including new information, updates, and special how-tos—can be found on that page.

And for general information about myself, fun quizzes, trivia, and a list of other books I've written and stuff, go visit:

`http://www.wambooli.com/`

Now you're ready to go forth, read, and enjoy your Naked Microsoft Office!

PART 1

From Word to Paragraph to Document

1 Life beyond the Basic Word

The biggest slice of the Microsoft Office Pie goes to Word, the word processor program pretty much all of mankind uses to compose their thoughts, jot down lists, create new ideas, or write that Great [insert country here] Novel. I've been using Word for over 23 years now, and there's one thing I've noticed: The program is horribly misnamed.

The original version should have been called Microsoft Letter, because that's what the program originally did best: put letters together. (Microsoft Letter would have been based upon an old DOS program called Microsoft Alphabet, which was purchased from an old PL1 programmer who wrote Quick-Cuneiform.) Then, with minor improvements, they could have introduced Microsoft Word, Microsoft Sentence, Microsoft Paragraph, and finally Microsoft Document—not to mention the companion program from Symantec, the Norton Microsoft Document Recovery Kit. Ah, but I digress...

Pretty much anyone can use a computer and figure out how to use Word. The program has been so successful that it's essentially unchanged from its Word 97 version. The name of the game is to get your stuff down on paper and make it look good. The rules are easy. This chapter here elaborates on some of the more basic concepts you may not know, plus a few new rules and tricks designed to help you make your word processing chores all the easier.

Dangerous and Useful Information Found Here:

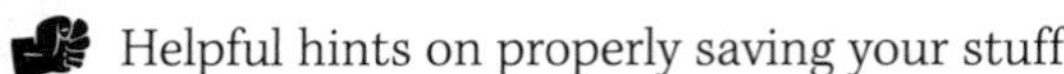

- Helpful hints on properly saving your stuff
- Password protection advice
- Better ways to cut and paste and search and replace
- Resetting defaults without messing with NORMAL.DOT
- Making the spell checker behave
- Printing a document backwards
- Setting margins for printing on three-hole-punch paper
- Printing two pages per sheet

Saving and Opening Your Documents May Seem Simple, but It Can Be Sheer Torture if You Don't Know a Few Things

Save now! Save early! Save often!

The three biggest issues whenever you save a document (in Word or in any application) are:

- The document's name
- The document's location
- The document's type

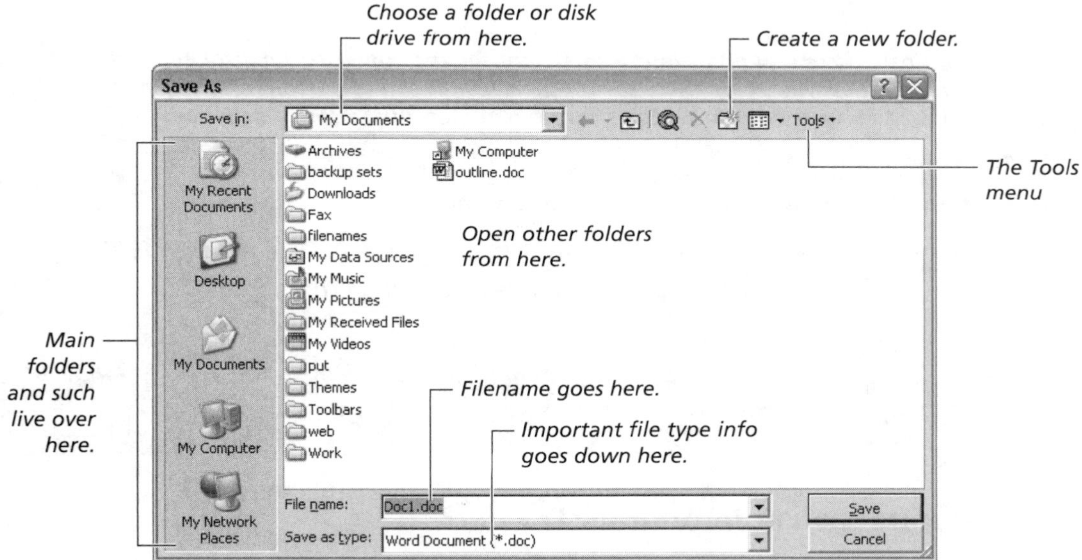

Figure 1.1 Your typical Office Save As dialog box

The Save As dialog box (Figure 1.1) handles all these details for you, which is basic baby Windows stuff. Of course, that doesn't mean you can't screw them up. So heed these words of advice before getting into the intermediate-level knowledge nuggets:

First, the document name must be descriptive of the contents. You have up to 200 characters to use for the name, including numbers and letters and a smattering of symbols, but brief is best.

Second, be thoughtful of the file's final folder destination. Don't just shove everything into the My Documents folder. Organize. Use subfolders. In fact, the filename can be simpler if the folder it lives in is more descriptive. Consider this: The file is named `14.DOC`. But it lives in the October folder. And that lives in the 2004 folder. And that lives in the Letters to the Editor folder. Consider:

```
Letters to the Editor/2004/October/14.doc
```

Versus a single file in the My Documents folder:

```
Letter to the editor on October 14.doc
```

Finally, there is the document file type, which is found in the bottom part of the Save As dialog box. You can use that list to save or *export* your document into a variety of different word processor formats. Most often you'll be using the Word Document format (thus a `.doc` extension on the file), but be careful not to neglect the power that drop-down list gives you—or the confusion that can result should you choose the wrong option.

You Must Know This: Making a Longer Recently Used File List

Without otherwise scolding Word into action, the recently used file list keeps track of only the last four files you've opened, saving their names at the bottom of the File menu. You can adjust the number of filenames Word remembers up or down, depending on your whim:

1. *Choose Tools ➢ Options.*
2. *In the Options dialog box, click the General tab.*
3. *Adjust the value by the "Recently Used File List" item (which must be checked on).*

   Values can go from 1 through 9. To choose zero, just un-check the box.
4. *Click OK.*

I personally like having only four items, though when I'm doing a big project and shuffling files quite a bit, six seems like a more logical value.

Why Save a Document in Another Format?

The primary reason for *not* using the Word Document file format is to share your stuff with some loser, uh, I mean someone who doesn't have Word as his or her word processor. For example, if they have WordPerfect, you can choose one of the WordPerfect file formats from the Save as Type drop-down list (Figure 1.1).

Another instance may be where you have to save a document in plain text format. For example, say you deleted something important in Windows and you have to replace it by creating a list and saving it to disk as an ASCII or text file. If so, choose "Plain Text (*.txt)" from the Save as Type drop-down list.

The best non-Word format to choose is the Rich Text Format (`*.rtf`). That format is the most common among all the major word processing applications for most computers. In fact, I would save a document as RTF instead of attempting to save in WordPerfect or even HTML format; it's just that much more common—and better.

Should I Ever Have to Save a Document as a Web Page?

My advice is never to use any web page or HTML format in the Save As dialog box, and by all means avoid the File ➤ Save as Web Page command. These options are designed for those who use Word as their web page editor. The problem with that is that Word is not a very good web page editor. (I've even gotten Microsoft personnel to admit that—off the record.)

If you want to create a web page, then use a decent web page–creation tool. The FrontPage program comes with most configurations of Microsoft Office and it works similarly to Word and other Office products. Try that instead of Word for your HTML/web page document needs.

Now, I'll admit. There may be some time when you need to "share" your precious Word document with others, and the suggested format may just be that HTML. If so, then go ahead and use the File ➤Save as Web Page command to create the HTML document. I suppose if your hands are tied doing that, then doing that you must. But don't make it a habit if you can help it.

Why Does the Document Open All Weird?

Again, you can blame the Save as Type drop-down list for any weirdness that happens when you open a document, though in this case the weirdness takes place in the Open dialog box with the Files of Type drop-down list, as shown in Figure 1.2.

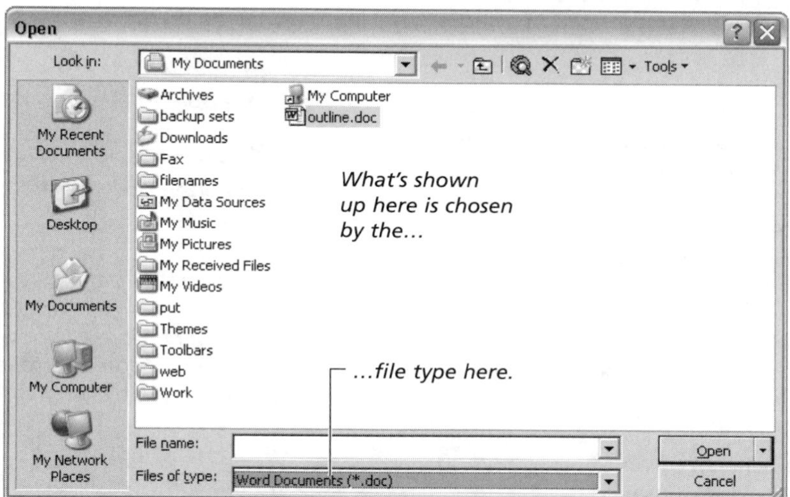

Figure 1.2 The typical Open dialog box for Office

The Files of Type drop-down list not only tells Word which types of files to display in the Open dialog box, but it tells Word how to open the files as well.

For example, if you choose the option "Recover Text from Any File," then Word dutifully does that—even to its own files. So if that option is chosen and you open a Word document, you will see junk on the screen.

The solution is to pay attention to the file type choices in the Open dialog box. If the document looks like junk, then follow these steps:

1. Immediately close the weird document; do not save it to disk.
2. Choose File ➤ Open to bring up the Open dialog box again.
3. Confirm that the proper type is chosen in the Open dialog box.
4. Open the file.

Be careful not to save the file if it's opened in a weird format. If you do so, then you cannot recover the original. Uh-oh! (As a suggestion, consider using Windows to make a copy of the original; then work on the copy only.)

KEYBOARD MASTER

Just Your Basic Open and Close Keyboard Commands

Here are the commands used in Word, as well as other Office and Windows applications, for the standard operations of opening, closing, and saving documents:

Ctrl+S

Save the document to disk, or summon the Save As dialog box if the document has yet to be saved.

Alt+F, A

Specifically summon the Save As dialog box.

Ctrl+O

Open a document previously saved to disk.

Ctrl+W

Close a window, prompting to save the document if it's unsaved.

When used with the Shift key, the commands apply to all open Word windows:

Shift+Ctrl+S

Save all open documents.

Shift+Ctrl+W

Close all open windows.

Finally, from before Windows was standardized, there are some leftover keyboard commands from the very early days of Word:

F12

Summon the Save As dialog box (even for an already-saved document).

Shift+F12

Save the document to disk.

Ctrl+F12

Summon the Open dialog box.

Can I Password-Protect My Document?

Certainly! After summoning the Save As dialog box, use the Tools menu to modify the way the file is saved to disk. (Refer to Figure 1.1.)

1a. In Word 2003/XP, choose Tools ➤ Security Options.

1b. In Word 2000, choose Tools ➤ General Options

The Save or Security dialog box appears, such as shown in Figure 1.3. It's very similar for all versions of Word, though the location of the open and modify password text boxes is different.

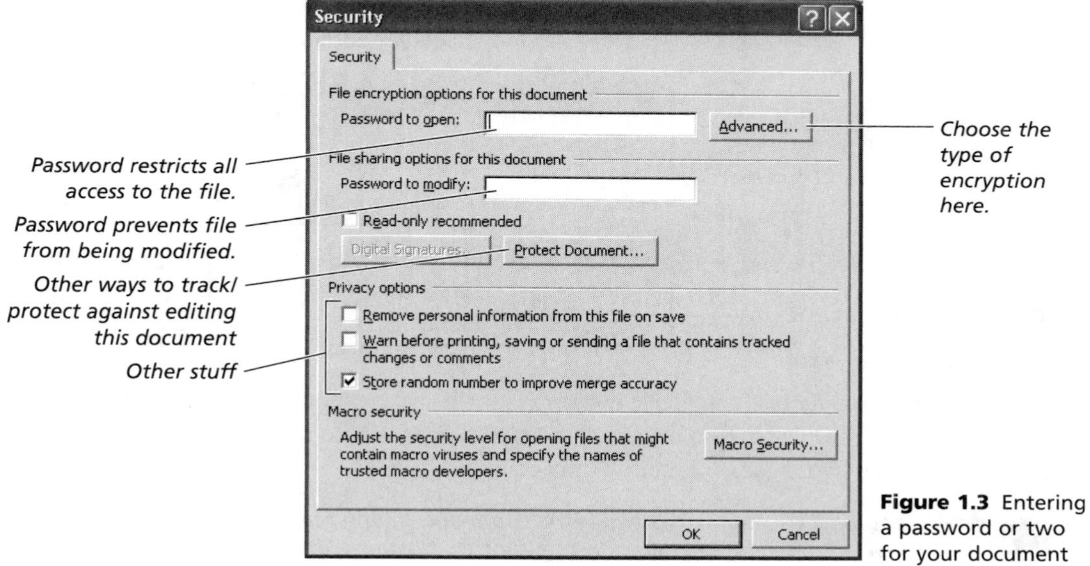

Figure 1.3 Entering a password or two for your document

2. If you like, enter an open password.

This password prevents the document from being opened unless the person knows the password.

3. If you like, enter a modify password.

This password allows the file to be opened as a "read-only" document. If they know the password, however, then they can modify the document.

Passwords are case-sensitive. They consist of up to 15 letters and numbers. Do not forget them or you're screwed!

4. Click OK after entering one or both passwords.

If you don't enter any passwords, then the document is not protected.

5. Confirm the password(s).

   Type them again to ensure that you remember them. Don't forget them!

6. Continue using the Save dialog box to save the file to disk.

The password-protected file doesn't look any different on disk, nor does it look any different when you're working on it in Word. But once you close the document, the password encryption takes over, and only by knowing the password can you get at the document's contents.

When you go to open a password-protected document, either in Word or by double-clicking the document's icon in Windows, you'll be presented with a Password dialog box or two. The first may be required for merely opening the document—that's the open password.

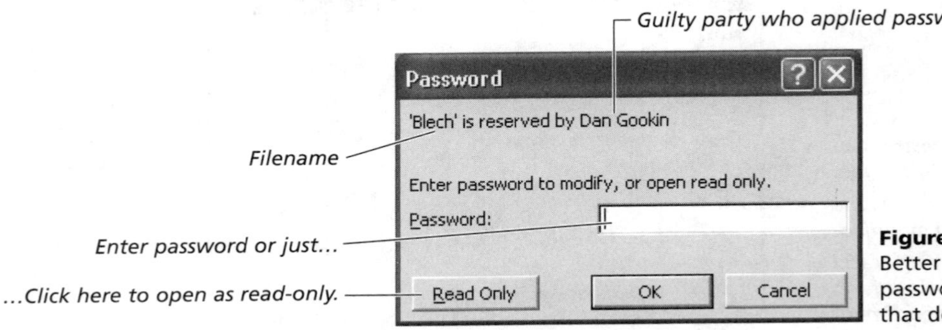

Figure 1.4 Oops! Better know the password to modify that document!

A second dialog box, such as the one shown in Figure 1.4, is the modify password dialog box. Note that there is a "Read Only" option in that dialog box in case you do not know the password; only by entering the password can you modify the document.

Actually, you can use the Save As command in any read-only Office document to save that document to disk using another filename. Then you can open that second document for editing. (Sneaky, but it works.)

Can I Remove the Passwords from a Password-Protected Document?

To remove the passwords, simply repeat the steps from the previous section, but leave both password input boxes blank. Click OK, and that resets the passwords back to nothing, and there are no more restrictions on opening or modifying the file.

But I Forgot the Document's Password!

You're screwed.

Don't Be Dumb and Ignore These Handy Password-Remembering Rules

If you feel you're going to forget your password, then write it down! But don't write it down on a sticky note and stick it on the monitor. Instead, put it in your day planner, perhaps on the bottom of the page with your birthday. But whatever you do, write that password down so you can at least find it later.

Shorter, memorable passwords work best.

Passwords mixing letters and numbers are also good, such as the number and street where you used to live or where a relative lives.

There is also a school of thought that absurdity often makes a memorable password. For example, stick together two obnoxiously unrelated words like "baby-meat" or "armored-nun."

Finally, there is really no hope if you forget your password. Microsoft cannot help you, nor are there any secret tools or tricks available on the Internet. So remember that password!

I Can't Find My Document!

If you're missing a document, then you have a few tricks you can pull before you consider tossing the computer before an oncoming train.

First, check the File menu. Is your document down near the bottom, in the list of recently used files?

Second, check the Documents or My Recent Documents submenu from the Start button. Is the file listed there?

Third, you can use Window's Find or Search command to look for the document, but you can also use the Find or Search command in the Open dialog box to help you quickly find your document based on its contents. Follow these steps for your version of Word.

Finding a Wayward Word File in Word 2003/XP

1. Summon the Open dialog box.
2. From the Tools menu, choose Search.

   The File Search dialog box appears, and like its ancestors it's too vast and ugly to reproduce on these pages. But fortunately it's not as complex or weird as the Word 2000 variation.
3. Make sure that the Basic tab is showing, not the Advanced tab.
4. Type some words from your document into the Search text box.

   For example, that letter to the editor you wrote comparing the snow plow driver to Adolph Hitler. If you lost that document, then consider searching for the words "Hitler" and "snow plow" to find what you want.

Fortunately, all the other settings are made for this type of search (the most common), so...

5. Click the Search button.

   Eventually a list of matches appears, which you can sift through.

6. Click the file you want to check out.

7. Click the OK button.

8. Back in the Open dialog box, click the Open button to open the file.

If the list appearing in the File Search dialog box is *way too long*, then you'll need to re-think your approach. Try using more specific words, or click on the Advanced tab and heed these instructions:

1. From the Property drop-down list, choose Contents.

   Not "Comments" but "Contents."

2. Enter the words you're searching for in the Value text box.

   For example, "Hitler" and "snow plow."

If the words appear together in your document, then surround them with double quotes. "Snow plow" searches for the word "snow" followed by "plow." But if you type each word individually, then the document can contain either word in any order any number of words apart.

3. Click the Add button.

   Now you can enter another bit-o-information to search for.

4. From the Property drop-down list choose "Creation Date."

5. From the Condition drop-down list choose an option.

   Such as "On" or "On or After" or "This Week."

6. If you chose a condition that requires a date, then enter the date in the Value text box.

7. Click the Add button.

   Now you have two search criteria, which should be enough.

8. Click the Search button.

   And off Word goes to look for the document matching your specifications.

Locating Lost Documents in Word 2000

1. Summon the Open dialog box.
2. From the Tools menu, choose Find.

   The Find dialog box appears, but it's much too complex and obtuse to show here in a figure.
3. From the Property drop-down list, choose Contents.

   The Condition drop-down lists self-modifies to say "Includes Words."
4. Type some words from your document into the Value text box.

   For example, if you lost the document about how you cheated the Brundlemans at cards, then searching for the words "Brundleman" and "cards" would most likely yield successful results.
5. Click the Add to List button.

   Ah-ha! This is the step everyone forgets (and the reason they changed all this with Word XP). If you forget to click the Add to List button, you'll be reminded to do it later.
6. Optionally choose a location from the Look In drop-down list.

   It already shows you the My Documents folder, which is an ideal place to look. But if you feel the file is on a disk in another drive or a specific folder, then choose it from the list as well.

   To search the entire computer, select My Computer from the list.
7. Put a check mark by "Search Subfolders" so that the search expands down into the very depths of your disk drive's folder structure.
8. Click the Find Now button.

   Word scurries around the folders you told it to look in and finds all files matching your search criteria. They appear in a tree structure that unfolds in the Open dialog box.

If a multitude of files were found, then consider re-doing the search with more specific information, or even repeating steps 3 through 5 and adding a range of dates to narrow the search.

9. Ctrl+Click to select all the files found.
10. Click the Open button to open all the selected files.

    Now you can sift through each of them in Word until you find the one you want.

Yes, it's possible to open more than one file at a time in the Open dialog box. The Open button opens any and all selected files shown in the list.

You Must Know This: Fixing the Stupid Menus!

Tired of the menus in Office changing size on you? Sick of having to click the "show more" chevron to see the entire menu? Me too! A program should never conceal its options. So to fix Word's timidity of its own menus, follow these steps:

1. *Choose Tools ➢ Customize.*

2. *Click the Options tab in the Customize dialog box.*

3a. *In Word 2003/XP, click to select "Always Show Full Menus."*

3b. *In Word 2000, remove the check mark by "Show Full Menus after a Short Delay."*

4. *Click OK.*

That way the menus stay open and visible all the time. It's also the way I prefer to use Office applications, and the way they're shown using the screen shots in this book.

How Do I Save a Document to Drive A?

You can save a document to any disk in your system, whether it's another hard drive or a removable disk such as a floppy disk or Zip disk. The secret is to choose that disk from the Save In drop-down list at the top of the Save As dialog box (see Figure 1.1).

Please don't try to save to Drive A—or any removable disk—as opposed to using the hard drive. The hard drive is designed to be your primary file storage location. Use it! Then, after the file is safely saved on the hard drive, consider using the Save As command to save a *copy* of the file to a removable disk. Or you can use Windows to simply copy the document to a removable disk.

Floppy disks are notoriously unreliable. They're fine for backups or for moving files between computers, but not for permanent storage.

Word Crashed! What Can I Recover?

Word is smart about document recovery. If there is anything to recover, then you'll see that file appear in a window the next time you start up Word. The window will have the original file's name followed by the text "(Recovered)."

In Word 11/XP, point the mouse at the recovered file, and a menu button appears. Click that button to select a recovery option.

In Word 2000, use the Save As dialog box to save that recovered file back to disk and overwrite the original.

Yes! It's okay to overwrite an original file with a recovered version. I would say 99 percent of the time that's the option I've chosen. (The other 1 percent of the time the recovered file was no different from the original.)

Of course, to make Word recover files, you need to turn on the AutoRecovery feature:

1. Choose Tools ➢ Options.
2. Click the Save tab.
3. Put a check mark by "Save AutoRecover Info Every" (if a check mark isn't there already).
4. Enter a time interval to save the AutoRecover information.

   Ten minutes is okay for most people.
5. Click OK.

Now your computer is semi-protected against bad things happening. Word will automatically save your documents (whether you do or not) every 10 minutes or so. Of course, nothing gets hurt by your pressing the Ctrl+S key combination every few minutes just to be safe.

If there are no recovered documents after a crash, then don't worry. Your stuff was probably all up-to-date and there was nothing necessary for Word to recover.

A Gaggle of Nifty Word Formatting and Editing Tricks

Just when you think you know every Word trick there is, some doofus pops up and shows you something new, something useful, something you wish you would have known for the last project you did. Well, for the next few pages I plan on being your personal doofus and showing you what I think are some handy, unknown, or under-used tools in the Word toolbox.

How Can I Select Only One Sentence of Text?

A sentence is an irregular beast, not a single word or paragraph. Therefore selecting it using the mouse or the keyboard requires tedious skill...unless you know this trick: Press the Ctrl key and click the mouse somewhere in the sentence. Zloop! The entire sentence is selected and ready for action!

And for your passing enjoyment, Table 1.1 lists other quick and nifty ways of instantly selecting text.

Table 1.1 Selecting Chunks of Text in Word

To Select This Chunk of Text	*Take This Action*	*Or This One*
Word	*Double-click the word.*	*With the insertion point in the word, press the F8 key twice.*
Sentence	*Ctrl+click the sentence.*	*With the insertion point in the sentence, press the F8 key thrice.*
Line	*Click in the margin to the left of the line.*	
Paragraph	*Double-click in the margin to the left of the paragraph.*	*With the insertion point in the paragraph, press the F8 key four times.*

Is There Any Way to Quickly Change the Capitalization without Retyping the Whole Stupid Sentence?

The easiest way to change capitalization of a word is to put the insertion point in the word and press Shift+F3. That changes the capitalization to one of three modes:

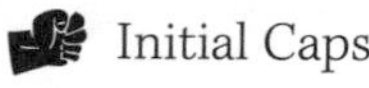 Initial Caps

 ALL CAPS

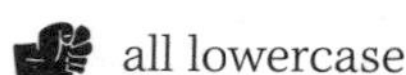 all lowercase

Keep pressing Shift+F3, toggling back and forth until you get the capitalization you want.

As an alternative, you can select the text you want to re-capitalize and choose Format ➤ Change Case from the menu. Doing so displays five options for changing the case of the selected text, as shown in Figure 1.5. Select an option and click OK.

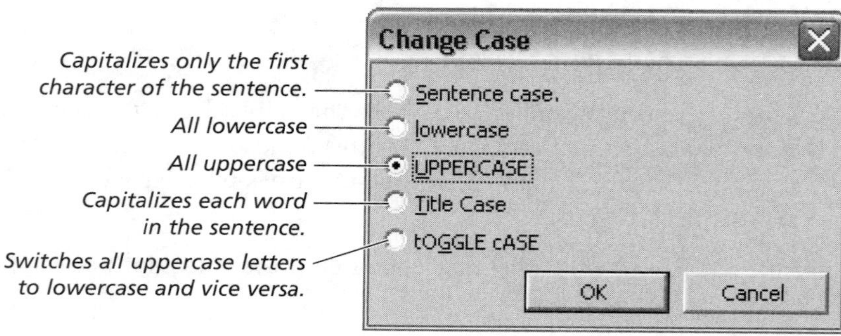

Figure 1.5 Even more ways to change the case

Despite the earnestness of the Change Case command (Shift+F3), referring to its Initial Caps command as "Title Case," do note that it is a common convention not to capitalize prepositions, articles, or conjunctions in a title. So, words such as of, in, and, on, by, with, for, *and so on are not capitalized, well, unless they appear at the start or end of the title. (I asked my editor about this issue and she trembled in fear, citing some obscure tome called the* Chicago Manual of Style. *But then she also mentioned about 1,600 exceptions. So I suppose whatever you capitalize in your title is okay with me.)*

How Can I Paste in Text without Pasting in All the Formatting?

I suppose it's handy that when you normally paste text into Word, all the text's original formatting follows along like so much emotional baggage. For example, if you copy text from a web page into Word, you'll notice that any formatting the text had on the web page automatically follows that text into Word.

If you don't want the formatting to follow the text—for example, you want the text to appear in the document using the document's own formatting styles (just as if you had manually typed the text yourself), then you need to know how to *Paste Special*. Obey these steps:

1. Choose Edit ➤ Paste Special.

   The Paste Special dialog box appears.

2. Choose "Unformatted Text" from the list.
3. Click the OK button.

   And the text is pasted into the document *minus* any formatting it may have had.

The end result is text that appears as if you've typed it yourself.

In Word 2003/XP, you can choose the Unformatted option *after* you paste the text by clicking the Paste Options button that appears after the text has been pasted. Choose "Keep Text Only" from the pop-up menu, and it's the same thing as pasting in unformatted text.

If there isn't an "Unformatted Text" option, then there is no text in the Clipboard to paste. Also note that you can Paste Special only from the Paste Special dialog box, not from the Clipboard task pane in Word 2003/XP.

What the Heck Is Wrong with This Formatting?

Most of the e-mail questions I get regarding Word deal with some sort of weird formatting, such as a blank at the start of each line or a border following random paragraphs. Fortunately, nothing in Word is truly hidden from you. And while Word lacks a Reveal Codes command (that I so loved back in the days of DOS WordPerfect), it does have a Show Formatting command.

To see what evils lurk in a paragraph's formatting, press the Shift+F1 key combination. This has two different effects, depending on your version of Word.

In Word 2000, the mouse pointer changes to a question mark–arrow, which you can use to point-and-click at any text in Word. Doing so displays a pop-up cartoon bubble that lists the formatting for whatever text you clicked on, as shown in Figure 1.6.

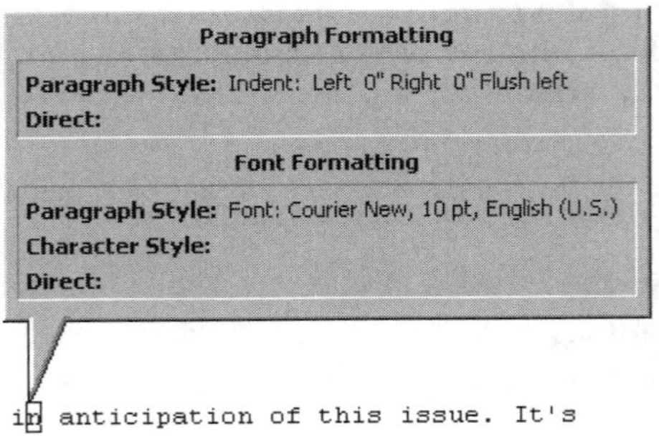

Figure 1.6 Checking the text formatting in Word 2000

The problem here is that only information is displayed. It's up to you to figure out where the problem lies, not only from the terms used in the description but from knowing which Word commands control those formatting options. (Fortunately all formatting options exist in the Format menu.)

In Word 2003/XP, information about the formatting appears in the reveal Formatting task pane, as shown in Figure 1.7. This is very similar to the information shown for Word 2000, but with the advantage that you can click the underlined (blue) links to get at the proper dialog boxes required to fix things.

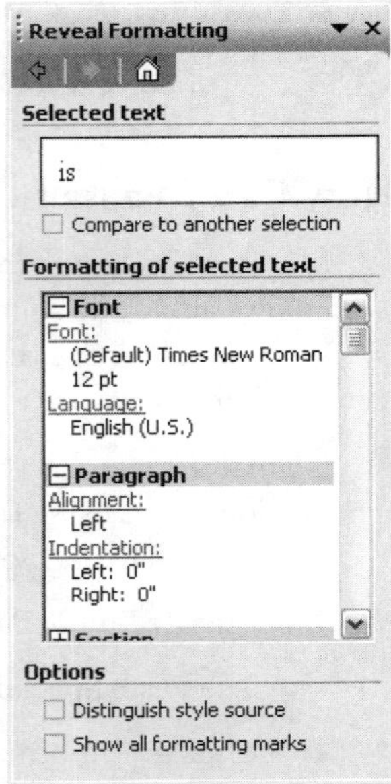

Figure 1.7 Checking the formatting in Word 2003/XP

How Come Changing the Format of One Paragraph Changes the Formatting of Them All?

I encountered this problem a while back and it bugged the bejoobies out of me: whenever I made one line of text bold, every other paragraph in the document bolded up. Very annoying, until I figured out that it was a Style issue.

Styles can be programmed to be automatically updated. So when you modify a paragraph in a document, all other paragraphs formatted with that style also change. This can be handy if you like to mess with styles after they're created, but it can also be a pain in the butt. To fix it, you must visit the Style dialog box:

1. Put the insertion pointer in the paragraph having the style you need to fix.

2a. Choose Format ➤ Styles and Formatting in Word 2003/XP.

2b. Choose Format ➤ Style in Word 2000.

3a. Choose Modify from the drop-down list next to the highlighted style in the Styles and Formatting Task Pane in Word 2003/XP.

3b. Click the Modify button in the Style dialog box in Word 2000.

The Modify Style dialog box appears.

4. Un-check the item that reads "Automatically Update."

5. Click OK.

With the Automatically Update option disabled, your document's paragraphs can be modified without changing the underlying style. Or, conversely, if you want styles to be updated on the fly, then you can check that option so that changes to one paragraph affect all other paragraphs of the same style. (But either way I find it annoying.)

You Must Know This: The Mighty F2 Key

One of the easiest ways to copy or move a block of selected text in Word is to employ the handy F2 key. Unlike any of the other 10,000 ways to copy or move text, F2 is a breath of fresh air, giving you an immediate command versus a combination of commands or windows or prayers and incantations. It works like this:

1. *Select the text you want to move or copy.*
2. *Press the F2 key to move that text, or press Shift+F2 to copy.*

   You'll see "Move to Where?" or "Copy to Where?" appear on the status bar.
3. *Click the mouse where you want the text moved.*

   You can scroll to anywhere else in the same document, but you cannot use this trick to move or copy between two different documents.
4. *Press the Enter key to move or copy the text.*

Note that moving or copying text in this manner does not *place that text into the Clipboard for re-pasting. No, the F2 command is more of a quick-move/quick-copy command than a traditional copy- or cut-and-paste operation.*

Why Would I Want to Search and Replace Styles?

Word's Search and Replace function is powerful enough to wreak havoc on even the most innocent of things, such as a style. So suppose you discover that for some arcane legal reason all your *italic text* has to be changed into boring old underline. Here's how you can do that without wasting a ton of time by using the Search and Replace command:

1. Press Ctrl+Home to zip to the tippy top of your document.

2. Choose Edit ➤ Replace.

The Find and Replace dialog box appears, ready to "Find What" and "Replace With." But you need more information than that, right?

3. Click the More button.

   More stuff appears!

4. Click the Format button.

5. Choose Font from the pop-up menu.

   The standard Font dialog box appears.

6. Choose Italic in the Find Font dialog box.

   Or select whatever font attributes you're searching for.

7. Click OK.

   Now notice in the Find and Replace dialog box how the text "Format: Font: Italic" appears below the Find What text box. That means Word is searching for a format, not a specific chunk of text. The format it's searching for is any text that's italic.

   Time to select what to replace the italic text with:

8. Click the mouse in the Replace With text box.

9. Click the Format button.

10. Choose Font from the pop-up menu.

11. Choose the solid underline from the Underline Style drop-down list.

    That's the replacement style.

12. Click OK.

    Now under the Replace With text box you'll see "Format: Underline." You're searching for italic text and replacing it with underline—a style search and replace instead of a text search and replace.

13. Click the Replace All button to convert all your document's italic text into Underlined text.

You can search and replace any formatting attribute with any other formatting attribute, including text color, paragraph formatting, even styles you've created. Just choose the proper formatting command from the Format button.

Word remembers the last formatting item you searched and replaced! To clear the formatting information from the Find and Replace dialog box, click the No Formatting button. If you forget to do this, then Find and Replace will not behave as you expect it to.

Where Was I Last Editing?

A handy key to remember is the Shift+F5 combination. Pressing Shift+F5 returns the insertion point back to the place in your document where you last edited. So if you're scrolling through text reading, or bouncing from here to there editing, remember Shift+F5 to return to where you once were.

Is There an Easier Way to Edit a Document Full of Pictures?

Word doesn't do desktop publishing very well. Instead of forcing too many pictures into Word, I recommend using a "real" desktop publishing program, such as Microsoft's Publisher or Adobe's InDesign. But anyway...

If you're suffering through a document that has lots of pictures and it seems to be slowing things down, then shift into this mode:

1. Choose Tools ➤ Options.
2. Click the View tab in the Options dialog box.
3. Put a check mark by "Picture Placeholders."

   That replaces the images in your document with placeholders, which makes scrolling around work a lot easier.

When you're done editing, simply repeat the above steps to re-activate the pictures.

Why Would I Need the Document Map?

The Document Map is one of those seldom-used features that can really save you time both navigating a larger document and getting "the big picture" on what you're writing.

To switch on the Document Map, choose View ➤ Document Map from the menu, or click the Document Map button on the toolbar. A slice of the screen is split off to show you the various headings in your document, as illustrated in Figure 1.8.

Alas, if your document lacks headings, doesn't use the Headings styles, or is too short, then the Document Map isn't of much help.

Choose View ➤ Document Map again, or click the toolbar button, to make the Document Map view vanish.

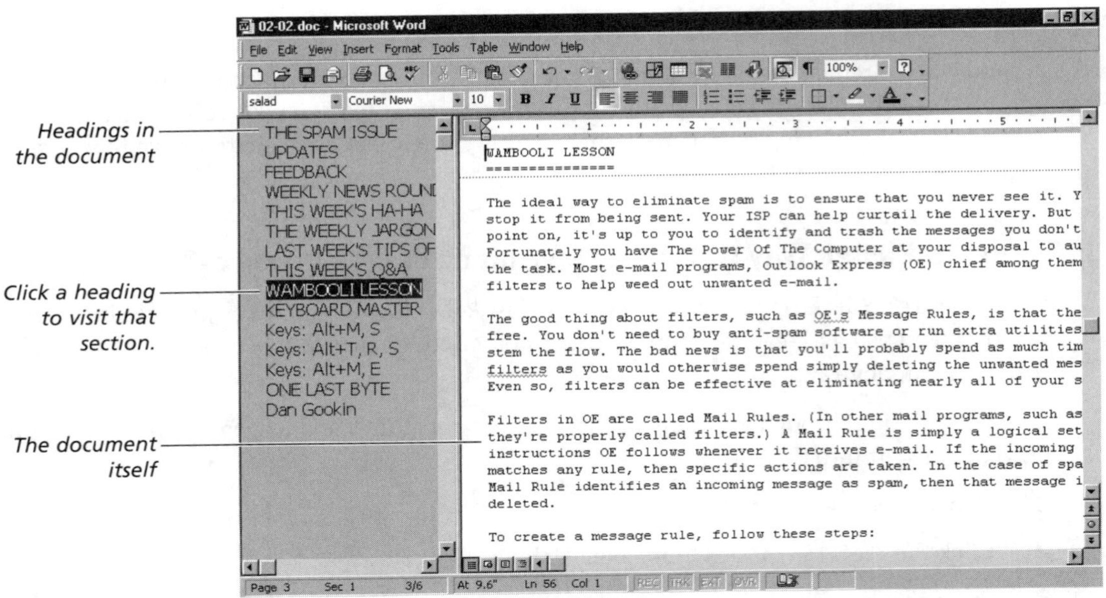

Figure 1.8 Viewing the Document Map

What's the Point of NORMAL.DOT?

`NORMAL.DOT` is a template file, not a document. As such, it is the standard (or "default" if you want) template used by Word whenever you open a new document and don't specify any other template. It contains the standard settings for any new document, such as Times New Roman font at 12 points, single-spaced, and so on. (See Chapter 5, "Using Styles and Templates to Save Oodles of Time," for more information on templates.)

If you want to change the way Word starts new, blank documents, then you merely need to edit the `NORMAL.DOT` template and update the settings. `NORMAL.DOT` can be opened like any template file in Word, edited, then saved back to disk. The secret is to choose "Document Templates (*.dot)" from the Files of Type drop-down list in the Open dialog box.

A better way to make subtle changes in the `NORMAL.DOT` file is to take advantage of the various Default buttons located in many of Word's dialog boxes. These buttons can be used to modify the `NORMAL.DOT` template without having to go through the ordeal of trying to find it on disk and opening it.

For example, say you want all your new documents to be in the Bookman font at 10 points. Just choose Format ➤ Font and select Bookman as the font and 10 points as the size. Then click the Default button. Word asks if you want to save that change to the `NORMAL.DOT` template, making it stick for all new documents you open (Figure 1.9). Click Yes to make it so.

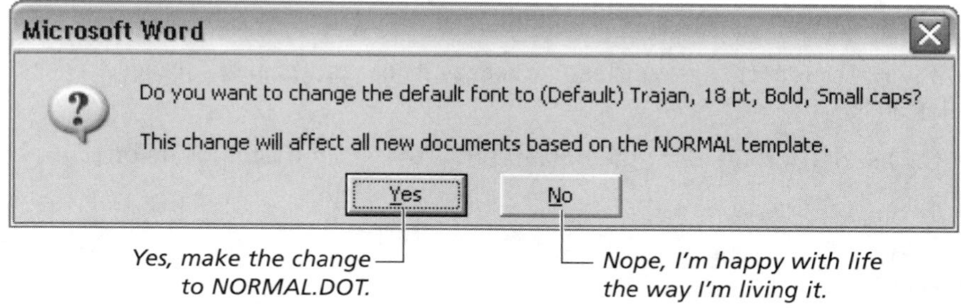

Figure 1.9 Changing the default font

There are other Default buttons in other formatting dialog boxes as well. These also modify the settings of the NORMAL.DOT template. Use them to change the settings for your new, blank documents.

NORMAL.DOT *also contains any modifications you make to the toolbars or other aspects of Windows. So if you modify the toolbar and are eventually asked to "Save the Changes to* NORMAL.DOT,*" click the Yes button to keep your modifications.*

It's a bad idea to over-modify the NORMAL.DOT *template. If you find yourself making too many modifications, consider moving them all from the* NORMAL.DOT *template into another, custom template file you create. That way you can leave* NORMAL.DOT *basically "nude," which may come in handy. Refer to Chapter 5 for information on copying and deleting information in a template file.*

What's the Best Way to Alphabetically Sort a List of Items?

Word is entirely capable of sorting text. The problem is that the Sort command is hidden in the Table menu. I suppose that's because Sort is a more powerful tool when it comes to messing with tables. But in any event, you can also use the Sort command to sort just any text. Here's how:

1. Select the text you want to sort.

For example, it can be a list of items, each on its own line. If you sort paragraphs, then only the first word in the paragraph is used for the sort.

2. Choose Table ➤ Sort.

The Sort Text dialog box appears, but you needn't pay any attention to it; it's already set up to sort alphabetically, A to Z.

3. Click OK.

And your text is sorted.

Oftentimes what you want to sort is an inline list of items. For example:

```
My favorite fruits are apples, oranges, bananas, pears, grapes, cherries
and peaches.
```

To sort the list of fruit, first edit the paragraph so that each fruit appears on a line by itself:

```
My favorite fruits are
apples,
oranges,
bananas,
pears,
grapes,
cherries and
peaches.
```

Now follow the steps above, selecting the fruits only and sorting them by name. You'll end up with:

```
My favorite fruits are
apples,
bananas,
cherries and
grapes,
oranges,
peaches.
pears,
```

Now re-edit the paragraphs back into a single sentence, moving the "and" and the punctuation into the proper positions, and you have a sorted list.

This Chunk of Text Is in Latin; How Can I Tell the Spell Checker to Ignore It?

The easiest way to avoid spell-checking foreign words is to format that chunk of text with the foreign language's attribute—yet another seldom-used feature of Word. Here's how:

1. Select the portion of text in a foreign language.

   Or select a chunk of text that you merely don't want Word to spell-check, such as a code listing, filler block, or whatever you tire of seeing flagged as "misspelled."

2. Choose Tools ➤ Language ➤ Set Language.

   The Language dialog box appears, described in Figure 1.10.

3. Scroll through the list until you find Latin.

4. Click OK.

   Now the Latin text will be identified as such. In fact, if you had the optional Latin dictionary installed, Word would spell-check the Latin text.

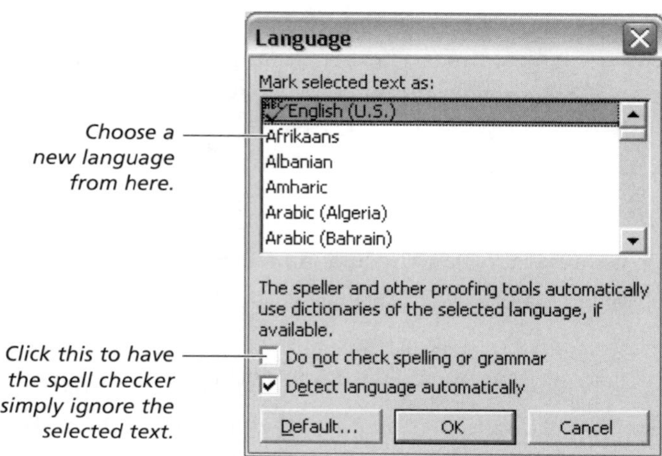

Figure 1.10 Setting a new language for the spell checker

Optional dictionaries exist for all the languages listed in the Language dialog box. Alas, I've had a heck of time trying to find or order them from Microsoft. So unless you meet with better luck, I would merely suggest using the Language dialog box to mark your foreign language text as "Do Not Check Spelling or Grammar." That way, you won't have to suffer through all the red and green wavy lines.

Printing Fun

The final step to the word processing process is getting your stuff down on paper, the hard copy, the printing part. This normally doesn't even receive a second thought. That is, until you come across one of the issues covered in the following sections.

KEYBOARD MASTER

Printing Keys

The printing keyboard shortcut is one of the basic Windows shortcut keys:

Ctrl+P

Another handy keyboarding combination worth knowing is the command to quickly summon the popular Page Setup dialog box:

Alt+F, U

The F is from File and the U comes from the word "Setup." Try to remember those special words as opposed to any others that the F-U combination might make you think of.

Note that some of the items here are printer-specific. Your printer's manufacturer, not Microsoft, creates the printer driver, the software used to control the printer. Printing is the spot where Word hands over control to that other software. So how your printer works may be subtly different than what's described below.

How Can I Stop Printing?

I find the most satisfying way to stop printing is to stand up and immediately yell at the printer, "Stop you idiot!" This is quite satisfying, but sadly this method has been found to be less than effective in most situations.

First, use your printer's queue list to try to stop the document from printing.

Because your printer is printing, there should be a tiny printer icon that appears in the System Tray/Notification area on the right end of the taskbar. Double-click that little printer icon to open your printer's window and view the queue list.

Click to select your document in the list. Then choose Document ➤ Cancel from the menu (or Document ➤ Cancel Printing, depending on your version of Windows).

Wait patiently. Eventually the document will stop printing.

If the document doesn't stop printing, and the printer keeps spewing out page after page, then consider turning off your printer. Do this only as a last resort: Turn off the printer. Wait a few moments, and then turn the printer on again. Eject a page from the printer just in case a page was "stuck" in the printer when you turned it off.

How Come the Document Comes out of the Printer Backwards?

Many ink printers and a few laser printers spew out their documents face up in the printer tray. The result here is that page 1 is always on the bottom of the stack, meaning that you have to re-shuffle your printer's output. *And aren't computers supposed to save you time!?*

Anyway, it's entirely possible to have your printer send out its pages in reverse order, providing that you remember these steps in Word:

1. Bring up the Print dialog box.

   Choose File ➤ Print or press Ctrl+P.

2. Click the Options button.

   This summons a second Print dialog box with a few special options custom to Word.

3. Click to check "Reverse Print Order."

   That's the secret!

4. Click OK.
5. Click OK to print in reverse order.

   And the pages come out of the printer backwards!

Now the last page prints first. If your printer spits out pages face up, then on top of the last page comes the next-to-last page, and so on all the way down to page 1, which prints on top the pile.

Can I Print on Both Sides of the Page?

Printing on both sides of a page is tricky. Well, it's tricky unless you have a printer that's capable of printing on both sides of the page. If you do, then you'll see the "Print on Both Sides" option deep in the printer's Properties dialog box.

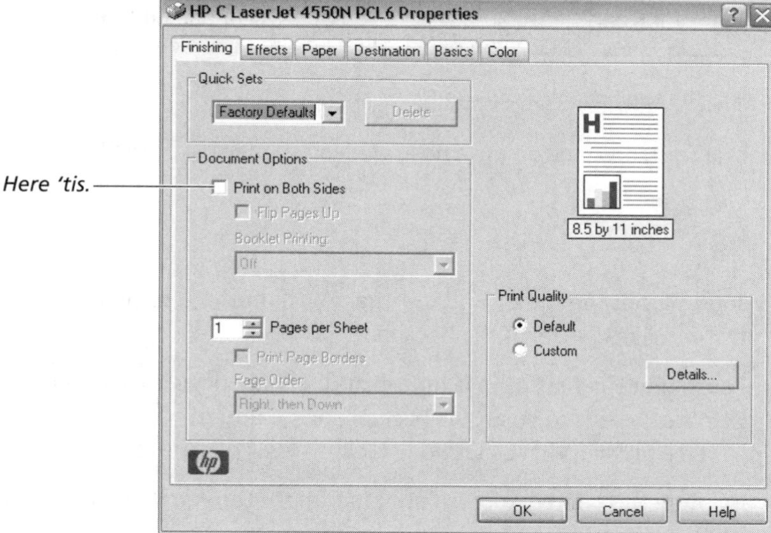

Figure 1.11 An option for printing on both sides of the page

For example, in Figure 1.11 you see the Properties dialog box for my HP color LaserJet, which has a dual-sided printing option attached. Alas, most printers lack this option, so you'll have to do things like this:

1. Save your document to disk, all nice and neat and ready to print.
2. Summon the Print dialog box.

   Choose File ➤ Print or use the handy Ctrl+P keyboard shortcut.
3. In the Print dialog box, choose "Odd Pages" from the Print drop-down list.

   Figure 1.12 shows where to find this.

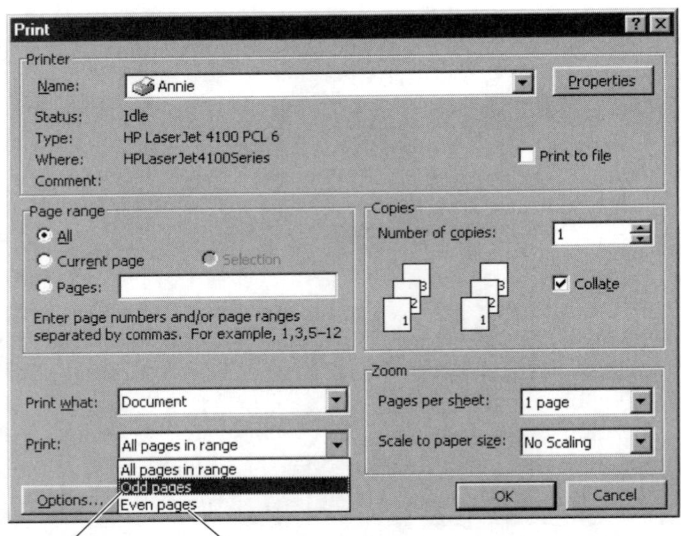

Figure 1.12
Printing odd pages, then even pages

First you want to print pages 1, 3, 5, and so on. Those will go on one side of the paper.

4. Click OK to print.

   And the printing goes on....

   When the printing is done, gather the sheets and put them back into the printer's paper tray, but oriented so that printing takes place on the back side.

   Further, you need to ensure that the first page is on top and the last page is on the bottom of the stack. That's because page 2 needs to go on the back of page 1, and so on. (See the previous section on printing in reverse order, if that helps you stack up your pages properly.)

   When the odd pages are properly ordered and oriented in the printer, you're ready to print on the even side.

5. Choose File ➤ Print.

6. Choose "Even Pages" from the Print drop-down list.

7. Click OK.

   And page 2 prints on the back of page 1, and so on for the rest of your document.

Yes, this can be a pain. It takes a bit of practice and patience to get it right. I recommend starting with a simple two-sided, one-page document. Then move up into longer documents. And if this is something you plan on doing often, look into buying a printer that has a dual-sided or duplex printing option built in. That certainly saves a lot of time and guesswork.

Any Way to Print This Color Document in Black Ink Only?

Setting the printer's colors is done using the printer's Properties dialog box, which is outside of Word's control: In the Print dialog box, click the Properties button. This displays your printer's Properties dialog box. Remember, each printer is different; this is not a Word thing.

Click the Color tab in your printer's Properties dialog box. Look in there for an option to print in black ink only. The option might be "Print in Grayscale" or "Black-and-White Only" or even "Don't Use Color." Also, the option might be found in the Graphics tab or be hidden in another dialog box or accessed through a Color button.

By printing in black ink only, you won't be wasting color ink on draft copies. That saves money in the long run. The only problem is that this is a non-standard option, so locating the black-ink-only setting takes time.

Is There a Better Way to Print on Three-Hole-Punch Paper?

I prefer printing out lots of stuff on three-hole-punch paper. Rather than mess with a paper punch, I prefer to buy my printer paper pre-punched. As long as the paper is properly oriented when you stick it into the printer, everything comes out fine—unless you forget to adjust the margins.

Generally speaking, I prefer a ½" margin on the left side of three-hole-punch paper. That gives enough room so that my text isn't too close to the holes. To set the margins that way, you use the Page Setup dialog box:

1. Choose File ➤ Page Setup.
2. Click the Margins tab (if you need to).

   Figure 1.13 shows you what's up with the Page Setup dialog box.
3. Adjust the Gutter margin up to .5".

   The "gutter" is a typesetting term for the edge of a page that is used for binding. Also note in Word 11 that you can set the Gutter Position for a document, though for three-hole-punch paper the position is Left, which is already defined.
4. Click OK.

   And the margins are properly set for three-hole-punch page printing.

The margins you set for the page are different from the margins set for individual paragraphs. In fact, the values you use for a paragraph's margin are all relative to these page margins. (Paragraph margins are set by using the Format ➤ Paragraph command.)

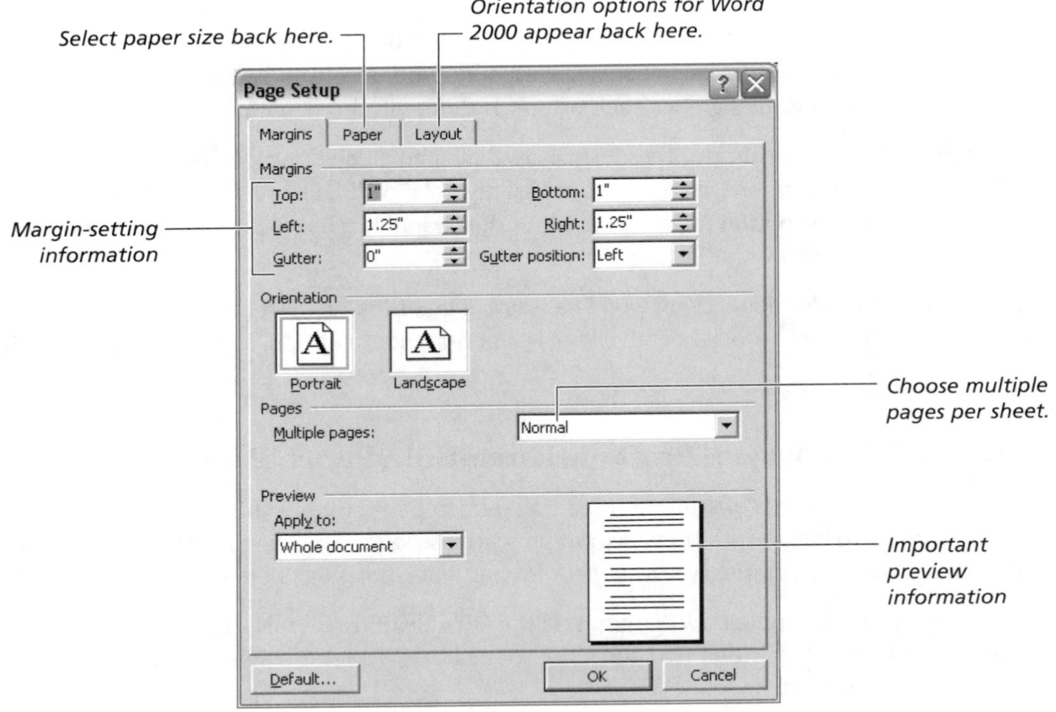

Figure 1.13 The Page Setup dialog box

How Can I Print Two Pages on an 11 x 14 Sheet?

It's simple to direct Word to print two or more "pages" on a sheet of paper. The problem comes, however, when you want to fold the paper in some way to make a book. Word lacks the smarts to intelligently print for binding purposes. (For that task you need a desktop publishing program, such as Microsoft's Publisher or Adobe's InDesign.) In any event, you can print more than one page on a sheet of paper if you follow these steps:

1. Choose File ➤ Page Setup.
2. Click the Paper or Paper Size tab.
3. Select Legal size paper from the Paper size drop-down list.
4. Change the Orientation to Landscape.

   Note that this is done in the Paper Size tab for Word 2000, but in the Margins tab for Word 2003/XP.
5. Click the Margins tab.

6a. In Word 2003/XP, choose "2 Pages per Sheet" from the Multiple Pages drop-down list.

6b. In Word 2000, put a check mark by "2 Pages per Sheet."

7. Click OK.

Now your document will print two pages on a single sheet. In this case, an 11 x 14 sheet of legal paper.

Again, the big problem here is binding. While Word can print two pages on a sheet of paper, it's very difficult to glue or staple the multiple pages together to make a book. If you attempt it, then the pages will be out of sequence. In fact, it's just better to print the pages, cut them out (with a scissors), then paste them (with glue) into a book form.

2 Alas, There Is No Such Thing as a "Simple" Document

The art of word processing is a fairly easy one. In fact, I know a great many people who get by in Word using just a few basic features. That's fine. Yet, by not understanding some of the other basic features, folks are missing out on some wonderful shortcuts and terrific insights. I know the argument is, "Why waste tricks on a basic boring document?" But my answer is, "Why not?"

It's shameful the amount of time people waste overdoing things that can be done automatically by the computer. I could offer example after example, but instead I thought I would present this chapter full of simple document sins and solutions. Yeah, it's more solutions than sins, so don't expect anything racy. The purpose here is to expose some of the more basic things Word does, tricks that will help you save time when you work on the typical document or letter.

Treasure Unburied and Miracles Revealed:

- Understanding a document's margins
- Properly formatting paragraphs (a variety of choices)
- Paragraph spacing: before, after, and in the middle
- Some tips for writing so-called simple letters
- Fudging your document's length without affecting word count

Measuring Your Way around a Document

One of the secret keys to unlocking the mystery of Word is to know how the frustrating program measures things in a document. It's enough to drive you mad! In fact, writing this chapter did drive me mad. I had to spend several days in a nice soft room to recover. But when I came out, I had an epiphany. It was one of those undiscovered truths that helps us understand the universe. And that is that it doesn't really matter how Word measures things in a document. What matters is the results. When you know what it looks like, then you can work backward to get those results while freely ignoring any details.

Where the Hell Are My Margins?

They say that the computer HAL went nuts in *2001: A Space Odyssey* because it was given two sets of conflicting instructions. Well, the reason most Word users go insane is that you're given two sets of margins to deal with: the page margins and the paragraph margins.

Making Sense of Page Margins

The page margins define the area where stuff appears in your document, as illustrated in Figure 2.1. These margins tell Word where to offset the text in your document from the edge of the paper.

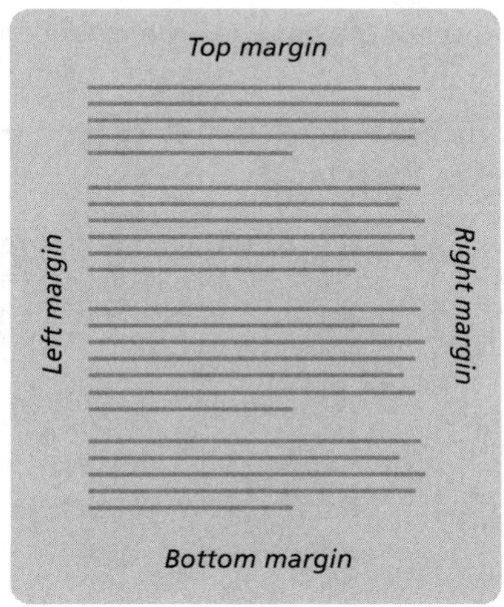

Figure 2.1
Here the hell are some of your margins.

And there is the key word: paper! Page and paper go hand-in-hand in Word. Whenever you think of something on a page, consider it as part of the piece of paper that prints. In a way, that's utterly different from your document, which consists of words in paragraphs. Those paragraphs have their own margins as well.

Page margins are set in the realm of the Page Setup dialog box, Margins tab. To get there, choose File ➤ Page Setup.

KEYBOARD MASTER

Changing the View

I'll admit that the easiest way for me to change the document's view is to use the wee little buttons in the document's lower-left corner. But the keyboard ways are certainly the fastest:

Alt+V, N

This switches you to Normal view faster than you can sneeze.

Alt+V, P

And off you go to Print Layout view.

Alt+V, O

Finally, the O takes you to Outline view.

It helps if you think of Alt+V as meaning "View" (which it does because Alt+V activates the View menu). After that, it's the first letter of the View mode you want: Normal, Print Layout, or Outline. Cinchy.

Keep in mind that most printers have absolute margin limits. For example, most laser printers cannot print on the outside half-inch of a page. Also, most inkjet printers need a larger margin at the top or bottom of the page in order to feed the paper through the printer.

Get Your Mind out of the Gutter!

The gutter margin is used to create extra space on any given edge of the page for binding purposes. So, for example, if you're planning on sticking the pages into a folder, then you probably want a little extra room on the binding side, so that the text doesn't "run into the gutter."

If your document needs a gutter, then Word lets you set one in the Page Setup dialog box. You can specify whether to put the gutter on the top or left edge of the page; then you set the gutter's depth by using the Gutter gizmo.

Headers and Footers: The Ugly Exceptions

Unlike all the other text in your document, headers and footers are not bound by the box created from your page margins. Nope, they're set differently, normally outside (above and below) the page margins. This is an odd exception, specifically because your header or footer can grow larger (top to bottom) depending on how much junk you place there.

To set the header and footer margins on a page, follow these steps:

1. Choose File ➤ Page Setup.

2a. In Word 2003/XP, click the Layout tab to find the Header and Footer settings.

2b. In Word 2000, locate the Header and Footer settings in the bottom of the Margins tab.

The measurements "From Edge" refer to the top edge of the paper for the Header and the bottom edge for the Footer.

3. Click OK after changing these settings, if need be.

For example, if you really, *really* want a one-inch margin all the way around your page, you'll need to change the settings for Header and Footer to 1.0" instead of the 0.5" (half an inch).

Also note that large headers and footers do push into the text. So if your header has a huge graphic in it, that header pushes *down* and causes the top margin for text on the page to go down as well. (The best way to see how this affects your document is in Print Layout view.)

You Must Know This: Several Ways to View a Document

Word offers several ways to view the document you're working on. Choosing one or another depends on your mood or, more accurately, what it is that you're doing with Word at the time.

Normal

I prefer to write in this mode. There are few distracting things on the screen, so I can concentrate on the text.

Web Layout

A poor choice: Don't use this option because it is best used for Word as a web page editor. I do not recommend using Word to edit web pages.

Print Layout

This is also a good writing mode to use, but it works best when you need to see elements such as page breaks, columns, and images in your text. For editing and page layout, I prefer to use Word in this mode.

Outline

This mode works best for using Word as an outline editor. This is covered in Chapter 6, "Writing That Great American Novel or Screenplay."

Reading Layout

This mode is available only with Word 2003. It's used only for reading documents, similar to the way Adobe's Acrobat Reader is used, though I'm certain Microsoft is unaware of any unintentional similarities.

Paragraph Margins

Most Word users become confused with paragraph margins rather than page margins. This is most likely for two reasons:

- The paragraph margin measurements are relative to the page margin on the left.
- The Ruler tends to distort things by putting a zero-inch mark where the paragraph starts. Stupid Ruler.

Figure 2.2 shows the Ruler with all the important features labeled.

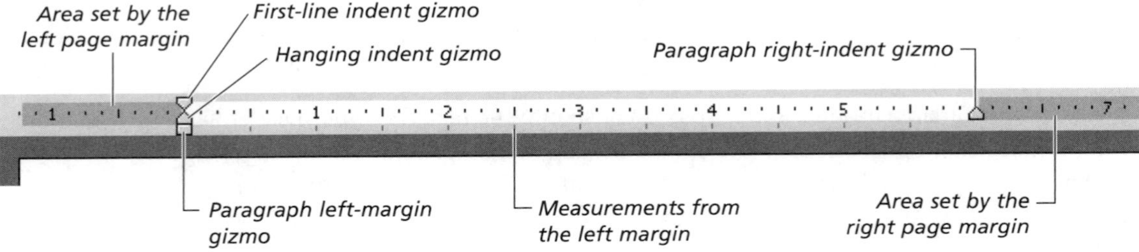

Figure 2.2 Uncovering the mystery of the paragraph margins

To best see how this works, switch to Print Layout view by choosing View ➤ Print Layout from the menu. Further, you may have to choose a Zoom value less than 100% to see the full page (left to right) on your monitor.

Print Layout view shows both horizontal and vertical rulers. The gray area is defined by the page margins. The white part of the ruler is what's used when setting paragraph margins.

Note that the paragraph's left margin is set at zero inches, which is *not* the edge of the page but rather the left margin offset. This is where most Word users get confused; paragraph measurements are from the *margin*, not the edge of the page!

Don't Be Dumb! Use the Preview Windows and Page Preview Command.

Setting margins here and there and testing how things look can be a major pain! First, I recommend writing your text and worrying about margins and all that later. But second, and most importantly, take advantage of the various Preview panes in the margin-formatting dialog boxes. Use them to get an idea of what kind of formatting you're getting into.

Finally, don't forget about the Print Preview command (File ➤ Print Preview). It uses both horizontal and vertical rulers to show you just how your document will lay out on a page—a very valuable tool, not to be overlooked by any margin-manipulating maven.

The indent gizmos on the ruler are used to control the paragraph's margins manually. Otherwise, you use the Format ➤ Paragraph command to summon the Paragraph dialog box and set things up there by entering measurements. The next section discusses all the options and such.

I Want to Indent My Paragraph Like This!

Say hello to my handy visual formatting guide for soothing your paragraph ills!

The problem with paragraph formatting is the terminology: hanging, indent, offset, justified. These terms, like the fine print when you lease a car, mean nothing! So instead of trying to fool your brain into understanding them, I've come up with the visual sample formatting guide for the next few pages. Hopefully there's a paragraph format here that you like and want to use. If so, then follow the handy steps required to format your paragraph that way.

Figure 2.3 illustrates a sample preview paragraph. This gives you a quick idea of what the paragraph formatting should look like, complete with the approximate settings of the paragraph margin gizmos on the ruler.

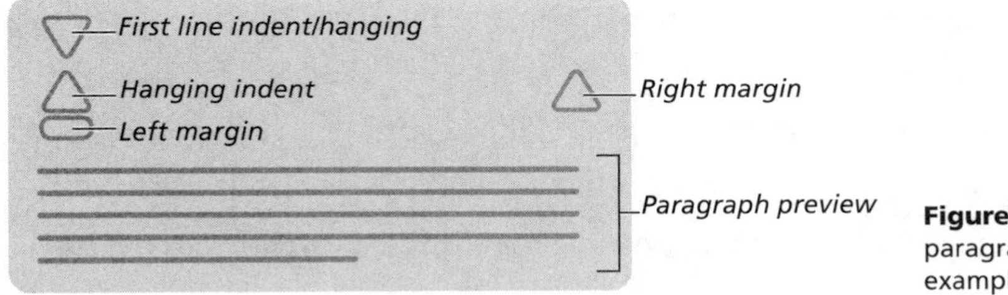

Figure 2.3 The sample paragraph-formatting example

Figure 2.4 shows the settings required inside the Paragraph dialog box, which you can access via the Format ➤ Paragraph command. Note that these measurements apply only to the Indentation part of the dialog box (which is why only it is shown). And you can adjust values to exact amounts other than those shown in the figure (but you should get the general idea).

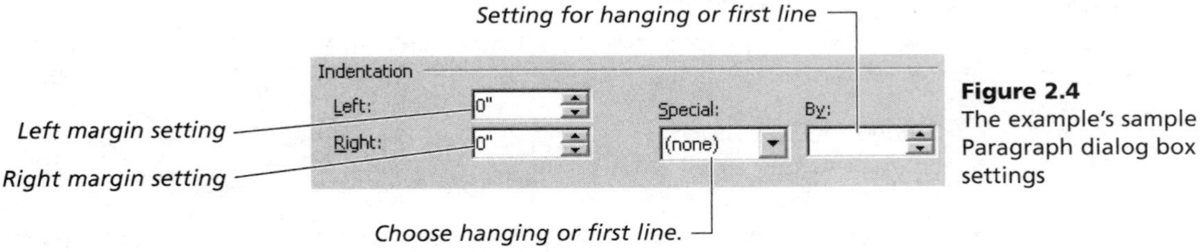

Figure 2.4 The example's sample Paragraph dialog box settings

Finally, ensure that the Ruler is visible when you use Word. Choose View ➤ Ruler if you don't see the Ruler on your screen.

The following sections do not cover the basics of paragraph alignment: Left, Right, Centered, or Justified. Most of these operations take place on paragraphs that have been formatted either with Left or Justified alignment.

You Must Know This: Paragraph Formatting Lingo and Gizmos

Can't tell the formatting players without a scorecard? Here's a quick rundown of what the heck all these things are.

Alignment: Left

The paragraph is lined up on the left margin but not on the right.

Alignment: Centered

Each line of the paragraph is centered on the page.

Alignment: Right

The paragraph is lined up on the right margin but not on the left.

Alignment: Justified

The paragraph is lined up on both the left and right margins.

Indentation: Left

The left edge of the paragraph is offset from the page's left margin by a given amount.

Indentation: Right

The right edge of the paragraph is offset from the page's right margin by a given amount.

Indentation: Special: First Line

The paragraph's first line is indented by the given amount.

Indentation: Special Hanging

The paragraph's first line is offset ("out-dented") from the rest of the lines by a given amount.

▽ *Set the first-line indent.*

△ *Set a hanging indent/right margin for the rest of the paragraph.*

□ *Set the paragraph's left margin, or move both the first-line and hanging indent marks together.*

△ *Set the right indent.*

What's the Point of the Dull, No-Format Paragraph?

The point is that this is the prototype paragraph. It's the one you want to recover to when your paragraph modifications have gone berserk and you need a small dose of sanity.

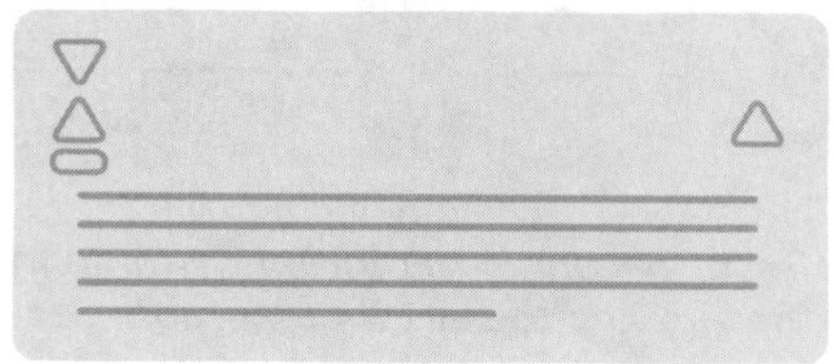

The typical paragraph the way Word starts out has both the left and right margins offset at zero (even with the page margins). There is no first-line indent or hang. Yawn.

To compensate for the lack of first-line indent, most of these style paragraphs are typically followed by a space. That's done either by tapping the Enter key twice after typing the paragraph or by adding space after the paragraph in the Paragraph dialog box. (This is covered later in this chapter.)

Also note that this formatting is what's required to undo some of the more complex examples that follow. So when you want to return to plain and boring, reset your paragraphs margins as described in this section.

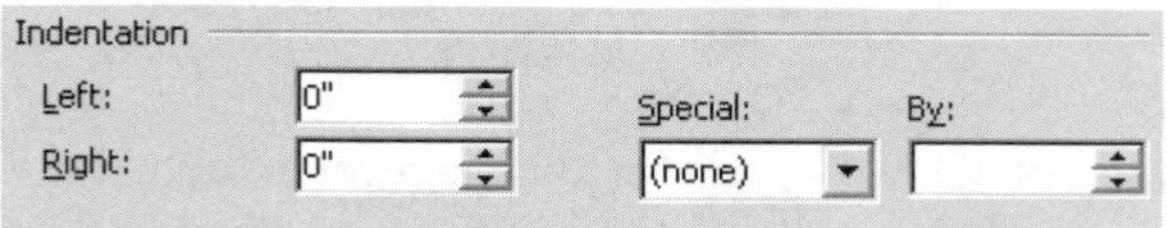

Why Would I Want to Indent the First Line?

If you don't have any spaces between paragraphs, then indenting the first line tells the reader where the new paragraph starts. Otherwise your document will be one long Great Wall of Text and potentially intimidate your readers into a state of unconsciousness.

The first-line indent is a popular alternative to no first-line indent. By using a first-line indent, you also avoid the necessity of having to double space between paragraphs; the indented first line makes it easier to see paragraph breaks on a page.

The typical first-line indent is half an inch, as shown below. You can make the indent as wide or as narrow as you like.

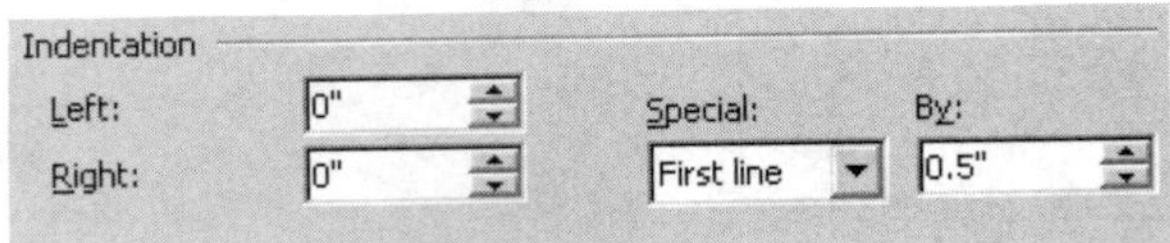

By automatically formatting a paragraph with an indented first line, you no longer need to press the Tab key to start a paragraph. See? Computers can make your life easier!

What Is a Hanging Indent and Why Would I Need One?

Hanging indents aren't common, but they can be ideal for certain types of lists, descriptions, or special items because the unusual paragraph formatting is appealing—especially how it stands out on the page.

A hanging indent paragraph looks like the first line is reverse-tabbed over beyond the margin, but that's not the case. Essentially, a hanging indent is where the first line is *not* indented but the rest of the paragraph is, as shown above.

KEYBOARD MASTER

The Instant Hanging Indent

Amazingly enough, Word has a keyboard combo to instantly create a hanging indent paragraph.

Ctrl+T

Press Ctrl+T once, and the paragraph is hung-indented one-half inch. Press Ctrl+T again to indent another half inch, and so on. But if you go too far, there is companion key:

Ctrl+Shift+T

This key combination un-hangs an indent by half an inch or merely undoes what's been done by the Ctrl+T key combination. (This keyboard shortcut has no effect on a paragraph without a hanging indent.)

Note especially how the left margin (shown below) is not changed by the hanging indent. Even though the indent gizmos on the ruler (above) look different, the margin indentation in the Paragraph dialog box has not changed. This has been known to drive people nuts.

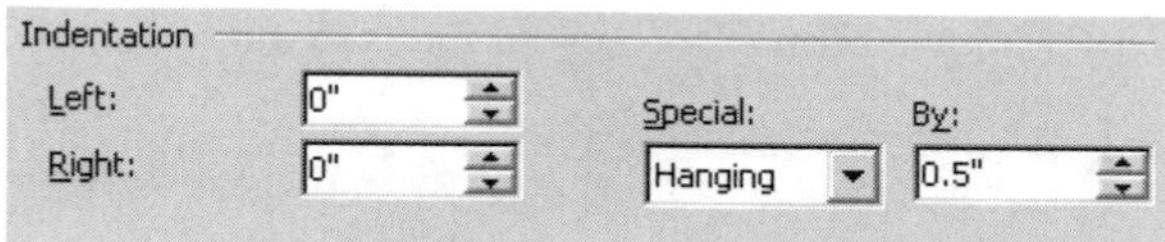

Can the Indent Also Hang beyond the Page Margin?
Okay. Sure. Whatever.

The quick way to hang an indent into the page margin is to drag the top first-line indent gizmo on the ruler to the left, into the gray area. That leaves the other items set on the left margin (as shown above).

The harder way to do this is in the Paragraph formatting dialog box, shown below. In that case you must enter a negative value for the Left indent that is equal to the positive value of the hanging indent. Me? I can't understand that while I'm not intoxicated.

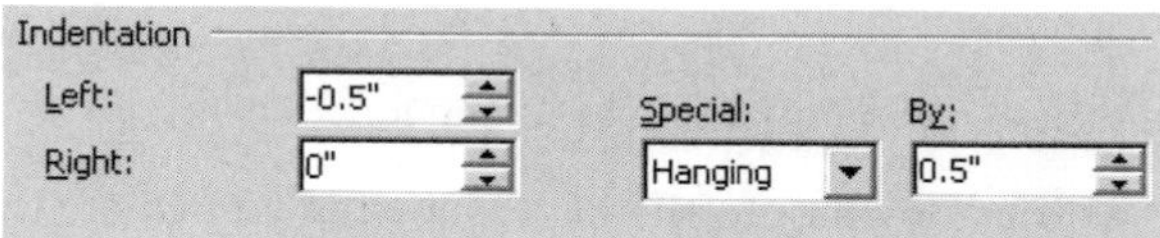

Come on: Is There a Real Need to Have a Hanging Indent?
The true advantage of hanging indents comes when you create lists of things, what I call "item-tab-paragraphs." Figure 2.5 illustrates how the example looks on the page.

To make this happen, first type your paragraphs:

1. Type the item.

   It can be a date, location, term, or whatever.

2. Press the Tab key.

   Don't worry if the paragraph looks ugly at this point; you need the tab there for when you finally create the hanging indent.

3. Type the rest of the paragraph.

   Again, it won't line up right at this stage. Don't worry! You're just getting information down. Formatting comes after.

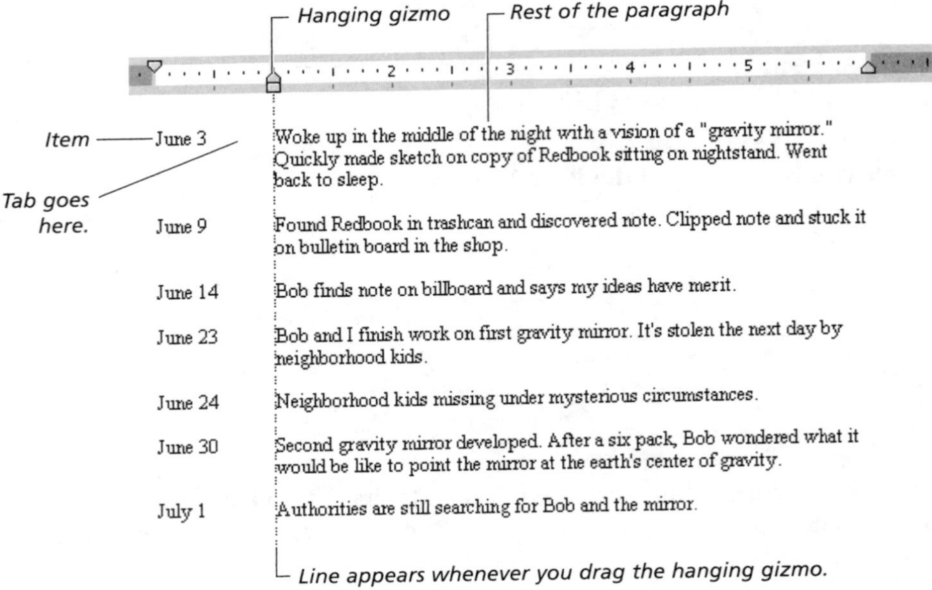

Hanging gizmo
Rest of the paragraph
Item
June 3
Woke up in the middle of the night with a vision of a "gravity mirror." Quickly made sketch on copy of Redbook sitting on nightstand. Went back to sleep.
Tab goes here.
June 9
Found Redbook in trashcan and discovered note. Clipped note and stuck it on bulletin board in the shop.
June 14
Bob finds note on billboard and says my ideas have merit.
June 23
Bob and I finish work on first gravity mirror. It's stolen the next day by neighborhood kids.
June 24
Neighborhood kids missing under mysterious circumstances.
June 30
Second gravity mirror developed. After a six pack, Bob wondered what it would be like to point the mirror at the earth's center of gravity.
July 1
Authorities are still searching for Bob and the mirror.
Line appears whenever you drag the hanging gizmo.

Figure 2.5 An example of an item-tab-paragraph

When you've finished typing all your paragraphs, you're ready to format:

4. Select all the paragraphs.
5. On the Ruler, drag the hanging gizmo over to the left.

   As you drag, a line drops down onto the page, showing you where the indented paragraph's left margin will fall. Use that as a guide as you drag the hanging gizmo. Wait until all the paragraphs are lined up properly.

6. Release the mouse button to view your paragraphs.

   If you need to adjust the indent, drag the hanging gizmo farther to the right or back to the left. Or if you're picky, find a half-inch tick to line the gizmo up with.

The end result looks something like Figure 2.5. Note that even in that figure, the hanging indent could be moved farther to the left to tighten up the space after the item.

The worst way to accomplish this same thing is by using spaces instead of the Tab key. Never use spaces! Any time you have to use more than one space, you should be using the Tab key instead! See Chapter 6 for more information on tabs.

What If I Need a Follow-on Item-Tab-Paragraph without an Item?

Then just press the Tab key to start the line; then type the paragraph. Any text before the tab lines up at the left margin. Otherwise, when you press the Tab key, you slide the rest of the text over to the hanging indent margin.

How Can I Right-Align the Item and Then Left-Align a Paragraph?

This is a tough one to explain, but visually compare Figure 2.6 with Figure 2.5. Notice how in Figure 2.6 the items are lined up along their right edge, whereas in Figure 2.5 they're lined up along their left edge? This trick can easily be accomplished by following these steps:

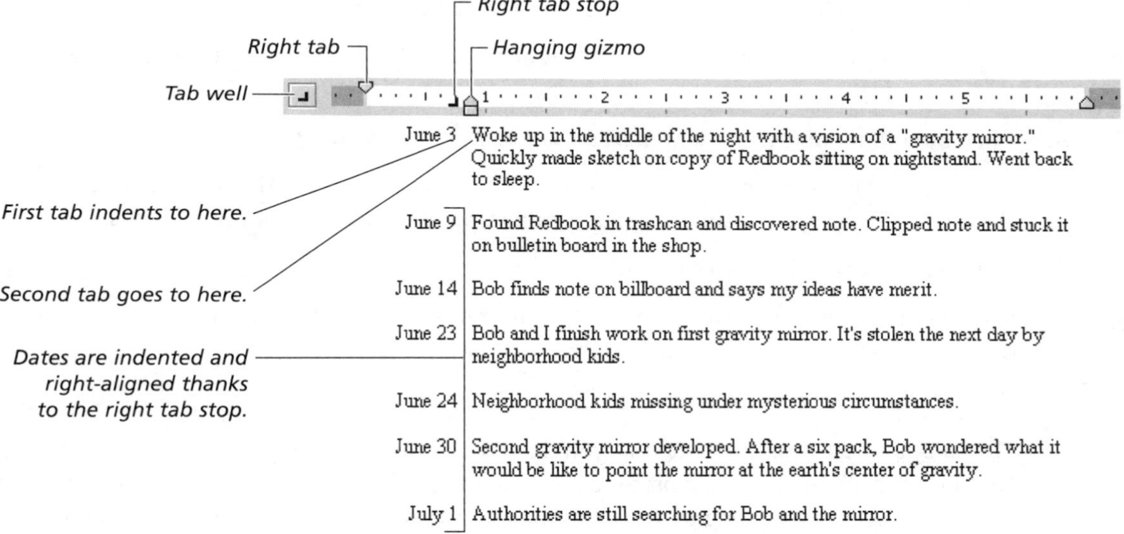

Figure 2.6 Say hello to the tab-item-tab-paragraph.

Start by typing your paragraphs. Always do this first before you format, but note how the tabs are laid out:

1. Start each paragraph with a tab.
2. Type your item.

   And remember these items must be short; otherwise the paragraphs will be too narrow and the whole thing will look damn ugly.
3. Press the Tab key again.

   Note that sometimes when you press the Tab key it appears as if the text doesn't move much. That's okay! Avoid the temptation to press the Tab key twice. Once is enough! The tab is in there, even if you can't see it. Trust me.

4. Type the rest of your paragraph.

   Yes, it will look ugly at this stage. But this is the best way to set up for the rest of the formatting.

After entering all your paragraphs, you're ready to format. This is where the ugliness clears up, but it also requires a bit of eyeballing and some finesse. Pay careful attention:

5. Select all the paragraphs.
6. Drag the hanging gizmo over to about the 2" mark on the ruler.

   No, this isn't where you want it; it's just temporary.

7. Click the Tab well on the Ruler until you get the right tab symbol.

   The Tab well is found on the far-left end of the Ruler. The right tab symbol is a backward "L."

8. Click the mouse on the 1" mark on the ruler to set the right tab there.

   You'll notice that the formatting is now better than it was before. All you need to do is adjust the offset of the right tab and hanging gizmo to perfectly line up your paragraphs.

9. Slide the right tab gizmo to the left.

   Slide it over as far as you can without shoving your items over to the left margin. For the dates in Figure 2.6, I chose the .75" mark.

10. Click the hanging gizmo over to the left.

    You can put it as close to the text as you like, such as one tick away, as I chose in Figure 2.6. Or you can back the text off a bit for a more dramatic effect. But don't back the text too far over to the right or the paragraphs will scrunch up and wreck the right-align effect of the items.

The key to making this work is remembering the tab-item-tab sequence when you type the initial paragraphs. Then keep the right tab and hanging gizmo close together, as shown in Figure 2.6, and it can look pretty neat.

Is There Such a Thing as an Item-Tab-Item-Tab-Paragraph?

You can have as many items sitting on the first line of a paragraph as you have room for. Generally speaking, however, if you have more than two items at the start of a paragraph, then what you really need there is a *table* and not a paragraph. Refer to Chapter 6 for information on creating a table. Otherwise, you can set up the items as shown in Figure 2.7.

The idea here is that you start your paragraph with an item, press the Tab key, type the next item, and then press Tab again to type your paragraph. The first tab stop sets the position of the second item, and the hanging gizmo sets the position of the rest of the paragraph.

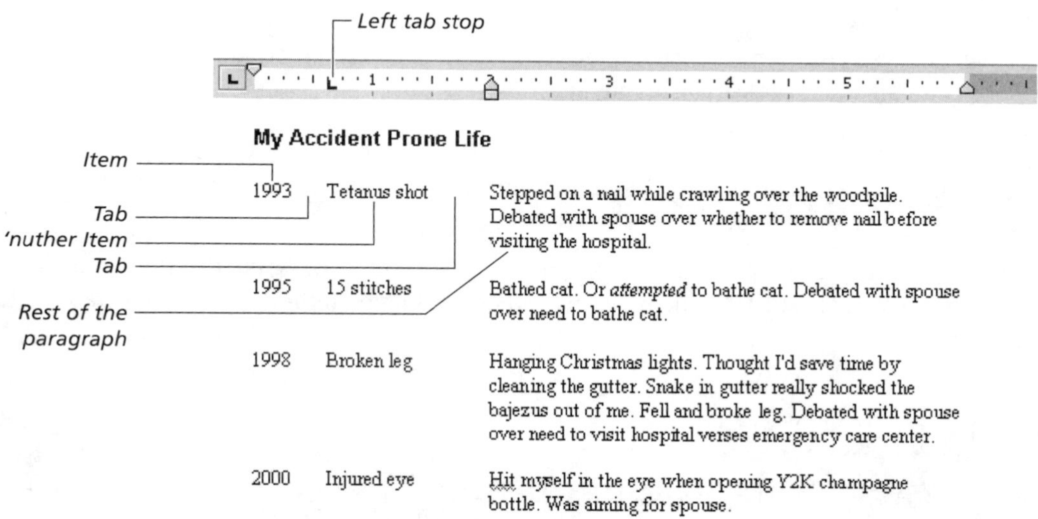

Figure 2.7 The item-tab-item-paragraph thing

Start, as with previous examples, by typing your paragraphs ahead of time:

1. Start each paragraph with the first item.
2. Press the Tab key.
3. Type your second item.

   Both items must be short, as shown in Figure 2.7. Anything longer and you really need to use a table instead of this paragraph-formatting trick.
4. Press the Tab key again.
5. Type the paragraph.

   Forget that it looks ugly! This job you're doing with the Tab key makes it all line up better in a second.

When you've finished typing the paragraphs, you're ready to format them:

6. Select the paragraphs that you want to format.
7. Choose a left tab stop from the Tab well.

   L The left tab stop looks like a fat letter "L." You may have to click the Tab well a few times until you get this symbol.
8. Click the Ruler at the 1" stop to set the left tab stop there.

This indents the second item in each paragraph. If you need to adjust the tab stop to the left or right, do so by dragging it with the mouse. (It's an eyeball thing; set the tab stop where it looks good for whatever list you're making.)

9. Drag the hanging gizmo to the 2" spot on the ruler.

That lines up the paragraph text (the third item). You can slide the hanging gizmo to the left or right to adjust how it looks with the rest of the text.

In Figure 2.7 I set the tab at .625" and the hanging gizmo at 2" exactly. Again, this is an eyeball thing, which is why it's best to use the Ruler instead of messing with the Tabs and Paragraph dialog boxes.

NERD'S CORNER

Cocktail Party Trivia, Part I

LOIS: All this talk of tabs makes me crave a one-calorie diet cola beverage!

MARK: Me too! With gin!

JOHN: Oh, ha-ha, you are silly. But doesn't anyone here know where the Tab key came from?

BILL: A typewriter.

MARK: Duh! Everyone knows that.

LOIS: Yes, but on the typewriter, the key was often called the Tabulator.

JOHN: Indeed, Lois, you're correct. But there still is a root to that word that you're all familiar with: That's "table."

EVERYONE: Oh....

JOHN: The word "tab" and even "tabulator" comes from the same root as "table." So even back in the old typewriter days, tabs were used to assist in the organization of information into tables.

BILL: Well, as best as they could in the linear analog style of the typewriter.

EVERYONE: Ha-ha-ha!

I Want to Have the Paragraph First and Then the Items on the Right Side of the Page.
Then what you need is a table. See Chapter 7.

When and How Would I Use a Block Quote?
Specifically, you block-quote any chunk of text that's too long to stick in double quotes in the middle of a paragraph. So when you decide to stick the "Gettysburg Address" into your document, you block-quote it to make it stand out special.

The block-quote text is simply a paragraph with both the left and right margins sunk in, typically one inch.

To move the left margin, use the left-indent gizmo; otherwise you have to move both the hanging and first-line gizmos separately.

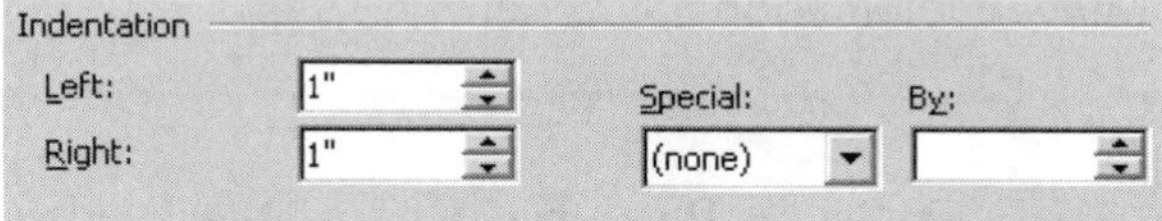

When you use a block quote in a document, you do not have to put quotation marks around it. Simply introduce the quote, such as, "Here is what James Madison had to say about tyranny," and then contain the entire quote in the block or blocks that follow.

How Do I Make a Block Quote with the First Line Indented?

It's unusual, but it can be done just as it would with any paragraph of text.

Indented block quotes simply share the same formatting as shown in the previous section, but with the addition of a half-inch (or less) offset with the first line of text.

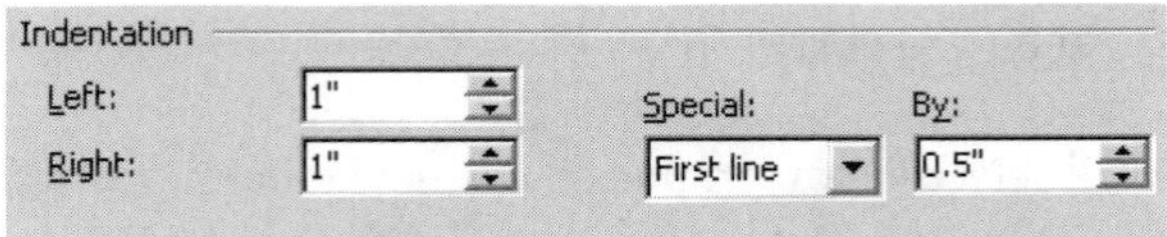

Is There Such Thing as a Double-Indented with Hanging First-Line Paragraph Monster?

Not in this book.

Indenting a Paragraph

Word has a handy keyboard combo for indenting a paragraph one-half inch on the left margin. This isn't the same as a block indent, but it's close:

Ctrl+M

Each time you press Ctrl+M, the paragraph's left margin is indented one-half inch. (The right margin is not affected.)

Ctrl+Shift+M

Pressing this key combination un-indents the left margin by one-half inch, effectively undoing whatever the Ctrl+M key combination has done.

Which Is Better: To Indent Each Paragraph or Double Space between Paragraphs?

Deciding how to format your paragraphs depends on your mood. There are no hard-and-fast rules; in professional publishing, it's up to the "house style" as to which way to go. But, generally speaking, all documents are formatted one way or the other, rarely mixed.

To format indented paragraphs, simply set the first-line indent to .5" or whatever you like. This can be done on the Ruler or in the Paragraph formatting dialog box, which is covered earlier in this chapter.

To automatically follow a paragraph with a space, you need to use the Paragraph dialog box:

1. Choose Format ➤ Paragraph.
2. In the Spacing part of the dialog box, set the amount in the After text box.

   By working the gizmo in the After text box, you can set a space of 6 pt (six points) or 12 pt (12 points) after each paragraph you type. This is automatic, so you don't need to double-press the Enter key at the end of a paragraph.

   Oh, and you can also manually type in any point value you like. For example, some twisted individuals prefer to follow fancy headings with only 3 pts of space.
3. Click OK.

This change applies to all selected paragraphs or any new paragraphs you type. Word automatically inserts the given number of points of "air" after each paragraph.

You can also use the Spacing: Before item in the Paragraph dialog box to add that much more space between your paragraphs. However, I typically use only the Spacing: After item to keep all my paragraphs consistent and to keep myself sane when I try to track down weird formatting errors.

The best way to ensure that the blank space follows all your paragraphs is to create a style in Word and apply that style to all your paragraphs. See Chapter 5, "Using Styles and Templates to Save Oodles of Time."

You Must Know This: Making Points

The pt abbreviation in Word stands for points. This is a typesetter's measurement, but you're already familiar with it in that Windows uses points to measure how large fonts are.

Typical values for points between paragraphs are 6 and 12. If you truly want a "blank line" between paragraphs, then choose a point size to match the point size of whatever font you're using. For example, if you're using 12 pt Times New Roman, then a 12-point space after each paragraph will give you your blank line.

I Hate the Way This Paragraph Breaks Up!

One way to control (or at least attempt to control) the way a paragraph breaks up between two pages is to take advantage of the Line and Page Breaks tab in the Paragraph dialog box, shown in Figure 2.8. Use the options there, described in the figure, to help you keep your paragraphs from being mangled between two pages.

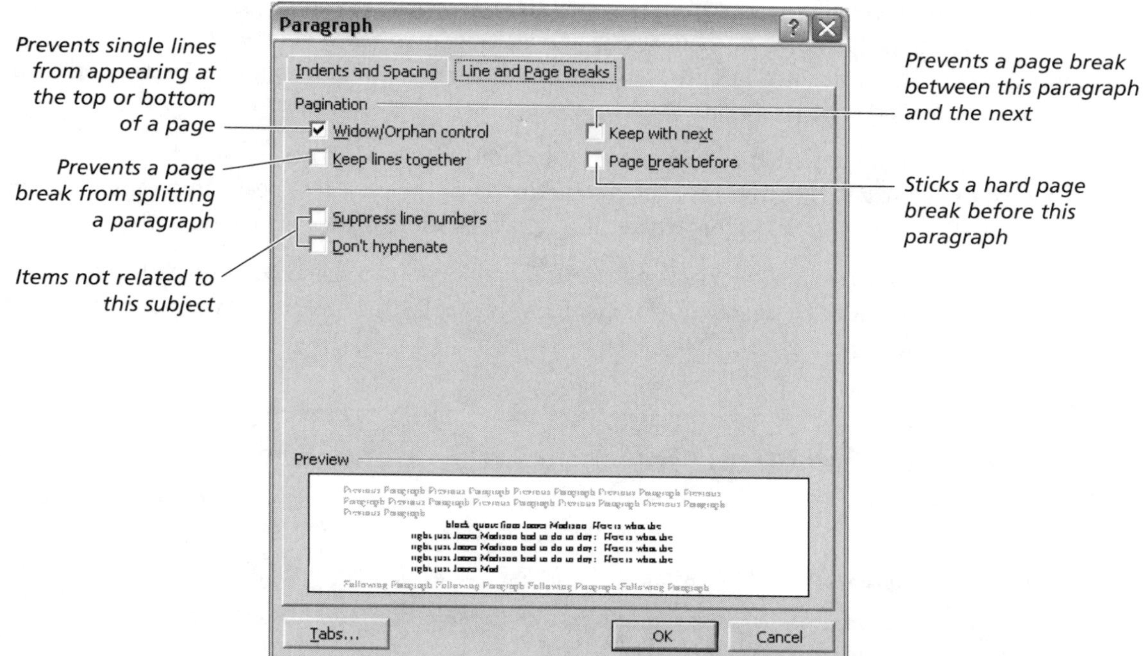

Figure 2.8 The other side of the Paragraph dialog box

Word does try its best to heed your instructions about not breaking up paragraphs. However, there are some cases where breakup must occur.

Stuff You Can Do Better When You're Writing a Simple Letter

While desperately trying to think up things you can do with a word processor, software developers inevitably claim, "You can write a letter." Sometimes there's more detail: "You can write a letter home" or "You can write a letter to a long-lost friend." Whatever. In the age of e-mail, do people still write letters?

Yes, you bet they do! And they write them as badly as they compose their e-mail. My favorite letter is the quasi-legal-sounding letters I get from annoying neighbors and political enemies. I'd happily list one here as an example of "what not to do," but that would spawn a whole raft of new quasi-legal-sounding letters, so I shall be more bland in the examples that follow.

Where Does My Address Go on a Simple Letter?

Honestly, it does not matter where you put your address on a letter! Such things used to fall under the guise of *etiquette*. Remember Ms. Manners? Ha! You thought I had her killed, but I didn't. She's still with us and as full of recommendations as ever. Of course, back when we had social classes and an aristocracy, you could get into serious trouble when writing a malformed letter. Today, in the age of e-mail, no one really cares. (Sorry, Ms. M.)

Still, according to the information I've dug up, the traditional way to format a simple, personal letter is shown in Figure 2.9. Note that neither your address nor their address needs to go anywhere on the letter. (Even so, I've seen letters where the recipient's address goes above the salutation.)

A typical business letter is shown in Figure 2.10. Your address is considered to be part of the letterhead (which is included in the document header in Figure 2.10). If not, then your address follows the closing. Otherwise, Figure 2.10 holds all the secrets.

Common Greetings for Your Correspondence

For familiar recipients, using "Dear" is the proper way to start a letter, as in "Dear Francis." If it's a personal letter, then you can even say "My dearest Christina."

For non-casual relations, "Dear Mr. Manfredi" or "Dear Ms. Johnson" is preferred.

For situations when the person's name is not known, you can use "Dear Sir or Madam," or if you know the title, then use "Dear Product Manager" or something similar.

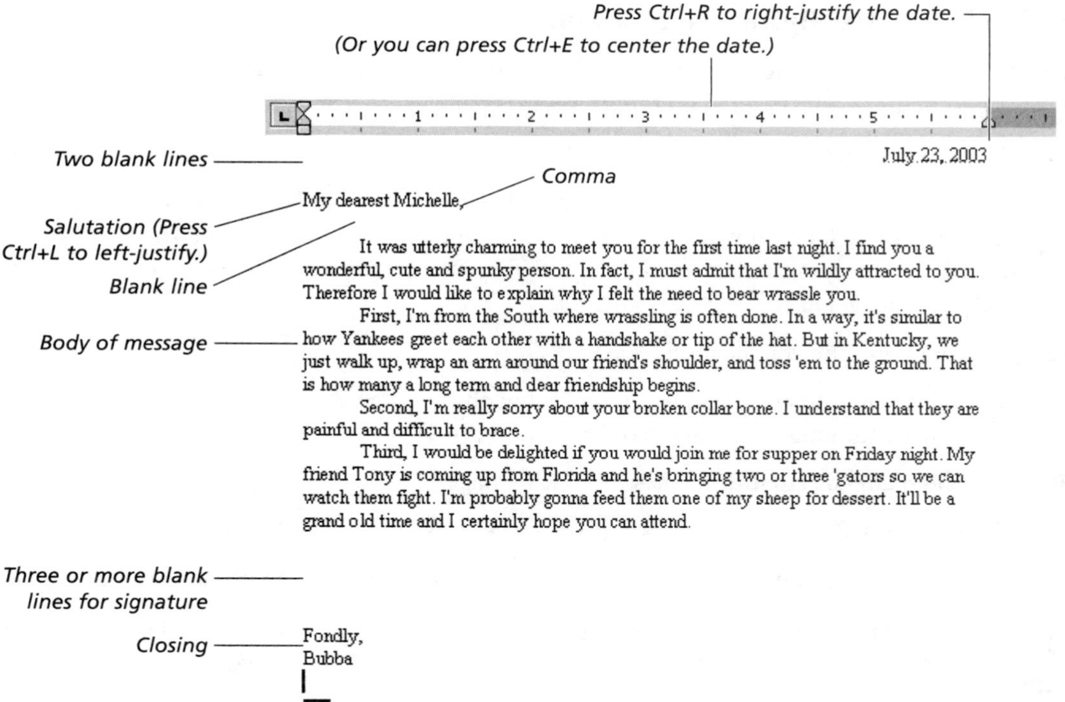

Press Ctrl+R to right-justify the date.
(Or you can press Ctrl+E to center the date.)
Two blank lines
July 23, 2003
Comma
Salutation (Press Ctrl+L to left-justify.)
My dearest Michelle,
Blank line
It was utterly charming to meet you for the first time last night. I find you a wonderful, cute and spunky person. In fact, I must admit that I'm wildly attracted to you. Therefore I would like to explain why I felt the need to bear wrassle you.
Body of message
First, I'm from the South where wrassling is often done. In a way, it's similar to how Yankees greet each other with a handshake or tip of the hat. But in Kentucky, we just walk up, wrap an arm around our friend's shoulder, and toss 'em to the ground. That is how many a long term and dear friendship begins.
Second, I'm really sorry about your broken collar bone. I understand that they are painful and difficult to brace.
Third, I would be delighted if you would join me for supper on Friday night. My friend Tony is coming up from Florida and he's bringing two or three 'gators so we can watch them fight. I'm probably gonna feed them one of my sheep for dessert. It'll be a grand old time and I certainly hope you can attend.
Three or more blank lines for signature
Closing
Fondly,
Bubba

Figure 2.9 A sample piece of personal correspondence

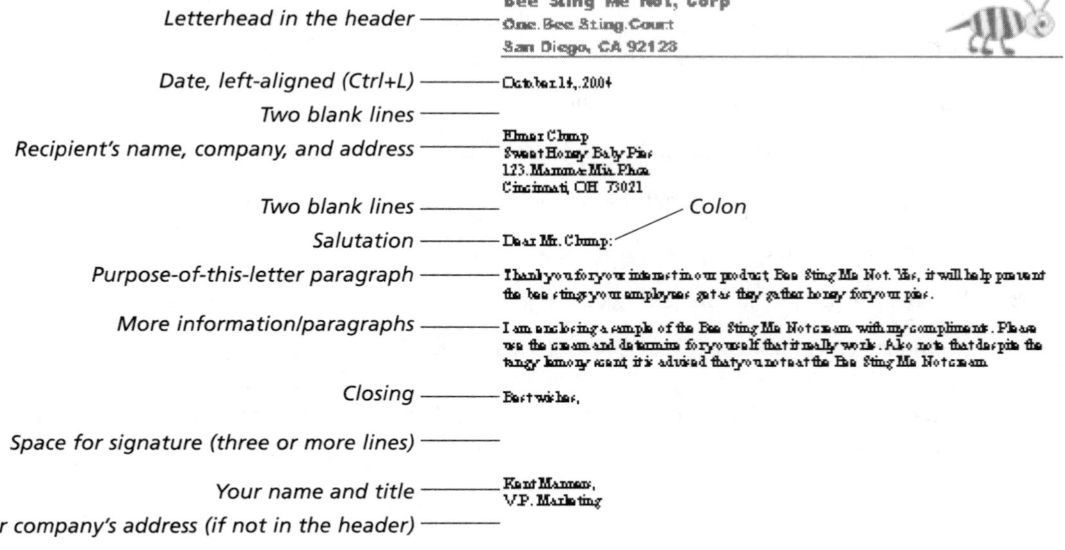

Figure 2.10 A sample piece of business correspondence

How Can I Add My Signature to a Letter?

The easiest way to add a signature to a letter is to print the stinking thing out and sign it. But, no: This is a computer and you must do things electronically.

1. Write your signature a few times on a white piece of paper.

   Use black ink. In fact, use a fat black marker, like a Sharpie pen. Feel free to write larger than normal or extra fancy. If you sign your signature the same every time, then there's no reason to write it out more than once. Me? I'm different every time, so I have to keep writing until I find a signature I like.

2. Scan the signature you like best.

   Set your scanner to grab a grayscale (not monochrome) image. Set the pixel depth to 256, but not higher. Scanning at about 150 dpi should do the job.

3. Save the scanned signature to disk as a TIFF image.

   The TIFF format is universal, allowing you to use the signature file in a number of applications.

   Save the image in your My Pictures folder, or some other folder where you can easily find it.

The signature's size on the screen is not important at this point. In fact, larger is better, since you may have to re-size the signature to look best on the page.

When you need to stick your signature into a document, then follow these steps in Word:

4. Position the insertion pointer where you want the signature to be plopped down.

   The signature appears in your document just like any other chunk of text. So if you want it at the start of a new line, press the Enter key to start a new line.

5. Choose Insert ➢ Picture ➢ From File.
6. Use the Insert Picture dialog box to browse for your signature file.
7. When you find the file, select it and click the Insert button.

   The signature image appears in the document.

8. Re-size the signature image if necessary.

   To re-size the signature, click it once to select it. The image grows "handles" on the corners and sides, as shown in Figure 2.11. Use the mouse to grab the lower-right handle and drag upward and to the left to make the picture smaller, or drag downward and to the right to make it larger.

Inserting a signature like this places that "picture" into the document just like any other character. So if you end up with extra space before or after the signature, simply select and delete those lines. Likewise, because the picture is like any character, you can indent or align it as necessary.

Also see Chapter 3, "Making Fancy Documents and Reports," for more information on playing with images in documents.

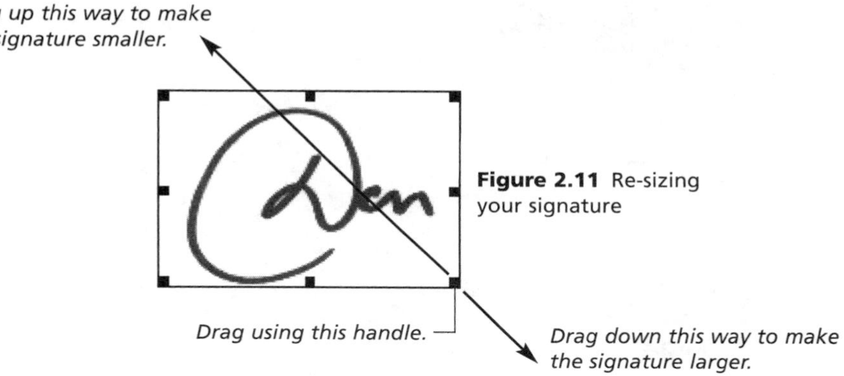
Drag up this way to make the signature smaller.
Drag using this handle.
Drag down this way to make the signature larger.

Figure 2.11 Re-sizing your signature

Properly Signing Off a Letter

There are many ways to end a business or formal letter, depending on how you feel: "Best wishes," "Sincerely," "Yours truly," and so on. My favorite cold-shoulder ending is "Cordially." For personal letters, you can use "Love," "Fondly," "Cheers," "All my best," and so on, with the closing proper for the recipient.

This closing should be followed by ample space for a signature (I use three lines) and then your full name and, if applicable, company title.

If it's a familiar or casual letter, then writing only your first name is considered fine, but proper etiquette guides recommend against using a casual sign-off such as "Yours" or anything other than those mentioned above.

The only time you don't need to type out your name at the bottom of the letter is if your name already appears as part of the letterhead. You still need to sign the letter, however.

Don't Letters Also Need Envelopes?

After writing your letter, tell Word to print a corresponding envelope. To do that, ensure that the letter document is on the screen, and then open the Envelopes and Labels dialog box:

- In Word 2003/XP, choose Tools ➢ Letters and Mailings ➢ Envelopes and Labels.
- In Word 2000, choose Tools ➢ Envelopes and Labels.

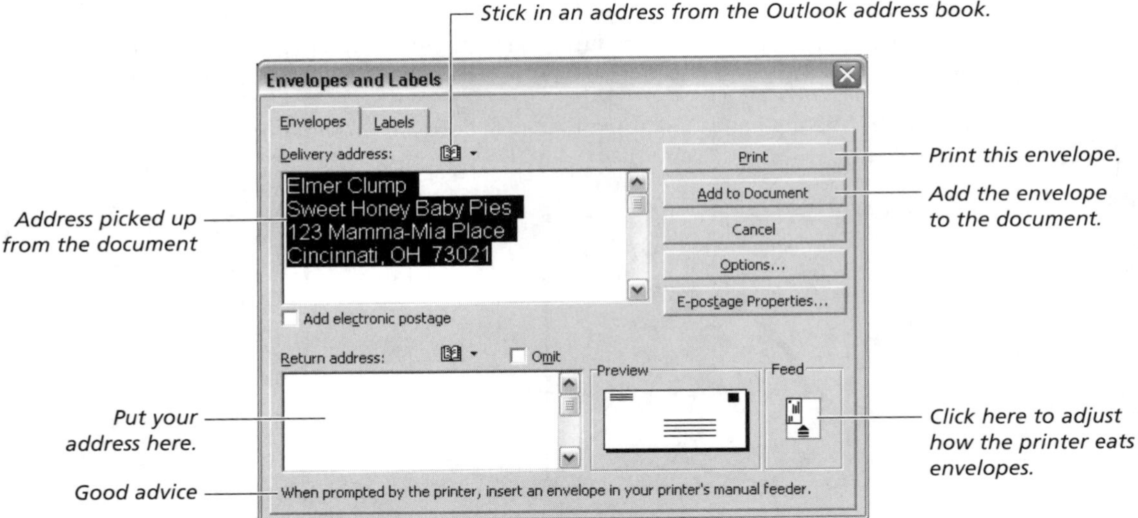

Figure 2.12 Adding an envelope

As if by magic, Word picks up the recipient's address and places it into the Envelopes and Labels dialog box, shown in Figure 2.12. If you don't see the proper address there, then Word probably couldn't locate it: Select the address in the document before you open the Envelopes and Labels dialog box. (Or you can always manually type in the address.)

What's the Difference between Inserting Today's Date and the Current Date?

Ah! A logic puzzle: The difference between today's date and the current date is that tomorrow, today's date will be yesterday's date and the current date will again be today's date.

Confused?

Let me put it another way: If you want the document to always have the date it was written, then type in *today's date*: clackity-clack-clack-clack. But if you want to have the document's date change depending on when the document is printed, then use the *current date*.

Oh, bother! This needs more explaining!

To stick today's date into a document, choose Insert ➤ Date and Time. This displays the Date and Time dialog box, shown in Figure 2.13. Pick out a date or time format, and then click the OK button.

To insert the date the document is printed, you need to use an updating *date field*. That way the document always displays the current date, no matter what. Print it today, it shows today's date. Print it in a year, it will show the date a year from now. Here is how to add such a date field to your document:

1. Position the insertion point at the spot where you want the date to appear.

2. Choose Insert ➤ Field.

3. Choose "Date and Time" from the Categories list.

4. Choose PrintDate from the Field Names list.

5a. In Word 2003/XP, choose a date format from the Field Properties column that appears.

5b. In Word 2000, click the Options button and set a format for the date in the Field Options dialog box. Click the Add to Field button, then click OK.

6. Click the OK button to insert an updating date field.

Don't be alarmed if the date field appears "blank." That's because the date value won't actually be entered until you print the document. Then, when you print, only today's date will be inserted into the document.

To delete the field, you must select it and then press the Delete key.

Also refer to Chapter 6 for more information on fields in Word documents.

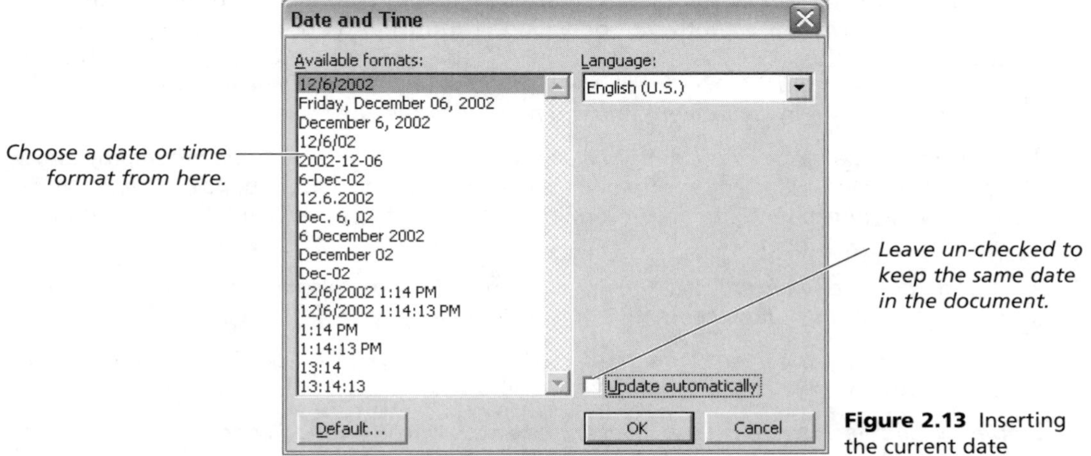

Figure 2.13 Inserting the current date

What Can I Do If I Have to Send the Same Type of Letter Over and Over?

If you find yourself re-writing the same type of letter, consider creating a document template for the letter. This is covered in Chapter 5.

If the letter merely has small parts that change, such as the recipient's personal information and perhaps a few other items, then you should do a mail merge to produce a stack of similar letters. Alas, this book does not cover mail merge; it's just too radically different for each release of Word.

For Word 2003/XP, you can refer to my web page for help on mail merge: `www.wambooli.com/help/Word/2002.mailmerge/`.

Various Spacing Tricks for Making Your Document Longer or Shorter

I'm sure you've been there. I have. It's the point where some idiot teacher or professor wants a 2,000-word report on how hairstyles influenced political reform in seventeenth-century Mongolia. Or you may be asked to write a five-page dissertation on how hip-hop music affects the mating habits of the North American honeybee. Whatever!

The following sections divulge some of what I think are the sneakiest tricks on getting more crap on the page than you could otherwise do with a typewriter. If you've ever written a two-page report and needed three pages, or needed to whittle down that five-page report to four, then this is the place to look for the best size-changing tricks.

Don't Be Dumb and Forget These Simple Re-sizing Tricks

1. *The first trick you can pull to change your document's page count is to subtly change the font size. The key is* subtly, *not obnoxiously. Most Word documents use 12-point type. Change it to 11 or 10 if you need fewer pages. To beef up the page count, change it to 13. Forget changing the font size to 14, however, as that's a dead giveaway. (Note that you can type in "between" values directly into the Font Size box.)*
2. *Switch to a smaller or larger font. Not all fonts are the same size. Some are slightly larger or smaller than others. For example, Bookman at 10 points looks about the same size as Times New Roman at 12 points. Reformatting your text to Bookman 12 pt makes the document look longer.*
3. *Adjust your page margins. Use the Page Setup dialog box to squeeze the margins in or out by quarter-inch increments.*
4. *To make a short document longer, select all the text and press Ctrl+5 to change the line spacing to ½.*
5. *Mess with the character spacing. Select the entire document and choose Format ➤ Font. Click the Character Spacing tab. From the Spacing drop-down list choose Expanded to slightly increase the document length, or choose Condensed to tighten things up. Then enter an amount to expand or tighten in the By box. Use the Preview window at the bottom of the dialog box to ensure that you don't go overboard.*
6. *Try using both paragraph-formatting techniques: Start each paragraph with a first-line indent, but also put a space between each paragraph.*
7. *To expand, use a block-quote format for quotations instead of putting the quotations inline. Or, vice versa to tighten.*
8. *To make a document longer, break it up with titles. Each title has space before and after.*

Discover the True Word Count!

Only writers care about word count, and that's because we're often paid by the word. Unlike school, when you're *paid* by the word you can never seem to find any shortage of them. In school, however, words are as rare as a full set of teeth in a Montana tattoo parlor.

To find out how many words are in your document, choose Tools ➤ Word Count. This displays a dialog box, similar to Figure 2.14, which enlightens you as to a number of document-measuring facts.

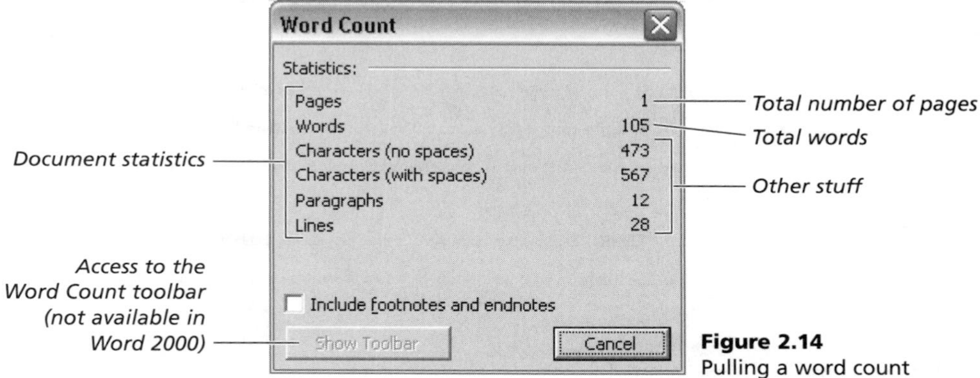

Figure 2.14
Pulling a word count

If you have Word XP or Word 11 and become grossly concerned over your document's word count, then you can use the Word Count floating toolbar to keep a constant tab on how your document is faring. To do so, choose View ➤ Toolbars ➤ Word Count. The Word Count floating toolbar appears, which you can move to any part of your document window or "dock" it next to another toolbar or the edge of the window. Figure 2.15 shows how to work the floating toolbar.

Figure 2.15 The handy Word Count floating toolbar

Does Hyphenating Help?

I recommend against using Word to hyphenate your documents. Hyphenation may, on the whole, tighten up a document. However, hyphenated documents are more difficult to read, plus it becomes more of a bother to edit the document, as well as to export the text to another application, should you ever need to do so.

What's the Difference between Adding Spaces between Lines and Adding Spaces between Paragraphs?

There are two ways to "space out" a paragraph. The first is by changing the paragraph's line spacing; the second is by adding space before or after the paragraph proper.

When you change a paragraph's line spacing, you're adding "air" between each line of the paragraph, as well as air between paragraphs. Figure 2.16 illustrates an example of double spacing, where one space is inserted between each line of the paragraph. This is setting is made in the Paragraph dialog box, as shown in Figure 2.17.

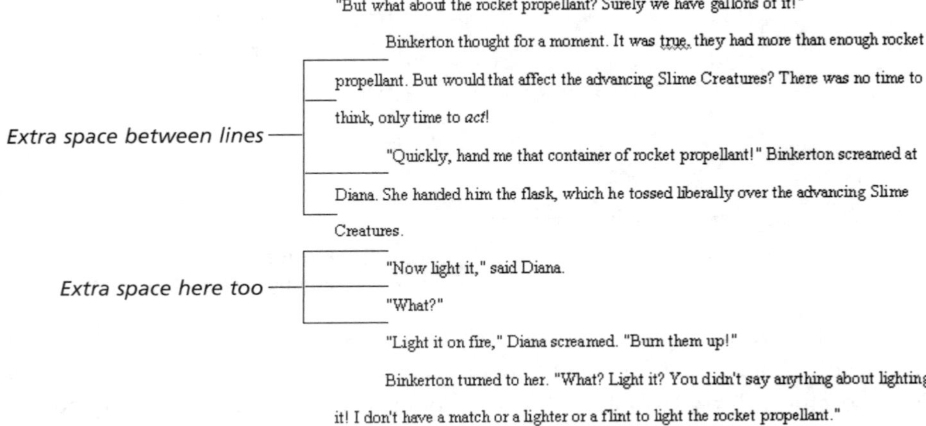

"But what about the rocket propellant? Surely we have gallons of it!"
Binkerton thought for a moment. It was true, they had more than enough rocket propellant. But would that affect the advancing Slime Creatures? There was no time to think, only time to act!
"Quickly, hand me that container of rocket propellant!" Binkerton screamed at Diana. She handed him the flask, which he tossed liberally over the advancing Slime Creatures.
"Now light it," said Diana.
"What?"
"Light it on fire," Diana screamed. "Burn them up!"
Binkerton turned to her. "What? Light it? You didn't say anything about lighting it! I don't have a match or a lighter or a flint to light the rocket propellant."
Extra space between lines
Extra space here too

Figure 2.16 How double spacing affects a paragraph's look

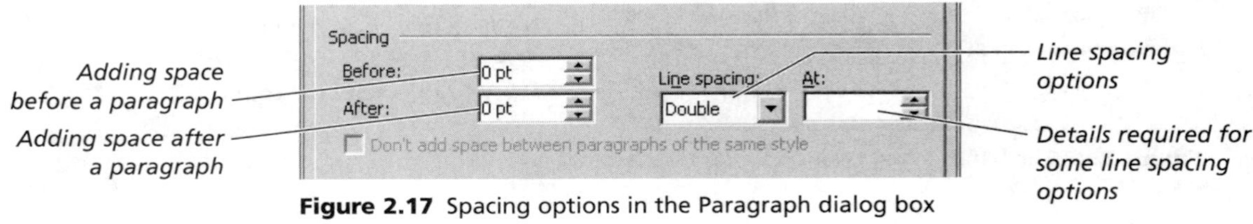

Spacing
Before:
0 pt
After:
0 pt
Line spacing:
Double
At:
Don't add space between paragraphs of the same style
Adding space before a paragraph
Adding space after a paragraph
Line spacing options
Details required for some line spacing options

Figure 2.17 Spacing options in the Paragraph dialog box

The Line Spacing drop-down list provides several options for changing line spacing, which are listed in Table 2.1.

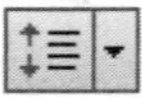

Also note that Word in Office 11 sports an interesting Line Spacing toolbar button menu, which you can use to select the line spacing for your document.

***Table 2.1** Various Line Spacing Definitions*

Line Spacing	*Keyboard Shortcut*	*Description*
Single	*Ctrl+1*	*Each line of text is on a line by itself; no blanks follow the line.*
1.5 lines	*Ctrl+5*	*Each line of text is followed by a blank line half the size.*
Double	*Ctrl+2*	*Each line of text is followed by a full-sized blank line.*
At least		*Specify a point size for spacing between the lines.*
Exactly		*Specify a point size for spacing between the lines.*
Multiple		*The At gizmo is used to select the line spacing. For example, choosing 3 from that box sets triple spacing in the document.*

Adding line spacing to the start or end of a paragraph merely adds "air" between paragraphs, not in the middle (as line spacing does). Contrast Figure 2.18 with Figure 2.16 to see an example.

"But what about the rocket propellant? Surely we have gallons of it!"
Binkerton thought for a moment. It was true, they had more than enough rocket propellant. But would that affect the advancing Slime Creatures? There was no time to think, only time to *act*!
"Quickly, hand me that container of rocket propellant!" Binkerton screamed at Diana. She handed him the flask, which he tossed liberally over the advancing Slime Creatures.
Space before appears here.
"Now light it," said Diana.
Space after comes down here.
"What?"
"Light it on fire," Diana screamed. "Burn them up!"
Binkerton turned to her. "What? Light it? You didn't say anything about lighting it! I don't have a match or a lighter or a flint to light the rocket propellant."

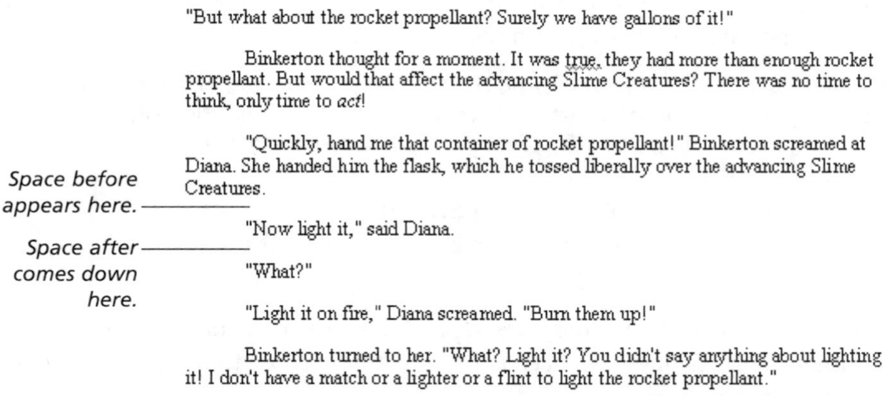

Figure 2.18 Adding air between paragraphs

Setting line spacing before or after a paragraph is done using the Spacing: Before or Spacing: After gizmos in the Paragraph dialog box (Figure 2.17).

There is no right or wrong choice with space between the lines (line spacing) or space before or after. It's more of an artistic decision on which to go for.

How Can I Quickly Change My Document from Single to Double Spacing?

The easiest way to change paragraph formatting is by using styles. When you modify a style, you modify all the paragraphs that use that style. Otherwise, you have to adjust your paragraphs manually:

1. Press Ctrl+A to select all the text in your document.

   Or you can use the mouse or any common selection technique to select the text you want to reformat.

2. Press Ctrl+2 to apply double spacing.

   Or you can use the Format ➤ Paragraph command and the Paragraph dialog box to change your text's formatting.

What's the Difference between "At Least" and "Exactly" Line Spacing?

The "At Least" option can be fudged a bit when Word needs to, whereas "Exactly" always stays the same. The only time such a difference comes into play is when you have two different fonts or two different type sizes in the same paragraph. In that case, with the "At Least" option, Word may add more space between the lines to accommodate the larger text. However, if you specify "Exactly" instead, then Word will not monkey around with the line spacing.

If it ever seems that Word is cutting off the top of your text or, more obviously, the top of a graphic, then it's most likely that the paragraph has been formatted with "Exactly" line spacing. The cure: Switch to any other form of line spacing.

Which Is Better, Space before a Paragraph or Space After?

I prefer setting extra space *after* a paragraph and not before. After all, that's how the line-spacing function operates in Word.

The only time I specify extra spacing before a paragraph is when the paragraph is a header or contains graphical or other elements that I feel need extra "breathing" room to separate themselves from the rest of the junk on the page.

Why Is There No Shortcut for Adding Space after a Paragraph?

While Word has shortcut keys for line spacing, there is no shortcut key for adding space before or after a paragraph. Sometimes I wish there was. Commonly I add six points between paragraphs. Selecting a paragraph of text and pressing, say, Ctrl+6 to add those six points would be a handy shortcut. In fact, you can create such a shortcut if you follow these steps:

1. Choose Tools ➤ Macro ➤ Record New Macro.

   The Record Macro dialog box appears. Alas, I consider macros to be an "advanced" topic, and though they are mentioned in this book, you really need a book on Office Basic or Word Basic or Visual Basic for Applications (or whatever they're calling it this week) to fully understand the bizarre complexity of macros.

2. Type `Add6pt` into the "Macro Name" text box.

   That means "Add six points after a paragraph."

3. Click the Keyboard button.

   The Customize Keyboard dialog box appears. This is where you can assign the new command—the shortcut for adding space after a paragraph—to a key combination.

   Because Ctrl+1, Ctrl+2, and Ctrl+5 each mess with a paragraph's line spacing, why not use Ctrl+6 to add six points after a paragraph?

4. Press Ctrl+6.

   The shortcut key "Ctrl+6" appears in the "Press New Shortcut Key" box. Note that Ctrl+6 is already assigned to the UnlinkFields command. That's no big deal; I don't know anyone who places a priority on that obscure command over a paragraph-formatting command.

5. Click the Assign button, then click the Close button.

   And now Word is ready to record your actions for the Macro.

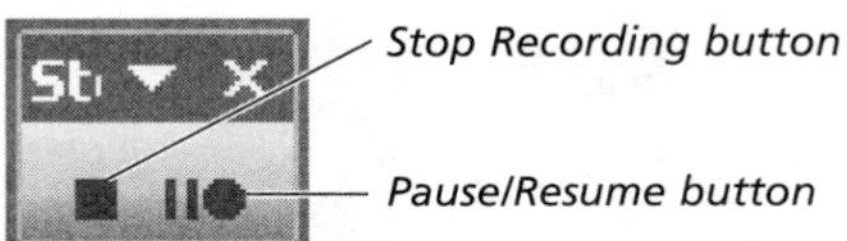

Figure 2.19 The Record Macro floating toolbar dealie

The Stop Recording floating toolbar appears, as shown in Figure 2.19. Also the mouse pointer has grown a cassette tape icon. All this reminds you that your activities in Word are now being recorded. Proceed:

6. Choose Format ➤ Paragraph.
7. In the "Spacing: After" gizmo, choose 6 pt.
8. Click OK.
9. Click the Stop button on the Stop Recording floating toolbar (Figure 2.19).

   Now the macro has been recorded and assigned to shortcut key Ctrl+6. But before leaving it at that, you need to (unfortunately) go in and clean up all the crap Word put into the macro:

10. Choose Tools ➤ Macro ➤ Macros.

    The Macros dialog box appears with a list of available macros. Unless you've messed with macros before, you should see only one, Add6pt.

11. Select the Add6pt macro.
12. Click the Edit button.

    Word runs the Microsoft Visual Basic editor, which should shock and appall you, but that's okay; remember this book is not about macros.

    The problem with the recorded macro is *too much freaking information*, which is typical of many things Office applications create. (Don't get me started on the excess information that happens when you save a Word document as a web page!)

    The idea here is to trim out the unneeded information and leave the macro with only the instructions required to add six points to the butt end of a paragraph. To meet that end:

13. Edit the macro down so that it looks like this and only this:

```
Sub Add6pt()
'
' add6p Macro
' Macro recorded 4/8/04 by Dan Gookin
'
    With Selection.ParagraphFormat
        .SpaceAfter = 6
    End With
End Sub
```

    Just delete all the other crap. If it's not listed above, delete it. (Do note that the line about the macro recorded will be specific for your computer; there's no need to change it.)

14. When you've finished with the changes, choose File ➤ Close and Return to Microsoft Word.

And now you've finished!

To demonstrate the macro, click on a paragraph or select several paragraphs. Then press Ctrl+6. That changes the paragraph's formatting so that it's followed by six points of space—a great trick to use when trying to provide more breathing room on a page full of paragraphs.

3 Making Your Documents and Reports More Fancy

Sure, anyone can word process. It's just like anyone can use a typewriter. In fact, typing class traditionally did not teach you how to operate the typewriter. No, it taught you how to operate it *quickly*. Any old dolt could figure out how to jam a sheet of paper into a typewriter, how to type, and that the "ding" of the little bell meant you had to start a new line—and even that aspect of the typewriter was easy to figure out.

Word processors lack all the moving parts of a typewriter. Even so, just about anyone can cobble together a document by using the alphanumeric keys on the keyboard, plus Backspace and Enter. Oh, and the Tab key (if they're clever). But you bought this book because you suspected there was more. And there is!

But now, after reading this chapter, you'll be able to spruce up your boring old report or document with some spiffy new pages, the kind of things that would take those casual word processing folk *years* to figure out. But you don't need years, only the handy information contained in this chapter!

Myths Exploded and Fantasies Unfolded:

- Getting the special page thing to happen with sections
- Using sections to control page formatting
- Creating title pages
- Working with page numbers
- Sticking relative page numbers into a document
- Renumbering, un-numbering, and generally becoming numb

How Do You Know a Special Page When You See One?

Special pages are easy to spot *after* they've been created. They give you that sense of "how the heck did they do that?" The answer is "simply." But the reason is, "Because I took some vaguely defined Word commands and put them to use so I could create something unique in my document to make it look better than your document." That's when you go "Oh!" and scurry off to try the trick for yourself.

But don't scurry off just yet! The following sections demonstrate how to create those special pages in any document. They use some obscure or obscurely named Word commands to do it—stuff you may already be familiar with but never new the full potential of.

Why Do I Need to Know about Sections?

When you scratch Word's formatting abilities just below the surface you'll find boundaries. Character formatting, for example, applies only to text: Font, size, attributes, and all that are applied only to characters.

Beyond character formatting is paragraph formatting. There are certain formatting commands that apply only to paragraphs: Center, Justify, Indent, and so on.

Above character formatting is page formatting, where you set page margins, headers, footers, and other formats applied to the page.

Above the page formatting? Is there anything there?

You bet! It's where you'll find *sections*. By using sections, you can divide up your document's pages by shifting the page format. So if you need a page centered here, you create a new section. If you need a page printed in landscape orientation there, then you apply a section.

Sections are the largest chunk you can format in any document.

Figure 3.1 illustrates a document with several sections in it. It's tiny, but still you can see how each section holds its own page formatting. The formatting for the page in one section doesn't affect the formatting in another. Once you know this, then you can take advantage of it to really spice up your documents.

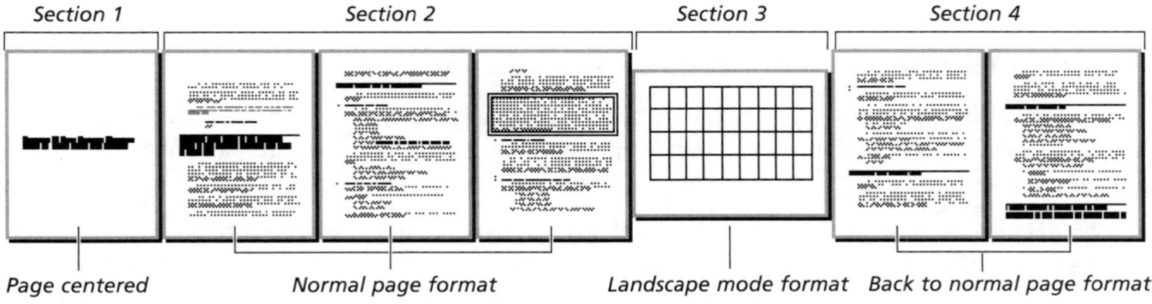

Figure 3.1 Various sections in a document

How Can I Create a New Section?

Sections are created using the Break dialog box. It's weird that a computer program would have a Break dialog box? You'd think the idea would be to *not* break things, but no. Or could it be "break" as in break up the text into chunks? Hmmm...

Choose Insert ➤ Break from the menu, and you'll see a dialog box similar to the one shown in Figure 3.2. There you have a choice of page or section breaks, as described in the figure.

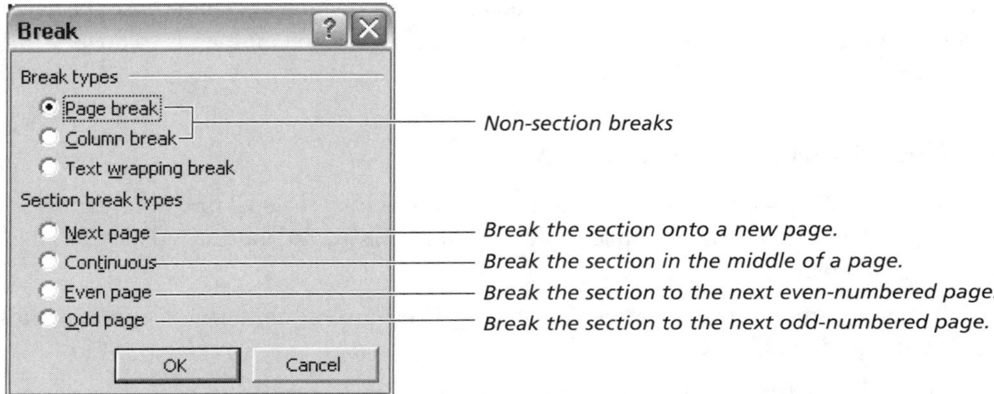

Figure 3.2 Sections are created here.

Only the Continuous option doesn't create a hard page break. And the Even and Odd section breaks will insert blank pages to line up the section break properly. (The Even and Odd options are best used when you're creating documents with different even and odd page formats.)

Of course, the key question is "Why bother?" but that's covered over the next few pages of this chapter.

How Can I Tell Which Section I'm In?

Page 2 Sec 2 2/2

Sections are listed on the status bar with the abbreviation *Sec*. Normally documents have one section, Sec 1. But when you mess with sections, your document can have a bunch of them. That Sec thing on the status bar lets you know which one you're working in.

How Can I Center My Title Page Top to Bottom?

The ideal title page appears as its own section in a document. That way you can use the page-formatting command that centers text from top to bottom on that page and not have it affect other pages in your document. Yes, indeed, a title page is a *special page*.

The typical yet incorrect way to create a title page is to first write the page, insert a hard page break, and then write the rest of the document. The result looks like Figure 3.3, which may be what you want. Alas, many Word users attempt to manually center the text by whacking the Enter key until the title looks more or less centered. In a word processor, that's a "bad thing" to do.

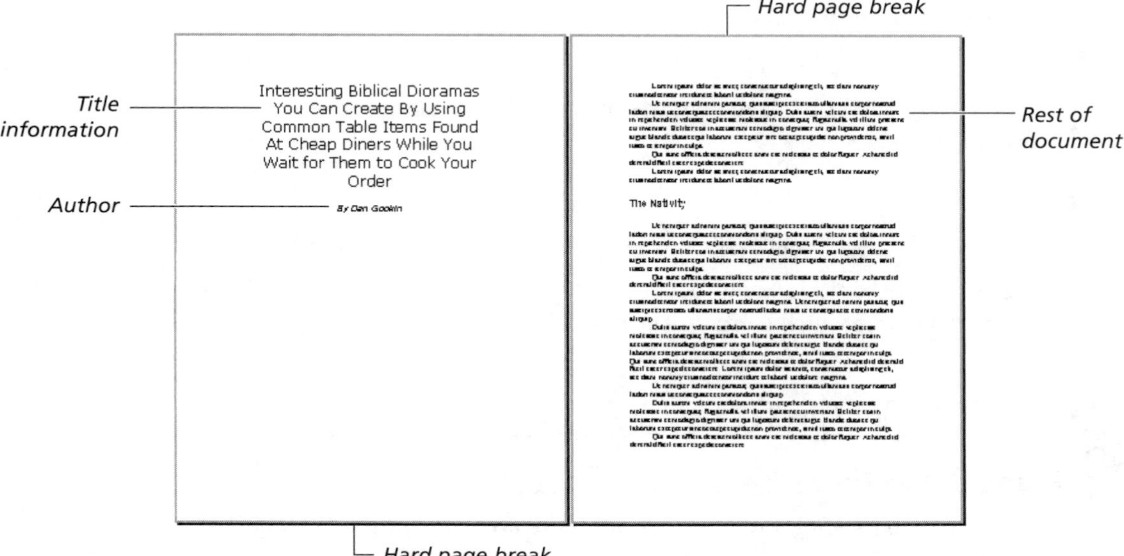

Figure 3.3 A typical title page

The good thing to do is to use a section break to separate the title page from the rest of the document. This is so close to what most people attempt to do that the difference isn't worth mentioning, but the benefits are huge. Here's how it works:

1. Type the title page.

   Just type the text.

   If you've already typed the title page, then delete it (and the hard page break, if there). Start over.

Most titles are centered. Use the Ctrl+E shortcut to center a paragraph. To double-space the paragraph, use Ctrl+2.

2. After typing the title, choose Insert ➤ Break.
3. Choose "Next Page" to create a page break and a new section.
4. Click OK.

   So far the section break is merely the same as a page break. Only by applying a different page formatting to the title page will the section break really help with formatting.

5. Click the mouse on your title page.

   You're about to reformat the page attributes for the title page.

6. Choose File ➤ Page Setup.

7. Click the Layout tab.
8. In the Page: Vertical Alignment area, choose Center from the drop-down list.

   It will likely say "Top" there now, which is how Word aligns text on the page, from the top down.
9. Click OK.

   And now the title is centered. You can use Print Preview to confirm this.

Because you built the title page into its own section, its attributes (centered) are not carried over into the next section, which contains the bulk of your document's text.

KEYBOARD MASTER

Some Title Page Keyboard Shortcuts

Whether you're heeding my advice or not, here are some of the keyboard shortcuts you can use to help you create a title page:

Ctrl+Enter

A "hard page break," this keyboard shortcut forces an immediate new page in the document. (It can be deleted using Backspace or Delete just as any other "character" can be removed in a document.)

Ctrl+E

Center a paragraph of text.

Alt+I, B, N, Enter

Insert a Next Page section break; better than using Ctrl+Enter when you want to set a title page.

Ctrl+F, U

Display the Page Setup dialog box, where most page setting options are made, the options that can affect only one section if you wish them to.

But I Don't Want a Page Number, Header, or Footer on My Title Page!

Like the ancient word processing nobles they are, page numbers, headers, and footers are wise and respect the section break boundaries. As long as your title page is created as its own section in a document, then you can halt any headers, footers, or page numbers from appearing on that page.

To suppress a page number on the first page, follow these steps:

1. Click the mouse on the first page.

2. Choose Insert ➤ Page Numbers.
3. Remove the check mark by "Show Number on First Page."
4. Click OK.

If that doesn't work, then the page number probably lives on a header or footer, so you'll need to suppress the header and footer for the first page/section. Here's how that works:

1. Choose View ➤ Header and Footer.

   The Header and Footer floating palette appears over your document (Figure 3.4), and the Header or Footer window appears on your document inside of Word.

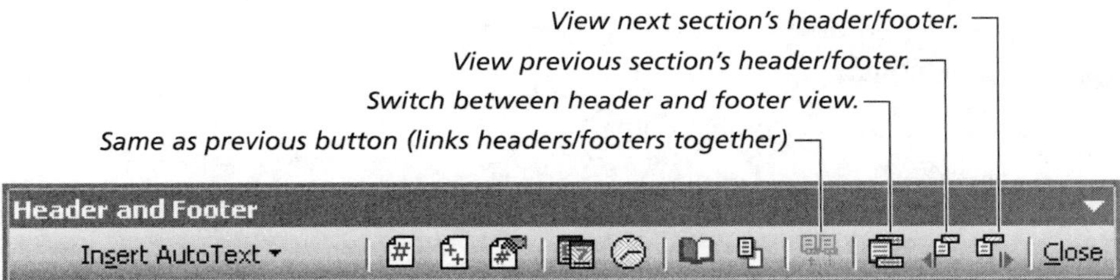

Figure 3.4 The Header and Footer floating palette thing

   Right now, the header is probably the same for all sections. Which means the header for Section 1 (on the title page) is also used for Section 2.

2. Visit the Section 2 header.

   Click the Show Next button to see "Header - Section 2". If it says, "Same as Previous," then you need to copy the header (and footer) from Section 1 into Section 2. That can be involved, so carefully follow these steps:

   a. Click the Show Previous button to return to Section 1, where the title page lurks.
   b. Select all the text in the header (use Ctrl+A).
   c. Cut the text from the header (with Ctrl+X).

   d. Click the Show Next button on the toolbar.

   e. Click the Same As Previous button. This "unlinks" the header text between the two sections.
   f. Press Ctrl+V to paste the header text into Section 2's header.

The reason these extra steps (above) are required is that otherwise the header is lost when you click the Same as Previous button. Therefore you must cut and paste it before you unlink.

g. Repeat steps A through E for the footer as well. Click the Switch Between Header and Footer button to do this.

If the Header doesn't say "Same as Previous," then follow these steps:

a. Click the Show Previous button to see Section 1's header.

b. Delete all the text in Section 1's header.

c. Switch to view the footer.

d. Delete any text in the footer.

3. Close the Header and Footer toolbar when you've finished.

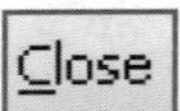

I've never seen such a mess as can be created with the Same as Previous button in a header or footer. While that option may seem nice—and it is most of the time—it does create problems when you have to suppress the header and footer for a section and then resume it. In those cases, as outlined above, it's best just to copy the entire header (and footer) from one section to another and avoid using the Same as Previous trick altogether.

How Can I Put a Border around Just the Title?

Want a border around your title to make it look sharp? Try these steps:

1. Select your title text.

2. Choose Format ➢ Borders and Shading.

The Borders and Shading dialog box appears, detailed in Figure 3.5.

3. For a quick border, double-click one of the options on the left side of the dialog box: Box, Shadow, or 3-D.

Otherwise, you can mess with the settings in the Borders and Shading dialog box to get the kind of effect you want.

4. Click OK and see how it looks.

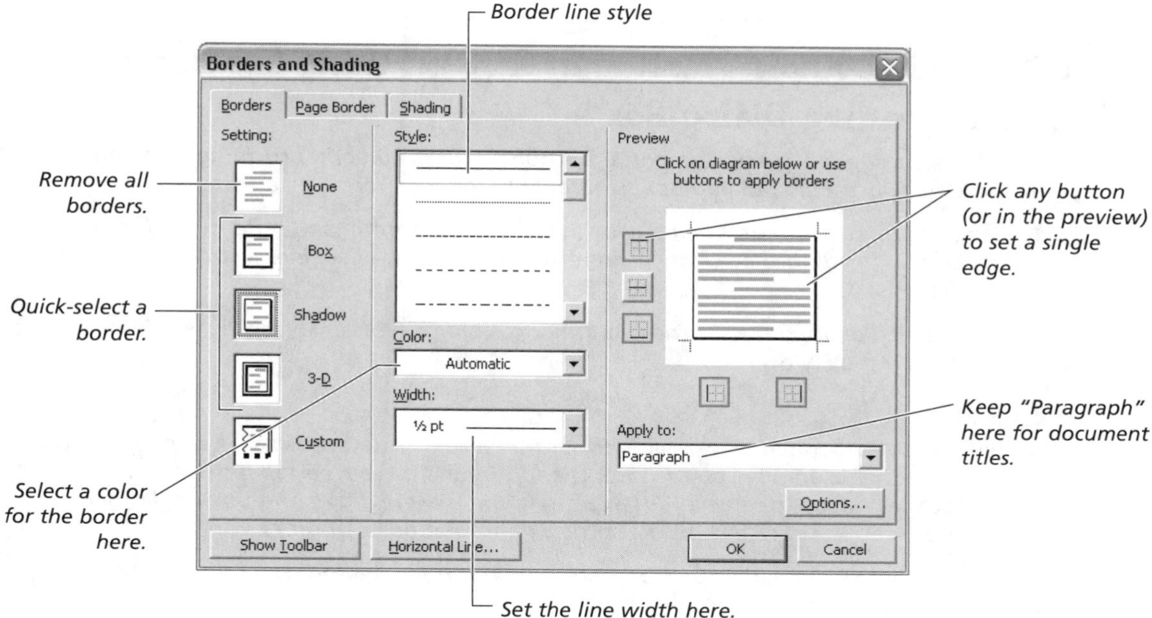

Figure 3.5 Applying a border to your document's title

Don't Be Dumb and Load Up Your Headers or Footers with Useless Junk.

True, you can put a lot of information into a header or footer—even graphics. I've done that myself when I run out of letterhead, but for complex documents it's best to keep the header or footer information limited.

If you haven't noticed, Word automatically formats each header and footer with left, center, and right tabs. So you can use these tabs to automatically position a page number or other information without having to redo the formatting. Instead, just use the Tab key.

The most complex header/footer arrangement I've used is like this:

Header: My name, [tab], Project name, [tab], Date

So my name is on the left, the project name is centered, and the date is flush right in the header. And then:

Footer: Chapter name, [tab], [tab], Page number

The chapter name is on the left, nothing is centered, and the page number is on the right.

Obviously, you can mix and match this information anyway you see fit. Just keep in mind that Word has already set the tabs up for you.

You Must Know This: Handy Tips on Using the Borders and Shading Dialog Box

You can get quite fancy with the borders around your document, providing that you work the Borders and Shading dialog box (Figure 3.5) properly. Here's my advice:

1. *Select a line style. There are many of them to choose from, and note that all four sides of the text need not have a style. For example, you can have lines just on the top or bottom.*
2. *Choose a color, if you wish. The "Automatic" color is typically black, or whatever color is defined by the Style.*
3. *Select a width or thickness for your border.*
4. *Click a button around the Preview to set the border. You can click one or more buttons at a time. For example, you can click the top button to set the top border and then repeat these steps to select a different style for the left, right, and bottom borders. Likewise, you can click a button a second time to remove a border.*

Most importantly: Remember that borders need not be on all four sides and that borders can be of different styles, if you wish.

Can I Color the Space inside the Border?

To add color to the box around your border, click the Shading tab in the Borders and Shading dialog box (Figure 3.5). Choose a color from the Fill area, or use a pattern from the Patterns: Style drop-down list.

Note that when you color the background of an area, you may also want to color the text. If so, select the title text and choose Format ➤ Font. Then use the Font Color drop-down list in the Font dialog box to color your text something that offsets the background color.

Any Way to Have a Block of Color without the Border?

After coloring the border's contents (according to the previous section), select your border text and return to the Borders and Shading dialog box. In the Borders tab of the dialog box, choose white from the Color drop-down list. (Or choose whichever color matches the paper color.) That effectively hides the lines around the border and leaves you with just a color block of text around your document's title.

How Do I Remove the Border When I Sicken of It?

To remove the border and all its attributes, select your document's title text and choose Format ➤ Borders and Shading. In the Borders tab of the dialog box, choose None from the left side; then click OK.

To remove color, you'll need to re-visit the Borders and Shading dialog box, click the Shading tab, and choose "No Fill" as the Fill color. Click OK.

Is There Any Way to Make the Title Border Box Taller or Wider or of a Different Shape?

The simplest way to put a box around any text is to use Word's Drawing toolbar and just draw a stupid square, rectangle, or other shape in your document, and then shove that shape "behind" the text. This eases a lot of the hassles associated with drawing a border using the Borders and Shading dialog box. For more information, refer to the Chapter 4, "O the Sacrilege of Drawing in a Word Processor," which covers drawing things in a document.

Why Can't I Put a Border around the Entire Page?

The secret to putting a border around a page in Word is to measure the border from the *text* and not the edge of the page. That's where most people screw up.

For example, most people can figure out how to put a border around a page using these steps:

1. Put the insertion pointer thing on the page you want to border.

   It works best if the page is its own section, though that's not a hard-and-fast rule.

2. Choose Format ➢ Borders and Shading.
3. Click the Page Border tab.
4. Work the dialog box's controls to configure what type, style, and color of border you want on the page.

   Refer to Figure 3.5 for the details.

5. Click the Options button.
6. Choose Text from the Measure From drop-down list.

   Ah-ha! This is the secret. If you choose "Edge of Page," then often the page border won't print. (Don't ask me why.)

7. Click OK to close the various dialog boxes.

Now your page has a proper border around it.

The Page Border tab in the Borders and Shading dialog box is a close duplicate of Figure 3.5. Note that there is also an Art drop-down list that allows you to create a border out of cutesy little images in addition to boring lines.

How Can I Paste This Excel Worksheet into Its Own Page?

To make the pasted Excel information, or really any information—an image, table, or what have you—appear on its own page, simply create that page as a section unto itself.

Start the page by choosing Insert ➢ Break and choose "Next Page" as the section break. Then put whatever information you want onto that page.

End the page by choosing Insert ➢ Break, then "Next Page" to create the end of the section and the continuation of the rest of your document.

The section sits by itself, like the Section 3 example shown in Figure 3.1. Any page formatting you change for that section applies only to that single page.

There's a Wacky Landscape Mode Page in the Middle of This Document!

Because each section in a document can contain its own page formatting, you can easily swap page orientation by selecting a Landscape layout from the Page Setup dialog box and applying it to that section only. Refer to the previous section for an explanation of why this is so. To change your page orientation, choose File ➤ Page Setup, and then choose Portrait or Landscape from the Margins or Paper Size tab, depending on your version of Word. Remember to choose "This Section" from the Apply To drop-down list before you click OK!

NERD'S CORNER

Cocktail Party Trivia, Part II

MARY: Oh, Phyllis is so loopy!

MARK: What has she done now?

MARY: She read that bit about putting a Landscape mode page in the middle of a document, and do you know what she did instead?

MARK: No, I still don't know.

MARY: (Gasping for air.) It's so funny! You tell, John!

JOHN: Okay.

MARK: John, what is it that Phyllis did that Mary is asphyxiating herself over?

JOHN: Rather simple—she used a section break to change the paper size in the middle of a document. So halfway through her document, the paper size changes from letter to legal and then back again.

MARK: Oh, that Phyllis is so loopy!

JOHN: Actually, Mark, she isn't. It's yet another thing you can do with section breaks. After all, paper size is a page attribute and can be set (somewhere) in the Page Setup dialog box.

MARY: Okay. Then tell me this, how will the printer stretch the paper to suddenly create legal size?

JOHN: Ha-ha. Now you're being silly, Mary. Most of today's printers are smart enough to recognize the change. They will prompt the user to change paper sources in the middle of the print run, either through an intelligent control panel or by beeping.

MARK: So Phyllis isn't such a loop after all?

JOHN: Certainly not! Ha-ha.

EVERYONE: Ha-ha.

The Woes of Numbering Pages

One of my most dreadful word processing memories occurred when I saw a friend working painfully on a report. "I thought you were finished with that," I remarked. He said he was, but "I had to change something so I'm going through and renumbering the pages."

ARGH!

Yes, he manually numbered each page at the bottom. When he added text, he had to go through and wiggle every sentence so that the new page numbers fit. What agonizing torture! I'd rather be forced to sit through nine hours of ballet than manually renumber pages in a word processor!

I certainly hope that no one out there is manually numbering pages. Heaven forbid! If there were a Top Ten list of word processing crimes, then manually numbering pages would be in the top three. Fortunately, you know more than the average user, right? If not, then the following sections of page-numbering tips and information will most definitely help.

How Can I Put the Page Number Right Here?

The key to blissful page numbering in Word is the Insert ➤ Page Numbers command, which summons the highly useful Page Numbers dialog box, shown in Figure 3.6.

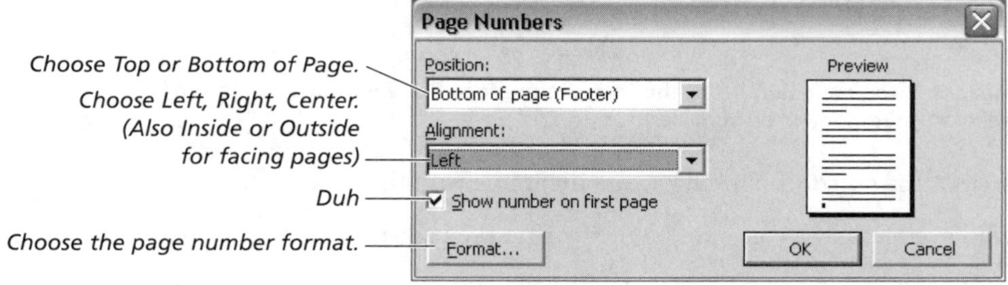

Figure 3.6 Setting the page number, the simple way

So if you want the page number to be in the bottom center, you choose "Bottom of Page (Footer)" from the Position drop-down list, then Center from the Alignment drop-down list. Click OK and you're finished. Simple.

But I Want the Page Number to Have Little Hyphens on Each Side!

No problem! The Insert ➤ Page Numbers command really—and this is top secret—simply sticks the proper header or footer commands into your document. To "fix" the page number, you merely have to edit the header or footer after you insert the page number (per the previous section's instructions). Here's how:

1. Follow the steps in the previous section.

   Even though the steps weren't numbered, they're in there.

2. Choose View ➤ Header and Footer from the menu.

   The Header and Footer toolbar appears, you're switched to Print Preview mode (if you weren't in it before), and the header area for the page is highlighted.

3. If the page number is in the footer, then click the Switch button on the toolbar.

   The page number appears in the header or footer as you specified it. But note that the page number is not plain text. No, it appears inside a *frame*, which is Word's way of protecting the page number from the rest of the header or footer. It's not a problem, but it helps if you recognize this deception before you get all kooky trying to figure it out on your own.

4. Click on the page number to select its frame.

   The page number appears within the frame's shaded box, as shown in Figure 3.7.

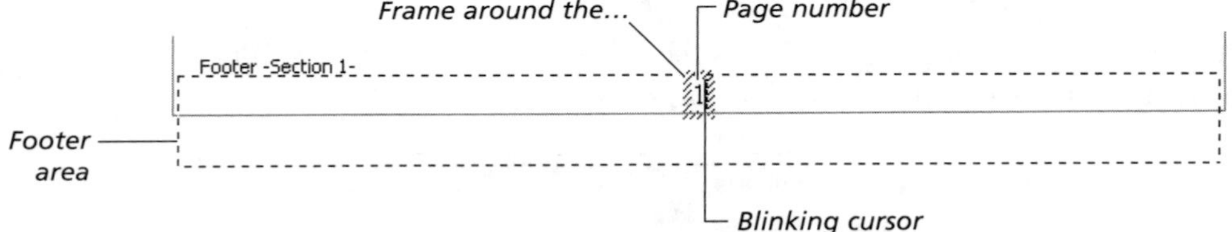

Figure 3.7 The page number in the frame in the footer in your document on the screen on your monitor on your desk

5. Click so that the cursor is blinking inside the frame with the page number.

6. Type whatever gewgaws you want before or after the page number.

   Such as hyphens or underlines or whatever. You'll notice if you move the cursor over the page number that it becomes shaded. That's because it's not a number at all, but a *field* designed to show the current page. So it's really a page number in a field in a frame in the footer in your document on the screen on your monitor on your desk.

7. Click the Close button on the Header and Footer toolbar to return to your regularly scheduled document.

For any further fancy page-numbering stuff, I recommend that you simply create a page number in a header or footer. That way you can add whatever text you want around the page number without having to bother with frames and fields and such. Refer to the section later in this chapter titled "How Do You Do the 'Page X out of N Total Pages' Thing in a Document?" for an example.

Is There Any Way I Can Put "This Is Page Number X" in the Middle of a Document?

Page numbers need not be limited to headers or footers. For example, if you want to say, "Here you are, gentle reader, on page 63 and you still haven't fallen asleep!" Then all you need to do is stick a page number field into your document at the proper spot. Obey these steps:

1. Choose Insert ➤ Field.

   Ah, the secret: fields. Love fields.

2. Choose Numbering from the Categories list.
3. Choose Page from the Field Names list.
4. Click OK.

Because the page number is a field and not just a number you stick into the document, it updates itself as you add or remove text. The page number field *always* reflects the current page number, regardless of what else you do.

I Need to Refer to Something on Another Page by That Page Number, Whatever It Will Be!

Referring to a page number is best done by inserting a field. But in this case, if you're referring to a page other than the current one, you must refer to something interesting on that second page. In this case, that something interesting can be a bookmark.

After setting a bookmark on a page, you can then reference the bookmark's page number with a field. You can stick that field on any other page, which is—in a roundabout and illogical way—exactly what you need!

Okay. It sounds complex, but it's really not—providing you follow these steps:

1. Go to the page that has the text you're referencing.

   For example, it's a citation from Evil Lord Cromth, who states that he will suck all the atmosphere from planet Jaredollo.

2. Select the text you're citing.

   Or if it's a lot of text, just click the mouse so that the insertion point is blinking at the start of the text.

3. Choose Insert ➤ Bookmark.
4. Name the bookmark.

   Argh! No spaces in a bookmark name! So be clever when you name this reference—especially if you have other bookmarks in the document. Be brief and concise, just as Lord Cromth was when he threatened the Jaredollons.

5. Click the Add button.
6. Return to the page where you need to reference the bookmark's page.
7. Choose Insert ➤ Field.
8. Choose "Links and References" from the Categories list.
9. Choose PageRef from the Field Names list.

10a. In Word 2003/XP, choose the bookmark name from the Bookmark Name list.

10b. In Word 2000, click the Options button, and then click the Bookmarks tab. Select your bookmark from the list, and click the Add to Field button. Click OK.

11. Click OK.

    A page number is inserted into the document, which references the bookmarked text you have elsewhere in the document.

When bookmarking in Word, mark the start of the text. So if you're flagging a particularly long section of information, simply place the bookmark where that text starts. The start of the information is typically what a reader is interested in locating, not the middle or end of the text.

I Need to Restart Page Numbering Here!

Restarting page numbering is simple—providing that you've already inserted page numbers into your document and you create a new section break where you want the page numbering to restart. Observe these steps:

1. Move to the top of the page where numbering is to restart.
2. Choose Insert ➤ Break.
3. Select Next Page.
4. Click OK.

   This creates a new section break to start your page renumbering. Page renumbering will not work unless you stick a new section in there. And that makes sense because numbering is a page-formatting deal, and sections break up page formatting.

   (You may optionally have to "clean up" after inserting a section break. If so, place the insertion point at the start of the section's text, and then press the Backspace key until the start of the text aligns with the top of the new page/section break.)

5. Choose Insert ➤ Page Numbers.
6. Click the Format button.

7. Click the Start At button.

8. Enter the new page number.

   For example, if you want to start over with page 1, type a 1 into the box, as shown in Figure 3.8.

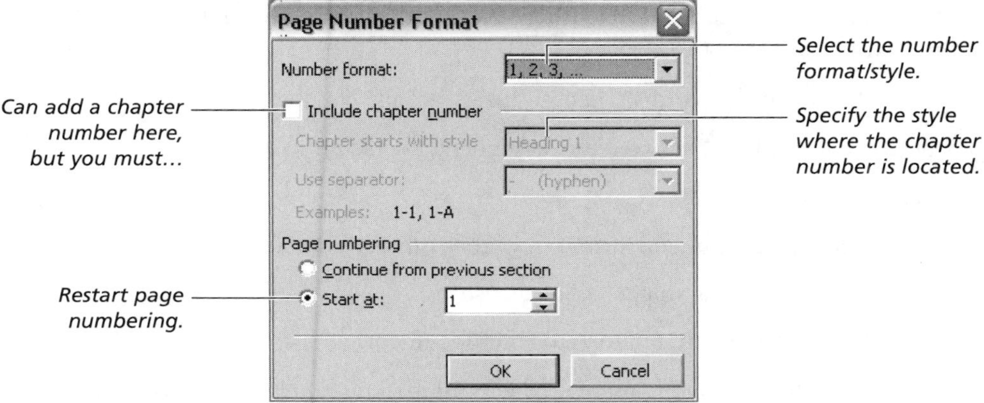

Figure 3.8 Formatting your page numbers

9. Click OK, then OK again to return to your document.

The new page number values appear in the header/footer, or in any page number fields you may have in that section of your document. Do note, however, that the status bar still reflects absolute page numbers from the start of your document.

How Can I Start My Document at Page 72?

Documents can start page numbering at any value. Doing so doesn't even require any sections:

1. Choose Insert ➤ Page Number to place the page numbers in your document's header or footer.

   This is how it's normally done. But then:

2. Click the Format button.

3. Click the Start At button.

4. Enter the starting page number in the Start At button's box.

   Type in a number or use the gizmo to select a number with the mouse. (It's quicker to just type in a number, such as 72.)

5. Click OK, then OK again to get back to your document.

Now your entire document starts page numbering at whatever number you chose.

How Can I Number the First Six Pages with Roman Numerals and Then Number the Rest of My Document Normally Starting with Page 1?

It's common to number a document's introduction using Roman numerals and then restart numbering when the "real" text starts. This is easy enough to do in Word, providing you use the Roman numerals in one section and then restart the page numbering with regular numbers in the next section. Easy peasy lemon squeezy:

1. At the start of your document, choose Insert ➤ Page Numbers.
2. Choose the page number's position, alignment, and so on.
3. Click the Format button.
4. Choose the Roman numeral format from the Number Format drop-down list.

   That would be i, ii, iii in upper- or lowercase.
5. Click OK, then OK again to return to your document.

   Now the document is being numbered with Roman numerals, which is cute up to a point. (Do you realize that only up until a few hundred years ago that all math was done with Roman numerals?)
6. Move to the point in your document where you want to restart numbering with non-Roman numerals.
7. Insert a section break on the next page.

   Choose Insert ➤ Break, and choose Next Page as the break's location. Click OK.

   You'll notice that the new section automatically resets the page numbers back to 1, or "i" in this case.
8. Choose Insert ➤ Page Numbers and click the Format button again.
9. Choose the standard 1, 2, 3 page numbers from the Number Format drop-down list.
10. Click OK, then OK again to return to your document.

And now the second section of your document has standard numbering.

NERD'S CORNER

The Horror of Roman Numerals!

You think math is bad now? Consider doing math in Roman numerals! That may seem insane, but it was the way most math was done in Europe until about the seventeenth century or so. And the practice continues: Witness the copyright date on many important documents (and even films) is still done using Roman numerals.

How Do You Do the "Page X out of N Total Pages" Thing in a Document?

I typically show the "page X out of N" thing in a document's footer, as opposed to using the Insert ➤ Page Numbers command. So if you've already started with the Page Numbers command, go back and remove the page numbers, and then follow these steps to stick the page number into a document's footer:

1. Choose View ➤ Header and Footer from the menu.

   The view switches to Print Layout view, the Header and Footer toolbar shows up (Figure 3.4), and you see the header for your document outlined on the screen.

2. Click the Switch button to see the document's footer.

   Or skip this step if you want to put the page numbering in the header instead.

3. If you want the page number centered, press the Tab key.

   Or if you want it right-justified, press the Tab key twice.

4. To insert the current page number, click the Insert Page Number button.

   If you need to type any text before this, then type the text before clicking the button, such as `This is page`, followed by a space; then click the Insert Page Number button.

5. Type any text you want to appear between the current page number and last page number.

   For example, `out of`, as in "This is page X out of N." Or sometimes I just use a slash to separate the values, as in "3/9."

6. Click the Insert Number of Pages button.

   And that inserts the final page number of your document, whatever that number may be.

7. Type any extra text you want.

8. Click the Close button when you've finished.

If you want to include information similar to this in the body of your document, then you merely need to use the NumPages field, which is found in the Document Information category. NumPages is equal to the total number of pages in a document. Combine that with the Page field (from the Numbering category), and you can include the text "This is page X out of N" anywhere in your document.

4

Oh the Sacrilege of Drawing in a Word Processor!

It's a left-brain/right-brain thing. On the left side you have logic, calm, and collected. It's words. Colorless, plain, formal, and stiff on the page, the words march relentlessly from sentence to paragraph to page, expressing ideas using cool intelligence expressing rational ideas. It is order. It is peace. It is calm, clear-blue waters.

Then there's the wild party that's taking place in the right brain, just a hemisphere away. It's loud. It's exploding with color. It's a daring psychic roller coaster with manic highs and accelerated screams, dipping into the dismal darkness of despair painted with the mud-colored ink of the despondent artist. It is chaos. It is insanity. It is the churning, hot frothy blood of passion erupting into a boil.

Obviously, mixing the two sides of the human brain would be like pouring matter into antimatter, yielding the explosive power that hurtles the USS Enterprise through the far reaches of space. Or it could just be one of those rare and interesting things that Word does when it attempts to cross the synaptic boundary between the left-brained word processor and the right-brained art program. This chapter shows you how to use those tools to improve the way your stuff looks.

Logic Explored and Passions Exploded:

- Breaking up text with boxes, circles, and shapes

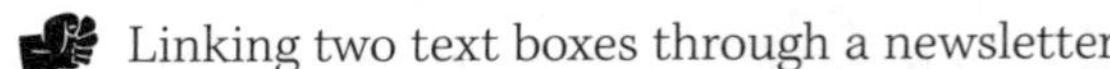

- Linking two text boxes through a newsletter
- Carefully wrapping text around an image
- Using captions
- Rotating, cropping, resizing, and relocating images
- Making more interesting document titles

Adding Pizzazz with a Text Box

The text box is one of those cute little things you can stick into a document that just blows people away. They're totally unaware that Word is capable of sticking text into a tidy square container, separate and free from the rest of the document. It's a handy trick to know, and one that if used well can really impress your friends and foes alike.

How Can a "Pull Quote" Make My Documents More Interesting?

Figure 4.1 illustrates what I refer to as a *pull-quote*. It's a box of text in the middle of an otherwise boring page of text. It usually contains a quote pulled from somewhere else on the page (get it?), but the quote is larger, bolder, and more prominent than the boring text around it. Pull quotes serve the dual function of breaking up a solid page of text as well as drawing attention to the text from someone who may just be skimming.

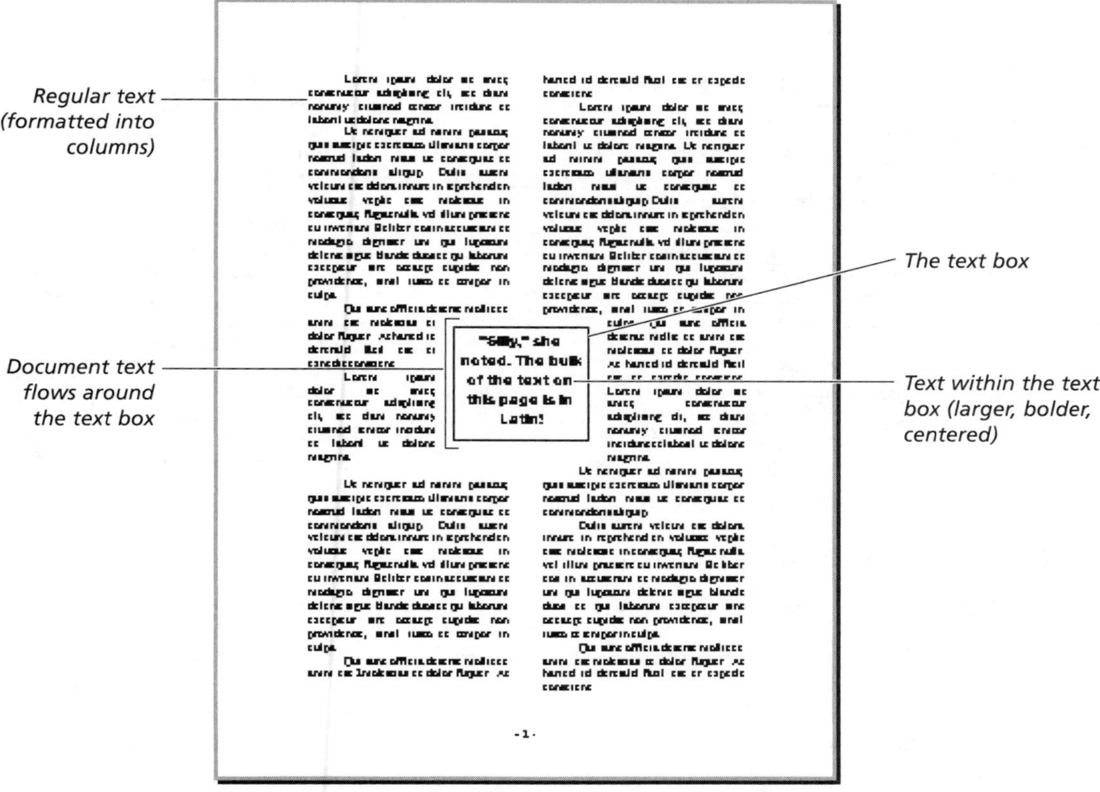

Figure 4.1 A pull quote in the middle of a page of text

Follow these steps to splash down a text box in your document, similar to what you see in Figure 4.1:

1. Choose Insert ➤ Text Box.

   The view switches to Print Layout, which is best for dealing with the taboo of non-text items in a document.

2. In Word 2003/XP, press the Delete key to remove the Drawing Canvas.

   The Drawing Canvas allows you to place several text boxes or other graphical objects into the same area for easy control, but it's unnecessary (and bothersome) for a single text box.

   + Note how the mouse pointer is now a large plus sign.

3. Draw the text box by using the mouse.

   Drag the mouse to make the text box appear in the size and position you desire. Don't worry about specifics just yet; it can be sloppy.

   When you release the mouse button, the text box appears right over the top of the text, as shown in Figure 4.2. This is okay.

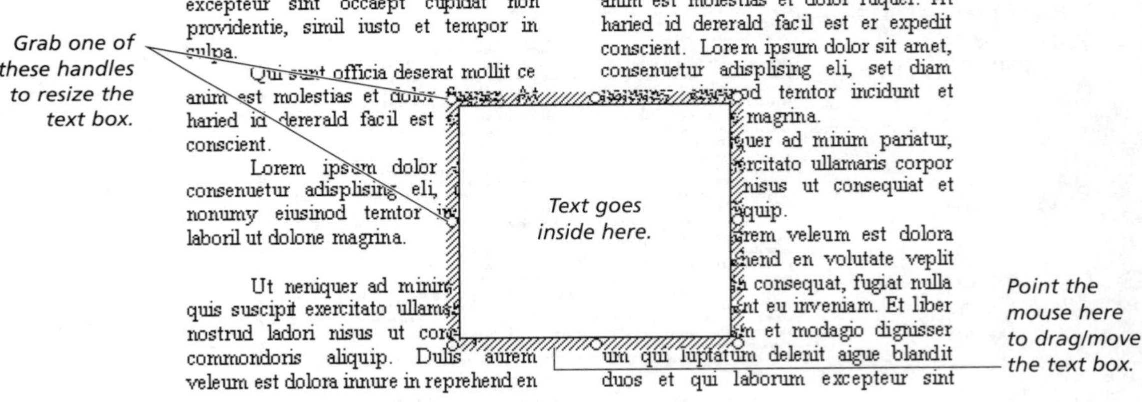

Figure 4.2 The text box awaits action in your document.

4. Type and format the text inside the box.

   Pull quotes are brief, just a few lines.

   Typically pull quotes are formatted larger, bolder, and centered.

   If you need to resize the box to make room for more text, do so. But remember that pull quotes are supposed to be short—and enticing. They're a trick designed to get people interested in the details of your text.

5. Resize the box to better fit your text.

   Use the top, bottom, left, or right handles to resize the box.

6. Move the box so that it's positioned where you want it.

   Point the mouse at the text box's fuzzy border. The mouse pointer grows a four-way-arrow thing, which means you can grab and drag the box.

7. Double-click the mouse on the edge of the text box.

   This brings up the Format Text Box dialog box. (If it doesn't, then try again; double-click when the mouse pointer sports the four-way-arrow thing, shown above.)

8. Click the Layout tab.
9. Choose Tight from the list of dogs.
10. Click OK.

    Now the text wraps tightly around your text box, looking a lot like Figure 4.1.

What's a Better Way to Make a Text Box Stand Out?

I find that printing white-on-black text often makes something stick out a lot more than a mere text box can. After creating your text box, follow these steps:

1. Double-click the text box border to bring up the Format Text Box dialog box.
2. Click the Colors and Lines tab.
3. Choose the black color from the Fill: Color area.

   Oftentimes choosing a gray color instead of black may have more of an impact. (It also saves on printer ink.)

4. Click OK.

In Word 2000, you'll have to select the text in the text box, and then choose Format ➤ Font to change the text color to white. Word 2003/XP does this automatically.

The end result? An inverse text box in your document.

You can also apply a background color to the text box by choosing something other than black in Step 3 above.

Any Way to Get Rid of This Text Box?

To zap away a text box, click its border with the mouse, and then press the Backspace key. Or the Delete key. Work isn't picky.

You Must Know This: The Difference between a Text Box and a Frame

If you want to stick text into a box in Word, then you use the Insert ➤ Text Box command. However there is a command that seems similar, which is the Frames command. Don't confuse them!

Frames are used primarily for formatting Web pages in Word, which is something I do not recommend. Therefore, do not mess with the Frames command! If you want text in a box, then use the Text Box command as discussed in this section.

How Can I Do a Sidewards Title?

Unlike text in your document, text in a text box doesn't always have to be right side up. It can also go sideways this way and sideways that way, which makes a text box an interesting tool for adding what I call a "sidewards title" to a document. Figure 4.3 shows what I'm talking about.

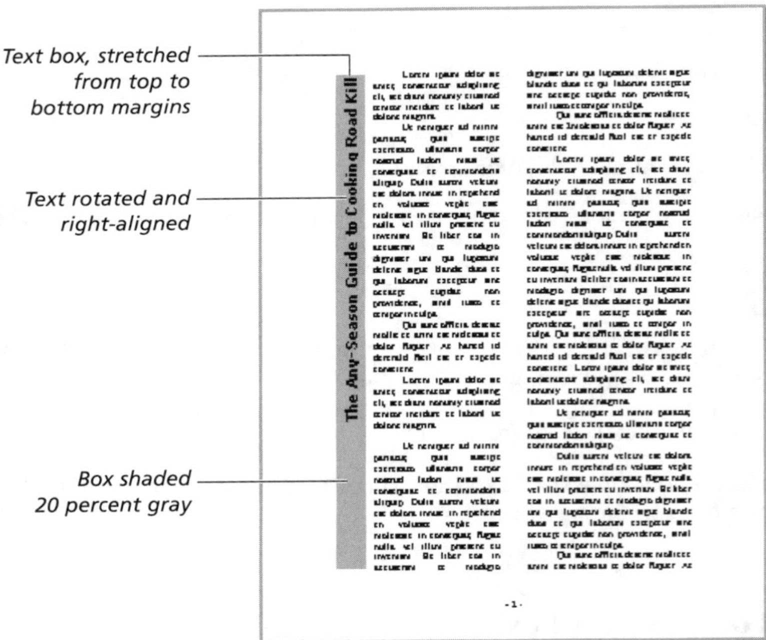

Figure 4.3
The sidewards title

To build this type of text box, follow the steps in the section, "How Can a Pull Quote Make My Documents More Interesting?" Then resize and drag the text box so that it stretches the entire length of the document, from the top of the text to the bottom.

Rotate the text by clicking the Change Text Direction button in the Text Box toolbar (Figure 4.4) until the text reads properly.

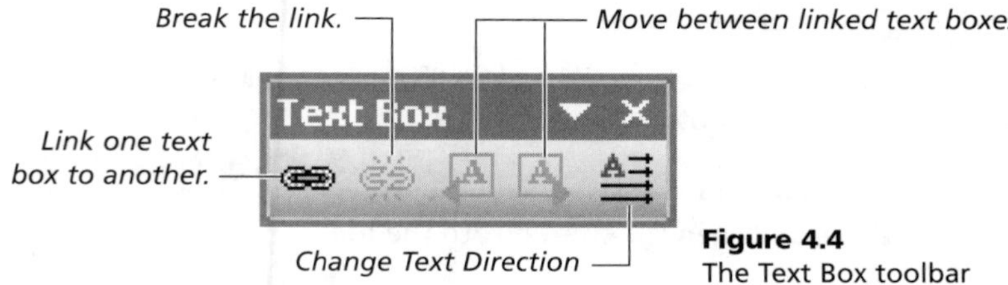

Figure 4.4
The Text Box toolbar

Optionally add a color background using the instructions found in the section "What's a Better Way to Make a Text Box Stand Out?" Note that in Figure 4.3, the background is set to 25 percent gray and no line is used to outline the box.

Why Do I Want to Link Text Boxes Together?

By linking text boxes together you can flow text from one into another. Obviously, for small boxes that makes no sense. But with larger boxes, it's possible to create a newspaper column–like effect. In fact, many folks attempt to put together newsletters using text boxes exclusively. Personally I think this is nuts; a desktop publishing program, such as Adobe InDesign or Microsoft Publisher, does a far better job with text boxes. But if you want to attempt such a thing with Word, you can. At your own peril.

Figure 4.5 illustrates how you could use text boxes to snake text through a newsletter. In fact, it seems like you could snake text using text boxes exclusively. The problem with that is Word slows to a crawl when you attempt it. Therefore, I recommend linking only one set of text boxes per document. If you try anything more, be sure to save often!

To link two text boxes, heed these loose steps:

1. Create both text boxes.

Follow the instructions earlier in this chapter. Note that the text boxes need not be on the same page.

2. Click to select the first text box.

This is the text box that contains the start of your flowing text.

3. Click the Create Text Box Link button on the Text Box toolbar.

The mouse pointer changes to a strange thing that I can only describe as a Pyrex measuring cup full of caustic acid. Okay, then.

4. Click the mouse on the second text box, the one the excess text from the first box is to flow into.

   When you move the mouse pointer into the text box, the Cup Of Acid "spills," displaying the initials of the Microsoft employee who designed the thing.

Now the two text boxes are linked. Text that overflows from the first box will miraculously appear in the second.

You can even add a third or fourth text box, simply by repeating the above steps and linking the second box to the third, and then the third box to the fourth.

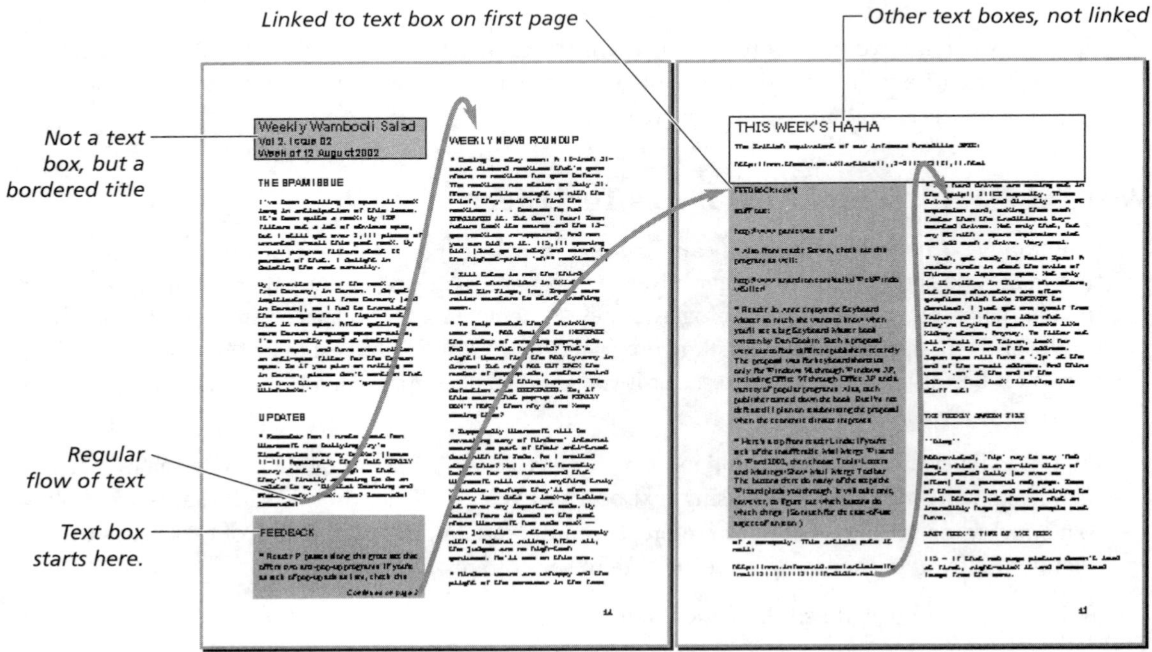

Figure 4.5 Linking text boxes in a newsletter

You can use the Next Text Box and Previous Text Box buttons to move between text boxes. This comes in handy, especially when the two text boxes are several pages apart. (Refer to Figure 4.4.)

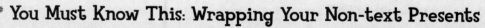

You Must Know This: Wrapping Your Non-text Presents

Text boxes, pictures, and graphics in your Word document can fit in with the text in a variety of ways. These are controlled by the Layout tab in the object's Format dialog box, where you can set the way text wraps around the image in one of five exciting ways:

Inline

In this mode, the graphic behaves just like any other character in the text. It sits "in line" with the other text in a paragraph. I rarely choose this option as, well, it looks dumb on the screen. The only time I've used it is when pasting in a sample text image, such as Chinese characters in the middle of a paragraph.

Square

Word puts a box around the image. Text flows around the image from top to bottom and hops over the image in the middle. My favorite choice.

Tight

This is similar to Square, but it allows the option of editing the wrapping points around the image to make text wrap even closer or, in some cases, in a shape identical to the image you've placed in your document—a circle, for example.

Behind Text

The image floats behind the text, making the image or object appear to be printed on the paper before the text was printed.

In Front

The image floats atop the text, just as if some wanton four-year-old pasted it on the page right over everything beneath it.

Toss In an Image or Two?

Oh, why not? Text is so boring. I mean, consider Tolstoy. Page after page of text and on and on and everyone has four different names and they all spend several pages internalizing dialog. I mean, KILL THE LANDLADY AND GET IT OVER WITH!

I'm sorry. That was a college flashback.

No doubt if Tolstoy had used Word instead of a grubby pencil, he probably would have delighted in brightening up his tireless tomes with a few splashy images here or there. It's just too easy.

Don't Be Dumb! Tips on Saving Images to Disk

There are three important things you must remember when you save a graphic to disk. Whether the image's source was the Internet, a scanner, a digital camera, or something you created with a painting program, know these things:

The File Format

Word works best with images saved in these formats: TIF or TIFF, GIF, JPG or JPEG, and BMP. Of these graphic image file types, TIFF is the best one to use. The files are larger than the other formats, but TIFF is very common and produces a good end result.

The Image's Size

Images look best when you don't have to enlarge or reduce them. Try to save your images in the exact physical size they will end up on the page.

The Folder or Location on Disk

Be sure you save your images in a proper folder on disk. Windows XP tries to save new graphics images to the My Documents ➤ My Pictures folder. However, if you're working on a large project, consider saving the images into the same folder that contains your Word document files. That way you can keep everything together.

The Filename

Be sure to give the image file a descriptive or specific name. When I create a document, I usually put in a placeholder for the image until I'm ready to paste it in. So I'll name the placeholder FIGURE1 and the image is named `FIGURE1.TIF` *on disk. Or, if the placement isn't important, I'll name the figure relating to its content, such as* `DADDY FUNNY HAT.TIF`.

How Do I Get This Image into My Document?

The key to getting any image into Word is to first *save it to disk*. Seriously! No matter where the source, first get the image from wherever it is now to a file on your computer's hard drive. Know the file's name. Know where you saved the file. Once it's there, then the rest is pretty easy:

1. Choose Insert ➤ Picture ➤ From File.
2. Use the Insert Picture dialog box to browse for the picture you saved to disk.

   You do remember the picture's name and its location, right?
3. Select the picture and click the Insert button.

   And the picture is stuck into your document.

Word sticks pictures into your document as inline text. That means the picture acts basically like any other character in the text, which is probably not what you want. Keep reading in the next section.

How Can I Make the Text Wrap around the Picture?

Your picture can float above, behind, inline with, or inside of your text. The different options are discussed in the earlier section "Wrapping Your Non-text Presents." To get at those options, follow these steps:

1. Switch to Print Layout view, if necessary.

   It's much easier to see your document's layout from Print Layout view than Normal view. Choose View ➤ Print Layout.
2. Right-click the picture you want to format.
3. Choose "Format Picture" from the pop-up menu.
4. In the Format Picture dialog box, click the Layout tab.
5. Choose your layout from the options listed.

   The one I prefer is Tight.
6. Click OK.
7. If necessary, reposition your picture in the document.

   Use the mouse to drag the picture around so that the text flows around it the way you want.

Of course, you may discover that you need to resize or even crop the image at this point. If so, keep reading in the appropriate sections that follow.

It may help to "zoom out" to get a better idea of how the picture works in with the rest of the text on the page. Use the Zoom drop-down list on the Standard toolbar to zoom out to 75% or 50%.

How Can I Wrap This Circle with a Circle?

To make text wrap around an image in a pattern not shown on the Text Wrapping menu, you have to be creative. What you do is choose the Tight option to wrap the image as tightly as you can; then you create your own wrapping image by making, moving, and editing various wrapping points about the image. Here's how it's done:

1. Click the picture to select it.
2. If the Picture toolbar doesn't appear, then choose View ➤ Toolbars ➤ Picture.

   The Picture toolbar is shown in Figure 4.6.

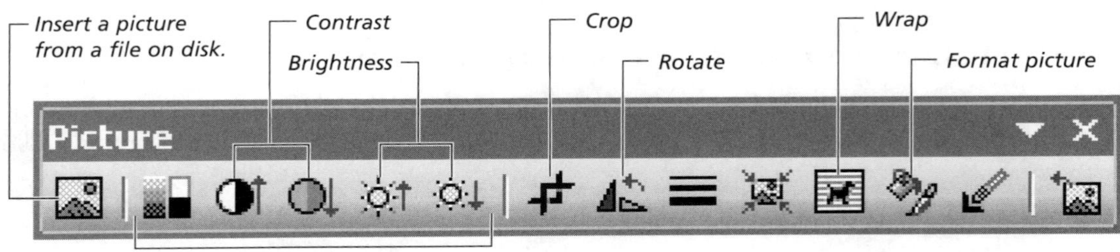

Figure 4.6 The Picture toolbar helps you edit a picture.

3. Choose Tight from the Text Wrapping button/menu on the toolbar.

   Click the "dog" button to see the menu.
4. Choose "Edit Wrap Points" from the Text Wrapping button/menu.

   The image is now surrounded by a rectangle with red dashed lines. Four wrapping points appear on the corners.

   The red dashed lines demark the boundary to where text will wrap. The wrapping points tell the lines where to go. Figure 4.7 shows you how to set these points so that you can wrap text around an odd-shaped image, such as a circle or oval.
5. Click the mouse on the red dashed line to create a new wrapping point.

   You may have to press and hold the mouse pointer on the red dashed line and then drag the pointer a wee bit to create the new wrapping point. (This takes some practice.)

   When the mouse pointer is in position to create a new wrapping point, it changes to look like a plus symbol, as shown in the margin.

   When you move a wrapping point, the mouse pointer changes again, as shown in the margin.

6. Drag the wrapping point to best wrap the red dashed line around your image.

You may need to insert more than one wrapping point to properly move the red dashed line around your image.

7. Keep repeating Steps 5 and 6 until your image is properly wrapped.
8. When you've finished, just click on the image or in your text.

If you need to edit the wrapping points later, just repeat these steps and use the mouse to add or move the points.

There is no way to delete a wrapping point once it's been added. However, you can change the layout option back to Inline or some other option that "forgets" the wrapping points.

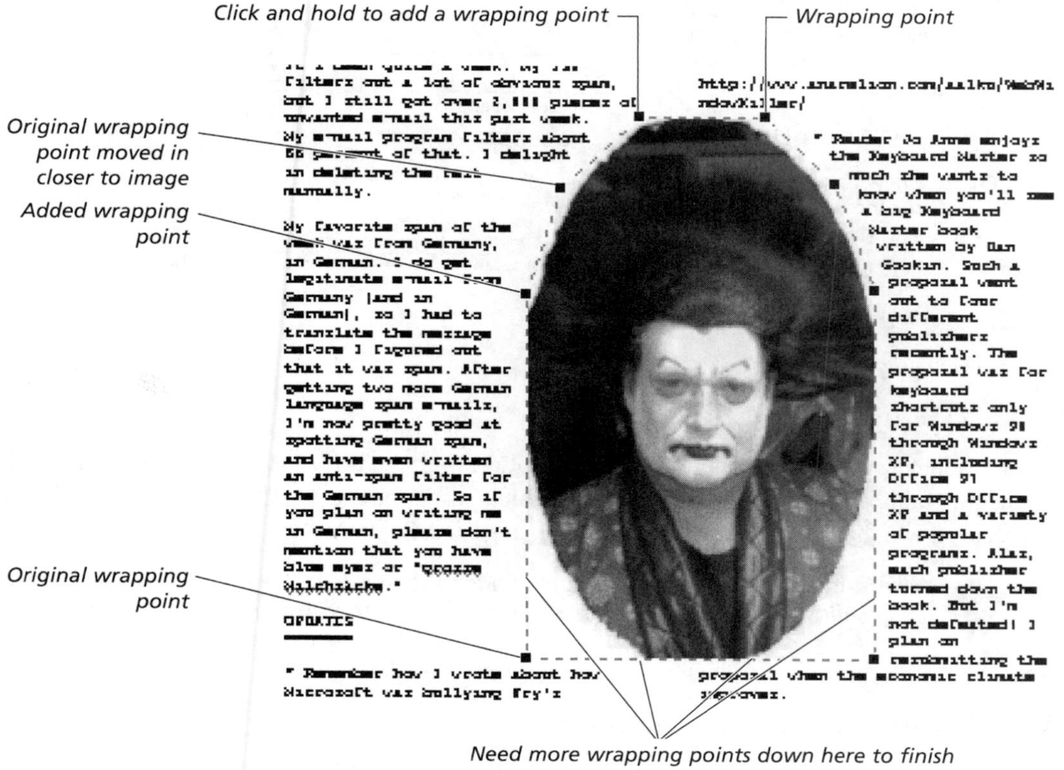

Click and hold to add a wrapping point

Wrapping point

Original wrapping point moved in closer to image

Added wrapping point

Original wrapping point

Need more wrapping points down here to finish

Figure 4.7 Editing the wrapping points

Any Nifty Way to Add an Image Caption?

Nifty methods abound for slapping a caption onto your figure. The best way is when the picture is placed into your document with the Inline layout—that is, without any text wrapping. In that case, you can add a caption by following these steps:

1. Right-click the image.
2. Choose Caption from the pop-up menu.

   The Caption dialog box appears, looking similar to Figure 4.8. (The gizmos have different positions in different versions of Word.)

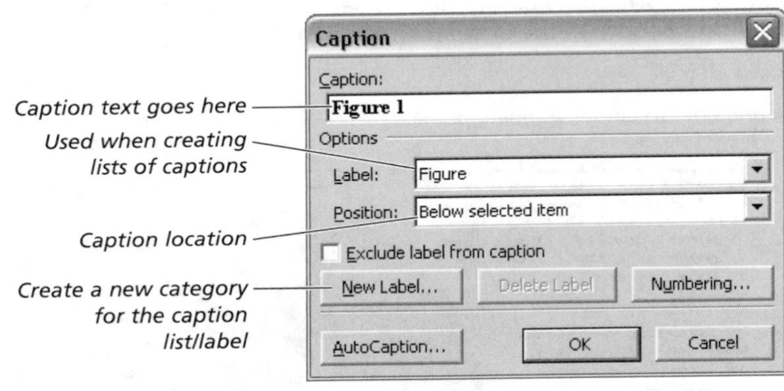

Figure 4.8
Slap down a caption on that puppy.

3. Type the caption text.
4. Click OK.

   The caption text is inserted below the picture.

The chief advantage of inserting a figure caption this way is that Word lets you later create a list or "table" of figures and captions and which pages they're on. This is part of Word's indexing feature, which is covered in Chapter 6, "Writing That Great American Novel or Screenplay."

Another way to create a caption is to stick a text box just below the image. That allows you a bit more formatting freedom than using the Caption command.

Any Way to Make the Image Smaller?

Reducing or enlarging an image is known as *scaling*. It's not "blowing up." No, you do that to old buildings. But to scale an image in Word is cinchy:

1. Click the image once to select it.

   Note how the image grows "handles," as shown in Figure 4.9? They are the key to scaling the image.

2. Grab the image's lower-right handle.
3. Drag the mouse upward and to the left.

   The image resizes proportionally as you drag the mouse, scaling it smaller.

To stretch in two directions at once, hold down the Ctrl key as you drag a handle with the mouse.

4. Release the mouse to keep the image at that new size.

You can drag any of the eight handles to resize an image, though the handles on the edges stretch the image non-proportionally.

These changes affect only the image as it appears in your document; they do not alter the original image saved on disk.

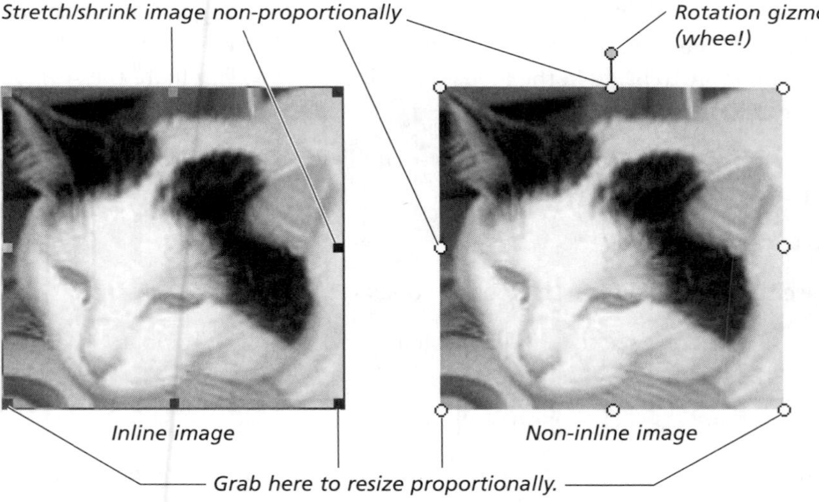

Figure 4.9 Selected inline and non-inline images

KEYBOARD MASTER

Various Picture Inserting Things

Working with graphics favors the mouse over the keyboard, so there aren't that many quick shortcuts. In fact, there's only one I use frequently:

Alt+I, P, F

This is pretty easy to remember for Insert ➢ Picture ➢ From File.

I Need to Rotate the Image?

Rotating the image is done by dragging it with the rotation handle, shown in Figure 4.9. Note that the image cannot be inline; it must have a certain type of wrapping selected other than Inline. After that, you can click the image and you'll see the topmost "green" handle: Point the mouse at that handle, and then drag to the left or right to rotate the image in that direction.

You can use the Ctrl or Ctrl+Alt keys while you drag the image to have it pivot around a certain point or rotate around the image's center as you drag the mouse.

To rotate by specific 90-degree increments, use the Picture toolbar's Rotate Left 90° button.

What Is Cropping All About?

Cropping is a way of resizing an image smaller without shrinking the image. It's like what Aunt Betty does with all her pictures; she whips out a pair of scissors and cuts out the less-meaningful parts. That's one way to bring in the focus on an image, or to eliminate the stuff you don't want others to see, specifically stuff on the edges.

Suppose Marsha really wants to crop ex-boyfriend Dougie out of that picture of her in the taffeta dress. To do so, she obeys these steps:

1. Click to select the image.
2. Choose the Crop tool from the Picture toolbar.

   If you don't see the Picture toolbar, choose View ➢ Toolbars ➢ Picture from the menu.
3. Drag one of the picture's eight handles inward to crop the image.

   To eliminate the top part of the image, for example, grab the top handle and slide the mouse downward. Or to crop in two directions at once, grab a corner handle and drag inward diagonally. (Refer to Figure 4.9 for information on the handles.)

   In Marsha's case, Dougie is standing on the right side of the picture, so she uses the right edge handle, dragging the mouse inward until most of Dougie is gone.
4. Click the Crop tool button again when you've finished cropping.

There is no way to undo cropping errors. Well, there is always the Undo command, Ctrl+Z. However, if you utterly screw things up, remember that you can always delete the image and reload it into the document.

Can I Crop the Image into a Circle?

No. Cropping works only along the edges of an image. If you want the image to be cropped into a different shape, then you'll have to use photo-editing software that sports some type of non-linear cropping tool.

What about Crop Circles?

Definitely aliens.

NERD'S CORNER

Cocktail Party Trivia, Part III

BILL: Cropping is merely an admission that you didn't properly frame the image when you took it.

MARY: Yeah, right.

JOHN: Well, not exactly.

BILL: And what do you know?

JOHN: I know that I prefer to work with more information than with little information. For example, a reduced image looks better than one you have to enlarge. That's because the reduced image has more information in it, so that the computer can better approximate a smaller version. However, when you enlarge, sometimes the computer has to approximate information that isn't there, which doesn't look as good.

BILL: What about cropping?

JOHN: If I'm going to crop, I'd prefer to do it in the final document, where I can see the image with the text and get a better idea of what and how to crop. Otherwise, I'm just guessing. And, again, I'd rather have the extra sides of a picture to crop than be forced to live with what has been pre-cropped for me.

MARY: And don't cut off the heads!

JOHN: Well, correct. In fact, in a portrait, the head should be in the upper part of the image, not in the center. You have to look at the picture as a whole, which helps you to crop it properly.

FRED: My favorite crop is corn.

BILL: Oh, Fred!

EVERYONE: Ha-ha.

Can I Put the Image in the Background?

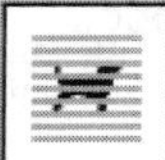

Setting an image behind the text is done by choosing the Behind Text layout option when the image is selected. This option can be chosen from the Picture toolbar's Text Wrapping button/menu or from the Layout tab in the Format Picture dialog box.

If you do set an image in the background, consider washing it out so that it doesn't detract too much from your text:

1. Click the image to select it.
2.  Click the Color button on the Picture toolbar.
3. Choose Washout from the Color button's menu.

   The image fades sufficiently so as not to detract from the text floating above.

You can undo this option by selecting Automatic from the Color button's drop-down menu.

Putting an image behind your text makes it harder to select the image for editing. Cheat a little bit by positioning the image just a hair to the left or right of the text's margin. That way you'll always have a piece of it to grab should you need to edit.

Why Does Word Slow Down with All These Images?

Hey! Word gets *tired* when you tax it too much! After all, it's a *word* processor, not an all-in-one document-formatting, data-manipulation, number-crunching, figure-editing jack-of-all-trades. (Though it tries to be.)

My best advice is to always add pictures, images, and foo-foo *last*. Save after adding and adjusting each image. And just cross your fingers that Word doesn't crash after you push it too far.

The best way to work with words, text boxes, pictures, and artwork is with a desktop publishing program. They're not as well suited to writing as Word is, but if you collect your words in a file and all your images in other files, then desktop publishing software can sew them all together with a minimum of fuss.

Simple Drawing Stuff

The final thing Word lets you mix into the text salad is *drawing stuff.* This includes lines, shapes, colors, and strange things that you can place into your text like pictures. Word also lets you illustrate your text or create your own figures or what have you. Honestly, I could write an entire book by itself on Word's drawing abilities (which are also shared by Excel). But instead, I'll just wrap up this chapter with some simple drawing basics. It's just enough to entice you without being so much as to overwhelm you.

Just Tell Me the Basics about Drawing in Word because I Don't Have a Lot of Time to Waste on This.

Let me introduce you to the amazing Drawing toolbar, shown in Figure 4.10, the source of most of the non-text things you can stick into a Word document. And it's so happy to be there, it even has a shortcut button on the Standard toolbar for instant appearances. Otherwise, choose View ➤ Toolbars ➤ Drawing.

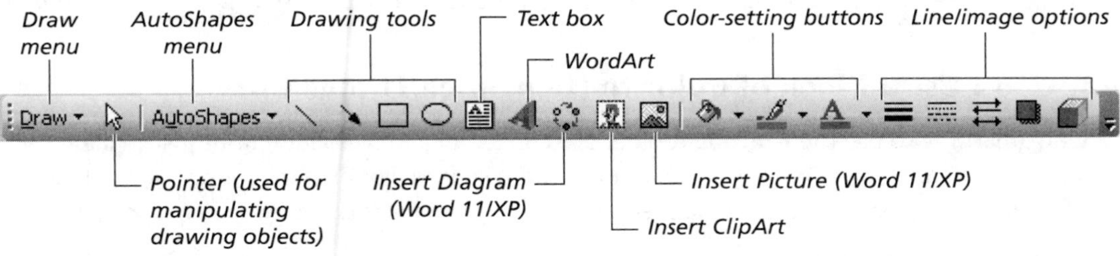

Figure 4.10 What's what on the drawing toolbar

The Drawing toolbar typically appears on the bottom of Word's window, below the document's horizontal scrollbar. (It might already be there; many Word users forget to hide it after they've finished using it.) Also, summoning the Drawing toolbar shifts you into Print Layout view if you're not already in that view.

Drawing works like this:

1. Summon the Drawing toolbar.
2. Click to select the type of object you want to draw.

   Say you need a circle to illustrate what the sun looks like to people who live only on the dark side of the planet. In that case, you click the Oval tool.

In Word 11/XP, a Drawing Canvas appears in your document. You can use this canvas to help group drawings together and to wrap text around the drawings. Otherwise, you can press the Backspace key to delete the canvas.

In Word 2000, you always draw items on top of the text where they first appear in a document.

3. Drag to draw the object in your document.
4. Optionally select a line style, line color, and fill color for the object.
5. Optionally use the mouse to reposition the object or resize or rotate the object using its various handles.

   See Figure 4.9.

You can continue to add objects to the document. As you do, be careful to save as you go; the more non-text junk you add to a Word document, the less stable it becomes. So saving often is important.

My best advice: Experiment! Play! Have fun!

Don't bother stringing together various lines to create more complex shapes. For example, don't try to link three lines together to make a triangle. Instead, use the AutoShapes pop-up menu and its palettes to select a predefined shape. That will save you some time.

How Can I Use a Block of Color to Help Spice Things Up?

One great way to use the Drawing toolbar is to break up a long document or just make it more visually appealing by adding some color or random shapes. For example, suppose you have a page of solid text. Consider adding a blue rectangle in the middle of the page to help break it up:

1. Summon the Drawing toolbar.
2. From the Zoom drop-down list on the Standard toolbar, choose "Whole Page."

   If you don't see the "Whole Page" option, then choose View ➤ Print Layout.

   This displays your document's entire page on the screen, allowing you to better place the color block.
3. Choose the Rectangle tool.

   If the Drawing Canvas appears in your document, press the Backspace key to delete it.
4. Drag to draw the rectangle in the middle of your document.
5. Choose Blue from the Fill Color button's menu.
6. Click the Draw button and choose Text Wrapping ➤ Tight.

   Or select another wrapping option to match your desire.

And now there's a blue square in your text. True, that does help break things up. But how about putting the page number in there as well? Continue with these steps:

7. Right-click the blue square.
8. Choose "Add Text" from the pop-up menu.
9. Choose Insert ➤ Field.
10. Choose Numbering from the Categories list, then Page from the Field Names column.
11. Click OK.

Now the page number sits in the blue square. But it can be better formatted:

12. Choose a fancier font.

    Such as Algerian or something very decorative.
13. Increase the font size to something larger, say 24 or 36.
14. Center the page number.

    Press Ctrl+E to do this.

Now to reformat the box to match the number:

15. Adjust the text box's vertical size to more accurately match the page number.

    And there you have a custom page number.

You can add text to any object you draw by simply repeating the steps above. In that case, the object becomes a specialized form of text box, into which you can place any text or a field, as was done in Step 9.

What About a Few Objects on the Corner of a Dull Page?

Figure 4.11 illustrates how I've placed three color blocks in the corner of a dull page just to help break things up.

Here's how I did that:

1. Summon the Drawing toolbar.
2. Select the Rectangle tool.

   (In Word 11/XP, delete the Canvas.)
3. Drag to draw the first rectangle.
4. Color the first rectangle red.
5. Repeat to draw a yellow rectangle.

6. Repeat again to draw a blue rectangle.

To bring the yellow rectangle forward, I'll need to rearrange them:

7. Right-click the yellow rectangle.
8. Choose Order ➢ Bring to Front from the pop-up menu.

Now to treat all three rectangles as a unit, I need to group them:

9. Ctrl+Click all three rectangles to select them.

   Press and hold the Ctrl key as you subsequently click each rectangle. This selects all of them.

10. Right-click the selected rectangles.
11. Choose Grouping ➢ Group.

    This allows you to work with all three objects as a single unit.

Next you need to wrap the text around your group:

12. Click to select the grouped items.
13. Click the Draw menu on the Drawing toolbar.
14. Choose Text Wrapping ➢ Tight.

    And the text wraps around the distraction in a non-distracting way, as shown in Figure 4.11.

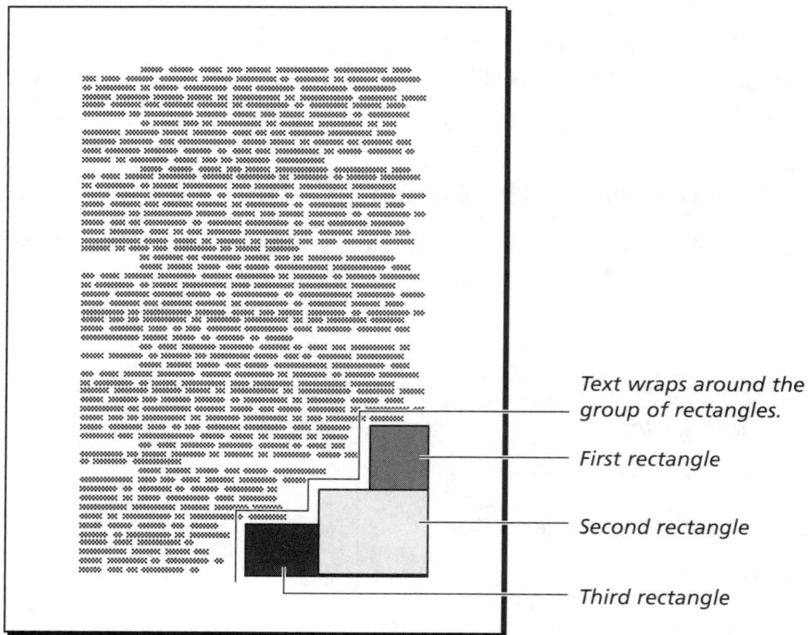

Figure 4.11 Blocks to break up a dull page

If color blocks seem silly, then consider that you can use the drawing tools to perhaps illustrate something described in the document. For example, the flow-chart tools may help you summarize a character's line of thinking. Or you may be able to draw a crude map or even a stick-figure diagram of the murder scene. Be creative!

How Can I Point Out a Specific Item in a Picture, Like with an Arrow?

Pictures are great for illustrating text, but often you need to call attention to a specific detail within that picture. That's where the arrow-drawing tool comes in very handy.

1. Insert the picture you want to reference with an arrow.

Stick the picture into your document; adjust its size, crop, and so on until it's perfect.

2. Optionally add a text box call-out.

You need to label the arrow, after all. Sometimes you can get away without arrows. For example, in the caption or text you could just say, "Arrows point to suspected obscene sculptures." Otherwise, use the text box instructions from earlier in this chapter to create a text box call-out, similar to the one shown in Figure 4.12.

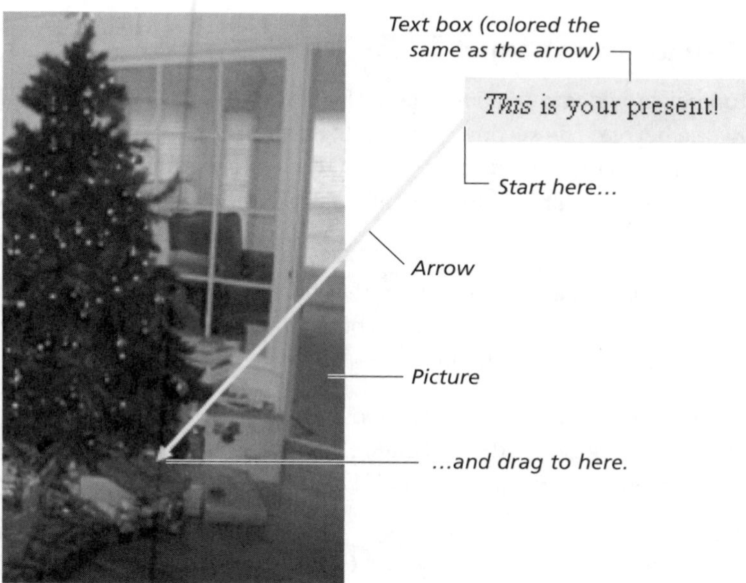

Figure 4.12 Using the Arrow tool

3. Choose the Arrow tool from the Drawing toolbar.

4. Drag to draw the arrow.

Keep in mind that the arrowhead appears at the *end* of the line, not the start.

5. Make adjustments as necessary.

   Move, color, resize, create.

I always have to mess with the arrow's color after I've added an arrow. This is to help make the arrow stand out from the image. In Figure 4.12, the arrow is colored yellow, which helps it stand out from the picture as well as show up on the page. (The text box is also colored yellow to match.)

Don't Be Dumb and Ignore the Two Different Types of Arrows.

There are two different types of arrows on the Drawing toolbar. The first is the Line tool with an arrowhead attached, or the Arrow tool. You can also use the Arrow style button (on the right end of the Drawing toolbar) to select a specific style for your arrow.

In addition to those line arrows, you'll also find a palette of "block arrows" on the AutoShape button's menu. Unlike line arrows, the block arrows have a width and depth to them and come in a few interesting variations.

Why Would I Use an AutoShape?

The Drawing toolbar provides you quick access to a few handy drawing tools: the line, square, and oval. But, as anyone beyond the second grade realizes, there are far more shapes than those available to the human imagination. So rather than try to cobble together a triangle, star, or trapezoid, Word gives you those shapes already formed, all neatly categorized on submenus in the AutoShapes menu.

For example, to add a cartoon bubble to that hilarious image of Aunt Courtney getting tackled by the dog, click the AutoShapes button and then choose the appropriate cartoon bubble from the Callouts submenu.

To use a star shape for your text box, choose AutoShapes ➤ Stars and Banners and then pluck out the old five-pointed star. Drag to create the star in you document; then right-click the star shape in your document and choose "Add Text" from the pop-up menu.

Avoid choosing the "More AutoShapes" item at the bottom of the AutoShapes pop-up menu. Selecting that item forces Word to venture out onto the Internet to look for more shapes on Microsoft's web page. I've found that more of an exercise in frustration than any handy tool I could really use.

I Need to Add a Curly Bracket to the Margin.

It just so happens that a curly bracket is one of those AutoShapes that the Drawing toolbar provides for you. I've used the curly bracket often when I write a script to indicate that several people are talking at once, as shown in Figure 4.13.

Here's how to add such a thing to your document:

1. Write your text first.

   After all, you can't bracket what you don't see.

2. Summon the Drawing toolbar.

3. Choose AutoShapes ➤ Basic Shapes ➤ Left Brace from the Drawing toolbar.

   "Left Brace" is the second-to-last item on the last row of the Basic Shapes menu.

4. Drag to create the brace in your document.

5. Adjust the brace: Resize and reposition as necessary.

You've finished.

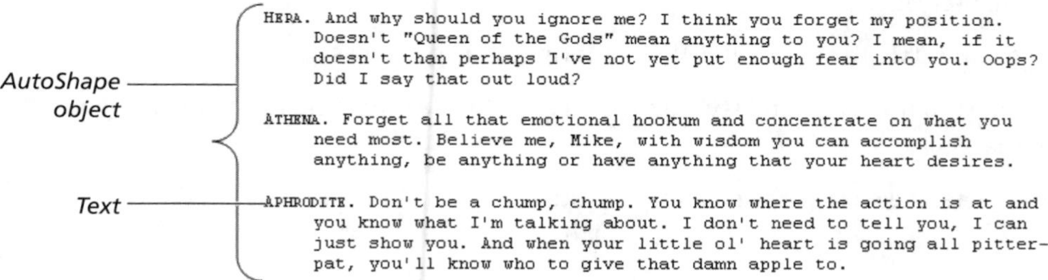

Figure 4.13 A curly bracket (or "brace") in the margin

What's Better Than a Square for Showing a Part or Chapter Number?

Oh, anyone can be clever with two dimensions. Consider the following steps for putting your chapter number into a three-dimensional doodad:

1. Type your chapter first.

2. Go back to page 1.

   Press Ctrl+Home to do that.

3. Summon the Drawing toolbar to create your chapter heading.

4. Select the Rectangle tool.

   Word 2003/XP, optionally delete the Drawing Canvas.

5. Drag to create the rectangle for your chapter title.

6. From the Draw menu (on the Drawing toolbar) choose Text Wrapping ➤ In Line with Text.

   This lets Word treat the box like a large character as opposed to an image floating above or below the text.

7. Position the rectangle so that it's on a line by itself.

   Click the mouse (or use the keyboard arrow keys) to put the toothpick cursor right after the rectangle; then press the Enter key.

8. Click to select the rectangle again.

9. Optionally add color to the rectangle.

   I use a light gray, say 25 percent.

10. Right-click the rectangle and choose "Add Text" from the pop-up menu.

11. Type the chapter title.

12. Apply a heading style to the chapter title, or format it as you please.

    It's a good idea to use a heading style on the chapter title, as this helps you organize your document later.

13. Adjust the rectangle so that the chapter title fits nicely within its bounds.

And now for the fancy stuff:

14. Choose a 3-D style from the 3-D button's pop-up menu.

This may take some experimenting because the text doesn't warp into three dimensions like the box does. But with practice, you can get it to look like part of the box, as shown in Figure 4.14.

What you end up with is more than just a fancy title in a box. It's…art!

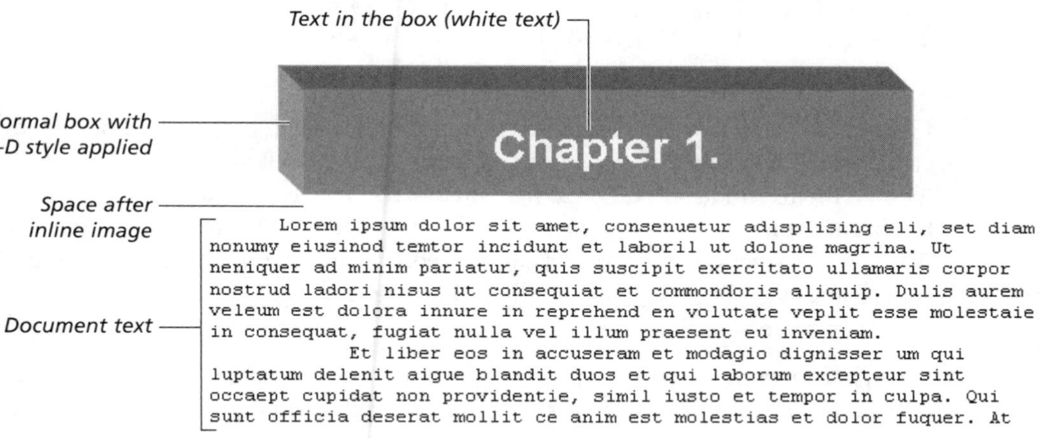

Text in the box (white text)
Normal box with 3-D style applied
Chapter 1.
Space after inline image
Document text
Lorem ipsum dolor sit amet, consenuetur adisplising eli, set diam nonumy eiusinod temtor incidunt et laboril ut dolone magrina. Ut neniquer ad minim pariatur, quis suscipit exercitato ullamaris corpor nostrud ladori nisus ut consequiat et commondoris aliquip. Dulis aurem veleum est dolora innure in reprehend en volutate veplit esse molestaie in consequat, fugiat nulla vel illum praesent eu inveniam.
Et liber eos in accuseram et modagio dignisser um qui luptatum delenit aigue blandit duos et qui laborum excepteur sint occaept cupidat non providentie, simil iusto et tempor in culpa. Qui sunt officia deserat mollit ce anim est molestias et dolor fuquer. At

Figure 4.14 A fancy title in a 3-D box

The Best Drawing Friend You Can Have

If you're into illustrations, then I recommend purchasing a separate drawing program for your computer. Popular applications include Corel Draw and Adobe Illustrator. These are professional-level drawing programs that give you far more control over your drawings than the Drawing toolbar in Windows.

5 Using Styles and Templates to Save Oodles of Time

I remember when styles were first introduced to PC word processing, way back in the early 1990s. My reaction to styles was the same as just about any Word user; I freely ignored them. I understood how styles could make formatting a document easier, but like most folks, I found it much easier simply to use the formatting buttons and commands to work with my text. That worked, of course, until I needed to change something. Only then did I discover the true value of using styles and how much time they could save.

For a short document, you don't need styles. But for anything longer than a page, or anything you expect to look professional, you should consider using styles and using them well. They aren't that difficult to understand, so this chapter doesn't concentrate too much on style basics. Instead, I thought I'd dish up about 14 years' worth of style tricks and tips to help you understand and use styles better than anyone else on the block. (Well, at least anyone else who doesn't have this book!)

Rudiments Explained and Gordian Knots Hewn:

- Creating a style the easy way
- Automatically applying styles
- Taking advantage of heading styles
- Discovering the power of styles
- Creating a palette of styles
- Working styles into templates

Why Bother with Styles?

A style is nothing more than a collection of formatting commands, all of which can be applied to text in one swift movement. And, honestly, if your document isn't that complex, then you don't need to bother with styles.

When it comes to creating or modifying styles, Word 2003/XP and Word 2000 handle styles differently. Word 2000 uses a special Style dialog box. Word 2003/XP uses the Styles and Formatting Task Pane. Both methods accomplish the same thing. And specific differences will be noted in the text.

The Type of Formatting Things Applied with a Style

A single style can contain commands that format text in any or all of the following ways:

Font

Select typeface, size, text attributes, color, and anything in the Font dialog box.

Paragraph

Choose various paragraph-formatting options, as found in the Paragraph dialog box.

Tabs

Set tabs.

Borders and Shading

Specify any borders or shading or anything else than can be done in the Borders and Shading dialog box.

Language

Select a language for the text, to be used for the spell and grammar check.

Frame

Stick the text in a frame (for Web publishing).

Numbering

Apply a bullet or number to the paragraph, per the Bullets and Numbering dialog box.

When Do I Need to Create Styles?

Suppose your document has a simple chapter heading and then a lot of text. If so, you probably don't need styles. (Though if you've used styles before, you'll probably use them even in that case.)

Otherwise, if your document contains any or all of the following, you're better off creating styles:

- A headline or headings to break up sections of text
- A header or footer
- Block-quoted text or any specialized text, such as `computer screen text` or quotations
- Specialized text, such as text in a table or foreign-language text

Essentially, any document that contains anything other than one style of text probably needs a few styles created to help you format.

What's the Best Way to Create a Style?

The best way I've found to create styles is to write your document's text first. Format as you go: If you have a header, format it with a bolder font, centered, bordered, or however you feel it looks right. Just use the formatting tools you have to create the look you want as you go.

The first time you need to reuse a style is when you need to cement the style's attributes and save them as an official Word style.

For example, suppose your document starts out with an A-head, or first-level heading. Then you write a few pages of text and you need another A-head. The first A-head is already formatted as you like. You merely want to copy all that formatting into a style so you can instantly apply it to the second (and any future) A-heads. Here's how:

1. Click the mouse on the paragraph containing the formatting you want to squeeze into a new style.

   Say you've already formatted a heading. It's bold, a fancy font, larger than the body text, and so on. You've created this look by manually selecting the various formatting commands.

2. Click the mouse in the Style drop-down list on the Formatting toolbar.

   This selects the text already there, illustrated in Figure 5.1.

3. Type a name for your style.

   Use a unique name, such as "A-head" or "First head." Try not to use one of Word's already-created style names, such as "Normal" or "Heading 1."

4. Press the Enter key to lock in that style name.

   And the style is created.

You can now apply the style to any paragraph of text in your document. So:

5. Scroll down to where the next header can be found.

Or go to the spot where you have text that is to be formatted in that same style.

6. Select the text with the mouse.

7. Choose your style from the Style drop-down list on the Formatting toolbar.

And in an instant, that style is applied to the text. The same style, exactly.

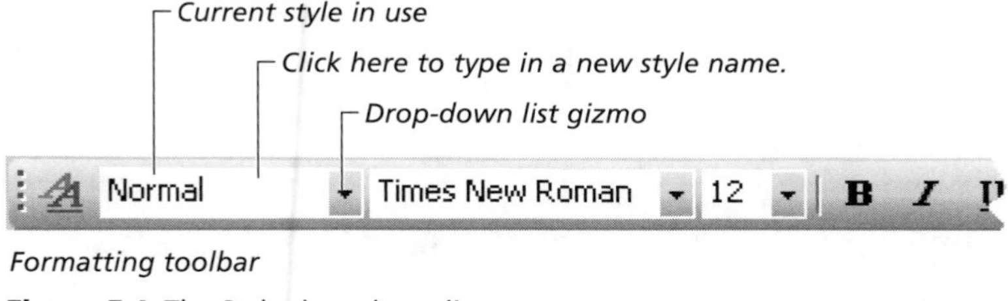

Figure 5.1 The Style drop-down list

Do I Need to Create a Style for Every Bit of Text?

If you don't create a style for every bit of text in your document, then your document uses the Normal style, which in Word is Times New Roman at 12 points, nothing else added or fancy. If that's what you want for your document, grand! Otherwise, create a style based on however you're formatting your text.

What about Plain Text? Does It Need a Style?

I always create a style called "Body" for the body of my document's text. Even though this style is typically just a typeface and a type size, I create it and apply it to the entire document. In fact, I often do it first to all the text and then go back and create other styles as needed.

To create a style for the majority of text in your document, follow these steps:

1. Select a typical paragraph of text.

The paragraph is formatted how you want all the text in your document to look: the font, size, typeface, style, paragraph options, and so forth.

2. Click the Style area on the Formatting toolbar.

Refer to Figure 5.1.

3. Type in a name for the body text style.

I use the word "Body." Do not use "Normal" or "Plain Text" as they are predefined styles used by Word.

4. Press Enter.

Now the name is locked in, and you can apply the style to all your document's body text.

If your entire document is Body text, then press Ctrl+A to select the whole thing, and choose Body (or whatever style you created) from the Style drop-down list. That applies that style to all the text in your document.

To apply the style to individual portions of text, select those portions with the mouse, and then choose Body from the Style drop-down list.

To reapply formatting to a chunk of text, press the F4 "repeat" key. For example, after applying the body style to a chunk of selected text, select a new chunk of text and then press the F4 key. This applies that same formatting (style) over again.

You Must Know This: Document Headings and Their Levels

Documents that are divided into sections are organized by using various headings or header levels. This is merely part of the outlining and thought-organization process—the stuff they tried to teach you in school by using 3 x 5 cards that never really sank in. But in real life, when you need to organize your thoughts into a paper, it's best to use various heading levels.

The first heading level is Heading 1, which is also the name of a predefined style in Word. That's the top-level heading or A-head, as it's known in the publishing industry.

Below Heading 1 is Heading 2, which is the second level of organization, or the B-head. Then comes Heading 3, or the C-head, following by Heading 4, or the D-head, and so on. Though, in practice, I've rarely seen a document with anything below Heading 3 used.

The purpose of the headings is purely organizational. Heading 1 defines a broad category. Heading 2 is a specific example of the Heading 1 category. And Heading 3, if needed, is a specific example of what Heading 2 represents. It works kind of like this:

Heading 1: Animal
- Heading 2: Dog
- Heading 2: Cat
- Heading 2: Vermicious Knid

Heading 1: Vegetable
- Heading 2: Tomato
- Heading 2: Carrot

Heading 1: Mineral
- Heading 2: Sapphire
  - Heading 3: Red
  - Heading 3: Blue
- Heading 2: Carbon

Also note that you must have at least two headings on each level, though this is debatable. In academic circles, however, they feel that if you have only one header, then there is no need for any header at all. (At least that's what they tell me.)

Why Not Just Use the Normal Style?

You can use the Normal style, if you like. You can even change the Normal style. For example, say that you prefer to have *all* of your documents formatted with the Bookman typeface at 10 points. If so, all you need to do is modify the Normal style:

1. Choose Format ➢ Font to open the Font dialog box.

2. Select the attributes for the Normal style's font.

For example, choose a typeface other than Times New Roman, a specific size, and so on. I changed the Normal font on my business correspondence computer so that all my new documents are 12-point Book Antigua font.

3. Click the Default button.

This is a special button in most formatting dialog boxes. It takes the changes you've specified and updates the `NORMAL.DOT` template file with those changes, which effectively changes the Normal style.

4. Click the Yes button in the confirmation dialog box.

And the Normal style has been updated.

Alas, you cannot update other styles using the Default button; they're keyed into the Normal style specifically. So if you want to use another style in your document, you must create it yourself.

When you quit Word, you may be asked to save the updates to the `NORMAL.DOT` *template. Click the Yes button to do so, which makes your changes permanent.*

Can I Use Information from My A-Level Head Style to Create a B-Level Head Style?

It's possible in Word to base a new style upon the attributes of an existing style. This way the two styles are related. In fact, if you change the attribute of one style, it can affect the attribute of the related style. But before I get into that, here's how to create a B-level head style based on an existing A-level head style in your document:

1a. In Word 2003/XP, choose Format ➢ Styles and Formatting.

The Styles and Formatting task pane appears.

1b. In Word 2000, choose Format ➢ Style.

The Style dialog box shows up.

2. Click the New or New Style button.

   The New Style dialog box appears, as shown in Figure 5.2. (The dialog box looks different between Word XP/11 and Word 2000; differences are pointed out in the figure.)

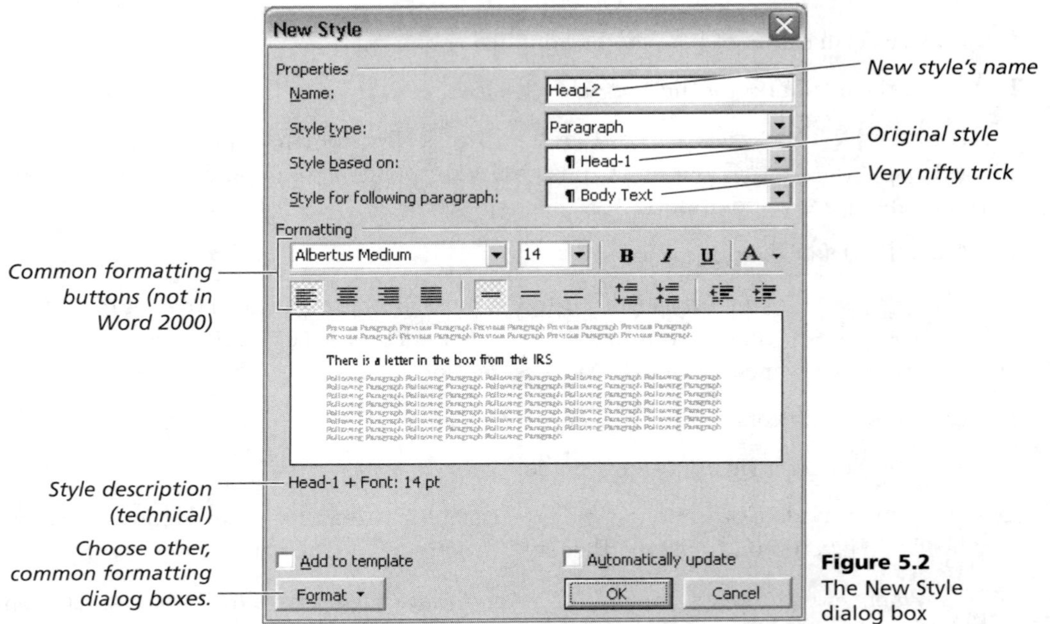

Figure 5.2
The New Style dialog box

3. Type a name for the new style, such as `Head B` or `B-head`.

   Be descriptive, yet brief.

4. Keep Paragraph as the style type.

   Character styles are covered later in this chapter.

5. Choose the original style, the one this style is based on.

   For example, Head A would be the style that Head B would be based on. Also note in the description area how this style is defined as the original style *plus* whatever options you change.

6. Select whatever body text style you're using as the style for following paragraph.

   That way, when you press the Enter key after typing your heading style, Word automatically switches to the body text style for the following paragraph. This is a very handy trick.

7. Adjust whatever formatting changes need to be made between the styles.

   In my documents, heading B is merely a smaller font size than heading A, so I'll just adjust the font size down to 14 from 18. Or sometimes I'll make the B head small caps or italics. Whatever is required to differentiate between an A and B head, make those changes.

8. Click OK to create the style.

Note that the style is *not* automatically applied to any selected text in your document.

To apply the style, choose it from the Style drop-down list. Or in Word 11/XP, select the style from the Styles and Formatting task pane. (Or you can close the task pane if, like me, you feel it's a waste of screen space.)

How Will Changes in One Style Affect a Related Style?

Suppose you have two related styles, such as Head-1 and Head-2. Head-2 is based on Head-1, with the only defined difference being that Head-2 is a smaller font size.

What happens if you change the font for Head-1? How will that affect the document? Try this to find out:

1. Click to place the blinking toothpick cursor inside a paragraph formatted with the original style.

It must be the original style, not a style "based on" another style.

2a. In Word 2003/XP, choose Format ➤ Styles and Formatting.

2b. In Word 2000, choose Format ➤ Style.

3a. In Word 2003/XP, locate the style in the scrolling list.

3b. In Word 2000, click to select the style in the scrolling list.

4a. In Word 2003/XP, point the mouse at the style, click the down-arrow that appears, and then select Modify from the menu.

4b. In Word 2000, click the Modify button.

For all versions of Word, the Modify Style dialog box appears, which is very similar to the New Style dialog box shown in Figure 5.2.

5. Click the Format button.

6. Choose Font.

7. Select another font or typeface for the style by using the Font dialog box.

8. Click OK.

9. Click OK to close the Modify Style dialog box.

10a. In Word 2003/XP, optionally close the Styles and Formatting task pane.

10b. In Word 2000, close the Style dialog box.

Observe your document. You'll notice that the typeface has changed for the style you modified. *Plus* the typeface for any styles based on that style also have changed. In the previous section's example, both the Head-1 and Head-2 style's font has changed. That's because Head-2 is based on Head-1, and any changes made in Head-1 are reflected in Head-2.

The only time a change in one style does not appear in another is when that second, based-on style redefines a specific formatting attribute. For example, you could change the point size of Head-1's font to 36, but because the point size for Head-2 is fixed at 14, that wouldn't change.

I Need to Change My Entire Document's Style from 12-Point Text to 10-Point.

Again, here is the magic part about using a style: Because all your document's text is defined by a style, all you need to do is change the point size for that style and every bit of text formatting with the style changes.

To modify any style, follow the steps in the previous section. Use the Modify Style dialog box to make your style changes.

(In the previous section, two styles were modified at once because one was based on the other. If no other style is based on the style you're modifying, then the changes you make affect only the current style.)

What's the Point of a Character Style?

Character styles are rarer than paragraph styles but still valuable in the scheme of things. Unlike paragraph styles, character styles affect only character formatting, not paragraphs or tabs. Because of that, there are few types of documents that even need to concern themselves with character formatting.

For example, when I write small computer how-to booklets, I use a special character style for the stuff people are supposed to type into their computer. That text is formatted with the Courier New font, at 10 points, and colored blue.

To make such a style, use the New Style dialog box, shown in Figure 5.2. Follow these steps:

1. Choose Character from the Style type drop-down list.

   Note that this limits other options in the dialog box to those that specifically cover character formatting.

2. Choose your character-formatting options.

   In Word 2003/XP, I can do all these with the gizmos present in the dialog box. For Word 2000, I need to click the Format button and choose Font from the menu.

   In my example, I choose the typeface Courier New, size 10 points, color blue.

3. Name the character style.

   Don't worry about specifying it as a character style; all character styles show up in lists with the tiny letter *a* by them, whereas paragraph styles appear with the paragraph symbol, the backward *P*.

4. Click OK.

   And the character style is created.

To apply the character style, select a chunk of text with the mouse, and then choose that style from the Style drop-down list.

Again, the advantage to creating such a style over just formatting text is tremendous. For example, in one of my documents I discovered that the blue-colored text didn't look right when printed. So it was a simple matter to modify the character style and change the text color to red. That one simple change was then reflected on all the text formatting with that style in the document, saving me a lot of time.

Some Style Tricks, Tidbits, and Advice

The beauty of styles is that once you create them, you simply have to use them. That's it! There's no more dinking or re-creating involved, unlike formatting everything manually.

Even though styles are relatively simple things, I've collected a bunch of tidbits, trivia, and other advice to freely dispense, giving you a bit more knowledge on the subject than a cursory tour would do otherwise. So here they are, my style tricks, in no particular order.

Can I Modify a Paragraph That's Already Formatted with a Style?

Any text in a document can be changed. Styles cannot "lock" a paragraph's formatting. For example, if you want *italic* text in the middle of a styled paragraph, you can do that, right? Similarly, you can change the font or color of the text or edit or anything.

If the modifications are common, then consider creating a new style. For example, say you need to change three paragraphs into a bulleted list. If so, then simply create a new style based on the existing one, but a style with bulleted paragraphs.

The problem you run into if you don't create a new style based on an old style is that if you modify the old style, you may lose your on-the-fly changes to a paragraph.

Why Bother with Heading Styles?

If possible, try to let Word identify your heading styles. This is important because Word uses the heading levels for many things, such as creating an outline, a table of contents, or the Document Map. But the key is to identify the heading style as such. Here's how you do that:

1. Modify the style you want to be the first-level heading.

   Refer to instructions earlier in this chapter for getting to the Modify Style dialog box for your heading style.

2. From the Format button, choose Paragraph.

   This displays the Paragraph formatting dialog box.

3. Select an Outline Level for the heading style.

   In the upper-right corner of the dialog box is a drop-down list of Outline Level options, shown in Figure 5.3. For the first heading-level style, choose Level 1. For the second, choose Level 2, and so on.

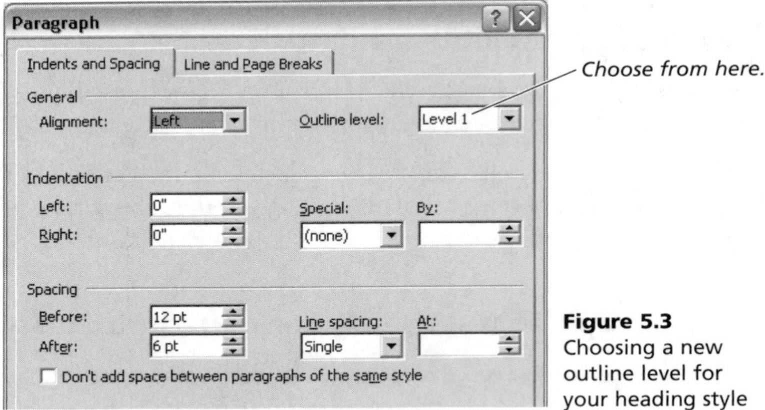

Figure 5.3 Choosing a new outline level for your heading style

4. Click OK to make the change in the Paragraph dialog box.
5. Repeat this change for other heading styles in your document.

   Assign to each of them the appropriate outline level value.

6. Close up various dialog boxes and windows when you've finished.

With these changes made, your made-up styles hold the same power over your document as the built-in Heading styles. You can use them to see an overview of the document with the Document Map command, or when switching to Outline mode, or when creating a table of contents.

What's the Benefit to Having One Style Follow Another?

To save time and energy when creating a document, it helps to have one style automatically follow another. For example, as was shown earlier in this book, a heading style should be automatically followed by a body text style. Indeed, the built-in Heading styles all specify that after pressing the Enter key, the following paragraph should be formatted with the Normal style.

This "Style for Following Paragraph" option comes in handy for documents with lots of formatting in specific order. For example, consider a document that starts with a heading, then a subheading, then an initial paragraph that's not indented, followed by paragraphs that are indented. That's *four* styles, but by specifying which style follows which, you can make all the changes take place automatically.

A style needs to be created before you can specify it to follow an existing style.

For example, assume that the first style is Title. That must be followed by the Subhead style, as shown here:

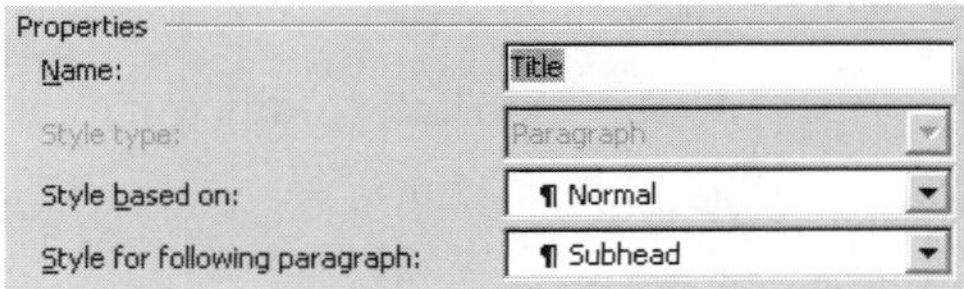

Then the Subhead style is followed by the Body-first style, which is the first paragraph of the document:

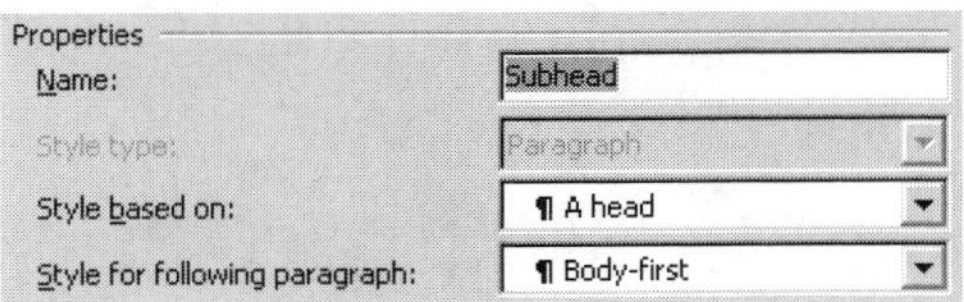

Finally, the Body style (indented paragraph) automatically follows the Body-first style (unindented paragraph):

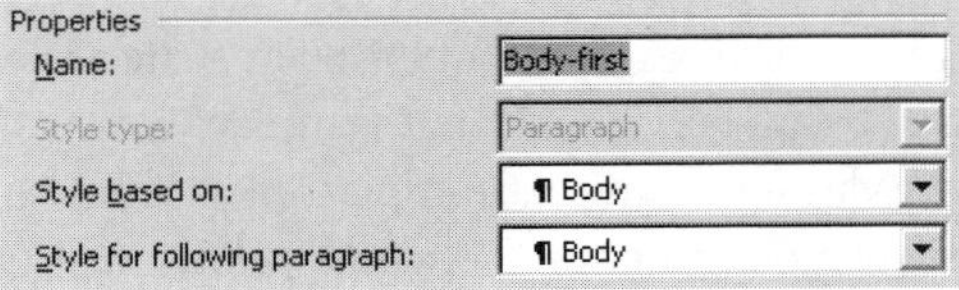

After that, the Body style simply follows itself.

To add a new heading, you must manually select it from the Style drop-down list or Style and Formatting task pane.

How Can I Quickly Restore a Style That's Been Reformatted in the Document?

As long as the style itself hasn't been modified, you can reapply it to any chunk of text. This is easier to do in Word 2003/XP than in Word 2000. In Word 2003/XP, any style that's modified appears as such in the Style drop-down list, as shown in Figure 5.4.

In Word 2000 there is no visible way to tell that a style has been messed with. There are, however a few tricks you can pull in all Word versions to restore a modified chunk of text.

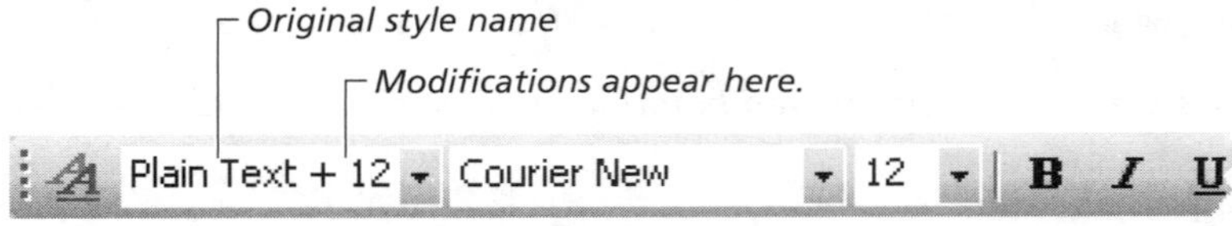

Figure 5.4 The style has been messed with, oh no!

Can I Modify the Standard Styles?

Certainly. Would that be a permanent or temporary modification?

If you merely want to change the styles for a specific document, then feel free to modify them as you would any other style.

To permanently alter the built-in styles, open the `NORMAL.DOT` template file, go into each style, and modify it as you see fit. Save the `NORMAL.DOT` template when you've finished. That way, those styles will be used any time you start a blank document in Word. They'll also be inherited by any other document that uses those styles.

A good reason not *to modify the built-in or standard styles is that some templates do rely on them being of a certain style. Therefore I do insist that you consider creating your own styles as opposed to modifying the built-in ones.*

How Can I Copy Styles from One Document to Another?

The easiest way to share styles is to create a template using the styles. Then you can start any new document with those styles. Or you can attach that template to any document and, presto-chango, that document inherits the styles found in that template. But I'm assuming here that your objective is merely to copy styles between documents and not actually mess with templates. Yes, there is a way. (If you do want to mess with templates, there's a whole section coming up.)

Before you start, it helps to have both files saved to disk. For example, if you're copying styles from `INVASION.DOC` to the current document, then obviously `INVASION.DOC` must be saved to disk. And then, if you haven't yet saved your current document to disk, do so! (Save! Save! Save!)

When both files are saved to disk, then you can copy styles between them, thusly:

1. Choose Tools ➤ Templates and Add-ins.
2. Click the Organizer button.

   The Organizer dialog box, Styles tab appears, as shown in Figure 5.5. This is where you can copy styles between documents or templates, as described in the figure.

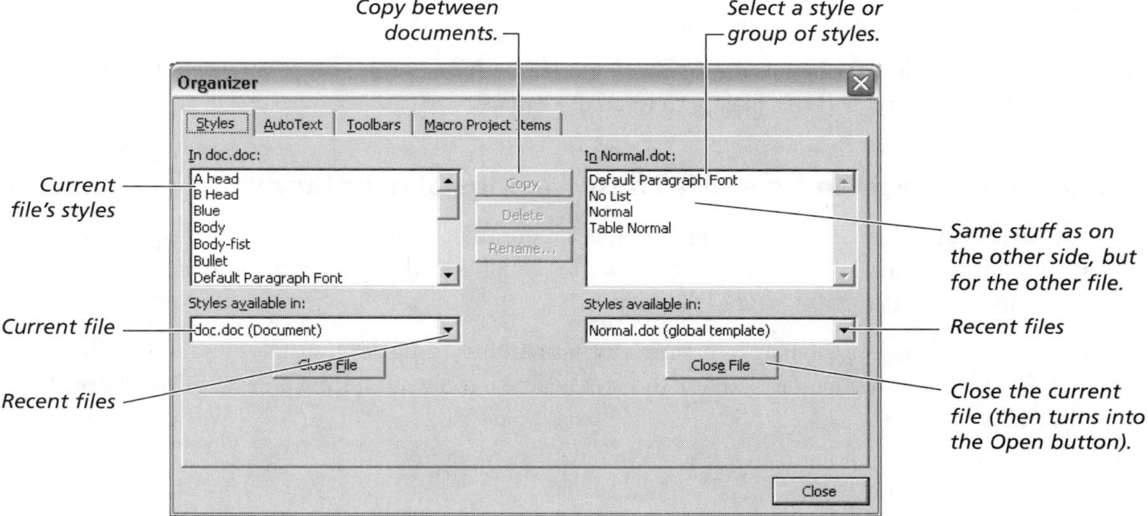

Figure 5.5 Copying styles from one document to another

   To keep sane, I keep the current document on the left and the document from which I'm copying styles on the right—though this isn't a hard-and-fast rule.

3. Click the Close File button on the left.

   The only time you don't need to do this is when the open file, such as `NORMAL.DOT`, contains the styles you want. Most of the time, however, that won't be the case.

4. Click the Open File button to locate the file containing the styles you want to thieve, or copy.

   Or, if you're lucky, the file may be available in the drop-down list above the Open File button.

5. Use the Open dialog box to locate the Word document or template file containing the styles you want.

   When the file is opened, you'll see a list of its styles appear in the wee li'l scrolling window on the right side of the dialog box.

6. Click to select the styles you want to copy.

   Or press Ctrl to click, click, click and select more than one style.

7. Click the Copy button.

   And the styles are copied from that file into the current document.

   If styles have the same name, you'll be warned about overwriting them, as you would expect.

8. Click the Close button when you've finished.

Ah! Thieving styles! Nothing to be embarrassed about. It's a handy way to move common styles between documents without having to re-create things.

What's a Nifty Way to Keep All These Various Styles Handy?

The Style drop-down list is okay—until you get more than a screen's-height list of styles and scrolling through them is like walking barefoot through a poisonous cactus nursery. And the Styles and Formatting task pane? What a pain!

When I have a project, such as a screenplay, that requires using several styles and manually switching among them, I just give up and create a new toolbar/floating palette full of styles. It's cinchy!

1. Choose Tools ➤ Customize.

   The Customize dialog box appears. It offers you more power than the mere mortal Word user should be allowed to mess with.

2. Click the Toolbars tab.

3. Click the New button.

   The New Toolbar dialog box appears, as shown in Figure 5.6.

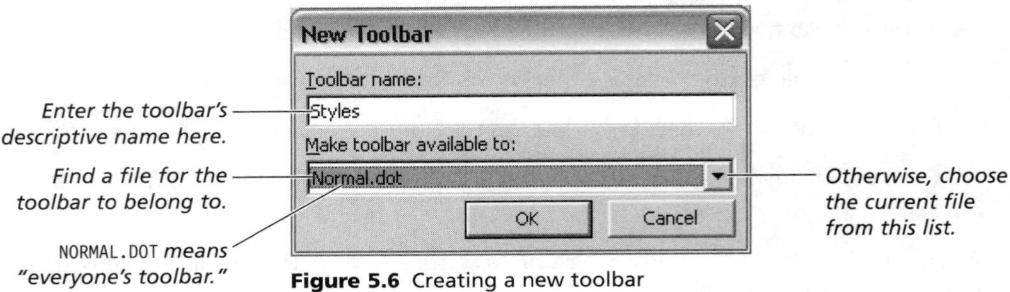
New Toolbar
Toolbar name:
Styles
Make toolbar available to:
Normal.dot
OK
Cancel
Enter the toolbar's descriptive name here.
Find a file for the toolbar to belong to.
NORMAL.DOT means "everyone's toolbar."
Otherwise, choose the current file from this list.

Figure 5.6 Creating a new toolbar

4. Enter `Styles` as the toolbar's name.

5. Choose a place to make the toolbar available.

   Choose `NORMAL.DOT` if you want the toolbar to belong to all your Word documents, or use the drop-down list to select the current document or its template. (If you can't decide, then select the current document or its template and not `NORMAL.DOT`.)

6. Click OK.

   The toolbar appears in two places. First, it shows up in the list of Toolbars in the Customize dialog box. But more importantly, look for its floating palette variation on the screen, similar to what you see in Figure 5.7. Yes, it will grow larger as you attach buttons to the palette.

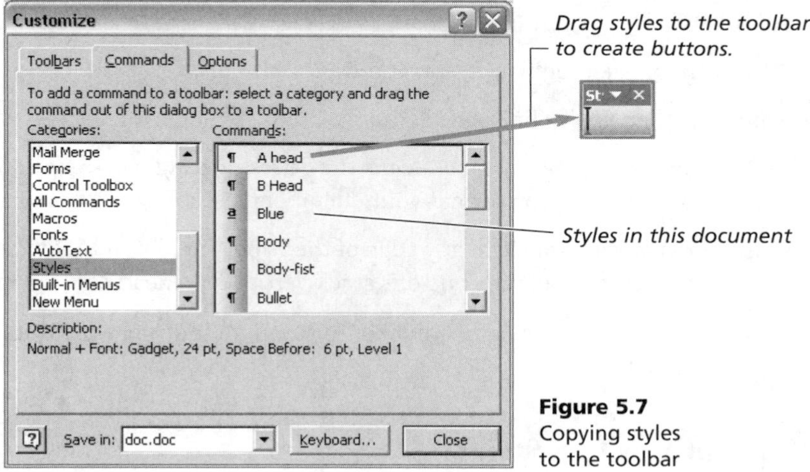

Figure 5.7
Copying styles to the toolbar

7. Click the Commands tab.

8. Scroll down the list of Categories and select Styles.

   The styles you've created for your document appear in the scrollable Commands list, as shown in Figure 5.7.

9. Choose a style to place on the toolbar.

   Make it a common style, one that you use often.

10. Drag that style to the toolbar.

    As you drag the mouse, the pointer changes to the "I'm dragging a style to the toolbar" pointer.

    When the pointer is over the toolbar, a hunky insertion pointer shows you exactly where on the toolbar the new button will be dropped. Release the mouse button to drop the style button at that location.

11. Repeat Steps 9 and 10 until you have your toolbar of styles.

Remember that you don't need to have all the styles on the toolbar, just the common ones.

When you've finished, you'll have a toolbar full of text: the blah-blah style and the so-and-so style. And style! Style! Style! It seems like a redundant word, so you can do some editing if you like:

12. Right-click a toolbar button to modify it.

A pop-up menu appears.

13. Enter or edit the toolbar button's name using the Name item.

It's the third item down. Click in there with the mouse and either edit the name or type something else that will appear on the toolbar. (I just edit the word "Style" from the name. Or if it's an "A-Head Style," I may just edit it down to "A.")

14. Repeat Steps 12 and 13 for each toolbar button you want to modify.

15. Click the Close button when you've finished.

That closes the Customize dialog box, which means the Styles floating palette is now locked into place and can be used to help you format your document.

As with any toolbar in Word, you can drag it to any edge of the window to "attach" it to that window. Or you can resize the toolbar to make the buttons stack vertically instead of horizontally.

You can close the toolbar to make it disappear if you like. To summon it again, choose its name from the View ➤ Toolbars submenu.

Can I Assign a Shortcut Key to a Style?

One of the fastest ways to apply any style is to give it a shortcut key. That way you can instantly apply the style's formatting with the press of a key. Or, actually, several keys because most of the handy Alt and Ctrl keys are already taken by various Word commands.

To slap a shortcut key combination to a style, follow these steps. It is assumed that the style has already been created:

1a. In Word 2003/XP, choose Format ➤ Styles and Formatting.

1b. In Word 2000, choose Format ➤ Style.

2. Locate the style you want to assign a shortcut key to.

3a. In Word 2003/XP, click the style's menu button (to the right) and choose Modify from the menu.

3b. In Word 2000, click the Modify button.

The Modify Style dialog box appears.

4a. In Word 2003/XP, choose Shortcut Key from the Format button's menu.

4b. In Word 2000, click the Shortcut Key button.

The Customize Keyboard dialog box appears, as shown in Figure 5.8. (In Word 2000 the items are arranged differently.)

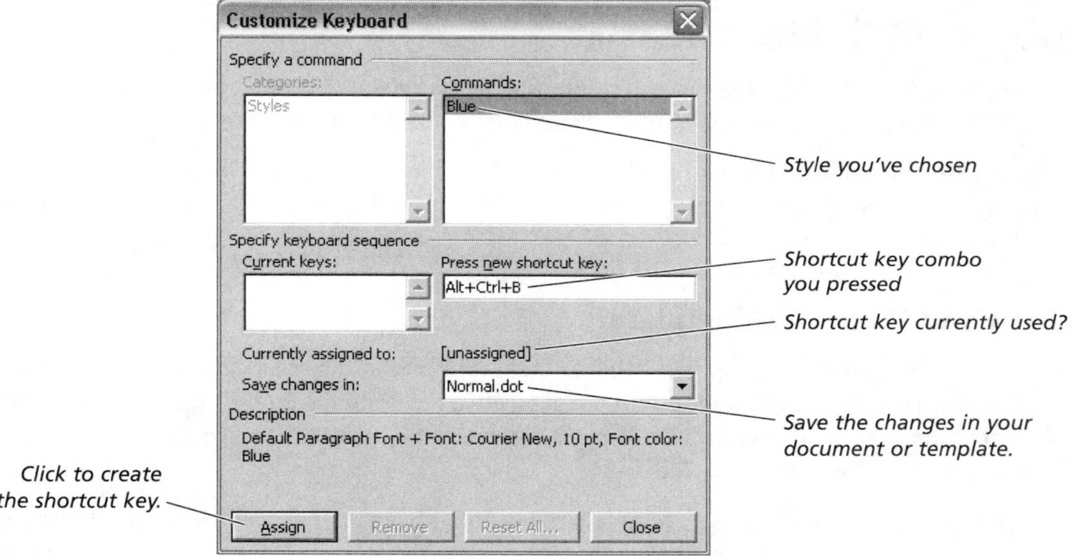

Figure 5.8 Assigning a shortcut key to a style

5. Type a key combination for your style.

It's best to use the Ctrl and Alt keys together, plus a letter key, such as the first letter of the style, as shown in Figure 5.8.

If the key combination is already used by Windows, you'll see the command listed in the dialog box. Try another command in that case.

6. Click the Assign button to assign that key combination to your style.

7. Choose your document's name or template from the "Save Changes In" drop-down list.

Try not to save the changes in `NORMAL.DOT`. If you do, you'll quickly run out of key combinations as you create more styles that can possibly have keyboard equivalents.

8. Click the Close button.

Now to apply that style, use the proper key combination.

I prefer using a palette of style buttons over assigning keyboard combinations to styles. That's because when I write I prefer to write first and format second. In that mode, it's easier to use a palette of buttons for formatting than to be messing with the keyboard again.

Holy Templates, Word Man!

Templates are handy files that let you create similar documents over and over again without having to build (or import) styles or copy and paste common chunks of text.

When it comes to word processing, the subject of templates is really a beginner-level one. Therefore I assembled a set of what I feel are suitable intermediate template topics to round out this chapter.

What Can I Put into a Template?

Templates are prototype documents that contain things that don't change. For example, if you create the same report every month, you can create a template file for that report. Include the headings and styles and headers and footers or whatever else is common to the report every month. Save that as a template file.

Beyond text (and even graphics), templates can contain your styles, toolbars, shortcut keys, and a smattering of other things you create. Those can all be specific to a template. (If not, then they're saved in the `NORMAL.DOT` file, which is why you're occasionally prompted to save `NORMAL.DOT` when it seems like you haven't done anything to it.)

To save a template, choose "Document Template (*.DOT)" from the drop-down list by "Save as Type," in the Save As dialog box.

To use a template, choose the File ➤ New Command. In Word 2003/XP you need to look under the "Other Templates" heading in the task pane. In Word 2000, just pluck a template from the New dialog box.

In Word 2003/XP, the "Other Templates" part of the New Document task pane lists any recently used templates. To see the rest of them, click the item that reads "On My Computer." That displays a Templates dialog box (like in the good old days).

I've Already Made a Document and Need to Make a Template from It.

To transform a document into a template, remove everything from the document that is specific. For a letter, keep only the parts that won't change from epistle to epistle. For a report, keep only the headings or whatever else doesn't change. Make the template brief, yet keep those items you know you'll have to type in anyway.

Once the regular Word document is pared down, use File ➢ Save As to save it as a template.

I generally create the document first, fumbling through creating styles and whatnot. Then I save that document to disk. Only after that do I open it again, delete most of the unique text, and save it to disk as a template.

I Need to Reassign This Document's Template!

There, you've done it! You've gone and created a document with a certain template only to find out that you really need to associate it with another template. Oh, drat!

Well, you're not entirely screwed. You can reassociate a document with a given template. You won't get the text from that template, but you will inherit the styles and any other template-y things:

1. Choose Tools ➢ Templates and Add-ins.
2. Click the Attach button.

   Use the Attach Template dialog box to find the real template you want the document to use.
3. Click the Open button.
4. Be sure to put a check mark by "Automatically Update Document Styles."
5. Click OK.

   And your document is now enjoying the benefits and graces of a new template.

Do Changes to a Template Affect Any Documents I've Already Created with That Template?

Yes. You won't see the changes until you open the document, but they'll be there.

Where the Heck Are the Templates Stored on Disk?

Ah, the sweet mystery of life! Where are those template files anyway? It used to be, back in the bad old days, that Word could hide its templates in any of three different places on the hard drive. It was maddening to determine which location Word was currently using. So if you had the full Microsoft Office installation, the files might be in one folder, but if you just installed Word by itself, the files might be somewhere else entirely.

Fortunately, sanity reigns and the location of the template files on disk depends on your version of Windows more than anything Word or Office is doing.

For Windows XP, templates are a personal thing. You can find them in your account's special area in the Documents and Settings folder:

1. Open Drive C, or wherever Windows is installed.
2. Open the Documents and Settings folder.
3. Open your account's folder.
4. Open the Application Data folder.

   This is a hidden folder, so you may not see it displayed. (Refer to my book, *Dan Gookin's Naked Windows XP,* for information on displaying hidden files.)
5. Open the Microsoft folder.
6. Open the Templates folder.

And if you do have Dan Gookin's Naked Windows XP, *refer to Chapter 8 on creating a custom palette of programs. You can use those same instructions to create a custom palette of Word document templates—another handy way to start Word!*

For Windows 98 and Windows Me, you can find the templates files here:

1. Open Drive C.
2. Open the Windows folder.
3. Open the Application Data folder.
4. Open the Microsoft folder.
5. Open the Templates folder

   And there they are!

Normally you don't need to know these "secret" locations for the templates. However, I remember quite a few times when I've tried to manually find this location on disk and was frustrated that it wasn't written down anywhere. Well...now it is!

6 Writing That Great American Novel or Screenplay

The word processor has completely overtaken the typewriter as the ultimate writing tool. After all, a typewriter cared not whether you were typing a school paper, a letter, a novel, or even one of those typing school exercises that, if you typed in all the characters correctly, looked like the Mona Lisa when held at a distance.

As that master of all things written, Word has no preference as to whether you're typing a government grant, a secret diary, or a list of chores for the kids to do while you're away on "business" in Orlando. It's designed to handle small tasks more than adequately, but Word has also been used to write novels, screenplays, and political treaties—heavy-duty stuff.

Where do you draw the line? It depends on what you want to do. For example, if you're writing something creative, such as a novel or screenplay, then you'll probably be using many of the Word tools described in this chapter. If not, then you can get by using a minimal amount of Word. But, for the moment at least, I'll assume that you want more from your word processor than just a letter telling the dentist that his payment will be late this month because alien robots stole your wallet.

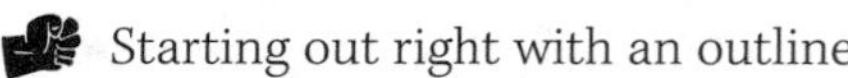

Thoughts Expressed and Misgivings Unfounded:

- Starting out right with an outline
- Manipulating your outline
- Managing your documents with a master document
- Building a table of contents
- Creating an index
- Cobbling together various creative projects in Word

What the Heck Is Outline Mode?

Outlining is the process of organizing your thoughts before you get them down on paper. For a long project, this is must. They tried to teach you that in school, but the problem in school is that they don't use a *long* project example. Instead, they try to have you outline a short project, which is a silly waste of time.

Whenever I write anything longer than three pages, or anything that must present issues, ideas, or solutions, I first craft an outline. That way I can ensure that my ideas progress logically and that I cover everything; Outline mode allows you to madly jot down simple ideas or splash words on the page and then rearrange them without worrying about the details.

In the old days, outlining was done on 3 x 5 cards. Then there was outlining software, such as Acta or the popular GrandView program. About a dozen years ago, Word incorporated an outlining mode into its basic program, so there's nothing more you need to do to start outlining like a pro.

I Have My Ideas, so How Do I Outline Them?

Outlining is done in the Outline view, yet another of Word's many ways of looking at a document. In this mode, the Heading styles take on special privileges, and certain keyboard and toolbar commands help you manipulate and hide a document's contents—all for the sake of easily organizing your thoughts. Yeah verily, outlining is not only a mode...it's a state of mind.

To begin outlining, choose View ➤ Outline from the menu. Or you can click the Outline button in the lower-left corner of the window. Two things happen: The screen changes to Outline view and the Outlining toolbar shows up, as shown in Figure 6.1.

The next thing to do is to organize your thoughts. You can do so by chapter, as shown in Figure 6.1, or by topic, subtopic, and even sub-subtopic. The idea is to rattle your brain and see what plops out. Then, in Outline mode, you can organize things to flow in whatever fashion you wish.

The Outlining toolbar is different between Word versions 2003/XP and Word 2000. Primarily it's missing the useful Outline Level button, though the Style drop-down list works similarly (when you select the Heading styles).

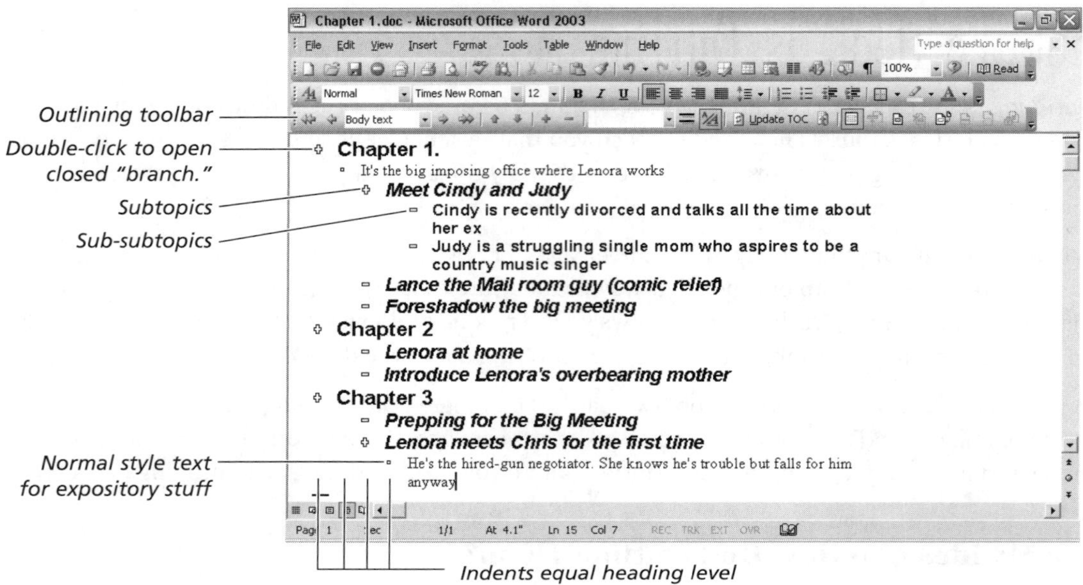

Figure 6.1 Outline mode in full bloom

How Do I Create a Topic?

A topic is any high-level heading or subject matter in your document. These are given the Heading 1 attribute in the outline window, and they appear farthest to the left.

To create a topic, type at the – (minus or hyphen) icon in the document. For a main topic, type less information. In fact, in most of my documents the main topic is a chapter title or scene or act from a play.

Remember that main topics are general! Your subtopics can contain more detail. (And for even more detail, I use the Normal style, but more on that in a few paragraphs.)

What's a Subtopic?

A subtopic is a specific aspect or element of the main topic. You create it like this:

1. Press the Enter key.

   This actually creates a sister topic, but what you want is a subtopic.

2. Press Alt+Shift+right arrow.

   This key command *demotes* the topic level to a subtopic.

3. Type your subtopic.

Hi-Ho! So Topics Can Be Jiggled Around?

Yes, and this is the beauty of an outline: You can shuffle things around easily. Here's how to move a topic or subtopic:

1. Click the topic's + or – icon.

   Note that this selects all the subtopics and any text belonging to that topic.

2. Now you can drag the topic up or down (or left or right) with the mouse, but a better way is to use the Outlining toolbar's arrow buttons:

   Instantly promote the topic to level 1. (This button isn't available in Word 2000.)

   Promote up (left) one notch.

   Level 1 — Select a specific level for the topic from the drop-down list (not available in Word 2000).

   Demote the topic (right) one notch.

   Convert the topic into body text (Normal style).

   Move the topic up (earlier in the outline).

   Move the topic down (later in the outline).

For example, refer to the quick outline I dished up in Figure 6.2. Suppose you need to move the subtopic "Pablo opens his taco stand amidst much celebration" up, swapping its position with "Maria finally agrees to marry Pablo." Here's how you'd do that:

Figure 6.2 A sample outline

1. Click to select the subtopic "Pablo opens...."

   This automatically selects any sub-subtopics or text below that subtopic, grouping the entire thing as a block, as shown in Figure 6.2.

2. Drag the subtopic upward.

   Drag by the + sign. As you drag with the mouse, a horizontal "here" line appears, showing where the moving topic(s) will be reinserted into the outline.

3. Release the mouse button to drop the subtopic.

   In Figure 6.2, it will be positioned just under "Opening number...." (And do note that you can have a sub-subtopic under a main topic.)

   You could also use the buttons on the toolbar to move the topic. In this case, first select the main subtopic so that all its own topics are selected (as shown in Figure 6.2). Then click the Up button twice to move the topic(s) earlier in the outline.

What's the Point of the + or – Icon?

The + and – icons are very handy, serving several purposes in the grand scheme of things. I can think of the following:

- The icon is a handle you can use to drag a topic with the mouse.
- The icon is a button you can double-click to select that topic and all its subtopics.
- The icon indicates whether or not a topic has subtopics. Only a topic with subtopics has the + sign.
- The icons relate to the corresponding keys on the numeric keypad, which can be used to open (expand) or close (collapse) a topic.
- The icons can also be clicked to expand or collapse a topic.

How Can I Split This Topic in Two?

Splitting a topic works like splitting any paragraph or sentence in word: Cleave the topic by clicking the mouse where you want the split and then pressing the Enter key. That creates two sisters where one stood before.

Can I Join Topics?

Yes, just as you would join paragraphs:

1. Put the cursor at the start of the second topic.
2. Press the Backspace key.

   The topics are now joined, but the words run together, so:

3. Press the spacebar.

   That sticks air between the last word of the old first topic and the first word of the old second topic.

I Need to Collapse All My Topics: Any Easy Way to Do It All at Once?

To see the Big Picture, you need to tell Word to hide all topic levels except for the first one.

In Word 2003/XP, choose "Show Level 1" from the drop-down list in the middle of the Outlining toolbar.

In Word 2000, click the number "1" on the Outlining toolbar.

Doing this is a great way to get a grand overview of your outline—to shove aside the details and concentrate on our major points or elements.

KEYBOARD MASTER

Faster Ways to Move Your Topics Around

There are a wealth of keyboard equivalents for manipulating your outline. In fact, I use the keyboard more than the mouse when I'm outlining. Here are my favorite keys:

Alt+Shift+arrow

The arrow can be any one of the four arrow keys on the keyboard: up, down, left, or right. Pressing this key combination moves an individual topic (but not the subtopics) in the direction of the arrow. Very handy.

Numeric Keypad –

Pressing the minus key on the numeric keypad collapses a topic, hiding any subtopics from view.

Numeric Keypad +

Pressing the + key on the numeric keypad opens a collapsed topic.

How Can I View Only Level 2 Headings?

I outline my books with the part levels at Level 1 and then the chapter titles at Level 2. So when I want to see all those chapter titles only, I do this:

In Word 2003/XP, choose "Show Level 2" from the drop-down list in the middle of the Outlining toolbar.

In Word 2000, click the number "2."

Whenever you choose a level to view, Word automatically shows you any levels "above" that level. There is no way to "hide" higher levels.

It's still possible to view details in this mode. For example, as I started this chapter, I brought up this book's outline and chose to view only the Level 2 headings, which are my chapter titles. Then I double-clicked the + by Chapter 6 to expand it and view the sections and subsections within this chapter.

How Can I See All the Levels Again?

In Word 2003/XP, choose "Show All Levels" from the drop-down list; in Word 2000, click the All button.

Why Bother with the Normal Style in an Outline?

Not everything you want to put into the outline will be a topic. For example, at some point you may want to write a bit of background or, heck, just start writing. In those instances, rather than waste a topic heading, you can just use the body text level to compose your thoughts.

To create a stretch of body-level text, click the Demote to Body Text button.

If you tend to be a little wordy with your body text stuff, and that gets in the way of your Big Picture view, then click the Show First Line Only button on the Outlining toolbar. That "hides" any second (or extra) lines of text in the outline. Click the button again to turn this feature off.

KEYBOARD MASTER

The Normal Style

Here's the quick way to get Normal.

Ctrl+Shift+N

To apply the Normal style to any paragraph of text, or to demote any outline topic to the body text level, use this keyboard shortcut.

Does the Outline Need to Be Saved as a Separate Document?

I always save my outlines as their own document. I typically give them the name `OUTLINE.DOC` or even `TOC.DOC`, where TOC stands for Table Of Contents. This file lives in the same folder as other documents for the same project.

For example, for this book there is a separate document called `TOC.DOC` that contains the book's entire outline. But you don't always have to do things that way.

In many cases, if you simply continue fleshing out an outline, then the outline document can eventually become your final document. Simply change the view back to Normal or Print Layout, start formatting, and your document is on its way to completion.

Organizing Your Work (after Outlining)

Some major projects will end up being more than a single document. While Word itself is capable of handing a document of any length, it works better with smaller documents. Plus, I believe you'll find that keeping the files separate reduces the chance that you'll lose information, and it makes it easier on Word (fewer crashes).

Is It Best to Create My Massive Word Project as One Document or as Several Documents?

It depends on how big your massive Word project is. In my travels, most writers put a chapter into each document. So a 42-chapter novel would consist of 42 separate files. Plus there may be separate files for appendixes, a prefix, a foreword, and other elements of a book.

For smaller works, keeping everything in one document makes sense. In fact, I keep screenplays or teleplays, which are from 30 to 120 pages, as their own documents. But for books and novels, I try to put a chapter into each document.

So I suppose the answer to the question is that it all depends on what you find easiest to work with.

If you're a professional writer, then check with the publisher to see which format they want. Publishers are very particular about how they want to see text submitted electronically. So ask!

Should I Worry about Binding Issues?

I would say no: If you're submitting a document to be published, then the publisher makes its own adjustments for binding. Only if you plan on printing out the document yourself should you concern yourself with binding or setting the gutters or using alternating headers and footers on separate pages. This is covered later in this chapter.

If you're getting into binding issues, then you're crossing the fuzzy line between desktop publishing and word processing. Consider your needs, and if you do plan on binding your stuff, then get a desktop publishing program and use it instead of Word.

How Do I Stick Multiple Documents Together?

To compile several smaller documents into a single mammoth document, you need to work with Word's Master Document mode, a kind of hybrid of Outline mode. This is optional, of course. I would bother with this only if you plan on printing your documents and want them all to have uniform page numbers, headers, and footers. Otherwise, you don't really need to mess with Master Document mode.

Assuming that you have all of your separate documents ready to be threaded together, and that you have the guts to go through with this, follow these steps:

1. Start a new, blank document in Word.

Click the New Blank Document button on the toolbar. This will become your new *master document*. Om!

2. Switch to Outline View.

Choose View ➤ Outline.

3. Activate the Master Document part of the Outlining toolbar.

Click the Master Document button on the Outlining toolbar. This extends the toolbar's length a bit to accommodate the Master Document buttons, as shown in Figure 6.3. (Note that the Master Document part of the toolbar may already be showing, in which case it's not necessary to click the button.)

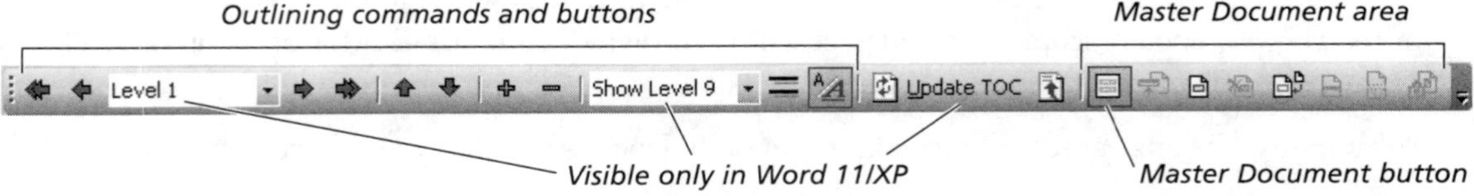

Figure 6.3 The Outlining toolbar, Master Document stuff

4. Click the Insert Subdocument button.

The Insert Subdocument dialog box appears. It's just an Open dialog box hybrid.

5. Use the Insert Subdocument dialog box to select your first chapter document or the document that you want to be first in your big master document.

So if it's front matter, an introduction, a foreword, or a preface, start with that. Otherwise start with Chapter 1.

6. Click the Open button to insert the document.

   The document is inserted into the master document á la a topic in an outline. The chapter appears in a box, complete with all its text and a subdocument doodad icon, as shown in Figure 6.4.

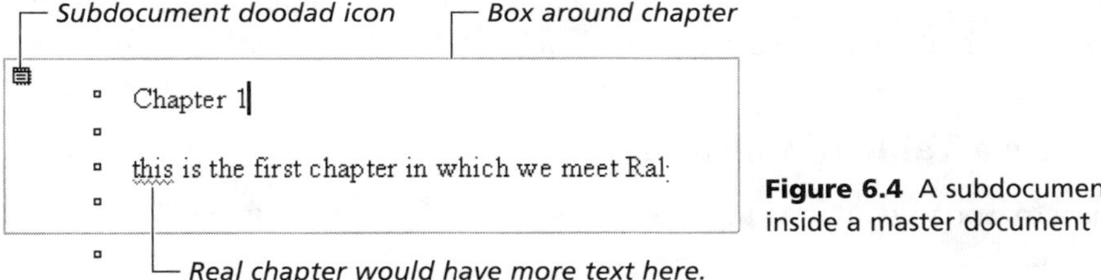
Subdocument doodad icon
Box around chapter
Chapter 1
this is the first chapter in which we meet Ral
Real chapter would have more text here.

Figure 6.4 A subdocument inside a master document

   You can use the doodad icon to move the entire chapter up or down in the sequence of events. Otherwise:

7. Repeat Steps 5 and 6 to continue to add your chapters or other subdocuments to the master document.

The idea here is to glue all the small pieces together into one big document, the master document. Once the pieces are in place, then you can do things like create headers and footers and page numbers for the *entire* document.

To prove how the master document works, use Print Preview to observe your entire document as it would be printed.

Save the master document! Be sure to save it! The thing is just as important as any other document you have. Save after inserting each new subdocument as well.

Do I Really Need to See All Those Subdocuments in the Master Document?

No. In fact, you can compress things so that the master document is easier to look at. To do so, click the Collapse Subdocuments button on the Outlining toolbar.

If you haven't saved, you'll be prompted to do so. Afterward, each document is replaced by a hypertext (Web page) link to its original file on disk. A little padlock below the subdocument doodad icon tells you that the subdocument is locked and can be edited only in the original file.

To go and visit a subdocument in the compressed state, just Ctrl-click its link. That opens the document in its own window, which is what you're used to in Word.

The subdocuments must be expanded before you can view them in Print Preview or print them all off.

What about Page Numbering across Multiple Documents?

All page numbering can be done in the master document. Just use whatever command you prefer to handle the page numbering.

Each subdocument appears in the master document in its own section. This allows for adjustment of the headers and footers so that, for example, a header doesn't print on a new chapter page. Refer to Chapter 3, "Making Fancy Documents and Reports," for more information on sections.

How Do I Create a Table of Contents?

You don't have to worry about creating a table of contents for any document! Word can do it automatically for you.

A table of contents can be created for any document, from a two-page treatise to a 300-page report. It doesn't have to be a master document or anything fancy. The only requirement for the table of contents is that you use styles, specifically Heading styles, in your document. If so, then Word can easily create a table of contents, complete with accurate page numbers.

To build a table of contents in your document, follow these steps:

1. Go to the place in your document where you want the TOC to appear.

If you're working in a master document, place the TOC at the front. For any other type of document, create a page or section break so that the TOC will appear on its own page. (See Chapter 3.)

Any document with the proper heading styles used can have its own TOC. Size is not an issue; merely applying the proper heading styles is all that's required.

2a. In Word 2003/XP, choose Insert ➤ Reference ➤ Index and Tables.

2b. In Word 2000, choose Insert ➤ Index and Tables.

The Index and Tables dialog box pops up.

3. Click the Table of Contents tab.

Figure 6.5 shows you what is what, though most of the settings are pretty much the way you want them. There is, however, only one thing you should check:

4. Click the Options button.

Word identifies TOC headings by your document's styles. Up front it assumes that you're using the built-in Heading 1, Heading 2, and Heading 3 styles for your document's headings. If you're using custom styles, such as A-head or Head1 or Title 1 or something unique, the Table of Contents Options dialog box is where you select the difference.

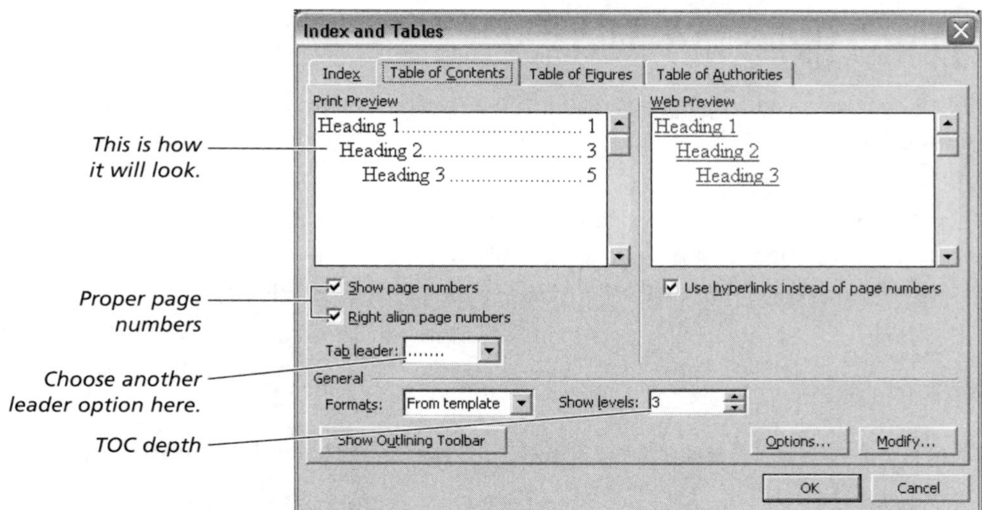

Figure 6.5 Creating the table of contents

5. Select the proper heading styles for the TOC.

For example, to have Word use style A Head as the first level in a TOC, scroll through the list to find A Head and assign that to TOC level 1. Assign B Head to TOC level 2, and so on. Or apply the levels to whatever heading levels you're using in your document.

If you've already set the proper outline levels for your styles, as described in Chapter 5, "Using Styles and Templates to Save Oodles of Time," then you won't need to go through this extra step.

6. Click OK.

7. Click OK to create the TOC.

And the TOC is filled in by using the text you formatted with the given styles in your document. Note that it's formatted using a standard body text type of style. You can, if you like, go in and reformat the TOC to look like whatever you want it to. Or you can delete parts of the TOC, edit certain headings, whatever you wish. Treat it like any other text.

Update TOC

Obviously the TOC should be the last thing you create for your document. Use a hard page break or section break to separate its page from the rest of the document. And if you have to update or change things, then simply click the Update TOC button on the Outlining toolbar, or just repeat these steps to rebuild the entire thing.

How Does Indexing Work?

In publishing, it's typically up to the author to index his own work. Even so, there are professional indexers and indexing services that go through books and, for a modest sum, do a far better job than an author can.

For your documents, you can index them yourself providing you remember to create the index entries. That is, you mark text in your document for inclusion in an index. Then Word can take all those marked-up bits of text and compile an index for you, all automatically.

As with a table of contents, you can stick an index into any Word document. It doesn't need to be a master document or, in the case of an index, even have fancy formatting or styles.

It Had Better Not Be Difficult to Mark a Bit of Text for Inclusion in an Index.

It's not. It helps if your entire document has been written and polished. Like the table of contents, the index is one of the last things you add to a document.

If everything is ready, then follow these steps:

1a. In Word 2003/XP, choose Insert ➢ Reference ➢ Index and Tables.

1b. In Word 2000, choose Insert ➢ Index and Tables.

The Index and Tables dialog box appears.

2. Click the Index tab.

3. Click the Mark Entry button.

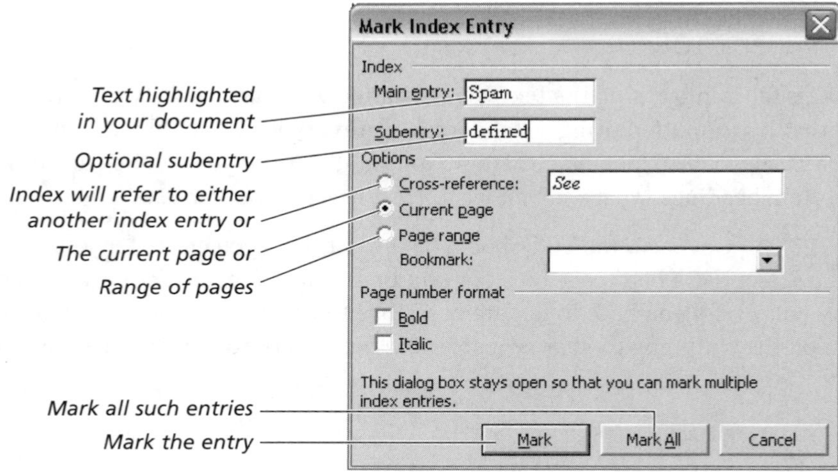

Figure 6.6 Creating an index entry

The Mark Entry dialog box appears, shown in Figure 6.6. It's a "modal" dialog box, which means you can keep it open while you work in your document. So your next task is to collect words and phrases that you want to appear in your document's index.

4. Select a bit of text in your document.

   Select something you want to appear in the index.

5. Click the mouse in the Mark Index Entry dialog box.

   The text you selected appears in the Main Entry.

6. Fill in the dialog box as needed.

7. Click the Mark button.

8. Repeat Steps 4 through 7 as needed until you've collected a cache of index entries.

   You can mark as much text as you like. You can even edit the entries you select. For example, if you select the text "Noted legal issues involving the abuse of a spatula," you can edit it down to just "legal issues" if you like.

Try to keep in mind what the reader is thinking. Oftentimes they don't use the same terms as you might. For example, in a cookbook consider indexing "Ladle" under "Spoon."

9. When you're absolutely sick of marking text, click the Cancel or Close button in the Mark Index Entry dialog box.

   Whew!

Note that marking a document puts special ugly, curly bracket field codes into the document and, well, while you're marking it, the document can look really gross. To make those marks go away when you've done, click the Show/Hide button on the Standard toolbar.

How Do I Put an Index into My Document?

After collecting and marking all the separate index entries, you merely need to order Word to build the index for you. Here's how to do that:

1. Go to the page where you want the index to appear.

   Yes, typically that's at the end of your document.

Don't worry about creating a separate section or page breaks for the index; Word does that automatically.

2a. In Word 2003/XP, choose Insert ➢ Reference ➢ Index and Tables.

2b. In Word 2000, choose Insert ➢ Index and Tables.

3. Click the Index tab, if needed.
4. Click OK.

   Sure, you could mess in the dialog box, but the settings are pretty standard. By clicking OK, you'll see the index sitting there in your document.

About the only thing you could do in the Index dialog box is to check the box that says "Right Align Page Numbers." That presents the index in a different format, but that's really about the only thing in the dialog box worth changing.

So Now I've Edited My Document and the Index Needs to Be Rebuilt. Help!

The hardest part about doing an index is building it. (Well, in the real world it's getting the stupid page numbers correct, but Word doesn't seem to have a problem with that.) So to rebuild your index, simply select and delete the old one (including the Continuous section breaks), and repeat the steps from the previous section to plop down a new index. Cinchy.

Ideas for Various Creative Projects

The following sections contain some ideas for styles you can put into templates and other tricks you can use when you work on some creative things in Word.

Microsoft has a wealth of Word templates you can use or "borrow" from the Internet. In Word 11/XP, on the New Document task pane, click the link for the Templates Home Page, and you'll be connected with a Microsoft computer that has dozens of interesting, handy, and useful template files you can download and use on your own computer.

The Great American Novel

Do you really need a template for the Great American Novel? Nope. Novels are mostly about content, not formatting or anything fancy. In fact, I know of no published author who has ever complained, "They just wouldn't read my stuff until I formatted with the proper heading styles." So rest assured, you don't really need a template to write a novel.

Even so, I do have a template I use for when I go into story mode. It contains the following styles:

Chapter This style has the chapter number or name in bold text, usually centered, with about three blank lines (36 pts) following it. It's automatically followed by the Body style, which is the main style for the document.

Body This paragraph style is usually 12-point Bookman, Palatino, or Book Antiqua, double-spaced with the first line indented one-half inch. No space follows or precedes the paragraph because it's double-spaced. And I use left justification instead of full.

Try to avoid making your novel look like a novel. Try not to use columns or full justification. If you plan on submitting the novel for publication, find out from your agent or the publisher in which format the novel should be. With that knowledge, you can easily adjust the style in your document and instantly reformat the entire thing.

That's it for styles. Occasionally I may have a sub-Chapter style that contains the text of the chapter title. So it looks like this:

```
8. We're back in the scary castle again
```

It's up to you whether your chapters have numbers, titles, or a combination of both.

For the template, I typically have it start with the Chapter style ready to go, so that when I open a new document with that template, I can type the chapter number or title and then start writing.

In the header I have my name, the novel's name, and the date. The footer contains the chapter number and the page number. This is all formatted in Arial 10-point bold, but it's part of the template so I don't really create a style for it.

Hurray for Hollywood and the Typical Screenplay

I've written both screenplays and stage plays. (Nothing published, however, mostly because nothing is finished!) Stage plays are easier because they lack the strict style guidelines set down for motion picture screenplays, teleplays, and video plays.

Writing a Typical Stage Play

Stage plays don't have much involved in the way of formatting or style. Aside from the stage directions, the lines make up the bulk of the document. They're formatted sort of like this:

```
LINDA: Take off my dress!
KYLE: Yes! At once!
LINDA: And don't let me ever catch you wearing my clothes again!
```

Most professionally published scripts have the character name in SMALL CAPS or often in **bold**. The text is formatted with a hanging indent of about 1/4 inch. Stage directions are in either italics or parentheses. There is no hard-and-fast style.

Professionally published plays do have a style, depending on the publisher. Even so, I've worked with local and amateur productions where the script is merely typed out any which way. The idea is merely to make it clear who is speaking which lines.

Don't go overboard on your stage directions. Most stage directors look for entrances and exits, plus key business regarding props and physical activity. Overloading your play with too many directions or descriptions merely slows down the reading process, which probably isn't what you want.

An alternative to the more traditional style is to format the text with the character's name centered above what they say, as in:

Bert

```
Molly! Uncle Cedric! What are you doing in that closet?
```

Molly

```
It's just a little fox trot. The closet is too small to tango.
```

In this case you can take advantage of styles, especially to follow each other:

ACTOR

This style contains the actor's name. It's centered with the text bold. Single-spaced, no space before or after. Immediately following this style is the Lines style.

```
Lines
```

This formats the text the actors say. It need not be anything interesting, though I would make it single-spaced with the paragraph followed by 12 points of "air" to separate it from the next bit of text. In fact, this style could automatically be followed by the Actor style in that lines in a play are not broken up into traditional paragraphs of text. (It goes Actor-Lines-Actor-Lines-Actor-Lines, only occasionally broken up by the stage directions.)

When writing a script, there is no need to break up what a character says into paragraphs.

Cobbling Together a Screenplay

Screenplays are strictly formatted. Word can handle it, but most of the "serious" Hollywood writers use a special word processor designed to build screenplays. For the casual writer, however (or until you get your big break), Word does just fine.

I have no idea why screenplays are so exactingly formatted (well, not being in Hollywood, how would I know?). I can guess that it's simply to weed out the less-than-serious from those who really pay attention. After all, if you have a slush pile of 100 scripts, it's easier to toss away something that's formatted improperly than it is to spend time reading the piece.

Figure 6.7 shows a page from a screenplay I worked on when I should have been working on some computer book.

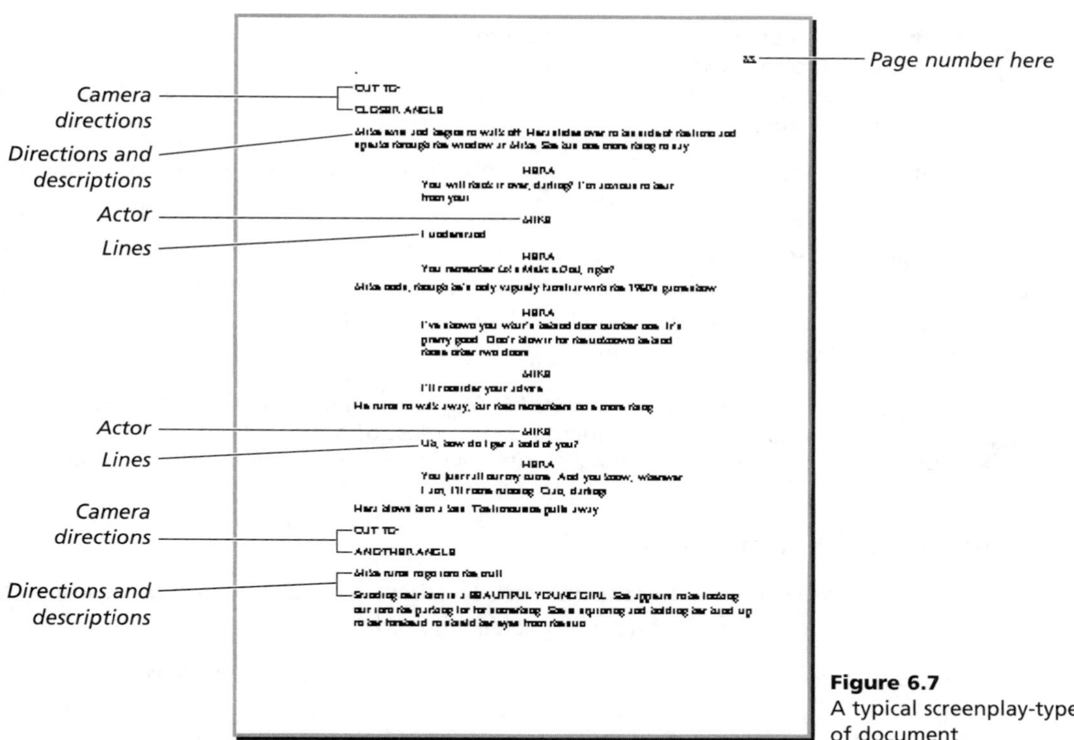

Figure 6.7
A typical screenplay-type of document

Here are the styles I use and their descriptions:

Scene Setting This is the style that introduces a scene, which is an INT (interior) or EXT (exterior), followed by a location and a time of day. It's also used for camera angles and such, though your script shouldn't contain too many of those. The style is ALL CAPS, right-justified, single-spaced, with a blank line following.

Stage Directions This is the expository style in the script, which explains a setting or situation or a character's mood or internal thoughts. It's single-spaced, with a blank line following each paragraph.

Actor The actor's name is formatted in ALL CAPS. Some scripts have the name centered, but I indent it 2.5 inches. This style is immediately followed by the Lines style.

Lines The Lines style is the format for the lines the actor speaks. It's indented one inch on the left and right (see Figure 6.7). A tab stop is set at position 2.5". It's used to include parenthetical directions in the middle of the line. The paragraph is single-spaced and followed with a blank line. The format for the next style is Actor, since dialog tends to go Actor-Lines-Actor-Lines. That way you can type dialog for a stretch without having to worry about formatting.

Unlike a stage play, actors in a screenplay don't talk much. Each block of text for them to speak should be at most five lines long. Longer exposition can be broken up by stage directions, but I would recommend against long exposition for your first screenplay.

In addition to these styles, the template should contain a page number. It's located in the upper-right corner of the page, and it shows the page number followed by a period. That's it!

The first page of the script should be its own section, without a page number. It contains the film's name and then your name as author, centered in the middle of the page. On the bottom left are your name, address, and phone number. If you have an agent, their name goes bottom center (below the lines containing your name).

Scripts are very tricky things to write! I recommend getting a book on screenwriting before you even attempt to submit a script. Most of them will tell you one specific truth: No one makes money by writing scripts for Hollywood. But don't let that stop you!

Hammering Out a Newsletter

Newsletters can be fun to do—after the first one. The first one is the toughest because it's where you end up making all the layout decisions and deciding what goes where.

The first thing I can recommend is *not* to worry about fancy binding. If you have a printer that can print on 11 x 17 paper, then you could create a four-page newsletter on one page that folds over. However, Word isn't really equipped to handle printing on such a thing. Ditto for folding over an 8 1/2 x 11 sheet of paper. Even though Word claims it can print two pages on a sheet of paper, it just can't arrange the pages so that you can fold the paper and have it print out nice and tidy.

And where do you find a program that can print out on folded paper nice and tidy? That's right: under the desktop publishing category.

So, for now, assume that you're doing a newsletter that is to be printed on both sides of a standard sheet of paper and then stapled together (if there are more than one sheet). That's about the best and easiest way to handle things.

Headings First

Start your newsletter with its heading. You can create a giant text block for this or use borders to put lines above and below (or around) the title text. Your title can be a graphic you paste in. But my favorite way to do things is to put the title into a table.

Figure 6.8 shows a table used as the potential header for a newsletter. Further modification can be done, such as removing the grid lines in the table and potentially shading in the different squares of text. And, of course, borders can still be added. (Refer to Chapter 7, "The Tough Stuff: From Labels to Tables," for more information on tables.)

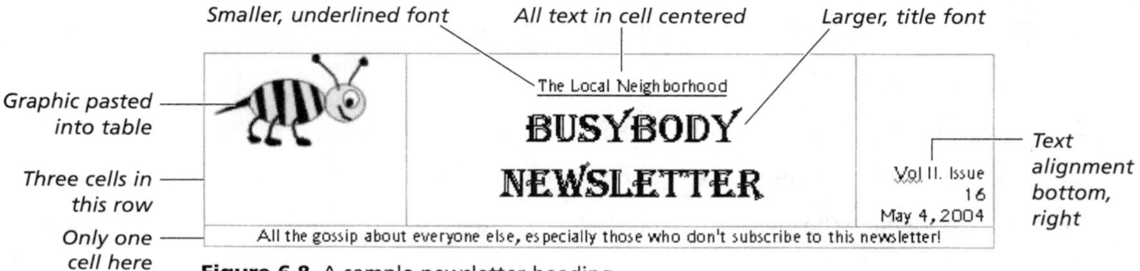

Figure 6.8 A sample newsletter heading

I'd Like to Lay Out Things in Two Columns.

After you do the heading, the rest of the newsletter is the *news!* Do you want it in columns or not?

To not use columns requires no skill: Just keep typing.

To use columns, follow these steps:

1. Stick the cursor right after the heading.
2. Choose Insert ➢ Break.

   The columns need to go into their own section.
3. Choose Continuous and click OK.

   Now you're ready for columns.
4. Choose Format ➢ Columns.

   The Columns dialog box appears.
5. Choose Two; then click OK.

And your document now has two columns. Write away your content! And spice it up! Refer to Chapter 5 for information on inserting graphics, images, pull quotes, and even random shapes!

Columns in newsletters are usually formatted fully justified. Also refer to Chapter 7 for more information on columns.

How Do I Stop a Column in the Middle of a Page?

Just as there are a page break and a section break, there is also something called a column break. If you want a column to stop at a specific location on the page, simply insert a column break.

To insert a column break, heed this procedure:

1. Position the cursor where you want the column to stop.
2. Choose Insert ➤ Break.
3. Select Column Break and click OK.

   And the text continues on the next column or page, whichever is closer.

The blank spot where the column used to be? Hey! What a great place for a picture or a text box with more information.

How Can I Start My Text with a Big Letter or Word?

To further draw attention to where text starts, production designers often make the first letter of that paragraph larger than the rest. If they want to get real fancy, they create a *drop cap*, shown in Figure 6.9.

Here's how you, too, can create a drop cap:

1. Click the mouse by the letter you want to drop.

   Or you can select the letter.

2. Choose Format ➤ Drop Cap.

   The Drop Cap dialog box contains some interesting options you can mess with later. But the Dropped option is the one pretty much everyone chooses.

3. Select the Dropped option and click OK.

   And the letter is transformed into a larger version of itself.

Be on the lookout for evil! While some vermin could be from legitimate businesses that just don't know how offensive evil is, other spirits can be down right illegal.

Figure 6.9 A drop cap

In a way, the drop cap is like a text box with the first three lines of the paragraph flowing around it. But don't be fooled: It is *not* a text box.

You can resize the drop cap, though you might just mess it up if you dink too much. To delete the drop cap, click to select it and press the Delete key.

And now, the secret to making a drop *word* instead of a drop cap: After you have the drop cap, click the mouse in the box. You'll notice the flashing cursor appear, which means that you can type. So go ahead and type the rest of the first word of the sentence to create a drop word. (Don't forget to edit the rest of the first word out of the rest of the paragraph, as shown in Figure 6.10.)

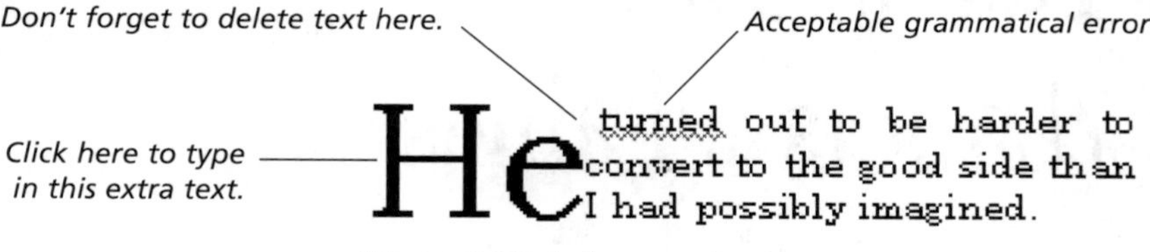
Don't forget to delete text here.
Acceptable grammatical error
Click here to type in this extra text.
He turned out to be harder to convert to the good side than I had possibly imagined.

Figure 6.10 A drop word

You can also drop a word by selecting the entire word in Step 1 (above) and then choosing Format ➤ Drop Cap. Same difference.

7 The Tough Stuff: From Labels to Tables

I'm so happy that I wrote the previous chapter on outlining. That way, when I got to this chapter here, I looked up at the title and I said, "Self, you're pretty clever with that rhyme up there. But you really need to teach *tables* before labels." And then I looked at the outline and said, "Self, you really need to teach tabs before tables." And then I realized that my clever rhyming title would no longer represent what was in the chapter. Nevertheless, I rearranged the outline (thanks to the last chapter) so that this chapter would retain its clever title and yet present information in a logical manner.

So with the door closed on my internal thinking process, I can now more properly introduce you to this chapter, which covers some of the esoteric and far-out things that Word attempts to do. About 15 years ago, certain peripheral items crept their way into word processing software. Starting with tabs, and then tables and envelopes and all sorts of not-really-word-processing tools, but yet handy things to have. These features were added to compete with other word processors that lacked such things. But today such competition is moot: Word does everything and, alas, there are no true competing word processors. (Well there are, but don't e-mail me with your pet list.)

This chapter covers the esoteric features with regard to how you can use them to make your documents all the more spiffy.

Enigmas Resolved and Impossibilities Mocked:

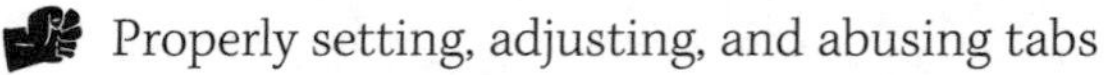

- Properly setting, adjusting, and abusing tabs
- Lining things up with tabs, left and right
- Discovering the best way to create a table in Word
- Converting from tabbed lists to tables
- Adjusting and formatting the table
- Doing math in tables
- Printing a sheet of labels
- Automating text with fields

Getting the Most from Tabs

Tabs are one of the most powerful features in Word, but sadly one of the most misunderstood. And what's misunderstood is not properly used. Alack! Alack! Alack!

Generally speaking, use a tab any time you really, *really* feel like using more than one space instead. The only time people feel compelled to use more than one space is when they have stuff to "line up." In that case, tabs work far better than spaces.

Also, tabs do not appear at the end of a paragraph. There they would do no good. And there is definitely no point in putting a tab in the middle of a paragraph. Therefore, tabs have a place only at the *start* of a paragraph. That limits their usefulness somewhat.

Hopefully the following sections will help drive all these points home.

You Must Know This: Tab Stop Basics

Tabs appear on the Ruler, along with the paragraph margin gizmos.

To set a tab, first click in the Tab well *to select a tab style. Then click on the Ruler where you want the tab to be set. You can drag tab stops to the left or right to reset them. As you drag, a line drops into the document to help you visualize how the text lines up. Dragging a tab stop upward or downward removes it from the Ruler.*

Tabs are also set using the Tabs dialog box, which you can get to using the Format ➤ Tabs command. The secret to the Tabs dialog box is to click the Set button to set a tab; clicking the OK button does not set tabs but merely accepts changes and closes the dialog box.

Oh, Come On: I Know All about Tabs! Tell Me Something I Don't Know!

Okay. Try this: Set a tab in the Ruler. No! That's not the trick. Now, point the mouse at the ruler and press *both* the left and right buttons. (Or you can Alt+click.) There you get a graphical distance chart, as shown in Figure 7.1.

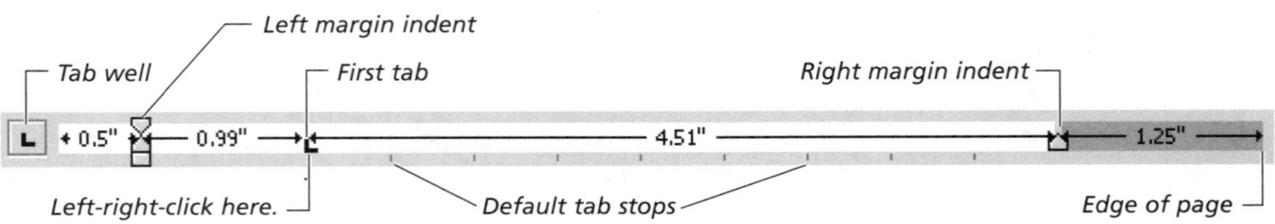

Figure 7.1 Measuring a paragraph's various widths

Unlike the normal Ruler, the distance measurements tell you how wide your tab and paragraph margin settings are, which can come in handy if your document is constrained by paper size or the size of an image or some other object. It's also easier than calculating widths via subtraction.

You can also drag the mouse left and right with the measurements showing, which may have some useful purpose but at least it's fun to do.

Doesn't Word Automatically Give You Tab Stops?

Yes. As can be seen on the Ruler in Figure 7.1, the ruler shows shaded ticks that hold the place of the default tab stops as preset by the Normal template (upon which all of Word's templates are built). If you don't define your own tab stops, then pressing the Tab key in Word hops the cursor over to the next default tab stop.

Notice, however, in Figure 7.1 how the one set tab stop removes the default stops? Any set tab stop overrides the default ones, as shown graphically on the Ruler.

Default tab stops are controlled in the Tabs dialog box. Choose Format ➢ Tabs, and then change the width for the default tabs by using the Default Tab Stops gizmo. (Refer to Figure 7.3.)

So What's the Advantage to Setting Your Own Tab Stops?

The advantage is that if you set things up right, you need only one tab to line stuff up. That's my rule about tabs. Otherwise, just as with spaces, if you have more than one tab in a row, you're not properly setting your tab stops.

This rule may not seem obvious right away. Where it saves you time is when you need to edit. Then, having only one tab stop makes realigning and retabbing stuff much easier.

Tabs for All Occasions

Word employs five tab styles. Here they are, along with information on when and how best to use them.

Left tab Moves text over to the next tab stop, left-aligned at the tab stop.

Center tab Centers text on the tab stop; used for single-line formatting tricks (see the section "What's the Point of a Center Tab?").

Right tab Moves text over to the next tab stop, but right-aligns the text.

Decimal tab Used to line up numbers on the decimal point (see the section "How Can I Line Up Numbers and a Total?").

Bar tab Inserts a vertical bar into your text (more of a graphical element than a true tab stop).

Where the Hell Are My Tabs?

Tabs are right the hell there on the screen! On the Ruler specifically, as shown in Figure 7.2. Before you get all steamed, however, recognize that tabs are a paragraph-level item. To see the tab stops in a paragraph, you must have that paragraph selected or the cursor must be blinking somewhere within that paragraph.

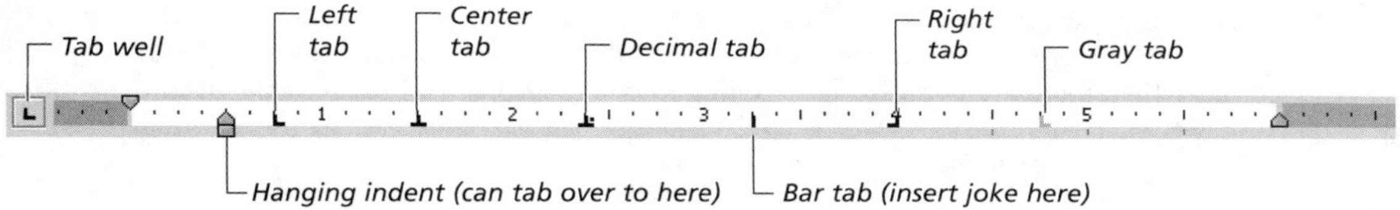

Figure 7.2 Tab stops on the Ruler

If a tab stop appears in gray, as shown in Figure 7.2, then that tab exists but not on all of the paragraphs you've selected. It's a rogue tab!

To be specific, of course, you should view your tab settings in the Tabs dialog box. Choose Format ➤ Tabs to see what looks like Figure 7.3 (it's subtly different in Word 2000). I prefer to set tabs visually using the Ruler after I write the text. But sometimes you need to be specific, in which case the Tabs dialog box makes an excellent choice.

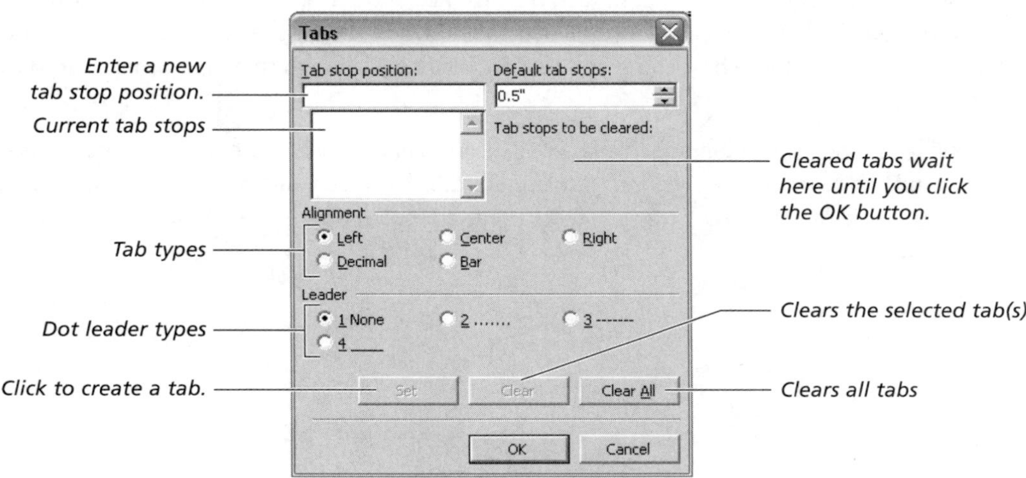

Figure 7.3 The Tabs dialog box

The secret to using the Tabs dialog box is to set the tab stop position, and then choose an Alignment option and finally (optionally) a dot leader. Then you click the Set button. Only after clicking Set should you click OK; otherwise, the tabs you picked may not be set properly.

The final way to find tabs is to reveal them inside your document. This is a great way to track down and fix the jiggly paragraph problem you get with a rogue tab in the middle of a paragraph.

To make tabs visible, click the Show/Hide button or press Ctrl+Shift+8 (not the 8 on the numeric keypad). This shows hidden codes in your document, as shown in Figure 7.4.

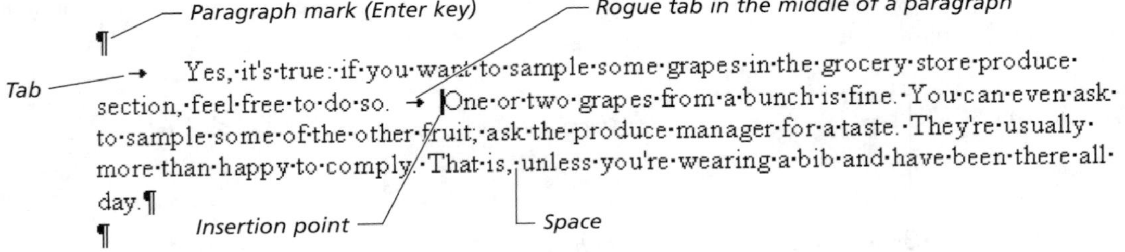

Figure 7.4 Tabs and other junk revealed!

In Figure 7.4, tabs appear as right-pointing arrows. That's the "tab character" produced when you press the Tab key. The type of tab stop you set determines its behavior, but the character itself can easily be removed the same way as any character in a paragraph: with the Backspace or Delete key. In Figure 7.4, pressing Backspace would rid your paragraph of the excess tab.

What Is Your Rule about Tabs?

Tabs are great for lining stuff up. In fact, the best use of them was demonstrated in Chapter 2, "Alas, There Is No Such Thing as a 'Simple' Document," inside the long section on indenting paragraphs. That's pretty much the best thing you can do with tabs, though there are other examples later in this chapter.

Outside of indenting paragraphs, tabs can be used to line up lists of items. However, thanks to Word's powerful Table command, even that function for tabs has pretty much gone by the wayside. Otherwise, my main rule remains: As long as you set the tab stops properly, you should never have more than one in a row.

How Can I Line Up Three Columns of Words?

A common use of tabs is to line up various columns of information, as shown in Figure 7.5. Here is the easiest way to format such a beast:

1. Type in the words, pressing Tab between each column.

   This will look yucky, as shown in Figure 7.5. *Live with it.* Bear with me until you set the tab stops. (You could set them beforehand, but you'd be just duplicating your efforts.)

2. Select your entire list.

   Very important. Don't forget this, or you'll be setting tab stops for only the current paragraph, not the entire list.

3. Set the first tab stop.

   Use that drop-down thingy, as shown in the figure, to help line up the tab stop beyond the end of the first column of words, as shown in Figure 7.5.

4. Continue setting tab stops.

   Set the next stop as you did the first one, dragging it over until the tab clears all the words in the column. Repeat this step for each column in your list.

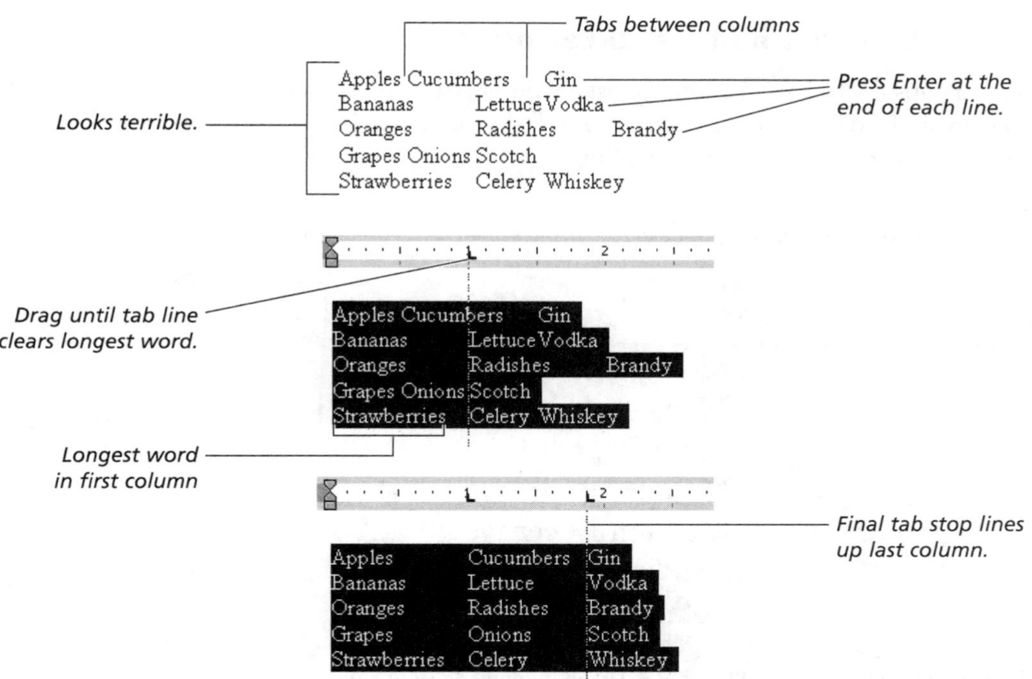

Figure 7.5 Columns of words

I Must Precisely Position My Tabs!

Suppose you need tab stops at 1", 2.5", 3.75", and 4.25". You can set those using the Ruler, but because of the precise measurements, you'd be better off setting them in the Tabs dialog box. Follow these steps:

1. Choose Format ➤ Tabs.
2. Enter 1 into the "Tab Stop Position" box.
3. Choose Left from the Alignment area.

   Unless Left is already chosen, in which case you don't need to click it.
4. Click the Set button.

   This is the task that actually sets the tab.
5. Repeat Steps 2 through 4 for each of the other values: 2.5, 3.75, and 4.25.
6. Click OK.

The key here is to use the Set button to actually set the tabs; do not just click OK or they won't be set. Only when the tabs are listed in the scrollable list (see Figure 7.3) are they truly set.

How Can I Line Up Numbers and a Total?

Decimal tabs are best used to line up lists of numbers, such as prices or quantities. By aligning the tab stop on the decimal, the Decimal tab creates a nice, even list, as shown in Figure 7.6. Here's how you'd go about setting up such a thing:

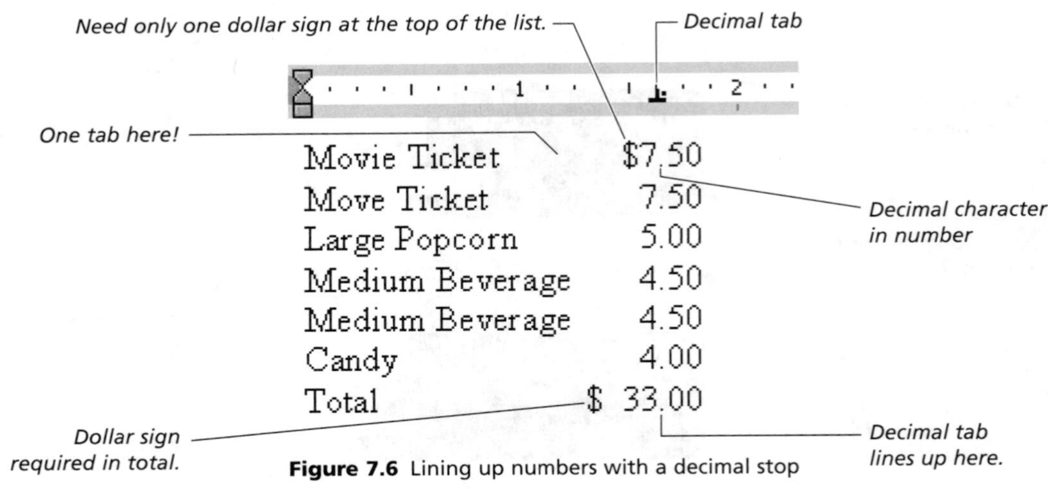

Figure 7.6 Lining up numbers with a decimal stop

1. Type your list. Type the item and then a tab and the amount.

   All amounts need a decimal point (period) in them.

2. Select your text.
3. Click the Tab well until the Decimal tab appears.
4. Click to place the Decimal tab on the Ruler.
5. Drag the Decimal tab to the left and right until things line up the way you want them to.

Again, the secret is to use only one tab. As long as you first type in the list (and can hold your breath through the ugly formatting), you can go back and set the proper tab. Then things will look just purty.

When you press the Tab key on a Decimal tab stop, the text will right-align itself until you press the period key. After that, the text left-aligns.

What Is the Right-Tab, Left-Tab Number-Alignment Trick?

Oftentimes when numbering a list, you discover that the numbers become too large and they bump into the text. To solve that problem, you need to right-align the numbers with a Right tab stop and then immediately follow it with a Left tab stop for the rest of your text.

The best way to see how such a thing works is visually. Unlike previous examples, you'll need to set things up in the Tab and Paragraph dialog boxes first and then type your paragraphs to see how this works:

1. Position the cursor at the start of a new paragraph, the one you want to number.

   Press Enter to do this.

2. Choose Format ➢ Tabs.
3. Create a tab stop at .25", Right alignment; click the Set button.
4. Click OK.
5. Choose Format ➢ Paragraph.
6. Create a Hanging indent at .38"; choose Hanging from the Special drop-down list and specify `0.38` in the box.
7. Click OK.

   The Ruler should now look as it does in Figure 7.7. You're now ready to type your numbered paragraph.

Right-align tab here — *Hanging indent here*

Numbers lined up on the right

Paragraphs lined up with hanging indent

99. Now, with the goat sedated and properly shaved, turn him over onto his back. You may have to prop it up with some pillows or blankets to keep it from rolling over.
100. Locate the bejeweled dagger.
101. Dip the dip of the dagger into the ceremonial oil, appropriate for the season and zodiac sign. (Though it's safe to substitute any oil, by specifying the proper oil you ensure a better reading.)

Figure 7.7 Formatting a tab for a numbered paragraph

8. Press Tab.

   Start the paragraph with a tab. That moves it over to the .25" tab stop where the number will be right-justified.

9. Type the number.

   Note how the number slides to the left as you type.

10. Press the Tab key to start typing the paragraph.

    Thanks to the hanging indent, the paragraph lines up just to the right of the number, as shown in Figure 7.7.

Unlike other ways to number paragraphs, with this style the number is always right-justified, which looks cleaner on a long list than having a left-justified number. This holds true especially if the numbers get rather large.

What's the Point of a Center Tab?

Center tabs have no use in life unless you're formatting something on a single line. That's because anything longer and you might as well just format the entire paragraph centered.

The most common place to find a Center tab is in the header or footer area. There you'll find a paragraph preformatted (by the Normal template) with a Center tab in the middle of the line and a Right tab on the right margin. That way you can type three items on the line, one left-justified, one centered, and one right-justified. Tabs separate each item. Figure 7.8 shows what's up.

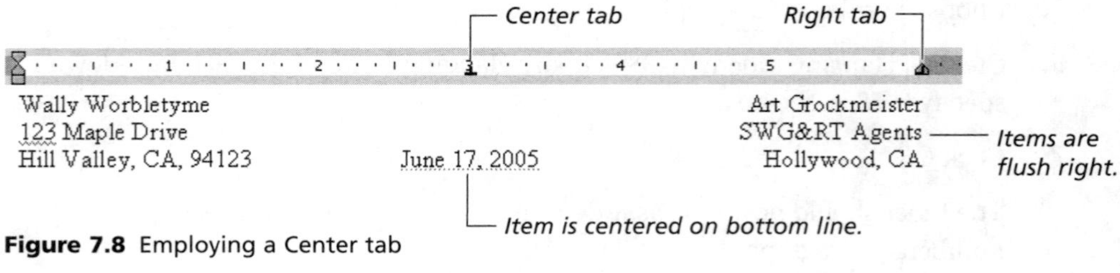

Figure 7.8 Employing a Center tab

The first two lines in Figure 7.8 sport only one tab, the Right-align tab at position 6" on the ruler. So to have the two addresses on opposite sides of the page, you type the first name, then press Tab, and then type the second name.

The last line has added a Center tab to place an item between the left and right sides of the page. On that line, I typed the address, pressed Tab, entered the date, pressed Tab again, and then entered the address for the agent.

What's the Best Way to Create a "Cast List" Type of Thing?

Being an old theater ham myself, I've done many a cast list. These employ dot leader tabs, which are simply tabs that shows periods, hyphens, underlines, or some other character instead of just space. The typical example is shown in Figure 7.9.

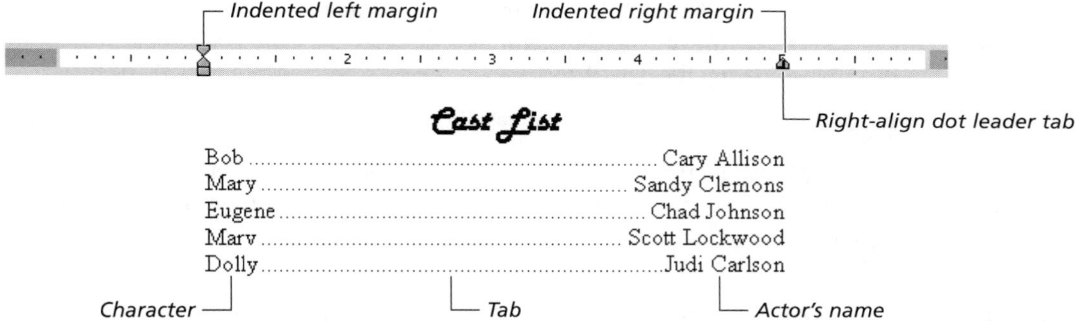

Figure 7.9 One of my favorite cast lists

Here's how to format such a thing:

1. Type in the cast list, pressing Tab between the actor's name and the character he plays.
2. Select the entire cast list.
3. Choose Format ➤ Tabs.

   To do a dot leader tab, you must use the Tabs dialog box.
4. Set the tab at the right margin.

   You'll notice in Figure 7.9 that I indented the margin 1" on both sides. My right margin is at 5".
5. Set a Right-aligned tab.
6. Choose a dot leader style.

   I like the period myself.
7. Click the Set button.
8. Click OK and the list is formatted as you see in Figure 7.9.

Remember that only *one* tab is required to do all this. Type the list, then format the tabs, and everything lines up nice and neat.

Figure 7.10 shows another alternative for a cast list, also using tabs. In this case the first tab is right-aligned and the second tab is left-aligned. So to type the list, you press Tab, type the actor's name, press Tab again, and then type the character's name. The Right tab and the Left tab (Figure 7.10) keeps things lined up with a wee bit of space in the middle.

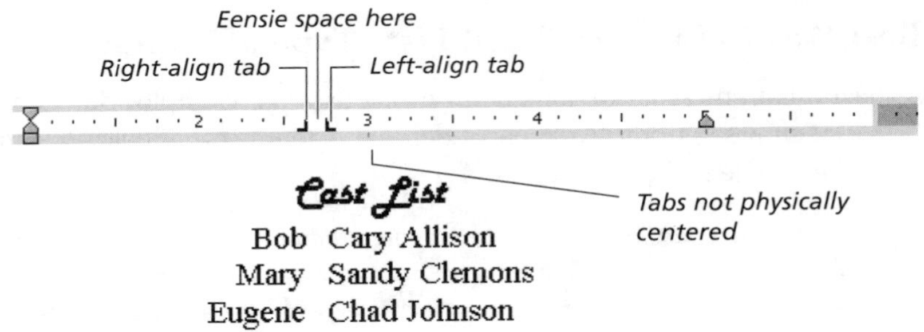

Figure 7.10 Yet another way to do the cast list

Notice also that the cast list is off-center for the title. That was a visual decision because it looked lopsided otherwise. It was a simple matter to drag the tab stops on the ruler over to a position that made things look more centered.

Can Tabs Be Part of a Style?

Yes. Tabs are part of a style just as paragraph and font attributes are. Technically, tabs are part of the paragraph format; however, to set tabs for a style you need to use the Tabs item from the Format button's menu. Refer to Chapter 5, "Using Styles and Templates to Save Oodles of Time," for more information.

How Can I Utterly Destroy These Tabs?

Tabs are fun to pluck off one at a time using the mouse: Point the mouse at the tab on the Ruler, then drag that tab down and into oblivion. You can do this with any tab, even the gray tab (see Figure 7.2).

A cleaner way to remove tabs is to use the Tabs dialog box. Heed these steps:

1. Select the paragraph(s) you wish to cleanse.
2. Choose Format ➢ Tabs.
3. Click the Clear All button.
4. Click OK.

Stumbling over Tables

Oh yes, I scoffed when they introduced the Table feature into Word. What folly, I chortled. But then it dawned on me: tabs and tables. They go together. Organizing things into columns with tabs is really like putting that stuff into a grid. And tables are essentially grids. In fact, I remember manually drawing in the table after I printed a document. Or resorting to using hyphens, underlines, and pipe characters (|) to cobble together a table.

So tables kind of sort of do have a place in Word. Any time you can think of a "grid" of information, slap down a table. You'll find the formatting commands much easier to deal with than trying to mess around with tabs or columns.

When Should I Use a Table?

Well, duh! Use a table any time you need tabular information in your document. You know, such as the results of last week's bedpan snow slide. That fits into a table. But at the bottom line, I generally move stuff into a table any time I have information in more than three columns. Or when the information in a grid includes not just single words but sentences and other information.

Bottom line: Any time formatting becomes hairy for anything more than two rows and two columns, get yerself a table!

Which Word Command Makes the Best Tables?

The best way to slap down a table is to use the Insert Table tool on the Standard toolbar. That's not really a button, but rather a menu.

Say you need a table that's four rows high by three columns wide. Follow these steps:

1. Click the mouse at the spot in your document where you want the table.
2. Click Insert Table button.
3. Drag down and across until you have a 4 x 3 grid, as shown in Figure 7.11.
4. Release the mouse button to create the table.

The table is then inserted into your document, filling the entire paragraph width, left to right. Figure 7.12 explores what's going on there.

To put information into the table, just start typing in a cell.

Check your paragraph formatting before you fill in a table. If you have left or right indents or a hanging or first-line indent, the text will be formatted that way in the table and cause you much grief as you type.

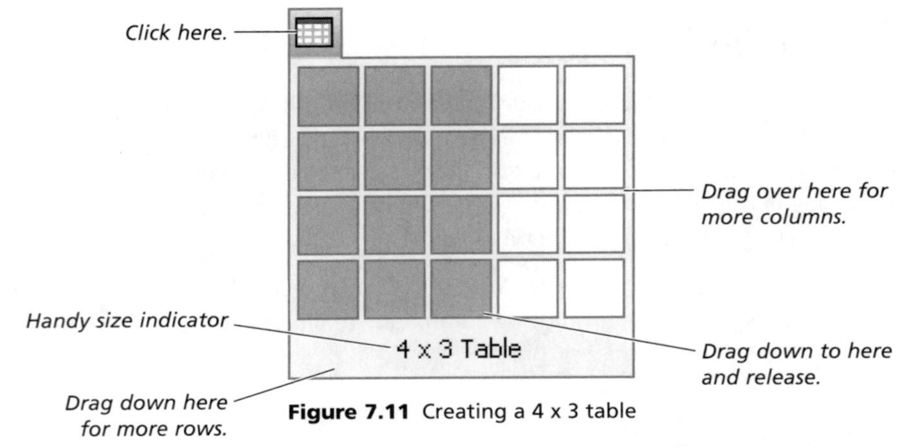

Figure 7.11 Creating a 4 x 3 table

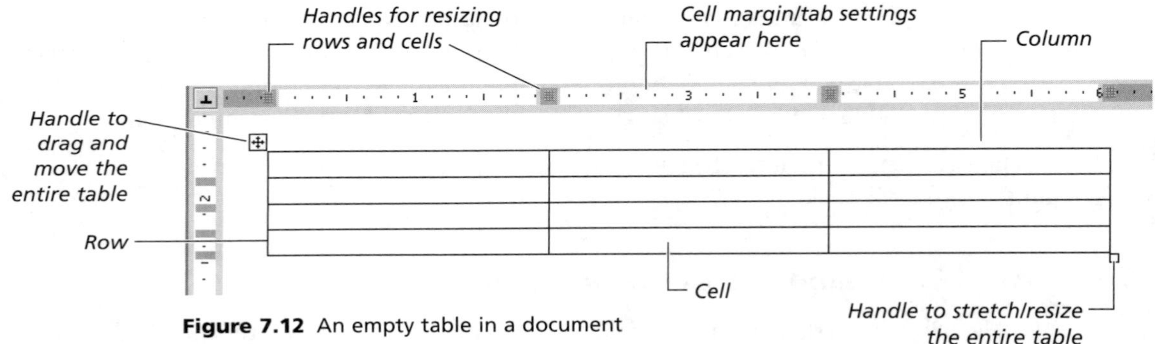

Figure 7.12 An empty table in a document

I'll Bet That There's Another Way to Insert a Table, Perhaps a Dialog Box-y Way to Do It, Huh?

Yes. The command is Table ➤ Insert ➤ Table. It displays an Insert Table dialog box and does everything described in the previous section but in far too many steps to bother with in real life.

How Does the Table Toolbar Fit into This?

The Table toolbar, along with the Table menu, provides all the handy Table tools you need in Word. In fact, anything you want to do with a table can be found in the menu or on the toolbar, which is one of the reasons working with tables in Word isn't such a pain—no, not like Mail Merge.

To quickly summon the Table toolbar, choose Table ➤ Draw Table from the menu, or you can click the Tables and Borders button on the Standard toolbar. This displays the Tables and Borders toolbar, shown in Figure 7.13. Note that only a few buttons there deal with table-making.

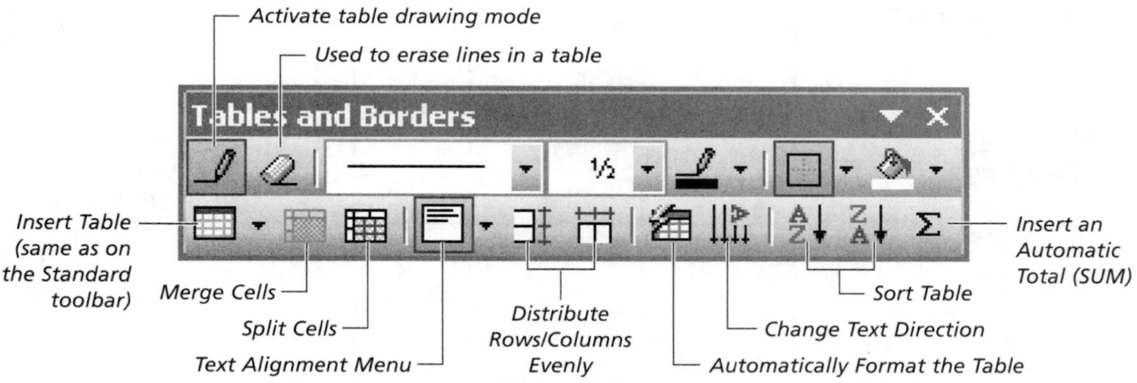

Figure 7.13 The Table toolbar is shared with the Borders toolbar.

You Mean That I Can Use the Stupid Pencil to Create a Table?

Being a right-brain person, I cannot fathom this concept, but yes, you can use the pencil button on the Tables and Borders toolbar to literally draw yourself a table in your document. Here's how to do that, should your left brain be so inclined:

1. Conjure up the Tables and Borders toolbar.
2. Click the Stupid Pencil button.

   It's officially the Draw Table button. Like I care.

   The mouse pointer changes into a pencil. This is a ham-handed way to let you know that you can now draw a table with it inside your document.
3. Slash a diagonal line through your document with the pencil-shaped mouse pointer.

   Drag the mouse as if you were drawing a box. This creates a large rectangle in your document, which is a one-celled table monster.
4. Draw some vertical lines in the table.
5. Draw some horizontal lines in the table.

   The lines don't even have to go all the way across the entire table, as shown in Figure 7.14. And nothing has to be even-steven. Why would anyone want such a contraption? I have no idea. Perhaps you want to shade each cell and create modern art. Who knows?
6. Keep drawing until the table looks like what you want.

   When you're done, click the Stupid Pencil button to leave Drawing mode and enter normal Word mode.

The eraser tool can be used to further modify your table by removing various lines. Click the button to select the eraser tool, and the mouse pointer turns into a bar of soap (though I suppose it's really an eraser). Click any line in a table to remove that line.

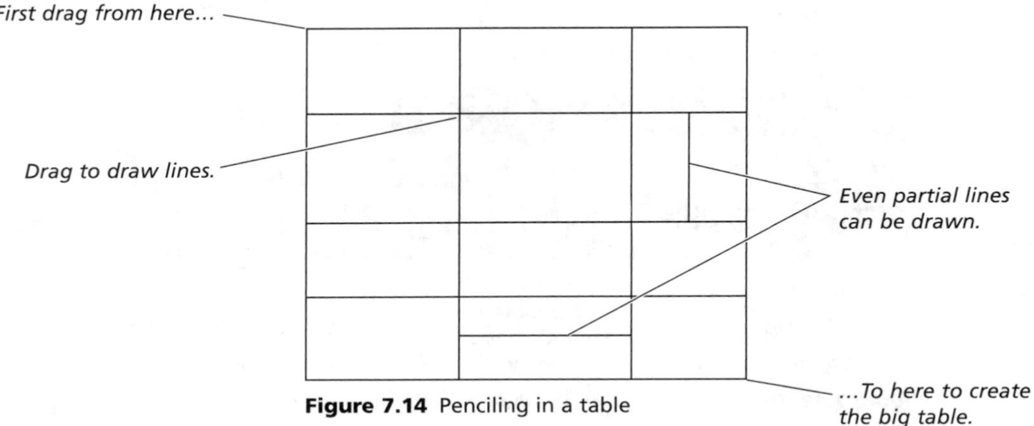
First drag from here...
Drag to draw lines.
Even partial lines can be drawn.
...To here to create the big table.

Figure 7.14 Penciling in a table

Note that removing lines from a table is not the same thing as deleting rows, cells, or columns. That information is covered later in this chapter.

You can use the pencil and eraser tools to modify any table, not merely one created by using the pencil tool.

I Was Dumb and Created a Table with Tabs, but Now I Want to Copy All That Stuff into a Table.

As long as your information is organized with each "column" separated by tabs, you can easily convert it into a table. Follow these incredibly easy steps:

1. Select the text you want to convert into a table.

   For example, a list of items, as shown in Figure 7.5.

2. Choose Table ➢ Convert ➢ Text to Table.

   A dialog box appears, though as long as you have tabs in your list, there's nothing to mess with there.

3. Click OK.

   And your text is now in a table.

You may need to further adjust the table's size or the column widths. To quickly make each column even, click the Distribute Columns Evenly button on the Tables and Borders toolbar, or choose Table ➢ AutoFit ➢ Distribute Columns Evenly from the menu.

The opposite of this command is Table ➢ Convert ➢ Table to Text, which takes any selected table in Word and lets you convert it back to plain text, separated by tabs (or some other character). This is useful when sharing Word documents with other applications that may not understand tables.

How Can I Add or Insert Rows or Columns?

This is cinchy: To add a row to the bottom of a table, put the cursor into the last cell on the right, in the bottom row. Press the Tab key. There's the new row!

To *insert* a row, put the cursor into a row above or below where you want the new row inserted. Then choose Table ➢ Insert ➢ Rows Above or Table ➢ Insert ➢ Rows Below to add your new row.

To add or insert columns, you must use the menu commands, either Table ➢ Insert ➢ Columns to the Left or Table ➢ Insert ➢ Columns on the Right.

I Need to Move Text from One Column to Another.

This is easier than it sounds:

1. Select the column you want to move.

   Point the mouse at the top of the column. The mouse pointer changes to a thick, down-pointing arrow. Click to select the column.

   Likewise, you can choose Table ➢ Select ➢ Column from the menu, but it's easier to use the mouse.

2. Drag the column to where you want it to go.

   If the destination already contains information, then the two columns are swapped. Otherwise, if the column is empty, the information you're dragging fills that empty column.

The same trick works when applied to rows as well: Select the row, then drag it up or down with the mouse to swap that text with any other row.

Sometimes with smaller tables it's difficult to swap the last row or column. In this case, it may pay to temporarily add an extra row or column, do the swap, and then delete the extra row or column.

I Need to Delete Just One Cell and Have the Rows Below Move Up Without Deleting the Entire Current Row.

This trick is so easy that I've often converted a list of tabbed items into a table, done this trick, then converted the table back into a list of tabbed items. Here you go:

1. Click the mouse to select the cell you want to delete.
2. Choose Table ➢ Delete ➢ Cells.

   The Delete Cells dialog box appears, as shown in Figure 7.15.

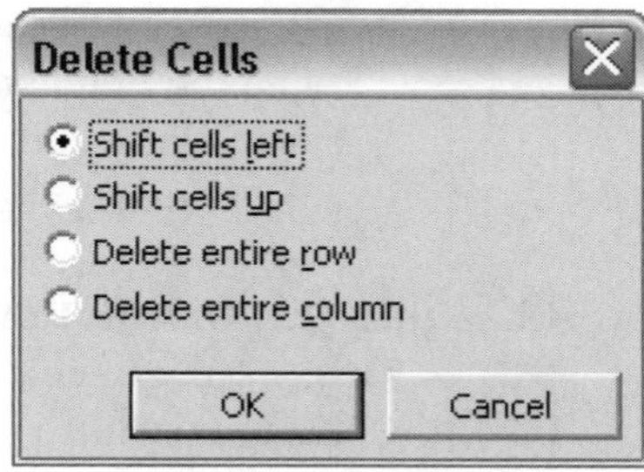

Figure 7.15 The handy Delete Cells dialog box

3. Choose an option.

   For example, I can choose "Shift Cells Up" to juggle all the cells below up a notch. (The other options are all self-explanatory.)

4. Click OK.

If you just need to delete the text in a cell and leave it blank, then simply select the cell and clear out its contents with the Backspace or Delete key.

How Can I Wrap Text inside a Cell?

Oh, let me count the ways!

Text inside a cell will wrap just as text in any paragraph in Word does. The cell will grow "taller" to accommodate the text. There are a few things you can do with the text in such a cell, as well as the cells in that same row or column.

Making the Cell Accommodate Text with Minimal Wrapping

To avoid a three-foot-tall cell in a table, you can tell Word to adjust the table's column widths to best fit the cells: Choose Table ➢ AutoFit ➢ AutoFit to Contents. That makes columns with narrow text narrow and widens columns with lots of text.

Adjusting Cell Width Manually

You can point the mouse at any column (or row) separator and drag it left or right to increase or decrease that column's width.

You can also use the "handles" that appear on the Ruler to adjust a table's column width.

Changing Text Alignment

A large chunk of text may make other cells in that row look dumb because of their alignment (top, bottom, left, right). You can change a cell's text alignment by using the Align button on the Tables and Borders toolbar. Clicking that button displays a drop-down palette of alignment options, as shown in Figure 7.16.

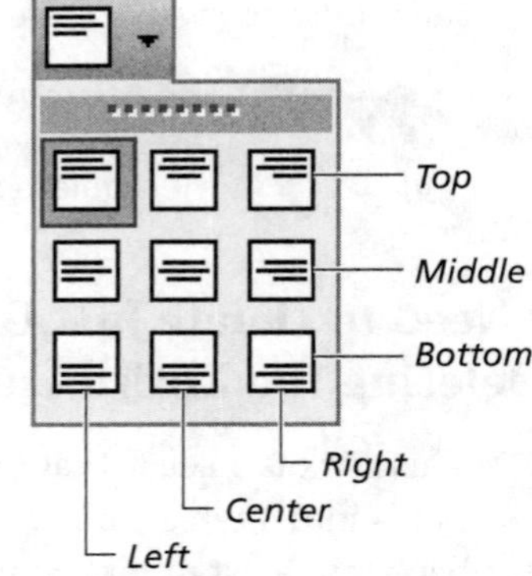

Figure 7.16 Select a cell alignment option from here.

Changing Text Orientation

Finally, you can change the text's orientation by using the Change Text Direction button. Clicking this button rotates the orientation of text in the selected cell counter-clockwise 90 degrees each time you click. (Alas, it does not orient the text upside down.)

But I Don't Want the Table's Gridlines to Print!

This is easy—and sneaky, too, because by not printing the gridlines, your table just looks like extra-special fancy-formatted text. Fool them all!

To hide the gridlines, obey these enumerated steps:

1. Select the entire table.

   I just click the table's handle to do this, though you can also choose Table ➤ Select ➤ Table.

2. Choose "No Border" from the Borders button on the toolbar.

   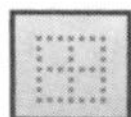

   The "No Border" item is the one that looks like a four-square court without any lines in it.

   Ta-da, the table's gridlines are gone.

To restore the lines, choose the "All Borders" item from the drop-down list in Step 2.

Why Would I Want to Do Math in a Table?

Tables in Word can incorporate a few handy math functions. For example, to total a column of numbers in a table, do this:

1. Click the mouse in the cell that is to have the total.

   Like in the bottom row of the column.

2. Click the AutoSum button on the Tables and Borders toolbar.

   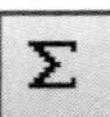

   And the total of the numbers in the cells above is put into that cell. Cinchy.

The AutoSum button sticks a Word *field* into the cell. The field basically says, "Total the sum of all the values in the cells above me." (Sigma, the Greek symbol on the button, is a mathematical doodad for "sum.")

The AutoSum button also totals values in a row, providing that there are no values immediately above the AutoSum cell.

There are a number of functions you can paste into cells for doing limited math. Here are the general steps you'll follow to insert a mathematical function into a table:

1. Click the mouse in the cell where you want the result to appear.

   For example, say you want the average of the values in the three cells on the left.

2. Choose Insert ➤ Field from the menu.

3. From Categories, choose "Equations and Functions."

4. From "Field Names" choose "= (Formula)."

5a. In Word 11/XP, click the Formula button.

Word 11/XP has a special Formula dialog box where you can paste in formulas. Oh, la-di-da.

6. By the = (equal sign) type `AVERAGE(LEFT)`.

The formula name is AVERAGE, and you're finding the average of the numbers on the left.

7. Click OK.

And the average of the numbers to the left of the cell is displayed.

This trick works as long as all the cells to the left are filled with numbers. Any blank cells halt the calculation at that cell.

There are other functions you can use in a table; however, I recommend using Excel instead of learning all the various fields and functions in Word. The only one I use occasionally is the SUM function, which has its own button. The other functions are just too weird to bother with.

Handy Field Codes for Use in Your Tables

Just because I'm a nice guy, here are some field formulas you can plug into a table to get some math happening.

To make the formulas work, put either `LEFT` *or* `ABOVE` *between the parentheses. That tells the formula to operate on the cells either to the left or immediately above the cell where the formula sits.*

AVERAGE()

Calculates the average of the numbers.

COUNT()

Returns the number of cells that contain data.

MAX()

Returns the highest value.

MIN()

Returns the lowest value.

PRODUCT()

Calculates the result of multiplying the values.

SUM()

Calculates the total.

These are only a few of the formulas available. There are several more and they can get quite complex. But remember, at that level you're better off using an embedded Excel worksheet as a table instead of messing with Word's own tables. I'll be getting to that in a minute.

I Changed the Table but the Math in the Cell Didn't Change!

Right-click the cell with the SUM (or other field) function and choose "Update Field" from the pop-up menu.

When Is Pasting In an Excel Spreadsheet Better Than Using a Table in Word?

Any time you have more than three or four columns, and especially when the cells need mathematical formulas or fancy formatting, you should consider using Excel as opposed to Word. In fact, it's this easy:

Inserting an Excel spreadsheet is also known as embedding.

1. Position the cursor where you want the Excel spreadsheet/table to appear.
2. Click the Insert Worksheet button on the Standard toolbar.

   Ah-ha! A select-o-grid drops down, similar to making a table the easy way, as shown in Figure 7.11.
3. Drag to select the size of table/worksheet that you want.

   Say, 3 x 4.
4. Click the mouse.

   And an Excel worksheet is secretly screwed into your Word document, as shown in Figure 7.17. Note how the toolbars are now Excel toolbars, not Word. Everything within the *rope of containment* is the domain of Excel.

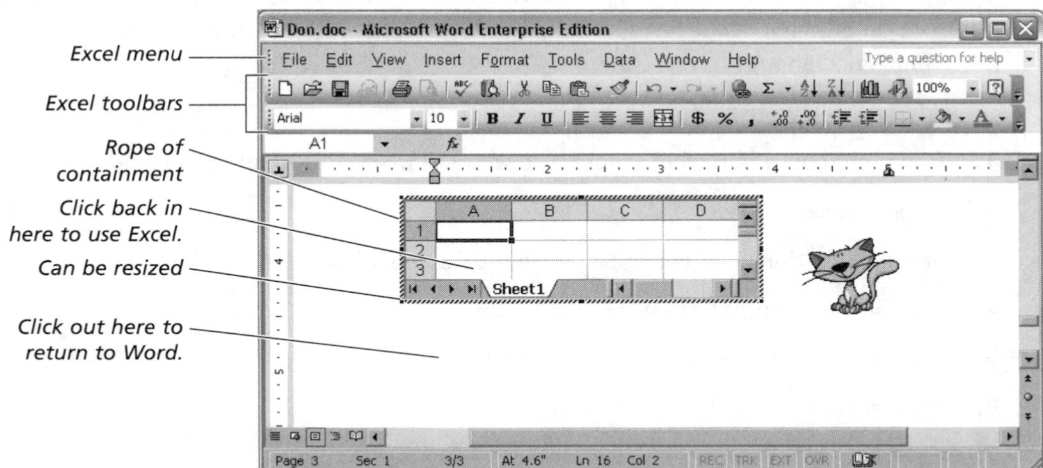

Figure 7.17 An Excel spreadsheet lurks in your document.

5. Work the worksheet.

   And now you're off using Excel, so refer to Part II of this book for the details.

6. Click back in your document when you're done.

   To return to Word, click outside the rope of containment (Figure 7.17). Note that the toolbar and menus change back to Word. To return to Excel, double-click inside the worksheet area.

Despite the wacky appearance of Figure 7.17, the Excel spreadsheet looks like a table in Word, prints like a table, and if it were possible, it would even smell like a table.

Will Sorting the Table Mess Up My Data?

As long as you carefully format your table, there's really nothing you can do to it that cannot be fixed, either by pressing Ctrl+Z (Undo) or just messing around. Consider Figure 7.18.

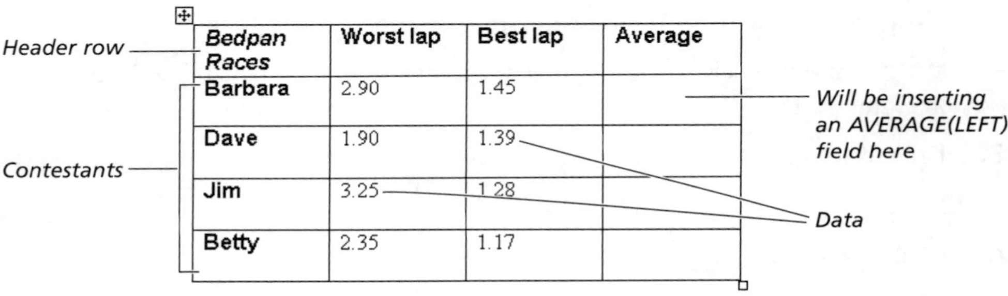

Bedpan Races	Worst lap	Best lap	Average
Barbara	2.90	1.45	
Dave	1.90	1.39	
Jim	3.25	1.28	
Betty	2.35	1.17	

Figure 7.18 A table, ready for action

The table shows the preliminary results of this year's bedpan races. The winner is determined by averaging the values of their best and worst laps. Your job is to figure that average (or let Word do it for you) and then sort the results alphabetically because last year they weren't sorted and everyone complained about it.

Gingerly, you follow these steps:

1. Click the mouse in the cell where you want the first AVERAGE(LEFT) field.
2. Choose Insert ➢ Field.
3. Select "Equations and Formulas" from the Category list.
4. Choose "= (Formula)" from the "Field Names" list.
5. Click the Formula button in Word 11/XP.
6. Type `=AVERAGE(LEFT)` as the formula.
7. Click OK.

And the average is calculated and placed into the cell. Time to repeat this action:

8. Click the mouse in the next cell to share that same formula.

9. Press the F4 (repeat) key.

   And the formula is inserted and calculated instantly.

10. Repeat Steps 8 and 9 for all the cells to share that same formula.

The F4 key is not a paste key, it's a repeat formatting key. You're reapplying the Field format to the cell, not pasting in a formula.

With all the cells filled, it's time to sort.

11. Click the mouse inside the table to select it.

    No need to "highlight" the table, just ensure that the insertion point is blinking away happily inside the table.

12. Choose Table ➤ Sort.

    The Sort dialog box appears, as illustrated in Figure 7.19.

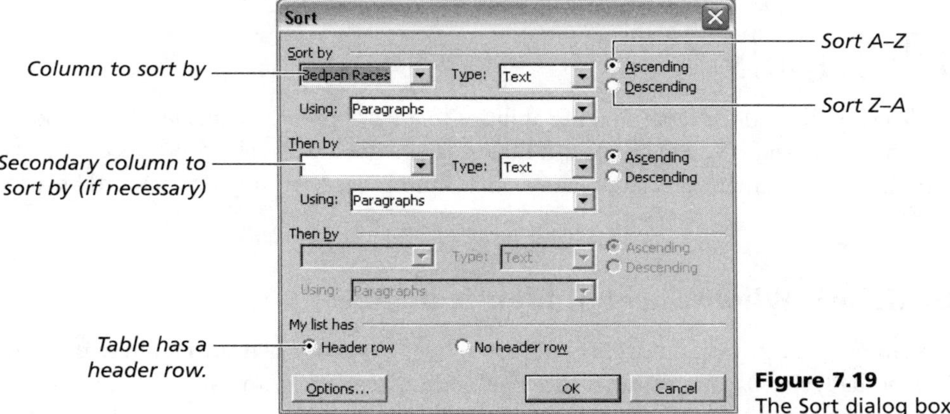

Figure 7.19
The Sort dialog box

13. Ensure that "Header Row" is selected.

    This is very important: It tells Word that your table has a header. If so, then Word will *not* sort that row. Also note how the table's header row appears in the "Sort By" drop-down list (as shown in Figure 7.19).

14. Click OK.

    And the table is sorted by the first column, which is labeled "Bedpan Races," but is actually the contestants' names.

Suppose you wanted to sort the list by who won? In that case, you would be sorting by the *lowest* score that appears in the Average column. Here's how to do that:

15. With the table still selected, choose Table ➤ Sort.

16. Ensure that "Header Row" is selected.

17. Choose Average from the "Sort By" drop-down list.

18. Choose Number from the Type drop-down list.

    There is a difference between sorting numbers (values) and text. In this case, you need to sort values, so you choose Number from the list.

19. Select Ascending.

    Lowest scores are best. If highest scores signified the winner, then you'd have to select Descending.

20. Click OK.

    And the table is sorted by who won, which is in the Average (last) column. Congratulations, Dave!

At Last: Labels

I've no idea why they added label-making abilities to a word processor. It may be because *labels* rhyme with *tables*. And if you're good with tables, you're good with labels. Because it's possible to fit a table on a document to match labels on a printed page, in which case Word becomes a label printer.

I Need to Make a Whole Sheet of Identical Labels

Every so often, I print myself out a sheet of labels. I use them as my return address on envelopes. It's a "tip" actually: Print yourself out a list of self-addressed labels, and you'll save yourself time over manually filling in the return address part of an envelope. This is especially handy if your handwriting is as lousy as mine.

Here's how to make a sheet of identical labels in Word:

1a. In Word 11/XP, choose Tools ➤ Letters and Mailings ➤ Envelopes and Labels.

1b. In Word 2000, choose Tools ➤ Envelopes and Labels.

2. Click the Tables tab in the Envelopes and Labels dialog box, shown in Figure 7.20.

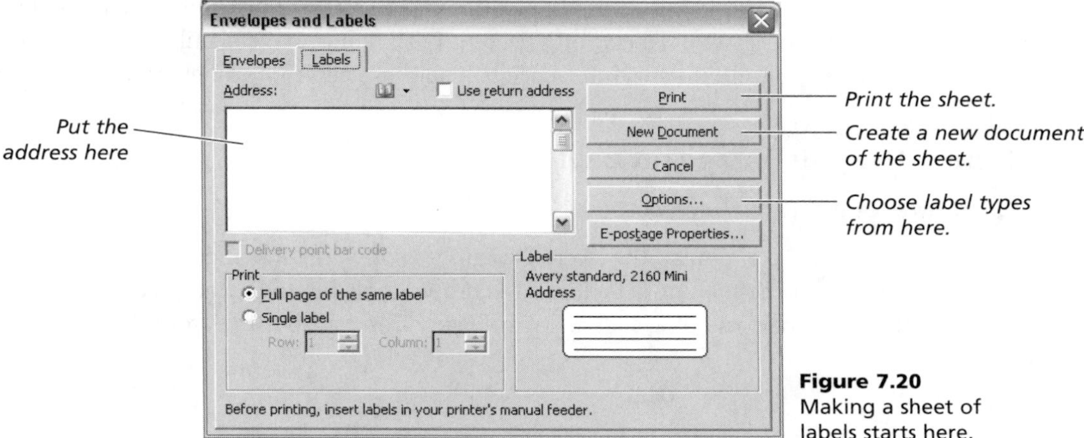

Figure 7.20
Making a sheet of labels starts here.

3. Click the Options button.

Your first step is to tell Word what type of sheet of labels you have. Word recognizes the common Avery label product numbers, as well as standards from other brands. Remember: You can't print out a sheet of sticky labels unless you have a sheet of sticky labels to print on.

4. Select your label brand and product number.

I print my return address on Avery 5160 labels.

5. Click OK.

6. Fill in the Address part of the dialog box.

Enter your own address or whatever address you want to fill a sheet with.

You can use the Enter key to end a line in the Address text box.

7. Choose the item "Full Page of the Same Label."

8. Click the New Document button.

And a new document is created, full of text that's ready to print on your sheet of labels.

The reason I have you create a document is so you can save it to disk and reuse it later. Save the document in a special Labels folder using a name that will help you remember the contents. After that, whenever you need a sheet of labels printed, conjure up the document and print it.

And now for the special treat: With your document of labels on the screen, choose Table ➤ Show Gridlines.

Ta-da! It's really a table! All the Labels dialog box does is to create a huge, one-page table that has dimensions equal to the sheet of labels you selected. Then it automatically fills in various cells in the table with the same (or different) information. And that's all Word's label printing is about.

Can I Put a Graphic Image on Each Label?

Yes, but it's a royal pain in the patoot.

As a suggestion, I can recommend the Avery Design Pro software for Windows, which is custom-designed to print labels or mailing lists. It has the proper tools for adding graphics to the labels without suffering the pain of doing such in Word. Avery Design Pro is free from the Avery website: `www.avery.com`.

Dreaming of Fields

And now, this chapter's dessert, which should be short and sweet: fields. Force fields. Fields of green pasture. Oh, to be outstanding in one's field. Or to be a field in Word, which means text that magically appears based on some condition or aspect of the document. Yes—that's right! Instead of calling them "fields," they should be called "Magic Text." At least more people would be interested in them that way.

What the Heck Is a Field?

A field is a bit of automatic text in your document. The text is variable; it can change as the document changes. So a field can reflect anything from the current page number to the document's printing date to text that jumps you from one location in the document to another. They're amazingly powerful but not widely used or appreciated.

What Are Some Fields Worth Knowing?

Most of the fields you can really take advantage of involve dates or page numbers. Even so, there are also fields that tell you who worked on a document, the number of times it was saved to disk, the document filename, and lots of other trivial stuff. The following sections explain some of the more useful fields.

Sticking the Document's Print Date into a Field

Some documents I prefer to have dated when they print, as opposed to when I wrote or updated them. To insert the print date field, follow these steps:

1. Choose Insert ➢ Field.
2. Choose the "Date and Time" category.
3. Choose PrintDate from the "Field Name" list.
4. In Word 2003/XP, you can select the date's format from the "Date Format" list.
5. Click OK.

In Word 2000, the date may look ugly if the document hasn't yet printed.

Specifying the Document's Filename

To stick the document's filename into a header or footer, or really anywhere in the document, follow these steps:

1. Choose Insert ➢ Field.
2. Choose the "Document Information" category.
3. Choose FileName from the "Field Name" list.
4. Click OK.

Entering How Long It Took to Create the Document

Curious about how long it took you to create your masterpiece? Or does such a thing fill you with anxiety? Here's how to find out:

1. Choose Insert ➤ Field.
2. Choose the "Document Information" category.
3. Choose DocProperty from the "Field Name" list.

4a. In Word 2003/XP, choose TotalEditingTime from the Property list.

4b. In Word 2000, type `TotalEditingTime` after DOCPROPERTY in the Field dialog box.

5. Click OK.

The value displayed is in minutes. Scary, huh? But it also grows if you leave your computer on all night and don't bother to close the document's window at the end of the day. So the value can be misleading.

Specifying the Number of Characters/Words/Pages in the Document

The document actually knows how much work you've done! In fact, budding writers should love this trick. When you're paid by the word, you can insert a field at the end of your document that accurately displays the document's word count. Or you can specify the number of characters or pages in the document. It's all very similar. Here's how:

1. Choose Insert ➤ Field.
2. Choose the "Document Information" category.
3. Choose one of the following from the "Field Name" list:

   NumChars, to display the number of characters in the document

   NumPages, to list the total number of pages

   NumWords, to list the document's word count

4. Click OK.

Specifying Your Name

Word knows who you are—yes you!—sitting there working on a document. In a large office where multiple people may work on a single document, it's possible to list the name of the author by specifying a field, as follows:

1. Choose Insert ➤ Field.
2. Choose the "User Information" category.
3. Choose UserName from the "Field Name" list.
4. Click OK.

Yes, you entered that name when you first installed Word or Office. Now it's stuck there.

If it's not your name, then you'll see the name of whoever installed Office or, in some cases, the original computer owner's name. Sometimes, if the copy of Office is stolen, you'll see the name of the person from whom it was stolen.

The Field Looks Gross!

Yes, fields can look gross. There are two ways to view them: as raw codes and output:

1. Right-click a field in your document.
2. Choose "Toggle Field Codes" from the pop-up menu.

And you now see the field in the raw. It's contained in curly brackets with the field code name followed by any options or settings. The MERGEFORMAT is a flag that prevents Word from messing with the field during certain internal processes.

Note that in the "Field Codes" option, you can edit the field manually, for example, to change a date format as described earlier in this chapter. But mostly you *do not* want to see a field look like this, so repeat the two steps above to get it back to normal.

Some fields can have no values, in which case they display "blank" or seemingly useless information. For example, the PrintDate field looks odd until a document is printed. After all, if a document hasn't been printed, what should that field display?

The Field Is Wrong!

So update it: Right-click the field and choose "Update Field" from the pop-up menu.

Unlike data in some programs, fields are not updated in Word all the time. Some fields update when you print, others when you save or open a document. To force an update, right-click the field and choose "Update Field." Works every time.

How Can I Change a Field?

Alas, only Word 2003/XP has an Edit Field command: If you right-click a field, you can choose "Edit Field" from the pop-up menu. This redisplays the Field dialog box, where you can make adjustments to a field's settings.

In Word 2000, you can right-click and choose "Toggle Field Codes" to update or change a field, but to make any radical changes, you'll have to backspace and delete the field and then reinsert a new field for what you want.

Formatting the Date Codes for Word 2000

If you have Word 2000, then you're not given the opportunity to format the date codes properly. Instead, Word just sticks in the 0/0/00 0:00 AM date format, which is ugly and probably ticks you off. To fix that, you can edit the field's codes to change how the date is formatted:

1. *Right-click the PrintDate field.*
2. *Choose "Toggle Field Codes" from the pop-up menu.*

   You now see the field "in the raw." It may look something like this:

   ```
   {PRINTDATE \* MERGEFORMAT }
   ```
3. *Edit the field's text to add the date.*

   Change the text so that it now reads

   ```
   {PRINTDATE \@ "d MMMM yyyy" \* MERGEFORMAT"
   ```

   You're adding the \@ thing, followed by a date/time format in double quotes.
4. *Right-click the field and choose "Toggle Field Codes" from the pop-up menu.*

   The field may still look ugly, but now it will print in format "25 March 2004."

You can build any date field using d *for the day of the month,* M *for the month name, and* y *for the year. Here are the patterns you can apply between the double quotes. You can also add hyphens, periods, slashes, and commas to the format:*

d	*The day of the month*
dd	*The day of the month as a two-digit number (with leading zero, if necessary)*
ddd	*The three-digit day of the week*
dddd	*The full name for the day of the week*
M	*The month's number*
MM	*The month's number as two digits (with a leading zero, if necessary)*
MMM	*The month's three-letter abbreviation*
MMMM	*The full month name*
yy	*The year as a two-digit number*
yyyy	*The year as a four-digit number*

If you want to specify the time, you can do so using h *for hours,* m *for minutes, and* s *for seconds. A colon can be used to separate the values:*

h	*The hour of the day*
hh	*The hour as a two-digit number (with a leading zero, if necessary)*
mm	*Minutes*
ss	*Seconds*
am/pm	*Append AM or PM to the time*

8 Sharing Your Work with Others

Writing is a solitary and silent art. Well, maybe not silent with the Office Assistant critter making all sorts of noise. Even if you like cats, don't use the Cat Office Assistant. Its purring will drive you nuts at 2:00 A.M. And the keyboard (on my PC at least) sounds like a machine gun going off. Nope, writing may not be so silent. And it may not be solitary, either.

Few writers have the extreme luxury of writing all their own stuff by themselves. Even published authors have to put up with various stages of editors. There was one publisher I worked for where my document had to pass through five editors. Each of them felt compelled to put at least three marks on the page in their own color. It helped keep them employed, but it did nothing for my manuscript's readability.

So I'll pop the myth: Writing is a group activity that makes lots of noise. Fortunately, if you're the kind of writer who likes their stuff enough to protect it, Word has the tools you can use. Further, Word has tools that let you see who has changed what in your document. Then, if you don't like what they've done, you can change it back swifter than a mere copy editor can say "dangling participle."

Treats Discovered and Tricks Abounding:

- Adding a comment outside of the text
- Reviewing and wantonly deleting comments
- Recording an audio comment
- Finding out what others have changed in your document
- Accepting or rejecting the changes
- Protecting against unwanted changes

Collaboration Tools

Whether you want to or not, someday you're going to work with others on the same document. Oh, joy. The idea is not to sit at the keyboard together and type (though you can do that if you *really* like the person). It's instead a chance to share ideas and provide feedback within the document, all without ticking the other person off. Word has plenty of tools to do that.

I Want to Tell My Collaborator That Something Sucks. How Can I Best Do That?

From a distance. Otherwise, I find the Insert ➤ Comment command works just fine. Here's how I relate such information to a co-author or weary editor:

1. Highlight the text that concerns you.

Be specific here, though I've often highlighted an entire paragraph and added the comment "pointless."

2. Choose Insert ➤ Comment.

Various things happen here, depending your version of Word and how you have it configured.

In Word 2003/XP, the Reviewing toolbar shows up, as shown in Figure 8.1. It's a great tool to use when editing someone else's stuff or when you have to review edits others have made to your stuff.

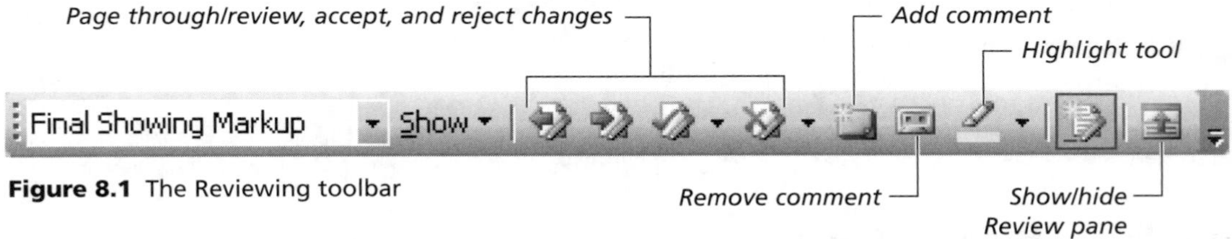

Figure 8.1 The Reviewing toolbar

In Word 2000, you can summon the Reviewing toolbar by choosing View ➤ Toolbars ➤ Reviewing from the menu. Note that the Word 2000 toolbar lacks some of the buttons found in Figure 8.1.

If you're in Print Layout view in Word 2003/XP, then a comment balloon appears, as shown in Figure 8.2. That's where you write your comment regarding the highlighted text.

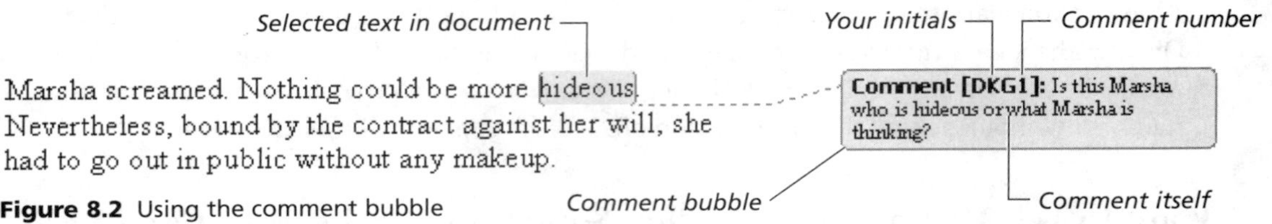

Figure 8.2 Using the comment bubble

Word 2000 has a similar feature: When you insert a comment, the Comment frame opens up, where you can type your comment, as shown in Figure 8.3.

3. Type your comment.

Be nice.

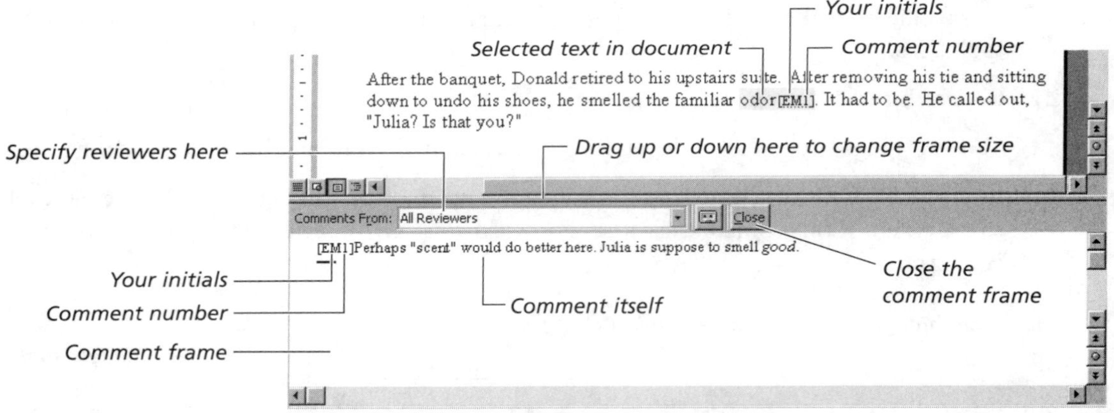

Figure 8.3 Adding a comment in Word 2000

Any Way to Hide the Comments?

What? You fear feedback? Oh, for shame!

In Word 2003/XP, you can always switch to Normal view to hide the comments: View ➤ Normal. In Print Layout view, you can hide the comment bubbles using the Show menu on the Reviewing toolbar: In Word 2003, choose Show ➤ Balloons ➤ Never Use Balloons; in Word XP choose Show ➤ Comments.

In Word 2000, click the Close button on the Comment frame to hide your comments.

Note that these steps do not delete the comments. The text is still highlighted on the screen, so you know that there is a comment available.

Any Way to Rapidly Scan the Comments?

This is my favorite, but it requires the presence of the Reviewing toolbar to work best, so choose View ➤ Toolbars ➤ Reviewing if you haven't already.

In Word 2003/XP, use the Previous and Next buttons to hop between comments. Note that these buttons also hop between edits and changes made by other authors when that option is turned on.

In Word 2000, there are Previous Comment and Next Comment buttons you can use. These buttons specifically move between comments and not any other gunk in your document.

And, of course, an easy way to review the comments is to open up the Reviewing pane and just read them all, as shown in Figure 8.4.

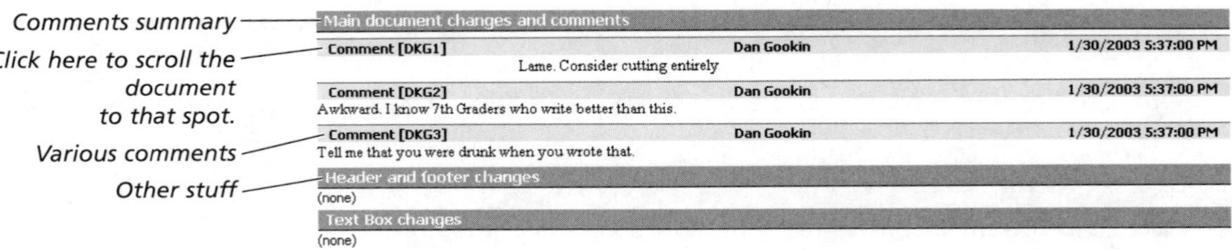

Figure 8.4 Reviewing comments all at once

Note that Word 2000's Comments frame works similarly, though it lacks the extra information shown in Figure 8.4.

I've Read That Nasty Note from My Collaborator. How Do I Delete It?

Right-click and choose Delete Comment from the pop-up menu. This removes the comment and renumbers any remaining comments in the document.

Can I Review Comments by Collaborators One at a Time?

Certainly. In fact, I find this is a good way to approach things when different collaborators are looking for different things. For example, say Jay is looking only for technical goofs, while Phyllis is looking for gross abominations of English. To view only Jay's comments, from the Reviewing toolbar choose Show ➤ Reviewers ➤ Jay.

Or if you want to see only Phyllis's comments, choose Show ➤ Reviewers ➤ Phyllis.

To see them all, choose Show ➤ Reviewers ➤ All Reviewers.

In Word 2000 you can make similar adjustments. The list of reviewers is found at the top of the Comments frame, as shown in Figure 8.3. Just choose your foe from that drop-down list.

It's Not Enough That I Delete the Comment; I Also Want to Comment Back!

You can comment on a comment simply by clicking the comment and inserting a new comment, as shown earlier in this chapter. Simply type in your remarks.

I've also gone into the Reviewing pane and written my comments after the original jerk's comments: Just click after their comments, press Enter, and then type away. Sometimes I select a new color for my add-on thoughts, such as bright red or hot pink, depending on my mood! Use the Font color button on the Formatting toolbar to set your comment's text color.

NERD'S CORNER

Cocktail Party Trivia, Part IV

DOUGLASS: I do say, Fred, being a published author, do you often argue with your editor using comments?

FRED: I used to. Then I found out that they never read them. It was pointless to reply when the document was never returned!

EVERYONE: Ha-ha!

MARY: Do professional editors really use Word's Comment feature?

JOHN: Alas, no, Mary. It depends on the publishing house. Some of the older houses still mark up text right on the page.

MARY: Oh, like with sticky notes?

JOHN: No. Sticky notes can fall off, so editors just mark up the page, la-di-da.

FRED: That's not very high tech.

JOHN: No. But they can often add comments using a special style. The editor may have a style, and the author may have a style, and they can send messages back and forth. Fortunately, the styles don't print.

FRED: Well, sometimes they do. And that can be really funny!

EVERYONE: Ha-ha!

I'm Inserting a Lot of Comments. Any Way to Make It Easier?

Yes, fire the original author and rewrite the entire thing yourself.

Now if that is out of the question, then here's what I do:

In Word 2003/XP, I turn off the comment bubbles or switch to Normal view. I find the comment bubbles distracting, especially for text I'm really commenting on.

Next, I open the Reviewing pane (or Comments frame thing in Word 2000). That way I can click the Insert Comment button (on the Reviewing toolbar) and then type in my comments down at the bottom of the window.

KEYBOARD MASTER

Alt+I, M

To quickly insert a comment, you can try these accelerator keys, which are faster than any mouse method of inserting a comment:

What's the Tape Recorder Thing For?

The tape recorder is used with the cooperation of Microsoft and the FBI to gather important bowling league information from your computer. Seriously, it allows you to insert audio files into your document—which is something Word does anyway, but in this case it's specifically to create vocal comments. I suppose that's for when your writing just can't blossom with the same expression as your voice. Or perhaps you want to sing your comments—who knows?

Adding approximately 10 seconds of audio commentary to your document bulks up the document's file size by at least 200K.

Because this isn't a PC hardware book, I'm going to assume that you have a microphone properly connected to your computer and that you know how it works. To add a bit of screaming audio as a comment, follow these steps:

1a. In Windows 2003, summon the Reviewing toolbar.

1b. In Word 2000, display the Comments frame with View ➤ Comments.

1c. Word XP, alas, does not have this feature, so you can go to the fridge and get some cookies.

2. Select the text you want to vocally comment.

3. Click the Insert Voice button.

Look for the tape recorder button, shown in the margin. This works just like the Insert Comment button/command; however, in addition to adding a comment, it also displays the Windows Sound Recorder program, shown in Figure 8.5.

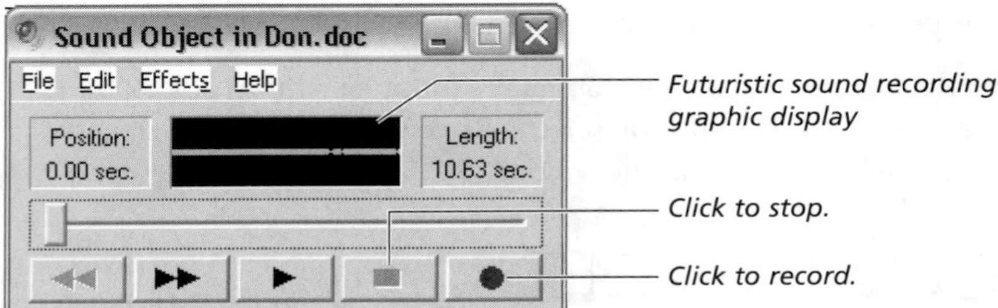

Figure 8.5 The Sound Recorder application

Technically, what you've done is to insert a *Sound object* into Word. In this case, the Sound object is stuck into a comment. But you can also stick a Sound object into any Word document, as covered in the sidebar nearby.

4. Click the Record button.

5. Speak the comment into your microphone.

According to the Sound Recorder program, you have up to 60 seconds.

6. Click the Stop button to stop recording.

You should see a graphic display of your voice as you speak. If not, then you'll need to troubleshoot the microphone. The most common problem is that the microphone has been software muted in the Master Volume Control Panel.

Double-click the Volume icon in the system tray/notification area on the taskbar to see the Master Volume Control Panel. There you can unmute the microphone, if necessary.

7. Close the Sound Recorder program window.

A speaker icon appears in your document, telling you that there is an embedded Sound object there.

To hear the sound, double-click the speaker icon. The sound plays back (the Recorder program does not appear). Remark to yourself, "Damn, this is a modern way to communicate updates to my co-author."

You Must Know This: Inserting a Sound Object

Word gives you the ability to insert just about any type of program "object" into a document. This includes multimedia objects, such as sounds and videos. If you want to insert a sound file—or audio anything—into a document just as you inserted an audio comment, follow these steps:

1. *Locate the spot in the document where you want the Sound object to appear.*
2. *Choose Insert ➢ Object from the menu.*
3. *Scroll through the list of Objects in the Create New tab until you find "Wave Sound."*
4. *Click OK.*
5. *Record the sound; click the Record button on the Sound Recorder application and speak into the microphone.*
6. *Click the Stop button when you're done.*
7. *Close the Sound Recorder program.*

The speaker icon in your document shows you where the embedded sound lives; double-click it to hear the sound.

Can Hidden Text Be Used for Comments?

No, not effectively. While there are many uses for hiding text, making your comment using the hidden text format is a rather awkward way to do it—especially given the power of the Insert ➢ Comment command.

The biggest problem with using hidden text is that, well, it's *hidden*! To display hidden text, you have to either search for it or tell Word to display it outright:

1. Choose Tools ➢ Options.
2. Click the View tab.
3. Put a check mark by "Hidden Text."
4. Click OK.

Hidden text now appears in the document; it shows up with a dotted underline. That text won't print, and it can be hidden again by repeating the steps above to remove the check mark.

To format hidden text, use the Font dialog box; put a check mark by Hidden, and any selected text in the document is hidden.

Alas, this is just too much work when the Insert ➢ Comment command is so much slicker.

To remove all hidden text from a document, select the entire document with Ctrl+A. Press Ctrl+D to bring up the Font dialog box. Clear the check box by Hidden. Click OK.

My Dumb Co-author Doesn't Know Which Part of the Text I'm Referring To. How Can I Point It Out without Changing the Formatting?

The best way to do that is with the Highlight tool. Like going crazy with a yellow marker, the Highlight tool lets you mark up text that concerns you without having to comment every tidbit. Figure 8.6 gives an illustration.

Highlighted words (supposed to be yellow)

So there we all were, alone in the middle of the creepy woods. So Josh gets the idea that we should light a campfire. I said no, that we should stick together. But others wanted that dumb fire, so six of them headed off into the woods. Do I need to say what happened next?

Figure 8.6 Highlighting offensive or questionable text

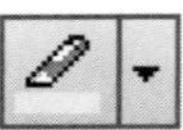

To go nuts and highlight text in your document, use the Highlight tool, which is found on both the Formatting and Reviewing toolbars. Click that tool once, and the mouse pointer turns into the Highlight tool. Then just drag over text to highlight it. Click the tool again to exit this scribbly mode of operation.

If you don't like the Highlight color, click the down arrow by the button and choose from one of 15 exciting colors.

To erase the highlighting, you must select "None" as the color and then use the Highlight tool to drag over the text and erase it. Because highlighting is *not* a part of the font formatting, you cannot use font commands to remove it.

Another quick way to remove highlighting is to re-select the highlighted text and just click the button on the toolbar again.

Will These Offensive Comments and Markups Appear in My Document if I Print It?

Indeed they will—if you tell Word to print them. Deep inside the Print dialog box is an option called "Print What." From that option's drop-down list you can select whether to print the comments or markups or whatever you like. If you want just the document to print, select Document from the list.

What's the Point of Online Collaboration?

There is none. It's stupid.

Revealing the Offenses of Others

Sadly, you release your document to a friend, coworker, or the most feared individual of any writer: the dreaded *editor*. Who knows what infectious jealousy may possess that person? Will they ruthlessly claw away at your treasured text until nothing of your wit and verve remains? How can you tell? Why, simple! Just review the changes to your document. It's simple. It's easy. And it's the best way to know what was changed and to give it your final thumbs-up or thumbs-down.

I Really Don't Trust My Collaborator and Would Like to Know How to Tell What's Been Changed and What Hasn't.

First, give your collaborator a *copy* of your document. Keep the original. That's very important.

Second, before you fork over the copy, turn on the Track Changes option. Now, normally that would be *their* responsibility. But sometimes they forget. Here's how to turn on Track Changes, which depends on your version of Windows:

Word 2003/XP Choose Tools ➢ Track Changes.

Word 2000 Slightly more complicated:

1. Choose Tools ➢ Track Changes ➢ Highlight Changes.
2. Click to select the option "Track Changes While Editing."
3. Click OK.

How Do I Know That Track Changes Is On?

You can see the TRK on the status bar. That means that all edits to the document from this point on will be marked.

A quicker way to activate Track Changes is to merely double-click the TRK thing with the mouse.

How Are the Changes Marked?

With Track Changes on, go back to your document and delete a word, change some formatting, and then add some text. Here is how such changes are marked, depending on your version of Word:

In Word 2003/XP, in Print Layout view, bubbles appear marking deletions or formatting changes. They describe the changes, and the colors used are specific to different reviewers; to see which reviewer is responsible, simply point the mouse at a bubble, and the reviewer's name will appear along with the date and time of the revision.

New text appears in color as well, double-underlined, as shown in Figure 8.7.

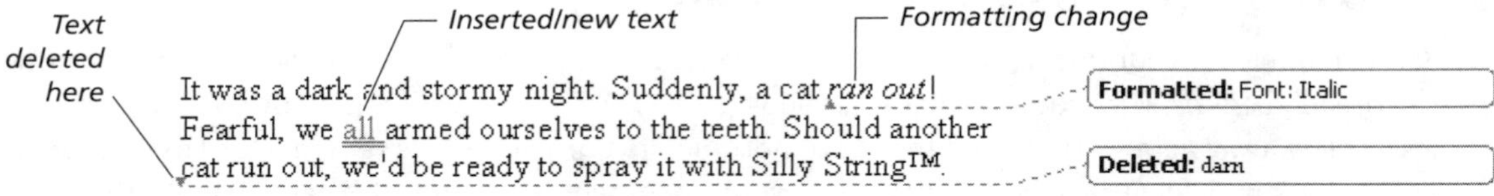

Text deleted here
Inserted/new text
Formatting change
It was a dark and stormy night. Suddenly, a cat ran out!
Fearful, we all armed ourselves to the teeth. Should another
cat run out, we'd be ready to spray it with Silly String™.
Formatted: Font: Italic
Deleted: darn

Figure 8.7 Marked changes in Print Layout view

In Word 2003/XP Normal view, as well as in Word 2000, no bubbles are displayed. Instead, deleted text appears colored red with the strikethrough attribute. Inserted text is shown as double-underlined in Word 2003/XP and colored in Word 2000. Formatting changes are not specifically marked.

The color of the text changes depending on who has reviewed it. Normally, changed text is red. But if a second person edits the document, their changes may show up in blue. Add a third person (annoying, I know), and you get another color, maybe purple or green. These colors are set in the Options dialog box: choose Tools ➢ Options and click the Track Changes tab.

What's That Annoying Line on the Left Side of the Document?

When you're in Track Changes mode, a vertical line appears on the left side of any modified text. That allows you to quickly locate where changes appear. And in Normal view or in Word 2000, it's the only way to tell that text has had its formatting modified (though you still cannot tell specifically what the modifications were).

To remove the line, tell Word not to show you the changes, or simply accept or reject each one. To hide the changes, see the section, "I Just Got My Document Back, but I Cannot See the Changes!"

Will the Changes Print?

Certainly, if you want them to.

In Word 2003/XP, in the Print dialog box there is a drop-down list by "Print What." You need to choose "Document Showing Markup" from that list so that the marked changes appear on the hard copy. (This is similar to printing comments, which was covered earlier in this chapter.)

In, Word 2000 go to Tools ➢ Track Changes ➢ Highlight Changes and select "Highlight Changes in Printed Document." The changes will print in color.

I'd Like to Reorient the Document to Landscape Mode for Printing the Comment Bubbles.

You can direct Word to print out in Landscape mode to display the comments only—this trick doesn't affect your document's true page layout.

To pull this stunt, and it works only in Word 2003/XP, follow these steps:

1. Choose Tools ➤ Options.
2. Click the Track Changes tab.
3. In the bottom of the dialog box, choose "Force Landscape" from the drop-down list by "Paper Orientation."
4. Click OK.

Oops! I Forgot to Turn on Track Changes!

Man, oh man, are you screwed!

Seriously, if you forget to turn on Track Changes, you still have an ace in the hole: It's your pristine document—the original—still on your hard drive. What you need to do is compare that original with the edited copy. Word will then mark any changes on the screen for you. This isn't as elegant as turning on Track Changes before you hand off a document, but it's the next-best thing.

Comparing Documents in Word 2003/XP

Here's how to compare a document with a modified copy in Word 2003/XP:

1. Open your original document.
2. Choose Tools ➤ Compare and Merge Documents.

   An Open dialog box, disguised as the Compare and Merge Document dialog box, appears.

3. Locate your document's mangled copy.

   Find the edited or changed copy using the dialog box.

4. Click Merge.

   Word compares the original with the copy on disk. Changes between the two appear in the copy—the document you selected with the Compare and Merge Document dialog box—on the screen.

Now you can see exactly what was done. Your original document is still safe in another window. But the copy has been marked up and presented to you, similar to what you see in Figure 8.8.

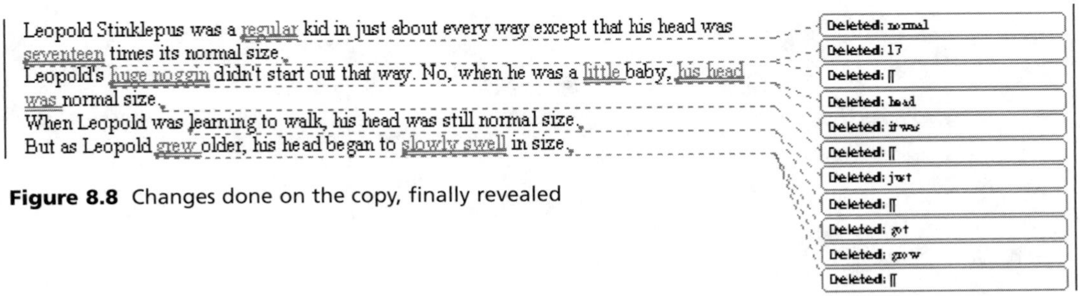

Leopold Stinklepus was a regular kid in just about every way except that his head was seventeen times its normal size.
Leopold's huge noggin didn't start out that way. No, when he was a little baby, his head was normal size.
When Leopold was learning to walk, his head was still normal size.
But as Leopold grew older, his head began to slowly swell in size.

Deleted: normal
Deleted: 17
Deleted: ¶
Deleted: head
Deleted: it was
Deleted: ¶
Deleted: just
Deleted: ¶
Deleted: got
Deleted: grow
Deleted: ¶

Figure 8.8 Changes done on the copy, finally revealed

Comparing Documents in Word 2000

Things are different enough with Word 2000 to warrant its own section. Pay attention, as this is different from the Word 2003/XP instructions in a sinister way:

1. Open the *copy* of your original document.

   You want the edited version on the screen, not your original.

2. Choose Tools ➤ Track Changes ➤ Compare Documents.
3. Use the dialog box to locate and select the original file.
4. Click the Open button.

   Word compares the original on disk with the copy on the screen. Any changes are noted in the copy on the screen. The original, still on disk, is left untouched.

The markups appear similar to those shown in Figure 8.8, with the exception of the bubbles off to the right. You can point the mouse at any specific change to read more information about it.

I Just Got My Document Back, but I Cannot See the Changes!

Changes can be hidden, if you like. To make them visible (or to hide them), follow these steps:

Revealing Changes in Word 2003/XP

From the Reviewing toolbar, choose Show ➤ Insertions and Deletions. Optionally you may also have to choose Show ➤ Formatting. That shows or hides the changes made to your document.

Revealing Changes in Word 2000

Choose Tools ➤ Track Changes ➤ Highlight Changes. In the Highlight Changes dialog box, remove the check mark by "Highlight Changes on Screen." That hides the changes in your document. Or you can repeat these steps to show the changes again.

To quickly display the Highlight Changes dialog box, right-click the TRK thing on the Status bar and choose "Highlight Changes" from the pop-up menu.

Okay, I See the Changes. Now What Do I Do?

As the writer, you always have the final say over what goes into your text. Even if an editor demonstrates flawless English logic, you can still overrule that mini-tyrant with a click of your mouse. It's called Reviewing and Accepting, and Word lets you accomplish this task in a number of ways.

To individually accept or reject a change, point to it and right-click: Choose Accept or Reject from the pop-up menu.

It's important that you get the Accept/Reject jargon down: If you Accept a cut, the cut is made. If you Reject a cut, the cut is restored. On the other hand, if you Accept an insert, then the inserted text is kept. To remove the inserted text, you must Reject it. Weird.

You can also use the buttons on the Reviewing toolbar to hop between changes and then to accept or reject them. Here they are:

 Hop to the next change in a document.

 Accept the change.

 Reject the change.

The buttons look slightly different in Word 2000, but you'll be able to figure them out from these.

Any Way to Just Accept All the Changes?

Giving up? If you tire of accepting all those wonderful suggestions that the charming editor has made, so much more enhancing your document, then you can blissfully accept them all. Here's how:

Accepting All the Changes in Word 2003/XP

1. Click the down-arrow by the Accept Change button on the Reviewing toolbar.
2. Select "Accept All Changes in Document."

Now if you'd rather reject them all, then just click the down-arrow by the Reject Change button and choose "Reject All Changes in Document."

Accepting All the Changes in Word 2000

Word 2000 has a handy dialog box you can use for reviewing the changes as well as accepting or rejecting everything en masse. To see the dialog box, choose Tools ➤ Track Changes ➤ Accept or Reject Changes. The toolbar appears, as shown in Figure 8.9.

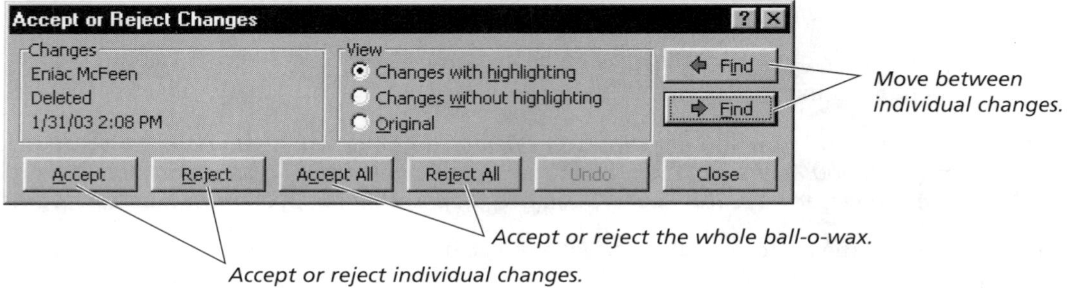

Figure 8.9 Reviewing changes in Word 2000

When you elect to accept or reject all the changes, a dialog box appears to confirm your choice. My insiders tell me that Microsoft was forced to put that in there by the United Editors Union.

How Can I More Vigorously Protect My Document against Unwanted Insertions and Deletions?

If you must share, then you must subject yourself to the changes made by others. That's what tracking changes (and the techniques presented in the past few sections) is all about. Even so, there are more drastic steps you can take.

In addition to giving a document an open or read-only password (see Chapter 1, "Life beyond the Basic Word"), you can further protect it by forcing whoever edits the document into Deletion Tracking mode, Comments-Only mode, or whichever options you select. You do this by choosing Tools ➤ Protect Document.

In Word 2003, a Document Protection task pane appears; in Word XP, a Protect Document dialog box shows up. Either way, you can restrict the way the document is edited. For example, to force people into Deletion Tracking mode, choose "Tracked Changes" from the drop-down list in item 2 and put a check mark there. Then click the button "Yes, Start Enforcing Protection." Enter a password twice and the document is protected.

In Word 2000, select an option from the Protect Document dialog box. For example, choosing "Tracked Changes" forces Deletion Tracking on; it cannot be turned off unless an editor knows the password. Enter the password into the box, shown in Figure 8.10. Another dialog box confirms the password, and you're set.

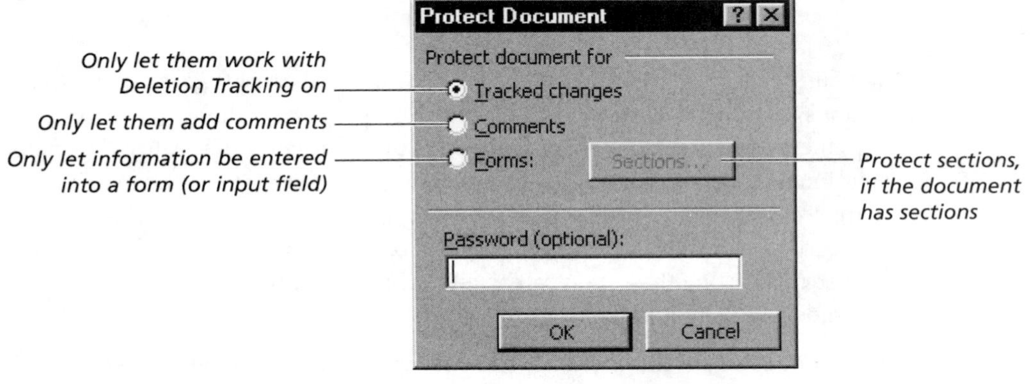

Figure 8.10 Adding protection in Word 2000

Unlike a password-protected document, anyone can open a document protected in the above manner. However, they'll be forced into Deletion Tracking mode or only be allowed to add comments or whatever restrictions you've set.

To remove this protection, you need to choose Tools ➤ Unprotect or Tools ➤ Unprotect Document. Then you enter the password, and Word behaves as normal.

9 Making Your Own Custom Word

You suffer from too many choices in Word. I think Microsoft gave you too many options with the idea that you'd be happy. The problem is that you can't realize happiness until you first accept that you're unhappy and then realize that there is a solution or a path to happiness. The situation with Word is that many of its commands, options, and presentation are confusing and overlapping. What you're not being told is that all that junk is optional. You can choose to see it or not. And if you choose to see something, you can always customize it to show what you want to see and hide what you don't.

Yes, Word can be customized beyond your wildest dreams. You are free to do this. It's entirely possible. Cyber storm troopers won't break down your door and accuse you of sedition if you modify or change things from the way Word looked out of the box. So please, by all means, feel free to wrestle Word's interface to the ground, dust it off, and then grow something pleasing and personally useful instead. I encourage it!

Knowledge Revealed and Secrets Exposed:

- Doing Word full screen!
- Customizing your toolbars
- Creating your own toolbar from scratch
- Making buttons where only text existed before
- Creating new commands with macros

To Hell with the Interface!

Love it. Hate it. The remarkable thing about the way Word presents itself on the screen is that it's utterly changeable. You can make Word look like just about anything, from a button-filled hell with only one square inch of writing space, to the pristine and frightening blank page. It's all up to you.

Blank page? Tell me more!

Prefer to write staring at a blank page? Then try this: Choose View ➤ Full Screen from the menu. Word abandons its toolbars, menus, doodads, and window gizmos to give you a full screen of nothing but blank paper and text, as shown in Figure 9.1. If you're a traditional, typewriter-style author, you should try this mode for a few days and you'll find it infectiously addicting.

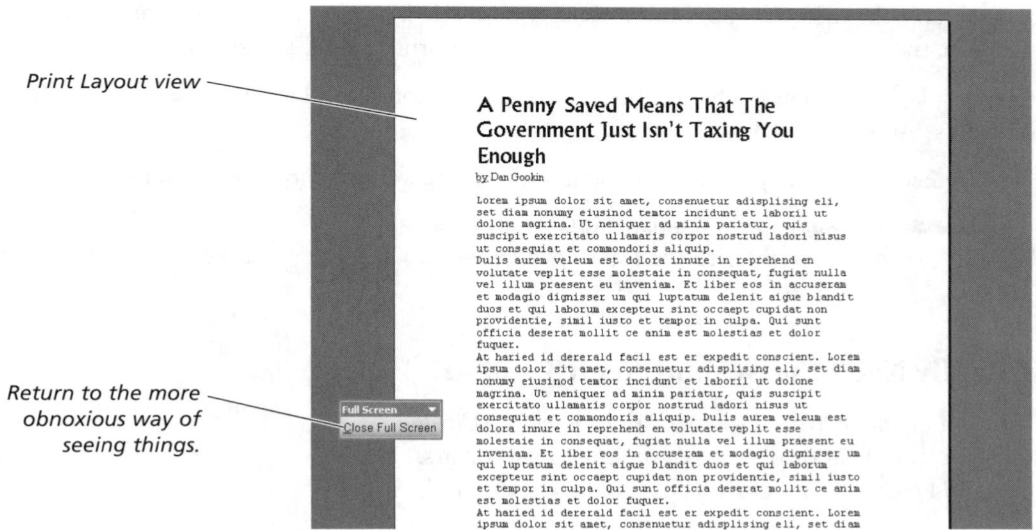

Figure 9.1 Word at its most minimal

Be careful where you drag the Full Screen floating palette. If it gets too close to the edge of the screen (any edge), it turns into a toolbar.

How Do I Get the Interface Back?

Easy enough: Click the Close Full Screen button, as shown in Figure 9.1. But note that you do not need to do this to use any of Word's commands.

KEYBOARD MASTER

Closing the Full Screen

With the Close Full Screen button visible, as shown in Figure 9.1, returning to Normal view is only one keystroke away:

Alt+C

This command is the same as clicking the Close Full Screen button, when that button is visible on the screen.

What If I Need to Use the Menus in Full-Screen Mode?

To have the menu bar temporarily displayed in full-screen mode, press the F10 or Alt key on your keyboard. Lo, the menu bar appears, allowing you to select a command. As soon as that command is chosen, the menu bar is hidden again and you're returned to full-screen mode.

For example, if you want to change the view to Normal from Print Layout, press Alt+V, N. To return back, press Alt+V, P.

Press the Esc (escape) key to hide the menu if you don't want to choose a command.

The menu also reappears when you slide the mouse pointer to the top of the screen.

But I Really Need the So-and-Such Toolbar!

To summon any of Word's toolbars, right-click the Close Full Screen button. That displays a pop-up menu of toolbars, as shown in Figure 9.2. Select the toolbar you want from the list.

Also refer to the sections later in this chapter on manipulating and moving toolbars, so that you can have more freedom on the display than with a fixed, unmoving toolbar.

Actually, the best way to do things is to create a custom toolbar, one that has the Close Full Screen button as well as other buttons for popular things you do. This is covered later in this chapter.

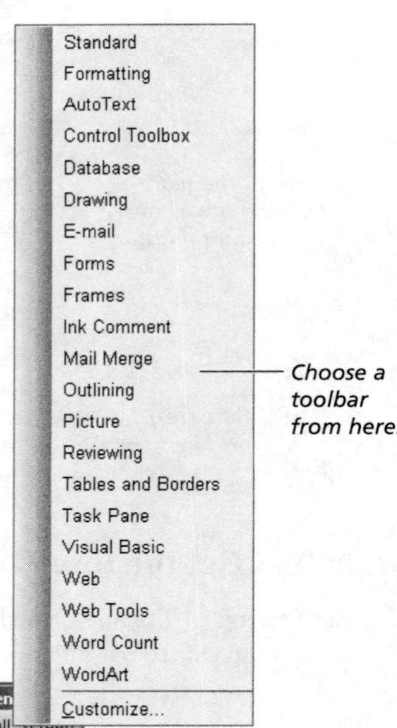

Figure 9.2 Conjuring up another toolbar

How Can I Get at the Windows Taskbar or Start Button?

To display the taskbar or Start button—which is part of Windows and not part of Word, press the Windows (Win) key on your PC's keyboard. Or you can press Ctrl+Esc if your keyboard lacks that key.

I Miss the Scrollbars!

Sorry, can't help you here. There are plenty of keyboard equivalents for scrolling your document up or down. If you have a wheel mouse, then you can use the wheel button to scroll up and down.

To scroll with the wheel mouse, press the wheel button and drag the mouse up or down to smooth-scroll the document up or down.

Can I Really Get Work Done in This Mode?

Most certainly! Many of the common Word commands have keyboard equivalents, most of which have been illustrated in the various Keyboard Master sidebars throughout this book.

Only a few of the less-common things you do in Word require the presence of the menu bar or specific toolbars. Even in those situations, it's often nicer to view a toolbar while you need it and then dispense with it when you're done.

For example, if you want to draw a table in full-screen mode, follow these steps:

1. Right-click the Full Screen toolbar.
2. Choose "Tables and Borders" from the pop-up menu.
3. Use the toolbar/floating palette to work on your table.
4. Close the toolbar when you're done.

Any toolbar can be made into a floating palette. Refer to the section, "What's the Difference between a Toolbar and a Floating Palette?" later in this chapter.

Belly Up to the Toolbar

It's debatable whether the toolbar is actually a productivity enhancer or merely crap junking up the screen. I vote for crap, myself. I feel no shame for doing that, seeing how the toolbar is ultimately customizable. Whether your changes are mild or extreme, toolbars are eager to have you beat them up.

How Can I Rearrange These Toolbars without Going Insane?

Like anything, toolbars are moveable. You just need to know where to grab them. Figure 9.3 shows the sweet spot.

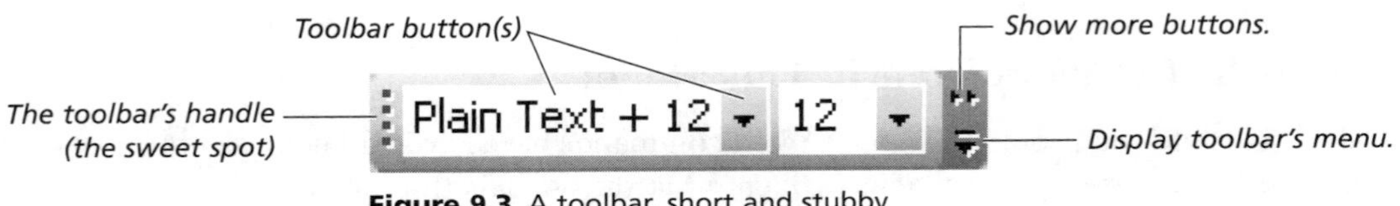

Figure 9.3 A toolbar, short and stubby

So point the mouse at the toolbar's handle; then you can drag it up, down, left, or right to rearrange it as you see fit.

Dragging toolbars must be done gingerly. Drag them too fast and you will go nuts.

Be careful of dragging the toolbar away from the edge of the window! If you do, the toolbar becomes a floating palette, as described in the next section.

The Standard and Formatting toolbars have a special item on their toolbar menu, "Show Buttons on Two Rows." When this item is chosen, Word automatically arranges the Standard and Formatting toolbars above each other and just under the menu bar.

What's the Difference between a Toolbar and a Floating Palette?

Location. Location. Location.

A toolbar is docked to an edge of the window. A palette is a little floating window. Just drag any toolbar (by its handle) into the middle of the screen, and it turns into a palette. Figure 9.4 shows the Standard toolbar as a floating palette.

To turn the palette back into a toolbar, drag it back to the edge of the screen, or just close it.

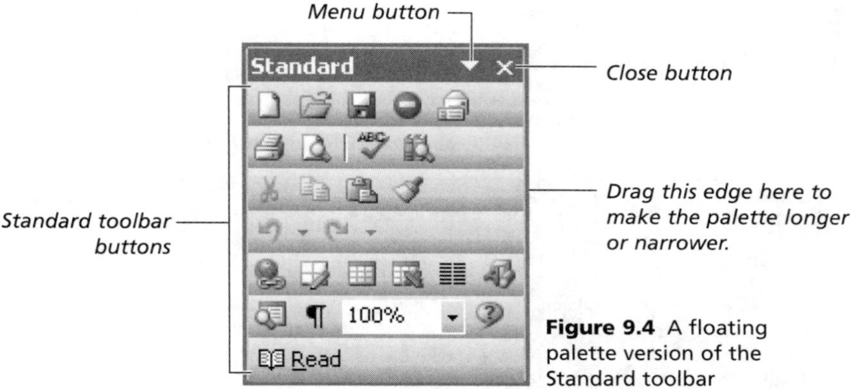

Figure 9.4 A floating palette version of the Standard toolbar

What about Putting a Toolbar down the Side of the Window?

This is possible: Simply grab the toolbar's sweet spot and drag it over to the edge of the window. In fact, I typically dock the Outline toolbar on the edge of the window when I'm working on outlines.

Can I Add a Small Caps Formatting Button?

Certainly. This is easier than you'd think:

1. Click the Menu button on the Formatting toolbar.
2. Point the mouse at the "Add or Remove Buttons" item.

   You don't have to click it.
3. Choose Formatting.

   A list of available options is displayed, common Formatting buttons and their functions. If one of them is what you want, then choose it. Alas, "Small Caps" isn't on the list, so you'll have to make a custom modification.
4. Choose Customize.

   The Customize dialog box appears.
5. Click the Commands tab.

   This lists all the commands in windows, organized into categories.
6. Choose Format from the list of Categories.

   "Small Caps" is a formatting command, found in the Font dialog box, which is part of the Format menu.
7. Scroll through the list of Commands until you find "Small Caps."

8. Drag the Small Caps icon up and drop it into the Formatting toolbar, as shown in Figure 9.5.
9. Close the Customize dialog box.

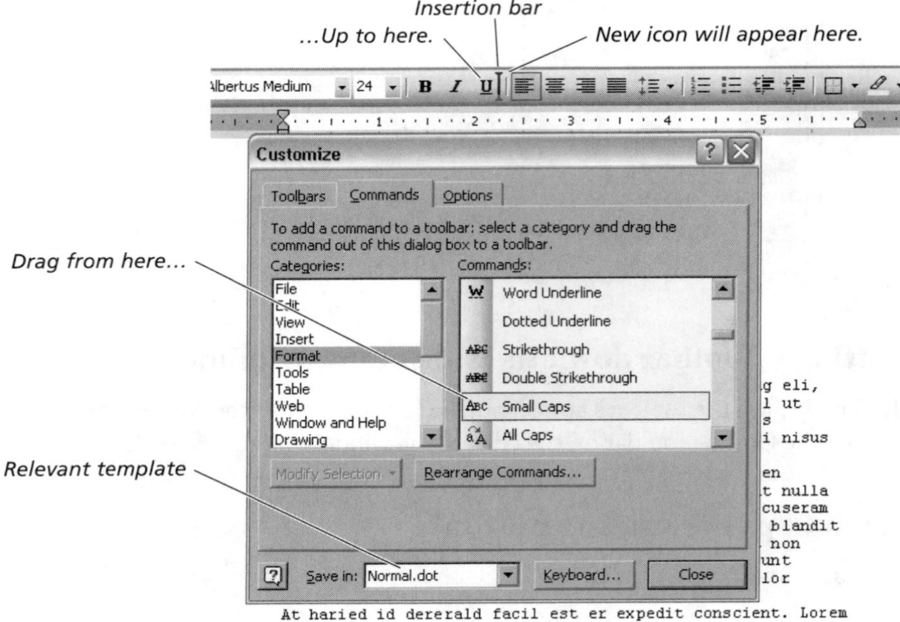

Figure 9.5 Adding a button to the toolbar

While the Customize dialog box is open, you can move, delete, or modify any of the buttons on any visible toolbar. This is done using the mouse. To insert a separator (group) bar, right-click the toolbar and choose "Begin a Group" from the pop-up menu.

Word must remember these changes, and the place it remembers them is in a template. So you can make these changes specific to a certain template or have them apply to all Word documents by specifying the `NORMAL.DOT` template, as shown in Figure 9.5. (To be specific, choose the current template being used from the drop-down list in the Customize dialog box.)

When you quit your document, you may be asked if you want to update the template. Say Yes; that cements the change so that it appears the next time you start Word.

What's the Point of the [Whatever] Button on the Toolbar When I Never Use It?

You're right! If you don't use that button, then why bother with it! For example, the Hyperlink button! I don't use it. I don't ever plan on using it. I should just send it straight to the fires of perdition by following these ecclesiastical steps:

1. Choose Tools ➢ Customize.

   There's the holy Customize dialog box, shown in Figure 9.5. When that dialog box is open, every button on every toolbar begs for mercy from the terror of your computer mouse.

2. Point the mouse at the toolbar button that offends ye.
3. Drag it off the toolbar and into damnation.

   Well, drag it down until the mouse pointer grows an X in a box, in which case you can release the mouse button. The toolbar button is gone.

4. Continue thy wanton ways of destruction.
5. Close the Customize toolbox when ye finisheth.

These changes are saved in the template specified in the Customize dialog box. So if you're asked to save the changes to the template file, click Yes to make your revised toolbar permanent.

To make the changes affect all your documents, specify the `NORMAL.DOT` *toolbar in the Customize dialog box.*

Can I Easily Restore the Toolbar back to the Way It Originally Was?

Of course:

1. Click the toolbar's menu.
2. Choose "Add or Remove Buttons."
3. In Word 2003/XP, choose Formatting.
4. Choose "Reset Toolbar."

This removes any added buttons and adds back any buttons you removed. The toolbar is restored to its original, out-of-the-box condition.

These steps must be done for each toolbar to restore it to its original look.

Which Toolbar Should I Use for Adding Things?

Try to keep your additions relating to the original function of the toolbar. For example, you add a Small Caps button to the Formatting toolbar, which is logical. Any formatting commands would work best on that toolbar. But, honestly, there are no hard-and-fast rules for any toolbar to add buttons to. In fact, if you plan on adding quite a few buttons, I recommend creating your own toolbar.

Why Would I Want to Create My Own Toolbar?

Simple: Because it would contain the commands you use most often and, therefore, it would be the only toolbar you need. So forget about customizing the other toolbars and create your own toolbar.

Here's how you can create your own toolbar in Word:

1. Summon the Customize dialog box.

   A quick way to do that is to right-click any toolbar and then choose Customize from the bottom of the pop-up menu.

2. Click the Toolbars tab.
3. Click the New button.
4. Enter a name for your custom toolbar.

   I named mine Danny's Own, even though it says "Bar None" in Figure 9.6. Other cool names are Unibar, Ultimate Bar, Candy Bar, Ba-Bar, and…you get the idea.

5. Select a template for the toolbar.

   If you choose `NORMAL.DOT`, then the toolbar will be available to all Word documents. Otherwise, you can link the toolbar to only the current document or to the current document's template by choosing either item from the drop-down list.

6. Click OK.

   The new toolbar appears in the list, but also as a floating palette off to the side of the Customize dialog box. Your next task is to fill it with buttons.

7. Click the Commands tab.
8. Select commands to add by choosing an item in the Categories list and then the individual command from the Commands list.
9. Use the mouse to drag that command's button to the toolbar, as shown in Figure 9.6.
10. When you're done, click the Close button.

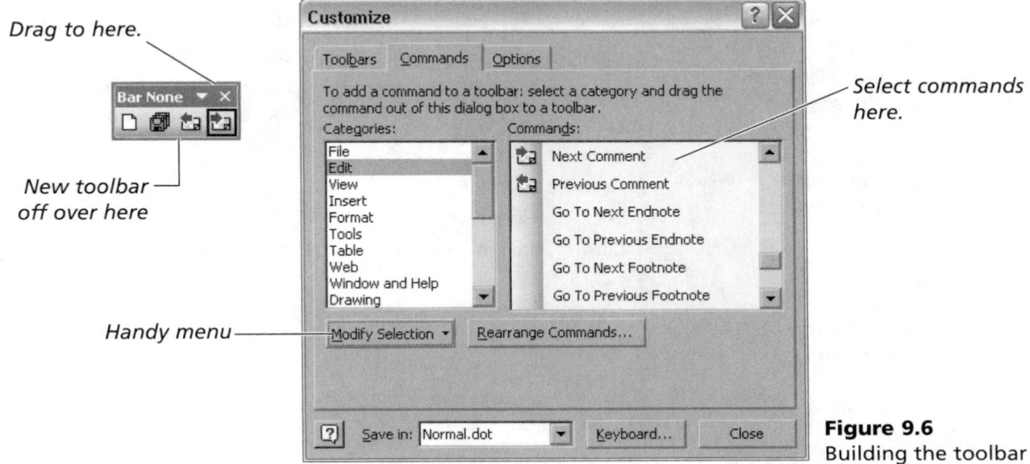

Figure 9.6
Building the toolbar

The toolbar can remain floating, or you can dock it on any edge of the screen. It appears as an optional toolbar to display in the View ➤ Toolbars menu, so even if you close it you can summon it back. In fact, it's now a permanent part of whichever template you chose in Step 5. You can show it, hide it, modify it, and so on, all as described in this chapter.

How Can I Make a Separator Bar to Group Commands in My New Toolbar?

Part of the Windows interface involves grouping similar commands on toolbars. You see this on the Standard and Formatting toolbars. On the Standard toolbar, the New, Open, Save, and E-mail buttons are a group. Then comes a separator bar, and then Print and Print Preview and so on. Separator bars visually group similar icons. To do that on your own toolbar, follow these steps:

1. Right-click your toolbar and choose Customize from the pop-up menu.

   It's the last command on the menu.

2. Click the Commands tab.

3. Click to select the button on your toolbar that starts a new group.

   Say the first three buttons are file commands and the next three are formatting commands. If so, click to select the fourth button, the first button in the second group.

4. Click the Modify Select button in the Customize dialog box.

   The Modify Selection menu appears, as shown in Figure 9.7.

5. Choose "Begin a Group."

   And the separator bar is inserted *before* the highlighted button.

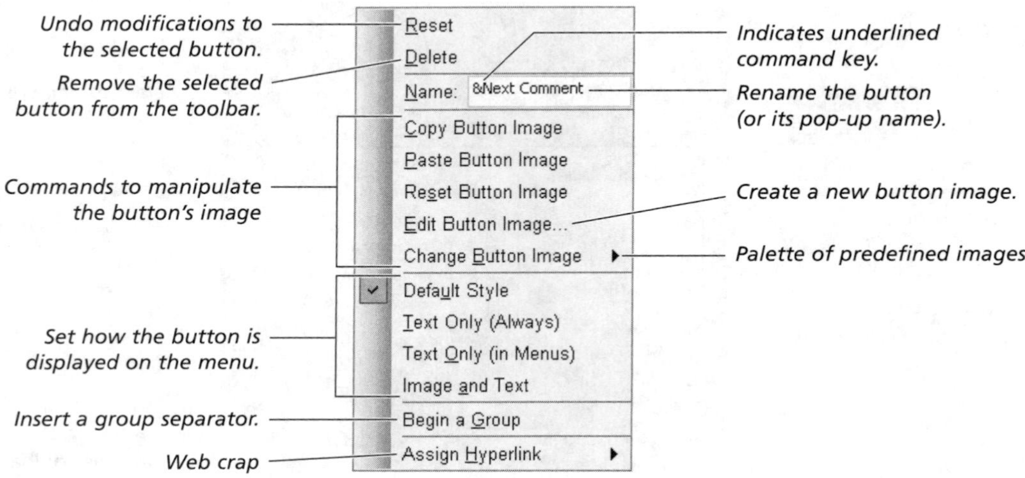

Figure 9.7 The Modify Selection menu

What Can Be Done for Commands That Lack Icons?

Say you're adding a button that lacks a specific icon. For example, in the Format category is a button called Tabs, which is designed to bring up the Tabs dialog box. It lacks an icon, so when you add it to your toolbar you get a text button that reads the name of the command, "Tabs" in this case.

If the text is particularly long, you can edit it. Here's how:

1. Select the text-only button on your toolbar.
2. Click the Modify Selection button in the Customize dialog box.
3. Use the Name command in the menu to rename the button.

   The Name command contains a text box, as shown in Figure 9.7. You can enter a new name for the button there, something shorter.

   Use an ampersand (&) to identify which letter of the command can be used with the Alt key as a keyboard shortcut.

   This is also the name of the button that appears if you point the mouse at the button.

   To display this name as well as the button's icon, also choose Image and Text from the menu.
4. Click the Close button when you're done editing.

Now you might want to dispense with the text and try slapping down your own icon instead. If so, follow these steps to display the icon instead of the text:

1. Click to select the text-only button.
2. Click the Modify Selection button in the Customize dialog box, Commands tab.
3. Choose "Change Button Image."
4. Select an icon from the palette.

   That is, select an icon if you find one that you like. For example, for the Tab command, the right-pointing arrow might be okay. Choose it.

   On my screen, Word has *both* the icon and the text. That can be fixed:
5. With the toolbar button still selected, click the Modify Selection button again.
6. Choose "Default Style" from the pop-up menu.
7. Click the Close button when you're done editing.

The right-arrow symbol for the Tabs dialog box is okay. A better symbol, however, would be the arrow/bar, which is shown on the Tab key on all PC keyboards. That symbol doesn't exist on the Change Button Image menu, so you'll have to create your own.

To create your own button image, in Step 3 above, choose the "Edit Button Image" command instead of "Change Button Image." This summons the Button Editor dialog box, which is where you can build your own toolbar button icon, as shown in Figure 9.8. There you can see how I created a button for the Tab command that looks like the icons on the Tab key.

Click OK when you're done creating the button image, and then continue working through the previous set of steps to convert your toolbar button into an image-only button.

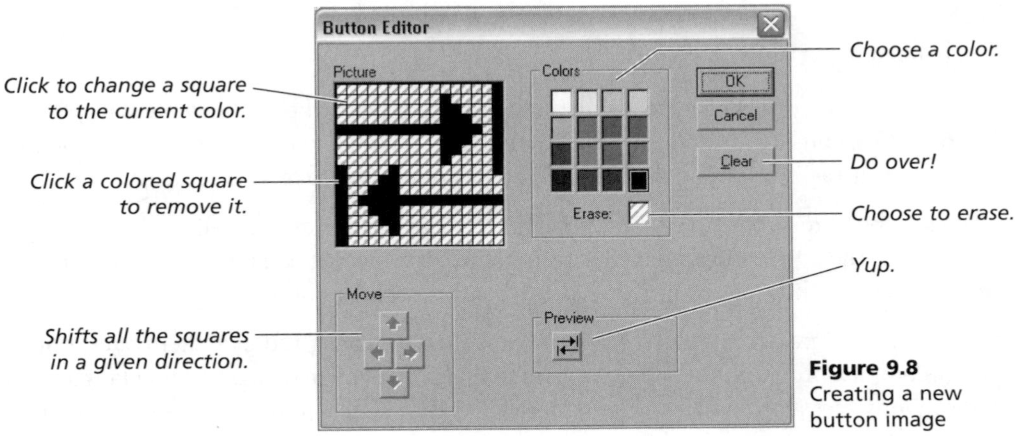

Figure 9.8
Creating a new button image

How Can I Create a Toolbar Full of Styles?

One special type of toolbar I often create is a formatting toolbar. Ever since Word messed up the Style drop-down list starting with Word 2000, I've enjoyed keeping my popular styles on a toolbar instead of using the drop-down list. I find that easier for switching styles because each style is a button I can easily click with the mouse.

You can create a style-only toolbar or you can add popular styles to your custom toolbar. It doesn't matter. The key is finding where the styles are hidden in the Customize dialog box. They're in there! You just have to scroll down the Categories list to the bottom, where you'll find Styles listed. Select that category, and the styles associated with the current document and current template are shown in the Commands list.

Simply drag the styles you want on the toolbar over to the toolbar itself, as covered earlier in this chapter.

Generally speaking, I always edit the style names because Word has the habit of tacking on "Style" to each style name. I don't generally apply icons to the styles, though you can do that if you wish; simply follow the instructions presented earlier in this chapter.

Remember that styles are associated with a given template, so you'll probably want to create your Style toolbar to belong to a given template only.

Have fun.

An Introduction to Macros

The more complex the program, the more there has been a need for automation within the program. To meet that end, a program will offer a feature such as macros.

Macros come in two flavors:

The first type of macro is the keyboard recording macro. That's where you can record your keystrokes or mouse commands and then play them back—just like you were watching a video recording of your tasks on the screen. That's one way to automate repetitive tasks.

The second type of macro is more complex. That's where macros are actually programming commands that tell the application what to do. In that aspect, macros can be used to program in new features, add commands, or customize and automate certain operations.

Word sports both type of macros. It will let you record keystrokes and play them back, but it also has richly complex programming abilities. Unlike the simple macro programming languages of yesterday, Word uses a programming language called Word Basic (or Office Basic), which is related to the Visual Basic programming language that Microsoft sells for writing Windows applications.

NERD'S CORNER

Cocktail Party Trivia, Part V

PHIL: John, I'll bet you didn't know that macro *is short for* macroinstruction.

JOHN: Wrong, Phil, I already knew that.

PHIL: Oh.

The following sections cover the use of macros for keyboard recording only. If you want to get into programming macros in Word Basic or Office Basic, then you are better off finding a book or tutorial specific to that subject. It's a pretty vast area and one I don't have time to get into in this book.

Alas, I am unable to recommend any advanced macro books for Word.

Any Way to Automate This Tedious Sequence of Keystrokes?

The problem with automating a tedious sequence of keystrokes is having the tedious sequence in the first place. Word is such a thorough program that there are few things it doesn't do or that aren't automated already. Still, those times do come up when you find yourself pressing the same key sequence over and over. When that happens, it's time to create a keyboard macro to save you some time.

The following is an example of a word-swapping macro. What it does is to take the first word and swap it with the second word. So if you type "brother irritated" and then run the macro, you end up with "irritated brother." Here's how to record that macro:

1. Make sure you have something to manipulate, some text or something to practice on.

   You need to set up an environment on the screen, in your document, so that you can properly record the macro. Otherwise, you'll have to stop halfway through and start over. It happens.

   In this case, type two words in your document. Put the insertion point at the start of the first word.

2. Choose Tools ➢ Macro ➢ Record New Macro.

   The Record Macro dialog box appears, as shown in Figure 9.9.

3. Give the macro a descriptive name.

   No spaces in the name!

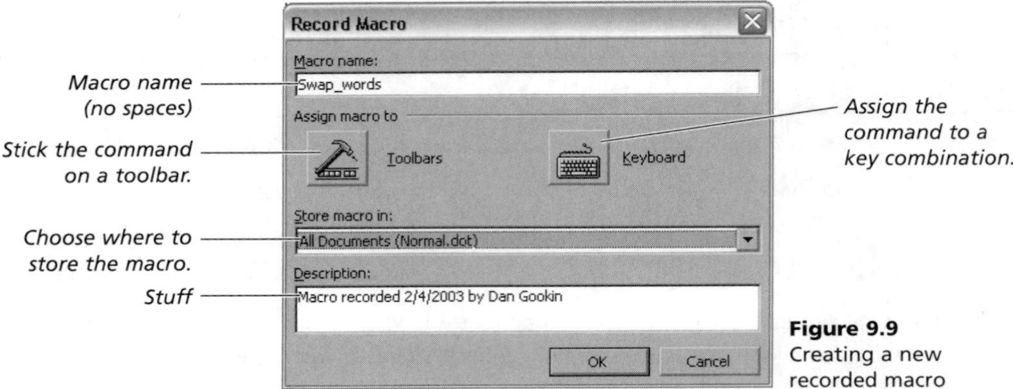

Figure 9.9 Creating a new recorded macro

4. Choose a location for the macro.

   If it's in `NORMAL.DOT`, then all your documents can use it. Otherwise, you can put the macro into the current document only or in the document template so that all documents using that template have access to it.

5. This is going to be a keyboard macro, saved to a shortcut key assignment, so click the Keyboard button.

   The Customize Keyboard dialog box appears, shown in Figure 9.10.

If you elect to add this macro as a button on a toolbar, you'll see the Customize dialog box (Figures 9.5, 9.6) with the macro you're recording listed as a command. From there you can drag it to any toolbar in Windows; skip ahead to Step 8.

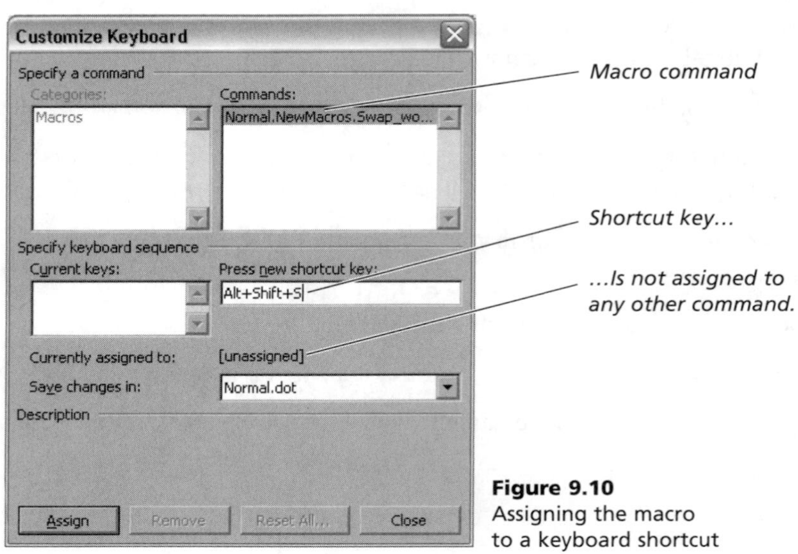

Figure 9.10 Assigning the macro to a keyboard shortcut

6. Press an appropriate shortcut key.

Choose a combination not used by any other command. For example, choose Alt+Shift+S for Swap_words.

*The Alt+Shift+*letter *keyboard combinations are the most open category for you to choose when assigning new keyboard commands.*

7. Click the Assign button.

8. Click Close.

Now you're ready to record. The mouse pointer grows a cassette tape icon, one sign that you're recording. Also the Stop Recording (yes, that's what it says) toolbar floats into existence, shown in Figure 9.11.

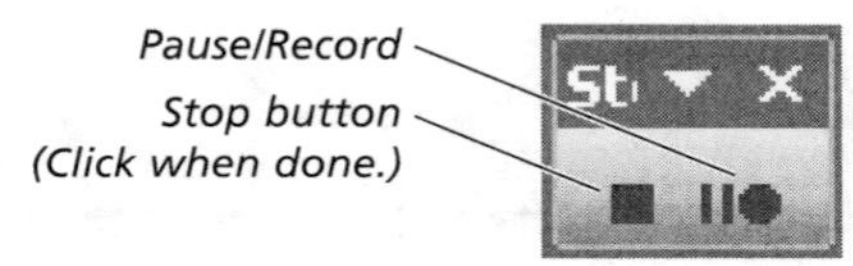

Figure 9.11
Control your macro recording from this toolbar.

9. Start working the commands to go into the macro!

In this case, you're swapping words. Here are the key commands I would use to swap the words, given that the cursor is blinking before the first word:

a. Press the F8 key twice. This selects the first word.
b. Press Ctrl+X. Cut the word.
c. Press Ctrl+right arrow. Move to the end of the second word.
d. Press Ctrl+V. Paste in the first word.

That effectively swaps the words. Time to stop recording.

In addition to any keyboard commands, you can also select menu commands or click toolbar buttons. Word records them all.

10. Click the Stop button on the Stop Recording toolbar.

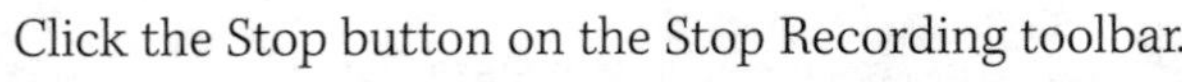

That's it. The macro has been successfully recorded.

Fortunately making macros to alleviate complex keystrokes is a rare thing. Most of the time what you want might easily be accomplished by the Replace command. For example, I used to have a macro that would find and delete excess spaces at the end of a paragraph. But searching for ^p^w and replacing it with ^p in Word now does the same thing. Still, for those times when the Replace command can't hack it, you can automate your task with a macro.

How Can I Test My Macro?

Simple: Find a spot in the document where your macro will play out; then issue the macro keyboard command or click the macro toolbar button.

In the case of the Swap_word macro, locate any two words in your document, put the cursor before the first word, and then press Alt+Shift+S.

Yes, of course it works!

NERD'S CORNER

Cocktail Party Trivia, Part VI

PHIL: But, I'm not done, John.

JOHN: So I see.

PHIL: Did you know that macroinstruction is actually supposed to be a simplified type of command?

JOHN: Yup. Knew that one as well.

PHIL: Macro means large. *And instruction means, well, instruction! So macroinstructions were supposed to be complex instructions, so that you wouldn't have to use many of them to create simple program modifications.*

JOHN: That was originally true, but over the years macros have evolved into things more complex than the simple instructions that they once were.

JILL: Maybe they should call them micros *now? Ha!*

JOHN & PHIL: ...

JILL: I'm sorry; I'm new here. I think I'll go check out that cheese ball.

Where Are the Macros Kept?

Macros dwell in the Macros dialog box. To get there, choose Tools ➤ Macro ➤ Macros. This shows the list of macros associated with your document or template, as selected in the Macros dialog box and shown in Figure 9.12.

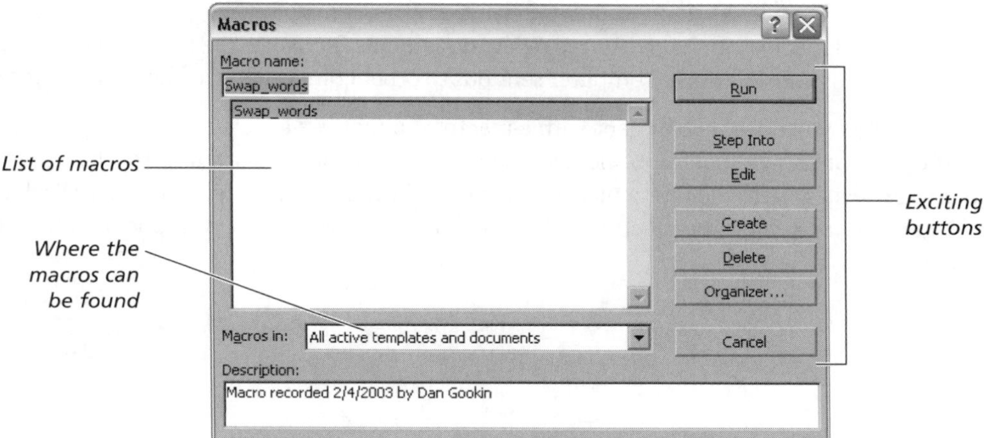

Figure 9.12 The Macros dialog box chock full of one macro

You can use the Macro dialog box to run a specific macro, edit a macro, create a new macro, delete macros, and so on, according to the exciting buttons on the side of the dialog box.

The Step Into button is used for debugging purposes. And the Edit button allows you to see the raw macro itself: If you select your macro and click Edit, you can see the Word Basic translation of your recorded keystrokes. It can be pretty complex, so do this only at your own risk. (Press Alt+Q to leave the Visual Basic Editor window and return to Word.)

Viewing the Macros Dialog Box

To quickly view the Macros dialog box:

Alt+F8

How Can Macros Be a Security Risk?

Word's macros have a lot of power. And, as you know from watching most science fiction television programs, with power comes a lot of responsibility. The problem with Word's macros is that they're powerful enough that the bad guys can write seemingly innocent Word macros that can do devastating things to your entire computer.

For example, Word macros can be written to delete documents on disk, to send out bogus e-mail, or to have vital information from your computer sent out to other computers elsewhere via the Internet.

Occasionally when you open a document with a macro, you may see a dialog box displayed explaining that there are unknown macros in the document. The dialog box gives you the option to disable the macros. Especially if it's a document you downloaded from the Internet, click that Disable button! You don't know what the macros could be or how they could affect your document. Better to be safe than sorry.

PART 2

Excel

10 Why the Hell Would Anyone Other than an Accountant Use Excel?

I love spreadsheets for three reasons and only one of them is that I'm a nerd. The other two are that I hate paying taxes and, most importantly, I understand the whole *grid* concept thing.

You see, Excel isn't about numbers. It's about tables. It's the grid thing! Any information you can stick into a table is probably best handled by Excel. That's the way it works. So where Word gives you the blank page to fill as your creative juices desire, Excel presents you with a massive grid full of thousands of cells. Anything you can picture in a grid—names and dates, city blocks, prisoners, quilting patterns, team rosters, or even (yes) financial data—goes into Excel.

Even though this book is intermediate in nature, I'm going to assume that you probably don't use Excel too much. Most people don't. They avoid it for reasons mathematical in nature. But if you study this chapter (and those that follow), you'll soon discover the secret most Excel mavens know: It's not just for accountants.

Puzzles Solved and Formulas Reproached:

- Introducing Excel
- Finding your way around the worksheet quickly
- Wrestling with formulas
- Referencing other cells directly, by name, or absolutely
- Decoding the various common and annoying error messages
- Busting an Excel table into a Word document

Some Information for Excel Newbies

The first spreadsheet software was called VisiCalc, short for Visible Calculator. The program's designer envisioned a calculator that had many different windows or locations, similar to an accountant's general ledger form. Because such a thing was made on a computer, the numbers on the form could be "live" and relate to one another, updating and changing as new information was entered. Oh, and those accountants went nuts over the thing.

While a spreadsheet has its foundation in numbers, the truth is that any information that goes into rows and columns can be more easily manipulated in a spreadsheet than in most other types of software. The key to your understanding of Excel is to stop thinking of numbers and switch your brain over to a mode where you see information presented in rows and columns. Once you see those rows and columns, you're ready to start using a spreadsheet.

The Cheap-Ass Tour of Your Basic Excel Window

Like all Office programs, Excel shares a common look and feel with its sisters and cousins and aunts. Figure 10.1 illustrates the basic big-picture things you see when you gawk at Excel after starting it the first time.

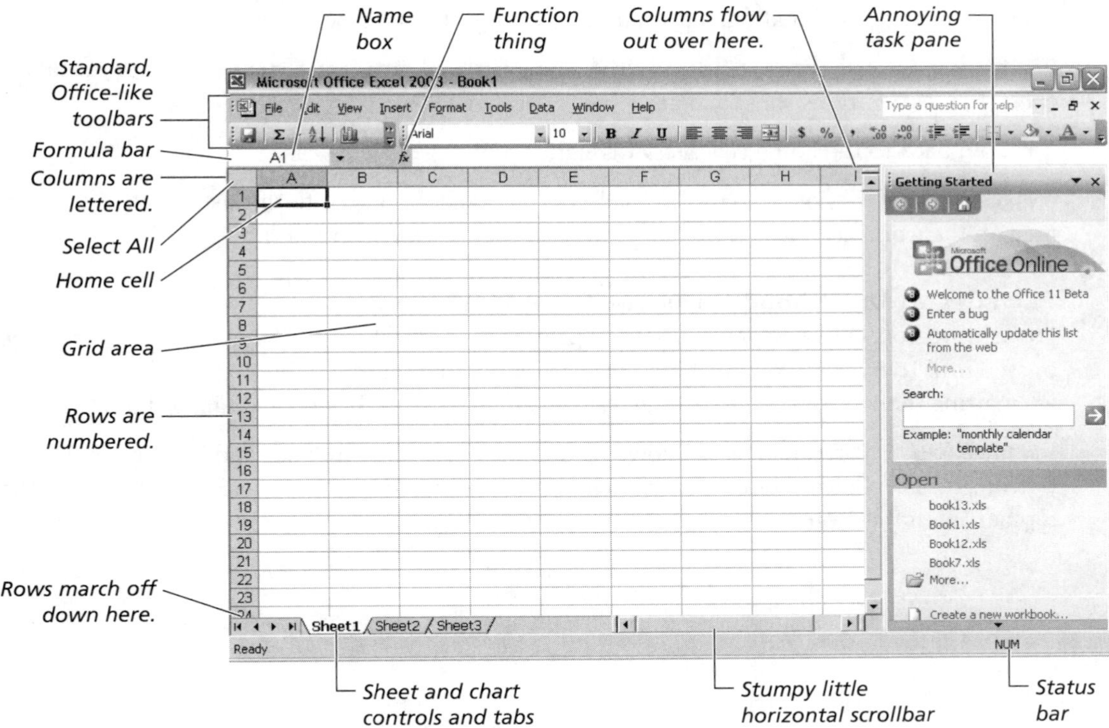

Figure 10.1 Excel, naked and exposed

How Many Rows and Columns Are There?

More than you'll ever use! Keep in mind that information doesn't need to fill every cell, however.

To find out the exact answer, locate the Select All button on the grid; see Figure 10.1. If you click that button once with the mouse, you select the entire worksheet. But if you click and *hold* the button, you'll see the worksheet's maximum size displayed in the Name box.

On my screen it says that the worksheet is 65,536 rows tall by 256 columns wide. That may seem like enough for anything, but rumor has it that there are massive worksheets in major corporations that are many times that size.

The larger a worksheet is, the more memory it consumes. Very large worksheets can bring a computer system to its knees.

Most of the worksheets you create will fit on a single screen or a printed page of text. Some may be longer, such as worksheets that track information over time, but only rarely will you see a worksheet that comes close to using every single cell.

I Want to Go Visit the Last Cell!

The first cell, or home cell, in the worksheet is named cell A1. That's from the A column and the first row. The very last possible cell in a worksheet is cell IV65536, which reads like some perverse Roman numeral combination, but it's not. It's column IV and row 65536.

To visit the last cell, type `IV65536` into the Name box and press the Enter key. There's nothing there, but it's a curious spot to look at.

To zoom back to the home cell, press Ctrl+Home.

(No, Ctrl+End does not go to the last cell in the worksheet; it goes to the last cell in your work area on the worksheet, which probably won't be that far down and to the right.)

Can I Get My Dumb Toolbars on Two Rows, Please?

For some reason, Office programs like to display the two usual toolbars, Standard and Formatting, on one row. To fix that, you must grab the second toolbar (on the right), which usually the Formatting toolbar, and carefully drag it down and to the left, below the Standard toolbar.

In Office XP/11, you can click the down arrow at the end of the toolbar and choose "Show Buttons on Two Rows" from the menu. That fixes the problem without making you wrestle the toolbars with the mouse.

Where the Heck Is the Office Assistant?

If you feel the urge to use the annoying, animated Office Assistant with Excel, then summon it from its locked vault: Choose Help ➤ Show the Office Assistant. Or if you tire of that dumb thing, choose Help ➤ Kill the Office Assistant. This command may not be found on all versions of Excel, so instead you'll have to settle for the Help ➤ Hide the Office Assistant command.

Do You Have Any Other Immediate Helpful Information That Will Soothe My Frayed Nerves?

Though it's stated in this book's introduction, again I'd like to remind you to turn off the Personalized Menu feature of Excel. That is, remove the options that keep "recently used items" at the top of the menu and occasionally shuffle menu items depending on how you use them.

To ensure that these options are properly set, follow these steps:

1. Choose Tools ➤ Customize.

2. Click the Options tab.

Here's where things get weird because Excel 11/XP is utterly opposite of Excel 2000:

3a. In Excel 11/XP, the top two items in the dialog box must be checked.

3b. In Excel 2000, the top two items in the dialog box must be unchecked.

4. Click OK.

Now Excel is set up to behave in a sane and predictable manner.

Don't Be Dumb: The Difference between a Spreadsheet, Worksheet, and Workbook

There are three general terms you need to know to use Excel:

Spreadsheet

This is the type of software Excel is; just as Word is a word processor, Excel is a spreadsheet.

Worksheet

This is the thing that Excel displays in its window. It's the grid full of cells, from A1 to IV65536.

Workbook

This is a collection of worksheets saved to disk, the equivalent of a document in Word. In Excel, you save a workbook to disk. You open a workbook previously saved on disk. You do not open a spreadsheet nor do you open a worksheet, though the terms may be improperly used that way.

How Do You Best Deal with the Task Pane?

The best way to deal with the task pane is to close it: Press Ctrl+F1 and it goes away in Excel 11, or you can choose View ➤ Task Pane to banish it (in both Excel 11 and Excel XP).

A more important question to ask might be, "How do I get the task pane *not* to show up when Excel starts?" The answer is to use the Options dialog box:

1. Choose Tools ➤ Options.
2. Click the View tab.
3. Uncheck the box by "Startup Task Pane."
4. Click OK.

Note that Excel 2000 does not use the task pane. Blessed be Excel 2000!

Do I Have to Start at Cell A1?

Heavens, no! Unlike a word processing document, there is no "first" cell. The first cell is literally A1, but the first cell into which you sling data can be any cell in the worksheet.

Logically, it makes sense to use a cell you can see on the screen. But the cell doesn't have to be at any specific location in the worksheet.

For example, when I start a new table of data in Excel, I typically start it at cell D5 or C3, as shown in Figure 10.2. There are no rules or traditions here; start wherever you like, even cell A1 if you need to.

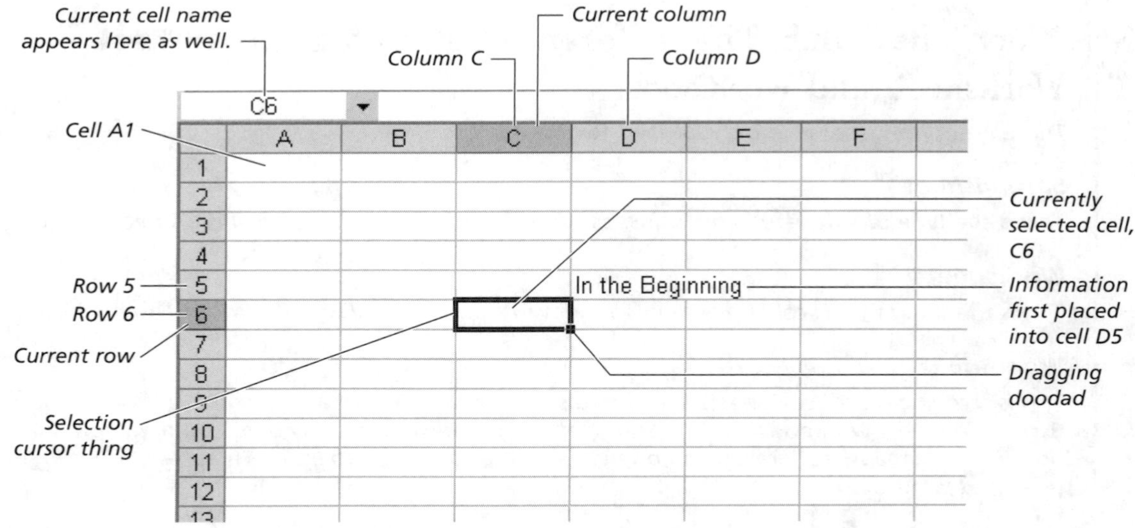

Figure 10.2 Picking a starting place for your Excel info

What Goes into a Cell?

Cells can contain three things:

 Text

 Values

 Formulas

In addition, cells can be formatted and shaded, and their size can be changed at a whim.

Also, as with other Office applications, you can draw objects on top of the worksheet to help illustrate things.

Typing in a Worksheet? No, It Just Doesn't Sound Right to Me.
Text has just as much of a right to exist in a worksheet as information. I suppose they figured this out early when the pioneer spreadsheet users discovered that numbers should often be *labeled* so that you know what they mean.

In Excel, of course, you can use text as titles to your worksheet, to add information and explain things. In fact, if you wanted to, you could put a lot of text into a single cell. Do remember, however, that Excel is a grid thing. Writing should be done in Word.

See Chapter 12, "Some Formatting Tricks," for information on formatting the text in a cell.

Something you may not know: All text you type is assumed to be text. Yeah, that seems dumb. But there is a prefix character you can type to ensure that Excel interprets what you type as text and not a label or anything else. That is the apostrophe key. Follow these steps:

1. Click cell C3.
2. Type `Pugsly School of Wart Removal`.
3. Press the Enter key.

   This moves you down to cell C4.
4. Type `'LaWanda Ridgeway, Chief Artist`.
5. Press Enter.

   And you're at cell C5.

Notice that the single tick before the text in cell C4 isn't displayed? That's because the tick is a prefix character that tells Excel to assume the cell's content is text. This is optional, of course; Excel is generally smart enough to know text when it sees it.

What's the Difference between a Value and a Number?

A value is a quantity or measure of something. Normally I would just call it a number, but in Excel there is also a numeric nonvalue. For example, your street address may be 4140. That's a number. It's not a value because you'll never use it to make a calculation.

For example, what happens when you add 15 to your Social Security number? Well, you get someone else's Social Security number, but the point is that the Social Security number is just a number, not a value. You don't ever need to add, subtract, multiply, or find the square root of that number.

So numbers are like text, but values are numbers you can play with and treat like they're measuring something.

As with text, you don't have to tell Excel that you're typing a value into a cell; Excel is smart enough to know. But you can flag a value as a number if you like. That's done by prefixing the value with a single quote mark, the secret text prefix tick. Follow these steps:

1. Click cell G1.
2. Type `1234`.
3. Press Enter.

   That's a value. Note how Excel automatically right-justifies a value in a cell?
4. In cell G2, type `'9876`.
5. Press Enter.

   That's a number. Actually it's text; note how it's left-justified.

   In Excel 11/XP, a green diamond appears in the cell's upper-left corner. That's the "This Cell Is Weird" warning that Excel gives. In this case, you're being alerted to the fact that you deliberately put in a number as text, and Excel thinks you're a dodo for doing that.

   a. Click the mouse in cell G2.

      A warning icon appears next to the cell.

   b. Point the mouse at the warning icon.

      A menu button appears!

   c. Click the menu button.

      A drop-down menu appears!

   d. Choose "Ignore Error."

      That gets rid of the green diamond.

   Meanwhile, back in cell G3...
6. Type `=5`.
7. Press Enter.

Like the tick, the equal sign can also be used as a prefix. In this case, when followed by a number, it means the contents of that cell equal that value. Dumb. Redundant. But it's an option and I'm required by the Computer Book Author's Code to demonstrate it to you.

Like the tick mark for text, the equal sign for values is optional. Excel is smart enough to know a value when it sees one. Unlike the tick mark, however, the equal sign cannot be used with text. If you do use it, you'll confuse Excel. And that makes sense because there is no numerical equivalent for "Brian's Bitchin' Tax Avoidance Scheme."

If you try to type = followed by text, Excel displays a #NAME? error. It believes the text to be the name of a specific cell or range of cells, which it's not. You'll have to edit the cell and remove the equal sign, promising yourself not to be so impertinent in the future.

Formulas? I Hate Chemistry Worse than Math!

No, not that kind of formula! In Excel, a formula is a mathematical or logical operation that takes place within a cell. This can involve numbers and symbols, as well as any of Excel's powerful and scary built-in functions. The formula's equation sits inside a single cell all alone, or it can reference other cells in the worksheet—or even cells in other worksheets or information on the Internet. It's very powerful. And scary.

Unlike with text or values, you *must* prefix a function in a cell with the equal sign. No options or cop-outs here. In fact, from the previous section, typing =5 is the simplest form of Excel function. The function is basically the value 5. It "equals five."

Wander through these steps, which assume that you have values in cells G1 and G3 per the previous section's instructions:

1. Click cell G5 to select it.
2. Type `=2+2`.

   Just like in the old Password game, imagine an off-stage voice whispering, "The formula is two plus two." Or you could say, "The contents of this cell are equal to two plus two."
3. Press Enter.

   Good! Two plus two still equals four. It's a simple formula, but Excel can handle it.
4. Into cell G6 type `=G1+G3-G5`.

   Now that's a formula! It reads "The contents of this cell are equal to the value of cell G1 plus the value of cell G3 minus the value of cell G5.

You don't have to type in G1 or G3 or G5; simply click the mouse on a cell, and it's address is automatically entered into the formula.

5. Press Enter.

   On my screen it shows 6543 as the result. Just kidding! It's 1235.

Of course, the most interesting thing about formulas is that they're *live* and change as information elsewhere in the worksheet changes.

6. Click cell G1.
7. Type 99.
8. Press Enter.

   Not only does cell G1 change its value, but also the formula in cell G6 updates to reflect the updated information. Nifty.

Beyond simple math, formulas also contain functions that let you manipulate values in incredible and often brain-numbing ways. But don't ever fuss over this: It's *the computer* that does the calculations. All you need to know is which function to use, which is where this book helps a lot.

What's the Trick to Editing a Cell?

You may notice that, unlike a word processor, the cursor keys move the cell selector and do not let you edit the contents of a cell—no matter how hard you stare at it.

There are two ways to edit a cell. The first is to select the cell and then use the Formula bar to change the cell's contents. The Formula bar always shows a cell's inner workings, whereas the cell itself merely displays the results (see Figure 10.3).

The evil that lurks inside the heart of a cell

Click the mouse up here to edit.

B14 fx =PI()*(B13/2)^2

	A	B	C	D	E
12					
13	Wheel diameter	18	inches		
14	Area is	254.469	inches		
15					
16					
17					

What the cell displays

Figure 10.3 How editing a cell works

A better way to edit a cell is to select it and press the F2 key, shown in Figure 10.4. This does the same thing as clicking the mouse in the Formula bar: It expands the cell to reflect its true contents (or formula), which you can then edit using the mouse or cursor keys.

To refer to another cell while you're editing, either type in that cell's name directly or use the mouse to click the cell (or select a range of cells), which inserts the cell(s) reference into your formula.

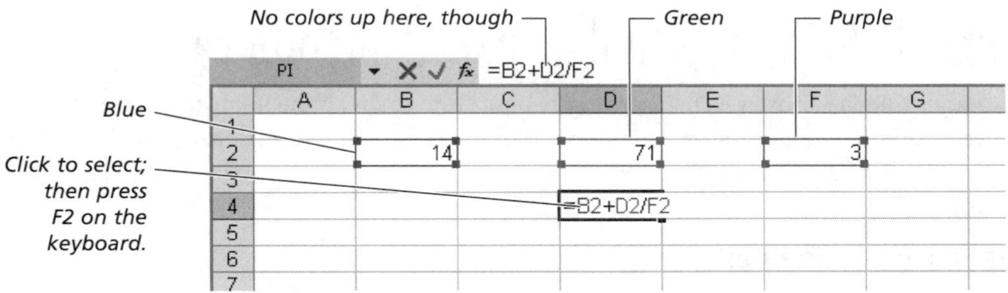

Figure 10.4 Editing a cell

Also notice that when you edit a formula, any cells referred to are highlighted in color on the screen. This is pretty cool, unless you're colorblind.

You can use the Cancel button on the Formula bar to weasel out of your edits.

Use the Enter button on the Formula bar if your arm is too heavy to lift and you can't press the Enter key on the keyboard instead.

KEYBOARD MASTER

Editing a Cell

While you can edit a cell using the Formula bar, I'm stuck in the old-fashioned keyboard-bound method of doing things, which includes using these keys:

F2

Press the F2 key to edit the cell's contents.

Esc

Cancel editing.

Ctrl+Z

Undo any editing changes.

Worksheet Tricks, Stunts, and Tomfoolery

The casual or briefly exposed Excel user may benefit from many of the following tips and suggestions. I've listed them in a somewhat random order to keep them interesting. Hopefully you'll find one or two that you didn't already know!

How Big Is My Worksheet?

All worksheets are the same size: a gazillion cells by a zillion cells. The actual numbers are listed near the start of this chapter, but what you really want to know is how big your *data region* is. That's the part of the spreadsheet that's populated with information.

To go to the southeast corner of your data region, press Ctrl+End. That selects the cell that is equal to the rightmost row and bottom-most column that's filled with something in your worksheet. Yes, it can be (and often is) an empty cell.

To hop to the last occupied cell in the current row, press Ctrl+right arrow.

To hop to the last occupied cell in the current column, press Ctrl+down arrow.

And, of course, Ctrl+Home always moves you to the A1 cell on the worksheet.

Where's the Cell Selection Thingy?

It's possible to scroll around and view a worksheet and lose where the cell selection thing is. The quick way to find it is *not* to scroll around madly, but rather press Ctrl+Backspace. That refocuses Excel's window on the location of the highlighted cell.

Any Spiffy Way to Jump to a Specific Cell off in the Yonder?

If you know the cell's address, just type it into the Name box on the Formula bar (see Figure 10.1). Press the Enter key and there you are.

To jump to a *named* cell, choose the cell name from the drop-down list on the Name box. You can also use the Go To command, Ctrl+G, which displays the Go To dialog box from which you can choose any of several recently visited places in your workbook, as shown in Figure 10.5.

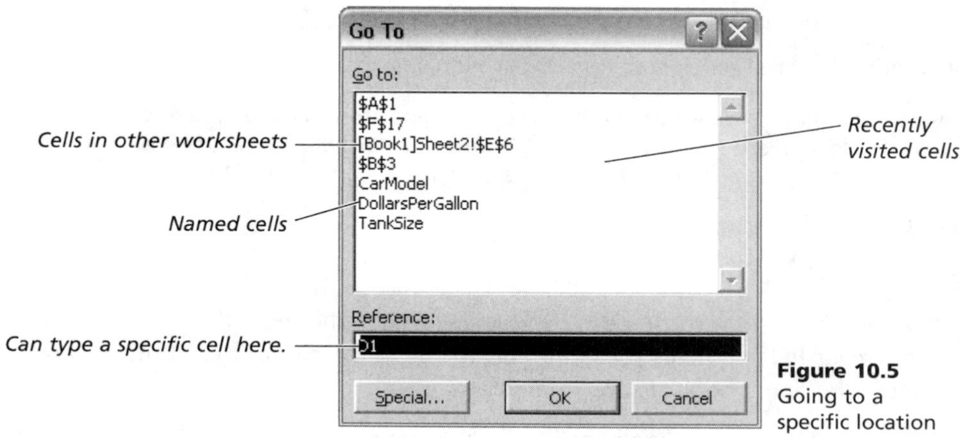

Figure 10.5 Going to a specific location

How Can I Better Remember Cell H34?

I find that I often remember specific cells if I keep on referencing them. However, that doesn't help if you insert or delete some rows or move portions of the worksheet around with Copy and Paste. Therefore, to be certain that you'll remember a specific cell or a range of cells, name it (or them).

To name a cell, follow these steps:

1. Click to select the cell you want to name.
2. Choose Insert ➢ Name ➢ Define.

   The Define Name dialog box appears, as shown in Figure 10.6.

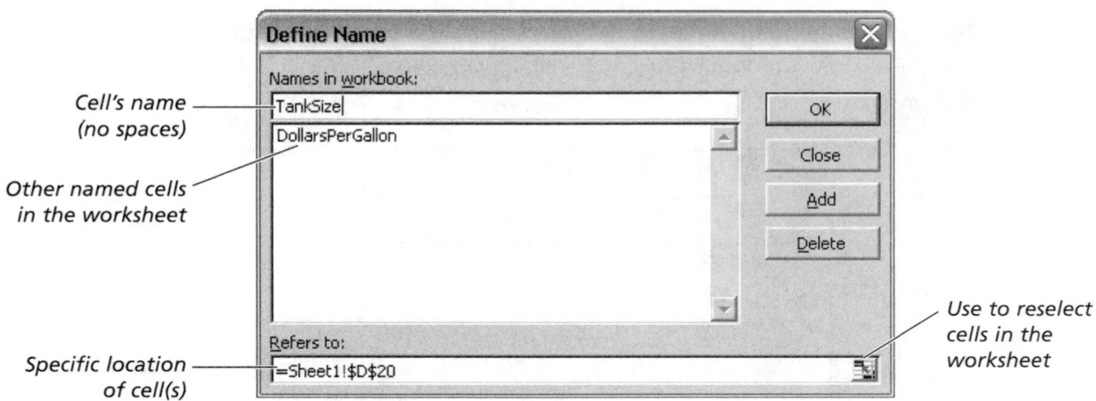

Figure 10.6 Naming a cell

3. Type a name for the cell.

   Be descriptive of the cell's contents. Also avoid using spaces.

*The more descriptive you are, the more your formulas can make sense. For example: =DollarsPerGallon*TankSize is obvious as a formula to calculate how much it may cost to fill up on gas. That's more apparent than =H21*G15.*

4. Click OK.

   And the cell is given that name.

The name sticks so well that you'll see it displayed instead of the cell's address in the Name box on the Formula bar. In fact, there's your shortcut: To quickly name a cell, click the cell and type the name into the Name box. That saves a few steps.

You can also name a range of cells or any cluster of selected cells. Simply select the cells, and then assign a name to them using any of the techniques covered in this section. The single name treats all the cells as a unit and can also be used in functions.

I'm in the Middle of a Function and Need to Recall a Name That I Forgot!

After you type that = sign, the Formula bar switches over to Function mode and the Name box disappears. So it's really difficult to recall the specific wording of the labels in your document. Fear not! There is an easy way:

1. Select a cell.
2. Press = to start entering the function.
3. Press the F3 key.

   This is the same thing as choosing Insert ➤ Name ➤ Paste. It brings up the Paste Name dialog box, shown in Figure 10.7, from which you can select any of the labels specified in your workbook.

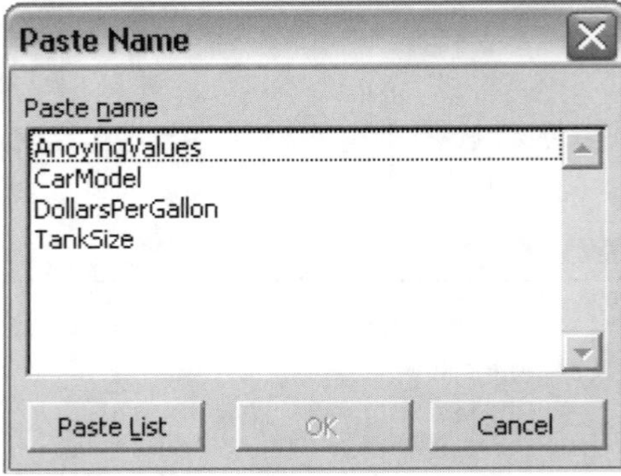

Figure 10.7
The Paste Name dialog box

4. Choose a name from the list.
5. Click OK.

   And that name (the cell it refers to) is slapped into your function.

What Is "End Mode?"

End mode is very stupid and not worth bothering with.

Okay: It's a holdover from a more ancient time in spreadsheets when the End key was used in an insane manner to navigate around the worksheet.

Pressing the End key activates End mode and highlights the End item on Excel's status bar. Now you can use the End key as a prefix to leap around your document. Pressing End, up arrow, for example, jumps up to the next chunk of data in the worksheet. End, left arrow does the same thing but to the left.

Pressing End by itself again quits this annoying and useless mode of operation.

KEYBOARD MASTER

Moving around the Spreadsheet

Hopefully, your worksheets won't be that huge or busy. Even if they are, you'll find these keyboard shortcuts handy for navigating regions near and far inside Excel:

Arrow keys

Move the selector one cell in the given direction.

Ctrl+Arrow key

Hop to the end of the data region or to the far edge of the worksheet (depending on how many times you press the keys).

PgDn

Move down one screen.

PgUp

Move up one screen.

Alt+PgDn

Move left one screen.

Alt+PgUp

Move right one screen.

Ctrl+PgDn

Display the next sheet in the workbook.

Ctrl+PgUp

Display the previous sheet in the workbook.

You Mean I Can Finally Use the Scroll Lock Key?

Spreadsheets are perhaps the only program in the universe for which your computer keyboard's Scroll Lock key comes into play. With the Scroll Lock key pressed, and its wee little light on, the four arrow keys actually slide the worksheet left, right, up, or down, depending on which key you press.

The cell selector does not move when Scroll Lock mode is on.

Pressing Scroll Lock again leaves Scroll Lock mode and returns the cursor keys back to normal. And the wee little light goes off as well.

Why Does the Text Get Lopped Off?

Text in a cell stretches out as far to the right as possible—until it bumps into something. So if there is nothing to the east of the cell, then the text goes on and on. But the first occupied cell "in the way" halts the meandering text in its tracks. Figure 10.8 kind of shows how this works.

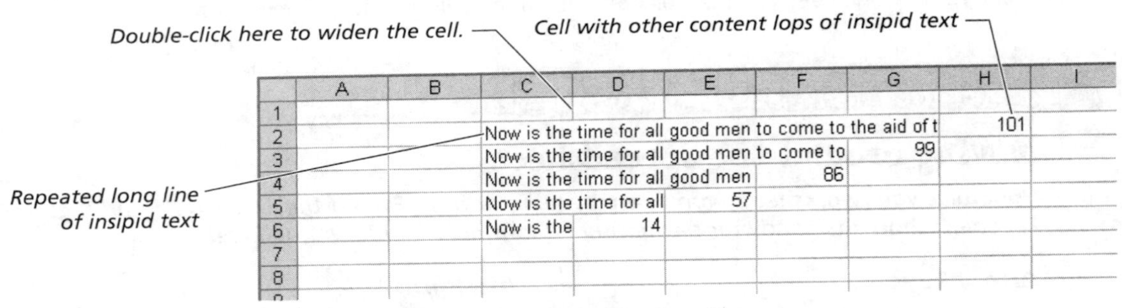

Figure 10.8 Various stages of text lopping-off-ness

There are a few tricks you can pull to prevent this from happening.

The Old Move-the-Data-Cell-Over Trick

The first trick is simply to cut the cell in the way and paste it over yonder where it doesn't get in the way of the text:

1. Select the cell you want to move.
2. Press Ctrl+X to cut.
3. Click the mouse in the cell you want to move to.
4. Press Ctrl+V to paste.

With practice, that moves the cell out of the way so that your text doesn't get cut off.

The Old Enlarge-the-Cell-with-the-Text-in-It Trick

You can also resize a cell so that it's wide enough to contain the long strand of text. The easiest way to do this is to double-click the mouse on the line separating the cell's column from the next column, such as between columns C and D shown in Figure 10.8. Double-click there, and the cell is automatically resized to fix the text length.

You can also choose Format ➢ Column ➢ AutoFit Selection to do the same thing as the double-click trick.

A drawback to this approach is that it widens all cells in the column. If that's a drawback.

The Old Format-the-Cell-So-That-the-Text-Wraps-in-It Trick

Think about it: When is it necessary for the text to march all the way across several cells in a worksheet? Probably only for titles and such. So as long as the text is what's important and not its position across the screen, you can format the text so that the cell consumes it all without crashing into other cells. Here's how:

1. Click the cell containing the long, winding text.
2. Press Ctrl+1 to format the cell.
3. Click the Alignment tab, as shown in Figure 10.9.

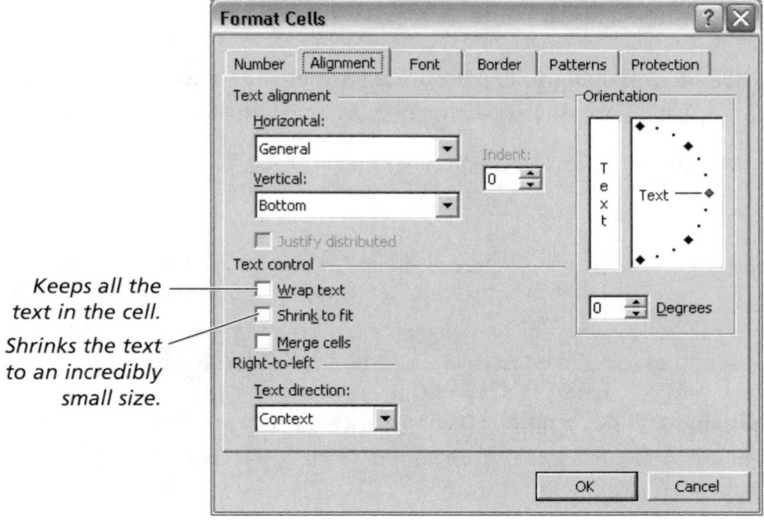

Figure 10.9
Various ways to mess with text in a cell

4. Check "Wrap Text."
5. Click OK.

Now the text wraps within the cell's left and right boundaries, but the cell gets incredibly tall; the cell's new height affects the entire row. That may be livable. Of course, you can always adjust the cell's width at this point as a sort of trade-off.

Wrapping text in a cell does not permanently alter the row height. If you delete or edit the cell, then the row's height changes accordingly.

Forget the Cell and Put the Text into a Damn Box.
The final way to stick a long bit of text into a document is to forgo putting it into a cell altogether. Instead, just use the Text Box drawing tool and put your text into there. Here are the details:

1. Click the Drawing button to bring up the Drawing toolbar.
2. Click the Text Box button on the Drawing toolbar.
3. Drag the mouse over your worksheet to create a rectangle for your text.

   Start at the upper-left corner and drag down and to the left to create the rectangle.
4. Type your text into the box.
5. Drag the mouse over your text to select it.
6. Format the text.

   Choose a font, size, attributes, and alignment from the Formatting toolbar. Or you can press Ctrl+1 to summon up a special Format Text dialog box that contains only the Font tab.
7. Drag the text box by its edge to the location where you want it.

   Refer to Figure 10.10.

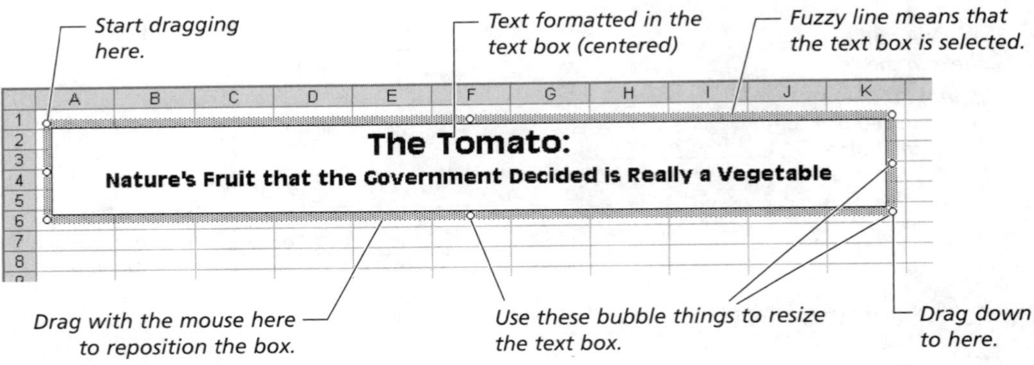

Figure 10.10 Using a text box for text

8.   Finally, you can use the Fill Color or Line Color icon on the Drawing toolbar to change the line or fill color of the text box.

Note that the text box floats over cells in the worksheet. Unless you want those cells hidden on purpose, try not to fill them in.

To remove the text box's border, choose "No Line" from the Line Color pop-up menu palette.

Be sure to close the Drawing toolbar when you're done with it.

Am I Spellling This Properly?

Unlike Word, Excel doesn't spell check on-the-fly. And why should it? Writing is the domain of the word processor. In Excel, you must specifically direct the program to check your awful spelling. This is done in one of two ways:

  Click the Spelling button on the toolbar.

 Press the F7 key

This starts the spell checking, which scours every cell in the worksheet for offending words. (You may be asked if you want to start or continue spell checking at the start of the worksheet; click OK or Yes.)

The Spelling dialog box for Excel 11/XP is shown in Figure 10.11. The dialog box for Excel 2000 has most of the same features but in different locations. (It also sports a handy and much-missed Undo Last button.) The operation of both generations of dialog box is the same: Locate the correct word in the list of suggestions, click it, and then click the Change button. Continue doing this until all the words in the worksheet have been checked.

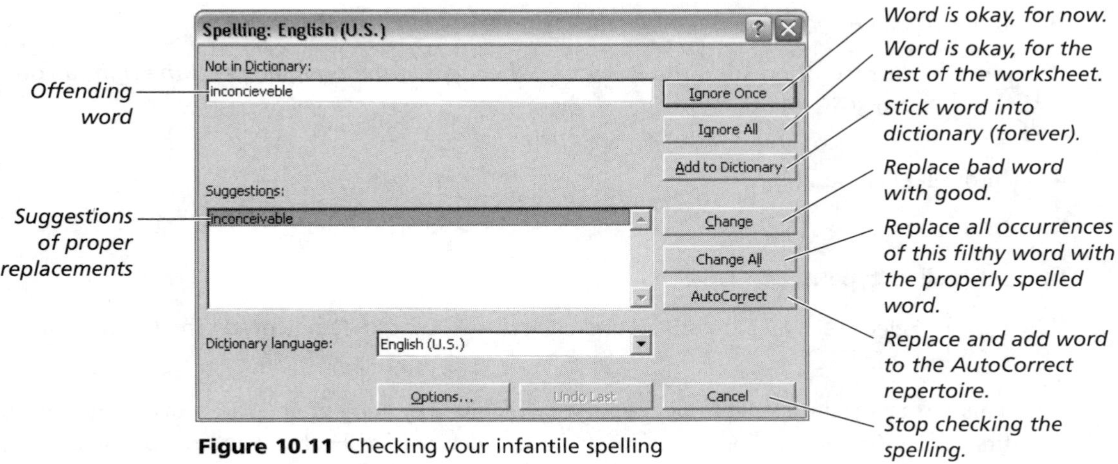

Figure 10.11 Checking your infantile spelling

Spell checking is a sheet-wide thing only. To check your spelling on a chart or on another worksheet, you must view that chart or worksheet.

Relative Addressing? Absolute Addressing? Why Should I Care?

When you refer to a cell in your worksheet, the reference is considered relative. Consider the worksheet snippet in Figure 10.12.

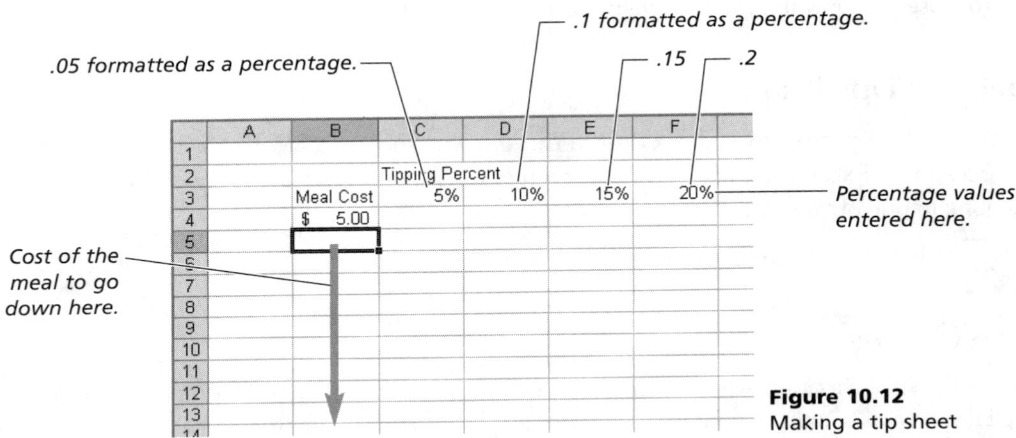

Figure 10.12
Making a tip sheet

Follow along by creating a similar worksheet in Excel. Enter the values shown in Figure 10.12 using the same cell locations by following these steps:

1. Into cell C2 type `Tipping Percent`.
2. Into cell B3 type `Meal Cost`.
3. Into cell C3 type `.05`.

Instead of pressing the Enter key after typing the number, press the right arrow key instead.

4. Into cell D3 type `.1`.
5. Into cell E3 type `.15`.
6. Into cell F3 type `.2`.
7. [%] Select cells C3 through F3 and click the Percent Style button on the Formatting toolbar.

   This formats the values into percentages, which is why you entered them as decimals in the first place: .05 is really 5% when formatted as a percentage. Had you entered 5 instead, then when you formatted it as a percent you would have gotten 500%, which is your first and most visual clue that you've screwed up something—or you're a really good tipper!

8. Into cell B4, type `5`.

In this case you want 5, which represents the cost of the meal in dollars.

9. Select cell B4 again and click the Currency Style button on the Formatting toolbar.

10. Click cell B5.

Now the screen should look similar to Figure 10.12. You're ready to use relative addressing to fill in the Meal Cost column. Relative addressing means that a cell refers to another cell in a nonspecific manner. For example:

11. Into cell B5 type `=B4+2.5` and press Enter.

You don't have to type B4 into the formula; use the mouse to click the B4 cell, and that address (B4) is automatically inserted.

This formula reads, "The contents of this cell equal the contents of cell B4 plus 2.5 (two dollars and fifty cents)." Pressing the Enter key yields the result, $7.50.

The formula you just entered uses relative addressing. The "B4" in the formula doesn't specifically mean "cell B4" but rather "the cell above the current cell." That's the way Excel normally does things, and it enables you to do fancy tricks, such as the following:

12. Select cell B5.

13. Fill down 15 cells.

Here's how to fill down if you're unfamiliar with it:

a. Point the mouse at the square on the cell selector's lower-right corner, shown in Figure 10.13.

The mouse changes to a solid + when you've found the sweet spot.

Figure 10.13 How to drag a cell into a series

b. Drag the mouse down 15 cells, to cell B20.

When you release the mouse button, the cells fill with the appropriate series. In this case, the series is "Add 2.5 to the number above"—relative addressing.

Now you have your tipping percentages in a row and various meal prices in a column. Time to fill in the rest of the sheet.

14. Select cell C4.

15. Type `=B4+(C3*B4)`.

The formula for the tip is equal to the price of the meal (B4) plus the tip. The tip is calculated as the percentage (C3) times the meal (B4). You should see $5.25 listed in cell C4, which is proper—for a 5 percent tip.

16. Use the mouse to drag and fill down from cell C4 to cell C20.

Theoretically, this should give you the 5 percent tip total for all those different meal costs. Alas, the result is, well—wrong!

The #### things means that the value is too large (wide) to display in the cell. But if you gander at cell C6, you'll see that it's the waiter's dream of a tip, nearly 50 times the meal cost! How did that happen?

Blame relative addressing! Click cell C5 and read the Formula bar. The formula reads =B5+(C4*B5). The B5 part is correct; that's the cost of the meal. But the C4 part is incorrect; that isn't the tipping percentage but rather the tip total for the previous line. Oops!

The solution is to use absolute addressing so that the tip value always refers to cell C3.

17. Click cell C4.

18. Press the F2 key to edit the formula.

19. Place a dollar sign ($) before the 3 so that the formula reads =B4+(C$3*B4).

The dollar sign tells Excel to focus on a specific cell—absolute addressing. In this case, it's not a specific cell but rather a specific row. The $3 means, "Always look in cell 3 for the value, no matter which row this is."

I could have written it as $C$3, which means, "Always look in cell C3, column C, row 3." But the $3 thing will come in handy as the formulas are copied off to the left into other columns.

20. Refill from cell C4 down through cell C20.

And the tip values should fill in rather nicely.

21. With cells C4 through C20 selected, grab the Fill gizmo and drag to the right to fill cells F4 through F20.

That should complete the table, but alas, things still don't add up right. The problem again is relative addressing.

22. Click cell D10.

As an avid restaurant goer, I know that the 10 percent tip on $20 is $2, for a total of $22. But the value in cell D10 shows $23.10. Look at the Formula bar and you'll see the cause:

=C10+(D$3*C10)

Relative addressing works with D$3 because it zeros in on the third row in the current column, accurately giving you the 10 percent value. But C10 is not the cost of the meal; the cost of the meal is in B10. The value $23.10 is the accurately calculated 10 percent tip on a $21 meal, not a $20 meal.

Time to fix relative addressing one more time!

23. Click cell C4.
24. Press the F2 key to edit the function.

    You know that C$3 means to address row 3 in the current column. Likewise, $B4 means to always look in column B in the current row.

25. Add two dollar signs into the function so that it now reads `=$B4+(C$3+$B4)`.

    This reads (and follow closely), "Take the value from column B in this row and add it to the value in row 3 plus the value from column B again." That's absolute addressing: specific rows and columns.

    You'll notice that pressing Enter doesn't change the value displayed in cell C4, also that adding the dollar signs doesn't move the color highlights from the proper cells.

    Now the tricky part:

26. Drag and fill from cell C4 down and right to cell F20.

    Drag down to cell C20 first, and then drag over to cell F20 to fill in the entire table. The values will now be correct for each entry in the table, thanks to absolute addressing.

If you're still having trouble with the concept, then click any cell in the table. For example, click cell E14, which shows a value of $34.50. Look at the Formula bar. You'll see = $B14+(E$3*$B14). If you mentally remove the dollar signs, you'll see the same raw formula as introduced at the start of this section. What the dollar sign does is keep the cells specific for drag-and-fill operations. That way, in this case, values are always referred to from column $B and row $3 no matter which cell is accessed in the grid.

Finally, if you need to access a specific cell, then you use two dollar signs, as in $C$3, which always refers to cell C3 from anywhere else in the worksheet. I could have used such an absolute reference in the tipping chart, but then I would have had to create new formulas for each column. So instead, I used a dollar sign.

Absolute Addressing Shortcuts with F4

You can use the F4 key in the Formula bar to "toggle" various absolute addressing options and shift the dollar sign ($) around inside a cell reference:

F4

With a cell address, such as B4, selected inside the Formula bar, pressing the F4 key toggles the address to an absolute address ($B$4). Pressing F4 again toggles it to an absolute row address (B$4); pressing it again toggles it to an absolute column address ($B4); and finally, pressing F4 a fourth time toggles it back to a relative address (B4).

I Don't Want My Data to Just Sit There! Any Way to Make Cells Do Things to Each Other?

Excel's reason for being is to have the cells and their contents interact with each other. It's not only math but also built-in functions that do so many calculations that your typical desktop calculator would hide in a drawer out of pure jealousy.

Why Bother with Parentheses?

Parentheses serve two purposes in a formula. The first is to contain the values required by a function; the second is to tell Excel in which order to make calculations. Calculations within the parenthesis take place first. That way you can ensure that the answer is calculated properly.

For calculations, it never helps to be too precise. For example:

1. In your worksheet, find a cell and type in `=24-4*3`.
2. In the next cell below type `=24-(4*3)`.
3. In the next cell below type `=(24-4)*3`.

The results in the first two cells are the same, 12. In the last cell, the result is 60, despite the same numbers being used. That's because the parentheses changed the order of the computation.

Excel normally evaluates equations from left to right, reading along as it goes. However, multiplication and division are higher priorities for Excel than addition and subtraction. So in the first example, =24-4*3, the 4*3 calculation is done first.

Now I probably explained that well and accurately, but my point here is that even I forget which things come first. I normally force the operation by using parentheses as shown in examples 2 and 3. So even though I know that examples 1 and 2 are identical, I'll still use the parenthesis to force the issue.

Bottom line: To ensure that the equations evaluate as you want, make liberal use of parentheses. What you put in the parentheses happens first.

I Need Help with a Long, Complex, Boring Formula!

My best advice is to keep your formulas as small as possible. The more you can separate things, and keep from having a formula that wraps itself twice in the Formula bar, the more you can split everything off into smaller bits.

Example 1: This Could Work Better in a Table Elsewhere!

I once had a formula in a travel expense report that had me input all my receipts into one cell, on one line. The formula looked like this:

=6.22+3.90+1.25+6.5+12.5+1.98+12.50+3.75+10.25+2.88+9.66

Don't ever do this yourself! It is *not* a formula. No, that looks like a list to me, and lists belong in separate cells, arranged either horizontally or, more often, vertically.

The solution here was to create elsewhere on the worksheet the same numbers but in a column with each value in its own cell, as shown in Figure 10.14. That way, the thing can be looked at "from a distance," and improper values can be replaced by editing a single cell instead of a foot-long formula sentence.

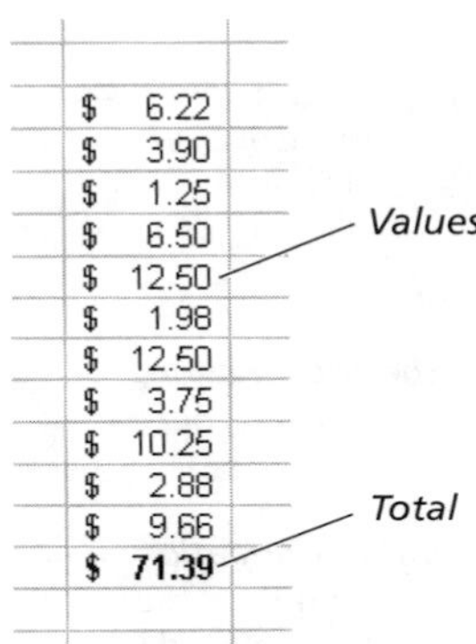

Figure 10.14 A small table elsewhere instead of a long formula

The total from those cells can then be used in whatever other formula you want or displayed in a single cell.

Example 2: The Formula Is Just Long and There's Nothing I Can Do about It!

Wrong! Formulas can *always* be broken up. Consider the following:

=A15+A22-(C3+C4+C7)

Granted, this formula isn't that long. Even so, it can be made shorter.

First, consider creating a cell where you add the contents of A15 and A22.

Second, create a cell where C3, C4, and C7 are added.

Finally, build the formula based on those two cells instead of the five original cells: =E14-E15.

If you name the cells properly (as covered earlier in this chapter), you'll end up with not only a smaller, more manageable function but a readable one as well:

=Income-Expenses

Where Are the Functions, Because I Can't Remember Them?

The easiest way to get at the numerous functions is to click the Function (Fx) button, located on the Formula bar in Excel 11/XP or found on the Standard toolbar in Excel 2000. This displays the Insert Function dialog box in Excel 11/XP (shown in Figure 10.15) or the Paste Function dialog box in Excel 2000. Regardless of the visual differences, the dialog boxes do essentially the same thing: Stick a function into the current cell.

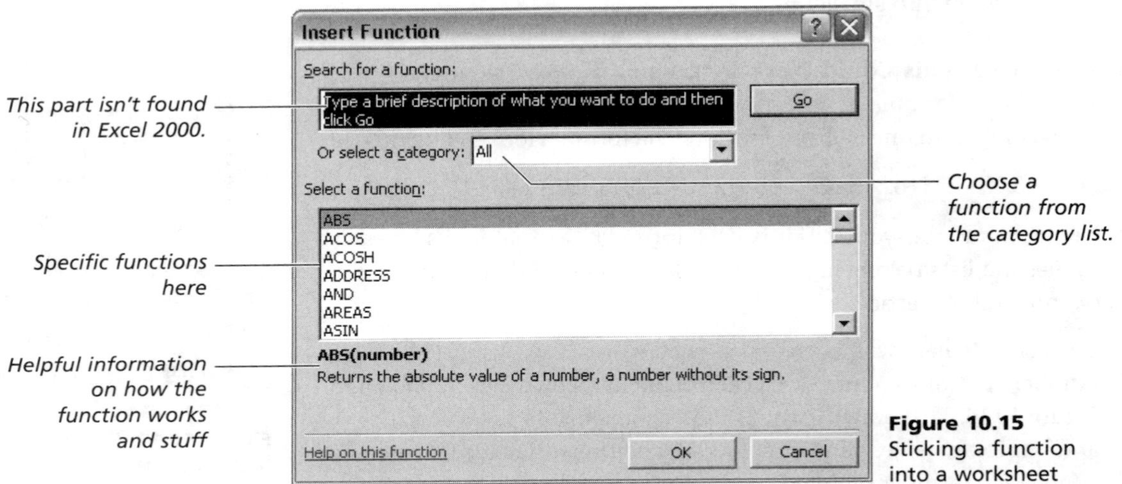

Figure 10.15
Sticking a function into a worksheet

Recently used functions are kept in the Formula bar's Name box. After you press = in a cell, the Name box lists the most recently used functions. To see the list, click the down arrow to the right of the Name box.

I Can Remember the Formulas but Not the Dajoobies That Go in the Parentheses.

Ooo! Me too! I can never remember in the ROUND statement whether the value or the number of digits comes first. Very annoying. Here's a solution:

1. Select the cell into which you plan on burying the formula.
2. Click the Formula bar.

   This trick works only if you type the function's name into the Formula bar, not into the cell directly.
3. Type = and the function's name.

   Such as `=ROUND`.
4. Press Ctrl+Shift+A.

Imagine in your head that Ctrl+Shift+A is the keyboard shortcut for "Automatically give me the guts!" You'll see the formula's secret bits displayed, as shown in Figure 10.16.

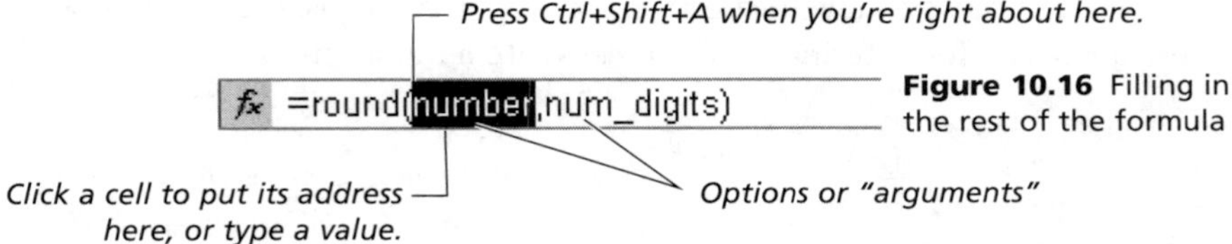
Press Ctrl+Shift+A when you're right about here.
=round(number,num_digits)
Click a cell to put its address here, or type a value.
Options or "arguments"

Figure 10.16 Filling in the rest of the formula

5. Enter the function's dajoobies.

You can manually type them in or click a cell or range of cells to place their references into the function. Do whatever is necessary to complete the function.

Remember that this trick works only when you're entering the function directly into the Formula bar.

Word 11/XP users don't really need to bother with this trick; as you enter the function into a cell, a "hint" bubble appears below the function to remind you of the dajoobies.

What Does the F9 Key Do in a Formula?

If you press the F9 key while the cursor is blinking in the Formula bar, then Excel translates the function displayed there to show the result. Now that's kind of a silly thing to do, since the cell in the worksheet already displays the result. But you can use the F9 key to evaluate portions of a formula or function to help you troubleshoot.

For example, suppose you have the following formula in the Formula bar:

=D4+D5+E4+E5+E6

To find out what the value of cells D5 and E4 calculates out to, follow these steps:

1. Select the portion of the Formula bar you want to evaluate.

So you would select D5+E4.

2. Press F9.

The text D5+E4 in the Formula bar will change to represent the total of those two cells—say, 42.

3. Press Esc to return to your formula.

If you don't press Esc, then the 42 becomes part of the equation and not D5+E4.

This is a great trick to check on the values in various cells, especially when the worksheet is large and you cannot see the entire thing at once.

How Can I Get the Function Calculation Thing Back?

One of the joys of choosing functions from the Insert Function or Paste Function dialog box is that Excel presents you with one of those handy function input dialog boxy things, such as the one shown in Figure 10.17. These are useful for entering values or cells into a function—a wonderful tool.

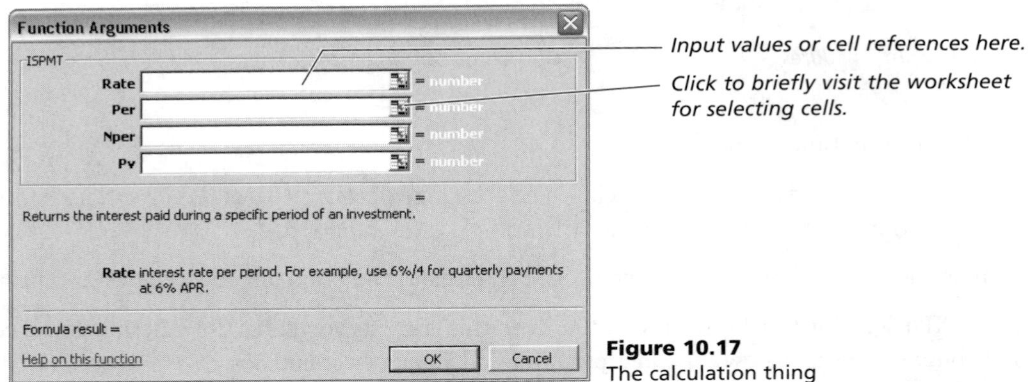

Figure 10.17
The calculation thing

So if you're lingering in the middle of a function and need the helper dialog box, click the Function button. You must have a function name in the cell for this to work. The cell must start with =, then a function name, and then whatever. Once that minimum is met, you can click the Function button and you'll see the dialog box displayed, similar to Figure 10.17 but specific to your function.

The Common "I Am Stupid" List of Excel Error Messages

Anyone using Excel for any length of time should be familiar with the common Excel error messages. I've written them down below mostly for their amusement value.

How Can I Fix the ###### Error?

This is the easiest Excel error to fix mostly because it's not really an error. The ### (nah-nah) things appear to indicate that the value for the cell is just too dern wide to display.

The immediate solution is to make the cell wider, which is the same thing as making the entire column wider: Position the mouse between the current column heading and the next, such as between the C and D column headings, as shown back in Figure 10.8, then double-click. That widens the column (C in the figure) to be as wide as the widest cell needs to be.

Another solution is to display the number in a different format—if that works. By removing the $ or the trailing .00, you can often squeeze a number into a cell without resizing:

1. Click to select the cell.
2. Press Ctrl+1 to bring up the Format Cells dialog box.
3. In the Number tab, choose General.
4. Click OK.

Sometimes this may render the number in *scientific notation*, that is, some monster like 1.23E+10. That's the way scientists fill in their tax forms, and while it amusingly drives the IRS bonkers, it's just not the way humans are used to seeing numbers portrayed.

What Does #REF! Mean?

The referee has obviously made a bad call: One team is full of anger and resentment, while the other is walking around innocently trying not to give away that they agree it was a bad call.

In Excel, #REF! in a cell means that you've referred to a cell that doesn't exist or has been deleted. This usually crops up after a copy or cut-and-paste operation, so be on the lookout. If you get a #REF!, then immediately undo the operation with Ctrl+Z and rethink your strategy.

Where Do You Get Off Calling Me That #NAME?

This is a simple error to fix: For some reason you typed in a word that is not the name of a cell, the cell's address, or the name of a function. No, it's a #NAME? name.

Most often you see #NAME? when you mistype a function's name. For example, instead of typing in SQRT to do the square root, you type in SQR (which is the name of the square root command in the BASIC language). So

=SQR(4)

gets you a #NAME? error, whereas:

=SQRT(4)

gets you 2.

Or it could be that you're referring to a named cell and mistyped the name. Use the Insert ➤ Name ➤ Paste command in that case, so that you are inserting a properly named cell or series of cells.

How Can I Fix a #VALUE! Error?

Typically the #VALUE! thing happens because you've attempted to do math on a cell that contains text.

How stupid!

But I Really Do Need to Divide by Zero!

Computers just cannot abide to divide anything by zero. I know that in algebra class, you (just like me) probably thought that dividing by zero was no big deal. After all, if you take 3 and divide it by nothing, you get 3, right? In my brain, dividing by zero is the same thing as not dividing at all. But in Excel's brain, it's the ugly #DIV/0! error.

There are two ways to handle #DIV/0! The first is to ensure that the denominator (the value on the bottom) is never zero. The second is to create an exception for the case when the value ends up being zero anyway.

For example, suppose you're tabulating results from a survey. You get the answers to questions and then determine the percentages. Say a number of people answer the question, "Do you like chocolate ice cream?" You present the results in a worksheet, as shown in Figure 10.18.

	A	B	C	D	E	F
1						
2		Do you like chocolate ice cream?			67	
3						
4			Yes	43	64%	
5			No	24	36%	
6						
7						
8						

Respondents to the survey
Results for each item
Results/Respondents

Figure 10.18 The sample survey where a dreadful and potential #DIV/0! error lurks in waiting

Here's how to create such a worksheet, complete with a safety check for dividing by zero:

1. Into cell D2 type `Do you like chocolate ice cream?`
2. Click the Right Align button on the Formatting toolbar to right-align the cell's text contents.
3. Name cell E2 "Respondents."

   The quickest way to do this is to select cell E2 and then type `Respondents` into the Name box on the Formula bar.

4. Into cell C4 type `Yes`.

5. Into cell D4 type `No`.

The number of respondents to the survey will go in cell E2. The number answering Yes goes into cell D4; the No response goes into cell D5. The formula to calculate the percentages goes into cells E4 and E5.

A percentage is calculated using the old "is over of" formula. In this case, what percentage *is* cell D4 *of* cell E2? Or use D4/E2 to calculate the percentage:

6. Into cell E4, type `=D4/E2` and press Enter.

   Oh, crap. There's the #DIV/0! thing. Now the way to avoid it, obviously, is to input some values. But it looks ugly without values, like something is wrong. To avoid some snoopy, nonspreadsheet person from thinking you've screwed up, you can fix the formula so that #DIV/0! doesn't show up.

7. Into cell E4 type `=IF(`.

   Don't forget that first paren!

8. Click the Function button.

   Now you can use the dajoobie to fill in the complex and often-confusing IF function's arguments.

   The Logical test is, "What if the value of cell E2 is zero?" Yes, that's a Logical test!

9. At the end of the Logical_test line, click the Go to Worksheet button.

   The dajoobie reduces in size to a Function Arguments dialog box.

10. Click cell E2.

    The word *Respondents* appears in the Function Arguments dialog box. Good. That's the name of the cell.

11. Type `=0`.

    So the Logical_test is "Respondents equals zero" or Respondents=0.

12. Click the Return to Dajoobie button.

13. In the Value_if_true box type `No Respondents Yet!`

    This is okay: You can put text in an IF function. Remember, the result is the *contents of the cell*, not some math function.

If you're manually entering the IF statement, then the text must be in double quotes.

14. In the Value_if_false box, type `D4/Respondents`.

You can use the buttons to select those cells, or you can type them in manually if you're careful.

So the whole logical IF statement reads, "If the value of the cell Respondents is equal to zero, then display the text 'No Respondents Yet!' in this cell. Otherwise, display the value of cell D4 divided by the value of cell Respondents."

15. Click OK.

And you'll see "No Respondents Yet!" displayed because there is no data in the worksheet at cell E2.

16. Drag to fill cell E5 with cell E4.

Drag the cell selector by its lower-right corner, down just one notch. That copies the same IF formula into cell E5. (Also, because the cell reference is relative to D4, the new formula in cell E5 properly references cell D5. However because cell E2 is named, it remains constant in both functions.)

17. Now fill in the data: Put `67` into cell E2.

And you see that with a value there, both cells E4 and E5 fill in with values (not errors).

18. Put `43` into cell D4.

19. Put `24` into cell D5.

And now your worksheet should look like Figure 10.18.

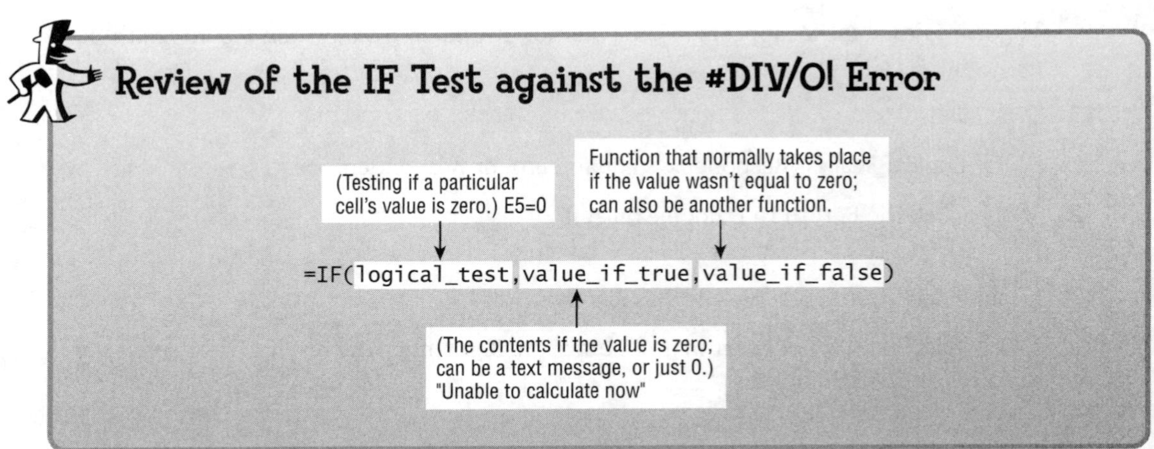

Review of the IF Test against the #DIV/O! Error
(Testing if a particular cell's value is zero.) E5=0
Function that normally takes place if the value wasn't equal to zero; can also be another function.
=IF(logical_test,value_if_true,value_if_false)
(The contents if the value is zero; can be a text message, or just 0.) "Unable to calculate now"

Plopping an Excel Thing into a Word Thing

Ah, the big trick you've been waiting for! Because Excel is so good at putting information into tables, you've probably been dying to do just that: Slap an Excel worksheet—or at least the good part of one—right there into a Word document. It's not that hard, but as you might suspect, there are several ways to do it.

At What Point Do I Give Up and Use Excel instead of Word's Table Feature?

One-word answer: math. Any time the table in Word requires math, switch over to Excel and do the table in there. For tables of text or smaller tables, using Word's table feature is fine. But also keep in mind that for tables of text, Excel has more powerful sorting features than Word does.

Another key thing people forget is simply that this trick is possible. I don't know how many meetings I've sat through where they handed out two sets of sheets, one the written report in Word and the other a random stapling of Excel worksheets. I ended up flipping back and forth between the two sets of sheets, agonizing that if only the poor slob would have bought this book, he would have saved everyone in the meeting a lot of time and paper-shuffling noise.

If I Need to Put a Worksheet into Word, Do I Start in Word or Excel?

Either way works fine. If you're clever, you'll start in Word and stay there. Otherwise, you can move data back and forth between the programs at any time. The following sections explain the details.

Building an Excel Worksheet from within Word

The secret to building an Excel worksheet in Word was covered in Chapter 7, "The Tough Stuff: From Labels to Tables." The secret is to click the Insert Worksheet button, which creates a worksheet of a given size inside the Word document. An example of that is shown in Figure 7.17.

Note that although you began in Word, since you inserted the Excel worksheet, the toolbars and keyboard commands all reflect Excel and not Word. Clicking inside or outside the Excel worksheet area is what switches you back and forth between the two programs.

Nerdily speaking, the Excel worksheet inside a Word document is *embedded.*

You can also insert an Excel worksheet by using the Insert ➤ Object command and then choosing "Microsoft Excel Worksheet" from the Object dialog box.

Been there. Done that.

Copying Part of a Worksheet from Excel into Word

The other way to get an Excel thing into a Word thing is to start Excel by itself as opposed to starting Excel in Word. (In fact, it's not very common to use the embedded type of worksheet covered in the previous section.) Supposing that you have a table in Excel that you want to shove into a Word document, here's how it's done:

1. Select the cells you want to copy.

   If the table has row and column headings, be sure to select them as well.

2. Press Ctrl+C to copy.

   Or you can use any of the other, numerous Copy commands.

3. Switch to Word.

   Or start Word if it's not started already.

4. Paste.

   And there's the table.

This variation, where the simple table is copied and pasted, basically creates a table in Word and copies the information from Excel into that Word table.

You'll notice that only data is copied; formulas and functions do not survive the simple copy/paste operation. So where your table may have originally contained complex formulas or relationships between the various cells, only the visible contents of the cells are copied into Word. If you want to retain the relationships, you have to do more than a simple copy and paste.

Copying a Live Worksheet from Excel into Word

Pasting a live table from Excel into Word is actually Word's responsibility. Instead of the standard Paste command, you have to use SuperPaste. Here's how:

1. Copy the table in Excel.
2. Switch to Word.

Press Alt+Tab to switch between two running programs in Windows.

3. Choose File ➤ Paste Special.

   The Paste Special dialog box appears, as shown in Figure 10.19.

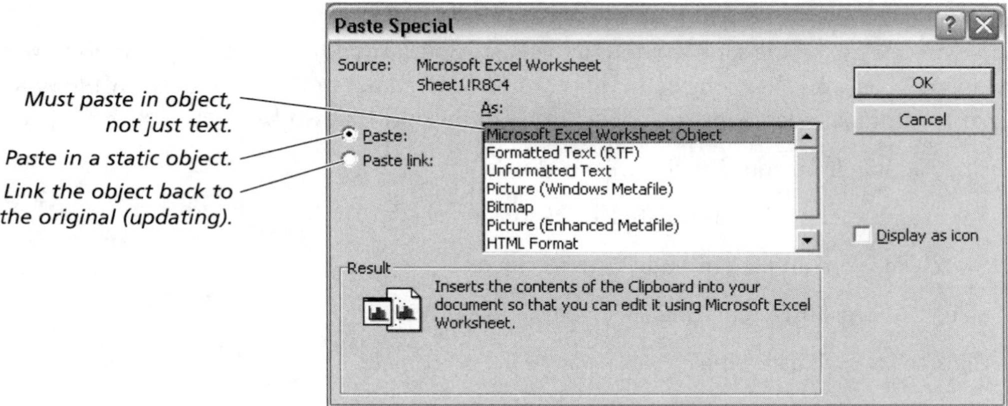

Figure 10.19 More than just pasting, it's *special* pasting.

4. Choose "Microsoft Excel Worksheet Object" from the list.

If this doesn't work at first, then return to Excel and reselect the table, copy it, and then return to Word.

And the table appears, but it is in fact an embedded Excel object, just as you would have gotten had you clicked the Insert Excel Worksheet button: Click inside the object to visit Excel; click outside to revisit Word.

The difference between this and regular pasting is, first, that you end up with a real Excel object and not a simple Word table. Second, the cells retain all their Excel formulas and functions and formatting. If you double-click inside the embedded worksheet, you can edit and modify the table just as if you were in Excel.

What's "Paste Link"?

You may notice the "Paste Link" option in the Paste Special dialog box. That's yet another way to paste in an Excel worksheet object. In this case, the embedded worksheet is actually *the same thing* as the original document you copied from. Here's how that works:

1. Copy a table from your Excel worksheet.

   For example, copy the Chocolate Ice Cream survey table.

2. Switch to Word and choose Edit ➤ Paste Special.
3. Select "Microsoft Excel Worksheet Object" from the list.
4. Click to select "Paste Link."
5. Click OK.

   So far, things look as you would expect; you've paste in an Excel worksheet object that is really like a tiny copy of the original worksheet. Because you selected "Paste Link," however, it is not a copy: It is the original.

6. Return to Excel.
7. Change the Yes responses in cell D4 to `1`.
8. Change the No responses in cell D5 to `66`.
9. Return to Word.

   And the results have changed there as well. This wouldn't happen otherwise, but you embedded a *linked* worksheet. So the information from it will always be reflected in both the Word and original Excel documents.

Of course this is a fancy trick, but I know of few people who actually use it. One potential drawback is that whenever you open the Word document with the link in it, it will ask you if you want to check the workbook document for updates. That's only a minor inconvenience, though.

You can manually update the linked item by right-clicking the table and choosing "Update Link" from the pop-up menu.

Can I Just Copy a Single Value from a Worksheet into a Word Document?

Sure. It works the same as copying a whole table of cells, as discussed in the previous sections. You're just copying a single-cell table in this case.

How Can I Copy a Chart from a Spreadsheet into a Word Document?

Charts copy over from Excel into Word just as portions of a worksheet do, as described in the previous sections. The only difference for pasting in chart objects is that you'll choose "Microsoft Excel Chart Object" from the Paste Special dialog box instead of choosing the worksheet object.

11 It's Super Dooper Grid Time!

Look! Up in the sky! It's a cell! It's a row! It's a column! It's a grid!

No, it's *super grid*. And it's the ability of Excel to do wondrous and strange things with the grid, beyond the normal cell-block approach to listing numbers and labeling them as "expenses this" and "income that." Yawn!

Beyond basic worksheet manipulation, this chapter explains a bit more about how to use Excel as a database. It's not as primitive as you might think. Excel can do amazing things with lists and tables (and without any math). Rounding that out is a visit to Bizarreland and the topic of the PivotTable, which most beginner books avoid the way Yuppies dodge trick-or-treaters. It's not that terrible, but not really that useful either.

All of it is covered here under the general guise of Super Dooper Grid tricks—more than what you would expect from your parents' spreadsheet.

Depths Explored and Murkiness Clarified:

- Managing worksheets in a workbook
- Moving data and worksheets between workbooks
- Exploring some automatic and automated things Excel can do
- Working with lists and tables
- Moving information between Excel, Word, and Outlook
- Sorting out the various database finding and sorting functions for tables
- Exploring the confusing PivotTable

Why Bother with the Extra Worksheets?

Bringing up the notion of "extra worksheets" summons the awful word combination "extra work." But it doesn't have to be that way. Multiple sheets are what makes a workbook document a workbook and not a single-worksheet document. Consider the extra sheets as bonuses, handy things to have, optional—or just ignore them.

Do you need them? Of course not! If all your stuff fits on one worksheet, great. If it all fits on the visible screen, even better. Worksheets are huge, so it seems tough to justify using more than one. However, I often find myself putting stuff into the extra worksheets.

For example, I may put all the main information or a summary on Sheet1, but then I use the other sheets to show raw data and how it was manipulated. That way, Sheet1 is kept clean and, if you plan things right, will all print on one sheet of paper.

Another example is keeping separate but related reports on each sheet. For instance, inflows on Sheet2, checks written on Sheet3, details on Sheet4.

Worksheets can also help add a third dimension to your tables. For example, Sheet1 could be data from 2001, Sheet2 from 2002, Sheet3 from 2003, and so on. Each worksheet is the same but contains data from different years.

Oh, the possibilities are endless! Just be thankful that there are extra worksheets. The following sections tell you how to mess with them.

Do I Have to Put Up with Sheet1 As a Name?

Absolutely not! Sheet1 is a dull, insipid name implying all that is bad with socialism. You can name your sheets anything! To wit:

1. Right-click a sheet's tab.

   Refer to Figure 11.1, not because it's necessary to do so, but just because I like the figure and need to put it on this page somewhere.

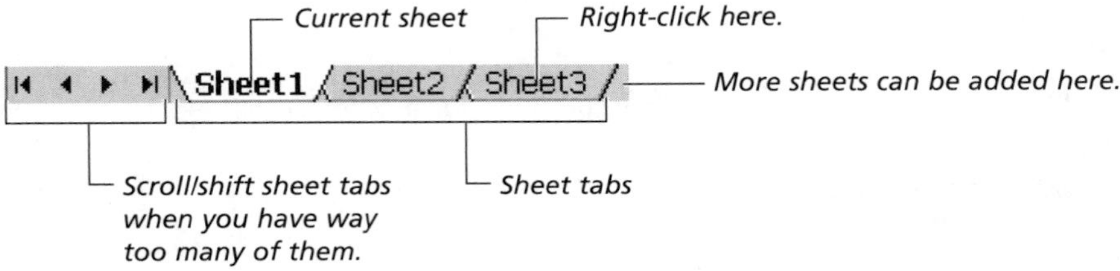

Figure 11.1 All the sheet you need to know

2. Choose Rename from the pop-up menu.

3. Type in a new name.

   Be short. Brief. Descriptive. Spaces are okay, but it's best not to use them as that can complicate formulas that cross between the sheets. (That sounds funky, but keep reading and you'll find out what I mean.)

4. Press Enter.

And you can always rename the sheets back.

I like to keep financial data and several reports all in one workbook with each worksheet labeled as a year. For the first year, I renamed Sheet1 to 1999. Then Sheet2 was renamed to 2000. Now I'm inserting new sheets and naming them for each year as it comes—yet another way to use the basic worksheet motif in Excel to help organize data.

The only problem you may run into when renaming sheets is external references to your sheets. For example, if another workbook or even a Word document references your worksheet, then changing the name may break the link. Therefore, if you're going to rename the sheets, do it first, before you enter any information.

KEYBOARD MASTER

Quick Sheet Tricks

I'm not certain how nifty-keen-o these tricks are, though I do use them. After right-clicking a sheet tab, you get the pop-up menu shown nearby. At that point, pressing the first letter of any command immediately selects that command. To wit:

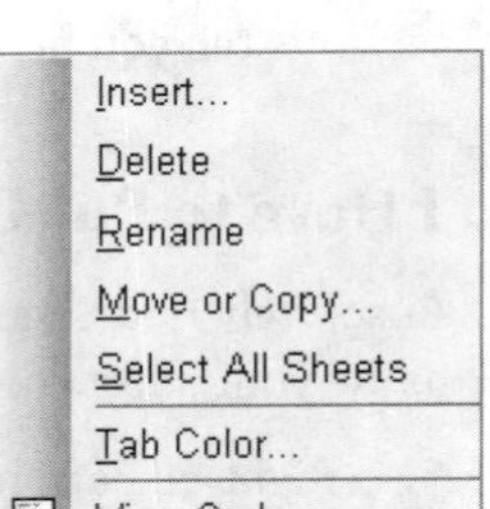

I

Insert a new sheet, chart, macro, or whatever.

D

Delete the current sheet.

R

Rename the current sheet.

M

Move or copy sheets to another workbook.

S

Select all the sheets (for moving, copying, deleting).

T

Change the sheet(s) tab color (Excel 2003/XP only).

V

View the code for a Macro tab.

Must a Sheet Have a Name?

Yes, but the name could be a single space or a set of underlines. That way, for example, if you wanted the sheet tabs to be colors instead of looking like text, you can do this:

1. Right-click the tab you want to unname.
2. Choose Rename from the pop-up menu.
3. Type a space for the new name.

   Or a single underline or a period—some unobtrusive character.
4. Press Enter to lock in the new name.
5. In Excel 2003/XP, right-click the tab and choose "Tab Color" from the pop-up menu.

   Yes, Excel 2000 lacks this feature. Boo-hoo.
6. Pick a color and click OK.

   The tab changes to that color—but only the bottom part. To see the tab filled with a color, you have to switch to the other sheet.

So, bottom line: Sheets must have names, but because you can rename a sheet with "space" as the name, it looks like they're not named. Also be aware that each tab needs a unique name; you cannot rename all the tabs to "space."

I Want My Sheet Color to Match the Tab's Color.

Okay. Say you have a light pink tab (created in the previous section) and want the entire sheet to be light pink. You can do that by selecting all the cells in the data region and filling them with the same color:

1. Press Ctrl+Home.
2. Press Shift+Ctrl+End.

   This selects all the cells in your worksheet's data region. If you want to select more than that, continue dragging the selector down and to the right.
3.  Click the Fill Color icon on the Formatting toolbar.
4. Choose a color to fill all those cells.

   Preferably choose the same background color as the sheet's tab.

Another way to do this would be to create a graphics file on disk the same color as the tab color. Then use the Format ➢ Sheet ➢ Background command to fill the worksheet's background with that color. Unlike using the Fill Color icon, that retains the worksheet's grid.

I Need Only One Worksheet, so Can I Kill Off the Excess?

Certainly:

1. Right-click the tab of the worksheet that offends you.
2. Choose Delete from the pop-up menu.

   Excel stupidly asks if you really want to delete the sheet, which somehow may contain data even though you know darn well that the thing is empty.
3. Click the Delete button.

   The sheet is gone!

You can use the Ctrl key to click and select multiple sheets for group deletion: Press and hold the keyboard's Ctrl key as you click, click, click several sheets. Then right-click any selected sheet and continue with Step 2 above.

The Edit ➢ Delete Sheet command also does the job of zapping a worksheet to kingdom come.

I Don't Want Anyone Else to See the Sheet So That My Dumb Employees Won't Mess with the Data There.

You can hide any sheet in the workbook. In fact, I recommend first renaming the sheet with another reference, which further helps throw naïve Excel users off the trail. Then to hide the worksheet:

1. Click to select the worksheet you want to conceal.

   It cannot be the only sheet in the workbook; the workbook must have at least two sheets and you must keep one sheet unhidden.
2. Choose Format ➢ Sheet Hide.

   And it's gone!

Actually, the sheet is still there and data on the sheet can still be referenced. But it's not visible, and unsuspecting Excel users will never know.

To get all the hidden sheets back, choose Format ➢ Sheet ➢ Unhide. An Unhide dialog box appears, and you can choose which sheet to unhide. Click the OK button, and the sheet falls back into the room like a drunken party guest stumbling out of a coat closet.

Must. Have. More. Sheets.

To add another sheet, choose Insert ➢ Worksheet or press Shift+F11. Thwoop! There it is! You can also quickly add a chart by choosing Insert ➢ Chart or pressing the F11 key.

If you need to use a template or macro, then you have to summon the Insert dialog box. Follow these steps:

1. Right-click any sheet tab.
2. Choose Insert from the pop-up menu.

   The Insert dialog box appears, with icons for inserting generic worksheets and charts, but also listing any templates you may have created.
3. Select what you want to add.
4. Click the OK button.

You'll notice that the sheets (or tabs) seem to be inserted in a rather haphazard manner. That's no problem. You can use the mouse to drag any tab to any position. Or you can Ctrl+click to select a group of tabs and move them as a cluster.

KEYBOARD MASTER

Adding a New Worksheet or Chart

Bringing in the sheets, bringing in the sheets. *For some reason, if you need a new sheet or tab in Excel, the F11 key is the one to drool over:*

F11

Stick a new chart into the workbook.

Shift+F11

Add a new worksheet into the workbook.

Alt+F11

Prepare to build a dialog in the ominous and scary Microsoft Visual Basic Editor.

Ctrl+F11

Add a new macro worksheet.

I Know You Can Click the Tab to Move to That Sheet, but What about a Nifty Keyboard Shortcut?

Use Ctrl+PgUp and Ctrl+PgDn to shuffle between the sheets via the keyboard.

Why Would I Want to Share This Sheet with Another Workbook?

Sometimes sheets are just so brilliant that they must be shared. For example, I copy a sheet from my tracking workbook into a year-end financial workbook. It's much easier than copying and pasting the entire worksheet—or even that copy-paste-link embedding nonsense. Here's how:

1. Open the other workbook, the one into which you want to copy a sheet (or chart).
2. Right-click the tab of your most beloved worksheet, the one you want to share with another workbook.

3. Choose Move or Copy from the pop-up menu.

   The Move or Copy dialog box appears.

4. Select the destination workbook from the "To Book" drop-down list.
5. Choose "(Move to End)" from the Before sheet list.
6. Click to put a check mark by "Create a Copy."
7. Click OK.

   And the sheet is copied over to the other workbook.

The worksheet retains the same tab name, so if there is a duplicate you'll see something dumb like "Sheet1(2)" displayed. Refer elsewhere in this chapter for information on renaming the sheet to something less insipid.

Any Way to Get Data from Another Worksheet into This One?

You can reference data in other sheets in a workbook just as you can reference cells in the same worksheet. It looks something like this:

```
='Sheet2'!$A$1
```

This refers to cell A1 over on Sheet2. If the worksheet was named Prince Harry, then you'd see

```
='Prince Harry'!$A$1
```

The nifty thing here is that all that's required of you is to recognize the format: sheet name in single quotes, exclamation point, cell reference. You never really have to type that exact thing in, just copy and paste the cells. To keep the reference linked to the other cell, use Edit ➤ Paste Special and be sure to choose the Link option. Or in Excel 2003/XP, click the Paste Options button and choose "Link Cells" from the pop-up menu.

There's one more doohickey that can appear here: If you're linking to a cell in another worksheet, then the format is

```
=[book1.xls]Sheet1!$A$1
```

The filename appears first, in square brackets. That links the cell back to the original worksheet in the original workbook document.

Okay. Enough of that nonsense for now.

Letting Excel Do the Work for You

Obviously, Excel is going to do the work for you; otherwise, you would have saved a few hundred dollars and bought an abacus instead. In addition to doing math, Excel recognizes that many elements in a worksheet are often the same: perhaps not the contents or values of the worksheet as much as common conventions, such as the days of the week or months of the year. These and other things appear in most common worksheets, and Excel has a bushel of tricks to help you enter such common things.

If I Have to Type Monday, Tuesday, Wednesday Again, I'm Going to Pull Out My Hair!

Save your hair and follow these steps:

1. Type a day of the week into a cell.

   It can be any day. And you can type the full day, such as Monday, or type the abbreviation Mon.

2. Reselect that cell.
3. Drag down or to the right to fill in a series of days.

   Figure 11.2 shows the sweet spot.

4. Release the mouse button when you're done.

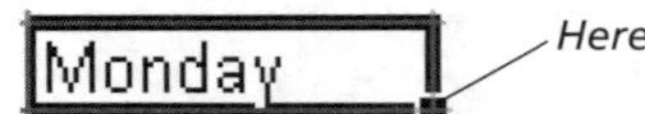

Figure 11.2 The sweet spot for dragging a series

Yes, you can drag in any direction, though down or to the right is most common. And you can drag more than seven cells.

In Excel 2003/XP, after you drag to fill a series, the AutoFill Options icon appears in the worksheet. Pointing the mouse at this icon produces a menu button that produces a menu with some options. One of them is "Fill Weekdays," which allows you to fill only Monday through Friday in your worksheet.

Can the Same Trick Work with Months?

Yes. Start with any month, January through December, or use the month's three-letter abbreviation, Jan through Dec.

What about Quarters?

Yes. Start with Q1 and then drag away. Excel automatically does the Q2, Q3, Q4 thing for you, repeating it if necessary.

How Can I Do a Series of Years?

Alas, there is no way to tell Excel which value is a year and which is just a number. So the best way to create such a row or column of years is simply to fill a series. Here's how:

1. Type the first value into a cell.

   Say, 1990.

2. Use the right mouse button to drag that value to the right or down.

   If you use the left (normal) mouse button, then 1990 fills the series. But if you use the right mouse button, you get a pop-up menu when the button is released.

3. Choose "Fill Series" from the pop-up menu.

   And the values in the selected row or column are all incremented by 1, giving you a series of years.

How about a Series That Skips by Threes?

There are two ways to do this. The first is automatic using a built-in Excel function. The second is a devious way I think you may prefer, especially if you're using the series as a basis for a table.

The Boring Excel Way

Here's how to create a series that skips by different values between the cells:

1. Select the starting cell.
2. Enter a starting value.
3. Reselect the starting cell.
4. Drag to the right or down to create a series.

   Use the sweet spot (Figure 11.2) to drag. The series will contain all the same number, but you're about to change that.

5. Choose Edit ➤ Fill ➤ Series.

   The charming and inviting Series dialog box appears, shown in Figure 11.3.

6. Choose Rows or Columns, depending on how your cells are selected.
7. Choose Linear.
8. Enter 3 into the "Step Value" box.
9. Click OK.

   And the cells are filled with values that bump up by three each time.

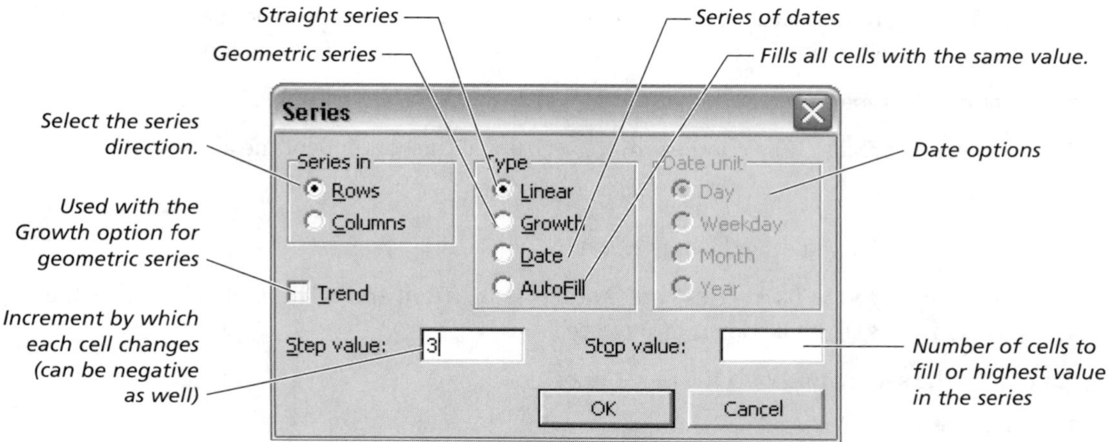

Figure 11.3 The exciting Series dialog box

Dan's Dirty yet Completely Ethical Way to Do the Same Thing

I prefer to have a wee bit more control over my tables when I build a series. And, let's be honest, what the series represents is one of two axes in a table. So suppose you want to build a table for your movie theater that shows ticket prices versus patronage, as shown in Figure 11.4. Here's one way to do that:

Values increment by .5.

	A	B	C	D	E	F	G	H	I
1		Ticket Prices							
2	**Patrons**	**$ 4.00**	**$ 4.50**	**$ 5.00**	**$ 5.50**	**$ 6.00**	**$ 6.50**	**$ 7.00**	
3	**0**	$ -	$ -	$ -	$ -	$ -	$ -	$ -	
4	**30**	$ 120.00	$ 135.00	$ 150.00	$ 165.00	$ 180.00	$ 195.00	$ 210.00	
5	**60**	$ 240.00	$ 270.00	$ 300.00	$ 330.00	$ 360.00	$ 390.00	$ 420.00	
6	**90**	$ 360.00	$ 405.00	$ 450.00	$ 495.00	$ 540.00	$ 585.00	$ 630.00	
7	**120**	$ 480.00	$ 540.00	$ 600.00	$ 660.00	$ 720.00	$ 780.00	$ 840.00	
8	**150**	$ 600.00	$ 675.00	$ 750.00	$ 825.00	$ 900.00	$ 975.00	$ 1,050.00	
9	**180**	$ 720.00	$ 810.00	$ 900.00	$ 990.00	$ 1,080.00	$ 1,170.00	$ 1,260.00	
10	**210**	$ 840.00	$ 945.00	$ 1,050.00	$ 1,155.00	$ 1,260.00	$ 1,365.00	$ 1,470.00	
11	**240**	$ 960.00	$ 1,080.00	$ 1,200.00	$ 1,320.00	$ 1,440.00	$ 1,560.00	$ 1,680.00	
12	**270**	$ 1,080.00	$ 1,215.00	$ 1,350.00	$ 1,485.00	$ 1,620.00	$ 1,755.00	$ 1,890.00	
13	**300**	$ 1,200.00	$ 1,350.00	$ 1,500.00	$ 1,650.00	$ 1,800.00	$ 1,950.00	$ 2,100.00	
14	**330**	$ 1,320.00	$ 1,485.00	$ 1,650.00	$ 1,815.00	$ 1,980.00	$ 2,145.00	$ 2,310.00	
15	**360**	$ 1,440.00	$ 1,620.00	$ 1,800.00	$ 1,980.00	$ 2,160.00	$ 2,340.00	$ 2,520.00	
16									
17	30								
18	0.5								
19									

Values increment by 30.

30

.5

Figure 11.4 A sample table with weird incrementing axes

1. Into cell A2 type `Patrons`.
2. Into cell B1 type `Ticket Prices`.
3. Into cell A3 type `0`.

   That's zero, not O.
4. Into cell B2 type `4`.

Now you're going to build a series of incrementing patron numbers and incrementing dollar signs to complete the two axes of the table. You'll be using Excel's formulas to create the series.

5. Into cell A4 type `=A3+30`.

   The formula reads, "The contents of this cell equal the contents of the above cell plus 30."

6. Press Enter.

7. Reselect cell A4 and drag down to cell A15.

   There is no need to fill a series here; AutoFill is in action and it automatically copies the [cell above]+30 formula down through cell A15.

Time to do the same thing with the ticket prices.

8. Select cell C2.

9. Type `=B2+.5`.

   That reads, "The contents of this cell equal the contents of the cell on the left plus point five." And point five is 50 cents here.

10. As you did with the column of patron numbers, drag-fill right with the ticket prices from cell C2 through cell H2.

    As you drag and fill, the formula [cell left]+.5 is copied to each cell, creating the series.

After creating the two series, some formatting is needed:

11. **B** Select cells A2 through A15 and format them as bold.

12. Select cell B1 and format it as bold.

13. **$** Select cells B2 through H2 and format them as bold and with the Currency style.

    Finally, it's time to fill in the table, the meat of the matter:

14. Into cell B3 type the formula `=$A3*B$2`.

    If you're not familiar with absolute addressing, then this formula says the following, "The contents of this cell are equal to the value of the cell in column A and in this row, multiplied by the contents of cell 2 in this column." The $ keeps the cell reference absolute. (Refer to Chapter 10, "Why the Hell Would Anyone Other Than an Accountant Use Excel?" if you need more information.)

15. Press Enter.

    Notice how smart Excel is to automatically format the cell as a dollar amount. Of course, the value is zero: Zero patrons at any price is zero. Prove it:

16. Select cell B3 and drag it out through cell H3.

Again you're filling a series, but in this case it's an AutoFill; the same formula is copied to each cell. Thanks to absolute referencing, the formula works out just fine.

17. With cells B3 through H3 selected, drag down to fill the entire table, from cell B3 down through cell H15.

Again, the absolute reference keeps all the values properly referenced and calculated.

If you see excessive ####s in your table, select the table (if you need to) and choose Format ➤ Column ➤ AutoFit Selection.

At this point your table should look just like Figure 11.4, but with two minor exceptions: the values in cells A17 and A18. Those are my incrementing updating values. You see, the table you created is in a beautiful number-crunching program called Excel. There's no reason to think the table is done or even static. Now you're going to find out how flexible this system can really be:

18. Select cell A17.

19. Name the cell Pincrement; type `Pincrement` into the Name box.

That's *P*, as in Patrons, *increment.*

20. Put the value `30` into cell A17.

21. Select cell A18.

22. Name the cell `Tincrement`.

That's *T*, as in Ticket prices, *increment.*

23. Put the value `.5` into cell A18.

Now you're ready to modify the table, though the results will still be the same (for now):

24. Edit cell A4 so that the formula reads `=A3+Pincrement`.

Replace the 30 by clicking cell A17, which inserts the name Pincrement into the formula.

25. Select cell A4 and drag-fill down through cell A15.

Nothing visible should change, though the formulas are all now linked to cell A17. More on that in a few steps.

26. Edit cell C2 to read `=B2+Tincrement`.

Again, replace the .5 by clicking cell A18, which inserts the name Pincrement into the formula.

27. Select cell C2 and drag-fill right through cell H2.

Still there is no visible change to the table or axis. Until you:

28. Put the value 1 into cell A18.

Ta-da! The table instantly updates with a new series of ticket prices. Similarly:

29. Put the value 25 into cell A17.

This goes along with some of my Excel philosophy presented in the previous chapter: As long as you can keep the values in functions separate, you'll find it easier to update and examine your worksheets. New results are easier to calculate when the values in a function can be adjusted without having to edit a formula and then refill that formula through a table.

KEYBOARD MASTER

Quickly Select Your Table

Tables, such as the one created in this section, are the meat and potatoes of Excel. To quickly select a table, click to select any cell in the table and then use this key combination:

Ctrl+Shift+8

You Know, the Rows Are Numbered—Why Can't I Just Use the Row Numbers in My Worksheet?

In the Page Setup dialog box, Sheet tab, there is a setting that tells Excel to print the row and column headings, 1 through whatever and A through whatever. But it's ugly, as shown in Figure 11.5.

Ugly

Ugly

	A	B	C	D	E	F	G	H
1		**Ticket Prices**						
2	**Patrons**	**$ 4.00**	**$ 5.00**	**$ 6.00**	**$ 7.00**	**$ 8.00**	**$ 9.00**	**$ 10.00**
3	**0**	$ -	$ -	$ -	$ -	$ -	$ -	$ -
4	**25**	$ 100.00	$ 125.00	$ 150.00	$ 175.00	$ 200.00	$ 225.00	$ 250.00
5	**50**	$ 200.00	$ 250.00	$ 300.00	$ 350.00	$ 400.00	$ 450.00	$ 500.00
6	**75**	$ 300.00	$ 375.00	$ 450.00	$ 525.00	$ 600.00	$ 675.00	$ 750.00
7	**100**	$ 400.00	$ 500.00	$ 600.00	$ 700.00	$ 800.00	$ 900.00	$ 1,000.00
8	**125**	$ 500.00	$ 625.00	$ 750.00	$ 875.00	$ 1,000.00	$ 1,125.00	$ 1,250.00
9	**150**	$ 600.00	$ 750.00	$ 900.00	$ 1,050.00	$ 1,200.00	$ 1,350.00	$ 1,500.00
10	**175**	$ 700.00	$ 875.00	$ 1,050.00	$ 1,225.00	$ 1,400.00	$ 1,575.00	$ 1,750.00
11	**200**	$ 800.00	$ 1,000.00	$ 1,200.00	$ 1,400.00	$ 1,600.00	$ 1,800.00	$ 2,000.00
12	**225**	$ 900.00	$ 1,125.00	$ 1,350.00	$ 1,575.00	$ 1,800.00	$ 2,025.00	$ 2,250.00
13	**250**	$ 1,000.00	$ 1,250.00	$ 1,500.00	$ 1,750.00	$ 2,000.00	$ 2,250.00	$ 2,500.00
14	**275**	$ 1,100.00	$ 1,375.00	$ 1,650.00	$ 1,925.00	$ 2,200.00	$ 2,475.00	$ 2,750.00
15	**300**	$ 1,200.00	$ 1,500.00	$ 1,800.00	$ 2,100.00	$ 2,400.00	$ 2,700.00	$ 3,000.00
16								
17	25							
18	1							

Figure 11.5 How a worksheet prints with row and column headings

A better solution is to just incorporate row numbers into your worksheet's cells. The key here is the ROW function, which returns the number of the current row. At one time I thought this was a silly function, but then I did something like this:

1. Click cell B3.
2. Type `=ROW()`.

   That's the ROW() function, which returns the current row.
3. Press Enter.

   The value 3 appears in the cell.

Now, most people who build worksheets don't typically start the worksheet at cell A1. No, you want room up there for headings and titles and other fancy foof. So if you wanted to show cell B3 as row 1 instead of 3, you would do this:

4. Select cell B3.
5. Press F2 and edit the function to read `=ROW()-2`.

   So the function now reads, "The value of this cell is equal to the current row number, minus 2." If the row is 3, then 3 minus 2 is 1.
6. Drag to fill the cell down through cell B12.

   And you have a series of numbers, 1 through 10 based on the rows.

The only time this can goof up is if you insert any rows above your ROW() function cells:

7. Select cell B2.
8. Choose Insert ➢ Rows.

   Oops! Now the table is numbered 2 through 11. You'll need to re-edit the function to `=ROW()-3` and then drag-fill in the rest of the cells to update them as well.

So I suppose the moral of the story is not to use the ROW() function unless you're dang sure you're not going to be inserting any new rows.

There is also a corresponding COLUMN() function that returns a numeric value representing the column the cell lives in. Column A is 1, Column B is 2, and so on.

What's a Great Tip for Entering a Whole Range of Cells with the Same Value?

It's the miraculous Ctrl+Enter key combination. And it works like this:

1. Select a range of cells.

   It can be a row. It can be a column. It can be a whole swath of cells.

2. Type something into the first cell.

   Text. Value. Function.

3. Press Ctrl+Enter.

   And every selected cell is filled with that text or value or function.

Is There Any Easy Way to Stick the Current Date into a Cell?

Yes, but I'd rather ramble on about dates for a few pages.

There is a problem with the date in Excel. Do you mean the current date or today's date? So do you want the worksheet to always say "May 5, 2005" or to say whatever date it is today? Big choice.

Unlike other programs, the date in Excel is a function. That function returns a number, not a date. The number can be formatted to look like a date, but otherwise all dates in Excel are really numbers. It's grossly complex how it works, so, like for gravity and time theory, just nod your head and hope that you're talented enough to fool others into believing that you understand this crap.

Here goes:

1. Select a cell where you want the date to be displayed.
2. Type `=DATE(2002,4,15)`.

   The format for the DATE formula is year, month, date.

3. Press Enter.

   Excel is smart enough to show the date in a date-like format, 4/15/2002, which happens to be the date my first divorce was final. The worksheet will always show that date because it's fixed. It's a number:

4. With the same cell selected, press Ctrl+1.
5. Click the Number tab.
6. Choose General from the list and click OK.

   37361. That's the real date. It's a number. Scary, huh? Try this:

7. Type 100 into a cell.

   It can be the same cell.

8. Press Ctrl+1 and format the cell as a date.

   It's April 9, 1900, back when a spreadsheet was something Grandma would quilt.

   Did you notice that the DATE() function disappeared, by the way? The only purpose of the DATE() function is to insert that magic number into a document. There is no record of the date kept, just the secret number. On the other hand, the NOW() function always returns the current date, no matter what day it is:

9. Edit the same cell so that its contents are `=NOW()`.

   And there is today's date, but:

10. Select the cell.

    Look in the Formula bar. It's still the NOW() function, which means that cell will always reflect the current date. Or time:

11. Press Ctrl+1.

12. Choose Time from the Category list and click OK.

    And now the cell shows the current time. Or, actually, the time when you updated the cell's format. The time doesn't update automatically. You must change a cell or edit something in the worksheet to see the time updated.

KEYBOARD MASTER

Oh Now He Tells Us Date and Time Shortcuts

There are two keyboard shortcuts you can use to instantly input the current date and time:

Ctrl+;

Inserts the current date as a value.

Ctrl+Shift+:

Inserts the current time as a value.

Why Do I Need to Know about Goal Seek?

Goal Seek is one of those weird descriptions of something you've probably wanted to use in the past but said something like, "I wish I knew how to juggle these numbers to get the result I want." That's Goal Seek.

For example, how much would you have to earn an hour to make $51 million dollars this year? Hmmm.

1. Create a worksheet similar to the one you see in Figure 11.6.

   The only formula is in cell F4, which is =B4*C4*D4*E4. That's shown in Figure 11.6, in the Formula bar.

   Also format cells B4 and F4 for Currency.

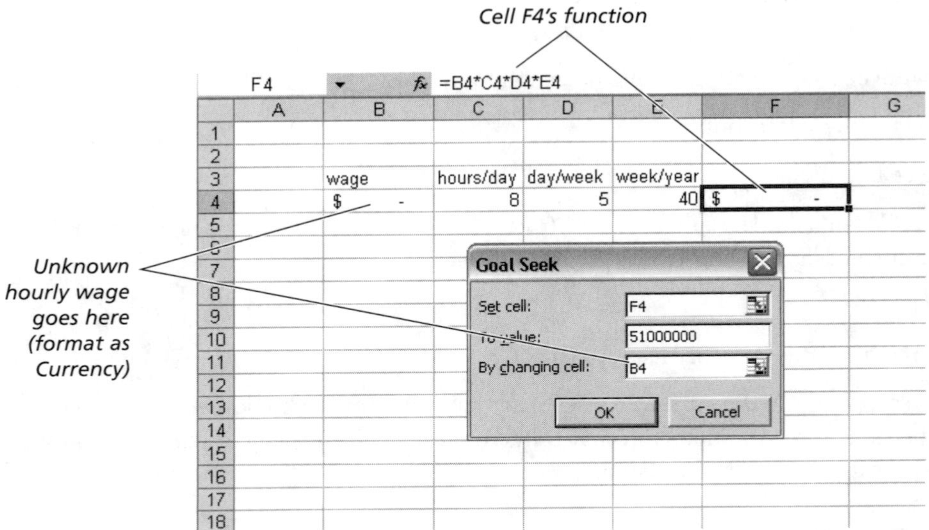

Figure 11.6 Working the Goal Seek thing

2. Choose Tools ➤ Goal Seek.

   The Goal Seek dialog box appears, as shown in Figure 11.6.

3. Enter F4 into the "Set Cell" box.

4. Enter 51000000 (51 million) into the "To Value" box.

5. Enter B4 into the "By Changing Cell" box.

6. Click OK.

   The values are filled in, but alas they're a little wide, so you'll have to make some adjustments.

7. Click OK to close the Goal Seek Status dialog box.

   Occasionally Goal Seek comes up with multiple solutions, which is possible in some situations. The Goal Seek Status dialog box helps you to weed through various solutions, should they be available.

8. Adjust the widths of columns B and F to see how much you need to make an hour.

   Boldly go forth and ask your manager for a raise.

I enjoy using Goal Seek because I often don't know how to phrase the mathematical question properly. Even in this example, if you take $51 million and just do division instead of multiplication, you get the results. So Goal Seek is there to help those of us who are not adept at seeing the mathematical possibilities all at once.

And thank goodness for that!

Letting Excel Be a Database of Sorts

Remember the grid thing? Excel isn't only numbers but also anything you put into a grid or table. For example, your vintage vinyl record collection or just your current CD collection. Or an inventory of all that paint in the basement, or your video disks, or video tape library. For my fellow Idahoans, it could be a list of the guns we own. Or maybe people you feel should die twisted, horrible deaths. In fact, there need not be any math associated with the thing at all. It can be just any old list.

Wow! Excel Is Good at Handling Lists. What Kind of Lists Is It Not Good At?

Excel can handle all sorts of lists but one: a list of contacts or people's names, places, and so on. That information is geared toward Outlook. In a way, Outlook is a custom database designed specifically for your "contact" information, or people and the loads of information that cling to people like barnacles on a whale.

Refer to Part III of this book for information on managing your people lists with Outlook.

Any Way to Import My Playlists into Excel from the Windows Media Player?

Yes, but not without extra software. As it stands, Excel cannot read the ASX file format that Media Player uses with its File ➤ Export command. The resulting file is a text file, but Excel can't make sense of it (nor should you).

The solution is to go to the Microsoft website and search for the Windows Powertoys. There is a Windows Media Player Powertoy "wizard" that converts the playlist ASX file into something that Excel can read and then display as a list database.

The address for the Windows Media Player Powertoys is

```
www.microsoft.com/windows/windowsmedia/download/bppowertoys.aspx
```

This address is current as this book goes to press.

Can I Use My Word Mail Merge List in Excel?

Absolutely. In fact, Excel is a better place to manipulate those lists because of all its fancy list features. The only weirdness here is that Excel 2000 lacks an easy way to import Word's mail merge *data source* (which is the official name).

Grabbing a Data Source in Excel 2003/XP

To grab a mail merge list you've already created in Word and stick it into Excel, follow these steps:

1. Choose Data ➢ Import External Data ➢ Import Data.

   The Select Data Source dialog box appears. It's focused on the My Data Sources folder, which is where Word 2003 or Word 2002 (XP) stores the data files created when you mail merge.

2. Choose the file from the list and click the Open button.

   And the Import Data dialog box appears.

3. Choose "New Worksheet."

   You can choose the "Existing Worksheet" option to stick the data source information into the current worksheet, though I like putting it into a new worksheet myself. (And that's work*sheet*, not work*book*.)

4. Click OK.

   And your imported data list appears in the worksheet.

The mail merge fields appear in the top row, in bold. In the rows below appear the data. Hey! It's a list! Now you can use Excel's powerful list management controls to work with the list. (These are covered later in this chapter.)

The Not-So-Slick Excel 2000 Way to Do This

Excel 2000 lacks the Import External Data command, so you'll have to rely on old-fashioned copy and paste to get the data source into Excel. Here's how:

1. In Word, open the data source file.

   Use the standard File ➢ Open command. The data source file is merely a table saved in a Word document. So the file appears in the Open dialog box like any other Word document.

2. Select the data source table.

   Click the mouse in the table and choose Table ➢ Select ➢ Table from the menu.

3. Copy the table.

   Press Ctrl+C to copy, or use any of the numerous Copy command equivalents.

4. Close Word and switch to Excel.

   Save the data source file, if you're asked to do so.

5. Select the cell that will be the upper-left corner of the table.

   I'll use cell A1 in a new worksheet.

6. Paste the table.

Use Ctrl+V or any Paste command; there is no need to Paste Special here—unless you want the tables linked.

Now you can use Excel's powerful list management toys to manipulate the table. Doing so is covered later in this chapter.

How Do I Save the Data Source Back to Disk?

You cannot save it back to disk as a data source; once the Word mail merge data source has been imported into Excel, it becomes a list or table in a worksheet. At this point, you should save it to disk as a workbook with a new workbooky name and everything.

If you want to use a table or list in the worksheet as a data source, then that is possible. I recommend saving the workbook to disk in the My Data Sources folder, which is where Word will look for it the next time you do a mail merge. This discussion continues in the next section.

The data source file in Word 2000 is nothing more than a Word document with a table, the table containing the data source. In Word 2003/XP, the data source file is an actual database file.

How Can I Create a List in Excel and Then Use It As a Word Mail Merge Data Source?

There is no direct way to export a list in Excel into the format used by Word as a mail merge data source. While you can create a list in Excel and save it to disk, the burden then falls upon Word to properly import that data for use in a merge operation.

Start by creating the list in Excel. It can be any sheet in a workbook, such as the one shown in Figure 11.7. Note that the list must have headers, as shown in the figure. This file must be saved to disk. It doesn't have to be closed, but it must be saved to disk.

Each header (column) corresponds to a field in Word's mail merge.

Headers

Different records in these rows

You can't see it, but this is in Sheet3 of the workbook.

	A	B	C	D	E
1	**Name**	**Age**	**Present**	**Parent's name**	
2	AJ	9	Walkie-talky	Barbara	
3	Ben	9	Action Figure	Stan	
4	Bonnie	8	Mouse pad	Susan	
5	Caitlyn	9	Toy bike	Brad	
6	Devon	10	Basketball	Steve	
7	Hayden	9	Ninja costume	Shauna	
8	Mike H	9	Aluminum bat	Steven	

Figure 11.7 A list in a worksheet

To save yourself time, save the file in the My Data Sources folder so that Word 2003/XP can easily locate it. For Word 2000, just save the workbook in a known location.

Now you're ready to use the list with Word in a mail merge.

When it comes time to select the data source for the mail merge, take these steps:

1a. In Word 2003/XP, Step 3 of 6 in the Mail Merge task pane, choose Browse to use an existing list.

1b. In Word 2000, Section 2 of the Mail Merge Helper, from the Get Data button menu choose "Open Data Source."

An Open/Select dialog box appears.

2. Choose "Excel Files" or "MS Excel Worksheets" from the "Files of Type" drop-down list.

That narrows the selection in the dialog box to only Excel worksheets.

3. Browse to the folder containing the worksheet.

4. Select the worksheet and click the Open button.

5. If necessary, choose the sheet or the location on the sheet where the list is located, as shown in Figure 11.8.

If there is no doubt, then only one item appears in the dialog box.

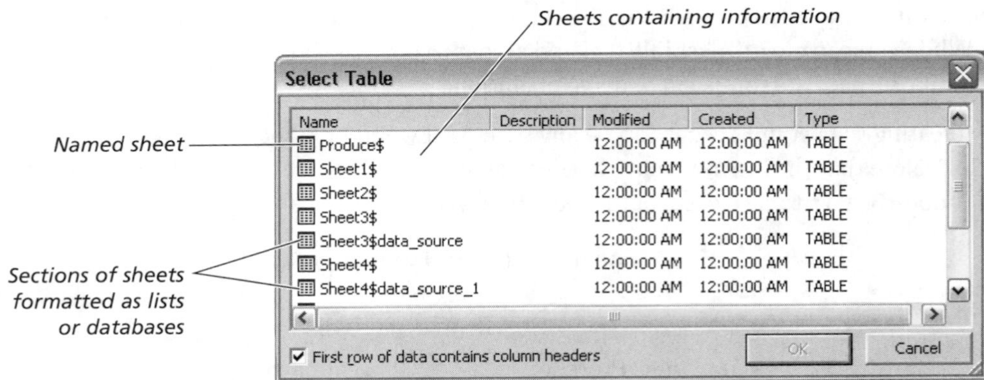

Figure 11.8 Word wants to know where the data can be found in the workbook.

6. Click OK.

In Word 2003/XP, you'll see the "List of Recipients" displayed in a dialog box, as shown in Figure 11.9 (which you can contrast with Figure 11.7).

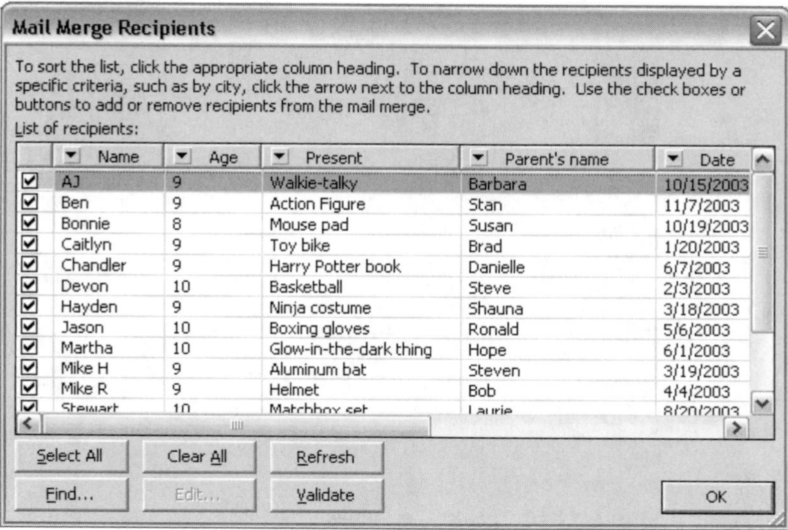

Figure 11.9 The final result for the data source (in Word)

7. Continue with the Mail Merge process.

Remember that the key here is to create the merge names as the list's "header" in Excel. Then use the rows beneath to fill in the list items. Save that file to disk; then you can use it as an external source for Word's mail merging.

To merge people and their associated information, you need to use Outlook. This information is covered in Part III of this book.

What's the Difference between a Table and a List?

The most important thing is first having the list; taking the time to write down information into rows and columns, and storing that information in the computer. In Excel, that stuff becomes a list, which you can manipulate—especially if you convert the table over into a list officially. Here's how:

1. Select the table.

Click any cell in the table, and then press the forgettable key combination Ctrl+Shift+8.

2. Choose Data ➤ Filter ➤ AutoFilter.

The table is now modified slightly (contrast Figure 11.7 with Figure 11.10). Each header has grown a drop-down menu button, which can be used to control the table in relation to the contents of that column.

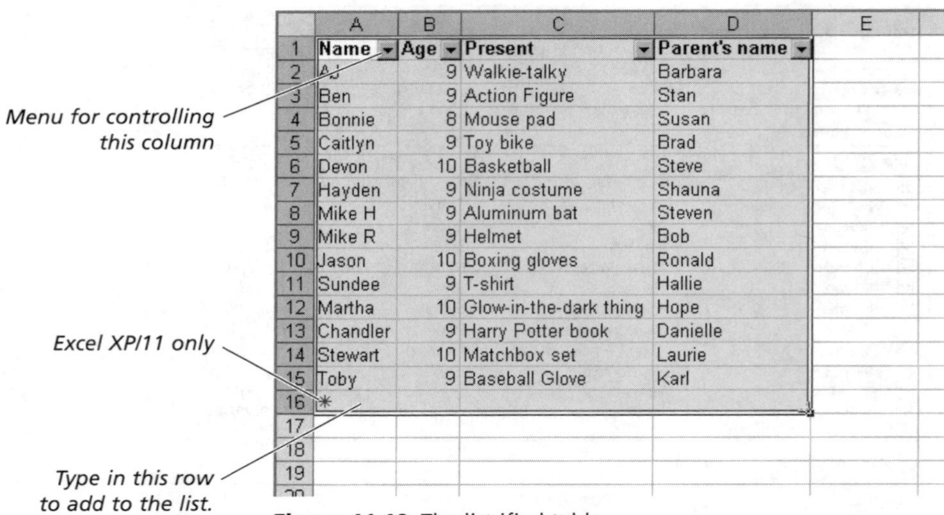

	A	B	C	D	E
1	Name	Age	Present	Parent's name	
2	AJ	9	Walkie-talky	Barbara	
3	Ben	9	Action Figure	Stan	
4	Bonnie	8	Mouse pad	Susan	
5	Caitlyn	9	Toy bike	Brad	
6	Devon	10	Basketball	Steve	
7	Hayden	9	Ninja costume	Shauna	
8	Mike H	9	Aluminum bat	Steven	
9	Mike R	9	Helmet	Bob	
10	Jason	10	Boxing gloves	Ronald	
11	Sundee	9	T-shirt	Hallie	
12	Martha	10	Glow-in-the-dark thing	Hope	
13	Chandler	9	Harry Potter book	Danielle	
14	Stewart	10	Matchbox set	Laurie	
15	Toby	9	Baseball Glove	Karl	
16	*				
17					
18					
19					

Figure 11.10 The list-ified table

So What the Heck Are Excel's Powerful List Management Controls?

The beauty of a list is that you can easily sort through it to get to the data you want. That's the key behind the menus, shown in Figure 11.10. A better example of this can be seen in Figure 11.11, which shows a list of names, teams, and bowling scores.

	A	B	C	D	E
1	Name	Team	Average	High Game	
2	Abdulla	Rolling Rollas	167	290	
3	Ayatollah	Rolling Rollas	175	255	
4	Bill Clinton	Expresses	126	157	
5	Che	Los Locos	155	220	
6	Danny Ortega	Los Locos	167	296	
7	Fidel Castro	Los Locos	156	210	
8	Gerald Ford	Expresses	162	267	
9	Gomez Addams	Jokers	202	300	
10	Herman Munster	Jokers	162	300	
11	Jimmy Carter	Expresses	145	198	
12	Madonna	Chix with Balls	145	208	
13	Mike Brady	Jokers	175	269	
14	Mullah	Rolling Rollas	182	260	
15	Patton	Old Faders	160	240	
16	Romell	Old Faders	157	229	
17	Roseanne	Chix with Balls	155	240	
18	Wynona	Chix with Balls	157	206	
19	Yamamoto	Old Faders	161	209	
20	*				
21					
22					

Figure 11.11 The infamous bowling team list

Say you want to view only the Jokers team members. To do so, click the menu button by the Team heading. The menu lists many options, as shown in Figure 11.12. Choosing the Jokers option limits the list to showing only those matching rows, as shown in Figure 11.13.

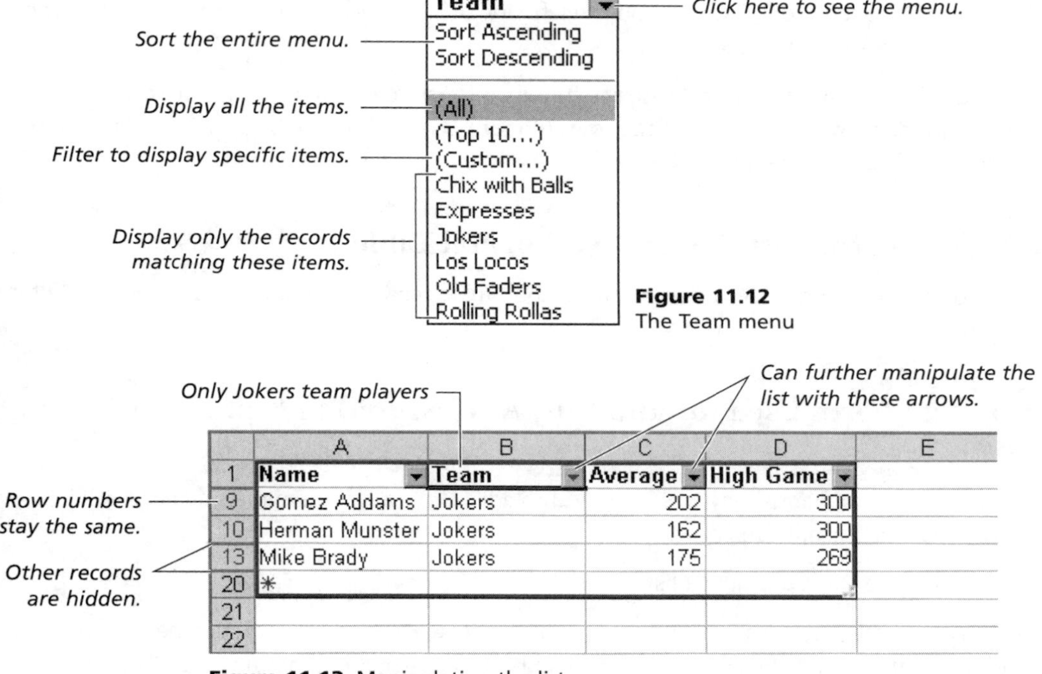

Figure 11.12
The Team menu

	A	B	C	D	E
1	Name	Team	Average	High Game	
9	Gomez Addams	Jokers	202	300	
10	Herman Munster	Jokers	162	300	
13	Mike Brady	Jokers	175	269	
20	*				
21					
22					

Figure 11.13 Manipulating the list

After the list is narrowed down, as shown in Figure 11.13, you can further manipulate things. For example, to find the Jokers team bowler with the highest average score, choose "Sort Descending" from the Average header's menu. (Though in this example it's easy enough to eyeball the highest score, imagine a table with hundreds of values.)

How Can I Find Duplicates in a List?

After spending all weekend entering your CD collection into an Excel database, you may wonder if you spent any time reentering the same albums. Or maybe you have two copies of one album and you *know* that you input it twice. Here's how to find out:

1. Select any cell in the table.
2. Choose Data ➢ Filter ➢ Advanced Filter.

   The Advanced Filter dialog box appears, plus it automatically selects your table. How nice.

3. Click to check "Unique Records Only."
4. Click OK.

Now the hard part: Any duplicate records have been hidden from view. The row the record is on isn't shown. You'll have to look carefully on the left side of the window for any missing rows (the line is thicker between the row labels).

Hiding the duplicate rows does not delete the items on those rows. To do so, you'll need to make a note of the hidden rows, then unhide the rows (choose Data ➢ Filter ➢ Show All). Finally, go back and manually delete the duplicates.

How Do I Convert the List Back into a Normal Table?

Playtime is over! Time to return to normal table-hood in Excel: Choose Data ➢ Filter ➢ AutoFilter and it's turned off.

What's the Data Form Used for and Why Am I Stupid to Build a List without It?

The Data Form is just a handy way to edit or add to a list. In fact, if you're making a list, it's just best to use the Data Form. Here's how:

1. Decide that you want to make a list.

   Do this over coffee and pastry, preferably at a downtown spot where you can be seen in the window. Combine your facial expressions and body language in a manner to let others know you're deciding to make a list. Do it in such an obvious way that even casual passersby would recognize your intent, despite your wearing dark glasses.

2. Create the labels at the top of each column.

   You must do this first. The labels must be created in a row by themselves. I typically format them bold and put them in the very tippy-top row (1) of the worksheet.

3. Enter the first record.

   I recommend this step because otherwise Excel gets confused and displays a bewildering warning dialog box. So go ahead and fill in the first record for your list.

Filling in the first record also ensures that you have all the fields you want; it's amazing what new fields you may think you need as you build the table.

4. Choose Data ➢ Form.

   And the input form, custom-designed for your list, appears. Shown in Figure 11.14, it makes it easy to add, remove, modify, and review all the junk in your list.

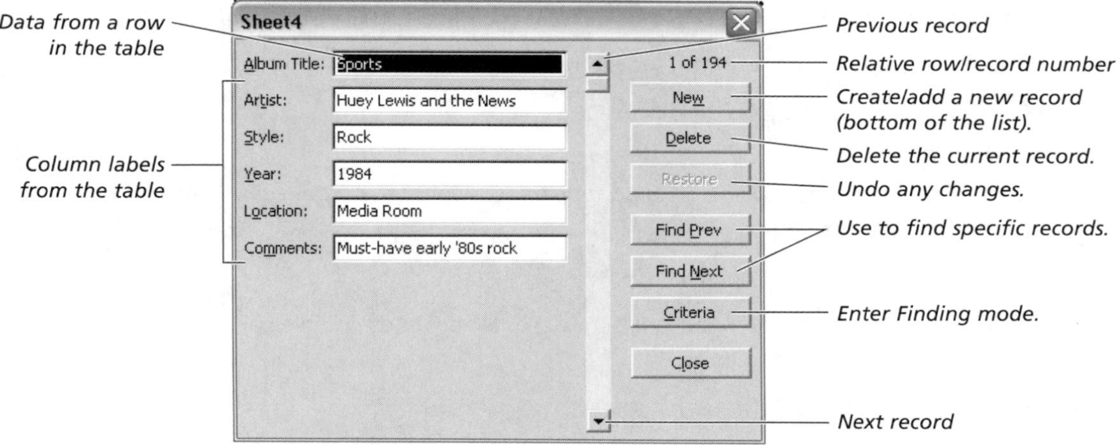

Figure 11.14 Using the Data Form

When modifying an existing record, use the New button to record the changes. Or use Restore to undo them. (The Tab key moves you between the fields.)

For information on using the Data Form to search through the records, see the next section.

I Can't Get the Data Form to Search; What's the Deal?

The secret to searching for information in a table with the Data Form is to click the Criteria button (Figure 11.14). That blanks out all the fields, allowing you to input information to match.

Say, for example, you had a table that listed record albums and you wanted to find all the albums from 1984. Here's what you would do:

1. Choose Data ➤ Form to display the data form for your table.
2. Click the Criteria button.
3. Type 1984 into the Year field.
4. Click the Find Next button.

Remember that you can also use the List mode's AutoFilter to have the list display only those records matching 1984. Refer to the section "So What the Heck Are Excel's Powerful List Management Controls?" earlier in this chapter.

Can I Select a Random Person from a List?

I use this function every time I hold a contest on my website. The list is an array of e-mail addresses. My job is to draw one name from the list on a random basis. This involves four functions and a named array of names. Sounds odd, but here's how to work it:

1. Select the entire range of names.

   They'll probably be in a column, for example, from cell B2 through cell B24. This range is known in Excel as an *array*.

2. Name the cells `names`.

   Click the mouse in the Name box and type a name for the array of cells. I chose the name "names" for this example.

3. Click to select some cell, such as D3.

   This is a calculation scratchpad cell, so it need not be on the visible part of your worksheet. I'm using D3 as an example.

4. Enter the formula `=ROWS(names)`.

   The function returns the number of rows in the array represented by "names."

5. Press Enter.

6. Into cell D4 enter the formula `=INT(RAND()*D3)+1`.

   Ah! A lovely complex formula. I'll start in the middle and work outward:

   `RAND()` This generates a random number between 0 and 1—a small fraction, so it must be multiplied by a larger number, in this case:

   `*D3` The random number is multiplied by the number of names in the list.

   `INT` The resulting number needs to be rounded to the nearest integer, which (in English) lops off the fractional/decimal part of the number. So instead of 7.8121216 you get 7.

   `+1` This adds 1 to the number so that the random value is between 1 and the number of rows. Otherwise, the value 0 could be returned as a result.

Of course, it could be best just to carefully copy the function and understand that this is a universal way in Excel to get a random number between 1 and whatever value is held in cell D3.

Now the value displayed in cell D4 is a row number, which might be enough to determine the random person in the list. But Excel is trickier than that. Keep moving along:

7. Into cell D5 enter the formula `= INDEX(names,D4,1)`.

   Here we go again: The INDEX function returns the contents of a cell in a table. In this case, it's the "names" array, or list of names, not a table. The second item, D4, is the cell containing the row number, randomly drawn. And the third item is 1, because the "names" array is only one column wide.

8. Press Enter.

   And as if by magic, the winner's name—randomly selected—appears in cell D5. A nifty payoff for some bizarre labor.

The RAND() function is an updating function, like the NOW() function. Any time anything changes on the worksheet, the function returns a new value. So if you type 1 into a cell and press the Enter key, you'll get a new RAND() random value, a new row number, and therefore a new result from the INDEX function. Be aware of this! Remember that when you save the worksheet and open it up again, a different name appears in the cell.

NERD'S CORNER

Are Numbers Really Random? Cocktail Party Trivia, Part VII

MARK: Oh, boy, Dan, you really worked them over with that RAND() function. Scary stuff.

DAN: RAND() is a great function. As long as you know the trick for generating specific values, you can use it to fill in sample worksheets and have them look like they contain real values. It's fun.

JOHN: But I'll bet you didn't know that the numbers aren't truly random.

DAN: That's right, John. They're pseudo *random.*

MARY: Like my pseudo *leather jacket?*

DAN: No. In this case, the numbers are merely as random as the computer can make them, which is random enough. But for scientists who really rely on the true random nature of a random number, computers cannot do the job. Despite the efforts of programmers, it's technically possible to predict a random number on a computer. Therefore, scientists and archvillains all over the world say that computers generate pseudo *random numbers, not true random numbers.*

MARY: That's right! I was talking with Lord Blothar the other day, and he quipped the same thing at one of his minions using Excel! Freaky!

How Can I Get Contacts from Outlook into Excel?

The best way is to use File ➤ Import and Export in Outlook. Choose "Export to a File," and then choose "Microsoft Excel" as the file format in which to save your data. Once the file is saved on disk, you can open the file in Excel and mess with it until the sun comes up and you realize you've spent another sleepless night slaving over the computer.

What's the Best Way to Sort a Table without Converting It into a List Thing?

Choose Data ➤ Sort. This command displays the Sort dialog box, but it's also smart enough to instantly select a table in your document. If the table has headings, then the Sort dialog box uses them, as shown in Figure 11.15.

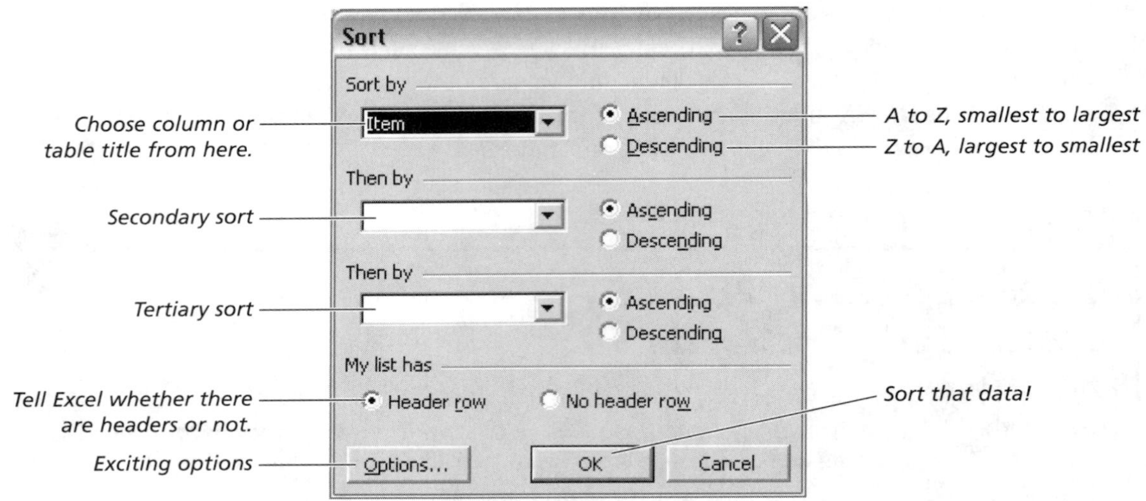

Figure 11.15 Sorting with the Sort dialog box

Because Excel is wise enough to see the whole table, items are sorted while the integrity of each record in the table is maintained. In other words, despite selecting only one column to sort, Excel sifts the entire table's data, not just the single column.

But I Need to Sort Only a Column.

If the column is all by itself, then simply use the Data ➤ Sort command on it. Otherwise, Excel feels bound to the table the column lives in. To sort that column away from the table, simply select the column, and then copy and paste it elsewhere in the worksheet. Then use Data ➤ Sort on that column.

Don't Be Dumb and Forget the Quick Sort Buttons on the Toolbar!

You can always rely on the Sort Ascending and Sort Descending buttons on the toolbar to do a quick sort in your worksheet.

If you have a table, then the Sort buttons sort by whichever column is selected in the table (or whichever column the cell selector is in).

For sorting a single column, just click to select any cell in the column. Excel is smart enough to find the top and bottom of the column, and Sort Ascending or Sort Descending does its job and sorts the column accordingly.

To All the Spreadsheets I've Loved Before

I'm a spreadsheet zany. Spreadsheet software and I go way back. I've probably used them all and owned nearly half a dozen. In fact, I still have data in older spreadsheet formats that no program can read today. Oh well. Here's my love list:

VisiCalc

The first spreadsheet. I got to play with it for only a few weeks on someone else's computer. Looking back now, I'm shocked at how limited it was, but it inspired others to do bigger and better things.

Multiplan

Microsoft's original spreadsheet, which came "free" when you bought the Microsoft mouse back in 1983. I did my original "tax planning" worksheet in Multiplan.

1-2-3

I never really got to use the grand 1-2-3 spreadsheet, and I never could figure out why everyone was all nuts over it. I do remember doing research on it once for a question someone had; apparently it was tough to print out only a portion of the worksheet.

Wingz

Installed it. Yawned. Forget why so many were so excited about this. My only memorable Wingz experience is that I saw the demo at Comdex and I still have the free vinyl bag they gave away.

Quatro Pro

One of the last, great text-based spreadsheets. Gave 1-2-3 a run for its money in the final days of DOS. I never really used it; at the time I was doing my spreadsheeting on the Macintosh with Full Impact.

Full Impact

My all-time favorite spreadsheet. From the dBASE people at Ashton-Tate, it was just dreamy to work in. Available on the Macintosh and with features that Excel still lacks today, I would love it if I could find a copy of this old antique. Just a well-thought-out product.

Improv

Developed by Lotus for the NeXT computer, a Windows version eventually came out. But it was too wild and unique for most spreadsheet users. No true grid was visible. Instead, you used a "dispenser" to pull out cells and place them on the work area. You could easily swap X and Y axes in the worksheet to manipulate data in several ways—a better version of what Excel now offers as the PivotTable.

PivotTable Is Designed to Make Me Go Insane, Right?

PivotTable is an ugly term for simply giving yourself a more flexible way to view information in a table. It would be wholly unnecessary if it weren't for Excel's last, great spreadsheet competition, a program called Improv.

Improv was created by Lotus (the 1-2-3 spreadsheet people) for the brand-new NeXT computer back in 1989. Improv wasn't like the traditional spreadsheet program. It was more of a build-your-own grid, but not just a grid, more like a cube that could be twisted and turned to see data in three dimensions. (Yes, I was a fervent Improv fan.)

It was the insane jealousy over Improv that caused Excel's designers to create this wild PivotTable utility for Excel. I'll run over the basics of this advanced feature in the next few sections. Yes, there is a point to it all. Don't give up on it yet.

What's the Key to Understanding the PivotTable?

Simple enough: The key to using the PivotTable is to have a table in your document that has more than one dimension to it. Keep in mind that PivotTables were inspired by the old Improv worksheet, which wasn't really a worksheet but rather a way to manipulate information in many directions.

Three dimensions to classify the data

The raw data

	A	B	C	D	E
1	**Product**	**Salesman**	**Zone**	**Sales**	
2	Plunger	Jones	East	121	
3	Plunger	Jones	West	35	
4	Plunger	Smith	East	46	
5	Plunger	Smith	West	190	
6	Mouthwash	Jones	East	22	
7	Mouthwash	Jones	West	64	
8	Mouthwash	Smith	East	97	
9	Mouthwash	Smith	West	182	
10	TP	Jones	East	36	
11	TP	Jones	West	78	
12	TP	Smith	East	145	
13	TP	Smith	West	12	
14	Fish Heads	Jones	East	96	
15	Fish Heads	Jones	West	41	
16	Fish Heads	Smith	East	57	
17	Fish Heads	Smith	West	86	
18					

Two zones

Two salesmen

Four products

Figure 11.16
A multidimensional table

Consider the table in Figure 11.16. This is actually a four-dimensional table, which is fine for a PivotTable. Here's how to look at it:

- The Sales column contains the data.
- Sales are divided between the East and West zones in the Zone column.
- Sales are further divided by salesman in the Salesman column.
- Finally, sales are broken down by the product sold, listed in the Product column.

The table may look like it contains a lot of repeated information, but it doesn't. It's just highly classified into different things, different *dimensions*.

So Then, How Does One Make a PivotTable?

A multidimensional table is the key to making and using a pivot table. Once you've determined that you have such table, building the PivotTable is a cinch. Witness:

1. Choose Data ➤ PivotTable and PivotChart Report. A funky dialog box appears.
2. Click the Next button.
3. Ensure that your multidimensional table is selected in the worksheet. If it isn't, then select the table now; drag over it with the mouse.
4. Click the Next button.
5. Click the Finish button.

   And the PivotTable is created in a new worksheet, as shown in Figure 11.17. Isn't it pretty? Well, actually not. It needs to be filled in and messed with.

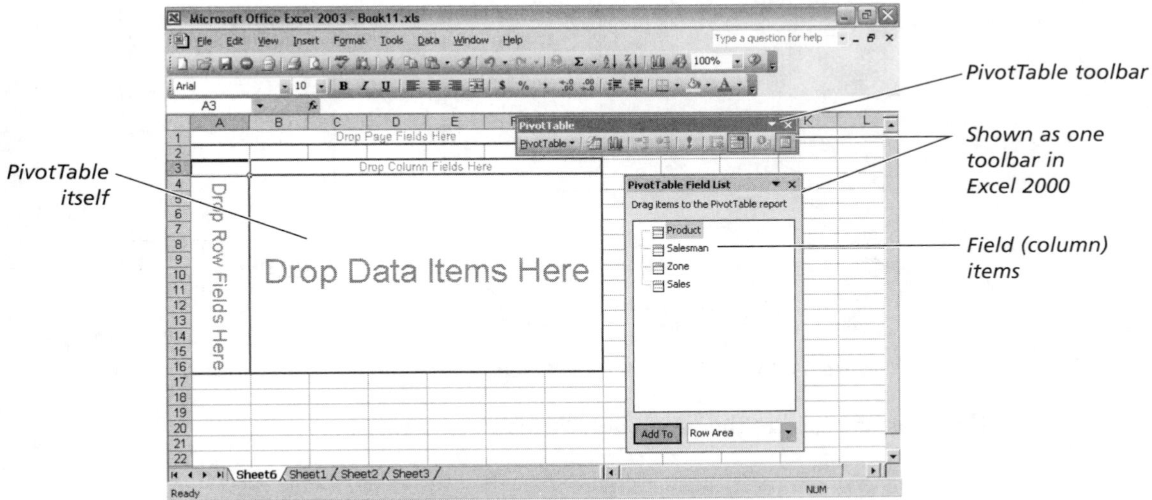

Figure 11.17 The PivotTable skeleton in a new worksheet

The PivotTable is now ready to be filled in and toyed with. That's done by dragging and dropping field names (column headings) from the list and into the PivotTable itself. The next section discusses this.

Any Necessary Rules about Dragging and Dropping Stuff into a PivotTable?

The key is to know *data* is. You'll notice that the PivotTable (Figure 11.17) has a large central area called "Drop Data Items Here." That's the meat of the matter and the key to using the PivotTable and dragging and dropping.

PivotTables answer questions. The questions are composed of the column headings or field names. For example, "How many plungers did each salesman sell in each zone?" Here's how to answer that question:

1. The table is about plunger sales. Plunger is a product, so drag the Product field up to the "Drop Page Fields Here" item.
2. Choose Plunger from the Product heading's drop-down list, as shown in Figure 11.18; click OK.

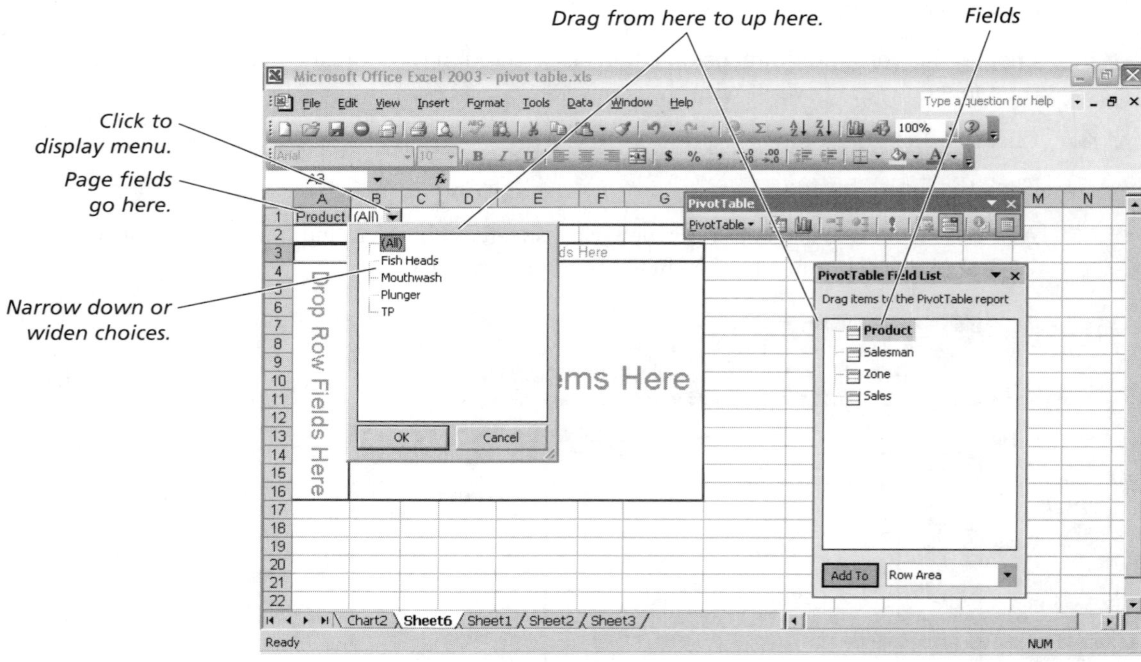

Figure 11.18 Setting up the PivotTable

3. Drag the Salesman field to the "Drop Row Fields Here" area.

4. Finally, drop the Sales field into the "Drop Data Items Here" part of the table (in the middle).

And there you see the sum of sales for plungers by each salesman, as shown in Figure 11.19.

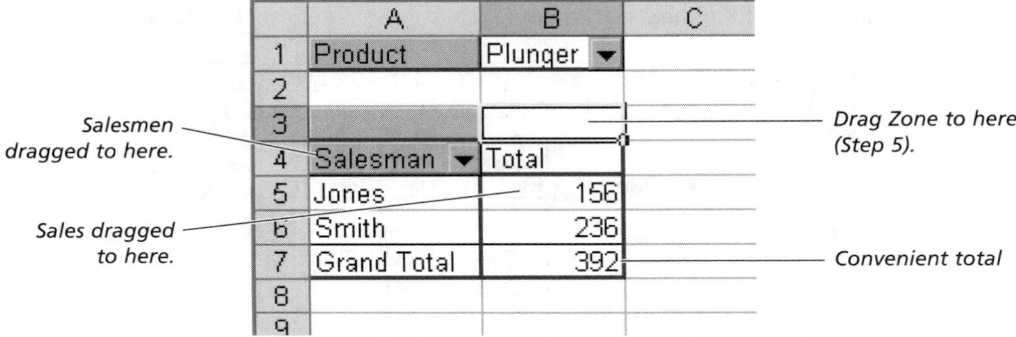

	A	B	C
1	Product	Plunger	
2			
3			
4	Salesman	Total	
5	Jones	156	
6	Smith	236	
7	Grand Total	392	
8			
9			

Figure 11.19 Summing up the sales of plungers

5. To see things broken down by Zone, drag the Zone field to the "Column Field" area in the table (shown in Figure 11.19).

Further manipulation can be done by simply choosing a specific item from each field's menu. For example, to see about sales of all the items, choose (All) from the Product field's drop-down menu, and click OK.

So What's So Magic about the PivotTable?

Continuing from the previous example (which you must have in order to get this magic stuff): Drag the Product field down from the top of the table and drop it right on top of the Salesman field. (As you drop, a fuzzy I-beam appears to the right or left of the Salesman field; ensure that the fuzzy I-beam is to the left of the salesman.)

	A	B	C	D	E
1	Drop Page Fields Here				
2					
3			Zone		
4	Salesman	Product	East	West	Grand Total
5	Jones	Fish Heads	96	41	137
6		Mouthwash	22	64	86
7		Plunger	121	35	156
8		TP	36	78	114
9	Jones Total		275	218	493
10	Smith	Fish Heads	57	86	143
11		Mouthwash	97	182	279
12		Plunger	46	190	236
13		TP	145	12	157
14	Smith Total		345	470	815
15	Grand Total		620	688	1308
16					

Figure 11.20 Sales by salesman and then by product

Now you have something that looks like Figure 11.20, with sales broken down by salesman and then by product.

Drag the Product field to the left of the Salesman field, and you get something like Figure 11.21. Or drag the Salesman field up next to the Zone field to get something like Figure 11.22.

	A	B	C	D	E	F
1	Drop Page Fields Here					
2						
3			Zone			
4	Product	Salesman	East	West	Grand Total	
5	Fish Heads	Jones	96	41	137	
6		Smith	57	86	143	
7	Fish Heads Total		153	127	280	
8	Mouthwash	Jones	22	64	86	
9		Smith	97	182	279	
10	Mouthwash Total		119	246	365	
11	Plunger	Jones	121	35	156	
12		Smith	46	190	236	
13	Plunger Total		167	225	392	
14	TP	Jones	36	78	114	
15		Smith	145	12	157	
16	TP Total		181	90	271	
17	Grand Total		620	688	1308	
18						
19						

Figure 11.21 Sales by product and then by salesman

	A	B	C	D	E	F	G	H	I
1	Drop Page Fields Here								
2									
3		Salesman	Zone						
4		Jones		Jones Total	Smith		Smith Total	Grand Total	
5	Product	East	West		East	West			
6	Fish Heads	96	41	137	57	86	143	280	
7	Mouthwash	22	64	86	97	182	279	365	
8	Plunger	121	35	156	46	190	236	392	
9	TP	36	78	114	145	12	157	271	
10	Grand Total	275	218	493	345	470	815	1308	
11									

Figure 11.22 Product sales by salesman and then by zone

How Can I Delete a Field from the Table?

Just drag the field down and off the table, until the mouse pointer grows a red *X* (meaning delete). Then release the mouse button, and the field is off the table.

Remember that you can always add the field back by dragging it over from the palette.

Does the PivotTable Update When I Change Data Elsewhere in the Worksheet?

No, you must manually update the PivotTable: Click the exclamation point button (Refresh External Data) on the PivotTable toolbar.

12 Some Excel-lent Formatting Tricks

Nothing makes me want to smash my head against the wall like a dull spreadsheet. It has the same effect on me as a jiggly column of text in Word, which was obviously lined up with spaces and not one even, well-placed tab stop. It's tacky and I know the person creating the spreadsheet could have done better—or at least deserves to be replaced by someone who can do better.

A well-formatted worksheet is the sign of refinement. Not only are the numbers properly formatted, but perhaps there is some playfulness with the fonts or a dash of color. Maybe there's a line here or there or a box. That's handy to have. But then, naturally, the whole thing is ruined because the last column of numbers—the most important one—prints on a separate sheet of paper. Now that's almost criminal.

This chapter covers a few of the elements of formatting: arranging cells, formatting them directly, and then working with the final, printed result. The idea is to get something on paper that looks better than it does now. The tricks are subtle, the hints are robust, and the tips are sublime.

Vagueness Clarified and Elements Enlightened:

- Adjusting column and row width and height
- Properly fitting information into cells
- Splitting and merging cells
- Creating and using styles
- Arranging text inside a cell
- Applying color
- Adjusting the way the pages print
- Fixing the document's headers and footers

The Narrow and Wide of Things

Don't be afraid to adjust the size of the cells in your worksheet! Instead, bask in the glory of the ability Excel has to change its cell size. Older worksheets had fixed cell sizes, which meant information might be only partially displayed or that you'd have to go through the agony of figuring a house payment displayed using scientific notation.

So relax! Take it easy. And understand that a cell can be any size you want!

How Can I Make All These Columns Wide Enough?

Oh, those narrow column blues....

Not all columns need to be the same width; some columns can be very wide, others very narrow or even nonexistent. To set the column width to be as wide as the widest item in all of the column's rows, follow these steps:

1. Select the columns you want to adjust.

   To select a column, point the mouse at the column header. The mouse pointer changes to a down arrow. You can then drag to the left or right to select a swath of columns.

2. Choose Format ➤ Column ➤ AutoFit Selection.

   Thwoop, and everything fits.

You can also instantly adjust any individual column's width by dragging the right edge of the column header, as shown in Figure 12.1. Or you can double-click that spot to resize the column to hold its widest cell.

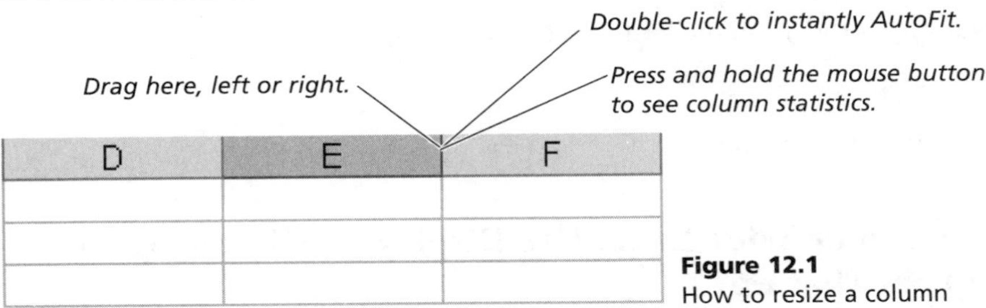
Double-click to instantly AutoFit.
Drag here, left or right.
Press and hold the mouse button to see column statistics.
D
E
F

Figure 12.1
How to resize a column

Selecting Rows and Columns

These keyboard shortcuts work for selecting an entire row or column. They cannot be used to select more than one row or column, unfortunately. The row or column is based on the position of the cell selector.

Shift+Spacebar

Select the whole row.

Ctrl+Spacebar

Select the whole column.

Any Easy Way to Make This Column's Width Match That Column's Width?

Without getting a ruler and measuring—or using the mouse to determine the exact column width, you can copy and paste column width values. Here's how:

1. Click to select the original column.

   Click in the column header; this is the column that has the width you want.

2. Press Ctrl+C to copy.

   Or choose Edit ➤ Copy.

3. Click to select the destination column.
4. Choose Edit ➤ Paste Special.

   Note that this is a special Paste Special dialog box, designed to paste column-width information, not specific values.

5. Choose "Column Widths" from the Paste Special dialog box.
6. Click OK.

   And the two column widths will match.

I'd Like the Column to Be Wide Enough to Display $1 Million, but Not Wider. How Can I Set That Up?

Column width values are measured by how many digits you can cram into a cell. Assuming that you're not messing with the standard font size (Arial 10), the column width required to hold 1000000 is 7. Go ahead and try this: Type 1000000 into a column, and then drag the column heading's right edge over until the width value equals 7. You'll find that 1000000 fits snugly in that space.

Of course, people don't write one million as 1000000; they use commas. That adds two digits to the column width, so you'll have to widen the column to 9: Drag the column heading's right edge over until 9.00 is shown for the width. Then click the Comma Style button on the Formatting toolbar to stick commas into the number: 1,000,000.

Ooops! Doesn't work, does it? That's because the Comma style button also adds a period and two zeros after the decimal place. So you really need a column that is 12 characters wide: Manually adjust the column width to 12. And it fits.

Adding the dollar sign? Widen the column to 13, one more place to hold that $ character.

And there you go.

How Can I Shrink My Column into Oblivion?

You can drag the column heading's right edge over to the left until the column shrinks into nothingness. When you try this, however, it often messes with the width of the column on the left. To prevent that, simply select the column you want to vanish, then choose Format ➢ Column ➢ Hide.

To resize the column back into the visible realm, choose Format ➢ Column ➢ Unhide.

You Must Know This: Painfully Detailed Information on Column Widths

When you squeeze the mouse on the right edge of a column's heading, you see a pop-up bubble that gives the column's width in both column width and pixel values.

Shown here, you see that the column has a width of 8.43 with a pixel size of 64—common for Excel.

Width: 8.43 (64 pixels)

The column width value is the left-right measurement of how many digits of the standard font will fit into a cell. The standard font is Arial 10 points. A digit is a number from 0 through 9. So the value 8.43 means that the column is wide enough to hold almost 8 and a half digits from the Arial font at 10 points. (If you change the default font, then the column width values change accordingly, but the cell size remains fixed at a certain number of pixels).

The pixel size is a hardware measurement. It's how many graphic dots (picture elements, or pixels) wide the cell is on the screen. This measurement is very consistent from PC to PC, where the monitor typically displays 72 pixels per inch.

When adjusting the column width manually (by dragging the column heading's right edge), you see the width and pixel values adjust accordingly. However the dialog boxes that control column width all use the width (character size) values.

Can Rows Be Adjusted, Grown, Shrunk, or Hidden Just Like Columns?

Yes.

Yes? That's Your Answer? Doesn't Your Editor Hate It When You Do That?

Of course.

Can You Tell Me More?

About my editor or the row height?

Okay. Let me assume "row height" before I get slapped into unconsciousness:

Row height, like column width, has two measurements: The first is points, which is relative to the height of the standard font (Arial 10), plus a few more points for wiggle room, things like commas and other items that float above or below the text. The second value is pixels, just as it is with column width.

You adjust the row height by dragging the row heading's lower border.

Standard row height is 12.75, or 17 pixels.

Do I Need to Adjust Row Height?

Rarely. Most of the time, things you do in the cells automatically affect the row height. For example, if you choose a larger font, that automatically adjusts the row height to accommodate the bigger text.

Or say you wrap text within a cell. If so, the row height grows tall enough to accommodate all the text in that cell.

I Need My Rows to Be "Yea" High.

As with formatting column width, to automatically adjust a row's height, double-click the row heading's bottom border.

If you need the row to be a specific height, choose Format ➤ Row ➤ Height and enter the character height value.

I Tried Wrapping Text in a Cell, but It Makes the Row Height Too Tall and Screws Up the Rest of the Worksheet. Anything Else I Can Do?

This is where the Merge Cells command comes in handy: It allows you to temporarily discard the boundaries between cells so that you can fit more information into a tight area without affecting the rows to the left or right of the cells.

It's really best to see this in action, so take these steps:

1. Select cells F3, F4, and F5.
2. Press Ctrl+1 to format the cells.
3. Click the Alignment tab.
4. Click to check "Merge Cells."

   This groups the cells into one, but it won't wrap the text in the cells. For that, you have to:

5. Click to check "Wrap Text."
6. Click OK.

   And now you have one big cell where you had three before.

Figure 12.2 shows how the merged cells form a single cell. Note the absence of grid lines.

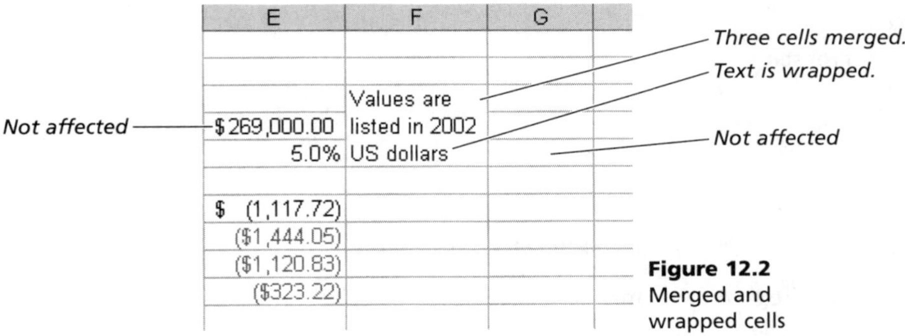

Figure 12.2
Merged and wrapped cells

The group of merged cells is referred to by the topmost cell in the group. In the case of Figure 12.2, all three of the merged cells are now cell F3.

You can also merge a group of cells, say a block of four by five cells. This doesn't affect any other cells, rows, or columns in the worksheet. The unit of merged cells is referred to by the cell in the upper-left corner.

Any Quick Way to Merge Cells?

To quickly merge a group of selected cells, click the Merge and Center button on the Formatting toolbar. This does not, however, wrap the text in the cells.

How Can I Unmerge the Cell(s)?

Unmerging cells is a snap: Click to select the massive cell, and then click the Merge and Center button. That undoes things rather nicely.

The contents of the merged cells are shoved into the top (or top-left) cell. The other cells are free again. Free! Free! Free!

Any Way to Split Cells?

No. But you can split up text across cells. This can be rather silly; for example, you wouldn't want to split a title, "Pan Dimensional Accounting," but you may want to split a list where the first and last names appear in one cell. That way the names could be split into two cells. Here's how to do that:

1. Type a list of names in cells A1 through A6.

   For example, U.S. presidents' names:

   ```
   George Washington
   John Adams
   Thomas Jefferson
   James Madison
   James Monroe
   John Adams
   Andrew Jackson
   ```

2. Select cells A1 through A6, the cells you want to split.
3. Choose Data ➢ Text to Columns.

   A wizard dialog box appears.

4. Select Delimited (if it isn't selected already).

   Choose the "Fixed Width" option only if all the text in every row has the same number of characters.

5. Click the Next button.

   The dialog box now wants to know what separates the items in your text.

6. Click to check Space.

Spaces separate the first and last names. After clicking the space, you'll see a vertical line drawn, showing how the text will be split, as shown in Figure 12.3. (You may uncheck the Tab option if you like.)

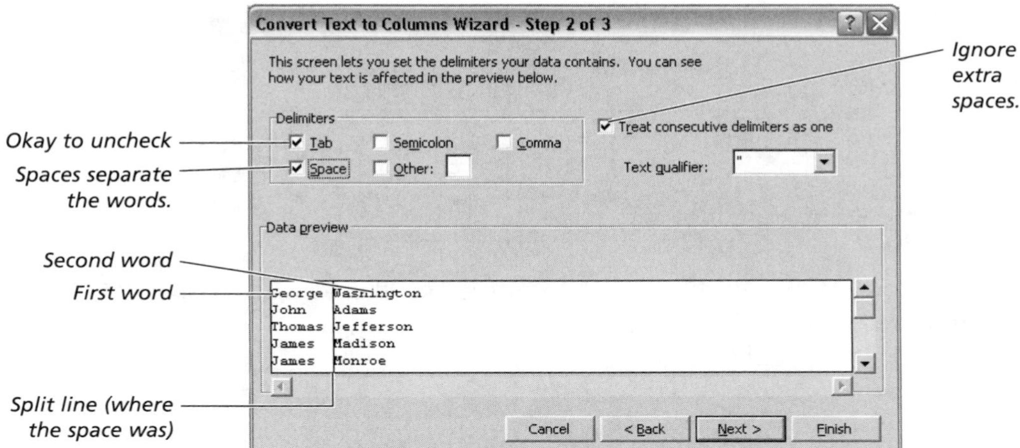

Figure 12.3 Splitting text between columns

7. Click the Next button.

In Step 3 of 3, the wizard lets you format each column, but for this exercise you're done. You could be finished, but you're done.

8. Click the Finish button.

First names in column A. Last names in column B.

If the cells to the right of the cells you're splitting contain data, a warning dialog box is displayed. The cells cannot be split without destroying any data in the cells to the right. Remember that before you set things up so you can move those cells out of the way.

Beyond Simple Formatting

Formatting your worksheet is fairly easy. Anyone who is familiar with Word—or even anyone who's bothered to format an e-mail—can manage to format text in a worksheet. There are, however, a few finer points I'd like to go over before you win your intermediate-level Excel scholarship.

How Can I Format All the Cells with the Same Style of Text?

This is an easy one: First select all the cells in the worksheet that you've messed with. A quick way to do this is to press Ctrl+End to move to the "end" of the worksheet (or merely the part that you're using). Then press Shift+Ctrl+Home to select all those cells as a unit.

With all the cells selected, choose your formatting commands. This can handily be done from the Formatting toolbar, or you can use the Font tab in the Format Cells dialog box: Press Ctrl+1 to see that dialog box, shown in Figure 12.4.

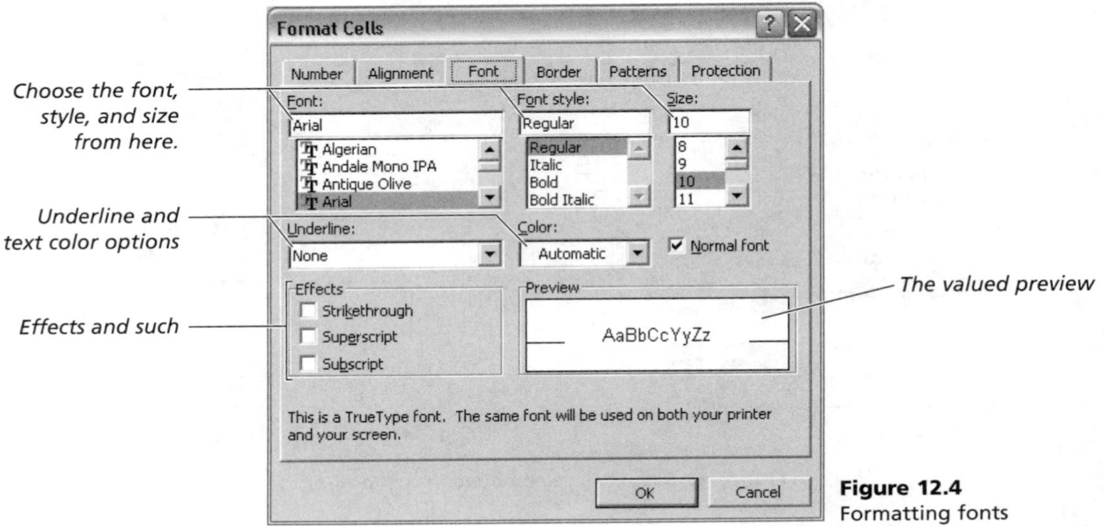

Figure 12.4
Formatting fonts

You Must Know This: A Style Covers More than Just the Cell's Font

Styles include information on all aspects of formatting a cell. From Figure 12.4, you see that each of the check mark items relates to a tab in the Format Cells dialog box. A style can use (or control) any setting from any of those tabs in the Format Cells dialog box. In addition to the font, that means you can have a specific number style with a certain alignment or perhaps a border. It can be any combination.

Why Should I Bother Selecting a Style? Can't I Just Change the Normal Style?

The Normal style in Excel defines how cells are formatted automatically for every sheet in the workbook. You can change this style if you like, but keep in mind that it does affect every worksheet.

To change the Normal style, mind these steps:

1. Choose Format ➢ Style.

   The Style dialog box appears, as shown in Figure 12.5.

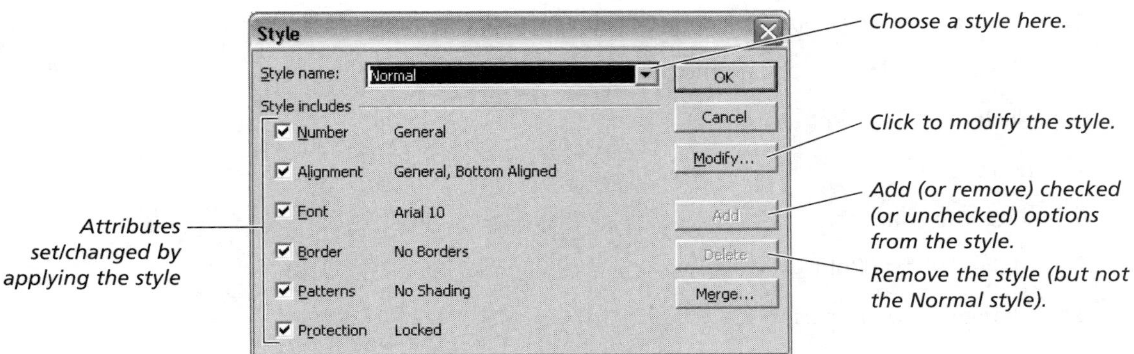

Figure 12.5 Using the Style dialog box

2. Click the Modify button.

   The Format Cells dialog box appears.

3. Click the Font tab.

4. Select the attributes for the new font you want to use for the entire workbook.

   Set the typeface, style, size, and other options.

5. Click OK.

6. Click OK to close the Style dialog box.

   And the new font is used as the Normal font for all worksheets.

You'll notice that the cells may adjust their size if you've chosen a larger font.

I do not recommend modifying the Normal style. Normal serves as a base—a plain, boring, nondescript format for a cell. By modifying it, you're removing a chance to unformat cells in the worksheet. Now that may be livable, but consider reading through the next few sections before you decide upon permanently altering the Normal style.

So How Can I Create a Style Other than Normal?

In Excel, Styles are created by example. While you can modify a style after it's created, no style itself is built from scratch in the Style dialog box.

Say you want to create a "Total" style, which you'll use to bring out the various cells that display totals (or grand totals) in your worksheet. The first step is to format the cell how you like it:

1. Select a cell to format as a Total.

2. Press Ctrl+1 to bring up the Format Cells dialog box.

3. Click the Number tab.

4. Choose Currency from the Category list.

   The total is always a dollar amount.

5. Click the Alignment tab.

   Looks good.

6. Click the Font tab.
7. Make the style Bold.
8. Change the point size to 12.
9. Click the Border tab.
10. Click that Outline button.

    Ooops! Maybe make the outline border thicker:

11. Select a thick, solid line from the Style area.
12. Click the Outline button again.

    There.

13. Click the Patterns tab.

    Nothing worthy there.

14. Click the Protection tab.

    Nope, nothing fun here.

15. Click OK.

    The cell is formatted as you like, but no style is created yet. Keep that cell selected.

16. Choose Format ➤ Style.
17. Type a name for the style, such as `Total`.

    Notice how when you start typing, you see your text replace "Normal" and your settings appear by the check marks in the dialog box, as shown in Figure 12.6.

18. Click OK.

    Now you could just click Add if you wanted to stay in the dialog box, but you don't. You want to apply the style.

19. Select the cells in your document that you want to apply the style to.

    You can use the Ctrl key and click the mouse to select several noncontiguous cells at once.

20. Choose Format ➤ Style.

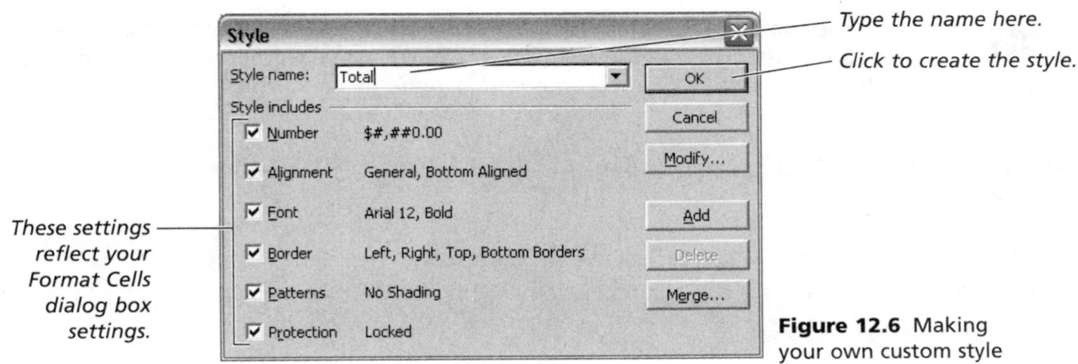

Figure 12.6 Making your own custom style

21. Select your style from the "Style Name" drop-down list.
22. Click OK.

    And the style is applied.

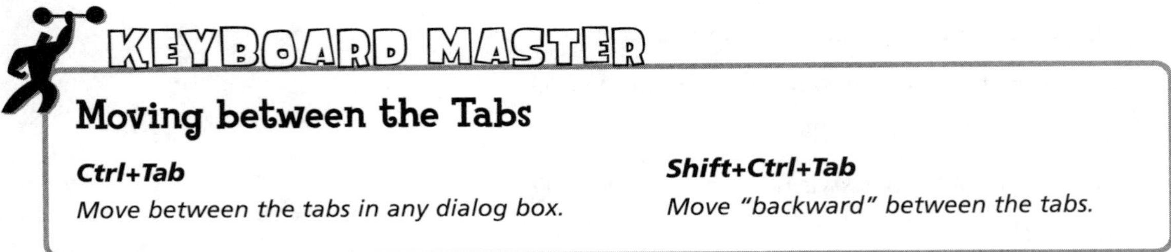

Moving between the Tabs

Ctrl+Tab

Move between the tabs in any dialog box.

Shift+Ctrl+Tab

Move "backward" between the tabs.

I Just Want to Copy the Formatting from One Cell to Another. Do I Need to Create a Style?

No, just use the Format Painter instead. Here's how:

1. Click the cell that has the style you want to copy.
2. Click to select the Format Painter button.

   The mouse pointer changes to a large + with a paintbrush by its side.
3. Click a cell to "paint" the original cell's format.

   And the original cell's formatting—all of it—is copied to the cell you clicked. If the original cell was formatted with a style, then the new cell also shares that formatting style.

You can also drag the mouse to paint a swath of cells with the Format Painter.

To undo the painting, press Ctrl+Z right away. If you're too late, then just click a normal, nonformatted cell in Step 1 and repeat the process to paint a cell Normal.

To continue painting after clicking a cell, double-click the Format Painter button on the toolbar. That keeps the Format Painter active so that you can paint/format many cells. Press the Esc key to end this mode of operation.

What's the Point of Creating a Style When I Can Just Use the Format Painter?

If you can remember from Chapter 5 on Word, "Using Styles and Templates to Save Oodles of Time," the advantage of a style is that when you modify the style, all the cells formatted with that style change at once.

For example, you can choose Format ➤ Styles. Choose your style from the list. Then click the Modify button to change some aspect, say, to color the text green or something. Clicking the OK button changes that style but also immediately changes all cells formatted with that style.

How Can I Strip Off the Formatting without Changing the Numbers?

The easiest way is to reapply the Normal style:

1. Select the cells you want to strip of formatting.
2. Choose Format ➤ Style.
3. Select the Normal style from the drop-down list.
4. Click OK.

And the cells are blandly formatted once again.

KEYBOARD MASTER

The Handy F4 "Repeat" Key

F4

Repeats the last formatting command given. This saves time from having to choose a style or use the Format Cells dialog box: Just select a cell and press the F4 key instead.

And Now for Some Basic, yet Common Formatting Q&A

Here is a smattering of other formatting questions I've received over the years. Keep in mind that there are no right or wrong ways to format things; there are only opinions as to what looks or works best.

I Need to Run My Text from Bottom to Top!

The Alignment tab in the Format Cells dialog box is where you can set your text direction, as shown in Figure 12.7. Text can appear tilted 90 degrees either clockwise or counterclockwise as set by the Orientation gizmo.

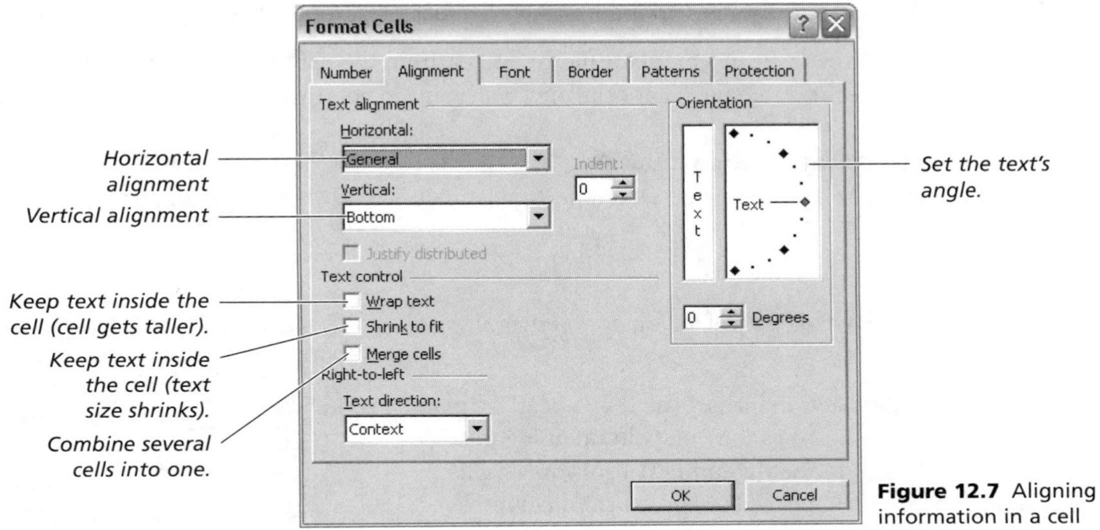

Figure 12.7 Aligning information in a cell

Figure 12.8 shows a worksheet with various text-alignment tricks, as explained in the figure.

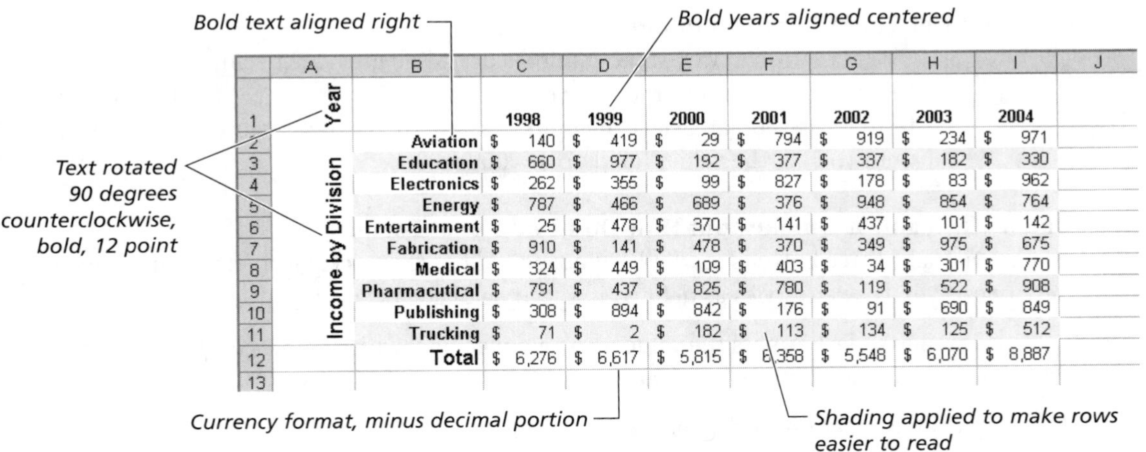

	A	B	C	D	E	F	G	H	I	J
1	Year		1998	1999	2000	2001	2002	2003	2004	
2	Income by Division	Aviation	$ 140	$ 419	$ 29	$ 794	$ 919	$ 234	$ 971	
3		Education	$ 660	$ 977	$ 192	$ 377	$ 337	$ 182	$ 330	
4		Electronics	$ 262	$ 355	$ 99	$ 827	$ 178	$ 83	$ 962	
5		Energy	$ 787	$ 466	$ 689	$ 376	$ 948	$ 854	$ 764	
6		Entertainment	$ 25	$ 478	$ 370	$ 141	$ 437	$ 101	$ 142	
7		Fabrication	$ 910	$ 141	$ 478	$ 370	$ 349	$ 975	$ 675	
8		Medical	$ 324	$ 449	$ 109	$ 403	$ 34	$ 301	$ 770	
9		Pharmaceutical	$ 791	$ 437	$ 825	$ 780	$ 119	$ 522	$ 908	
10		Publishing	$ 308	$ 894	$ 842	$ 176	$ 91	$ 690	$ 849	
11		Trucking	$ 71	$ 2	$ 182	$ 113	$ 134	$ 125	$ 512	
12		Total	$ 6,276	$ 6,617	$ 5,815	$ 6,358	$ 5,548	$ 6,070	$ 8,887	
13										

Figure 12.8 Various alignment tricks

Alignment works not only on text but on cells containing numbers as well.

Any Way to Do Upside-Down Text?

Nope.

Well, there is, but it's not a totally Excel solution: To create upside-down text, enter the text in a drawing program, such as the Paint program that comes with Windows. Use the text tool to create your text. Then use the painting program's drawing tools to rotate the text until it is upside down.

Save the upside-down text in a graphics file, or copy it from the painting program. Then place it into the worksheet as an image. That's the only way you can get upside-down text in a worksheet.

What's the Best Way to Align a Date?

Dates are generally hard to line up when the digits are not consistent. For example:

```
3/6/05
12/19/05
```

Obviously, those two dates will look ugly whether aligned left, right, or center.

For lining up days and months, I use the "6-Mar" format, right-aligned, as shown in the first column of Figure 12.9. The "6-Mar-2005" format (column 2) also works right-aligned, as does "March 6, 2005" in the third column. These patterns are chosen in the Number tab of the Format Cells dialog box.

6-Mar	6-Mar-2005	March 6, 2005
12-Mar	12-Mar-2005	March 12, 2005
24-Mar	24-Mar-2005	March 24, 2005
31-Mar	31-Mar-2005	March 31, 2005
1-Apr	1-Apr-2005	April 1, 2005
4-Apr	4-Apr-2005	April 4, 2005
8-Apr	8-Apr-2005	April 8, 2005
13-Apr	13-Apr-2005	April 13, 2005
1-May	1-May-2005	May 1, 2005

Figure 12.9 Good formats for lining up dates

How Can I Get These Numbers to Line Up?

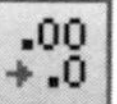

The main reason why some numbers don't line up is the decimal place. To adjust the decimal place, use the Increase Decimal and Decrease Decimal buttons on the formatting toolbar: Select the numbers, and then experiment with the buttons until you get the values lined up as you like.

I Can Make $ and % Quickly, but How Do I Undo That Format?

There are actually three buttons on the Formatting toolbar for quickly formatting numbers in three styles—yes, they are styles as defined in the Style dialog box:

Currency style: Formats the value using a dollar sign, with commas at the thousands place, and two digits after the decimal.

Percent style: Formats the value as a percent.

Remember that 1 is actually 100 percent. Percent values less than 100 percent are less than 1: .5 is 50 percent; .02 is 2 percent. This always goofs people up.

Comma style: Same as Currency style, but without the dollar sign.

One thing I don't like about Comma style is that it adds the decimal point and two digits. Of course, this can be fixed:

1. Choose Format ➤ Style.
2. Choose Comma from the drop-down list.
3. Click the Modify button.

   In the Format Cells dialog box, Number tab, reduce the number of decimal places to zero.
4. Click OK.
5. Click OK to close the Style dialog box.

   And the Comma style is changed for the entire workbook.

How Come Some Numbers Line Up Differently than Others?

What you're probably describing are numbers formatted in the Accounting format. That format uses parentheses to display negative values. Because of that, all the positive numbers are given a little extra space on the right, so that positive and negative numbers line up, as shown in Figure 12.10.

No space on the right — *Space on the right for parenthesis*

General	Number	Currency	Accounting
10000	10,000.00	$10,000.00	$ 10,000.00
1000	1,000.00	$1,000.00	$ 1,000.00
100	100.00	$100.00	$ 100.00
10	10.00	$10.00	$ 10.00
1	1.00	$1.00	$ 1.00
-1	-1.00	($1.00)	$ (1.00)
-10	-10.00	($10.00)	$ (10.00)

Figure 12.10 Numbers line up differently depending on the format.

So if you have a column of numbers, and one of the cells is formatted with the Accounting style and the others are in some other style, then yes, they will not line up properly. The solution is to use the same type of format for all numbers.

The Currency Style button on the Formatting toolbar actually applies the Accounting *style format. Weird, huh?*

Don't Be Dumb and Screw Up on These Common Number Format Misconceptions.

In addition to giving a little space on the right for the parenthesis, there are other subtle differences between the number formats.

For example, in Figure 12.10, notice how the Currency and Accounting formats display the currency symbol ($)? Accountants like the dollar sign off to the left of a cell, whereas the Currency format keeps it snug against the number.

Why Do Accountants Sometimes Put a Dollar Sign at the Top of a Column of Values but Not for Every Value?

I don't know. I suppose it's because they're trained or beaten that way. For example, in Figure 12.11 you see a column of dollar values formatted the way your typical accountant would format things: dollar values on the top and bottom, other values in the middle.

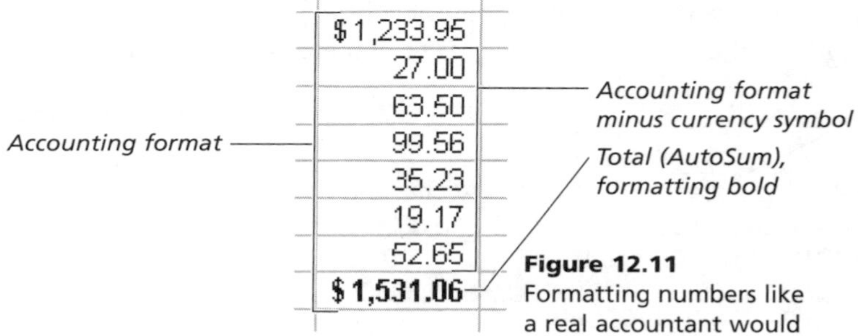

Figure 12.11
Formatting numbers like a real accountant would

Here's how to format such a column:

1. Type in all the numbers first.
2. Σ In the final, Total cell, click the AutoSum button on the Standard toolbar, and then press Enter.

   This automatically inserts the column's sum or total into the bottom box.
3. Drag to select the entire column, including the total.
4. Press Ctrl+1 and click the Number tab.
5. Select Accounting from the Category list.

   Ensure that two decimal places are selected, as well as the $ symbol.
6. Click OK.

   Almost there.

7. Now reselect the column, but not the top or bottom value.
8. Press Ctrl+1 again.
9. From the Symbol drop-down list choose None.
10. Click OK.

And your list is formatted in a manner that would make an accounting teacher weep bitter tears of joy.

In Figure 12.11, the total was also formatted in bold, so that it's more apparent it's a total and not just some burp in the column formatting.

How Can I Effectively Use Color?

Color can be used in many ways, but most importantly color can provide handy mental links to certain areas in the worksheet. For example, many of the number formats can display negative values in red text. That's one great way to draw attention to a certain part of a worksheet—even better if you have a color printer.

The Font Color button on the Formatting toolbar is used to color text fonts. One example of effectively using color would be to color similar items in a worksheet with similar text colors. For example, color code values by region or salesperson.

The use of color fonts is especially effective if they're scattered in a table. In Figure 12.12, the regions with the best results for the quarter are colored in red; the worst results are colored in blue (pretend you can see this on the grayscale figure.)

	A	B	C	D	E	F
1		**Q1**	**Q2**	**Q3**	**Q4**	
2	**North East**	226	417	212	411	
3	**East Coast**	415	131	619	667	
4	**South**	918	668	714	664	
5	**Southwest**	127	655	916	415	
6	**California**	56	96	202	924	
7	**Midwest**	97	412	212	37	
8	**Northwest**	112	606	208	266	
9						

Red text

Blue text

Figure 12.12 Using color to highlight elements in a table

Fill Color can be used to shade cells in the worksheet. This can be done for design purposes. For example, jump ahead to Figure 12.20, and you'll see how color is used to highlight design elements in the invoice. Better still, way back in Figure 12.8, color is used to help identify rows in a table.

Unless you just want a blob of color, be sure to choose a light shade to fill your cells. Darker shades make the cell contents harder to see.

How Do I Apply the Color?

Whether you're coloring text or filling a cell, the color is applied the same way:

1. Select the cell(s) to color.
2. Click the proper button on the toolbar: Fill Color to shade a cell's background or Font Color merely to color the font.

If you want to choose a new color, click the menu button by the icon to display a drop-down color palette. That shows 40 predefined colors you can use, or you can select the No Fill or Automatic option to remove the color.

Automatic merely resets the cell's text color to whatever color the current style defines.

What's the Difference between a Pattern and a Color?

You want to use colors; you want to avoid patterns.

Well, not all the time; patterns can be used as design elements. But as the background "color" for any cells with information, patterns tend to be too annoying to be useful.

Patterns are doled out in the Format Cells dialog box, Patterns tab, shown in Figure 12.13. But to set the patterns, you have to click the drop-down button, which displays the menu shown in Figure 12.14.

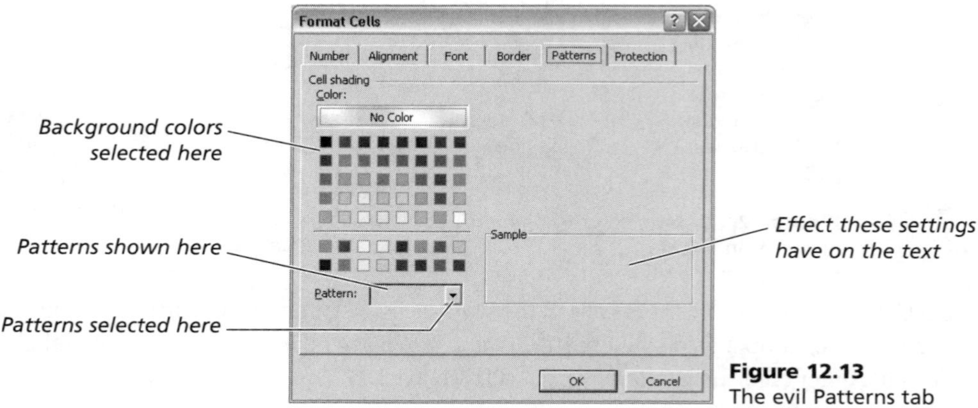

Figure 12.13
The evil Patterns tab

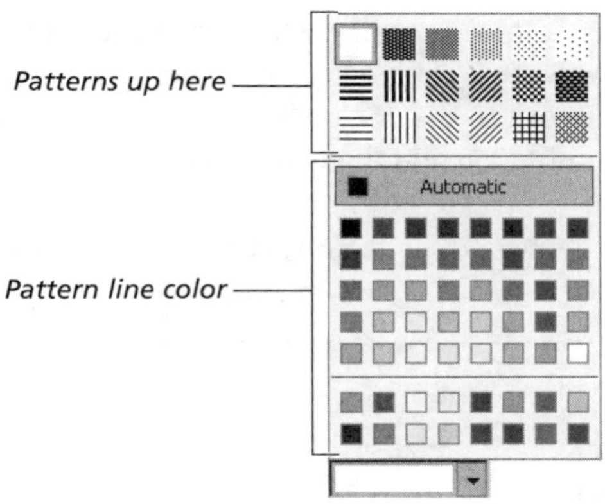

Figure 12.14
Selecting a pattern

Selecting a pattern is a two-step process. First, select the pattern from the top part of the pop-up menu (Figure 12.14). Then select a color from the bottom part. The color affects only the pattern. If you want to set a color for the cell's background, you have to do that from the main part of the dialog box (Figure 12.13).

Again, most people find the use of patterns to shade cells extremely annoying. Try to use them as design elements only.

What about Drawing Lines and Boxes and Stuff?

Excel shares the same Drawing toolbar as Word. For information on drawing various objects in Excel, refer to Chapter 4 on Word, "O the Sacrilege of Drawing in a Word Processor!" The instructions there apply to both Excel and Word.

Printing Woes and Worries

Despite this section's heading, it has nothing to do with the anxiety you can get over printing bad news. Ideally, you want the worksheet to be accurate and informative, regardless of the negative news it may feature. But that's not the point here: The point is printing the worksheet, which is actually quite painless—if it weren't for the minor quirks and worries solved in the following sections.

Is Printing Your Worksheet an Unwelcome Surprise?

Unlike other programs, worksheets don't rely on the paper's page size to create apparent printing boundaries. So you can never really tell how close you are to the edge of a page when you're working on a worksheet—which is okay, I suppose.

The trick I used to pull was using Print Preview. By choosing File ➤ Print Preview or clicking the Print Preview button, you can see how your document prints, one page at a time. But more important than that, when you return to the document, you can see dotted lines representing the page boundary (Figure 12.15) and then use those lines to help you keep a report or such all on one page.

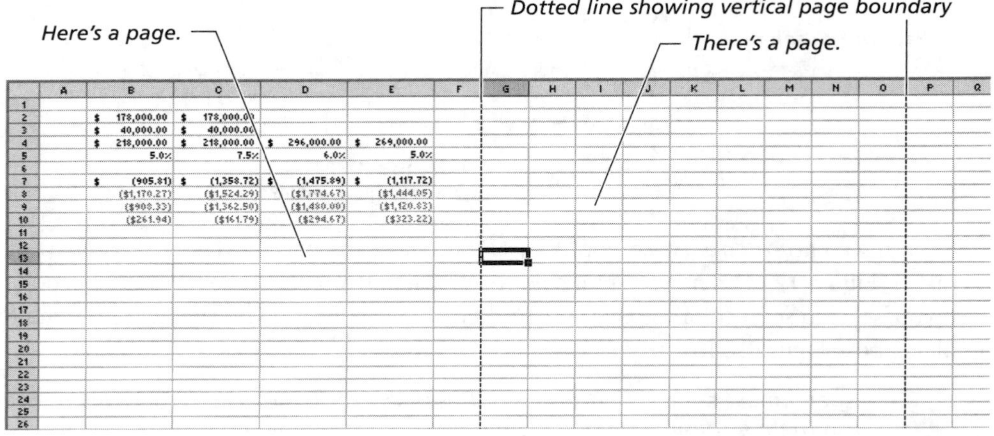

Horizontal page boundary down there (trust me)

Figure 12.15 Dotted lines appear in the worksheet after using Print Preview.

Alas, this is not the best way to deal with things.

Is There Any Other Way to See Where the Page Breaks Fall?

Of course! It's called Page Break Preview, a command that shows how there is an obvious need to know where page breaks are in a worksheet.

To view your entire worksheet and see its page breaks, choose View ➤ Page Break Preview. Instantly, or longer if you bought your computer locally, the screen shows a seriously scrunched up version of your worksheet with page breaks appearing as dotted blue lines, similar to what's shown in Figure 12.16.

Now you can see how the document can print—the big picture, if you will. But the best part is that you can manipulate the pages by dragging the page breaks or even adding new ones. Keep reading.

Do not try to edit your worksheet in Page Break Preview mode. You will go insane.

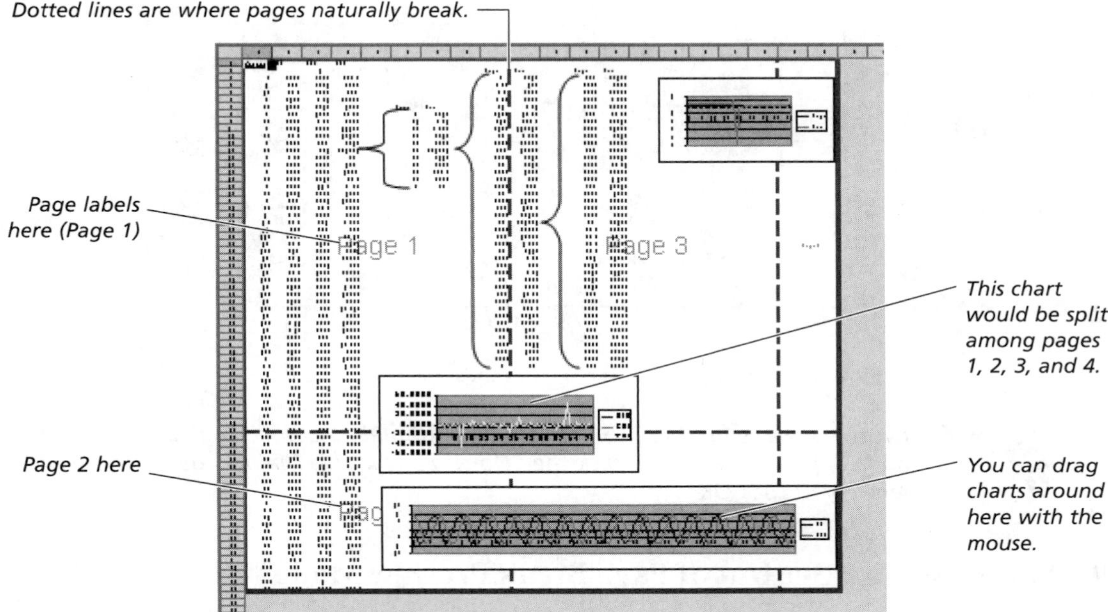
Dotted lines are where pages naturally break.
Page labels here (Page 1)
Page 1
Page 3
This chart would be split among pages 1, 2, 3, and 4.
Page 2 here
You can drag charts around here with the mouse.

Figure 12.16 Page Break Preview in action

When Do I Need to Move a Page Break?

First, before you decide you need to move a page break, determine whether the entire sheet can't print better in Landscape mode.

For example, in Figure 12.17 you see the Page Break Preview, but the paper is still printing in a Portrait representation. If you choose File ➤ Page Setup, choose Landscape orientation, and then click OK, the worksheet fits, as seen in Figure 12.18. There's no need to mess with the page breaks in that case.

Ooo! Nasty page break.
Page 1
Page 2

	A	B	C	D	E	F	G	H
1								
2		$ 5,600.00	$ 6,160.00	$ 6,776.00	$ 7,453.60	$ 8,198.96	$ 9,018.86	$ 9,920.74
3		$ 9,200.00	$ 10,120.00	$ 11,132.00	$ 12,245.20	$ 13,469.72	$ 14,816.69	$ 16,298.36
4		$ 15,000.00	$ 16,500.00	$ 18,150.00	$ 19,965.00	$ 21,961.50	$ 24,157.65	$ 26,573.42
5		$ 15,200.00	$ 16,720.00	$ 18,392.00	$ 20,231.20	$ 22,254.32	$ 24,479.75	$ 26,927.73
6		$ 1,900.00	$ 2,090.00	$ 2,299.00	$ 2,528.90	$ 2,781.79	$ 3,059.97	$ 3,365.97
7		$ 850.00	$ 935.00	$ 1,028.50	$ 1,131.35	$ 1,244.49	$ 1,368.93	$ 1,505.83
8		$ 17,600.00	$ 19,360.00	$ 21,296.00	$ 23,425.60	$ 25,768.16	$ 28,344.98	$ 31,179.47
9		$ 27,000.00	$ 29,700.00	$ 32,670.00	$ 35,937.00	$ 39,530.70	$ 43,483.77	$ 47,832.15
10		$ [illegible]	$ 16,940.00	$ 18,634.00	$ 20,497.40	$ 22,547.14	$ 24,801.85	$ [illegible]
11		$ 5,700.00	$ 6,270.00	$ 6,897.00	$ 7,586.70	$ 8,345.37	$ [illegible]	$ 10,097.90
12		$ 9,200.00	$ 10,120.00	$ 11,132.00	$ 12,245.20	$ 13,469.72	$ 14,816.69	$ 16,298.36
13		$ 36,000.00	$ 39,600.00	$ 43,560.00	$ 47,916.00	$ 52,707.60	$ 57,978.36	$ 63,776.20
14		$ 40,000.00	$ 44,000.00	$ 48,400.00	$ 53,240.00	$ 58,564.00	$ 64,420.40	$ 70,862.44
15		$ 198,650.00	$ 218,515.00	$ 240,366.50	$ 264,403.15	$290,843.47	$ 319,927.81	$ 351,920.59
16		5.0%	105.0%	205.0%	305.0%	405.0%	505.0%	605.0%
17								
18		$ (825.41)	$ (19,066.95)	$ (40,948.55)	$ (67,015.79)	$ (97,887.00)	$ (134,262.30)	$(176,933.78)
19		($1,066.40)	($19,120.06)	($41,062.61)	($67,202.47)	($98,159.67)	($134,636.29)	($177,426.63)
20		($827.71)	($19,120.06)	($41,062.61)	($67,202.47)	($98,159.67)	($134,636.29)	($177,426.63)
21		($238.69)	($0.00)	$0.00	$0.00	$0.00	$0.00	$0.00
22								

Figure 12.17 A nasty page break due to Portrait orientation

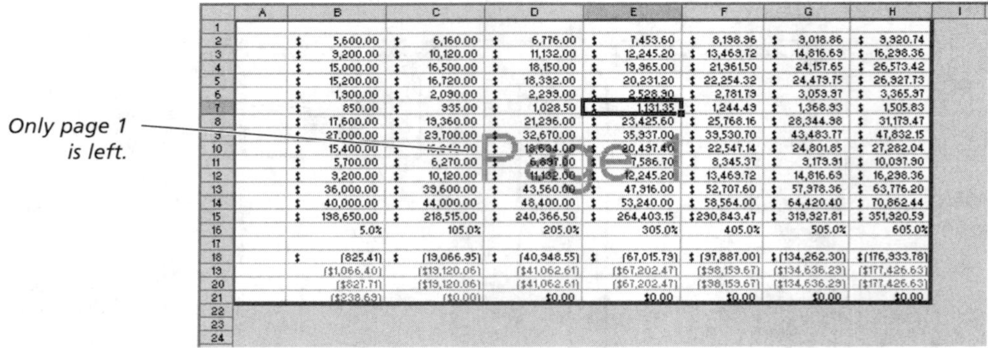

	A	B	C	D	E	F	G	H	I
1									
2		$ 5,600.00	$ 6,160.00	$ 6,776.00	$ 7,453.60	$ 8,198.96	$ 9,018.86	$ 9,920.74	
3		$ 9,200.00	$ 10,120.00	$ 11,132.00	$ 12,245.20	$ 13,469.72	$ 14,816.69	$ 16,298.36	
4		$ 15,000.00	$ 16,500.00	$ 18,150.00	$ 19,965.00	$ 21,961.50	$ 24,157.65	$ 26,573.42	
5		$ 15,200.00	$ 16,720.00	$ 18,392.00	$ 20,231.20	$ 22,254.32	$ 24,479.75	$ 26,927.73	
6		$ 1,900.00	$ 2,090.00	$ 2,299.00	$ 2,528.90	$ 2,781.79	$ 3,059.97	$ 3,365.97	
7		$ 850.00	$ 935.00	$ 1,028.50	$ 1,131.35	$ 1,244.49	$ 1,368.93	$ 1,505.83	
8		$ 17,600.00	$ 19,360.00	$ 21,296.00	$ 23,425.60	$ 25,768.16	$ 28,344.98	$ 31,179.47	
9		$ 27,000.00	$ 29,700.00	$ 32,670.00	$ 35,937.00	$ 39,530.70	$ 43,483.77	$ 47,832.15	
10		$ 15,400.00	$ [illegible]	$ 18,634.00	$ 20,497.40	$ 22,547.14	$ 24,801.85	$ 27,282.04	
11		$ 5,700.00	$ 6,270.00	$ 6,897.00	$ 7,586.70	$ 8,345.37	$ 9,179.91	$ 10,097.90	
12		$ 9,200.00	$ 10,120.00	$ 11,132.00	$ 12,245.20	$ 13,469.72	$ 14,816.69	$ 16,298.36	
13		$ 36,000.00	$ 39,600.00	$ 43,560.00	$ 47,916.00	$ 52,707.60	$ 57,978.36	$ 63,776.20	
14		$ 40,000.00	$ 44,000.00	$ 48,400.00	$ 53,240.00	$ 58,564.00	$ 64,420.40	$ 70,862.44	
15		$ 198,650.00	$ 218,515.00	$ 240,366.50	$ 264,403.15	$290,843.47	$ 319,927.81	$ 351,920.59	
16		5.0%	105.0%	205.0%	305.0%	405.0%	505.0%	605.0%	
17									
18		$ (825.41)	$ (19,066.95)	$ (40,948.55)	$ (67,015.79)	$ (97,887.00)	$ (134,262.30)	$(176,933.78)	
19		($1,066.40)	($19,120.06)	($41,062.61)	($67,202.47)	($98,159.67)	($134,636.29)	($177,426.63)	
20		($827.71)	($19,120.06)	($41,062.61)	($67,202.47)	($98,159.67)	($134,636.29)	($177,426.63)	
21		($238.69)	($0.00)	$0.00	$0.00	$0.00	$0.00	$0.00	
22									
23									
24									

Figure 12.18 Page break is gone in Landscape orientation!

If you see that stupid Welcome dialog box displayed before Page Break Preview mode appears, be sure to click the "Do Not Show This Dialog Again" check box before you click OK.

Uh, Now How Do I Get Out of Page Break Preview Mode?

You can't. You've permanently altered Excel and the program cannot be changed back. Sucker! Ha-ha!

Really?

No. Choose View ➤ Normal from the menu.

Printing in Landscape Mode Doesn't Help, So I'd Like to Know How to Move a Page Break.

Occasionally, despite your best efforts, the stuff you want printed on one page spreads into two, as shown in Figure 12.19. The solution is to drag the page break over until all your stuff fits on a single page, as shown in Figure 12.20.

Here is how you can do that:

1. Choose View ➤ Page Break Preview.
2. Point the mouse at the dashed, blue page break.

   The mouse pointer changes to a left and right pointing arrow, meaning that's the direction you can drag the page break.
3. Drag the vertical page break to the right, just outside column F on the screen.

   Refer to Figure 12.19.

   This still, unfortunately, leaves you with an extra blank page that prints, shown in Figure 12.20.

4. Drag the right edge of the page over one cell.

   Yes, you can drag the page edge. The final result is all set to print on one page.

In Figures 12.19 and 12.20, a better solution would most likely be to resize column D, which looks rather wide. Upon first glance, it doesn't appear that there's anything in the worksheet that requires that column to be so wide.

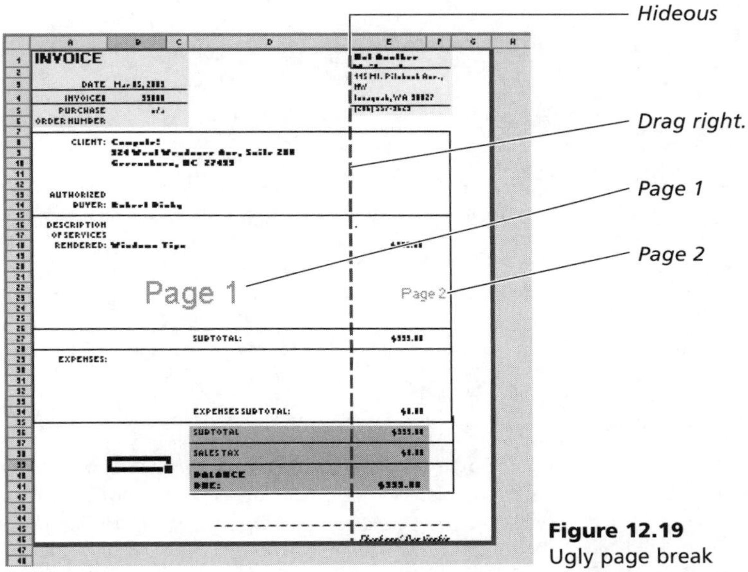

Figure 12.19
Ugly page break

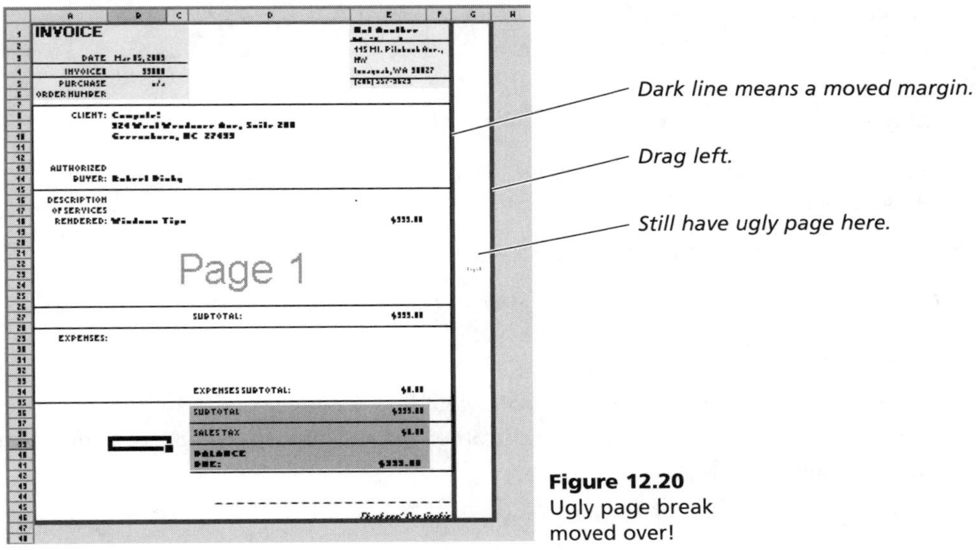

Figure 12.20
Ugly page break moved over!

These page break tricks are really printing tricks. Basically, Excel just scrunches up the worksheet, reducing its printed size a bit to help you fit it all on one page. (After all, it's not the paper that's changing size here.)

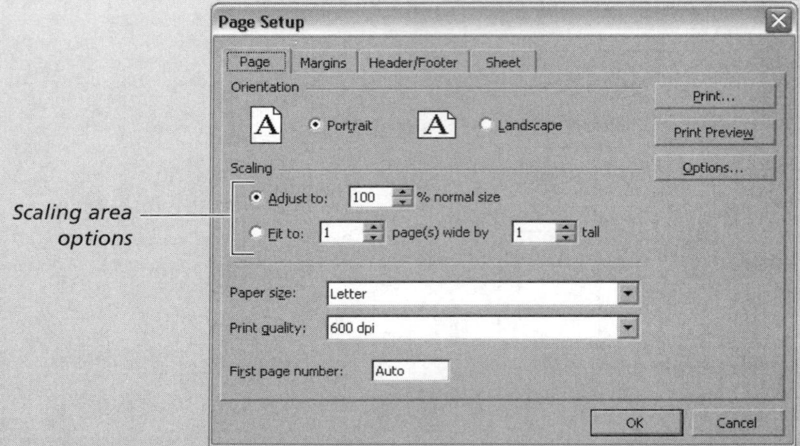

If you choose File ➢ Page Setup, you'll see a Scaling area in the Page tab, shown above. There are two options. The first, "Adjust To," is used to scale the entire document, reducing its printed size so that it fits on the page according to how you broke things up in Page Break Preview.

The second option, "Fit to," allows you to select how many sheets you want the entire worksheet to print on, regardless of size. So you could force the thing all onto one page if you like. Or choose two pages wide by one page tall to see it on two pages.

Can I Split One Page into Two?

Pages can be split as many times as you like, thanks to the handy Insert ➢ Page Break command. Here's how to work it:

1. Choose View ➢ Page Break Preview.
2. Click the mouse to select the page you want to break up.
3. Choose Insert ➢ Page Break.

   Instead of splitting horizontally, as Word would, your single page is split into fourths with two page breaks, one horizontal and the other vertical. Note that this does affect other page breaks in the document.

4. Move the page breaks to where you want them.

   Drag the page breaks around until your document looks as peachy and as keen as you like.

How Can I Remove a Page Break?

Two ways: First, you can drag the page break off the page.

Second, you can click the page break and choose Insert ➤ Remove Page Break from the menu—though oftentimes this command doesn't seem to show up.

I'm All Screwed Up with Page Breaks and Would Like to See Things Restored to the Way They Originally Were.

This is easy: Right-click in the print area and choose "Reset All Page Breaks" from the pop-up menu.

How Can I Get Rid of This Blank Page?

Suppose you have a setup such as the one shown in Figure 12.21. After adjusting the margins and moving a few of the charts around, you discover a blank page in the middle of the worksheet. According to Figure 12.21, it's page 4.

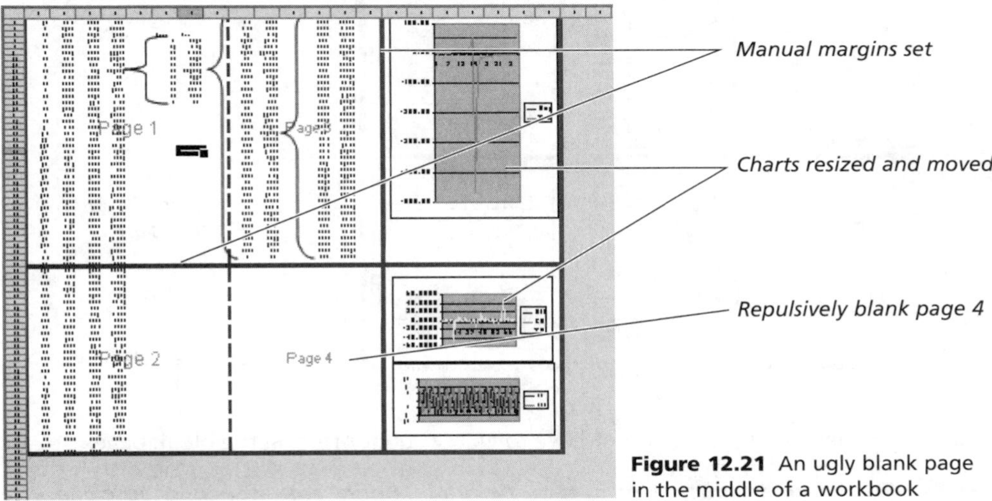

Figure 12.21 An ugly blank page in the middle of a workbook

The secret here is to use the Print dialog box and direct it *not* to print page 4:

1. Choose View ➤ Page Break Preview.

   And you'll see something like Figure 12.21.

2. Use the mouse to select a large chunk of the area you want to print.

   Yes, you can use the mouse to select things in Page Break Preview; just be careful that you select all of the text on the page and don't miss any rows.

3. Choose File ➤ Print Area ➤ Set Print Area.

This defines the area you selected as printable. Nothing else will print.

Now if you have a weird shape, as shown in Figure 12.21, then you'll need to add to the print area.

4. Select the next chunk of the worksheet you want to print.
5. Right-click the selection and choose "Add to Print Area" from the pop-up menu.
6. Repeat Steps 4 and 5 until all the pages you want printed are selected.

You'll end up with something like Figure 12.22, where the blank page is simply not selected as part of the print area.

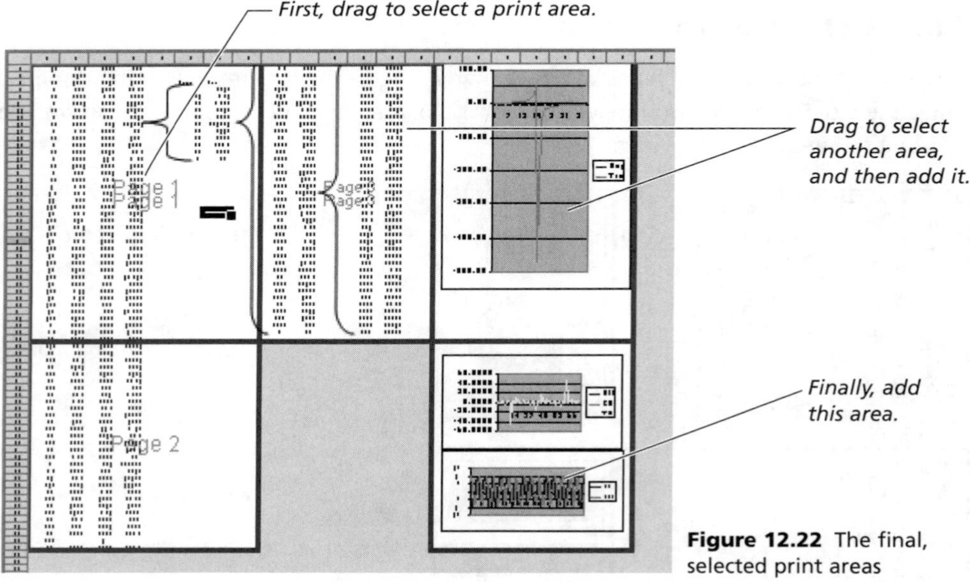

First, drag to select a print area.
Drag to select another area, and then add it.
Finally, add this area.
Page 1
Page 3
Page 2

Figure 12.22 The final, selected print areas

Now you can go ahead and print and not have to worry about printing the blank page.

To restore the document so that the original print area is seen, choose File ➤ Print Area ➤ Clear Print Area.

Can't I Also Use the Ctrl Key to Select Multiple Parts of the Worksheet?

Yes. You can hold down the Ctrl key while you use the mouse to select several cells or groups of cells at once. Then you can choose File ➤ Print Area ➤ Set Print Area to set the multiple portions of your document as a single print area, all at once.

Can I Change the Order of When Things Print?

Not really. In the Page Setup dialog box, Sheet tab, there is a section on "Page Order," as shown in Figure 12.23. Your only two options are listed in the figure. (Choose File ➤ Page Setup to see this dialog box.)

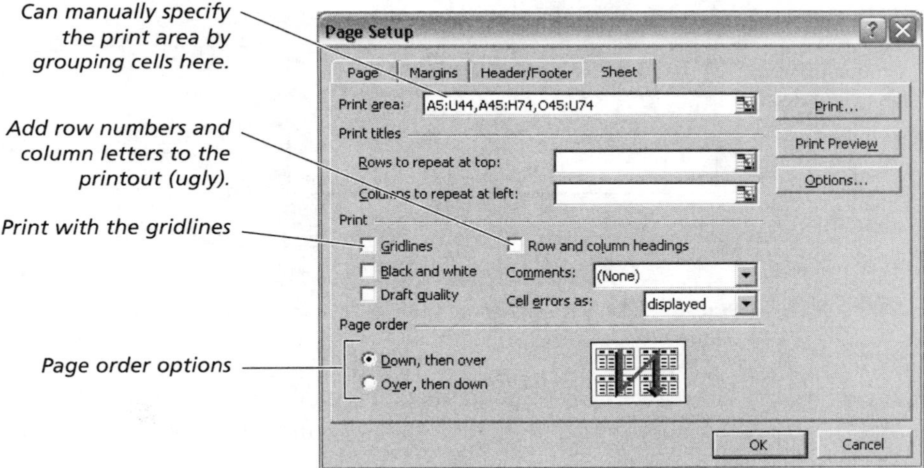

Figure 12.23 Various goodies in the Page Setup dialog box

How Can I Turn the Grid On or Off during Printing?

Refer to Figure 12.23: The grid can be turned on or off by clicking the Gridlines check box in the Page Setup/Sheet dialog box.

Note that sometimes what you may see as a grid may actually be borders or lines drawn in the document. Those must be manually removed (lines) or reformatted (borders).

I Need the Header to Include the Document's Title, Not the Filename.

The header and footer information for a worksheet is kept in the Header/Footer tab of the Page Setup dialog box. Choose File ➤ Page Setup, and then click the Header/Footer tab to get there. Figure 12.24 shows what it looks like.

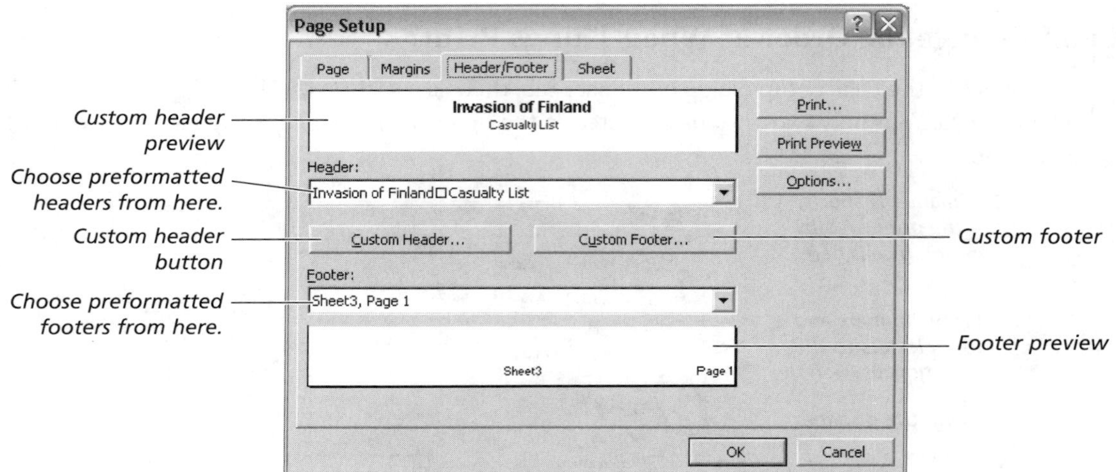

Figure 12.24 Setting headers and footers in the Page Setup dialog box

The drop-down lists by Header and Footer contain common information usually found in worksheet printouts, such as the sheet name, workbook filename, and other various and sundry things.

To create a custom header or footer, click the Custom Header or Footer button. You'll see a dialog box such as the one shown in Figure 12.25. As you can see, there are some buttons for automatically inserting information, plus formatting your text. And you have three positions in which to place things: Left (flush left), Center (centered), and Right (flush right), according to the figure.

To include a document's title in the header, click the Custom button and type the document's title into the "Center Section" box, as shown in Figure 12.25.

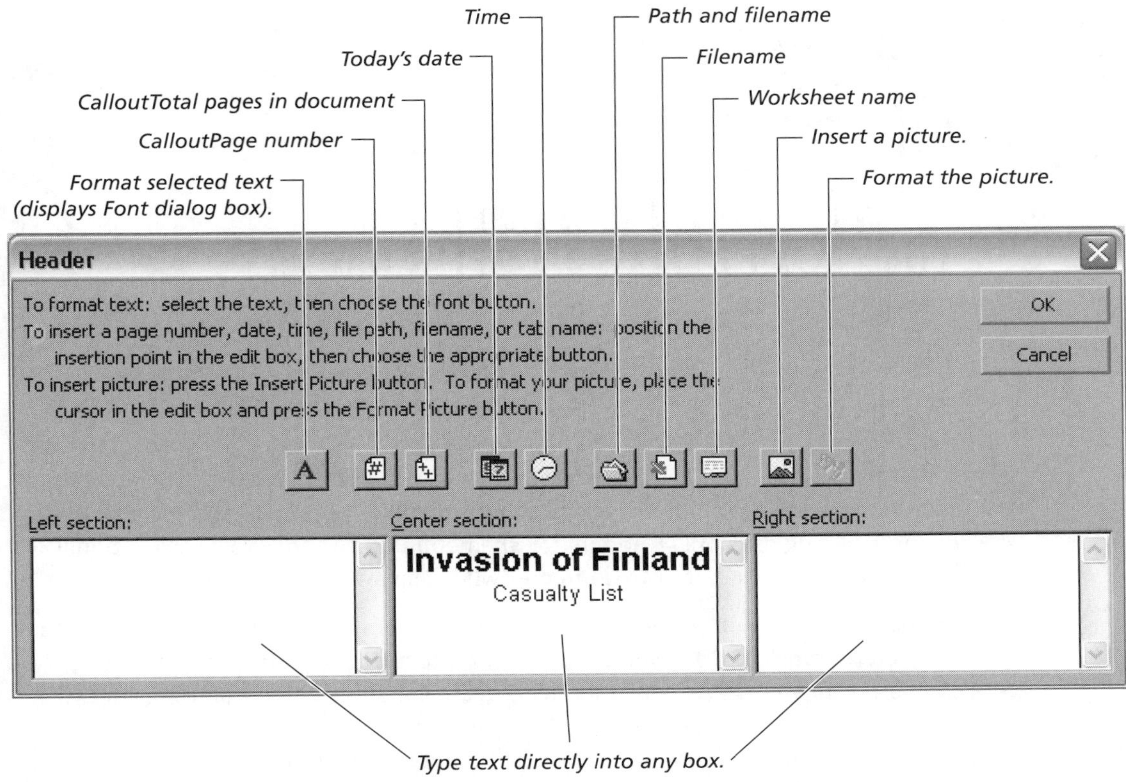

Figure 12.25 Creating a custom header

13 Oh No! The Horrible Math Chapter!

What better number for a math chapter than 13, huh?

Here's the whole deal with math on a computer. This is very simple, so you can rest your furrowed brow and release the tension in your shoulders. Ready? Good. The truth is that it's the *computer* that does the math, not you. Whew! No worrying about whether you still remember your multiplication tables or understand the subtle nuances of long division. Denominator, shemominator! Thanks to his exceptional mathematical abilities, it's Mr. Computer who deals with all of that tough stuff.

Of course, *you* are not off the hook. While it's the computer that does the math, it's your job to translate whatever it is you want into a language the computer understands. Fortunately, Excel is very forgiving and helpful to the point of being annoying. Combine that with the genteel way this chapter presents mathematical concepts necessary, useful, and obscure, and you're bound to actually enjoy doing math in Excel. Promise!

Quandaries Explained and Solutions Revealed:

- Properly using math symbols in Excel
- Raising to power and lowering to roots
- Going positive
- Finding the remainder
- Getting the total of a column, row, or chunk
- Finding uses for the COUNT function
- Mixing text with addition

Basic, Annoying Math

One day, should I live long enough, I am going to re-create the basic math primer for all humans in the galaxy. That's because it's almost universally accepted that math is one of the worst things you can force your brain to do (beyond, of course, trying to understand avant-garde art). There's a reason for this (see the sidebar nearby), and I won't dwell on any of that here. Just let me start out with the simple and you can take it from there.

Why Isn't the ÷ Symbol Used in Excel?

Quick answer: Because it's not on your keyboard.

Rather than make the keyboard this colossal, imposing, button-filled monster, the computer designers were forced to choose only a few limited keys. Because the / (slash) key can also be used to separate items, and it's used to set up a fraction, it was determined that it could double as the division symbol for a computer—just as * doubles for the x in multiplication.

The ÷ is the division symbol. In long division, the bracket around the numbers is known as a gazinta. *For example: $4\overline{)12}$ reads, "4 gazinta 12 how many times?"*

Don't Be Dumb and Forget These Basic Mathematical Symbols!

The key to remembering the computer's mathematical symbols is your keyboard's numeric keypad. Clutching the edges of the keypad like barnacles on a hull are the four basic computer math symbols, also used in Excel:

+	*Addition*	*	*Multiplication*
–	*Subtraction*	/	*Division*

Officially these are known as operators, *because they perform a mathematical operation on two or more numbers. Excel's pantheon also includes the following symbols:*

% *Calculate (display) the value as a percentage.*

^ *Express exponentiation, such as 2^3, which is the same as 2^3.*

– *Negation; makes positive numbers negative and negative numbers positive.*

You Must Know This: Why Math Is Made to Drive You Nuts

The first math book was written over 2,500 years ago by Euclid. Or it could have been someone else who was also named Euclid, seeing how Euclid was a common name back then and how others wrote books and often attributed the authorship to some great (and potentially dead) person.

There are several odd things about that first math book.

First, almost every textbook written today that purports to teach math is based on the same organization as that original book, written over 2,500 years ago.

Second, the book was written in ancient Greek, and some argue that it was never fully translated from ancient Greek into any modern tongue.

Third, and most curious, the book was never *intended to teach the average human being how to do math. (Does it all make sense now?)*

Euclid was a Pythagorean, a group consisting of followers of Pythagoras. You remember him? Pythagoras brought us the famous theorem about triangles, the Pythagorean theorem—which I'm not getting into here. Pythagoras was the first mathematician, and the Pythagoreans were those who followed him, that is, other *mathematicians.*

The Pythagoreans flourished in Egypt, principally in Alexandria. They were Greeks, not Egyptians, remnants of Alexander the Great's conquest of the world around 500 B.C. Euclid was a member of this group but was also the librarian of the great library that Alexander established on that Mediterranean coastal city. That's where the link between Euclid the Pythagorean and Euclid the author comes into play.

While you might think of the Pythagoreans as noble, philosophy-spouting Greeks, and that may have been true, when it came to math they mostly kept their mouths shut. That's because the Pythagoreans were pretty much a secret society, almost like a cult. Their purpose was to practice math and produce interesting mathematical things for others—like accountants do today. They did not exist to teach math to the unwashed masses. Far from it, their goal was to express math in some of the most cryptic manners possible, specifically to keep it from the masses and further solidify their position in society.

And there you have the problem: Today's math is being taught from a book written 2,500 years ago, a book whose author believed that no one outside a select group should ever learn math. Why does learning math hurt? Because Euclid wanted it to hurt! It's supposed to be awkward and cryptic and difficult to learn. The Pythagoreans didn't want it any other way!

So the next time you sit down and puzzle over some mathematical problem, accept the fact that clever Greeks two thousand years ago set you up for a fall. Now you can feel good when it comes to "not getting it" regarding math.

How Is the % Sign an Operator?

The % symbol serves both to format a value and input that value as a percent. For example, type 20% into a cell and you see 20% displayed. But the value entered into the cell is 0.2 (two tenths).

This can also happen when you're inputting a long formula. Say you need to calculate a price plus 8.2% sales tax. Here is the formula:

```
=10.99+(10.99*8.2%)
```

That is, the original price of the item, 10.99, plus the sales tax, which is the price of the item times 8.2 percent.

Remember that the parentheses specify order but also organize the items. Here you are talking about two different prices: the price of the item and the price of the sales tax. The price of the sales tax *is not* 8.2% (or 0.082). A percentage must be calculated on a value for it to work; otherwise it's not a percentage, just a value.

Also remember that I prefer to keep numbers listed in cells and have the formulas operate on cells instead of the numbers directly. In that case, consider Figure 13.1 as another potential solution to the sales tax problem.

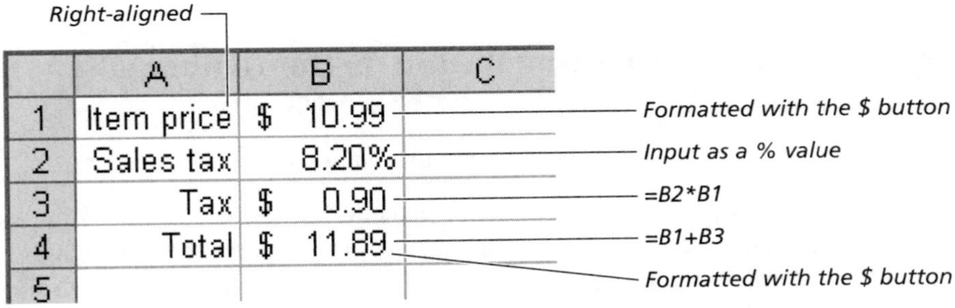

Right-aligned

	A	B	C
1	Item price	$ 10.99	
2	Sales tax	8.20%	
3	Tax	$ 0.90	
4	Total	$ 11.89	
5			

Formatted with the $ button
Input as a % value
=B2*B1
=B1+B3
Formatted with the $ button

Figure 13.1 Breaking out the sales tax percentage formula

Create such a thing to play with:

1. Fill in column A as shown in Figure 13.1.

   All items are right-aligned.

2.  Type a value into cell B1, such as `10.99`; format the value by clicking the Currency button on the Formatting toolbar.

3. Into cell B2, type `8.2%`.

   You do not need to use the equal sign, nor do you need to click the % format button. Entering the % operator automatically make the value a percent *and* formats the cell.

4. Into cell B3 type the formula =B2*B1.

   The added tax value is the sales tax percentage times the original price.

5. Into cell B4 type the formula = B1+B3.

   Or, the total purchase cost is the original price plus the added tax.

6. Select cells B3 and B4 and format them with the Currency button.

   If you want a homework assignment, consider naming the cells:

- Name cell B1 ItemPrice.
- Name cell B2 SalesTaxRate.
- Name cell B3 SalesTax.
- Now the formulas will read a little better. In cell B3 you'll have

  ```
  =SalesTaxRate*ItemPrice
  ```

- And in cell B4 you'll have the logical

  ```
  =ItemPrice+SalesTax
  ```

Why Does the % Formatting Button on the Toolbar Often Give a Wrong Amount in a Cell?

It, in fact, does not; you've entered the wrong value.

If you want to input a value as a percent, use the % operator. Otherwise, if you click the % button on the Formatting toolbar, you get the percent equivalent of whatever value is in the cell—which is usually wrong; the value 100 formats out to 10000%, which is true. The value 1 formats to 100%.

How Do You Do That "Raised-to-the-Power" Thing?

The raised-to-the-power thing—known as *exponentiation* in mathematician coffee klatches—is done with the caret symbol, Shift+6 on the keyboard, which produces the ^ thing.

If you ever need this doohickey, then it works like this: Suppose you're creating a table of holy computer numbers:

1. Enter the values 0 through 10 into column E.

   If you're clever, you'll remember how to fill a series so that this takes only one step. Otherwise, if you forgot how to fill a series—which happens—you'll happily take these substeps:

   a. Enter the value 0 into a cell.

   b. Select that cell.

c. Drag the cell (by its lower-right corner) with the mouse's right button; drag down 10 cells. That's to cell E11.

d. Choose "Fill Series" from the pop-up menu.

And there is your column, 0 through 10.

2. Into cell F1, type `=2^E1`.

This reads, "The value of this cell is equal to 2 'raised to the power' of the value in cell E1 (on the left)." Ah, yes: a *relative* reference.

3. Drag to fill cell F1 down through cell F11.

And the end result looks like Figure 13.2, with power values in column E and holy computer numbers in column F.

D	E	F	G
	0	1	
	1	2	
	2	4	
	3	8	
	4	16	
	5	32	
	6	64	
	7	128	
	8	256	
	9	512	
	10	1024	

Figure 13.2
A handy holy computer number table

Excel also uses the POWER function to raise a value to specific power. It works just like the ^, but as a function. So to modify column F in Figure 13.2, you could change the formula in cell F1 (Step 2) to be:

```
=POWER(2,E1)
```

Then drag-fill down to get the same results.

Is There an Opposite for the Raised-to-the-Power Thing?

Yes: The LOG function is essentially a backward raised-to-the-power thing. I realize how much logarithms pained you back in school, but they're essentially variations on the raised-to-the-power theme.

Continuing from the example in the previous section:

4. Into cell G1 type `=LOG(F1,2)`.

This reads, "The contents of this cell equal the value of cell F1 'unraised' to the power of 2."

5. Fill-copy the formula down through cell G11.

The results are the same as column E; the original number is raised to the power of 2 in column F. But in column G it's "lowered" back to the original value. So here are the two formulas as they stand opposed to each other:

`value=base^number` OR `value=POWER(base,number)`

That's like saying *value=base*^{number}, or raising number *base* to the power *number* gives you a *value*. That clever little twisty can be undone by

`number=LOG(value,base)`

Or to put it another way (and close your eyes here if you're utterly confoosed):

`number=LOG(POWER(base,number),base)`

This silly function reads that the same number will be returned when you raise it to the same power as you lower it with the LOG function. I assume there is some cosmic significance to this and that the first person who discovered it was probably called a "genius." For a while, at least.

Okay. Time for a beverage!

Where Does the SQRT Function Figure into All of This?

SQRT is simply the square root function, not the "squirt" function. It returns the square root value of a number, or whatever value multiplied by itself equals another value.

The SQRT function has nothing to do with exponentiation; it is a multiplication function.

You Must Know This: Various Power and Raising-To Functions

Again: Excel does the math, but it's up to you to know which formula to plug in. The raising-to-the-power-of function, or exponentiation, is handled by the ^ symbol:

 *=value^power*

The cell's contents equal the value raised to the power. Lord only knows when you'll need something like that in a financial statement.

There are four other power functions in Excel: EXP, LN, LOG, and LOG10.

 *EXP is the base e logarithm. So =EXP(1) displays the value of e, or 2.718282. Only geeky scientists will know how best to use that number (though it comes up all the time in many common calculations).*

 *LN is the natural logarithm. It's the inverse of the EXP function—if that helps.*

 *LOG returns the logarithm of a number in whatever base you specify.*

 *LOG10 returns the base 10 logarithm of a number. (It's the same as =LOG(value,10).*

Is There a "Cube Root" Function?

Thankfully, no.

But because this is math, and you suffered through math just as I did, you know that there's always *something* going on. In this case, although there isn't a cube root companion to the SQRT function, there is still the POWER function.

You may recall from math (or probably not) that the square root of a value is the same thing as raising that value to the 1/2 power:

$4^{1/2} = 2$

Now they probably have a SQRT function because most of us numskulls don't remember that 1/2 "power" is the same as a square root. But it is. This function

```
=SQRT(number)
```

gives you the same answer as this function:

```
=POWER(number,1/2)
```

The cube root then? It's the 1/3 power. So to get the cube root of a number you use this function:

```
=POWER(number,1/3)
```

And I can only pray that you never really have to use such a function in real life.

I'm Trying to Use SQRT but Keep Getting #NUM! Errors. Why?

Excel is unable to calculate the square root of a negative number. This opens up a wormhole in mathematics having to deal with imaginary numbers, flagged by the constant *i*. Excel doesn't really give a damn about *i*, so the solution is instead to filter out the possibilities of calculating the square root of a negative number.

To eliminate the possibilities of a negative number inside the SQRT function, you need to use the ABS function. ABS returns the "absolute value" of a number, or the value of any number minus the minus sign. So ABS(–15) is 15. And ABS(4) is 4. Here's how you would put such a thing to work:

1. Type the following values into cells J1 through J4:

   `16    -4    10    -25`

2. Into cell K1 type `=SQRT(J1)`.
3. Fill-copy down from cell K1 through cell K4.

   And you'll see something similar to Figure 13.3. Obviously something in the universe is out of whack.

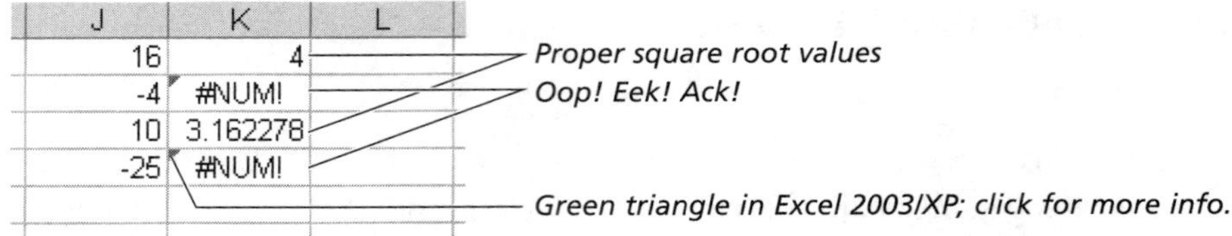

Figure 13.3 The dreadful result of finding the square root of negative numbers

Don't fret over the negative numbers. They happen. The solution is merely to make them non-negative and try again.

4. Edit the formula in cell K1 to read `=SQRT(ABS(J1))`.

Remember the F2 key to edit!

Formulas read from the inside out. So first you're converting the value of cell J1 into an absolute value—whacking off the negative part, if it exists. Then, with that guaranteed-to-be-positive number in there, you can safely and sanely calculate the square root, no errors possible.

5. Fill-copy down through cell K4.

And the values should happily be calculated, negative numbers be damned.

I've done woodworking and shop work enough to know that I do occasionally end up trying to calculate the square root of a negative number. It typically happens because I measure a distance in a manner that yields a negative number. By recalculating the distance, it's possible to come up with a positive number that doesn't cause the SQRT function to vomit all over the place, but, generally speaking, the ABS function ends up giving you a proper result despite the original negative numbers.

How Can I Get My Answer to Display to Two Decimal Places?

The number of decimal places displayed is controlled by the cell's number format: Select the cell(s) and press Ctrl+1; then click the Number tab. The Number, Currency, and Accounting formats all have a setting for the number of decimal places to appear in the cell.

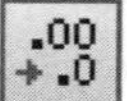

The decimal places can also be quickly set by using the Increase Decimal and Decrease Decimal buttons on the Formatting toolbar. Note that as the number of decimal places is changed, values are rounded up or down accordingly.

What's the Difference between Rounding and Truncating a Number?

The rounding functions take a number and bump it up or down to the next decimal place depending on which function you choose. Some functions round up, some round down, and some round depending on the number's value (like they taught in school).

Truncating functions are the executioner's axe: They just lop off part of a number, like WHACK! Leaving you with whatever is left over, again depending on the function.

There are various rounding and whacking functions available to you in Excel. Choose the proper one depending on how you want that value manipulated.

CEILING

Ceiling is a rounding-up function that lets you specify what to round the value up to. The format is

```
=CEILING(value,significance)
```

So if you want to round the value in cell A1 up to the nearest 10th spot, you would use

```
=CEILING(A1,0.1)
```

Or suppose they do away with the penny and everything has to be rounded up to the nearest nickel; then here is that function:

```
=CEILING(A1,0.05)
```

Or, worse, suppose they do away with the penny, nickel, and dime and you have to round everything up to the nearest quarter:

```
=CEILING(A1,0.25)
```

The companion function for CEILING is FLOOR.

The advantage to using CEILING is that it rounds up to a given digit or interval. The disadvantage is the function's spelling: I before E except after C.

EVEN

The EVEN function always rounds any value up to the next even integer (number without a decimal part). So

```
=EVEN(0.98)
```

produces the value 2, the next even number up from the value .98.

The companion function for EVEN is (logically) ODD.

FLOOR

The FLOOR function is the rounding-down version of the CEILING function. So when that day comes that they do away with the penny, pray that they use the FLOOR function to round *down* to the nearest nickel, not up. This would be that function:

```
=FLOOR(A1,0.05)
```

The above function takes the value in cell A1 and rounds it down to the nearest .05 value.

Both the CEILING and FLOOR functions can round negative numbers, but both values in the function must be negative or you get a #NUM! error. For example, if A1 is negative, then =FLOOR(A1,-0.05) must be used; both values must be negative.

INT

The INT function converts numbers of any type into integers. An integer is any number without a decimal or fractional part, including negative numbers.

For positive numbers, INT lops off any decimal part.

For negative numbers, INT lops off the decimal part and rounds *down.*

For example:

```
=INT(4.25)
```

The cell with the above formula displays the value 4—no fraction or decimal.

```
=INT(-11.01)
```

The cell above displays the value –12.

The most common reason I use the INT function is for generating a random number. The random number function, RAND, produces values in the range 0 to 1. So to get a value higher, you must not only multiply the RAND function's result but also lop off the fractional part. INT is handy for this.

My generic random number formula is

```
=INT(RAND()*value)+1
```

This formula produces a random number between 1 and *value.* So if you're trying to calculate rolls of the dice for some sort of Excel craps game, you would use this formula:

```
=INT(RAND()*6)+1
```

ODD

The ODD function is the companion of the EVEN function. It's job is to round any number up to the next whole odd number.

```
=ODD(0.98)
```

The cell with the function listed above displays the value 1.

ROUND

The ROUND function does the same rounding as they tried to teach you in school: It rounds up or down depending on whether the number ends in a 5 or not. Also, with this function, you can set which place before or after the decimal place to round. Here is the format:

```
=ROUND(value,precision)
```

The *value* is a cell or specific value. The *precision* is a positive or negative number that tells ROUND the number of digits to round to. Positive precision values round to the right of the decimal place; negative values round to the left.

The ROUND function is so much fun that I've devised a mini-worksheet for you to play with it, as shown in Figure 13.4.

Numbers to be rounded — Rounded results — Significant digits input here

	A	B	C	D	E
1					
2	Values	Rounded	precision=	0	
3	1.01	1.00			
4	1.05	1.00			
5	2.40	2.00			
6	2.50	3.00			
7	2.60	3.00			
8	10.20	10.00			
9	10.40	10.00			
10	10.70	11.00			

Figure 13.4 Toying with the ROUND function

Follow these steps to create the worksheet and experiment with the ROUND function:

1. Into cell A2 type `Values`.
2. Into cell B2 type `Rounded`.
3. Into cell C3 type `precision=`.
4. Into cell D3 type `0`.
5. Name cell D3 `precision`.
6. Type these values in cells A3 through A20, as shown in Figure 13.4:

   `1.01 1.05 2.4 2.5 2.6 10.2 10.4 10.7 14 15 16 45 55 65 109 115 154 155`
7. Format the cells in A3 through B20 to display two digits.
8. In cell B3 type `=ROUND(A3,precision)`.
9. Drag to fill the formula in cell B3 down through cell B20.

   Now your screen should look similar to Figure 13.4.

Right away you can see how the numbers in column A are rounded up or down in column B; most notable are 1.05, 2.4, 2.5, and 2.6.

10. Type 1 into cell D2.

Now the values in column B are rounded to the first digit after the decimal. This affects only the first two values, 1.01 and 1.05, which are rounded down and up, accordingly.

11. Type 2 into cell D2.

Nothing changes. Rounding to the second digit after the decimal doesn't affect any of the numbers in the table. That's because none of the numbers hold any digits that far out on the right.

12. Type -1 into cell D2.

Now the rounding happens on the left of the decimal. Note how the first five values in column B are now zero? They're all rounded down. Other values in column A are rounded up or down to the nearest 10, which is where –1 sets things.

13. Type -2 into cell D2.

Now the rounding happens to the nearest hundreds digit. To go any higher you'd need to restack column A with larger numbers.

ROUNDDOWN, ROUNDUP

These are two companion functions to the ROUND function, and they behave as their names imply: ROUNDDOWN always rounds down and ROUNDUP always rounds up. (The ROUND function rounds up or down depending on the value.)

Like ROUND, each of these functions has a precision value, which tells you which digit to the left or right of the decimal place is used for rounding. But unlike ROUND, the direction of rounding is set by the function, not the value of the digit rounded off.

TRUNC

The final rounding function isn't rounding at all; it's *truncating*, or lopping off, any given portion of a number. In its simplest format, TRUNC merely lops off the decimal part of any value:

```
=TRUNC(2.3)
```

The above function displays the value 2 in the cell. Whack! Off goes the .3.

TRUNC can also sport an optional precision value, which works like the precision value in the ROUND function:

```
=TRUNC(3.141,2)
```

This function displays 3.14 in the cell; the digits after the second decimal place are lopped off. Likewise:

```
=TRUNC(12345,-2)
```

This function displays 12300 in the cell; the two digits to the left of the decimal place are lopped off.

I don't use TRUNC myself. Then again, I drive a pickup truck and it doesn't have a TRUNC.

How Can I Assure That the Result of This Operation Will Always Be Positive?

This is the ABS function, which was discussed earlier in this chapter on how to deal with the square root of negative numbers ("I'm Trying to Use SQRT but Keep Getting #NUM! Errors. Why?").

What's the Word I'm Looking for That Means the Remainder of One Value Divided by Another?

The "leftover" value when dividing one number into another is known as the *remainder*. To determine what the remainder is you use the *modulus* function, named after evil Dr. Modulus who developed it.

As anyone who's ever struggled through division knows, not every number cleanly divides into any other number. Typically there is something left over. For example:

```
=22/7
```

The result displayed in the cell is 3.142857. So you could say that 7 goes into 22 three times "plus change." But back in math class, you most likely wrote, "7 goes into 22 3 times with 1 remainder." Alas, .142857 doesn't look anything like "1 remainder." So that's where the modulus or MOD function comes into play. Write this into a cell:

```
=MOD(22,7)
```

This reads, "What is the remainder of 22 divided by 7?" Press Enter and you'll see the value 1 displayed in the cell. Or try this:

```
=MOD(24,5)
```

Before pressing the Enter key can you guess what the remainder of 24 divided by 5 could be? Yup, it's 4.

When the MOD function returns 0, it means the number divides in cleanly:

```
=MOD(52,13)
```

The above function returns 0 because 13 gazinta 52 four times.

Use the MOD function in conjunction with dividing a value that cannot return a fractional number.

Why not write one of those old chestnut math problems to demonstrate how MOD works? Assume that there are three of you: yourself, Smelly Kelly, and Dirty Berty. You would like to split up the apples you stole from Mr. Magillicutty's tree evenly between you all. Any apples left over you're going to toss back at Mr. Magillicutty's kitchen window. Create a table that shows numbers of apples from 3 on up to 30 and how many apples for each value you would have left to throw back at the kitchen window.

Don't spaz! I've done this for you, as shown in Figure 13.5.

Apples stolen — *Left over after dividing them three ways*

A	B	C
Apples	Remainder	
3	0	
4	1	
5	2	
6	0	
7	1	
8	2	
9	0	
10	1	
11	2	
12	0	
13	1	
14	2	
15	0	

Continues down here (trust me)

Figure 13.5
The dreaded solution to the math word puzzle

It's really easy, thanks to the MOD function:

1. Into cell A1 type `Apples`.
2. Into cell B1 type `Remainder`.

   These are the apples you get to toss at the kitchen window (which is closed, so the intent here is to break the glass—but it's only a story so don't get all moral and ethical on me.)
3. Into cell A2 type 3, and then drag-fill with the right mouse button down to cell A 29; select "Fill Series" from the pop-up menu when it appears.
4. Into cell B2 type `=MOD(A2,3)`.

   This reads, "the remainder of dividing the value in cell A2 (the number of apples) by the 3 of you."
5. Copy-fill down from cell B2 through cell B29.

   And there you have it: Depending on the number of apples you stole, you will have a 2/3 chance that you'll get to throw one or two of them at the window.

The SUM of All Things

The handiest function of them all is the SUM function. It's one of the original functions from the very first spreadsheet, VisiCalc. And evidence of its importance is seen right there on the Standard toolbar; it's the only function that sports its own button. Golly! I suppose that merits the glut of interesting sections that follow.

Why Bother with the SUM Function When I Just Love Typing + Signs Over and Over Again?

The reason the SUM function exists is to handle the extremely common task of totaling a column of values, such as shown in Figure 13.6: Select the bottom cell, click the AutoSum button on the Standard toolbar, and achieve the total. Instant sum! Very smart.

Hooded cloak	$ 59.00
Amulet	102.00
Bejeweled dagger	250.00
Golden bowl	120.00
Marble altar	800.00
Goat (each)	40.00
Total	**$ 1,371.00**

Items right-justified
Column width set to widest item
Bottom border
Accounting style
Accounting style minus $ sign
Bold
=SUM(G5:G10)

Figure 13.6 Instant sum

The name of the function is SUM, which includes a range of cells that are totaled and displayed. The symbol for the AutoSum toolbar button is the Greek character Sigma, which could be the Greek word for SUM but probably isn't.

You Say the AutoSum Button Is Very Smart, but Sometimes It Can Be Very Stupid.

Actually, the AutoSum button knows only as much as it assumes. Sometimes you need to give it a little help.

Suppose you have a worksheet similar to the one shown in Figure 13.7. Go ahead and type it in, if you dare; that's the first part.

	A	B	C	D
1	**Hotel Expenses**			**Totals**
2		Basic rate	$ 594.00	
3		Taxes	$ 65.34	
4		Telephone	$ 24.98	
5		Other/Misc	$ 7.50	
6	**Total Hotel (non food)**			
7	**Hotel Expenses - Food**			
8		Minibar	$ 12.60	
9		Room Service	$ -	
10		Other/Misc	$ -	
11	**Total Hotel (food)**			
12	**Total Hotel**			
13	**Car**			
14		Rental	$ 175.00	
15		Gas	$ 34.00	
16		Other/Misc	$ -	
17	**Total Car**			
18	**Grand Total**			
19				
20				

Figure 13.7
Yet another sample worksheet

The second part is detailed below. This covers how you finish off the report by using the SUM function sometimes and not other times:

1. Click to select cell C6.
2. Click the AutoSum button on the toolbar.

   The SUM function is inserted and smartly selects the four cells above, C2 through C5. Smart. Smart. Smart.
3. Press the Enter key to lock in the formula.
4. Format cell C6 bold.
5. Click to select cell C11.
6. This time manually type `=SUM(`.

   Type only the first part of the function, as shown above.
7. Now select cells C8 through C10 with the mouse.

   And they're plugged into the function.

You can actually click and select individual cells or values for the SUM function; it doesn't always have to be a slew of cells.

8. Type the closing) and press Enter.
9. Make cell C11 bold as well.
10. Click to select cell C17.

11. Click the AutoSum button on the toolbar again.

    And the values are smartly selected. (Yes, spaces interfere with the cells the SUM command automatically selects. More on that in a second.)

12. Press the Enter key.

13. Make cell C17 bold.

    Now to do the Totals column:

14. In cell D6, type `=C6`.

    This copies the non-food Hotel subtotal over into the Totals column; no need to reuse the SUM function in D6 because it's already used in C6.

15. Format cell D6 bold.

16. Into cell D11, type `=`.

17. Click cell C11 with the mouse and press Enter.

18. Make cell D11 bold.

19. Click to select cell D12.

    Time to calculate the Hotel subtotal.

20. Click the AutoSum button on the toolbar.

    Oops! It selects only cell D12.

21. Use the mouse to drag from cell D6 down through cell D11.

    Now the formula reads =SUM(D6:D11), which is a few cells too many, but occasionally such lassoing of cells is necessary with the SUM command.

22. Press Enter and format cell C12 bold.

23. Into cell D17 type `=C17` and format that cell bold.

    Finally you come to the Grand Total.

24. Into cell D18 type `=SUM(D12,D17)`.

    Again, remember that the SUM function can accept individual cells. And they need not even be in the same row or column as the cell with the SUM function.

25. Press Enter.

26. Format cell D18 bold.

I Want the Sum off to the Left.

The best way to sum a row of cells instead of a column is to select a cell to the right of the row of cells and then click the AutoSum button on the toolbar.

Excel looks up, and then it looks to the left to see if there are any numbers needing to be totaled. Otherwise, you have to manually select the cells using the mouse, as shown in Figure 13.8.

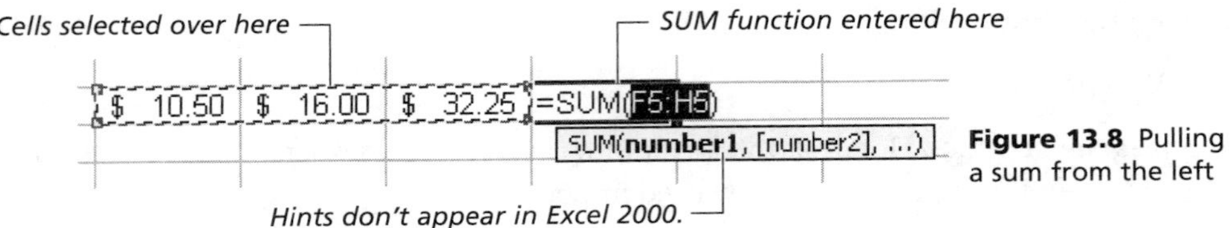

Figure 13.8 Pulling a sum from the left

Can I Use the SUM Function on More Than a Row or Column?

Sure: The SUM function can total up a whole block of numbers, as shown in Figure 13.9. It can even total up multiple blocks of functions, as shown in Figure 13.10.

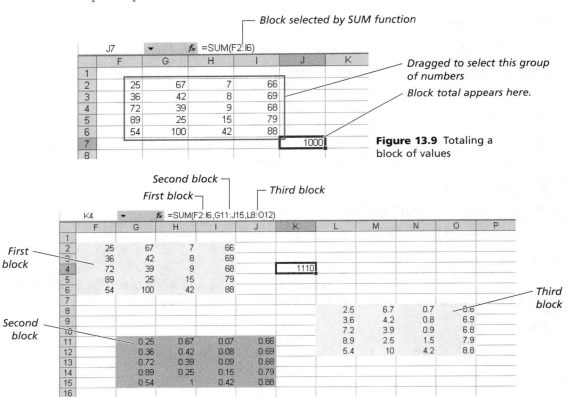

Block selected by SUM function

J7 =SUM(F2:I6)

	F	G	H	I	J	K
1						
2	25	67	7	66		
3	36	42	8	69		
4	72	39	9	68		
5	89	25	15	79		
6	54	100	42	88		
7					1000	
8						

Dragged to select this group of numbers

Block total appears here.

Figure 13.9 Totaling a block of values

Second block

First block

Third block

K4 =SUM(F2:I6,G11:J15,L8:O12)

	F	G	H	I	J	K	L	M	N	O	P
1											
2	25	67	7	66							
3	36	42	8	69							
4	72	39	9	68		1110					
5	89	25	15	79							
6	54	100	42	88							
7											
8							2.5	6.7	0.7	6.6	
9							3.6	4.2	0.8	6.9	
10							7.2	3.9	0.9	6.8	
11		0.25	0.67	0.07	0.66		8.9	2.5	1.5	7.9	
12		0.36	0.42	0.08	0.69		5.4	10	4.2	8.8	
13		0.72	0.39	0.09	0.68						
14		0.89	0.25	0.15	0.79						
15		0.54	1	0.42	0.88						
16											

First block

Second block

Third block

Figure 13.10 The Sum of three different blocks of values

Any Way to Subtract a Large Swath of Numbers?

Not with a function. The only way to subtract a column of numbers is to create a formula where you subtract the value of each cell from each cell, which you can do in the following steps:

1. Type the values `125`, `99`, `801`, and `191` into cells D1 through D4.
2. Into cell D5, type the formula: `=0-D1-D2-D3-D4`.

   You have to start with 0 because you're subtracting all the numbers, not just subtracting the last three from the first one. That way you get the proper answer, –1216 and not –966.

Of course, there's an easier trick, which is probably why there isn't a specific function for such a thing:

3. Click to select cell D5.
4. Σ Click the AutoSum button on the toolbar.

   And SUM naturally selects the four numbers above.
5. Press the Enter key.

   Did you notice anything about the result? Yes, it's 1216, which is the positive value of the result you got in step 2. Thus looms the question: How do you turn a positive value into a negative one in Excel?

   You should remember that you can use the ABS function to always return the positive value of a function or number. Is there a NEGS function?

   No, there is no NEGS function. Instead, there is the – operator. Like the % operator, it affects a number by making it negative. This is subtly different from the subtraction operator, –, though it's essentially the same symbol.
6. Edit the function in cell D5 to read `=-SUM(D1:D4)`.

   Press the F2 key to edit the cell and simply insert a minus sign before the SUM function. This negates the result and gives you the subtracted total of the column—or the end result you originally requested.

Keep the values in cells D1 through D4 for the next section's example.

Any Way to Subtract the Value of π from Numbers Using the SUM Function?

Don't be ridiculous; you can fashion any sort of function you want by mixing and matching formulas. SUM is unique in that it performs a common worksheet function. If it's not a common worksheet function, then it doesn't need to exist, right?

How about Multiplying All the Numbers in a Chunk?

Yup: That's done with the PRODUCT function. It works exactly like SUM, but it multiplies all the values of each cell with each other. So if you edit cell D5 from the previous set of steps to read =PRODUCT(D1:D4), you get a number so huge it has to be displayed in scientific notation: 1.89E+09. (But you can make the cell a little wider to see the value 1,893,263,625, which is how many dollars the U.S. government spends in just over five hours.

What's the Point of Using the AutoSum Button on the Toolbar Like a Menu?

If the AutoSum button is the king of functions, then it must have a royal court. In Excel 2003/XP (but not in Excel 2000) the AutoSum button has a drop-down menu, as shown in Figure 13.11. This menu lists four other functions similar to SUM and almost as popular. You can instantly insert these functions by choosing them from the menu. (Excel 2000 users can still manually type in each function.)

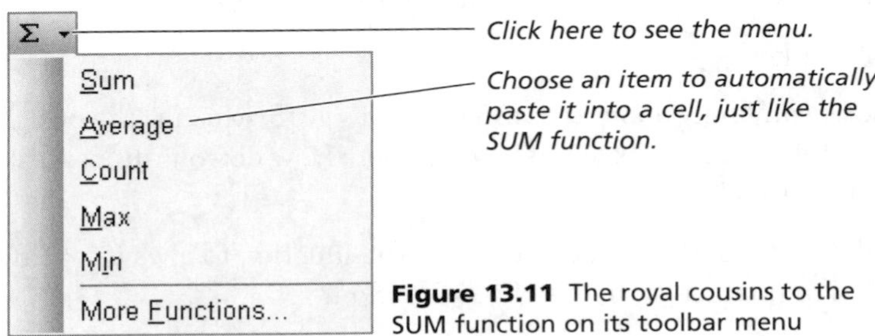
Σ
Sum
Average
Count
Max
Min
More Functions...
Click here to see the menu.
Choose an item to automatically paste it into a cell, just like the SUM function.

Figure 13.11 The royal cousins to the SUM function on its toolbar menu

Is AVERAGE Just an Average Function or Does It Really Calculate the Average?

You remember hating averages from school, right? The idea was to total up a bunch of numbers and then divide that result by the number of numbers. So:

125+99+801+191 = 1216

You know this from earlier in this chapter. Now to get the average you have to divide 1216 by 4 (the number of numbers). But screw that! Instead, and using the same values in cells D1 through D4 as shown earlier, complete these steps:

1. Click to select cell D5.

2a. In Excel 2003/XP, choose AVERAGE from the AutoSum button's menu.

2b. In Excel 2000, type `=AVERAGE(D1:D4)`.

3. Press Enter.

It's 304!

Now teachers can really figure out the class average, baseball nuts can do batting averages, and all of us below- or above-normal people can simply sit back and appreciate the AVERAGE function.

Though I'm not getting into them here, Excel has a surplus of statistical functions, logically kept in the Statistical category of the Insert Function dialog box. So if you need to cast a standard-deviation spell on a group of numbers, you'd use the STDEV function, similar to the way AVERAGE is cast above.

Why Would I Ever Use the COUNT Function?

You gotta figure: How does the AVERAGE function know how many numbers it's reading in? Obviously, somewhere in Excel's bowels must be a function that counts the number of numbers. That function is, logically, the COUNT function.

The COUNT function merely returns how many cells contain values. So if you select a swath of cells—say some huge block—COUNT tells you how many of those cells have values in them. It does not count any cells with text, nor does it count blank cells.

I can imagine a situation where there is some sort of tally being kept in a worksheet. For example, in Figure 13.12 results are posted for an election as they come in. A popular statistic on election night is the number of counties reporting. In Figure 13.12, that can be calculated in cell D2 by using the function =COUNT(B2:B17).

	A	B	C	D	E
1	County	Results			
2	A		Counties reporting:	6	
3	B	256			
4	C				
5	D				
6	E	109			
7	F				
8	G				
9	H	13			
10	I				
11	J				
12	K	27			
13	L				
14	M	1025			
15	N				
16	O	19			
17	P				
18					

=COUNT(B2:B17), or 6

Only six cells have values.

Figure 13.12
An example of using the COUNT function

The COUNT function reads the range of cells, B2 through B17, and counts how many have values.

A variation on the COUNT function is COUNTIF, which bases its results on the number of items in a group matching something specific. So suppose the election is over, and Figure 13.13 shows the winning results by each county according to political party.

	A	B	C	D	E
1	County	Results			
2	A	Rep	Counties reporting:	ALL	
3	B	Dem	Republican:		
4	C	Dem	Democratic:		
5	D	Rep			
6	E	Rep			
7	F	Rep			
8	G	Dem			
9	H	Rep			

Totals go here.

Either "Dem" or "Rep" text

Figure 13.13
Election results by party

To total them up without using your fingers, into cell D3 you would type this formula:

```
=COUNTIF(B2:B17,"Rep")
```

This reads, "Count the number of cells between B2 and B17 that match 'Rep.'" Or, actually, the "IF" implies to count the cells if they are equal to or match a logical expression that could be included in the function. More on that in a sec.

Into cell D4 enter the following formula:

```
=COUNTIF(B2:B17,"Dem")
```

And that displays the total number of counties that are represented by Democrats.

Mathematically, suppose you had a series of test results in cells D4 through D44 and you wanted to determine how many were above 60. If so, then you could use COUNTIF to determine that value:

```
=COUNTIF(D4:D44,">60")
```

Above, COUNTIF examines cells D4 through D44. If any are "greater than 60," they are counted and the total number is displayed in the cell.

Don't Be Dumb and Forget These Common Comparison Things!

Here are some more symbols you learned and have since forgotten since high school. These are comparison operators, primarily used in the various IF formulas:

=	*Is equal to; is TRUE if the values are equal.*
>	*Is greater than; is TRUE if the value on the left is more than the value on the right.*
>=	*Is greater than or equal to; is TRUE if the value on the left is equal to or more than the value on the right.*
<	*Is less than; is TRUE if the value on the left is smaller than the value on the right.*
<=	*Is less than or equal to; is TRUE if the value on the left is equal to or smaller than the value on the right.*
<>	*Not equal to; is TRUE if the values are not equal*

What Are the Advantages to MIN and MAX?

The MIN and MAX functions are used to find the lowest and highest values in a swath of selected cells, like this:

1. In cells F3 through F8, type the following values:

   `325     456     197     224     380     210`

2. Select all the cells, F3 through F8, and name them `scores`.

   Select the cells, and then type `scores` into the Name box.

3. Into cell G3, type the formula `=IF(F3=MAX(scores),"Winner!","")`.

   So if the cell on the left (F3) is equal to the highest value in the list of scores, the cell displays the text "Winner!" Otherwise, nothing "" is displayed.

4. Drag-fill to copy the formula down from cell G3 through cell G8.

   And we have a winna, as shown in Figure 13.14.

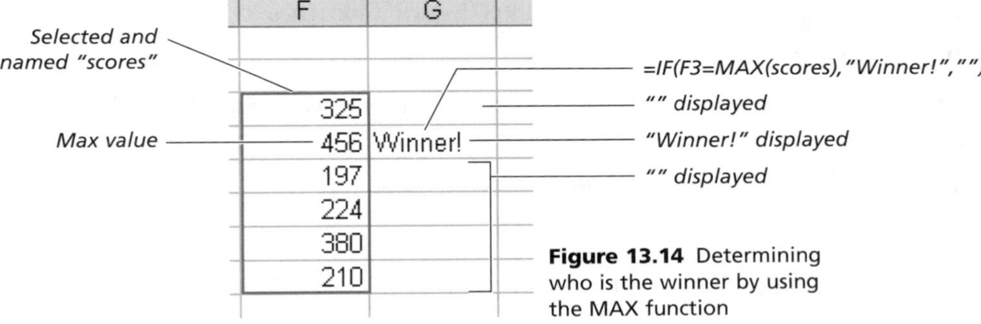

Figure 13.14 Determining who is the winner by using the MAX function

To determine the lowest score, MIN would be used: Simply edit the formula in cell G3 to read

```
=IF(F3=MIN(scores),"Loser!","")
```

Then drag-fill down to copy the formula into the rest of the cells.

And now the thought puzzle: How can you get both "Winner!" and "Loser!" to display, as shown in Figure 13.15?

No, the answer isn't to use a logical function, such as OR.

The answer is not to use two IF statements in the same cell.

The answer is to hide your work elsewhere and use text concatenation to create the illusion of too much work in one cell. Figure 13.16 explains it all.

F	G
325	
456	Winner!
197	Loser!
224	
380	
210	

Figure 13.15 The MIN and MAX values are highlighted.

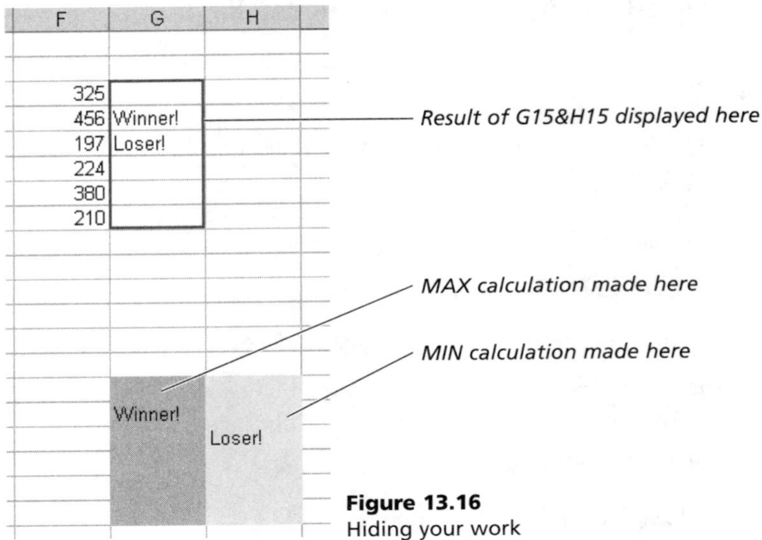

Figure 13.16
Hiding your work

First, the same "Winner!" formula is used in cells G15 down through G20:

```
=IF(F3=MAX(scores),"Winner!","")
```

This produces the same results, with the winner being displayed well below the original set of scores.

Second, the same "Loser!" formula is put into cells H15 through H20:

```
=IF(F3=MIN(scores),"Loser!","")
```

Again you get the same results, just away from the action.

At this point you have both the "Winner!" text and "Loser!" text displayed in the cells. Because they should never be the same cell (that would mean everyone tied), you can use the & operator to add the text from one cell to the text from another cell. So:

Third, the formula =G15&H15 is placed into cell G3. This tells Excel to display the text from cell G15 plus the text from cell H15 into cell G3. Because G15 and H15 are blank, nothing is displayed.

When the formula is copied down, however, the cells containing text are duplicated. So the result of cell G16 "Winner!" & H16 "" is "Winner!" And that is displayed in cell G4.

The result of cell G17 "" & H17 "Loser!" is stuck together and placed into cell G5. And so on.

That's one way you can get the MIN *and* MAX values to display in one column.

Yes, it's cheating. But it's a great way to lead into the next subject: text functions.

Another Way to Get "Winner!" or "Loser!" to Display

Yet another way to get either "Winner!" or "Loser!" to display is by "nesting" IF statements.

In a programming language there would be a companion ELSE statement for an IF. So you could say "IF this item is the maximum value, do this, ELSE (or otherwise) do that." The equivalent of this in Excel is the following:

```
=IF(F3=MAX(scores),"Winner!",IF(F3=MIN(scores),"Loser!",""))
```

What's being done above is that the "Value_if_false" part of the IF function is being replaced by yet another IF function—perfectly legal. That way a second comparison can be done in the same cell. The results come out the same as the example in the main part of the text.

There is no real limit on how many IF commands you can nest inside of each other, though I suppose after a certain number the logic would be hard to follow and tough to test.

If Math Gives You a Headache, Wait Until You Start Adding and Subtracting Text.

I'm kidding! Relax.

Excel has a number of interesting text functions, but they can't really do much unless you add in the power of macros to help make your worksheet hop, skip, and jump. Alas, this book does not cover macros, so there are only a few text functions I feel are worthy enough to take up your time with. In fact, one of the most useful is the & operator, which is covered in the previous section and also helps solve an interesting puzzle there.

How Can I Drag-Fill a Series of Letters?

You can have a series of days, months, values, and so on. But if you want to fill column A with letters A through Z you must use a text function to make that happen. Here's how:

1. Click to select cell A1.
2. Type in the formula `=CHAR(ROW()+64)`.
3. Press Enter.
4. Reselect cell A1
5. Drag the cell down to fill and copy it, down to cell A19 or so.

   As you drag, you copy the formula into each subsequent cell, which creates a range of letters, A through as low as you want to go.

The CHAR function is used to display a character in a cell—any character. You can enter values from 1 through 255, though only a few of those numbers display recognizable characters; most of the characters are "blank" or display foreign language letters or symbols.

The values used by the CHAR function are ASCII codes. ASCII is a common scheme for assigning letters, numbers, and other symbols to code values. It's used by almost all computers worldwide.

You don't need to know all the codes to use CHAR; only a handful are worthy of attention:

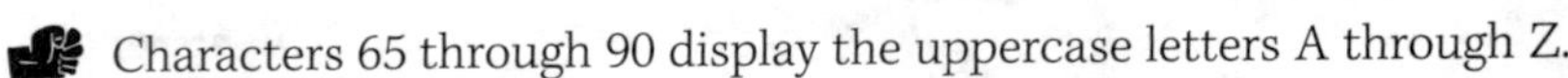

- Characters 65 through 90 display the uppercase letters A through Z.

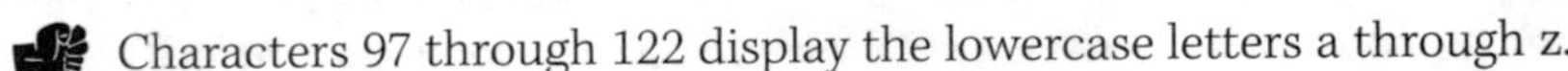

- Characters 97 through 122 display the lowercase letters a through z.

Pretty much everything else is some symbol or dingbat that you'd probably never want in a cell by itself. (And if you do, I'm certain that you're clever enough to figure out how to make a table in Excel to display all 255 variations of the CHAR function.)

In this function, =CHAR(ROW()+64)), I'm using the value returned by the ROW() function to help calculate the letter displayed in a cell. ROW() returns the current row number, or 1 for cell A1. That calculates out to =CHAR(65), which displays the letter A.

Alas, you cannot drag-fill with the CHAR function. Remember that CHAR displays text, not a value, so there is really nothing to fill (just as you cannot drag-fill text).

So if you want to display letters A through J in cells C8 through C18, you could do this:

1. Click cell C8.
2. Enter the formula `=CHAR(65)`.
3. Click cell C9 and enter the formula `=CHAR(66)`.
4. Repeat this for each cell down to C18, incrementing the value in the CHAR function by one each time.

BORING!

Or you could do this:

1. Click cell C8.
2. Enter the formula `=CHAR(ROW(A1)+64)`.

   Rather than have the ROW() function return the current row—which means you'd have to do math in your head (65-current_row)—you can simply have Excel calculate the row number for cell A1, which is always 1. Add 64 and you get an A.
3. Drag cell C8 down through cell C18 to copy and fill.

   As you drag, the relative reference A1 changes to the next row, which increases for each cell down and gives you the next letter in the alphabet.

How Can I Use CONCATENATE to Make My Worksheet More Polite?

Concatenation is the art of sticking two or more pieces of text together. It's a fancy term for what's basically "word glue." You already saw an example with the & operator earlier in this chapter. Basically & just takes text from one cell and combines it with text in another cell to create a longer, combined piece of text.

As an example, consider Figure 13.17. All the lines of text say basically the same thing, "Pay up or die!" The difference is in the formatting. In both cases, the second line of text looks better than the first. That's because the second line uses concatenation to build the line of text as opposed to stuffing the text and values into separate cells (which is how the first line does things).

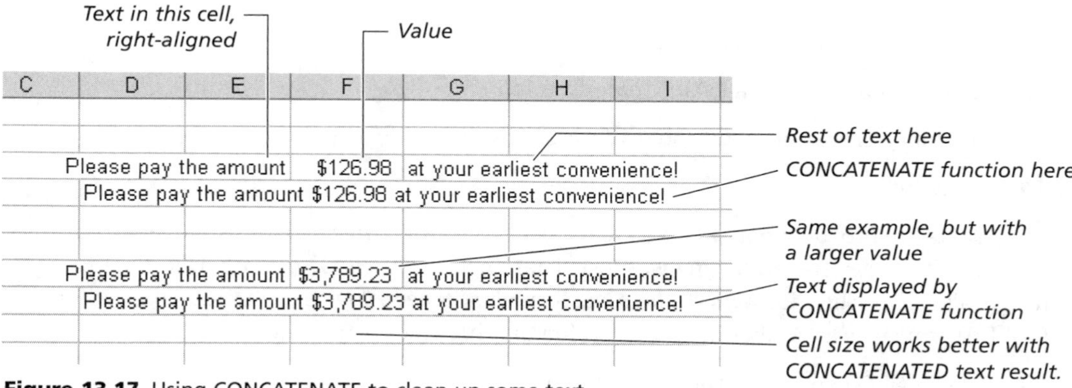

Figure 13.17 Using CONCATENATE to clean up some text

The following steps show you how to use concatenation by building the example in Figure 13.17:

1. Into cell E3, type `Please pay the amount.`
2. Right-justify cell E3.
3. Type `126.98` into cell E4.
4. Format cell E4 with the Currency format.

   Do not click the Currency button to do this; remember that the Currency button on the toolbar uses the Accounting format. You want the dollar sign close to the number to make it look good.
5. Into cell E5 type `at your earliest convenience!`

This is the way most folks would format a calculated dollar amount into a worksheet, such as an invoice or purchase order. But the cell containing the value still isn't wide enough to make the sentence appear continuous. Instead, it looks like one of those "You have won!" junk mails where your name has obviously been added after the fact.

Now you could adjust the cell's width for column F. But look at the second example in Figure 13.17. It still doesn't look as good as it could—not when compared to the two "perfect" sentences below the examples.

The way to clean up the situation is to concatenate everything so that one string of text is displayed, not two pieces of text and a value. That's done with the CONCATENATE function, as follows:

6. Into cell D4, type `=CONCATENATE(`.
7. Click cell E3. That's the first bit of text.
8. Type a comma.
9. Click cell E4 and type a comma.
10. Click cell E5 and type a closing parenthesis.

    The function should now read = CONCATENATE(E3,F3,G3).
11. Press Enter.

The results are probably not what you're expecting. Though the value did survive into the final sentence, it's ugly. The formatting was lost. That's because the CONCATENATE function merely reads values, not their formats. To fake the format, you need to use the DOLLAR function. DOLLAR converts a number into a text value that has the Currency format. Keep working:

12. Select cell D4 and press the F2 key to edit.
13. Replace the reference to cell F3 with `DOLLAR(F3)`.

    The function should now read = CONCATENATE(E3,DOLLAR(F3),G3).
14. Press Enter.

    Alas. Still not there. You need to add some spaces around the number. Spaces are merely text, and the CONCATENATE function accepts text in a cell or text you can type in directly. So:
15. Select cell D4 and press the F2 key to edit.
16. Insert blank spaces—" "—before and after the DOLLAR function as follows:

    ```
    = CONCATENATE(E3," ",DOLLAR(F3)," ",G3)
    ```
17. Press Enter.

    And finally the text looks good.

The moral of the story is that CONCATENATE, aside from being a booger to type, accepts text from a cell, values from a cell, or even text you directly type in, such as the spaces in this section's example. In fact, you could concoct a function like this:

```
= CONCATENATE("Please pay the amount ",DOLLAR(F3), " at your earliest convenience!")
```

This includes the text directly (plus the blank spaces), which may save you from crowding up your worksheet too much.

14 Fun with Charts and Graphs

Charts are fun.

Oh, no: I mean, charts are *hard work*. Toil! Dread! Endless effort! Some charts take *weeks* to create and tune. And the results are worth it: High and lofty, frequently overpaid individuals can look at a chart and rub their dour chins in deep, near-comatose contemplation. These overstuffed, overinflated, and overpaid individuals appreciate the frankness and honesty of an XY plot or pie graph over the pages of numbers—the "real work." That's because the aristocratic brain just isn't attuned to seeing the trees. No, they want the forest—preferably a National Geographic–type photograph of one.

Aw, what the heck: I just can't help myself. Charts are fun! Even when the data they illustrate is as dismal as Minnesota in February, there is just this certain joy that comes when playing with charts. Fortunately, there are really few secrets when it comes to charts, so this is going to be a fun chapter—probably a review for most because nothing induces the joy of play like charts in Excel.

Demons Tamed and Angels Praised:

- Cooking up a chart in Excel (review)
- Using the Chart Wizard and Chart toolbar
- Repairing a chart after it's made
- Adjusting chart fonts and colors
- Adding and removing chart chunks
- Changing the way the chart appears

NERD'S CORNER

Cocktail Party Trivia, Part VIII

MIKE: Charts and graphs are yet another reason why Lotus 1-2-3 triumphed over its competitors back in the last century.

PAUL: That and they cheated at poker!

MARY: Paul?

MIKE: I think he's drunk. But anyway, 1-2-3's charts, though primitive by Excel's standards, really prompted a lot of people to adopt 1-2-3 over other spreadsheets of the era.

PAUL: Stank razno, forbee the dong shangle of those guys mup nair.

MIKE: Then other spreadsheets started offering more powerful chart-making abilities, plus other features that 1-2-3 lacked.

PAUL: Dibno! Dibno graphics freen!

MIKE: Until Excel became the number one spreadsheet.

MARY: What about...

PAUL: Cornstarch.

MARY: What about...

PAUL: Corn. Starch.

MARY: Okay.

PAUL: Dibno onatalla. Dup lip snack frito oblong shangle graphics freen.

Basic Chart Tricks

Charts are rather easy to "get" in Excel. There are only a few basic things to remember, so if this is your first exposure—or even your first in-depth exposure—read over the next several sections to get up to speed. The next major part in this chapter, "Redoing the Chart," is where most of the common chart puzzles are solved and questions are answered.

What's the World's Second-Fastest Way to Create a Chart?

Aside from theft, the fastest way to create a chart is to lasso a group of numbers in a worksheet and click the Chart Wizard button on the Standard toolbar. When the wizard appears, click the Finish button. Voila: instant chart.

Okay, it's instant *ugly* chart, but it's a chart or "graph" of the numbers you lassoed. Now some answers to your deepest questions:

Q: Can you lasso only one number and make a chart?

A: Yes, but this is utterly stupid and produces a useless chart. Charts are designed for overview and comparison—the "Big Picture" thing. Charting only one value is hardly useful.

Q: What if I lasso a table of numbers?

A: Then you get a multidimensional chart.

Q: The chart looks ugly.

A: That's because you didn't work all the way through the wizard, so as a punishment Excel coughs up its ugliest chart.

Q: How can I fix things?

A: Keep reading.

How Can I Force the Chart onto a New Sheet?

To create a chart on a new sheet in Excel, you must use the first-fastest way of creating a new chart. Here are the quickie steps:

1. Lasso the numbers you want represented on the chart.
2. Press the F11 key.

Instantly a new sheet—a Chart sheet—is created in the workbook, as shown in Figure 14.1. It contains a graph of the numbers you selected. And, yes, it is a dumb graph, just as if you had used the second-fastest chart-creating method described in the previous section.

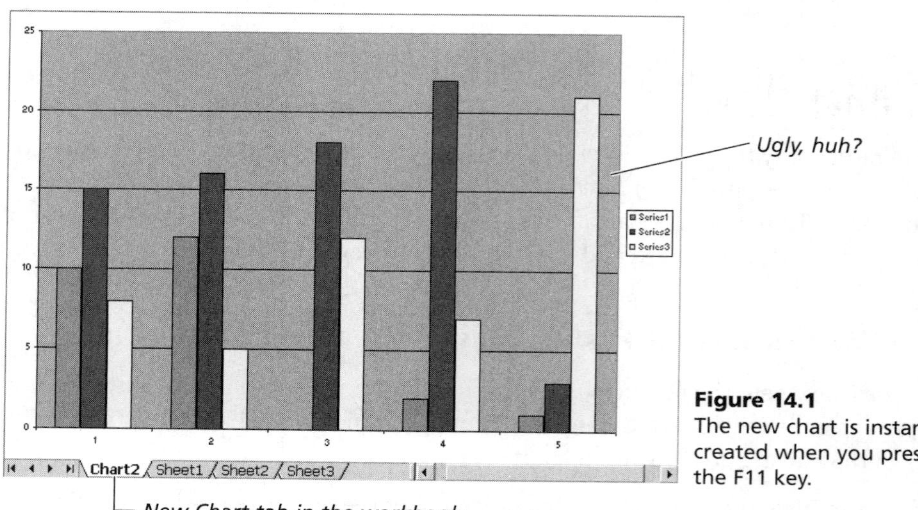

Figure 14.1
The new chart is instantly created when you press the F11 key.

KEYBOARD MASTER

Creating a New Chart

Here are the fastest and next-fastest ways to create a chart in Excel:

F11

Create new Chart sheet in the workbook based on selected cells.

Alt+F1

Same as F1, though not as easy to remember.

Alt+I,H,Alt+F

Using the wizard, places a chart in the current worksheet.

Can I Copy a Chart from a Chart Sheet Back into a Workbook?

Yes, but the results are ugly. It's much better just to create the chart in the workbook by using the wizard as opposed to copying the chart from the Chart sheet.

If you work the entire wizard through, then the final option lets you decide whether to put the chart into the current worksheet or create a new Chart sheet for it.

If You Use the Wizard Properly, Then You Won't Have to Redo the Chart.

Most of the advice in the next part of this book covers undoing things that could have been done right, had you paid full attention to the wizard. The problem is that the wizard just has so many steps, seemingly disorganized, that it's tough to tell where the bodies are buried. Therefore, the next few pages outline the wizard process, telling you what's where and what you might be missing. This should save you time when you next need to create a chart.

1. Create a nifty little table in your document.

To best test the various chart types, I created the table shown in Figure 14.2—just a simple silly thing. Note that it is labeled. The Chart Wizard will pick up the labels, as Excel's List commands did.

	Jordan	Simon	Jonah	Jeremiah
Breakfast	0%	100%	50%	100%
Lunch	75%	100%	25%	25%
Dinner	100%	100%	75%	100%

Percentages of meals consumed

Figure 14.2 A silly table I whipped up

If you want labels on the chart, then first put them on your data in the worksheet.

2. Select the table.

   You can select the whole table, labels and all, or just click one cell in the table 'cause Excel is smart and knows where the table is.

3. Choose Insert ➢ Chart.

   This is just another way to click the Wizard button. (I'm required by the *Computer Book Author's Handbook* to show all the variations.)

The wizard begins.

Step 1: Choose the Type of Chart

The first choice you must make in the wizard is the overall look of the chart. There are chart types and subtypes, as shown in Figure 14.3.

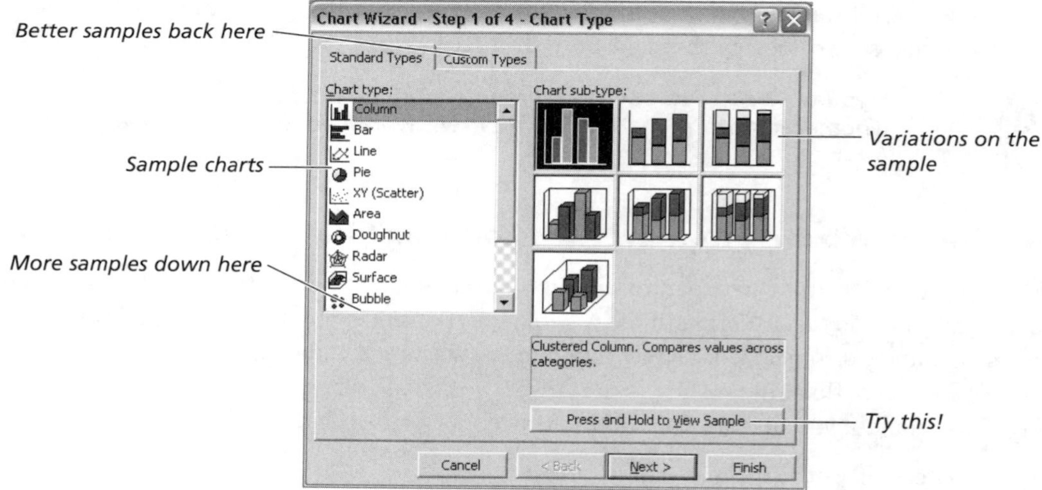

Figure 14.3 Selecting a chart type

Which type is proper? It depends on your data, but also your audience. The cool thing is the handy Press and Hold to View Sample button, which I recommend you use liberally before clicking the Next button.

Another buried treasure in this step is the Custom Types tab. It contains even more variations, though it lacks the Press and Hold to View Sample button as well as the subtypes.

You Must Know This: Three-Dimensional Charts in a Two-Dimensional World

Excel charts can fall into two categories: two-dimensional and three-dimensional. This has nothing to do with the graphics that appear on the chart. You can have a two-dimensional graph using three-dimensional objects, such as cones or cylinders. No, it refers to the dimensions of the graph itself.

A two-dimensional graph has an x-axis and a y-axis. The x-axis goes left and right. The y-axis goes up and down. This is just as you would expect from your nightmarish experiences in high school geometry class.

- *The x-axis is the* Category *axis, and it goes left and right.*
- *The y-axis is the* Value *axis, and it goes up and down.*

A three-dimensional graph has x-, y-, and z-axes. Here things get screwy:

- *The x-axis is the* Category *axis, and it goes in and out—the third dimension. (This would have been the z-axis in geometry glass.)*
- *The y-axis is the* Series *axis, and it goes left and right. (It would have been the x-axis in geometry class.)*
- *The z-axis is the* Value *axis, and it goes up and down. (The y-axis in geometry class.)*

Don't punish yourself trying to memorize this. If it's something you refer to often, then just dog-ear this page. (I've never bothered memorizing it.)

4. Select a chart type.

Do not worry if the chart is labeled or positioned properly at this point. You're just picking out a general type. The labels and axes can be fixed later in the wizard.

For my sample, I've chosen the "Area Blocks Chart" type from the Custom Types tab. I don't know why. I may change my mind later.

5. Click the Next button.

Step 2: Check Your Data

I suppose Step 2 is really required only if you were a ditz and didn't first select any data from your worksheet. But more importantly, it's also where you can change the way the data in the table runs in the chart, from XY to YX (so to speak), as shown in Figure 14.4.

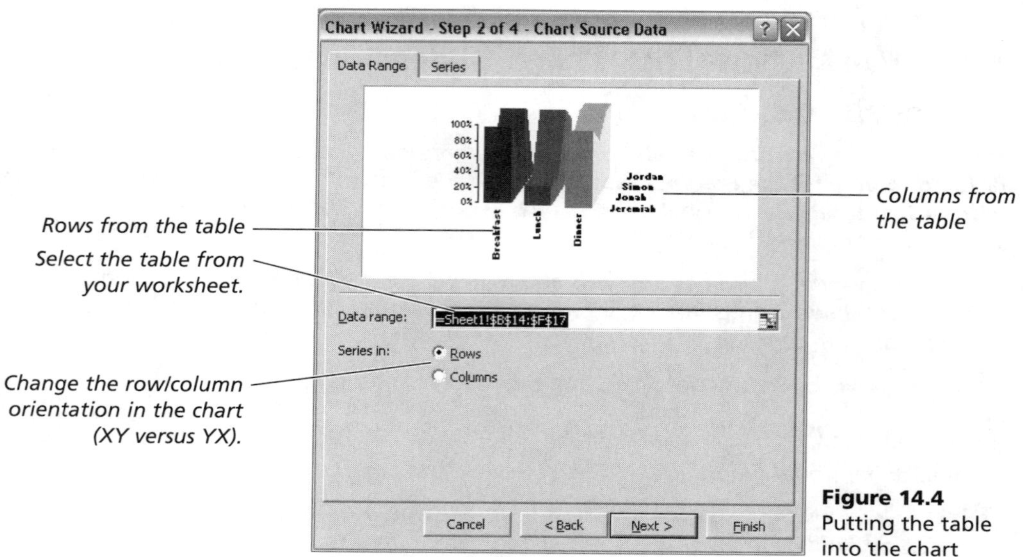

Figure 14.4
Putting the table into the chart

6. Click to select Columns or Rows, whichever isn't selected now.

Observe how this changes the perspective on your table.

The row values from the table are the key to the chart. They're the values that can be manipulated more than the column values. If the table wasn't set up properly, then you can swap the rows/columns as shown in Step 6.

7. Click the Series tab.

This part of the dialog box lets you add or remove rows from the chart. Remember: If you'd rather manipulate the columns, then return to the Data Range tab and swap the rows/column again.

Normally you wouldn't mess with this stuff. In fact, instead of manipulating the table here, do it in the worksheet instead. For example, if you notice that one row tends to block another (such as Simon blocking Jordan in Figure 14.5), then click Cancel to quit the wizard, and rearrange the rows in your table before re-creating the chart.

8. Click the Next button.

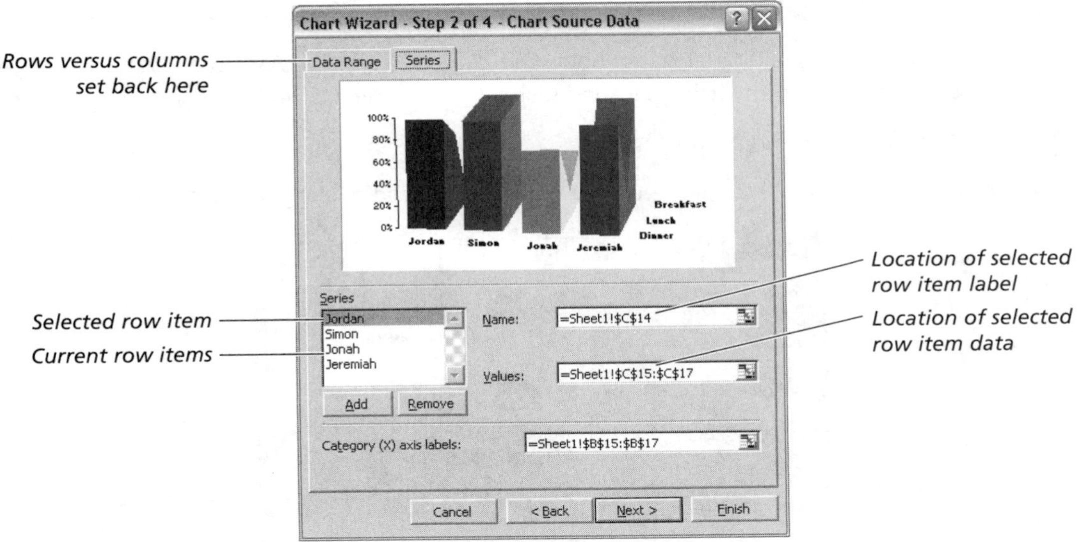

Figure 14.5 Messing with the rows in the chart

Step 3: Adjust the Chart's Appearance and Visible Options

Step 3 my butt! There are six tabs in this dialog box! Six different things to do. It's Steps 3 through 8 if you ask my opinion. Add another two steps for the other tabs in the other dialog box boxes and, dang it, I'm starting a letter-writing campaign!

9. Click the Titles tab (if you need to).

Here you can optionally add a title to the chart plus labels for each of the axes. (Three-dimensional charts have a z-axis; other charts just have x- and y-axes.)

If you want to give your chart a title and some labels, then this is the place to do it. It's much more difficult to do this after the chart has been created.

10. Type in a name for the chart into the "Chart Title" box.

The title appears over the chart, on the top, centered.

11. Optionally label the axis.

The number and variety depend on the chart type. Sometimes this makes sense. For example, if you have merely numbers on an axis, you can clarify them by saying "Part numbers" or "Sales districts" or whatever would help you make more sense out of the numbers.

On the other hand, if the chart already shows the months January through December, then there is no need to add a redundant "Months" label.

12. Click the Legend tab.

The Legend tab should be next, as shown in Figure 14.6, not the Axes tab. This is where you can save a little space by using a legend instead of labeling individual columns or pie slices.

13. Click the Show Legend button.

14. Optionally click the Placement buttons to put the legend where you want it in the chart.

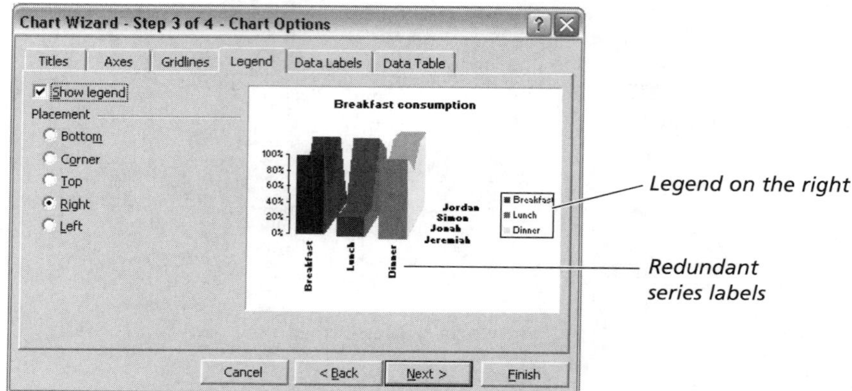

Figure 14.6 Adding a legend

In Figure 14.6, I've put the legend off to the right. But notice how the legend repeats the labels on the Series (bottom) axis? Even the colors in the legend match the block graphs in the chart. So the labels on the Series axis are now no longer needed.

15. Click the Axes tab.

16. Click to remove the labels on the bottom axis.

For 2-D charts that's the Category (x) axis; for the 3-D charts it's the Series (y) axis. But don't bother memorizing that: Just click the various check boxes until the bottom labels are removed.

17. Click the Gridlines tab.

Another place to play: Click to check and uncheck the various gridline options. I find the value gridlines come in handy.

18. Click the Data Labels tab.

This tab lets you put information right on the graph part of the chart, labeling individual bars or pieces of the chart. I think it looks too crowded with that information showing.

If it's too crowded now, don't fuss: You can always space the bars farther apart, which is covered in the section "How Can I Space the Bars Farther Apart?" later in this chapter.

19. Click the Data Table.

Only one job to tackle here: whether you want the original table from the worksheet to be included with the chart or not.

Clicking the "Show Data Table" item gives you a preview of how junky it looks. It looks less junky if you create the chart in its own sheet in the workbook. And you can always add the data table later.

20. Click the Next button.

Step 4: All Done Silly Last Step

It all comes down to this: Where do you want the new chart? As a new sheet or as an object in a worksheet? If you're printing off transparencies for a slideshow or incorporating the chart into another Office application, choose its own sheet, as shown in Figure 14.7.

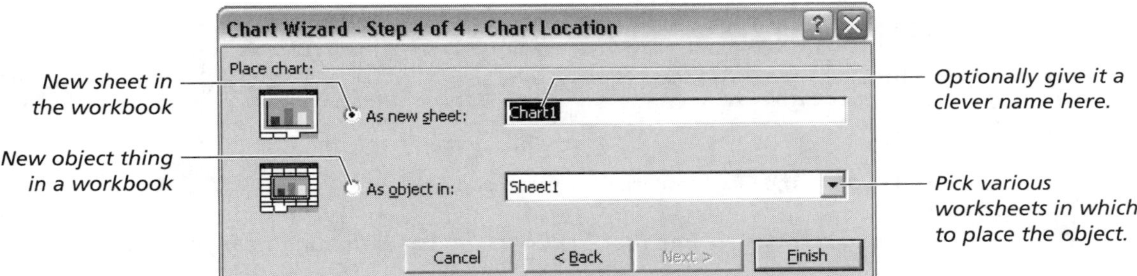

Figure 14.7 Picking a place for the new chart

21. Click the Finish button.

And you're done.

The chart sits lovingly in its new home—ready for you to mess with it further.

Yes, Indeed, I'm Grossly Unhappy and Must Redo the Chart.

Who ever are happy with their charts? And consider this: Modifying (or "playing") with a chart most definitely does fall under the category of "working." So if you have a slow afternoon, you can spend gobs of time honing and perfecting an Excel chart.

The best part of messing with a chart is that Microsoft understands the need. Therefore there are many, many tools available for hammering out new charty things. The following sections describe them all.

Don't Be a Fool and Ignore the Handy Chart Redoing Helper, the Chart Toolbar.

If you're lucky, then the Chart toolbar pops up after you slap down a chart into a worksheet. Hands down, the Chart toolbar is the best way to mess with a chart. Forget pocking and right-clicking with the mouse. If that's ever frustrated you, then the Chart toolbar is the answer you've been seeking.

To summon the Chart toolbar, choose View ➤ Toolbars ➤ Chart. Figure 14.8 tells you what's what on the toolbar. Between that and a few of the tricks in the next several sections, you can fix your chart in no time.

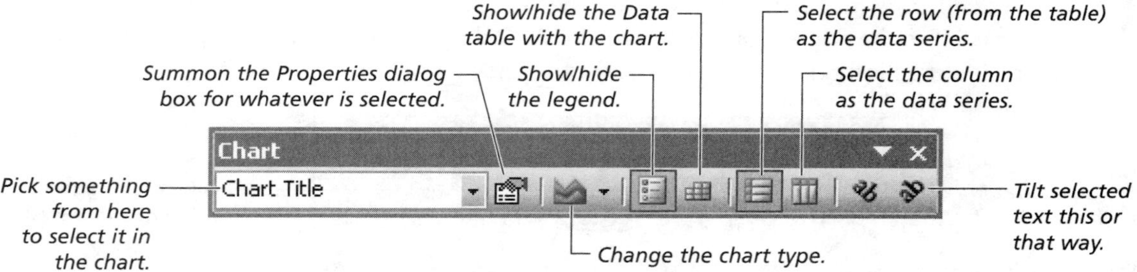

Figure 14.8 The Chart toolbar, your friend and pal

The following sections assume that the Chart toolbar is floating near your chart.

How Can I Quickly Convert the Chart into a Chart of Another Type?

Use the Chart toolbar's Chart Type button to quickly change the chart type. When you click this button (on the Chart toolbar), a drop-down palette of options appears, as shown in Figure 14.9. Just click one of the options to see your chart reformed.

Sadly, the options aren't as vast as in the Chart Wizard.

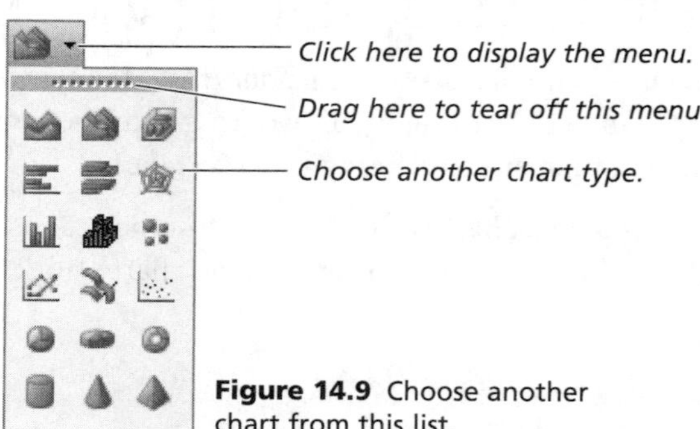

Figure 14.9 Choose another chart from this list.

If you really want to mess around, note that the drop-down palette can be "torn off" the Chart toolbar and dragged away to create the Chart Type toolbar. Point and drag the mouse as indicated in Figure 14.9.

Do I Have to Redo the Whole Wizard if I Don't Find a Chart Type I Like on the Wee Li'l Palette?

No. If you want the vast options from the Chart Wizard, then just right-click anywhere on your chart. Choose "Chart Type" from the pop-up menu, and you'll once again see the Chart Type dialog box, similar to the Chart Wizard's first step (Figure 14.3). That way, you can reset your chart to any of the examples Excel offers.

Now That the Chart Is Done, I Don't Like the Order of the Series. Do I Have to Redo Everything?

No. You can move the various columns or rows around whichever way you like. Follow these steps:

1. Right-click any column in the graph.

   If the graph doesn't have columns, click an element that represents the data, such as a dot in a scatter graph.

2. Choose "Format Data Series" from the pop-up menu.
3. In the Format Data Series dialog box, click the Series Order tab.

   Now you can rearrange the columns by selecting one and clicking the Move Up or Move Down button, as shown in Figure 14.10.

4. Click OK when you're done moving.

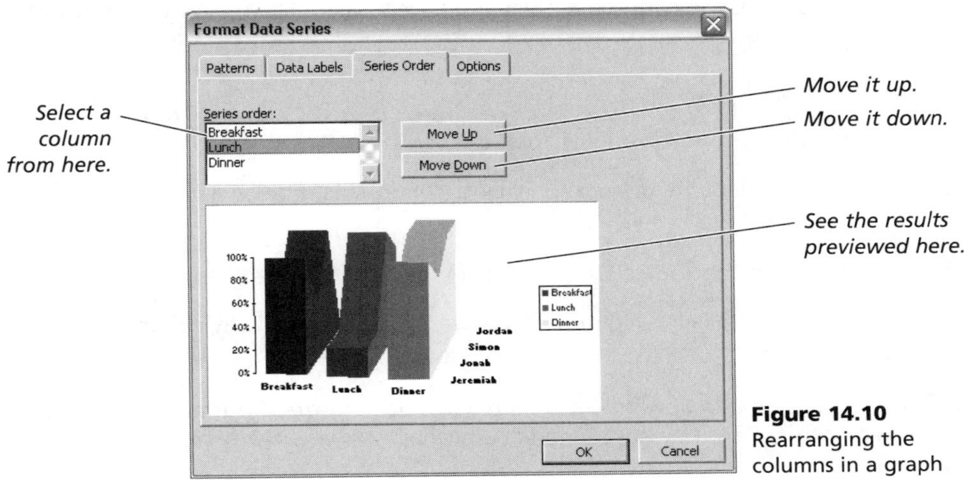

Figure 14.10
Rearranging the columns in a graph

What if I Want to Get Rid of a Column?

Cheating, huh? Seriously, it's easy to get rid of a column or any chunk of data in a chart. Use Figure 14.11 as an example.

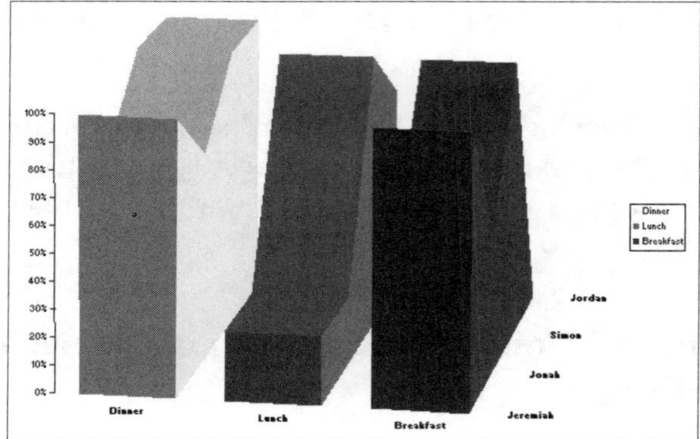

Figure 14.11
An example

Say you wanted to get rid of the Breakfast column in Figure 14.11. Follow these steps:

1. From the Chart toolbar, select Series "Breakfast" from the drop-down list.
2. Press the Delete key on the keyboard.

   It's gone.

You could also just right-click the thing and choose Clear from the pop-up menu, but with some charts removing a column or row can be tricky.

Now I Want My Column Back!

If you're too slow with the Undo command, then you have to manually re-add your row by telling the chart, once again, where to find its data. Heed these carefully worded steps:

1. Right-click the chart.
2. Choose "Source Data" from the pop-up menu.

   If you don't see that menu item, then try clicking again, this time on a column or other important bit in the chart.
3. Click the Series tab in the Source Data dialog box.

   You'll see something similar to Figure 14.12, where you can re-add any column you deleted from a chart.

You can also add new columns simply by selecting that information from any worksheet. This is a way to modify any chart you've already created.

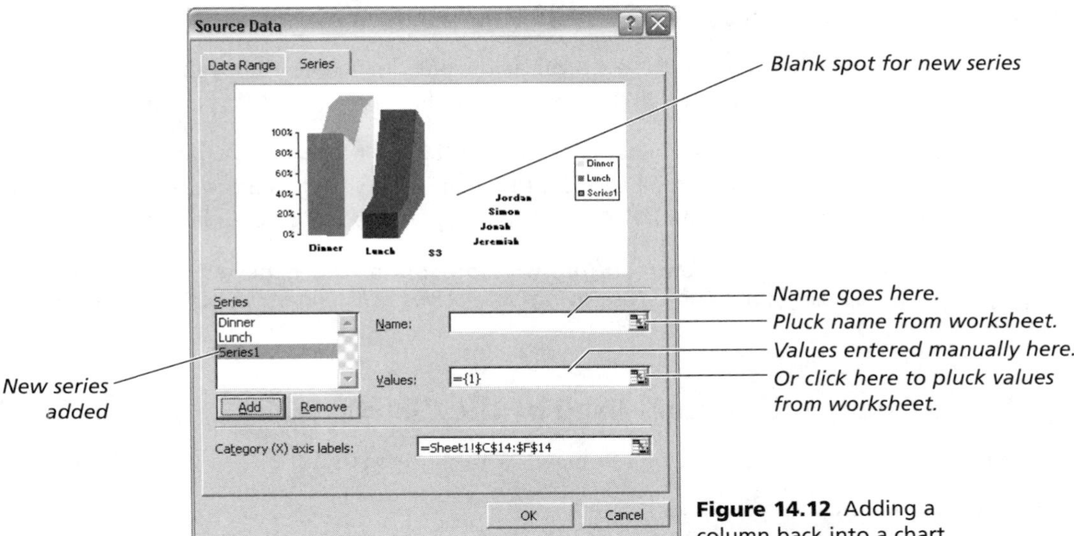

Figure 14.12 Adding a column back into a chart

4. Click the Add button.
5. Click the Go-get-her button on the right end of the Name box.
6. Click the tab of the sheet that has the chart's original table.

   You may think Excel is broken here. It's not. The dialog box is hidden, and you're looking at the chart underneath. You need to click a worksheet tab to return to the worksheet from whence the chart got its data.
7. Click the cell that contains the name of the column you zapped.

   In Figure 14.11 it was Breakfast, which happens to be in Sheet1, cell B15 on my screen.
8. Click the Return gizmo button.

   And you're back in the dialog box.
9. Click the Go-get-her button on the right end of the Values box.
10. Click the tab of the worksheet that contains the values you're looking for.
11. Select the cells containing the data for the new column.
12. Click the Return gizmo button.

    And that should be it.
13. Click OK.

    The chart is restored.

What About Deleting a Row of Data?

The data that series charts prefer to work with is the bottom, left-to-right values. If you want to work with values on other scales, you'll have to rotate the chart so that those values are in front.

For example, in Figure 14.11 the names are on the right side, not the bottom. To fix this, click the By Column button on the Chart toolbar. Then you can remove the item as outlined in the section, "What if I Want to Get Rid of a Column?" covered earlier in this chapter.

The By Row and By Column buttons will not work if you've messed with the chart too much. Especially, moving or removing data series will render the buttons useless.

Any Way to Change the Colors Used by the Chart?

If you don't like the color of a line or graph, follow these steps to fix it:

1. Right-click the offending line.

   Blue! How dare they. Especially this late in the spring!

2. Choose "Format Data Series" from the pop-up menu.
3. Click the Patterns tab in the Format Data Series dialog box.
4. Choose a new color from the Area area, as shown in Figure 14.13.
5. Click OK.

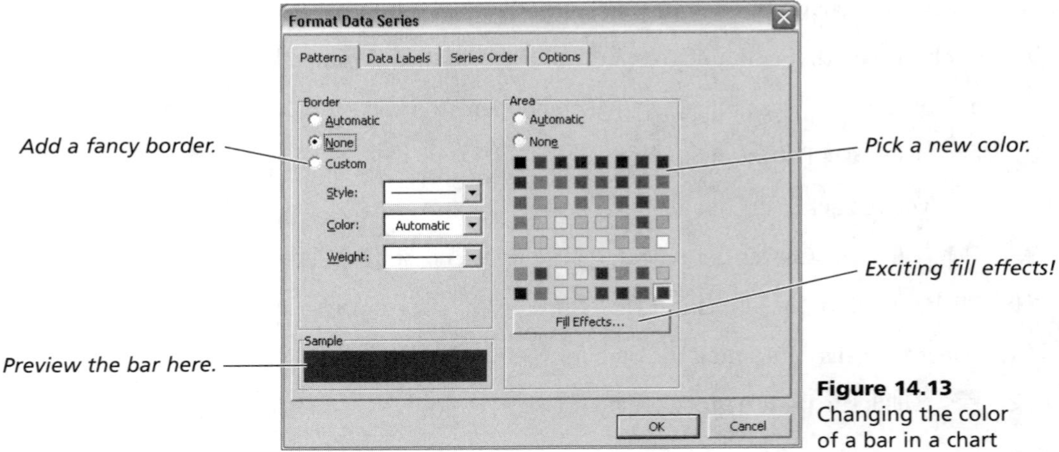

Figure 14.13
Changing the color of a bar in a chart

Rather than be boring by choosing another color, consider clicking the Fill Effects button in the Patterns tab of the Format Data Series dialog box. When you do, you'll find a great dialog box that lets you select gradients, textures, patterns, and even images from graphics files elsewhere on your disk for the chart.

For example, say you want your bar to look like it's faced with marble. If so, click the Fill Effects button and then click the Texture tab. Select a marble pattern from the list, and then click OK. Back in the Format Data Series dialog box, be sure to add a border to the artwork so that it can more easily be seen.

Figure 14.14 shows the results of reformatting the same chart from Figure 14.11, but using various types of fill styles for the data series.

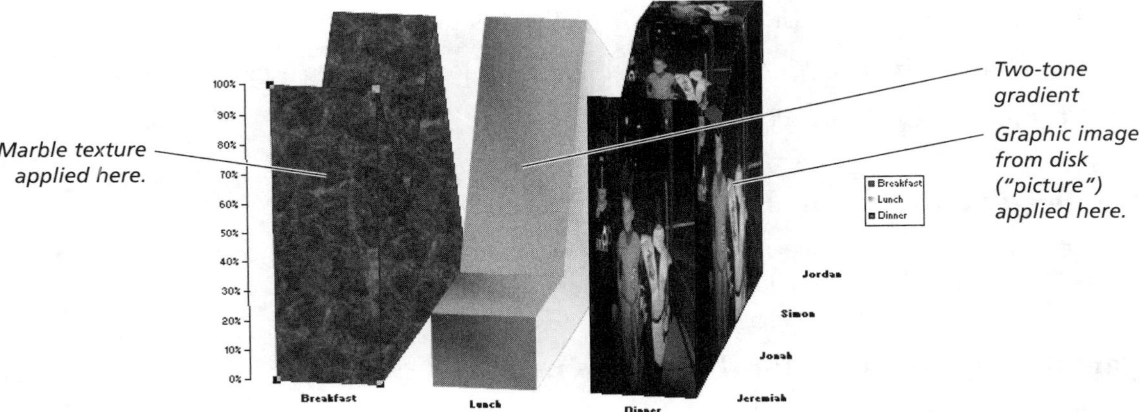

Figure 14.14 Way different colors for the chart

The availability of patterns, textures, gradients, and pictures depends on the type of chart selected.

I Forgot to Add a Title and Now I Want a Title!

This is easy to fix:

1. Right-click anywhere on the chart.
2. Choose "Chart Options" from the pop-up menu.

   If you don't see this command, then you clicked in the wrong place! In this case, unlike the previous sections, do not click on the chart's data.
3. The Chart Options dialog box appears.

   It looks similar to the dialog box you see in Step 3 of the Chart Wizard. In fact, anything you forgot to do back there can be redone or undone here.
4. Click the Titles tab.
5. Type the chart title into the "Chart Title" text box.
6. Click OK.

A problem now, and even back when you ran the Chart Wizard (if you did), is that you're given only a title and not really a chance to format it. If you want to format it, then continue with these steps:

7. Choose "Chart Title" from the drop-down list on the Chart toolbar.
8. Click the Properties button on the Chart toolbar.
9. In the Format Chart Title dialog box, click the Font tab.
10. Work the gizmos in the Font tab to select the title formatting you want.
11. Click OK when you're done.

I've Decided to Add the Legend.

This is cinchy, thanks to the Chart toolbar: Just click the Legend button on the toolbar. Ta-da! It alternately adds or removes the legend from your chart.

Can I Change the Font for the Chart's Labels?

Labels in the chart are referred to in the Chart toolbar's drop-down list as "Axis." These are the Category axis, Series axis, Value axis, and more (or fewer), depending on the type of chart.

To change the font, color, or other properties of these labels, choose the one you want from the Chart toolbar's drop-down list; then click the Properties button on the toolbar. Click the Font tab in whatever dialog box appears, and you're on your way.

How Can I Change the Label Names Used in the Chart?

The easiest way to do that is to return to the worksheet containing the original data table. Change the labels used on the table, and the chart will be updated instantly.

The Value Axis Is Displeasing Me to No End. Where Can I Modify It?

"Value axis" is the name given to the part of the chart that tells you what the bars represent, as shown in Figure 14.15. Here's how you mess with that part of the chart:

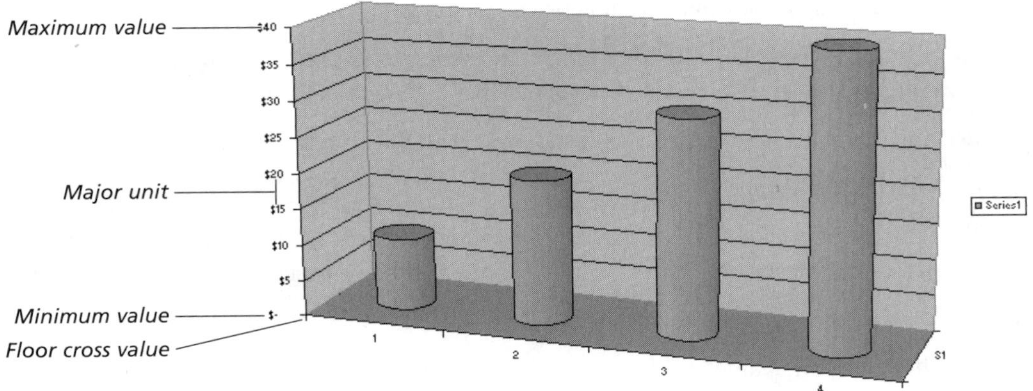

Figure 14.15 Things to play with on the Value axis

1. Choose "Value Axis" from the drop-down list on the Chart toolbar.
2. Click the Properties button.

   The Format Axis dialog box is displayed.
3. Click the Scale tab.

   And there is where you can mess with the axis, as shown in Figure 14.16.

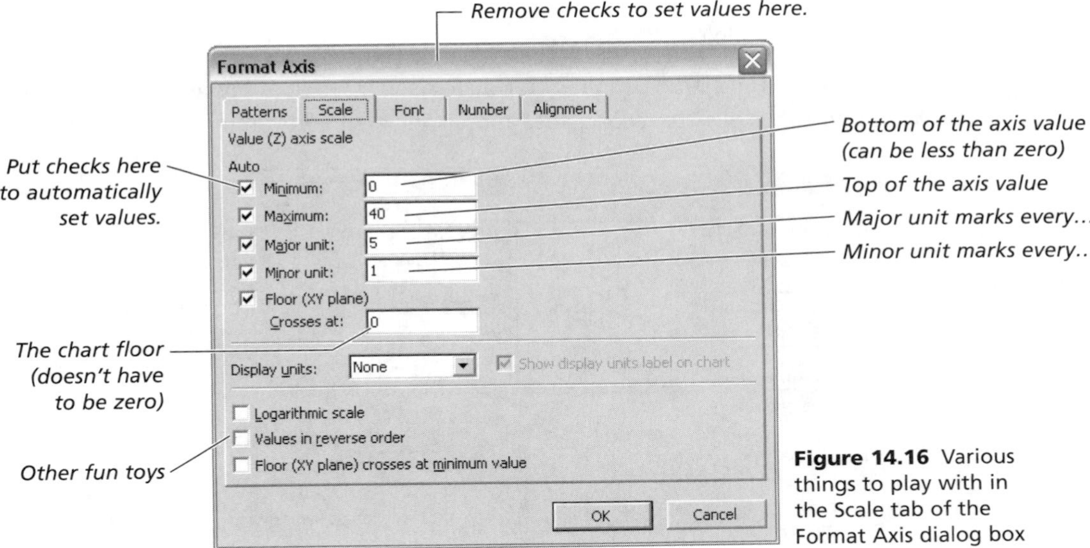

Figure 14.16 Various things to play with in the Scale tab of the Format Axis dialog box

4. Set the various options in the dialog box as please you.

   For example, if you want the Value axis to be shorter, uncheck the Minimum value and input something new. Or if you want it taller, put in a higher value.

   Leaving the check mark lets Excel decide where to put things.

5. Click the Patterns tab.

   Note the two areas for setting the Major and Minor tick marks. Normally the Minor tick marks aren't shown, so None is selected. But you can see them if you specify an option other than None.

6. Click OK.

   And hopefully the Value axis is formatted in a manner that does not tweak you.

Can I Redo the Angle of This 3-D Chart?

This is perhaps one of the most commonly asked of all the chart questions. That is, after you create a 3-D view on a graph, how can you move the "camera" that displays the graph. It's simple, providing you follow these secretive steps:

1. Right-click the chart.

   Not on any data, but just on the chart's background.

2. Choose "3-D View" from the pop-up menu.

3. Play with the 3-D View dialog box.

   Figure 14.17 shows you the gizmos, though this dialog box more than invites playtime. Note that the Default button is used to recover the original angle, should you really screw things up.

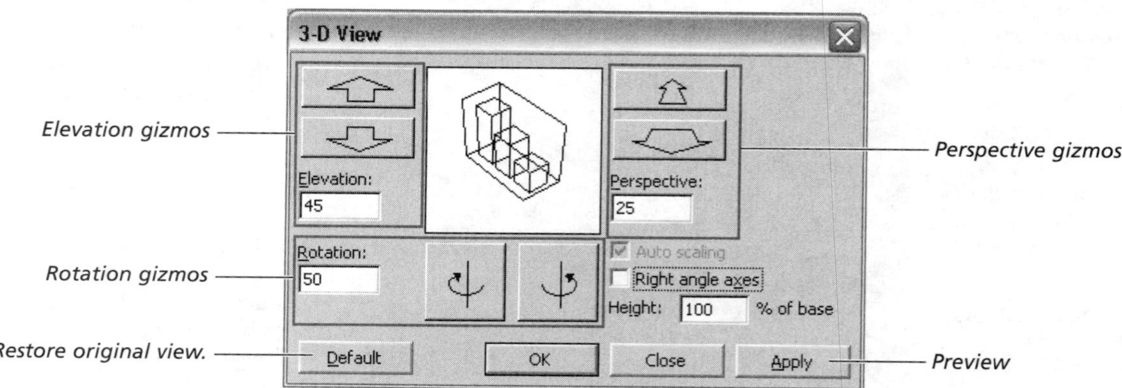

Figure 14.17 Adjusting your view

4. Click OK when you're done.

Note that the 3-D View dialog box is one of the rare ones in Office with an Apply button. Clicking that button allows you to see (in the background) the effect your adjustments have on the chart. That way you can preview without having to close the dialog box.

How Can I Space the Bars Farther Apart?

Some of those charts do get crowded. It really depends not only on how much data you're putting into the chart but also on the chart type. Some charts show a mess of data better than others; you just have to preview things to see which looks best.

There are some after-creation adjustments you can make to a chart to space out the bars. Compare Figures 14.18 and 14.19.

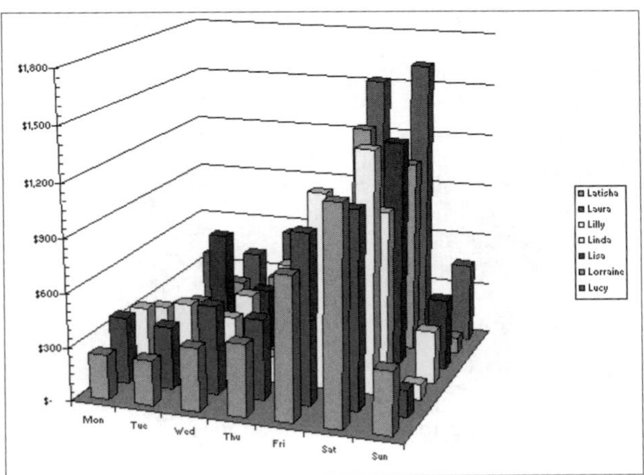

Figure 14.18
Bars too close together

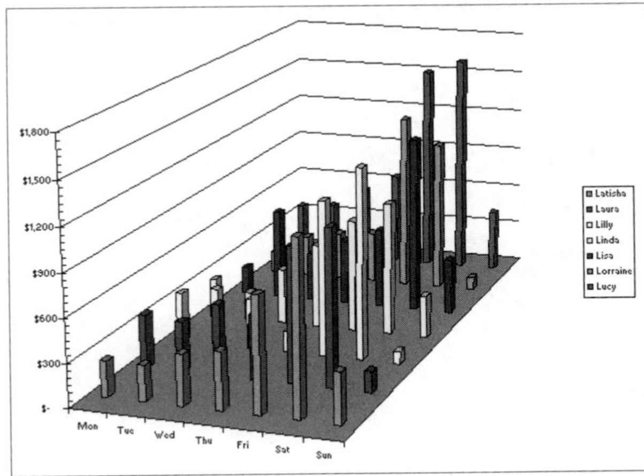

Figure 14.19
Bars just right

Here are the steps taken to make those bars appear farther apart:

1. Right-click the mouse on any bar.
2. Choose "Format Data Series" from the pop-up menu.

   The Format Data Series dialog box appears.
3. Click the Options tab.

   If there is no Options tab, then you have a chart type that cannot be adjusted in this manner.

   Figure 14.20 shows the dialog box and its pertinent parts.

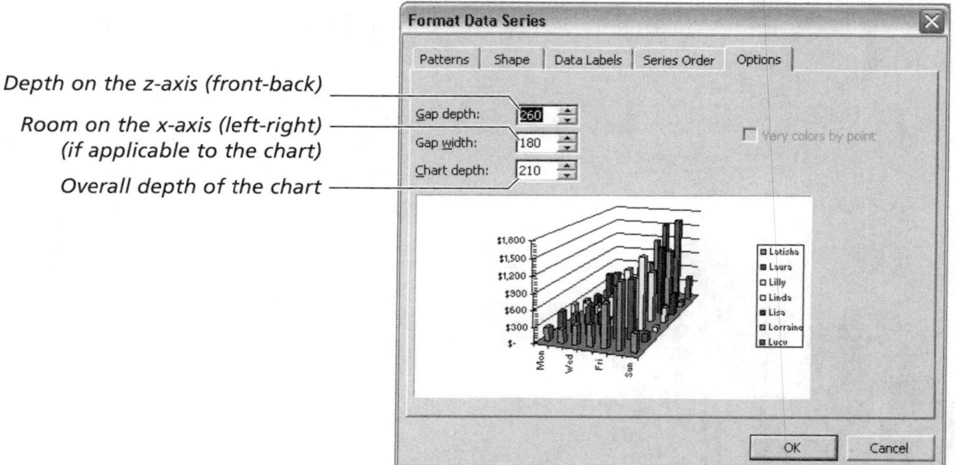

Figure 14.20 Adjusting the room between bars

4. Adjust the depths and widths.

   Refer to Figure 14.20 for how this works, though you can have fun just playing on your own.
5. Click OK when you're done.

Also consider combining the adjustments made here with the 3-D View adjustments described in the previous section to truly customize how your chart is presented.

Does the Chart Update if I Change the Values in the Worksheet?

Yes.

I Need to Paste the Chart into a Word Document!

The key here is to be able to select the chart properly. You must select the whole thing, the Chart Area. If not, you won't even be allowed to copy.

The quickest way to select the Chart Area is to choose that option from the Chart toolbar's drop-down list. Then copy, switch over to Word, and paste.

Beyond that basic move, everything that is mentioned about copying a worksheet into Word (from Chapter 10, "Why the Hell Would Anyone Other than an Accountant Use Excel?" the section "Plopping an Excel Thing into a Word Thing") also applies to charts.

15 Excel Templates, Samples, and Web Mischief

I like eating out, but I hate menus. For some reason, my brain never makes the connection between what's written on the menu and what the food eventually looks and tastes like. So I generally order something I don't want. That's unless I'm dining with someone, and then I'll have what they're having. Or unless I'm eating at Denny's or some restaurant with pictures on the menu. Then I'm okay.

This chapter has nothing to do with dining out. Instead, it's the "show me a picture" chapter. Sometimes it's just easier to point at the picture and say, "This is what I want!" So what I've done is concocted a few worksheet examples. Some of them illustrate concepts I haven't yet presented—things that I'd like to show you but that didn't fit into the other chapters. The rest of the examples are of some common worksheets. They're enough to build upon or at least inspire you to create bigger, better, and bolder worksheets in the future.

Rumors squelched and gossip silenced:

- Creating, using, and changing workbook templates
- Designing the special BOOK and SHEET templates
- Using the handy Split and Freeze commands
- Formatting rows and columns to create a calendar
- Importing data from the Web into a worksheet

The Document You Use Over and Over: The Template

The examples that dot the rest of this chapter may eventually form the basis for some common worksheets—stuff you use over and over. In Microsoft Office parlance, the stuff you use over and over is potential template material. After all, why keep rebuilding the same worksheet over and over when you can start with a basic template and get most of the job done ahead of time?

Saving a Template: Duh

You've built the basics. Formatted. Created styles even. Everything about the workbook is set for reuse. The only things you haven't entered are the things that change in specific cells: information that will be input later, such as dates, values, text, other numbers, and la-di-da. It's Miller Time! But before you walk into the sunset with your pals in a beer commercial, you need to save the workbook to disk as a template. Here's how your fumbling fingers would do that:

1. Choose File ➤ Save As.
2. From the "Save As Type" drop-down list, choose "Template (*.xlt)."

   When you do this, note that the folder changes. Excel saves the template in your own personal Templates folder. Its location varies depending on your version of Windows. See the sidebar, "Where the Templates Lurk on the Hard Drive" for the boring details.
3. Give them template a memorable filename.
4. Click the Save button.
5. Close the file.

   I recommend this step to cease any further modification of the template at this time. If you want to use the template, then it's best to start up a new document and do it that way.

A template can come from any source. You can build one off a workbook you've already created or you can make one from scratch. My advice is to create a workbook first, then customize it over time, and finally save it to disk as a template.

Saving a template focuses Excel's attention on the Templates folder. To return to the My Documents folder when you go to open another workbook, click the My Documents button on the left end of the Open dialog box.

You Must Know This: Where the Templates Lurk on the Hard Drive

Excel tends to save its template files in the most random of locations. It would take me a few paragraphs to describe these locations for each version of Windows. Instead of wasting your time reading that, here's a big tip:

Create a folder specifically for your Excel templates. For example, create a folder in the My Documents folder and call it `Excel Templates`*. Then store all your Excel templates there, instead of the place Excel uses—which, as I've said before, isn't easy to get to and varies depending on which version of Windows you're using (and whether you've upgraded Office or installed it new).*

And to Use the Template?

Templates ain't no good unless you can use them over and over. To create a new workbook based on a template, obey these steps:

1. Choose File ➢ New.

In Excel 2003/XP this action displays the New Workbook task pane. You're not done yet. However, if you do see the template you want to use displayed near the bottom of the task pane, you can click it now and get on with things. But that's not the point of these steps.

In Excel 2000, you'll see the New dialog box, similar to the Templates dialog box shown in Figure 15.1.

2a. In Excel 2003, click the "On My Computer" link in the task pane.

2b. In Excel XP, click the "General Templates" link in the task pane.

Now you see what your Excel 2000 brothers saw already (the price for upgrading), which is the Templates dialog box, shown in Figure 15.1.

3. Select a template to use and click the OK button.

And you're using that template.

Everything from the template is imported into your current workbook. With all that work done, you just need to fill in the missing parts. But do not forget to save! Give the file a new, proper name, and then save it in a logical location when you're done. Or, better still, do that first so you don't have to be reminded of it later.

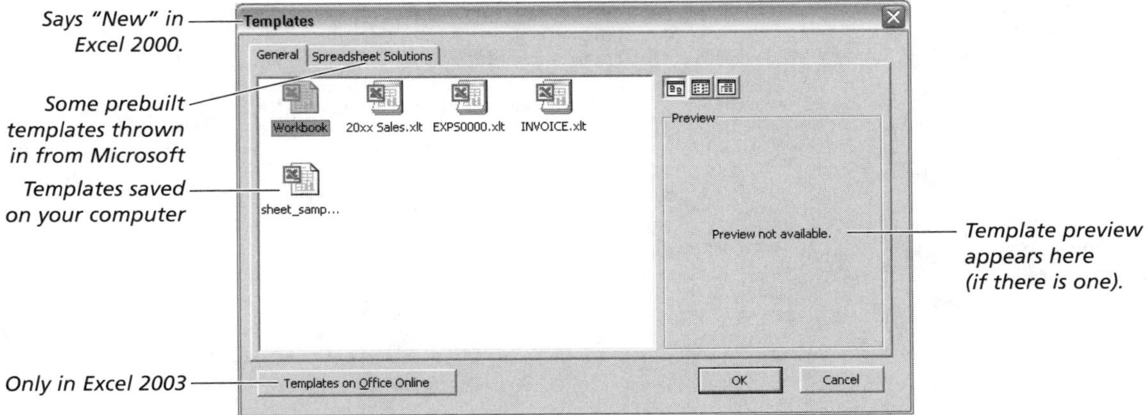

Figure 15.1 Pluck a template from this place.

What's the Best Way to Change a Template?

Rather than search all over the hard drive for a template you want to fix, just start up a new document using that template. Fix stuff. Then save the document back to disk as a template again, which is covered earlier in this chapter.

Rename the file back to the original template name! The file will probably have a "1" in it. Delete that 1, and then you'll have the original template name.

Be sure to answer "Yes" when you're asked if you want to replace the original.

How Can I Save a Template with a Preview Window?

Before you save the template file to disk, follow these steps:

1. Choose File ➤ Properties.
2. Click the Summary tab.
3. Put a check mark in the box by "Save Preview Picture."
4. Click OK.

   The template is now saved with preview information you can see when selecting the template.

This trick also works for any Excel workbooks. For example, to see the preview in the Open dialog box, click the Views button/menu in the Open dialog box (Figure 15.2). Choose Preview from the menu that appears, and then you can see the preview (for regular documents that have them).

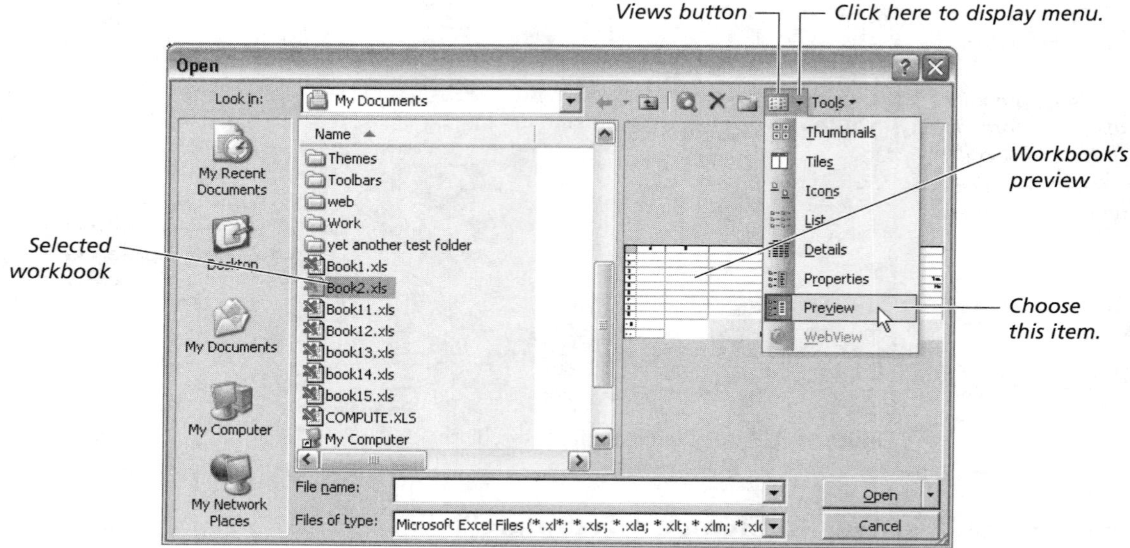

Figure 15.2 Preview documents in the Open dialog box.

Other Users on My Windows XP Computer Cannot Find the Template!

No, they can't! That's because each user on a Windows XP computer has their own account area, separate from other users and typically password-protected as well.

The least awkward solution is to copy the template files you want to share into the Shared Documents folder. Then have the other users copy them from the Shared Documents folder into their own folders.

Or if you want to be magnanimous, simply direct everyone on the computer to save their Excel templates directly into the Shared Documents folder (or a subfolder of Shared Documents).

What's the Equivalent in Excel to the NORMAL.DOT Template in Word?

Excel has two equivalents to `NORMAL.DOT`, which is the main document template in Word. One is called `BOOK.XLS`, and the other is called `SHEET.XLS`.

As an example, suppose that every sheet you add to your workbook must be the same. Say they are invoices or yearly financial summaries—whatever—the bottom line is that whenever you add a new worksheet, you'd like it to be preset with certain things. If so, then what you need is a SHEET template. Here's how to make one:

1. Start a new, blank workbook.
2. Delete Sheets 2 and 3.

So that you have only one sheet remaining. This is very important. If you don't delete the extra sheets, then this technique doesn't work.

3. Gussy up the one sheet as your single-sheet template.

   For example, you can set various styles, name ranges of cells, or preformat dates and times. Do whatever it is you want to appear in every new sheet you add to a worksheet. An example is shown in Figure 15.3.

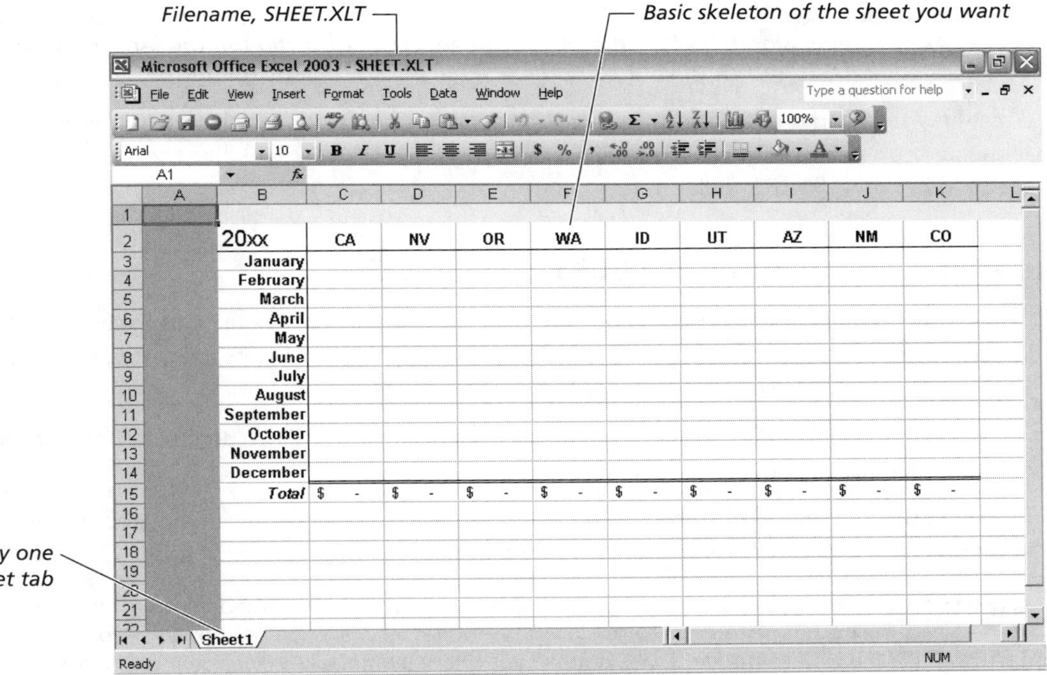

Figure 15.3 A sample sheet template

Obviously if you prefer not *to have preformatted sheets but blank sheets, you do not need to create a SHEET template.*

4. When you're ready, choose File ➢ Save As.

5. Choose "Template (*.xlt)" from the "Save As Type" drop-down list.

   You are saving a template to disk.

6. Name the document `SHEET`.

   So the full name would be `SHEET.XLT`, for Excel template.

7. Choose the folder `C:\Program Files\Microsoft Office\Office\XLSTART` from the "Save In" drop-down list.

   If you've upgraded Microsoft Office, then there will be several subfolders named Office inside the Microsoft Office folder. Choose the one with the highest number. Or perhaps the only folder there may have a number at the end of its name, such as Office10.

8. Click the Save button to save.

This resets Excel's working folder to the XLSTART folder. The next time you use the Save As or Open dialog box, click the My Documents folder button (on the left side of the dialog box) to return to your computer's main My Documents folder.

To test how this works, simply add a new sheet to any workbook; choose Insert ➤ Worksheet from the menu or press Shift+F11. All new sheets added to the workbook look like the `SHEET.XLT` file you saved in the XLSTART folder.

What's the Purpose of the BOOK.XLT Template?

The `BOOK.XLT` template provides a template for all new workbooks you create in Excel. It works like the `SHEET.XLT` template, though `BOOK.XLT` can contain multiple sheets formatted how you like them—or it may only need to contain some styles you enjoy using.

Like `SHEET.XLT`, the `BOOK.XLT` template must be saved in the XLSTART folder; refer to the previous section for details.

After `BOOK.XLT` is saved, all new workbooks you create will carry whatever features are found in the `BOOK.XLT` template—unless you use another template to create a workbook.

Remember that a `BOOK.XLT` *template need not contain any preformatted cells at all. Perhaps it just needs to contain some styles you like to use. However you format the* `BOOK.XLT` *template, that's how all your new workbooks will appear and work in Excel.*

I'm Painfully Tired of My SHEET.XLT and BOOK.XLT Templates.

To suspend the preformatting action of the `SHEET.XLT` and `BOOK.XLT` templates, merely move them out of the XLSTART folder and paste them elsewhere. For example, I moved them to the Shared Documents folder in Windows XP, which is a handy spot for anyone to get at them.

When the files are gone, then Excel behaves as it normally does: New workbooks are blank and contain three blank worksheets, and when you insert a new worksheet, it comes up blank as well.

Is It Safe to Use a Template from the Web?

Downloading anything from the Web involves two keywords, "reliable source." It's possible to download an Excel template that contains a virus, for example. So when you go web browsing for templates—and there are many out there—find a web page that you feel is trustworthy. If you're trustworthy-impaired, then just visit Microsoft's own web page, which has literally thousands of useful templates—a solution for just about every puzzle you could imagine.

To visit the Web for templates in Excel 2003, click the "Templates Home Page" link in the New Workbook task pane.

In Excel XP, click the link that says "Templates on Microsoft.com," also in the task pane.

For Excel 2000, visit the following page on the Internet:

`http://officeupdate.microsoft.com/TemplateGallery/`

From what I can gather, each version of Office appears to have its own home plate on the Microsoft web page. Yet I don't see anything that says specifically that templates from one version of Excel will not work on another.

What's the Need for the Save Workspace Command?

The File ➤ Save Workspace command can be very handy for the busy Excel user. What it does is to save the size and position of all your open Excel workbooks, charts, and what-have-you. That way, if you're a stickler for positioning your stuff "just so" on the screen, you can get that position back by saving the workspace.

To reload the workspace, simply choose the saved workspace file when you start Excel. Because of that, obviously, it helps to save your workspace using a memorable filename.

For example, Stella works at a major television production studio (not Fox) and every day she's e-mailed the overnight ratings. She likes to open up that window on the left and then enter data for her shows into a worksheet on the right edge of the screen. Rather than spend four or five minutes positioning each worksheet's window "just so" (and because her boss is too cheap to buy an 18-inch LCD display), she just uses the Save Workspace command. To start her day, she opens the workspace and the worksheets are already positioned, opened, and ready for her to report the "overnights."

Some Simple Sample Documents

The following sections show how to set up and use some sample documents. These could be future templates, or they could be handy examples of new things you didn't know about, or they may just show you a few tricks you haven't yet thought of.

The Big Worksheet with the Seemingly Stable Headings

Not every worksheet is going to fit neatly on the screen. Consider at the minimum that a worksheet with the months January through December requires 12 columns. That may barely fit on your screen. The problem isn't seeing them all at once; Excel scrolls over to display any part of a large worksheet. The problem comes when you use column or row headings. They disappear as you scroll into the meat of a worksheet.

Consider Figure 15.4. August through December are off to the left—just a scrollbar away—but when you scroll over that far, the row headings in column A disappear! Note that I've color-coded the major headings, so that's one helpful clue. But otherwise, there will be a lot of left-right scrolling going on as you fill in the months August through December.

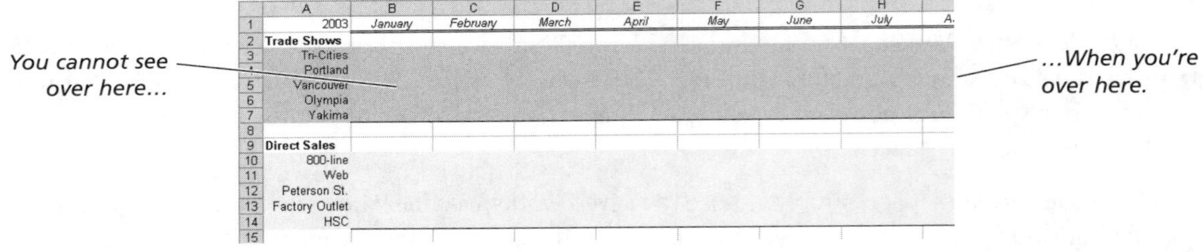

Figure 15.4 The wide problem

And that's just not my idea of a computer trying to save you time!

KEYBOARD MASTER

Scrolling in a Worksheet

Here are the keyboard keys you use to scroll in a worksheet:

PgUp
Scroll up.

PgDn
Scroll down.

Alt+PgDn
Scroll right.

Alt+PgUp
Scroll left.

Fortunately there is a handy solution, which I call split and freeze. First the split:

Excel lets you split a single worksheet into two or four panes. Each pane scrolls independently of each other pane, which is the key to seeing a larger piece of a worksheet without losing sight of another piece. Follow these peaceful steps:

1. Click a cell somewhere in the middle of your screen.

Say, cell E12, which looks middlish on the screen.

2. Choose Window ➤ Split.

Holy smokes! A cross is nailed to your worksheet, but what you actually see are split-pane bars that allow you to scroll each of the four areas individually. Figure 15.5 shows what's up.

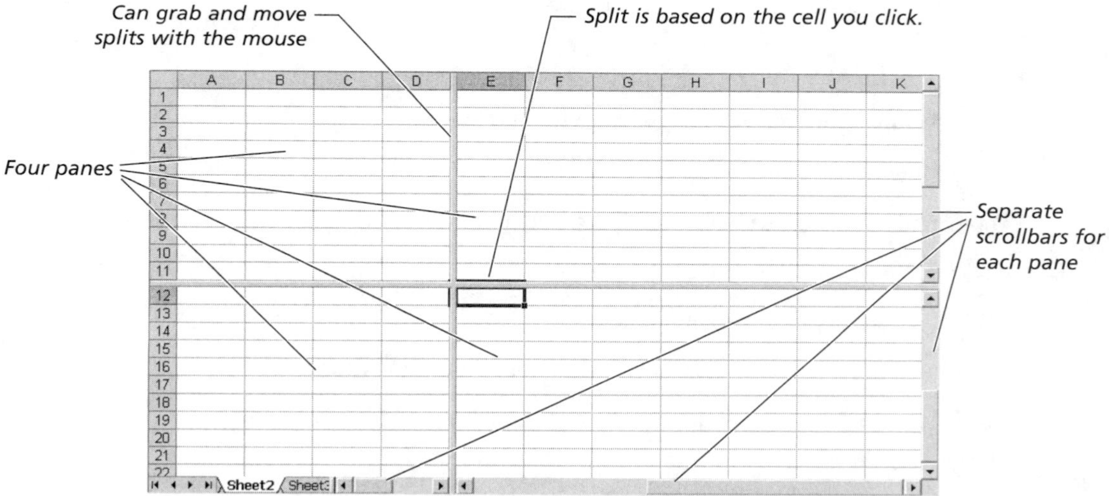

Figure 15.5 Not a banana split, but a worksheet split

Each pane shows you a different part of the worksheet. They're all scrollably independent. Or they can all show you the same view:

3. Scroll each pane so that cell A1 is visible in each.

4. Click to select cell A1.

5. Type `echo` into cell A1.

And what you see should look like Figure 15.6. Scary that you can click one pane and see three echoes.

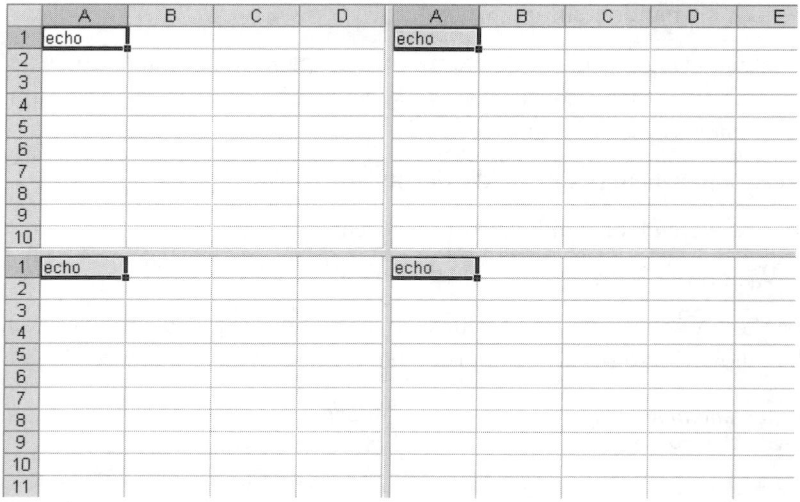

Figure 15.6 Four views of the same set of cells

Scary. Downright frightening.

You can also arrange to have the worksheet split manually.

6. Choose Window ➤ Remove Split.

   And the three bogus panes are gone.

7. Grab the horizontal split gizmo with the mouse and drag down.

   Use Figure 15.7 as your guide. When you're done moving the split bar, you'll have two views on the worksheet.

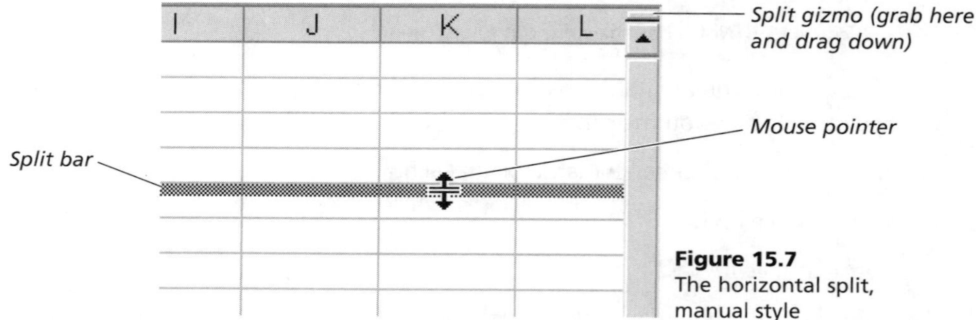

Figure 15.7 The horizontal split, manual style

To split vertically in a manual manner, use the vertical split gizmo:

8. Grab the vertical split gizmo and drag to the left.

Refer to Figure 15.8 for information on how this one works.

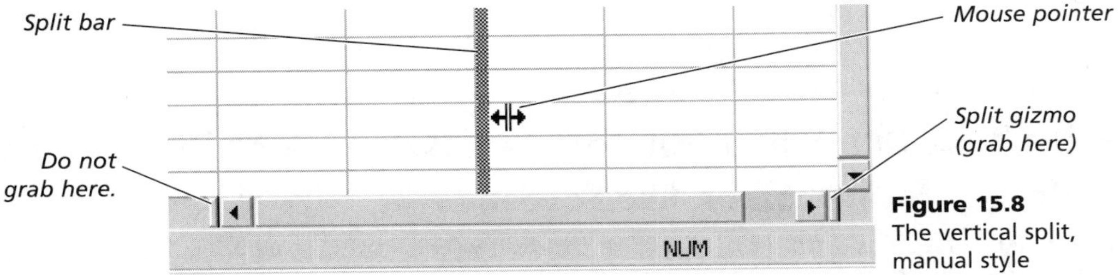

Figure 15.8 The vertical split, manual style

Returning the example in Figure 15.4, what's needed are split bars just below row 1 and to the left of column A. This solution is shown in Figure 15.9.

Year stays in this tiny pane.

Months stay up here.

Column A stays in this pane.

Scrolling data area

	A	I	J	K	L	M	N	O
1	2003	*August*	*September*	*October*	*November*	*December*	Totals	Percentage
2	**Trade Shows**							
3	Tri-Cities							
4	Portland							
5	Vancouver							
6	Olympia							
7	Yakima							
8								
9	**Direct Sales**							
10	800-line							
11	Web							
12	Peterson St.							
13	Factory Outlet							
14	HSC							
15								
16	**Wholesale**							
17	Wholesale							
18	**Special**							
19	Special							
20								
21	**Total**							
22								

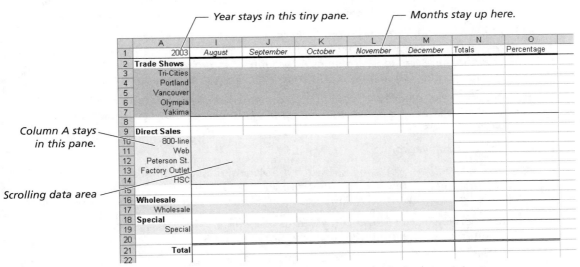

Figure 15.9 The split-screen solution to the large worksheet

See how part of the sheet can scroll over to display August through December? The rows and columns on the worksheet are still visible. But there's one more trick:

9. Choose Window ➤ Freeze Panes.

This command does two things. First it locks the split bars in place, which essentially freezes the top, top-right, and bottom-left panes. Those panes cannot be scrolled. Second, the split bars narrow so that they become less distracting.

Now you can use the worksheet, scrolling it around at your own whim, and not have to worry about losing the row or column headings.

To unfreeze the panes, choose Window ➤ Unfreeze Panes. Then optionally choose Window ➤ Remove Split to get rid of the split bars.

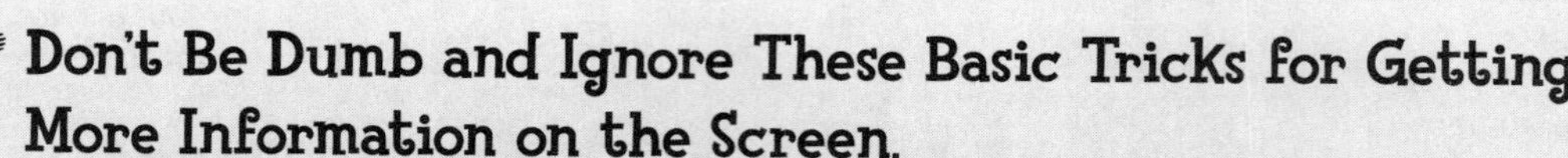

Don't Be Dumb and Ignore These Basic Tricks for Getting More Information on the Screen.

You may not be stuck with a tiny aperture through which you must view Excel's worksheet. There are many tricks for getting more information on the screen, all of which are basic computer tricks but which are also easy to forget. Here's my short list:

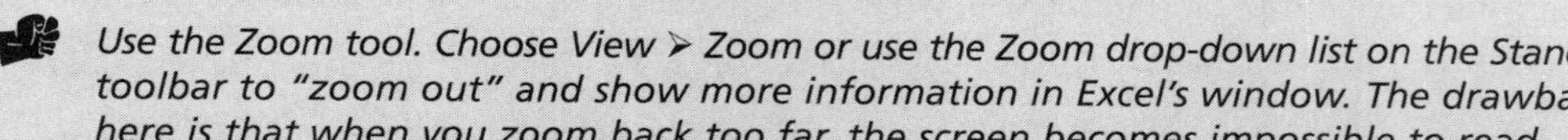

- *Use the Zoom tool. Choose View ➤ Zoom or use the Zoom drop-down list on the Standard toolbar to "zoom out" and show more information in Excel's window. The drawback here is that when you zoom back too far, the screen becomes impossible to read.*

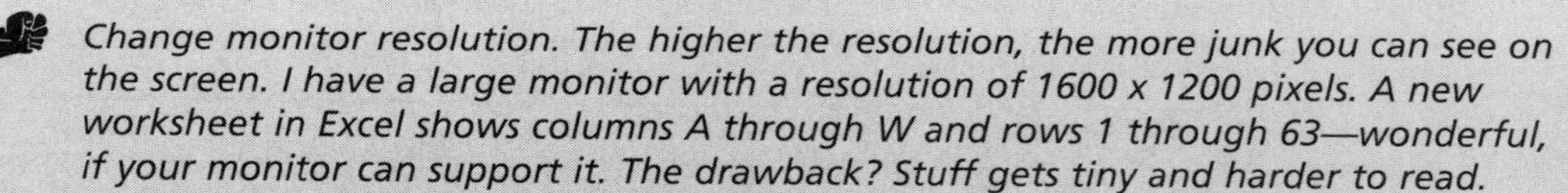

- *Change monitor resolution. The higher the resolution, the more junk you can see on the screen. I have a large monitor with a resolution of 1600 x 1200 pixels. A new worksheet in Excel shows columns A through W and rows 1 through 63—wonderful, if your monitor can support it. The drawback? Stuff gets tiny and harder to read.*
- *Adjust all the column widths so that no column is wider than it needs to be. Remember: Double-click the line between one column and the next to make the first column as wide as necessary.*

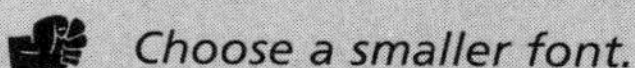

- *Choose a smaller font.*
- *Remove toolbars. You can also switch the Windows taskbar to Auto-hide, which can be a frustrating option, but it does give you at least two more rows on the screen. (Refer to your favorite Windows book for information on auto-hiding the taskbar.)*
- *Use the View ➤ Full Screen command to do away with all of Excel's gizmos. Refer to Chapter 9, "Customizing Word," for information on how this works with Word; the command is similar for Excel.*

The Travel Expense Report Example

There was one time when I was traveling quite a bit in my line of work, at least twice a month. For every trip, I had to fill out a report or my evil boss wouldn't reimburse me. That taught me a lot about worksheets, because my original quick-and-dirty expense report eventually grew to include all kinds of categories for things I could be reimbursed for. The final evolution of that worksheet is shown in Figure 15.10.

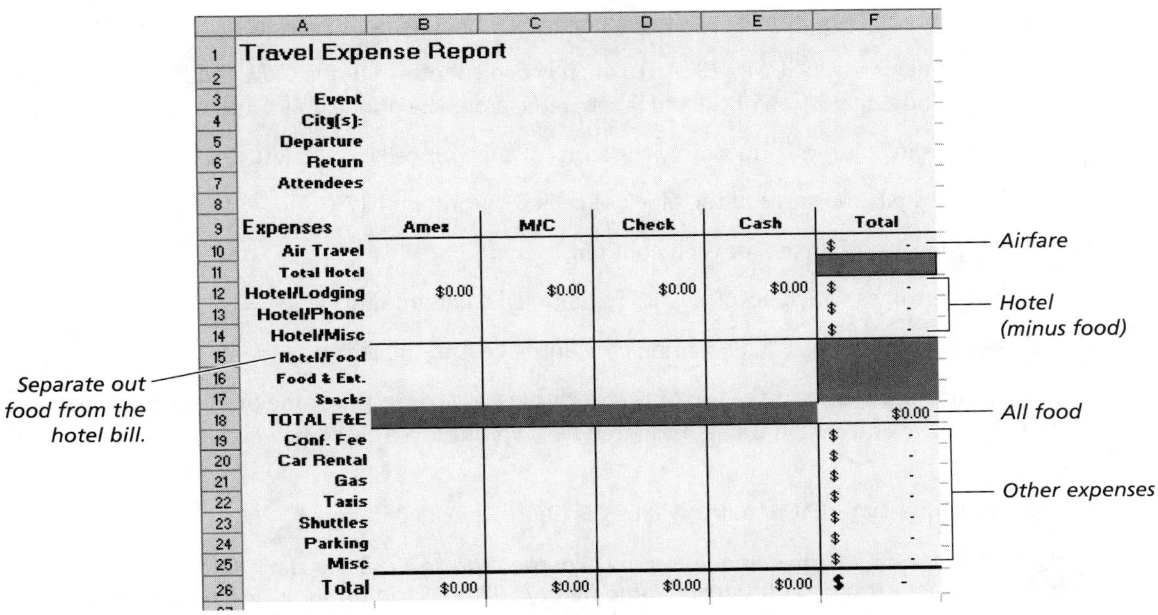

Figure 15.10 Crude but effective travel reimbursement report

It's the evil accountant who forced most of the "logic" in this travel expense report. The categories for reimbursement are all in column F. That's the key to the thing. Because of that, I had to devise some way to pull any food paid for on the hotel bill out of that part of the bill and onto a separate food bill. (Some companies make you do the same thing with the phone bill charges.) Here's how I did that:

1. The total hotel bill is input on line 11.

   There are four columns for inputting the expenses, depending on how the expense was paid: corporate American Express card, personal MasterCard, check, or cash. The source didn't matter to the company, but it did to me for when I filled out my expenses at home on the computer.

2. The total for all the phone calls is put into line 13.

3. The total for any miscellaneous charges is put into line 14.

4. Line 15 shows any food purchases made at the hotel.

   This included hotel restaurants, room service, the minibar, and those overpriced soda machines in the ice room.

5. The non-food, non-phone, non-misc part of the hotel bill is then calculated in line 12.

   The formula is =B11-SUM(B13:B15), which is copied into columns C, D, and E as well. That's how the lodging portion of the bill is separated from the phone, food, and whatever.

6. The totals in column F are simply the sums of the four cells to the left.
7. Cell F18 equals the sums of the block of cells B15 through E17.
8. The totals on row 26 are for each column.

   This determines which account gets reimbursed what amount.

9. And the final total cell, F26, contains the entire cost of the trip.

Note that there are spaces at the top of the worksheet to type in the name of the event, the cities visited, departure and return times, and attendees. For multiple cities, however, it's best to do one sheet per stay.

Now the only question that remains will be, "Is liquor considered 'food?'"

When it comes to naming my expense reports, I use the start date of the trip. So a trip on February 9 would be EXPS0209. A trip on June 17 would be EXPS0617. This naming scheme allows the files to be sorted in chronological order when the folder is sorted alphabetically.

Making a Calendar

Excel can make beautiful calendars, and I'm not going to waste any of your time here giving the step-by-steps when so many prebuilt templates exist. So if you want to use Excel to print out a pretty calendar (and even add pictures of the kids), visit the Web and browse through the many calendar templates available.

In my own experience, I'm stubborn and so I make my own calendars, but usually not the wall-hanging kind (which I can still pick up free at various car part stores around town—and some credit unions still hand them out). What I need calendars for is *scheduling*. I've used both linear and two-dimensional calendars for this purpose.

The Linear Calendar

A linear calendar is something most people would probably make in Word. I use Excel because it has better grid-management features such as Calendar, shown in Figure 15.11.

Basically I'm using Excel as a table here. The problem with putting such information into a standard calendar is that there's not enough room. The "cast" that needs to be present in Figure 15.11 (column D) would never fit in a standard calendar-sized square.

Date	Time	Subject	Who needs to be at the Theater!
Tue, March 23	7:00 PM	*Work Act 3*	Lys, Dem, Hermia, Helena, Quince, Snug, Bottom, Flute, Snout, Starveling, Oberon, Titania, Puck, Peaseblossom, Cobweb, Moth, Mustardseed
Thu, March 25	7:00 PM	*Work Act 4*	Theseus, Hyppolyta, Egeus, Athenians, Lys, Dem, Hermia, Helena, Quince, Snug, Bottom, Flute, Snout, Starveling, Oberon, Titania, Puck, Peaseblossom, Cobweb, Moth, Mustardseed
Sat, March 27	10:00 AM	*Set building!*	Entire cast!
	1:00 PM	Pizza Party!	
	4:00 PM	*Work Act 5*	Entire cast!
Wed, March 31	7:00 PM	*Work Acts 1 and 2*	Entire cast (all Fairies, Athenians, Indian Boy too!)
Fri, April 2	7:00 PM	*Work Act 3*	Lys, Dem, Hermia, Helena, Quince, Snug, Bottom, Flute, Snout, Starveling, Oberon, Titania, Puck, Peaseblossom, Cobweb, Moth, Mustardseed
Sat, April 3	10:00 AM	Painting	All Cast

Figure 15.11 A linear calendar done in Excel

The More Traditional Calendar

I typically use this linear calendar when I direct large-cast shows at my community theater. For smaller-cast shows, people are more familiar with—and actually use—the traditional calendar make-up, as shown in Figure 15.12. It's actually not that difficult to create, once you know a few shortcuts.

April 2003

Sunday	*Monday*	*Tuesday*	*Wednesday*	*Thursday*	*Friday*	*Saturday*
		1	2	3	4	5
6	7	8	9	10	11	12
13	14	15	16	17	18	19
20	21	22	23	24	25	26
27	28	29	30			

Figure 15.12 A more traditional calendar done in Excel

The key I've found when creating a traditional calendar is to allocate four cells for each date, as illustrated in Figure 15.13. That way you can stick a variety of information into a "date" by cheating. And it also helps to know how to squeeze text into cells using text wrapping and alignment tricks.

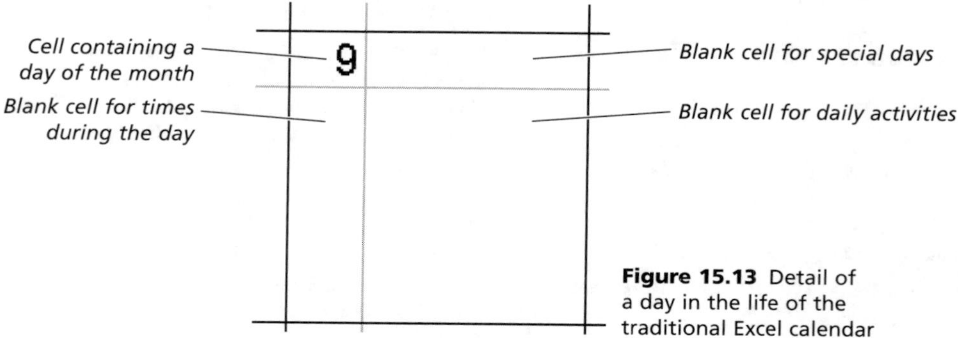

Figure 15.13 Detail of a day in the life of the traditional Excel calendar

To set up the calendar:

1. Start a new worksheet in Excel.

   First you format the columns:

2. Click the A heading to select all of column A.
3. Press and hold the Ctrl key to select columns C, E, G, I, K, and M.

   These are the cells that will hold the days of the month. Pressing and holding the Ctrl key ensures that you can select multiple things in Excel.

4. Choose Format ➢ Column ➢ Width.
5. Set the width to `2.6` and click OK.

   This works as long as you're using standard Arial 10 pt as your calendar's font. If you're not, it's easy to fix later by reselecting the columns and making the width wider.

6. Select columns B, D, F, H, J, L, and N.

   Use the Ctrl key to click and select the multiple columns.

7. Format their column width to `9`.

   That takes care of seven days a week. The next step is to format the rows for the dates. Most months can fit into a 7 by 5 grid, though occasionally there are months requiring a sixth row. The following steps do a five-week grid:

8. Click to select rows 4, 6, 8, 10, and 12.

   Use the Ctrl key to select multiple rows at once.

9. Choose Format ➢ Row ➢ Height.

10. Set the row height to 56.

    Now you enter the text for the calendar:

11. Type the month and year into cell F1.

To ensure that Excel accepts exactly what you type, prefix the month by a single tick (') or apostrophe. That prevents Excel from formatting the month and year as a time value.

12. Into cell A2 type `Sunday`.

13. Into cell C2 type `Monday`.

14. Into cells E2, G2, I2, K2, and M2 type the rest of the days of the week.

    Nope, you cannot drag-fill here because you're skipping every other cell.

15. Format the days of the week and the month and year as you see fit.

    I used *italics*. You can play around, but do be careful: The day text is supposed to hang over into the next cell. That may look wrong now, but it looks proper when printed.

    Next, the calendar dates:

16. Type 1 for the first day of the month in the proper column in row 3.

17. Continue to fill in the rest of the days of the month.

If you need an extra row for the last week of the month, select row 14 and set its row height to 56.

Finally, format the lines. There are numerous ways to do this, but you've got to be careful because you're surrounding four cells with a single border. Here's a quick way I did it, though this is by no means the only way:

18. Select the cells for one day of the month.

    For example, E3, E4, F3, and F4.

19. Press Ctrl+1 to bring up the Format Cell dialog box.

20. Click the Border tab.

21. Choose the thin line style.

22. Click the Outline preset button.

23. Click OK.

    Now to repeat this:

24. Select the next four cells that make up a date on the calendar.

25. Press the F4 key.

This reapplies the border command to those four cells.

26. Repeat steps 24 and 25 for the rest of the days of the month.

If you screw up, you'll have to return to the Format Cell dialog box and do steps 20 through 23 again. But you won't screw up, will you?

This by no means completes the calendar. There are still lots of fun things you can do with color, borders, text formatting, and even inserting pictures. But do keep in mind that Excel does have a nice selection of predesigned calendar templates on the Web, should you want to save some time.

If you're trying to create a personal calendar with due dates and appointments, stop! Microsoft Outlook has this ability built in, plus the ability to print its calendars in a manner much quicker than those 26 steps listed in this section. See Chapter 20, "Organizing the Rest of Your Life," for more information.

The Worksheet That Shows You How to Cheat on Your Taxes

You wish.

Can I Grab Data from the Web and Use It in a Worksheet?

Oh, absolutely. This all depends on the web page, however. Some web pages don't cough up Excel-friendly information. Some do. In any event, once you find the information, provided that it's held in a table on the web page (which most information is), you can easily import that table's information into your worksheet.

You cannot grab information from all web pages. Some web pages have only text or perhaps display their information in a format Excel cannot read. If that's the case, then try to find another web page that offers similar information. Or just give up.

Before starting out, you need to know that most, if not all, of the material you find on the Web is copyrighted. This means it cannot be taken and used for profit or distributed without permission. Even so, there is something called "fair use," which says that you can use information personally, but you cannot profit from it.

For example, if you want to make your own Larry King shrine on your hard drive, that's fine. But if you want to mass-produce Larry King memorabilia, you need his (or his owner's) permissions. Keep that in mind, and also understand that's why the following sections have fictitious websites as their examples.

Outright Web Theft with Excel 2003/XP

Be thankful you upgraded; the web connection in your version of Excel is dead sexy. It makes stealing, er, borrowing stuff from the Web as easy as cheating on your taxes. (Sadly, that section had to be cut from the chapter.)

Here you go:

1. Choose Data ➢ Get External Data ➢ New Web Query.

A very sweet dialog box opens displaying a mini web browser. Very cool, so I'm showing it to you in Figure 15.14. Just be amazed at its wonder.

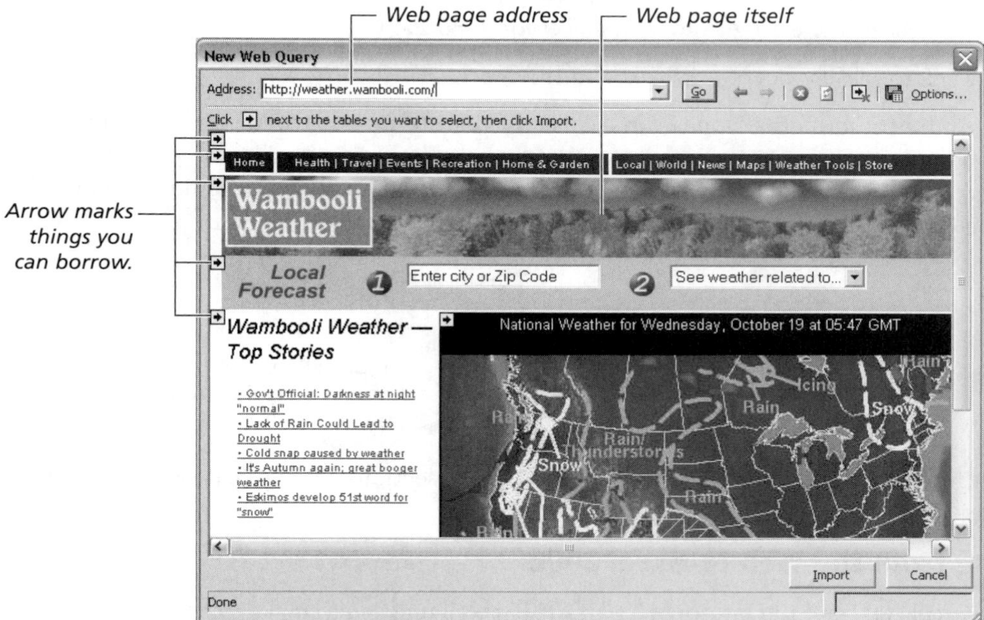

Figure 15.14 Web theft begins here.

2. Type in the address of the web page you want to thieve from and click the Go button.

For this example, visit any of the several online weather forecasting websites. (These are great examples of websites that have regularly changing information).

Once you're at the website, enter your zip code or take whatever steps are necessary to summon your local weather page.

When you see the local weather page, locate the local forecast. Or if you're borrowing from any web page, ensure that you're on the page you need to borrow from before continuing with the next step.

3. Click the arrow next to the item you want to stick into your worksheet.

   The arrow changes to a checkmark.

   You can select more than one item, though if you're doing this for the first time, pick only one to download, such as the current temperature on your local weather page.

If the arrows are having trouble showing up, click the Show/Hide Icons button on the toolbar in the New Web Query dialog box.

4. Click the Import button.

   An Import Data dialog box appears, letting you choose between sticking the data in an existing worksheet or creating a new worksheet for it. For now:

5. Click to select a new worksheet, and then click OK.

   And the information appears in a collection of cells in your worksheet. Actually it's a "table" because the table format was originally used on the web page. Also, no pictures or images are transferred, merely the pertinent text data—which may include hyperlinks. Figure 15.15 shows what the new imported worksheet looks like on my computer.

	A	B	C
1		37°F	
2	Partly Cloudy	Feels Like	
3		31°F	
4			

Figure 15.15 The final result for a typical April day where I live

Don't fuss over the format just yet. Skip ahead to the section, "Fixing That Ugly Web Data."

Stealing from the Web in Excel 2000

Alas! Excel 2000 and the Internet just aren't that well married to make this task as seamless as it is in the more recent versions of Excel. But who's complaining? Just follow these steps:

1. Choose Data ➢ Get External Data ➢ New Web Query.

   This opens the dreadfully dull New Web Query dialog box. Ignore it.

2. Click the Browse Web button.

   Your web browser starts up all bright and gay. Your job is to browse to a web page that contains data you want to steal. How about the weather?

3. Visit a weather forecasting web page.

4. Enter your zip code to look up your local weather.

Hopefully, without too many pop-ups or annoying ads or surveys to fill out, you will eventually arrive at a page that displays the weather for your locale. I'll assume that you can get there on your own. When you're at that page, continue:

5. Switch back to Excel.

   Press Alt+Tab to do this, or just click the Excel button on the taskbar. You'll be amazed to find that web page address listed in the New Web Query dialog box.

   The next steps are harder here because you're operating blindly:

6. Select only the tables from step 2 in the dialog box.
7. Click the OK button.
8. Choose "New Worksheet" from the new dialog box that appears.
9. Click OK.

   Excel attempts to load the pertinent information from the web page and place it into your worksheet. The problem here is that everything from that page will be loaded—not just the weather info you need but advertisements and other information as well.

As an example, the weather page for my home downloaded into a chunk of cells and some very wide columns. It took me a while to find the pertinent information, which ended up in cells B17 through C19. That's fine! It's the best Excel 2000 can do, but you can do better on your own, as covered in the next section.

Fixing That Ugly Web Data

Remember earlier on how I explained that not all the raw data in a worksheet needs to be seen? Some stuff you can put way off the normal viewing area and just pull in the SUM totals or other important information. That same philosophy must go with web information as well.

From Figure 15.15, the current temperature is stored in cell B1. (Excel 2000 put it in cell C17.) That's fine because that cell can be referenced by another cell in another worksheet, something formatted more to your liking: Simply copy and paste special the cell; paste it as a link, as shown in Figure 15.16. Then format it all nice and pretty.

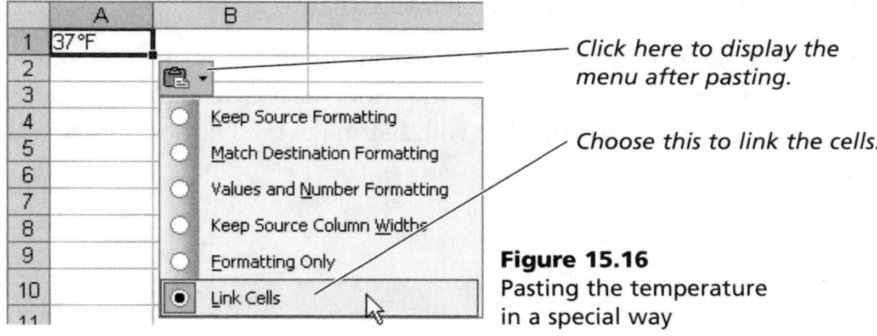

Figure 15.16
Pasting the temperature in a special way

In Excel 2000, you must choose Edit ➤ Paste Special from the menu to paste in the cell's value as a link; choose Paste Link from the Paste Special dialog box, and then click OK.

A better need for this type of reformatting would be if you're pulling in financial or stock data from some website. The stock data may appear in a vast table with other information, but you may just want the up-to-the-minute price quote. If so, you just select the proper cell in the imported data worksheet, and copy-paste special that cell's data into your main financial wizard worksheet—one you most likely have set up to better monitor such things.

It's Getting Hotter Out but the Temperature in My Worksheet Hasn't Changed.

While you can paste-link items from one worksheet to another on your own computer, hot-linking to the Web just isn't done yet. So instead you must manually set refresh times for your web data. If you don't, then the information is updated only when you open the worksheet after saving it to disk. And you can also force an update if you like. This applies not only to the weather example here, but also to stock quotes, news items, or whatever else you've imported that needs updating.

The secret here is the External Data toolbar, shown in Figure 15.17. To summon this toolbar, choose View ➤ Toolbars ➤ External Data.

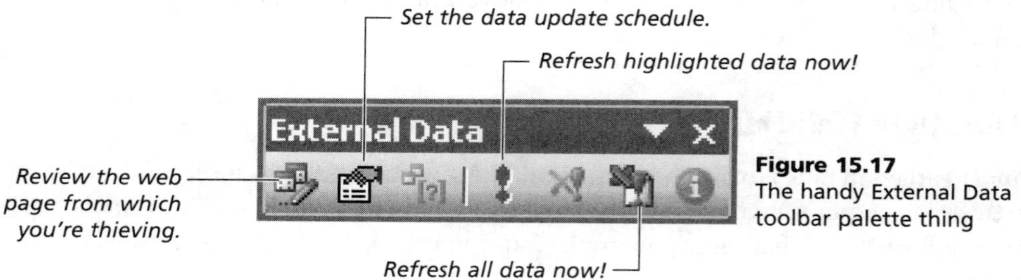

Figure 15.17
The handy External Data toolbar palette thing

To set a refresh schedule, first click to select a cell in the table imported from the web page. Then click the Data Range Properties button. This displays the nifty dialog box shown in Figure 15.18, where you can tell Excel how often to venture out to the Web. Refer to Figure 15.18 for what to set and what to ignore.

If you'd rather just quickly update, click the Refresh button. That way if the stock market is churning your soul with angst, you can view those near-real-time quotes in your worksheet as they're really happening. Boy, will that make the hairdos on CNBC seethe with jealousy!

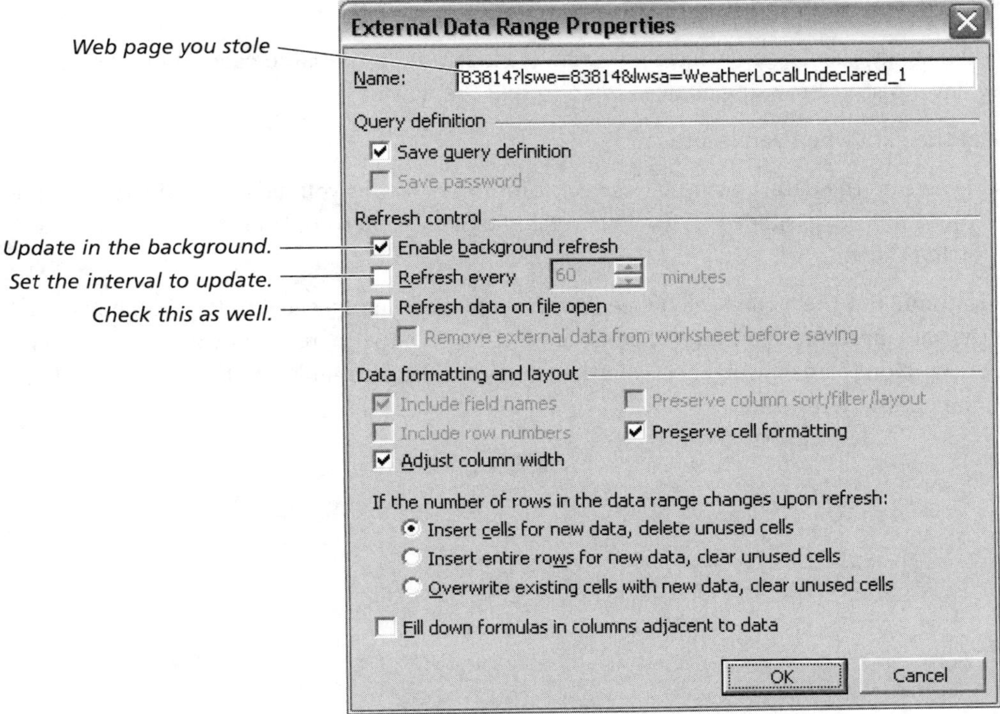

Figure 15.18 Set a web page update schedule here.

The Web Page Has Changed or Something, and I'm Not Pulling in the Data I Once Did.

Web pages do change. This is a constant truth of the Web. Because of this, linking to a web page means that one day you may open your favorite external data worksheet and discover something unknown or silly in place of the weather, the latest headline, stock news, or computer tip. When that happens, follow these steps:

1. Return to the worksheet that contains the imported information from the web page.

   Note that it's *imported* information now and no longer stolen.

2. Display the External Data toolbar.

3. Click the Edit Query button.

   This redisplays the original Web Query dialog box (Figure 15.14), showing the web page you're stealing from. (Now it's theft again.)

4. Use the dialog box to relocate the data.

   If you're lucky, the data may have just changed location on the same page. Otherwise, you may have to start browsing all over again to find the new data.

5. Select the data when you locate it.

   Once you find the data, continue to select it for importing as you did originally; refer to the section in this chapter specific for your version of Excel. Then continue with the steps for importing there.

Again this points out the advantage of keeping the web data on one sheet in the workbook and copying the valuable stuff to another sheet. Even if the web page changes, all you need to do is relocate the data on the new worksheet and then copy-paste special-link it to the "real" worksheet you use for examining the data.

PART 3

Outlook

16 Just Your Intermediate E-mail

I've written lots of beginner information about e-mail. I took my time. The text was carefully crafted, with steps logically explaining things—good gentle guidance. It was all given in a warm, friendly, avuncular tone that would remind readers of soft chocolate chip cookies fresh from the oven. Yet it was a grand waste of time. Little did I know that e-mail was no big deal. Hip grannies could latch onto e-mail and send their far-flung grandchildren messages without so much as referring to anything written. My efforts were in vain.

Apparently mankind has no problem figuring out e-mail. If hip grannies can get it, then anyone can. No, the problem with e-mail lies beyond the first layer of the onion. Sending. Receiving. Replying. Spell checking. Even attaching an image—all that is pretty basic e-mail stuff. What's the next level? Why, it's what's covered in this chapter, of course!

Outlook is Microsoft Office's e-mail program. It's more than that, which other chapters will get into. But central to the other things Outlook does is e-mail. If you've used Outlook Express, then you're ready to upgrade. This book helps make the transition, as well as introduces experienced Outlook users to the finer, more intermediate points of the program.

Traps Revealed and Ambushes Uncovered:

- Quoting and interposing an e-mail reply
- Cleaning up e-mail for replying or forwarding
- Understanding To, Cc, and Bcc
- Applying just enough formatting so as not to be annoying
- Using and abusing stationery
- Discovering the hows and whys of e-mail signatures
- Utilizing e-mail attachment tips and tricks

Some E-mail Propriety

Some e-mail doesn't deserve an answer. Someone sending you a "thank you" note, for example, doesn't warrant a "you're welcome" reply. And certain other courtesies that one would observe for written correspondence can also be overlooked in e-mail. But one offense bugs just about everyone: If someone sends you an e-mail and asks a question or somehow implies that a response is wanted, *RESPOND!* With the immediacy of e-mail, a delayed or absent response is considered really offensive by many people. (And sadly, it's computer industry "professionals" who are generally most guilty of not responding to e-mail.)

With that one peeve out of the way, I thought I'd open the Outlook chapter with some issues on e-mail propriety, or a few of those things you can do to with your e-mail that reflect the highest of electronic manners.

What's the Best Way to Respond to a Long E-mail?

It depends on the nature of the e-mail and, of course, your mood.

When I get a long story that requires no specific response, I'll reply to the message with a "thank you" or a quick note acknowledging that I have read and appreciate the message.

If a reply is required and you don't presently have the time, reply and state that you've read the message and will reply to it at a specific time. That's only polite; remember that e-mail is supposed to be an *immediate* medium.

KEYBOARD MASTER

Your Basic Outlook Key Commands

Here they are, in no particular order:

F9
Send and receive all e-mail.

Ctrl+N
Start up a new e-mail message.

Alt+S
Send the current message.

Ctrl+R
Reply to the current message.

Ctrl+F
Forward the current message.

Ctrl+D
Delete current message.

Ctrl+>
Display the next item.

Ctrl+<
Display the previous item.

Ctrl+Q
Mark a message as being read.

Ctrl+U
Mark a message as being unread.

NERD'S CORNER

To Read Receipt or Not—A Discussion

DAN: Personally, I don't mind receiving a Read Receipt message. In fact, I think many folks send them without knowing what they are. And when I get them, I rarely respond to the read receipt, sometimes just putting the e-mail away and then getting back to it later. But I know others have different opinions and experiences with them.

ACEY: I think that attaching a read receipt to an e-mail message has always been considered extremely impolite, at least in the circles that I run in. It's sort of an invasion of privacy in that if I want you to know that I read your e-mail, I will tell you. I learned this lesson early on when I sent an e-mail with a read receipt request to an author posing a question about a magazine article he had written. I quickly received a "How dare you ask for a read receipt!" response, and was promptly told to never contact him again.

DAN: The guy sounds like a dork anyway.

ACEY: Maybe he was the one oddball out there that doesn't like it, but I doubt it.

DAN: Where there is one, there are bound to be more.

ACEY: Make that one of two oddballs—I don't like it either and have flamed many a person for doing it.

DAN: Perhaps that's the lesson you learned from the Ziff-Davis magazine author. Did I say "Ziff-Davis?" I actually meant to say "Technical Magazine." Yes.

COLLEEN: I'm going to have to agree with Acey's evaluation of people who ask for read receipts. The only time I've used it was to "check up" on someone who wasn't answering my e-mails.

DAN: I think that's the whole idea. But in a way it actually begs for some sort of "Are you alive" Internet command, like a PING for humans.

COLLEEN: As far as voluntarily sending a read receipt, an inbox full of "I have read your message and will respond when I am able" would be annoying when what I really needed were answers. Besides, if people are like my sister, just because she's opened it, doesn't mean she's actually read it.

DAN: And I do the same thing, but I just don't respond to the read receipt.

What About the Read Receipt Thing?

Many e-mail programs have a return receipt requested feature. Outlook calls it a *read receipt*. Other e-mail may call it a return receipt. Whatever.

The read receipt is a great way to acknowledge that you've read a message without having to reply. In fact, it can be made automatic, and it's terribly polite. What happens is that when you open a message with a read receipt, Outlook displays a dialog box asking if you want to notify the sender that the message has been read; click Yes and a message is instantly sent back to the sender. Then you can go on reading the message.

Now if you're trying to be sneaky, click the No button. That means the sender won't know whether you've read the message or not. They may think that you're out of town or lying crippled in the hospital or dead. But my point here is to be polite, which doesn't require any effort—though consider that the sender does recognize that you've opened the message and are now merely dawdling over the reply.

You can click the Don't Ask Me About Sending Receipts Again button to avoid that dialog box in the future—a good idea.

To add such a feature to e-mail you send, follow these steps in a new message (Untitled Message) dialog box:

1. Options... Click the Options button on the toolbar.

   The Message Options dialog box appears.

2. Put a checkmark by "Request a Read Receipt for This Message."
3. Click the Close button.

Now your message will be sent with a read receipt as well. But please be sure to read the sidebar "To Read Receipt or Not" before you decide on making this a habit.

Isn't It a Waste to Send Back All That Text with Just a "Thank You?"

Yes, especially if the message is being sent to multiple recipients. It's much better to edit the message. For example, refer to Figure 16.1. In my reply, I kept the "Original Message" quote but deleted everything after it. To prove that this was intentional, I added "[snip]" to the message, to let the recipient know that it was cut on purpose.

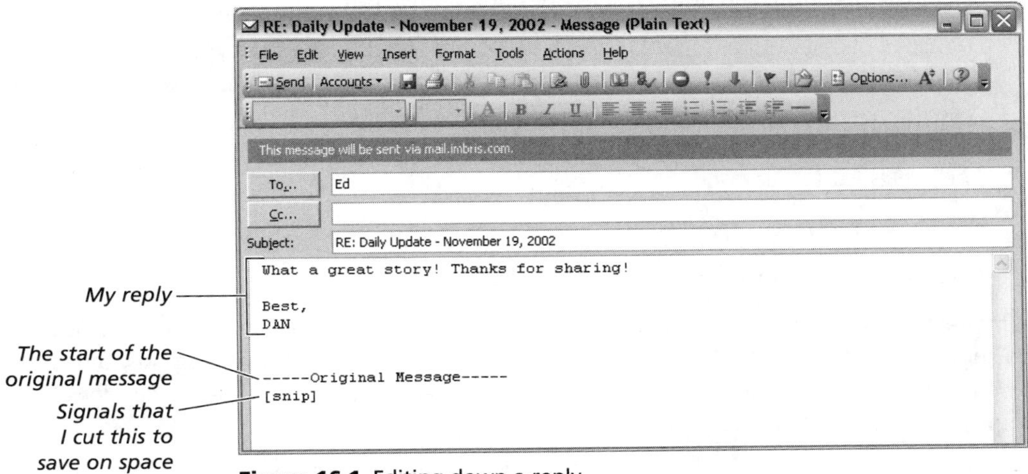

Figure 16.1 Editing down a reply

You Must Know This: The Issues About Wasting Bandwidth

When speaking of the Internet, bandwidth *is a term used to describe how much information can squeeze through a given sized information pipe.*

For example, consider sending 10 people a 20K e-mail message. That creates a lump of information nearly 200K in size. That would seem easy enough for the Internet to handle—and relatively speaking it is. The problem is that when more and more people do that, eventually the system becomes clogged—just like adding more and more cars to a freeway. Even if the freeway has eight lanes in both directions, eventually a certain number of cars will clog things up and snarl traffic into a jam.

The Internet's pipes are only so big—and getting bigger over time. However, the amount of traffic flowing over the Internet is increasing faster than the pipes are growing. To help keep traffic down, you can be smart about how you send e-mail. For example, instead of replying to 10 people with a 20K message, pare down the original message (through editing) to only 2K or less. That decreases the bandwidth required to send the message, making the Internet faster for everyone.

What? I Can Edit the Original Message in My E-mail Reply?

I'm surprised at how many people don't know this: After you click the Reply button, or press Ctrl+R to reply to an e-mail message, the text of the original appears in the bottom of your reply. Hey, it's open season on that text! You can edit it any way you like.

For example, say out of the entire original message, only a small part applies to you. Do this:

1. Press Ctrl+R to reply to the message.
2. Select the text from the original that does not apply to you.

   Don't feel bad about deleting the text. The sender should have a copy, and you will still have the original copy in the message you're replying to. So nothing is really lost here.
3. Press the Delete key.

   The irrelevant text is gone.
4. Write your reply.

   And you're replying to only the part that's left.

All the text you see in your e-mail reply, or even a forwarded e-mail, is yours to play with. Traditionally, you shouldn't edit a reply to make it appear that someone sent you something they didn't. In fact, any editorial cutting you do should be made obvious; keep in mind that the sender does have the original copy of the message.

What Is "Interposing" and How Will It Make Me Look Like Such an Experienced E-mail User?

Interposing is the art of inserting your comments into a message you're replying to. So rather than reply to the entire e-mail at the top of the message, you intersperse or insert your replies to the questions as they were asked in the original e-mail.

As an example, consider Figure 16.2. It shows an e-mail with a lot of questions. Some folks can remember all that and can answer them without having to scroll up and down to review the original. I detest that, so I interpose my answers, as shown in Figure 16.3. That way, the response flows more like a conversation, which not only helps you address many issues in a long e-mail but ensures that you cover everything.

```
Hello Dan!

I know you're busy, but was wondering if you had time to answer a few
questions about your projects? I hope so. And don't worry about
answering right away.

When are you going to be in Indy? I'd like to know because I have a
cousin there and she's really homely looking, but she really wants to
meet you.

Also you said you might stop by Kentucky when you're going to Memphis,
is that still in the works?

I'm glad that you got my package. Did you find the secret note? See? I
told you I would be sneaky!

All the best,
Lynn
```

Figure 16.2 The original letter

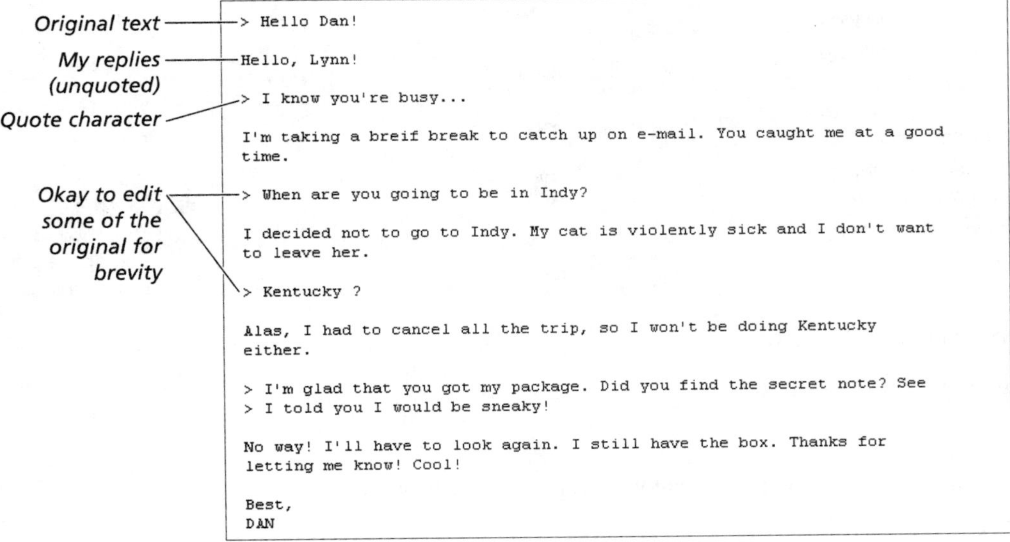


```
> Hello Dan!

Hello, Lynn!

> I know you're busy...

I'm taking a breif break to catch up on e-mail. You caught me at a good
time.

> When are you going to be in Indy?

I decided not to go to Indy. My cat is violently sick and I don't want
to leave her.

> Kentucky ?

Alas, I had to cancel all the trip, so I won't be doing Kentucky
either.

> I'm glad that you got my package. Did you find the secret note? See
> I told you I would be sneaky!

No way! I'll have to look again. I still have the box. Thanks for
letting me know! Cool!

Best,
DAN
```

Figure 16.3 An interposed reply

The best hint I can offer about interposing is to instantly reply to the message; don't read it first. Then, as you read the message in the Reply window, make your comments, similar to what's shown in Figure 16.3.

How Can I Get the Original Message to Be Quoted As Shown in Figure 16.3?

Normally Outlook just places the message you're replying to at the bottom of your reply. It doesn't have to be that way. The message can be quoted, indented, or even not included at all. The secrets here are found in the E-mail Options dialog box. Here's how to get there:

1. Choose Tools ➢ Options.
2. Click the Preferences tab (if you must).
3. Click the E-mail Options button.

   The E-mail Options dialog box appears, as shown in Figure 16.4. The bottom part covers the adjustments for responding to (and forwarding) e-mail.

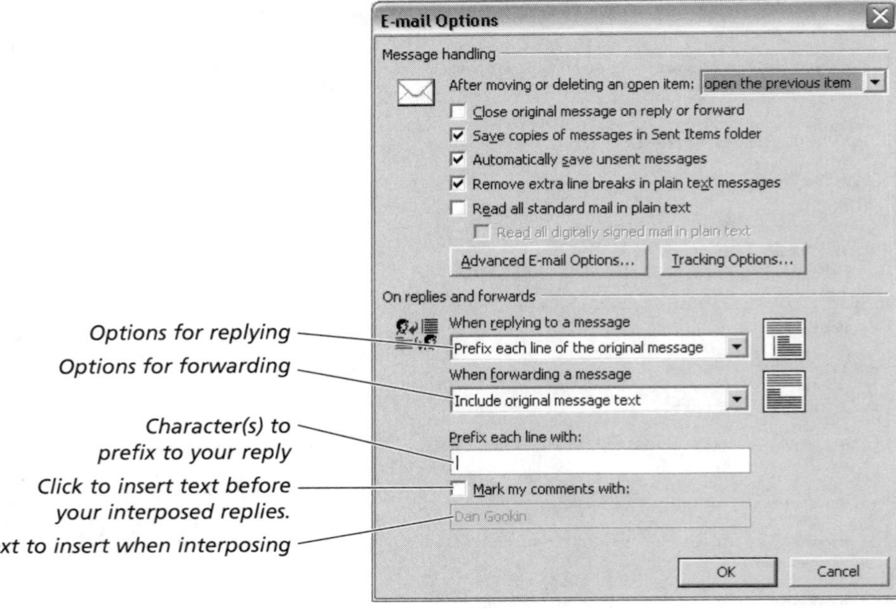

Figure 16.4 Adjusting how a message appears in a reply or forward

4. Make your adjustments.

   Use Figure 16.4 as your guide.

5. Click OK.

   The changes affect any new e-mail you respond to or forward.

For replying to a message, Outlook has five options:

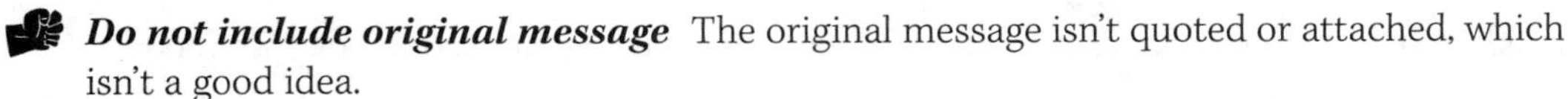

- ***Do not include original message*** The original message isn't quoted or attached, which isn't a good idea.
- ***Attach original message*** Also a bad idea; some e-mail programs (other than Outlook) have a problem with attachments. Why make things more complicated for the people who receive your messages?
- ***Include original message text*** This is the standard option, which boringly appends the original message to your reply, prefixed by "— Original Message —."
- ***Include and indent original message text*** One step closer to perfection, though there are e-mail programs out there that screw up the indented message.
- ***Prefix each line of the original message*** The best option, the traditional way messages are replied to on the Internet. You can even select which character to prefix, as shown in Figure 16.4.

I also recommend you avoid the "Mark My Comments With" option. That causes Outlook to insert the text (from the dialog box shown in Figure 16.4) before each and every new line you add. It looks gross.

Remember that the idea here is to make clear which comments are yours and which were in the original message.

How Can Color Be Used to Separate My Comments?

Another way to separate your interposed replies from the original message is to use color. For example, if the original message is in color text, simply reply in black text. Otherwise, you can color your text by using the Font Color button on the Message Reply toolbar:

1. Click the Font Color button and select a color from the drop-down palette.
2. Click within the message to start typing your reply in that color.

You can change the color of the text by selecting the text with the mouse and then choosing a new color.

This trick works only if you're sending an HTML or Rich Text Formatted message or replying to one. It will not work if you've chosen Format ➢ Plain Text from the menu; in fact, the Font Color button will not even be available.

If you want to get really fancy, you can go way out and waste time formatting your reply with a different font and even at a different size. Do keep in mind two things:

- Not every e-mail program will be able to read and understand your formatting.
- The e-mail may read well on your computer, but the text may be too small or faint to be read on another system.

Any Way to Preset Which Color My Replies Will Be?

Yes, and this definitely saves time if you're going to be using fancy fonts for your reply:

1. Choose Tools ➤ Options.
2. Click the Mail Format tab.
3. Ensure that HTML is chosen from the "Compose in This Message Format" drop-down list.
4. Click the Fonts button.

   The Fonts dialog box lets you preset fonts you'll use and see for composing, replying, and forwarding e-mails, as shown in Figure 16.5.

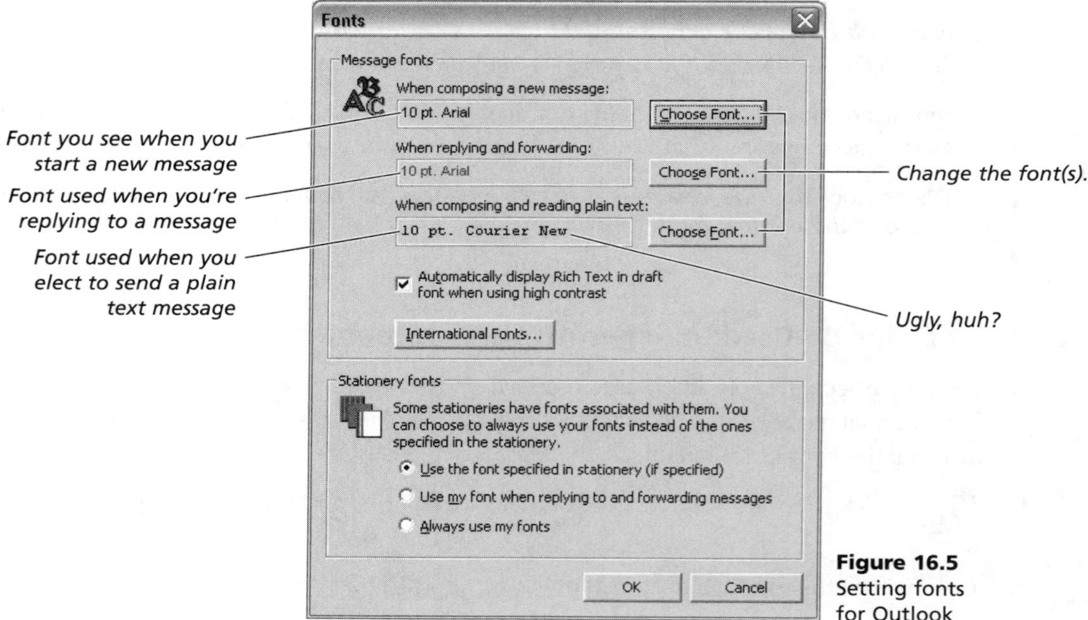

Figure 16.5 Setting fonts for Outlook

5. Click the Choose Font button by the "When Composing a New Message" option.
6. Use the Font dialog box to set a new font to use when composing a message.

   If you like larger fonts, colors, or fancy fonts, pick them here. Do remember that not everyone has the same fonts on their computer as you have on yours.
7. Click OK when you're done setting fonts.
8. Click the Choose Font button and select a new font for your message replies; click OK in the Font dialog box when you're done.

9. Click the Choose Font button by the "When Composing and Reading Plain Text" option.

   This is really necessary because the 10 pt Courier New font is just butt ugly and hard to read on the screen. Use the Font dialog box to change it to anything else.

Changing the font for plain text does not negate the plain text option; your message will still be sent unformatted. But by changing the font in Outlook, you'll keep your own eyes from bugging out of your head when you compose a plain text message.

I'm Using Word As My E-mail Editor and the Font Changes in Outlook Aren't Coming Through!

You must change your fonts using Word instead of Outlook.

By the way, I do not recommend using Word as an e-mail editor.

Is It Possible to Split Up an E-mail Reply?

The easiest way to do this is to reply to the message first, deleting whatever it is you don't want to reply to. Send that message.

Then reopen the original message and re-edit it, this time deleting and saving different chunks of the message. Reply to the new chunk; then send that message.

You can keep doing this all day long—and sometimes it works better than endlessly interposing comments. For example, interposing gets difficult to read after passing the same message back and forth twice. In that case, it's probably best to split the message into chunks and reply to each individually, as described above.

How Can I Clean Up a Forwarded E-mail Message?

It's those damn AOL users! They just don't know how to pare down a message. So their delight in forwarding you the current joke that's making the rounds is utterly washed away by the tower of e-mail names, Cc lists, and endless >>>>>>>>> quotations. The joke better be darn good...

Doesn't it seem like the length of the forwarded e-mail is inversely proportional to the impact of its message?

First, what causes those quotations is an endlessly forwarded e-mail. People forward a message without editing it. Sometimes their e-mail program (AOL) won't let them edit that stuff out.

Second, you can remove those >>>> things from your own message by simply telling Outlook *not* to quote a forwarded message. Here's how:

1. Choose Tools ➤ Options.
2. Click the Preferences tab.
3. Click the E-mail Options button.
4. In the drop-down list by "When Forwarding a Message," choose "Include Original Message Text."

   See Figure 16.4. Do not choose the "Indent" or "Prefix Each Line" option!
5. Click OK, then OK again to get back to Outlook.

Now when you forward the message, it will look something like Figure 16.6. You can delete the name of the original sender—even clean up the formatting or spelling—then click the Send button to send the forwarded message on to your gang.

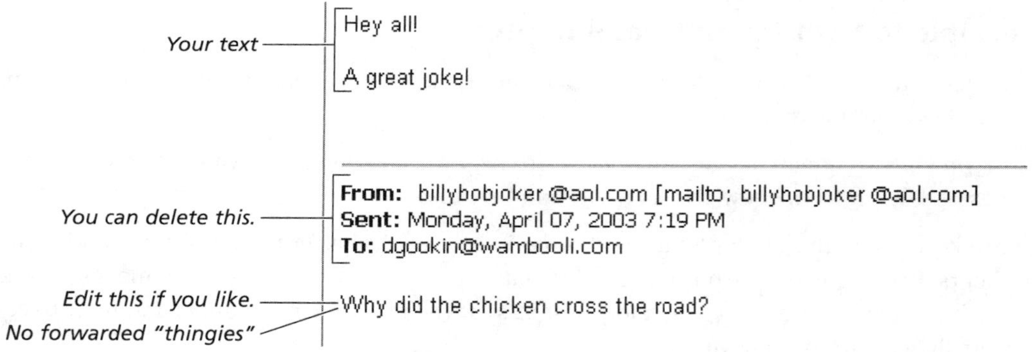

Figure 16.6 Forwarding a message (a suggestion)

Third, if the problem is really bad, then you have to do major surgery of a kind beyond the power and scope of Outlook. Follow these steps:

1. Select the original message.

   Don't even bother clicking the Forward button.
2. Press Ctrl+C to copy it.
3. Open Word.

   Ah, there's a text editor.
4. Press Ctrl+V to paste the message into Word.

5. Edit the message.

   For example, use the Find and Replace commands to remove any and all >>>>> things from the message. Spell-check it. Buff it out. But keep in mind that you're not really formatting it like it's going to go in a professional brochure.

   You might also want to reformat the message by removing the extra paragraph marks (Enter key presses) at the end of each line.

6. Select the entire message again.
7. Press Ctrl+C to copy.
8. Switch to Outlook.
9. Start up a new message.

   Press Ctrl+N.

10. Select your recipients and enter a subject—all the normal stuff.
11. Press Ctrl+V to paste the cleaned-up message into Outlook.
12. Continue sending the message.

    And don't forget to eventually switch back and close Word, should you need to.

Yes, I understand that these steps may seem involved and too much work for the timesaving computer. But that's the best that can be done now. Hopefully in the future Outlook may grow a new feature similar to Word's AutoFormat that will let you format an e-mail message and clean up a lot of the junk.

What's the Point of "Reply to All"?

The Reply to All command is used to send a reply to every one who got the original message—that is, everyone who is listed in the To field and also in the Cc field. Otherwise, the reply goes only to those in the To field, often just one person.

The idea here is to keep people "in the loop." That way, they can follow the conversation—reply, answer, reply—and you won't have to retype names into the To and Cc fields.

For example, if everyone on your team needs to be kept in the loop, you use Reply to All so that all the recipients of the original message will receive your reply to that message.

Is There Any Time When "Reply to All" Shouldn't Be Used?

Yes! This is part of that bandwidth issue covered earlier in this chapter. There is no need to reply to everyone if your reply is intended to only one person or is merely a "thank you" or "ha-ha" reply.

Also if your reply is of a sensitive or private nature, it might be a good idea to reply merely to the person who sent the message. In fact, you could manually delete anyone who is inappropriate from the To field: Just use the mouse to select the e-mail addresses and press the Delete key.

Any Way Not to Quote a Message When I Reply?

The first way is to simply select and delete the quoted message. This works best if you prefer to quote messages most of the time but only occasionally don't want the original in there.

If you'd rather not quote at all, refer to section "How Can I Get the Original Message to Be Quoted As Shown in Figure 16.3?" earlier in this chapter. Choose the option "Do Not Include Original Message" when setting up how you want replied messages to appear.

How Can I Reread an Original Message?

The New Message window is actually a separate window on the screen. Look at the taskbar and click the original Outlook button to return to Outlook and then reread the original message. Or you can use the Alt+Tab key combination to switch between the New Message and Outlook windows.

If the original message was written a while back, then you have to use Outlook's sorting abilities to help you track the conversation. Here's what I do:

1. Return to the Inbox, where you replied to the message.
2. Right-click the message.
3. Choose Find All ➤ Messages from Sender.

   This displays an Advanced Find dialog box, but you don't need to mess with it any further: Simply double-click the messages displayed on the bottom to open recent messages.
4. Close the Advanced Find dialog box when you're done.

I use this method to help me keep track of long conversations; not everyone pops back the same day with e-mail. So if I haven't replied to someone in a while, I can look up their old messages and then bring something up from a previous conversation. It's a simple trick, but it amazes people because they really think that you're paying attention.

What's the True Difference between a Cc and a To Recipient?

Technically, nothing. Both get the same message. The only difference is that the recipient's e-mail address is in either the To or Cc field.

On your end, the To recipients are listed in the To column of the Sent Items folder window. You'll have to open the message to see the Cc people.

There is also a certain (and subtle) psychological effect of the Cc field. Basically the To field is for people to whom the message is intended: "This is for you!" The Cc people are "by the way" people. Often their importance to the message isn't as central as the To people. So it's common in business to disrespect people by placing them on the Cc field instead of the To field. Again, this has no technical difference as far as the e-mail is concerned, but it can be considered a snub when a boss sends most everyone in the group a message on the To field but yet puts others in the group on the Cc field.

There is a limit to the number of names you can put on the To and Cc fields. But the value is so high that no dorky boss should use that as a reason why some people were put on the Cc field instead of the To field.

How Can I Send to a Bunch of People Without Them Seeing One Another's Addresses?

Ah! What you're talking about is the Bcc field, where Bcc means Blind Carbon Copy.

The Bcc field, shown in Figure 16.7, works just like the Cc (and To) fields. Just like e-mail addresses inserted into the other fields, those folks will receive the message. But there will be no record kept of the people in the Bcc fields. No one, not even the Bcc field folks themselves, will see their e-mail names in the final message.

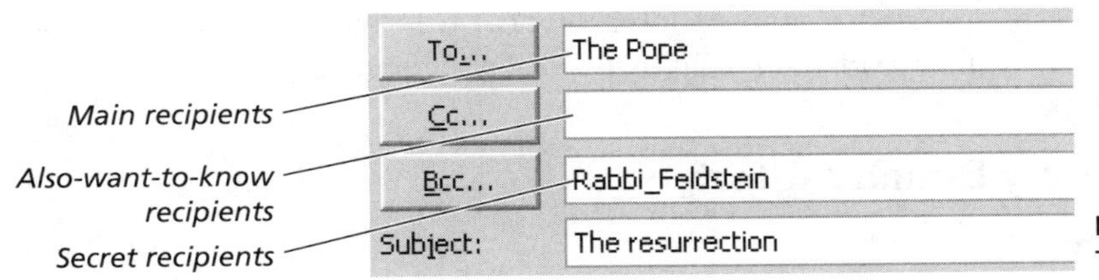

Figure 16.7
The Bcc field appears!

Yes, the Bcc field can be sneaky. For example, if you want to clue in a friend to a conversation taking place at work, just stick the friend in the Bcc field and they'll get the message, but no one will know any better.

Less-covert uses include putting another one of your e-mail addresses on the Bcc field so that you can keep extra copies of the messages you send. (Outlook does keep copies of all e-mail you send in the Sent Items folder.)

I also use the Bcc field when sending out jokes to "the gang." I put all their names in the Bcc field so the message header won't be a mile high, but also to protect their individual identities.

I Don't Have a Bcc Field in My Version of Outlook!

When composing a new message, choose View ➤ Bcc Field from the menu.

How Do I Know That I've Received an E-mail Where I Was on the Bcc List?

The only way you'll know is that you do not see your name in the To or Cc field. Then you can pretty much guess that you were privy to the message via the Bcc field.

Be careful when replying to a message you've been Bcc'd to. The sender knows that you were Bcc'd but, for example, if you accidentaly Reply to All or there is more than one person on the To line to reply to, then you may let the cat out of the bag.

Being on the Bcc field may present a problem as far as Outlook's spam filters are concerned. Because your e-mail address does not appear in the message, it's possible that your e-mail may be interpreted as unwanted. Refer to Chapter 19, "E-mail Rules!" for more information.

E-mail Formatting

I never format my e-mail. I use plain text. Most business people do. AOL, MSN, Hotmail, Incredimail—all that stuff is fun and the messages look friendly and all that. But Outlook is about business, and business people generally do not have animated butterflies flitting around their messages or Garfield waving bye-bye below their signature. But then who am I?

If you want to format your e-mail messages, go right ahead! Outlook has lots of formatting features, especially some beyond the basic text format. Before you go nuts, however, do remember that not all e-mail programs on the Internet can properly interpret heavily formatted messages. If you want to ensure that your e-mail will be read, then plain text is really the only way to go.

Must I Use Word As My E-mail Editor?

Heavens, no!

I do not recommend working in Word at all for e-mail. Word is for word processing. It can do e-mail, but that's more of a show-off feature they added to Word and not anything that really has a practical use or an advantage over using Outlook itself. No, just stick to Outlook for formatting your e-mail.

How Much Formatting Is Enough?

In the business world, no formatting is considered enough. Generally speaking, business people don't send out HTML e-mail. It's used rarely, but in general they don't.

For down-homey friendly e-mail, however, it's as much as you think is appropriate or whatever is required to get your point across. For example, you may be Aunt Velma, who "always sends her e-mail with violet-colored text." That's fine. If that's you, then that's great.

To remove formatting from your e-mail, choose Format ➤ Plain Text in the New Message window. If Outlook pops up a warning, click Yes; you do want to go with plain text.

NERD'S CORNER

Cocktail Party Trivia, Part IX

TOM: Back in the old days, when the Macintosh first came out, they found out that kids just loved to write reports in it. Something about the formatting just made them want to write.

MARY: So interesting...

BILL: Actually, that's not entirely correct.

TOM: Dang you, Bill! You know how to wreck a story!

BILL: My high IQ justifies my actions.

MARY: That's cool!

BILL: While it's true that the kids really did enjoy formatting their documents, what they did was overformat. They used too many fonts, different sizes, text effects, and so on. So their papers looked, well, interesting, but they utterly lacked content.

TOM: So the kids weren't writing as much as they were just toying with the various formatting commands?

BILL: Correct. Now if you'll excuse me, I have to go get into a debate about what the 37th digit of π is.

What's the Difference between HTML and Rich Text Formatting?

Both the HTML and Rich Text options let you send a formatted e-mail message, whereas the Plain Text option does not. Between the two, HTML formatting is more common than rich text; more e-mail programs can understand and display HTML messages properly, whereas rich text is less common. (In fact, to my knowledge, only Outlook uses rich text as a formatting option.)

Between the two, choose HTML if you want to send a formatted message. But remember that if you want to send e-mail that's universally readable by all e-mail programs, plain text is the only way to go.

Sometimes to switch between HTML and rich text formatting you have to first switch to plain text: Choose Format ➤ Plain Text first, and then choose Format ➤ HTML or Format ➤ Rich Text from the menu.

How Can I Change the Background Color?

After starting a new message, choose Format ➢ Background ➢ Color and select a color from the palette that appears.

If the Background item isn't available (it's "dimmed"), then ensure that you've chosen HTML from the Format menu and that you've clicked to select the message body.

If you'd rather have an image in the background, choose Format ➢ Background ➢ Picture. Rather than letting you select any image on the hard drive, Outlook displays a special Background Picture dialog box that gives you a limited selection of choices for the background image, shown in Figure 16.8. The pictures are stylized so that they won't interfere too obnoxiously with the text of your message.

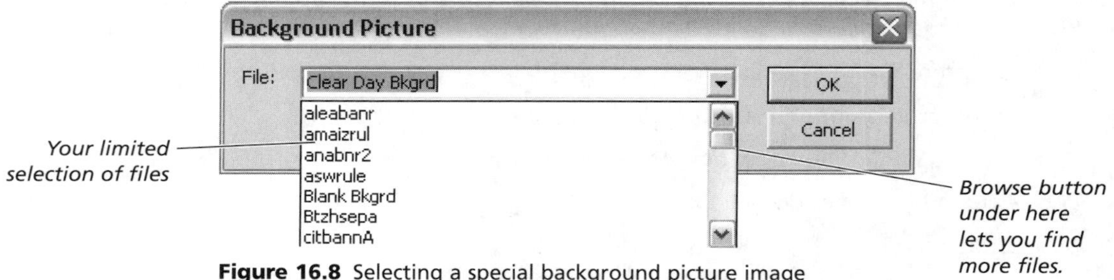

Figure 16.8 Selecting a special background picture image

If you do use the Browse button in the Background Picture dialog box, be sure that you select an image that won't overwhelm the content of your message.

What's the Difference between Inserting a Picture and Having a Picture As the Background?

An inserted picture is simply an image that appears in the e-mail when it's received—like pasting a picture into a Word document. Such an image does not become the background of the entire letter.

The last part of this chapter deals with e-mail attachments, which describes how to put such images into your e-mail message.

What Is Stationary?

It means not moving, standing still.

Okay, Then: What Is Stationery?

Stationery in Outlook is simply a preformatted e-mail message, much like a template in Microsoft Word.

To create a new e-mail message using stationery, follow these steps:

1. Choose Actions ➤ New Mail Message Using.

   This is important; you must use the Actions menu and not the File ➤ New ➤ Mail Message command, or Ctrl+N, or the New button. To use stationery, you must use the Actions menu, as shown in Figure 16.9.

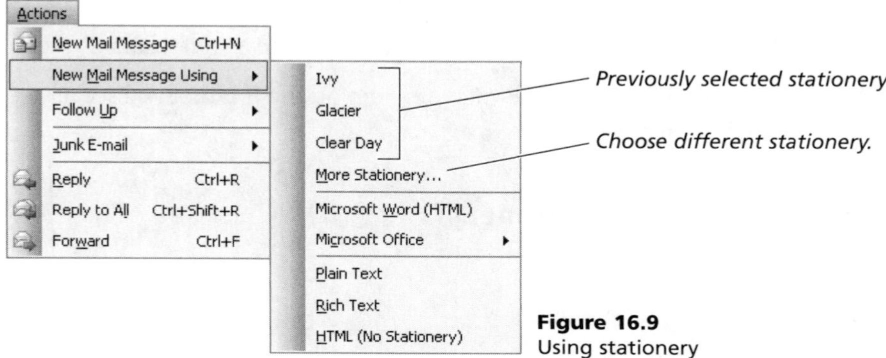

Figure 16.9
Using stationery

   On the menu you'll see some stationery you've previously used.

2. Choose some previously used stationery from the top of the submenu.

   In which case you're done, or:

3. Choose "More Stationery" to see the Select a Stationery dialog box.

   The Select a Stationery dialog box lists a variety of stationery templates, as shown in Figure 16.10.

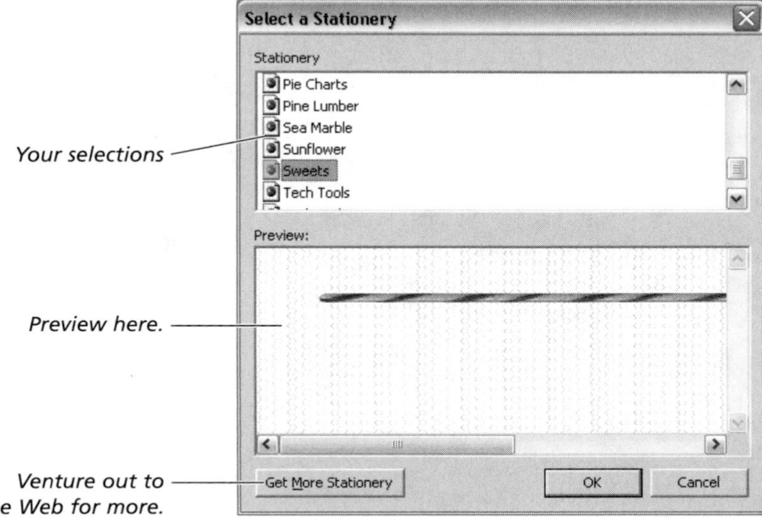

Figure 16.10
Choose more stationery from here.

4. Select a stationery style that intrigues you.

   Observe its preview in the dialog box.

Some stationery won't preview until it's been installed; to install it, select that stationery and then click OK. It's a rather roundabout way to preview, but it's the only option you have.

5. Click OK when you're satisfied.

   And a new message is started using that stationery's fonts, colors, and background.

Do keep in mind that not every e-mail program on the Internet will see all the fancy formatting you put into your message.

Can I Make My Own Stationery?

If you like, here's how:

1. Choose Tools ➤ Options.
2. Click the Mail Format tab.

   The Options dialog box, Mail Format tab is shown in Figure 16.11.

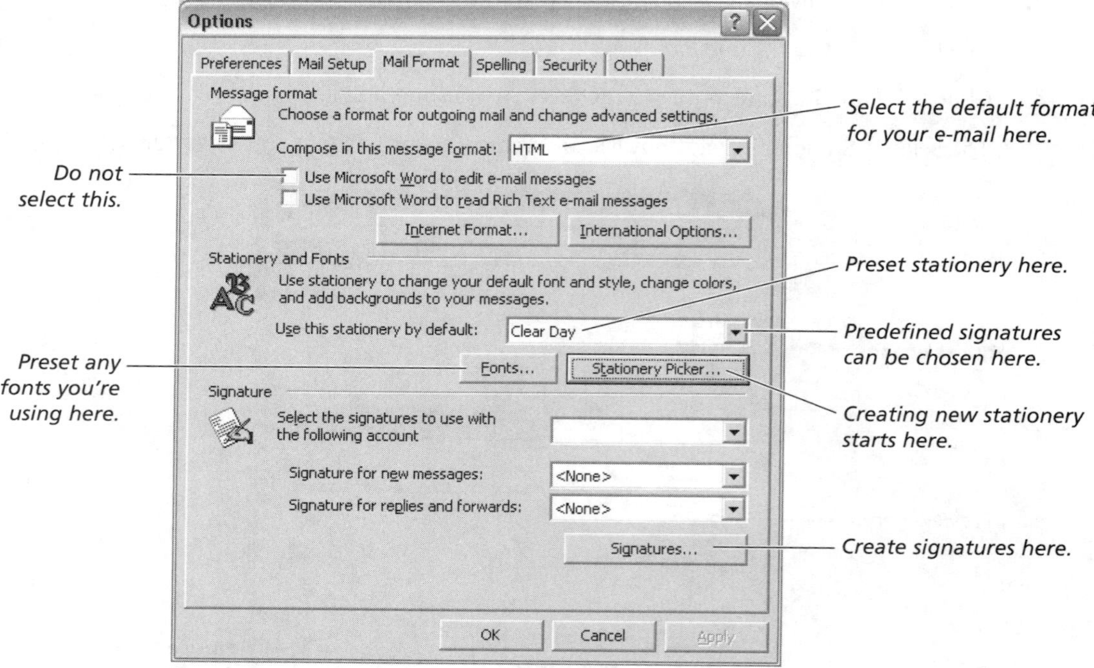

Figure 16.11 Various options for formatting your e-mail

3. Click the Stationery Picker button.

   If this button is unavailable, then select HTML as the message format, as shown in Figure 16.11.

   The Stationery Picker dialog box appears. It looks similar to Figure 16.10, but there are three new buttons: Edit, Remove, and New.

4. Click the New button.

   Now you start a Stationery Wizard of sorts.

5. Enter a name for your stationery.

6. Click to select "Start with Blank Stationery."

   Choose the other options after you're familiar with how creating stationery works.

7. Click the Next button.

   The Edit Stationery dialog box appears, as shown in Figure 16.12.

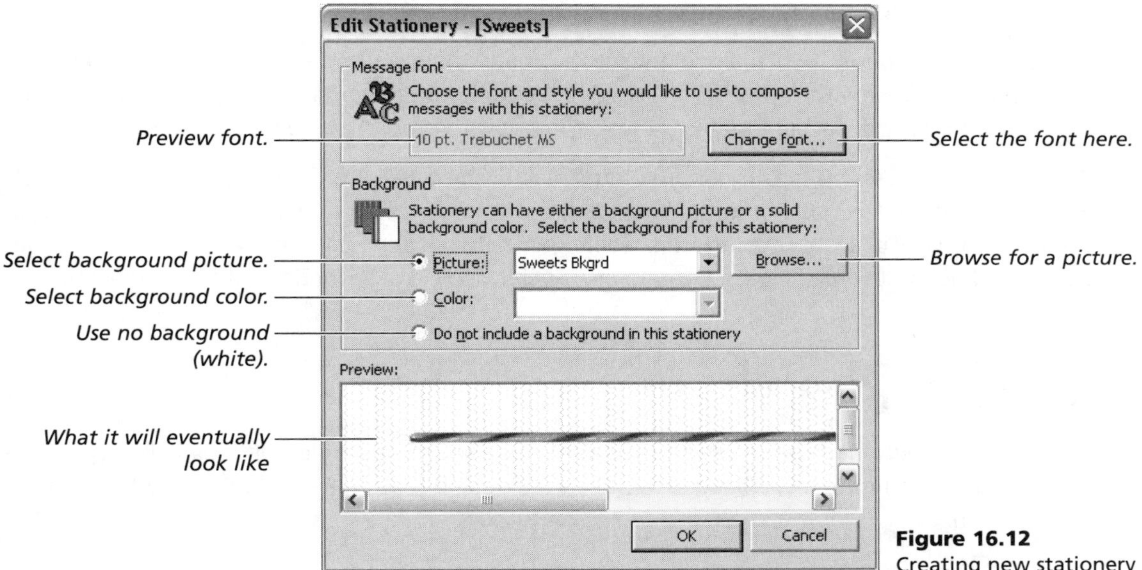

Figure 16.12
Creating new stationery

8. Work the Edit Stationery dialog box to create your stationery.

   Use Figure 16.12 as your guide.

If you elect to choose a picture, ensure that it does not overwhelm the message text of your e-mail.

9. Click the OK button when you're done.

   Your new stationery then appears in the Stationery Picker dialog box. Success, but you're not yet done.

10. Click OK to return to the Options dialog box.

   Note that the new stationery you created is now preset as the default (Figure 16.11).

11. Click OK.

   The new stationery is now ready for use.

If you need to edit the stationery to make changes, then repeat Steps 1 through 3 above, but in Step 4 select your stationery from the list and click the Edit button. That redisplays the Edit Stationery dialog box (Figure 16.12), where you can make adjustments.

Is There Any Way to Preset Text in Stationery?

You mean like boilerplating? Alas, no.

Some e-mail programs, such as Eudora, have the ability to preset text in stationery, in which case you can use stationery to contain often-used replies or common e-mail messages. Outlook doesn't exactly lack that feature, but creating new stationery with preset text just cannot be done.

To build preset messages in Outlook, you must master the concept of Forms. This is a terribly awkward and advanced feature not normally used by individual Outlook users. In fact, the best situation for using Forms is in a large organization where your network administrator has set up an Exchange Server and prebuilt some forms for you to use. Such a subject is beyond the scope of this book.

Sign This, Please!

One of the first automated aspects of e-mail was the signature, or the sign-off most folks type when they end an e-mail message. For example, when I'm done typing an e-mail message, I typically sign off with:

```
Cheers!
DAN
```

That's my e-mail "signature," or the way I sign a message.

Back in the early days of the Internet, when most of the computers were Unix-based, the users would put a special file into their home directories named `.signature`. This file contained text that was automatically appended to each e-mail message they sent.

Sometimes the `.signature` file was a simple signoff, sometimes it was a long, complex, detailed resume. No matter what, the contents simply reflected what the sender wanted.

Don't Be Dumb and Forget to Put Some of These Things into Your Signature

An e-mail signature is a personal thing. It can be as simple or as complex as you like. Here are some common things folks put into their signatures:

 *A famous quote or saying*

 *A web page*

 *Phone numbers and other contact information*

 *Their job title*

There is only one thing you don't need to put into a signature: your e-mail address. Your e-mail address already appears in the message heading, and the recipient can simply reply to the e-mail to get back to you. The only time you need to put an e-mail address into a message is when you have more than one address and would like the recipient to use the other e-mail address for the reply.

The Signature Overview

Signatures in Outlook are created and preset in the Options dialog box, Mail Format tab, as shown in Figure 16.11. Signatures are created by clicking the Signatures button. They then appear in the drop-down lists in the options for new messages and replies and forwards. That way you can have two different sets of signatures used depending on whether you're sending a new message or merely replying (or forwarding).

Here is how to create a new signature:

1. Choose Tools ➤ Options.
2. Click the Mail Format tab.
3. Click the Signatures button.
4. Click the New button.
5. Enter a name for your signature.

   For example, the signature I use when I send e-mail to close friends and family is called "Friends and Family."
6. Click the Next button.
7. Use the Edit Signature dialog box to craft a signature.

   Refer to Figure 16.13 for help.

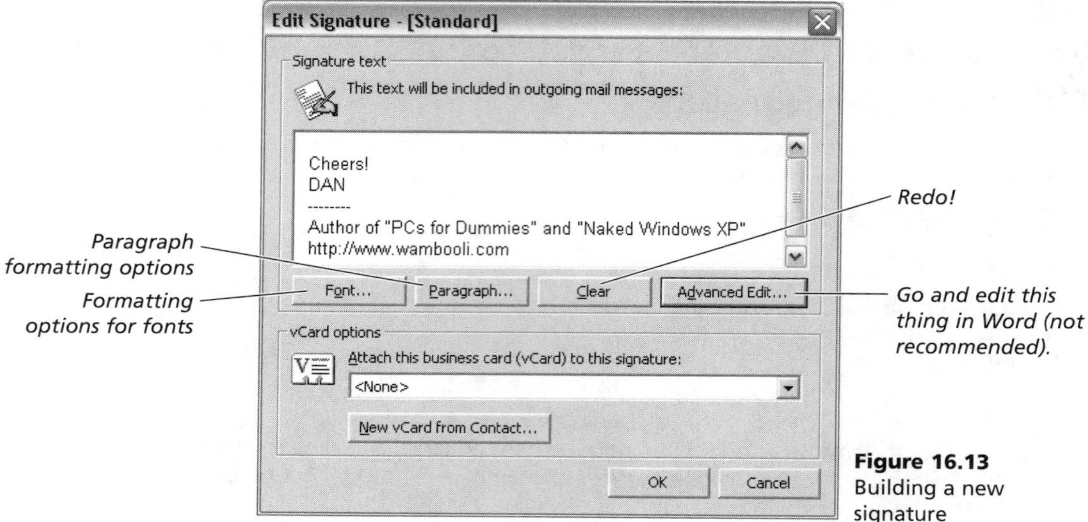

Figure 16.13 Building a new signature

8. Click OK when you're done.
9. Click OK two more times to back out of the other dialog boxes that you've opened.

There is no limit on the number of signatures that you can have. Only two can be preset for new messages and replies. And you can change your e-mail's signature on the fly, which is covered in the sections the follow.

Don't forget that you can always go back and edit old signatures to keep them up to date.

Why Would I Need More than One Signature?

I use a more complex signature for new messages than I do for replies. The reason is that new messages might be sent to someone who doesn't know me. So the signature offers details on who I am, what I do, which books I've recently completed, plus links to my web page and newsletter.

If I'm replying to a message, then I can assume that someone already knows a bit about me. Therefore, I create a briefer signature that may just be a farewell and not require all the information required by a new message. Brief.

How Can I Change Signatures after I Start a New Message?

Your message uses the signature you've chosen in the Options dialog box, Mail Format tab (Figure 16.11), so which one appears depends on whether you're creating a new message or just replying to someone.

To change the signature on the fly, choose Insert ➤ Signature from the new message's menu. You can pick a different signature from the submenu that appears, as shown in Figure 16.14, or you can choose the More option to display more choices (if you've created them).

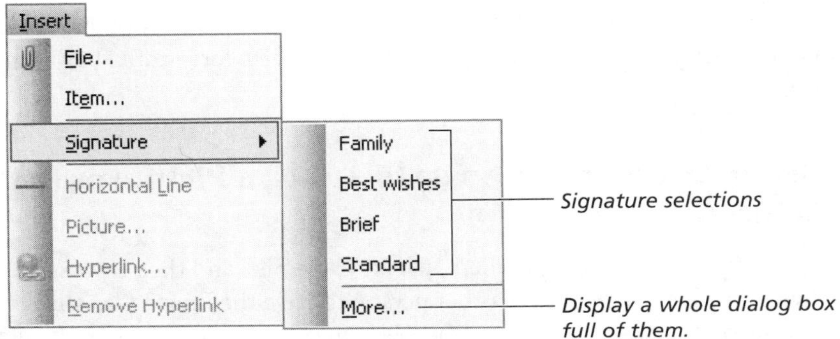

Figure 16.14 Changing a signature on the fly

What Is a Digital Signature?

It's a form of security designed to assure the recipient that you are, in fact, the person who sent the e-mail message. Also known as a digital ID, it allows you to encrypt your e-mail message for better security. That sounds great, but the problem is that you must obtain a digital signature from a company that sells them, such as VeriSign. They are not cheap.

To learn more, choose Tools ➤ Options to display the Options dialog box. Click the Security tab, and then click the Get a Digital ID button.

Attaching Various Things

One optional feature of e-mail that's become incredibly popular is its ability to send one or more files along with the e-mail message. Again, this is pretty common stuff, so much so that it's no longer considered an advanced or even intermediate concept.

The only thing to look out for with e-mail attachments is that they're a common way that computer viruses or worms are spread from PC to PC. The best way to avoid that is to use antivirus software. But because of the problem, you should be aware that people are on the lookout for unknown or unexpected attachments. If you decided to send something out, it's a good idea to first send an e-mail without the attachment, just to let the recipient know that an attachment is coming in the next message and, yes, it is indeed from you.

The following sections deal with some issues beyond the basics of attaching and receiving files via e-mail.

What's the Difference between Insert ➤ File and Insert ➤ Item?

The Insert ➤ File command is used to attach a file to your e-mail message.

The Insert ➤ Item command is used to take the text of any message from any folder in Outlook and stick that message's contents into the current message. It's a way of quoting or "stealing" text from one message and reusing it in another, kind of like forwarding but without clicking the Forward button.

Which Is Better, to Use Insert ➤ File to Attach a Picture or to Use Insert ➤ Picture?

To send a picture as an e-mail attachment, use Insert ➤ File, and then browse to find the picture. This what you do when you want the other person to have the image *file*, which they can then use as any other file on their computer. For example, you can send an image of the new baby to relatives, which they can then keep in their photo albums or forward along to their friends and relatives. That's the advantage of attaching an image as a file.

The Insert ➤ Picture command is used in HTML messages to *embed* an image into your e-mail, just as web pages often have images in them. The end result will be the same for the person receiving the mail. In fact, some e-mail programs receive both types of images as attachments regardless of how they first got into the message. But, generally speaking, Insert ➤ Picture is used to stick an image into an HTML message, not really to attach the image to the file.

What's the Best Way to Attach Multiple Files?

Outlook lets you attach a number of files to any e-mail message. There isn't an upper limit on the number of attachments, though many ISPs refuse to accept e-mail messages over a given size (say 5MB). But the best way to attach multiple files is to first copy them into a Zip or compressed folder archive.

Compressed folders are features of the Windows XP and Me operating systems. They're essentially the same thing as Zip file archives, but you don't need any third-party software to use them. For other versions of Windows, it's necessary to obtain a Zip file utility for creating compressed folders. The one I recommend is WinZip, which can be found at `www.winzip.com`.

The first step in attaching the multiple files is to create the archive file. Follow these steps:

1. Right-click the desktop.

   Or you can right-click any folder. Wherever you right-click, it becomes the location of the compressed folder or Zip archive. The desktop is just a handy place to get to.

2. Choose New ➤ Compressed (Zipped) Folder from the pop-up menu.

   Or if you have WinZip installed, choose New ➤ WinZip File.

You may not see this option if your copy on Windows XP does not have Compressed Folders installed. To install the Compressed Folder feature, refer to my book Dan Gookin's Naked Windows XP.

The new folder (or file) appears. Rename it:

3. Click the file to select it and press the F2 key.
4. Type in a new name, such as `sendme` or something more descriptive.

   You may be required to type the `.zip` filename extension. If you forget, Windows will warn you.

Now you have the archive file created. The next step is to collect all the files you want to e-mail and put them into the archive:

5. Open the folder containing the file(s) you want to send.
6. Drag the file(s) from that folder window and drop them onto the archive folder on the desktop.

   Figure 16.15 shows how this works. To select multiple files from a single folder, press the Ctrl key as you click to select each file. Then drag the group over and drop it onto the archive file.

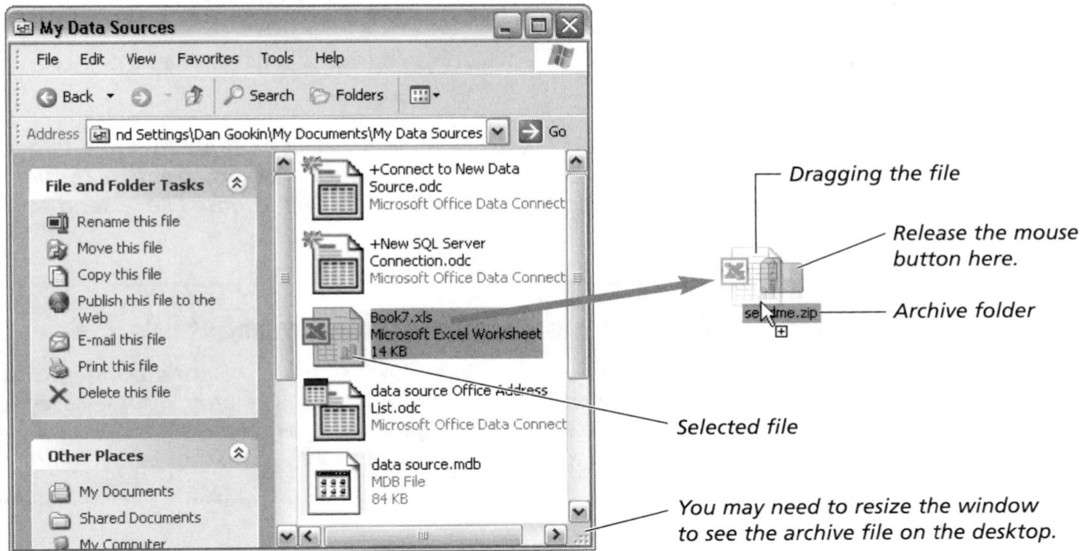

Figure 16.15 Dragging an icon from a folder onto an archive

7. Repeat Steps 5 and 6 for all the files you want to e-mail.

When you're done dragging and dropping and building the archive, the final step is to attach that archive file to an e-mail message and send it:

8. Return to Outlook.

9. Start a new e-mail message.
10. Choose Insert ➢ File.
11. Use the Insert File dialog box to browse to the desktop.

    From the "Look In" drop-down list, choose Desktop (the first item).
12. Select the archive file.
13. Click the Insert button.

    The file attachment appears on the new Attach line in the new message's header. You're ready now to send the e-mail message.
14. Finish addressing and composing the message.
15. Send the message.

    And along with the message you're sending the many files you packed into the single archive. Not only does this save time, but the archive file also compresses the files so they take less bandwidth to send.

When the recipient opens the file, they should save the archive to disk. Once it is there, they can open it up and extract the files, saving them on their own PC's hard drive. (If they don't have a version of Windows with the Compressed Folders feature, then they'll have to get a copy of WinZip to extract the files.)

As a shortcut, if you have WinZip, it's possible to select multiple files in a folder and then choose File ➢ Add to Zip from the menu to instantly create a Zip file from the folders you created. With compressed folders, choose File ➢ Send To ➢ Compressed (Zipped) folder.

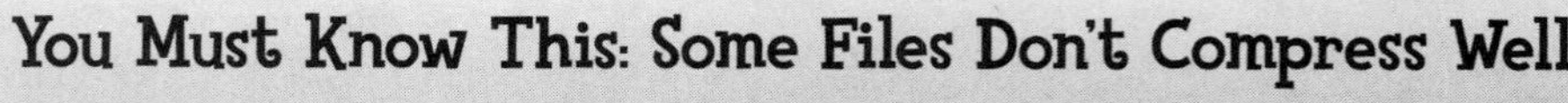

You Must Know This: Some Files Don't Compress Well

Using compressed folders or WinZip to send multiple files is simply a way of picking up several files, putting them in a box (so to speak), and just sending the box. In some cases, the files will compress and actually take up less disk space. In other cases, the files won't compress. That's fine! Remember that this trick is sending one file instead of many.

How Large Can an Attachment Be?

The limitation really depends on your ISP, and that of your intended recipient. Some cap the limit based on the size of your inbox, which could be 2MB or 5MB or 10MB. The only way to really know is to ask. But there is a practical limitation as well.

Not everyone uses the Internet at cable modem or DSL speeds. Most individuals are still using dial-up connections where downloading a hefty file can take a few minutes. In those cases, receiving a 2MB e-mail attachment may delay their day for a few healthy minutes. So the practical limit on e-mail attachment size depends a lot on your and the recipient's connection speed.

Above 5MB, however, I recommend creating a CD-R for the file and sending it through standard mail instead. Even if there is no file size limit on the account and your recipient has a T3 line into their house, sometimes it just makes more sense to burn a CD and fling it off through the regular mail.

Big file attachments include mostly MP3 music files and computer video. Generally speaking, if you're going to send video via e-mail, use video compression and keep the file size to several hundred kilobytes or less than 1MB.

What's the Quickest Way to Send a File Attachment?

The quickest way to send a file attachment via e-mail doesn't even involve running Outlook. From Windows itself, follow these steps:

1. Locate the file you want to send.

   Remember that it can be an archive collection of other files.

2. Right-click the file.

3. Choose Send To ➤ Mail Recipient from the pop-up menu.

   A new message window appears. This is part of Outlook, but note that the rest of Outlook need not start; this is a sending operation only.

4. Complete the message.

   Fill in the To field, the Cc field if needed, the Subject field, and write a message.

5. Click the Send button.

   And the e-mail and its attachment are off onto the Internet.

If you have WinZip installed, an even better trick is to right-click the file and choose "Zip and E-mail" from the pop-up menu. This compresses the file(s) you've selected, saving it (them) in a temporary Zip file, but then starts up a new message and lets you send the compressed file instantly as an attachment. Once it is sent, the temporary Zip archive is deleted.

Even though you can do this on-the-fly sending without opening Outlook, a copy of the message sent still appears in the Sent Items folder (if you have things set up that way). In other words, despite its quick-and-dirty nature, a record is kept of the e-mail being sent.

17 Managing Your E-mail

In passing one day, I overheard a relative say that if they printed out the complete contents of their e-mail inbox it would probably be 100 yards long. Gadzooks! I asked them if they'd ever bothered to clean up or organize their e-mail, and I was met by that familiar blank stare that paints its face on deer just before a truck plows into them, innocent taxpayers as the IRS comes to call, and unsuspecting computer users who never really bother to read the manual or any book on how to use their software.

Managing your e-mail boils down to one simple task: organizing your stuff into folders. It's not time-consuming. In fact, it's the opposite; you'll save time by keeping your e-mail in folders. You'll be able to find old things quickly, and your inbox will remain a thin or empty remnant of its former self. Oh, and you'll be taller and more attractive, small children will follow you skipping and singing songs, and you'll definitely start making more money.

This chapter is about one of the central and most forgotten parts of e-mail, organization. It's not beginner stuff because, honestly, they just don't know. But you know better. And after reading this chapter, you'll know more!

Beds Made and Floors Swept:

- Keeping that Inbox clean
- Organizing your e-mail into other mail folders
- Working with mail folders
- Using the Drafts folder
- Saving e-mail and folders to disk
- Archiving and restoring Outlook's information

After I Read My E-mail, Then What?

The mail comes in and it flows like a gentle stream into your Inbox. There Outlook displays it using bold text, which reminds you that you've yet to read the message. Oh, there may be some nonbold messages in there as well; you've already read those. But then what comes after that?

Okay: reading. Yes, you read your bold messages eagerly like the Broadway star reading reviews, ready to soak up adulation or blow up in a steaming tempest. But then, what comes after that? *What comes after that?*

Is It Okay Just to Keep Everything in the Inbox?

Sure. But it's sloppy.

Keeping old messages in your Inbox is like keeping empty milk cartons in the refrigerator. And we all know how some people just *hate* that!

The fewer items you have in Outlook's Inbox, the faster Outlook runs.

Oh Dear! I Don't Want to Be Sloppy! I Want Outlook to Run Faster! What Can I Do with My Already-Read Messages?

There are three things you can do:

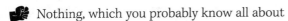

- Nothing, which you probably know all about
- Delete the messages, which is okay for some of them
- File messages away into appropriate folders

The worst of these is to just do nothing with everything. Even so, as long as you're deleting messages and moving others into appropriate folders, it's okay to keep a few messages in the Inbox—kind of like a to-do list or something. That way, by seeing those messages there, you can take action on them later.

Then again, if they hang around in the Inbox too long, you'll just ignore them after a while. So the idea truly is to leave Outlook with an empty Inbox at the end of the day (or at least once a day, if possible).

Deleting messages is also a great idea. Some messages just don't need to be kept: spam, acknowledgments, Ccs for things you don't really care about, jokes you've received a zillion times, and so on. Don't ever be fearful of deleting messages.

That leaves the chore of organizing and using appropriate folders.

What Are Appropriate Folders (As Opposed to Inappropriate Folders)?

As Outlook comes out of the box, it gives you five standard e-mail folders, as shown in Figure 17.1. A sixth folder has been added with Outlook 2003, though it's easy to create this in other versions of Outlook (more on that in a second).

Figure 17.1 The standard Outlook e-mail folders

But are six e-mail boxes enough? No, I say! You need more. You should have more! That folder list should be quite extensive—even if you consider yourself a light e-mail user. I'm a rabid e-mail user and I have 70 e-mail folders total, including folders within folders. The idea is to keep my e-mail organized.

For example, if you've done any online shopping, then you might want to create a Shopping folder. Here's how:

1. Choose File ➤ New ➤ Folder.

   The Create New Folder dialog box appears, as described in Figure 17.2.

2. Give your folder a name.

   Such as "Shopping."

3. Specify the folder's contents.

   This is "Mail and Post Items" for Outlook 2003/XP, or just "Mail Items" for Outlook 2000.

4. Select the location for the folder.

   In this case, click to select the "Personal Folders" item in the bottom of the Create New Folder dialog box, shown in Figure 17.2.

5. Click OK.

   The new folder is born and is ready for use and abuse.

You may be asked if you want to put a shortcut to the folder on the Outlook bar. I would say "Yes" if you plan on that e-mail folder being very popular. Otherwise, don't bother.

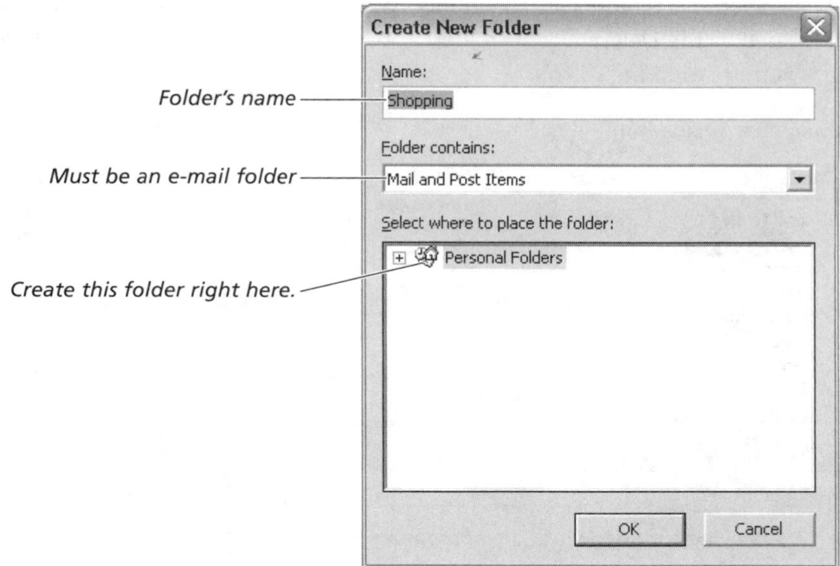

Figure 17.2 Creating a new e-mail folder

KEYBOARD MASTER

The Quick and Dirty Folder Shortcut Keys

There are only two sets of folder shortcut keys, both of which are fairly complex until you train your fingers to assume the proper "claw" pattern:

Ctrl+Shift+E

Summon the Create New Folders dialog box.

Ctrl+Shift+V

Copy the selected message(s) to a folder (displays the Move to Folder dialog box).

What's the Trick to Using a Folder?

Simple. After reading a message you have a decision to make: What do I do with this message?

For some messages you may leave them in the Inbox. For example, it's a long message and requires detailed attention—time you don't have right now. That's fine; just leave it in the Inbox—not to rot, but to come back to later.

Some messages, well, you just know that they're destined for the stank bowels of hell; delete them. Press Ctrl+D to zap them off to the infernal darkness of the Deleted Items folder.

A more satisfying way to delete messages is shown in Figure 17.3. You can use the mouse to drag a message into a folder, such as the Deleted Items folder. Apparently this is very painful for the message, so dragging it is more fulfilling to you.

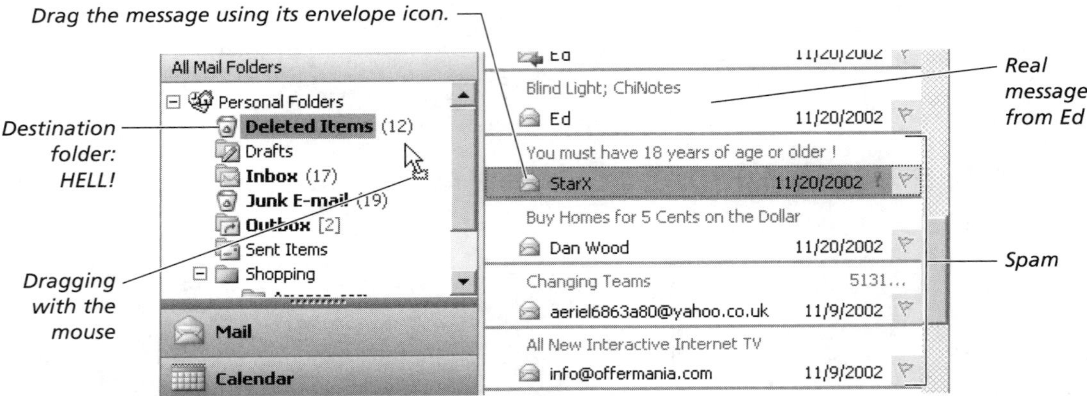

Figure 17.3 Moving a message into the appropriate folder

Just as you can drag a message to the Deleted Items folder, you can also drag it to another appropriate folder. For example, that wallet you bought on the Internet, the one that is made from duct tape? That's an Internet sale! When you receive the e-mail reply, drag it over into the Shopping folder to keep the receipt. The message is properly saved, plus it's out of the Inbox.

What About Viewing a Folder's Contents?

The folders you create work just like the folders Outlook already has set up: Just click to select a folder, and you'll see its contents displayed—just like the Inbox.

Dan, I Get a Lot of Jokes...

Some jokes are worth keeping. So why not create a Jokes folder? That way if the joke is something you want to have and hold forever, save it into the Jokes folder from the Inbox folder when you're done reading it.

Those bad jokes? Delete 'em.

Table 17.1 lists a bunch of suggested folders you might consider creating for organizing your incoming e-mail.

Table 17.1 The Vast Collection of E-mail Folder Suggestions and Selections

Folder Name	*Potential Contents*
Business	*E-mail from work*
Family	*E-mail from family members*
Friends	*E-mail from your friends and associates*
Internet	*E-mail from your ISP*
Jokes	*Funny e-mail*
Misc	*A general e-mail folder for stuff you don't really have another place for*
Shopping	*Online shopping receipts and such*

The suggestions in Table 17.1 paint a broad stroke. You may want to get specific. For example, I have individual folders for my mom and sister because they send me e-mail fairly often. Some friends send a lot of e-mail and they get their own folders as well. But other folks just get tossed into the generic folders.

How Can I Get the Message into a Folder After I've Read It?

If you have the message window open, then choose File ➤ Move to Folder or press Ctrl+Shift+V. This displays the Move Item To dialog box, shown in Figure 17.4. Pick a folder to store the message in, and then click OK.

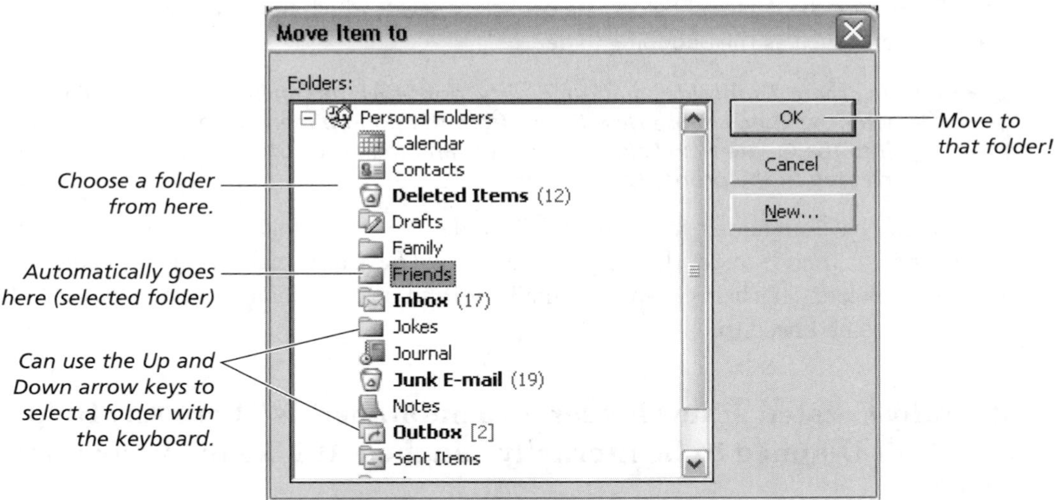

Figure 17.4 Finding a home for the message you've just read

My Folders List Is 18 Miles High!

The good news about having lots of e-mail folders is that you know you're keeping everything you've read organized. But rather than suffer scrolling through a long list of folders, you need to learn the art of organization on the subfolder level. Just as you can in Windows, you can further organize your e-mail by subfolder.

A subfolder is simply a folder inside another folder. For example, suppose you go online shopping at Amazon.com, Eddie Bauer, and eBay. Why not create separate folders for all of them. And while you're at it, why not create a subfolder for the online travel purchases you make? Figure 17.5 shows how such a thing looks in my Outlook folder list.

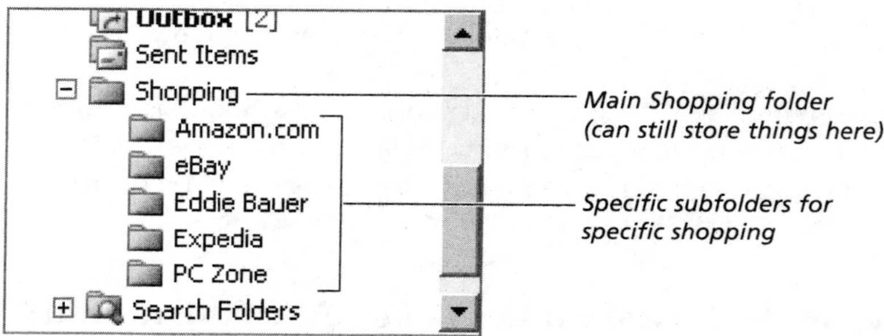

Figure 17.5 Super-organized subfolders to the rescue!

To create a subfolder, use the Create New Folder dialog box as described earlier in this chapter, in the section "What Are Appropriate Folders (As Opposed to Inappropriate Folders)?" In Step 4, instead of choosing the Personal Folders item, click to select which folder you want the subfolder to appear under—such as the Shopping folder.

To create a subfolder quick-and-dirty, right-click the main folder in the Folders window, then choose New Folder from the pop-up menu. Type the folder name into the Create New Folder dialog box, and then click OK. The subfolder is instantly created in the proper spot.

On my system I have subfolders for Mom and Sis under the Family folder. I have individual subfolders for specific friends under the Friends folder. And I have a special Dirty Jokes folder under the main Jokes folder. This helps keep the e-mail neat and organized, and it also helps me to find things quickly when I need to.

I Accidentally Created a New Folder As a Subfolder! Is There Any Help for Me or Am I Doomed to Be Eternally Laughed At Like the Incompetent Fool I Am?

Relax! Right-click the folder and you'll see a pop-up menu similar to the one shown in Figure 17.6. Use those commands to fix whatever is wrong.

For example, to move a folder, choose "Move *Folder Name*" from the menu. A Move Folder dialog box appears, in which you can select the proper location for the folder. To move a folder up to the top level, choose "Personal Folders" in the Move Folder dialog box. Otherwise, choose the proper "parent" for the folder.

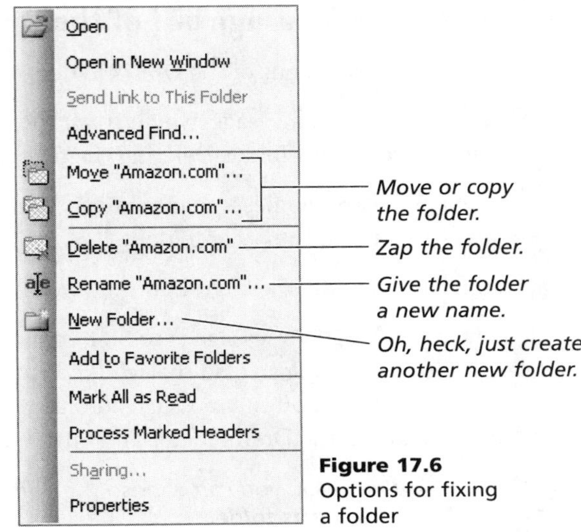

Figure 17.6 Options for fixing a folder

What's the Point of the Drafts Folder?

After all the information about creating new folders and organizing your e-mail with them, the basic question that comes up time after time is, "What's the point of the Drafts folder?"

Drafts is used to hold unsent and unfinished e-mail.

Messages get into the Drafts folder when you select not to send a message. For example, you start up a new message or a reply (or forward) and then close the window. Like closing any unfinished "document" in Office, you're asked if you want to save the changes. If you click the Yes button, the unfinished e-mail lodges in the Drafts folder. (If you answer No, the message is discarded; it isn't even saved in the Deleted Items folder.)

You can also save a message to the Drafts folder by choosing File ➤ Save from the menu. That puts a copy of the message into the Drafts folder without closing the New Message window. After doing that you can close the window if you want to; the message is saved.

Can I Use the Drafts Folder for E-mail I Write but May Want to Review Before I Send It Off?

Some e-mail shouldn't be sent. It should be sat upon and reviewed later when you're not angry or intoxicated or you're in a better mood. To do this you can take advantage of the Drafts folder. Here's how:

1. Choose File ➤ Save to save the message in the Drafts folder.
2. Close the message window.

Now the message sits safe—and unsent and unable to be sent—until you're ready to do so.

How Can I Get a Message out of the Drafts Folder?

There are many paths out of the Drafts folder:

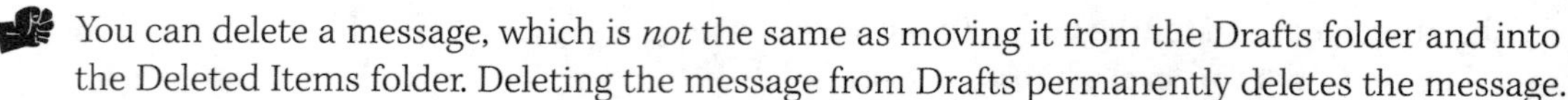

- You can delete a message, which is *not* the same as moving it from the Drafts folder and into the Deleted Items folder. Deleting the message from Drafts permanently deletes the message.
- You can move the message into another folder; just drag the message by its envelope icon and drop it into the other folder.
- You can open the message, continue working on it, or just send it.

The key to sending the message is to first open it. Then you can review it, edit it if you like, or delete it after becoming so glad that you didn't send it in the first place. But to send it, you simply click the Send button on the message's toolbar as you would for any new message. This transfers the message out of the Drafts folder and into the Outbox, where it will be sent.

If you're quick, you can choose the Edit ➤ Undo command to undo deleting a message from the Drafts folder.

Escape from Outlook: Getting Mail from Outlook to Your Hard Drive

One thing most folks don't understand about Outlook is that its folders are *not* the same as folders on disk. Even though they look the same. Even though they operate under the same philosophy. Even with the organization tools being roughly the same as the tools for organizing folders under Windows, they're just not the same. Accept it! Live with it!

All is not peril and doom, of course. There is a bridge between the e-mail stuffed into your Outlook folders and the "real world" inside the computer. That's the secret the following sections help you uncover: working between Outlook's folders and folders out there on the hard drive.

How Can I Save a Message to Disk?

The secret to getting a message out of a folder in Outlook and into a real folder on your computer's hard drive is to use the File ➤ Save As command. Here are the steps to take:

1. Open the message you want to save in the real world.
2. Choose File ➤ Save As from the menu.

   A standard Save As dialog box opens, beautifully illustrated in Figure 17.7.

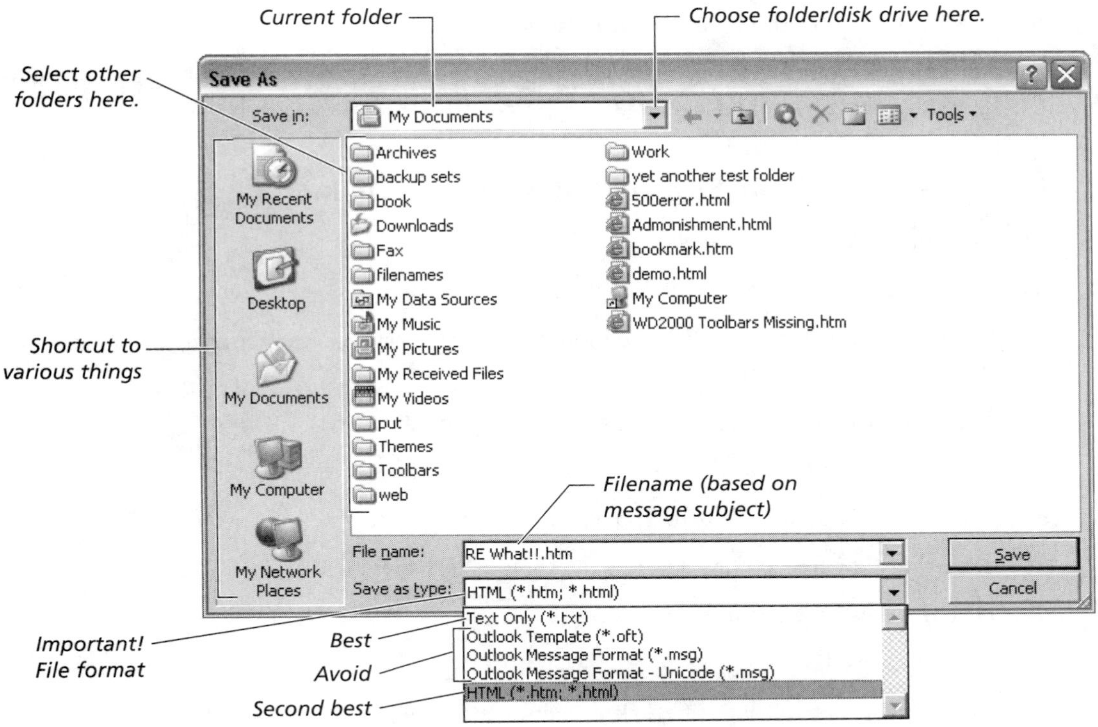

Figure 17.7 A beautiful illustration of the Save As dialog box

3. Use the Save As dialog box to decide where you want to place the e-mail file on disk.

This is important! If you plan on doing this a lot, then perhaps you should create a special folder (in Windows) for storing e-mail. If it's a temporary thing, then you can just use the My Documents folder, shown in Figure 17.7.

4. Carefully choose the e-mail file format from the "Save As Type" drop-down list.

The best format for your e-mail is plain text, Text Only. That's the most common file format available on any computer. Any software program can read the message that way. The plain text format will never go out of date. Trust me.

The next best format is HTML, which unlike the Text Only format will retain any fancy fonts, pictures, or other formatting applied to the e-mail. If you feel that stuff is important, then save the message in HTML.

HTML is also known as the Web page file format. Any web browser can open and properly display a file saved in the HTML format.

Avoid the other formats. While Outlook can read them, other programs cannot. To give yourself the fewest headaches in the future, I recommend avoiding those formats.

5. Click the Save button to save your message.

Once it's on disk, you can do whatever else you want with the message: save it to a floppy disk or CD-R, or just have and hold it handy.

I'd Like to Save a Whole Swath of Messages to Disk.

This is actually easier than it seems:

1. Select the messages you want to save.

   Press the Ctrl key as you click the mouse to select messages; each message you click becomes part of the group.

   You can select all the messages in a mailbox by pressing Ctrl+A.

2. Choose File ➤ Save As.
3. Use the Save As dialog box to find a location for the files.

   Note that they'll all be saved as one contiguous text file; there are no other file-saving options.

4. Give the messages a fine name.
5. Click the Save button.

   The messages are all saved to disk, one after the other, in a single text file.

This may seem nutty, but it's actually the same internal format that Outlook (and most e-mail programs) uses for storing messages. A mail folder is, in fact, a special type of text file. An index reaches into the file and pulls out where new messages start, along with the Subject, To, and Date fields. But otherwise, the e-mail folders Outlook works with are basically text files.

To prove this, open the file you just saved to disk. You'll see each mail message one after the other saved as a giant text file.

Note that some formatted e-mails have been truncated; the original HTML code is not saved to disk in the text file. That's good.

NERD'S CORNER

Some Trivia about the "From" in a Message

To find the start of a new message, look for any line of text that begins with the word "From." That's how e-mail programs do it. It also explains why when you send e-mail and you start a line with the word "From," your mail program inserts a > character before that word, ">From." The only "From" allowed at the start of the line in an e-mail message is the From field telling you who sent the message.

Can I Save a Folder to Disk?

Not directly, but you can *export* the folder's data. That's pretty much the same thing because exporting places the data into a usable format, such as delimited text or an Excel worksheet. Here's how you can manage that:

1. Choose File ➤ Import and Export.

Ta-da! It's the Import and Export Wizard. This wizard can also be used to read data from other applications into Outlook.

2. Choose "Export to a File" and click the Next button.

Now you get to choose the format for the data.

If you see the destination program listed, choose it. For example, choose Excel if you want to create a list of the folder's contents in Excel. The databases Access, dBASE, and FoxPro are also listed.

For general purposes, however, there are comma- and tab-separated values (formatted for DOS and Windows). These are "delimited text files," which are the most common type of data format, readable by just about any database or spreadsheet.

If you're unsure, choose "Comma Separated Values (Windows)."

3. Click the Next button.

4. Choose the folder you want to export from the list.

Yes, you can select only one folder from the list at a time. For my example, I'm exporting the Dirty Jokes subfolder beneath my main Jokes folder.

5. Click the Next button.

6. Enter a name for the file.

The file will be saved in the My Documents folder. To select a different folder, use the Browse button.

Do not save the file directly to a removable disk, especially a floppy disk. Save the file to the hard drive first. Then, after the wizard is complete and you quit Outlook, you can copy the file to a removable disk.

7. Click the Next button.

The next step looks scary, but it's not. You can use the Map Custom Fields button to rearrange the fields from the e-mail messages, but I wouldn't do that now; save such a thing for when you import the file to its final destination. For now, leave things pretty much as Outlook puts them.

8. Click the Finish button.

There's some churning and chugging. Eventually the operation is complete.

The Body field is the one that contains the body of the message. This is going to be the largest of the fields—and potentially the most difficult to view if you decide to import the data into Excel, for example. However, exporting in one of the delimited text formats, such as "Tab Separated Values (Windows)," produces wonderful results when read into Word; the entire mailbox appears readable as one long text document.

How Can I Back Up My Folders?

Saving a folder to disk is not the same as backing up. When you back up, you're creating a safety copy of your data, one you'll probably save to a CD-R for the future or to prepare for disaster.

Outlook is more than capable of backing up all your folders. The key is the Archiving command. Heed these steps:

1. Choose File ➤ Archive.

The Archive dialog box appears, as shown in Figure 17.8.

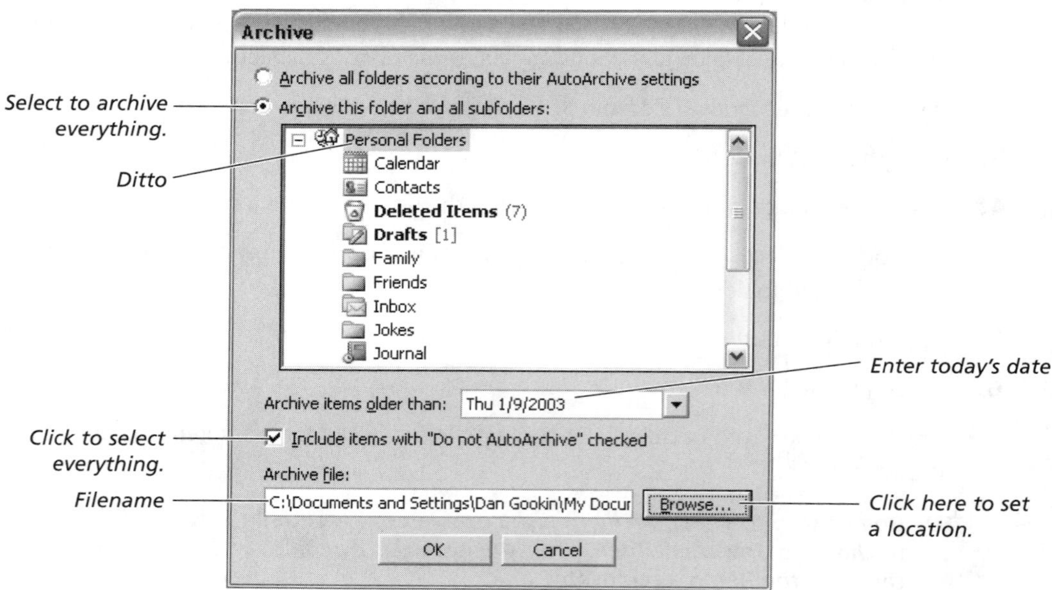

Figure 17.8 Creating a backup of your Outlook stuff

2. Select "Personal Folders" to archive all of Outlook.

You can select individual folders, but why not just select "Personal Folders" to archive the entire dang doodle?

3. Choose today's date.

You don't want to miss anything.

4. Click to check "Include Items with 'Do Not AutoArchive' checked."

   This way everything is archived.

5. Click the Browse button.

   Without otherwise expressing yourself, Outlook places the backup archive in an arcane folder you wouldn't normally suspect. Dumb. Dumb. Dumb. By clicking the Browse button, you can easily select another, more common folder.

6. In the Open Personal Folders dialog box, click the My Documents button.

   It's on the left end of the dialog box.

7. Click OK.

   Now Outlook is told to save the file in the standard My Documents folder location.

8. Click OK to create the archive backup.

   There. Quite painless.

The archive data file is pretty hefty; it contains all your Outlook stuff, so the more you use Outlook, the bigger it becomes. If you want to save it to a removable disk, use a CD-R; do not attempt to save this sucker to a floppy.

You Must Know This: Bizarre Folder Locations

In all cases, when you save things to disk you should know where you're saving them. I prefer the central location of the My Documents folder as somewhere that's well known and easy to get to. However, if you make it a habit to back up, archive, or export your e-mail, consider creating a special E-mail Backup subfolder inside the My Documents folder. Then you can save everything nice and tidy in there.

Without specifying otherwise, meaning that you ignore all those Browse buttons Outlook offers you, the files end up being saved in what Microsoft refers to as the Application Data folder. This folder exists in the Windows folder on some versions of Windows. In other versions, it's found in your personal account's folder and then in the Application Data folder. The problem here is that this Application Data folder is found under the Local Settings folder—which is hidden. So if you don't have Windows Explorer configured to display hidden folders, you'll end up beating the bushes on your hard drive all the doo-da-day until you find the folder.

To sum it up, with Windows 98/Me, you'll find Outlook's secret folder on this path:

```
C:\Windows\Local Settings\Application Data\Microsoft\Outlook
```

In Windows XP, you'll find the secret folder located on this path:

```
C:\Documents and Settings\[your account name]\Local Settings\Application
Data\Microsoft\Outlook
```

What's This AutoArchive Option For?

Rather than manually archive your Outlook stuff, you can configure Outlook to archive—even to clean up folders—automatically for you. It's cinchy. Here's how:

1. Right-click the e-mail folder you want to manage.
2. Choose Properties from the pop-up menu.
3. Click the AutoArchive tab in the mailbox's Properties dialog box.

   Figure 17.9 shows what's up. There are many fun folder-management options to choose from.

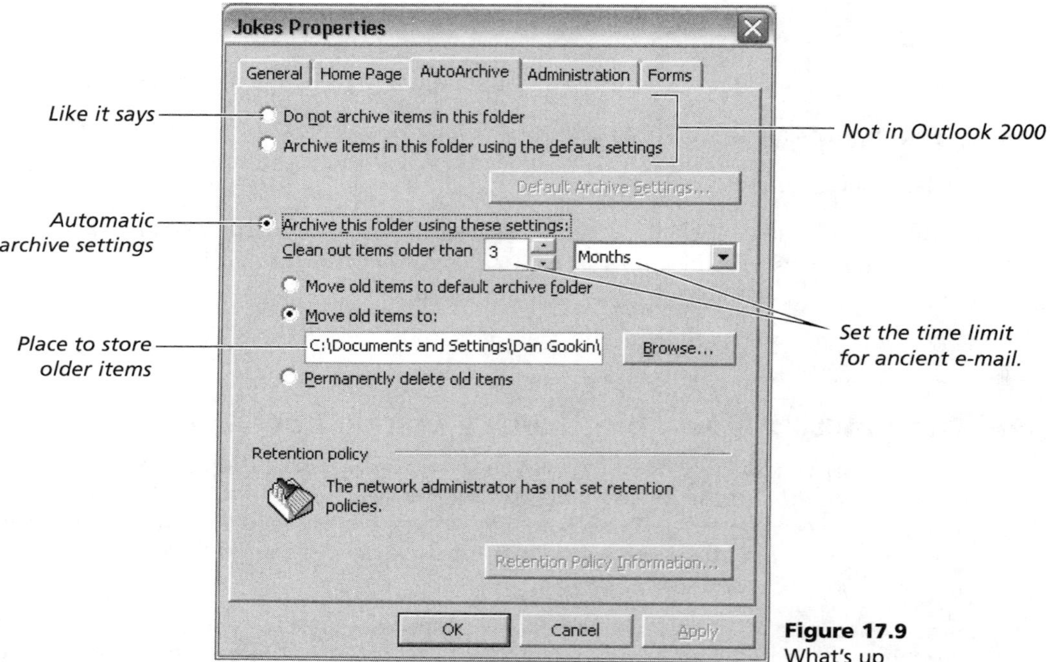

Figure 17.9
What's up

4. To prevent the folder from being archived, click to select "Do Not Archive Items in This Folder."

   For example, say it's just a junk or temp folder. Why bother wasting disk space with it? Note that this option is not available in Outlook 2000.

5. My advice is to choose the option "Archive This Folder Using These Settings."

   This option is found only in Outlook 2003/XP.

6. Enter an expiration date for old e-mails in the folder.

   You can specify months, weeks, or days to wait. After that time the old e-mail can be automatically archived or just blown to bits.

7. Click "Move Old Items To" and select a folder to back them up to.

   I prefer this option as it backs up different folders separately, which I can then restore individually.

8. Choose a file for the backup by clicking the Browse button.

9. Use the Find Personal Folders dialog box to locate a folder for your backups.

   You can keep the bizarrely located folder for this operation; Outlook remembers its location well.

10. Enter a name into the Filename box. Make it specific to the folder that you're archiving.

11. Click OK to set the archive folder.

12. Click OK to close the folder's Properties dialog box.

As an alternative to archiving the folders, in Step 7 you can merely elect to delete any older items; choose "Permanently Delete Old Items" instead. But if the contents are worth keeping long term, then archive them.

How Can I Use an Archive I Previously Saved to Disk?

Obviously, saving something to disk isn't worth the trouble if there's no way to read the data back after it's been saved. Boy, would that be some hellish torture! Windows XP version 2: The Cruel Version. But I digress.

Should you need to dig up and use an archived folder, follow these laborious steps to retrieve it:

1. Choose File ➢ Import and Export.

2. Choose the option "Import from Another Program or File."

   Weird choice, but that's what you have to choose.

3. Click the Next button.

4. From the next list choose "Personal Folder File (.pst)."

5. Click the Next button.

   Outlook automatically selects the generic `BACKUP.PST` file saved in the secretive Outlook folder hidden somewhere on your hard drive, shown in Figure 17.10.

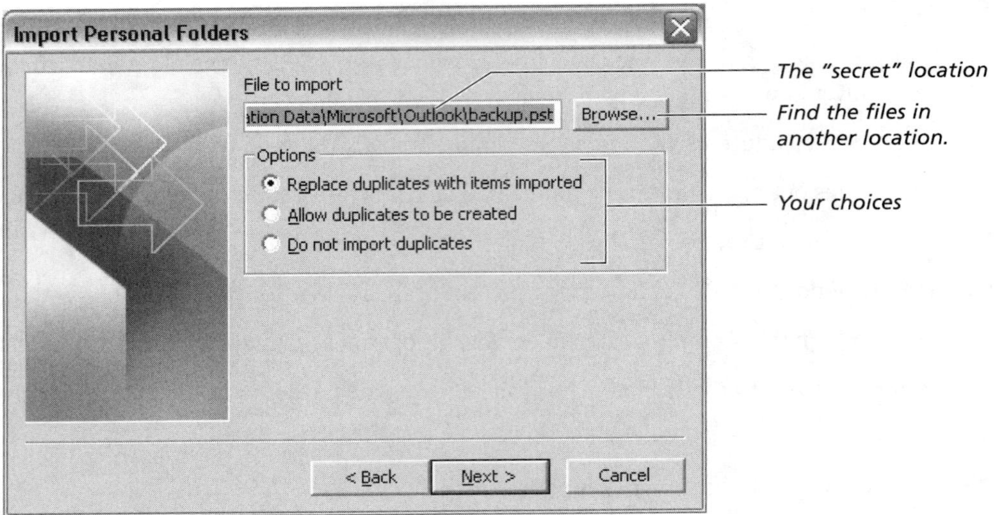

Figure 17.10 Reading in a backup file

6. Click the Browse button to locate specific folders if you've selected another location for them.

For example, if you're backing up stuff to the `\My Documents\E-mail Backup` folder, use the Browse button to locate that folder and then select the specific backup file you want to restore.

7. Choose "Do Not Import Duplicates."

This is the best way to just import the differences between the folder backup and the current folder. Use the other options if you think they make more sense.

8. Click the Next button.

9. Click the Finish button.

Sure, there are a lot of options in that final panel, but most of them are set up fine for importing what you need. Otherwise refer to Figure 17.11 for your choices.

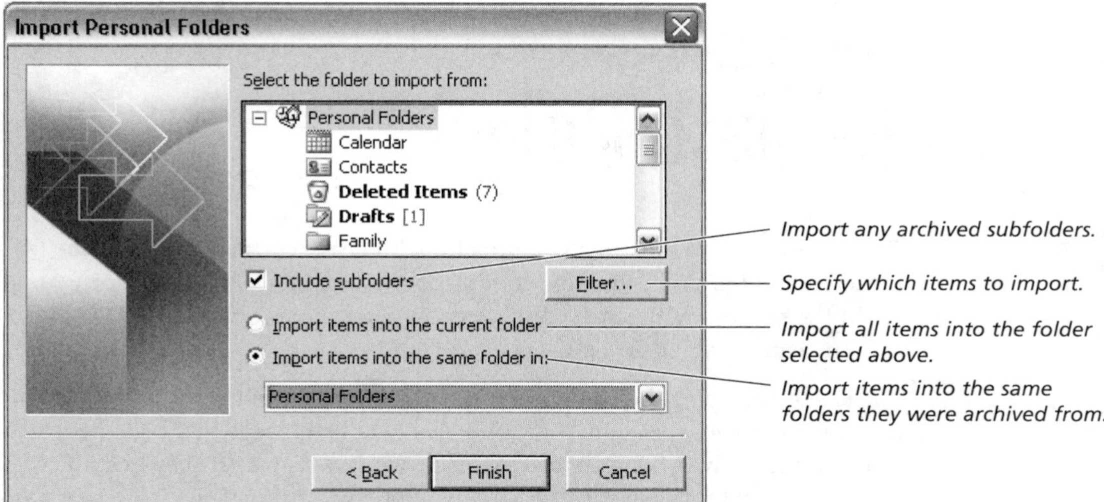

Figure 17.11 Insane last-minute options

If disaster ever befell your system and you had to import old e-mail information, the steps here would help you do it by recovering files from an archived backup. That's really the entire point of the exercise. However, you can get picky with restoring older files that were backed up after the AutoArchive limit (described in the previous section.) My advice is that if you find yourself doing that often, then either up the interval for archiving older messages or just don't do it at all.

18 E-mail Rules!

Computers live and breathe for automation. Endless, repetitive tasks are the PC's bread and butter. Unlike minions in fast food restaurants, computers don't complain about the monotony. By gum, computers *strive* for monotony. They live for the day to be repeated over and over again.

The key to supplying the computer with enough mundane monotony to keep it happy is to properly program that thing. The problem here is that most people just program themselves. Some folks don't really witness that what they're doing with a computer is, in fact, repetitive. So a connection must be made between that tedium and the computer's ability to lighten the load.

So it is with much joy and anticipation that I present you with the "E-mail Rules!" chapter. This is where you can direct Outlook to take immediate action on e-mail based on who is sending the e-mail, the message's subject, or a number of other factors. It's telling the computer do to automatically what you've probably been doing manually in the past. And it's a great step up from average e-mail user to Super E-mail Human.

Powers Given and Tricks Unveiled:

- Creating Mail Rules to organize your e-mail
- Modifying the Mail Rules
- Blocking spam
- Automatically forwarding your e-mail
- Searching for individuals in your mail folders
- Flagging e-mail with colors

Making a Mail Rule

In other e-mail programs they call them *filters*, but in Outlook they're called *Mail Rules*. Still, I prefer filter, which is a database term. In a database, you use a filter to select specific members of the database and create custom lists or subgroups of a main group, say a group of all men between the ages of 44 and 65, or a group of folks you send birthday greetings to, and so on. Mail Rules work along those lines.

A Mail Rule is an instruction to Outlook to first look for e-mail matching specific characteristics—sent from a specific person or organization or having a certain word in the subject—and second to do something with that e-mail, such as file it in a specific folder, play a sound, or just delete the e-mail. All that can be done automatically, provided you create the proper rule.

How Can I Create a Mail Rule That Automatically Files E-mail from a Specific Person into a Specific Folder?

Suppose you have a Family folder, which you've designed to hold e-mail you receive from family members. Start with Uncle Joe, who is joe@yahoo.com. Here is how you can create a mail rule to automatically file his e-mail into the Family folder:

1a. In Outlook 2003, choose Tools ➤ Rules and Alerts.

1b. In Outlook XP/2000, choose Tools ➤ Rules Wizard.

2a. In Outlook 2003, click the New Rule button.

2b. In Outlook XP/2000, click the New button.

The Rules Wizard finally appears, shown in Figure 18.1. The 2003 version is shown in the figure; the XP/2000 version is slightly similar.

3. Click to select the item that begins "Move Messages from Someone."

It ends with "to a Folder" in Outlook 2003.

4. Click the Next button.

Now you get to review conditions, or specifics about the e-mail. There's a whole swarm of them, but what you want are messages from Uncle Joe or joe@yahoo.com. Figure 18.2 explains this.

5. Ensure that the top item is checked, "From People or Distribution List."

A distribution list is a collection of people's e-mail addresses—such as a gang you can e-mail all at once. More on this in Chapter 19, "Making the Best of Your Contacts."

Now here's where things in the wizard stop making sense. You would normally be under the spell to click the Next button—but that's not the case! Instead, you need to go to the bottom part of the Rules Wizard dialog box and choose some names.

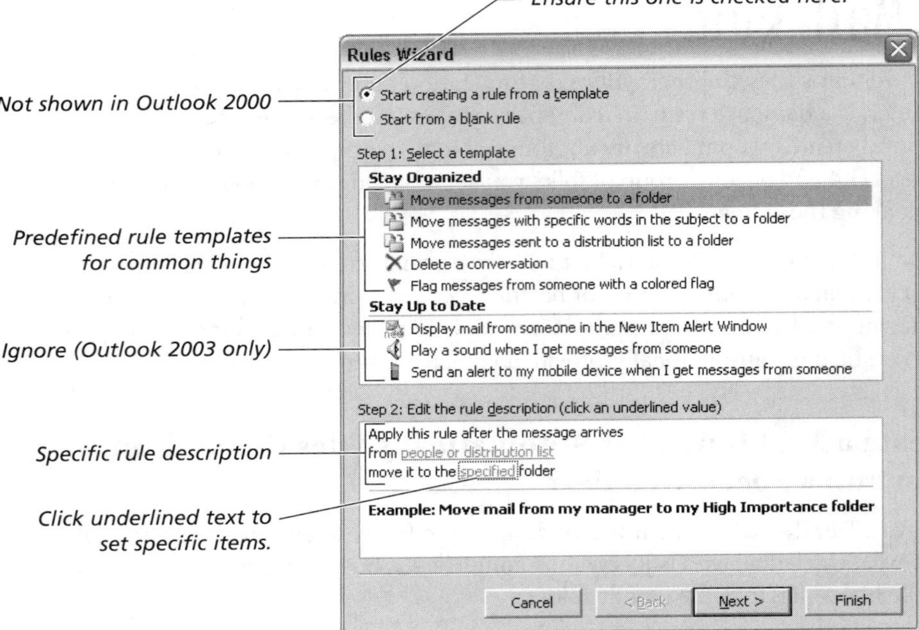

Figure 18.1 The Rules Wizard, ready to automate for you

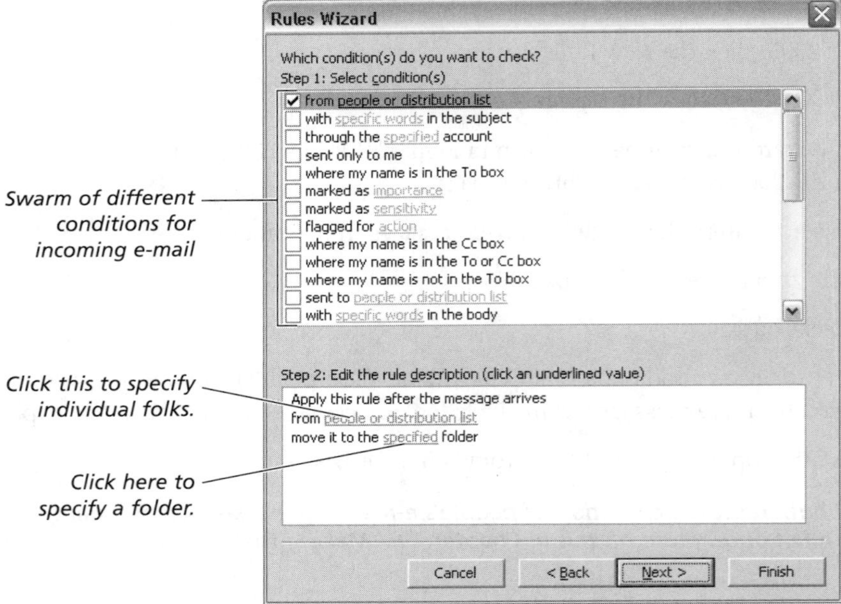

Figure 18.2 Crafting the rule

6. Click the underlined text, "People or Distribution List."

This is where you pick the name, "Uncle Joe," for example. You do this in the Rule Address dialog box, shown in Figure 18.3.

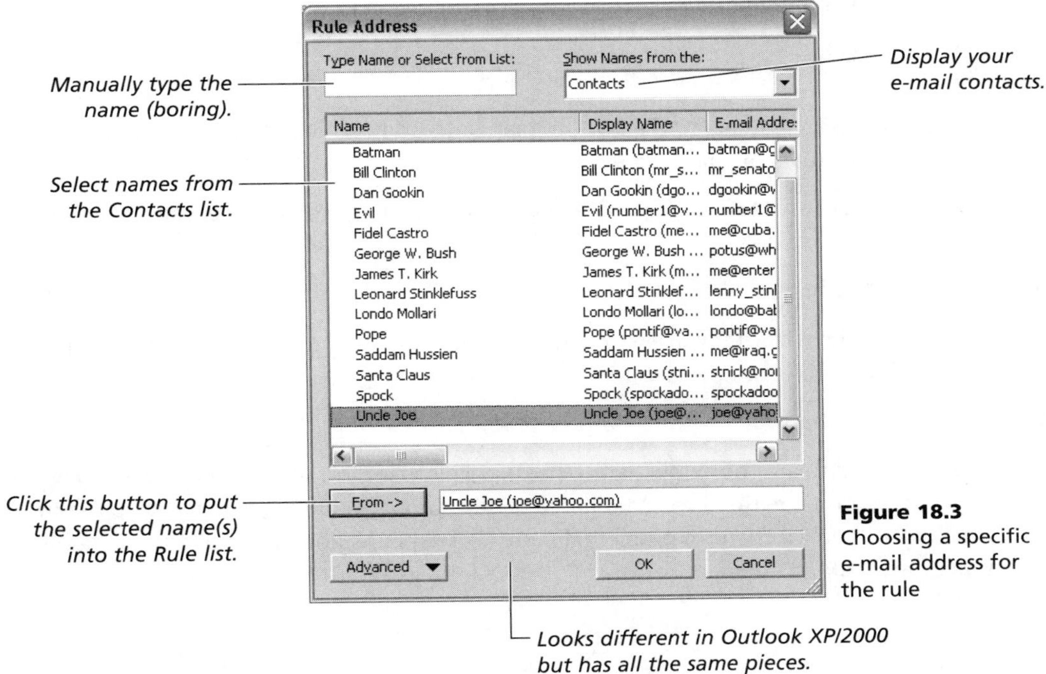

Figure 18.3
Choosing a specific e-mail address for the rule

7. Select the e-mail address or name from the Rule Address window.

You can select more than one, as shown in Figure 18.3.

8. Click the From button.

9. Click OK.

Back in the Rules Wizard dialog box, note how the name you selected replaces the underlined text "People or Distribution List" (see Figure 18.2).

10. Click the Next button.

Now you have to choose what to do with messages from Uncle Joe when they arrive. A slate of choice is displayed, but the wizard is already predisposed to move the message to a specific folder (as shown in the bottom part of the dialog box).

11. Click the underlined text, "Specified."

A list of folders is displayed.

12. Choose the Family folder.

Or whichever folder is appropriate for this rule.

You can even create a new folder here by clicking the New button. Oh, they think of everything. Mostly.

13. Click OK.

Now the rule should read, in the bottom part of the Rules Wizard dialog box, just as you want it to automatically perform:

`Apply this rule after the message arrives from Uncle Joe (joe@yahoo.com) move it to the Family folder.`

14. Click the Next button.

This step of the wizard involves exceptions to the rule. That doesn't really apply here, though there will be other examples later in this chapter.

15. Click the Next button.

Now you need to appropriately name the rule. This is important because not all rules are perfect when they're first created. Therefore you want to name it properly so you know which one to edit if there's a problem. Figure 18.4 explains how the final step of the Rules Wizard works.

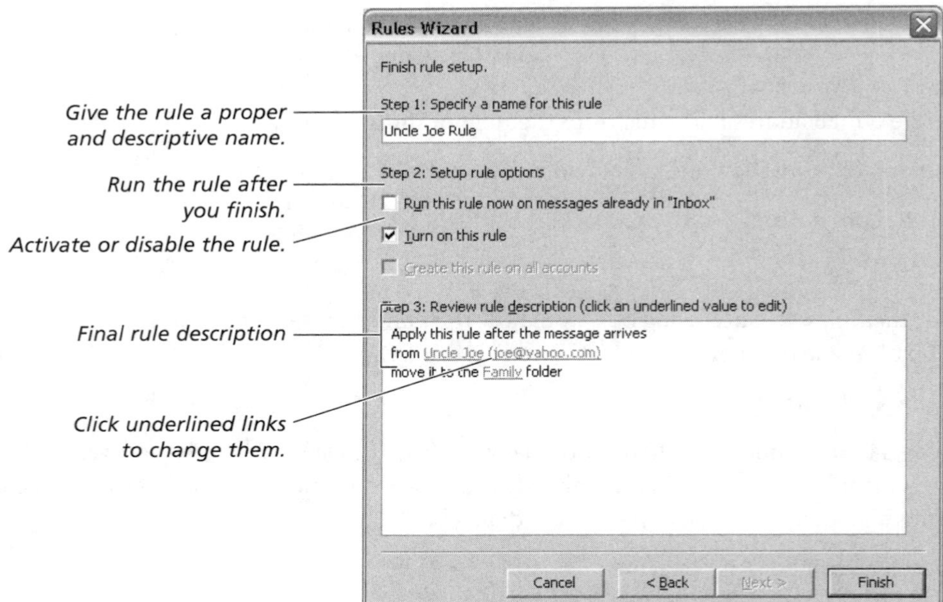

Figure 18.4
The final step

16. Enter a name for the rule.

17. Click the Finish button.

    The rule is created and ready to run.

18. Close the Rules and Alerts or Rules Wizard dialog box.

The only way to test the rule is to go out and fetch new mail. If you're lucky, a message from Uncle Joe (or whomever) will arrive. When it does, the rule is kicked into action and that message is properly—and instantly—filed away into the proper mail folder.

By the way, your clue that you have new mail from Uncle Joe is that the Family mailbox will become bold after you pick up new e-mail. That bold text means that the mailbox holds unread messages. That's your clue to open it and read what's up.

I Think Filing Uncle Joe's E-mails Away Is Cruel. I Demand a Better Example!

Rather than instantly shove all of Uncle Joe's e-mail into the Family folder, a better option for this type of rule concerns legitimate e-mail you may get from various robots on the Internet.

For example, whenever you order something from Amazon.com, you get a receipt. It's possible to set up a Mail Rule that simply files all Amazon.com e-mail into the Shopping\Amazon folder for you. Or your online stock trading confirmations from E*trade can also be automatically filed into the E-Trade folder.

In these automatic cases you can shove the e-mail directly into a folder and even mark it as being "read." Here's how:

1. Follow the steps in the previous section for running the Rules Wizard and creating a new Mail Rule in your version of Outlook.

   No sense in repeating that stuff here.

2. Choose the option that begins, "Move Messages from Someone" or "Move Messages from Someone to a Folder."

   Again, you're going to be automatically filing your incoming mail.

3. Click the Next button.

4. Un-check the text, "From People or Distribution Lists."

5. Check the text, "With Specific Words in the Sender's Address."

   This is necessary because otherwise you would have to create an account for "Amazon.com" or "E*trade" or "FancyPotHoldersRUs" or whichever online vendor you're dealing with—and Outlook cannot create such generic contacts.

6. Click the underlined text, "Specific Words."

This is located in the bottom part of the dialog box.

7. Type the word in to the Search Text dialog box.

For example, type **amazon.com**.

8a. In Outlook 2003/XP, click the Add button, and then click OK.

8b. In Outlook 2000, click OK.

9. Click the Next button.

10a. In Outlook 2003/XP, in addition to checking the "Move It to the Specified Folder" option, put a checkmark by the item "Mark It As Read."

You want to both mark the message as being read as well as move it to the folder you'll specify in Step 12.

10b. In Outlook 2000, you can only select "Move It to the Specified Folder"; there is no option to mark the message as being read.

11. Click the underlined text, "Specified."

It's in the bottom of the dialog box.

12. Click to select the folder you want to shove the message into.

13. Click OK.

14. Click the Next button.

No exceptions this time.

15. Click the Next button.

16. Enter a name for the rule.

For example, **Amazon.com - automatic filing**.

17. Click the Finish button.

And you can close the Rules and Alerts or Rules Wizard dialog box as well.

Yes, unfortunately, there is no rule in Outlook 2000 to flag a message as already being read. That means anything automatically filed using this rule shows up in bold text in the folder list. You can tolerate that.

By setting the "Mark It As Read" option in Outlook 2003/XP, you are preventing the mail rule from being exported and then imported into Outlook 2000. Eh, big deal!

What's the Difference between Selecting "Delete" or "Permanently Delete" for a Mail Rule?

The Delete option merely moves the message into the Deleted Items folder. The Permanently Delete option removes the message at the server level, preventing it from even being downloaded into your computer. You'll never see it. On the other hand, you'll never be able to recover it, should you want to.

Yes, unwanted e-mail can be copied out of the Deleted Items folder.

Can I Modify a Rule So That It Plays a Sound When Specific Mail Arrives?

Any mail rule can be modified. The tricky thing is creating it perfectly. Because few people manage that the first time, you can always go back and spruce up a rule, changing it or even disabling it altogether.

To add a sound to a rule as it executes, follow the steps listed below, which assume a rule has already been created.

Modifying a Rule in Outlook 2003

Here's one reason you can be glad you upgraded to Office 2003: Outlook 2003 makes it easier than anything to modify any existing Mail Rule. Here's how:

1. Choose Tools ➤ Rules and Alerts.
2. Select the rule you want to add a sound to from the list.
3. Click the Change Rule menu button and choose "Play a Sound" from the menu.

   This is shown in Figure 18.5.
4. Use the Select a Sound to Play dialog box to find and choose a sound.

To preview a sound, right-click the file in the Select a Sound to Play dialog box and choose Play from the pop-up menu.

5. Click OK to select that sound.

   And the sound is added to your rule, as can be seen in the bottom part of the Rules and Alerts dialog box (the text description) and by the speaker icon to the right of the rule.
6. Close the Rules and Alerts dialog box, if you must.

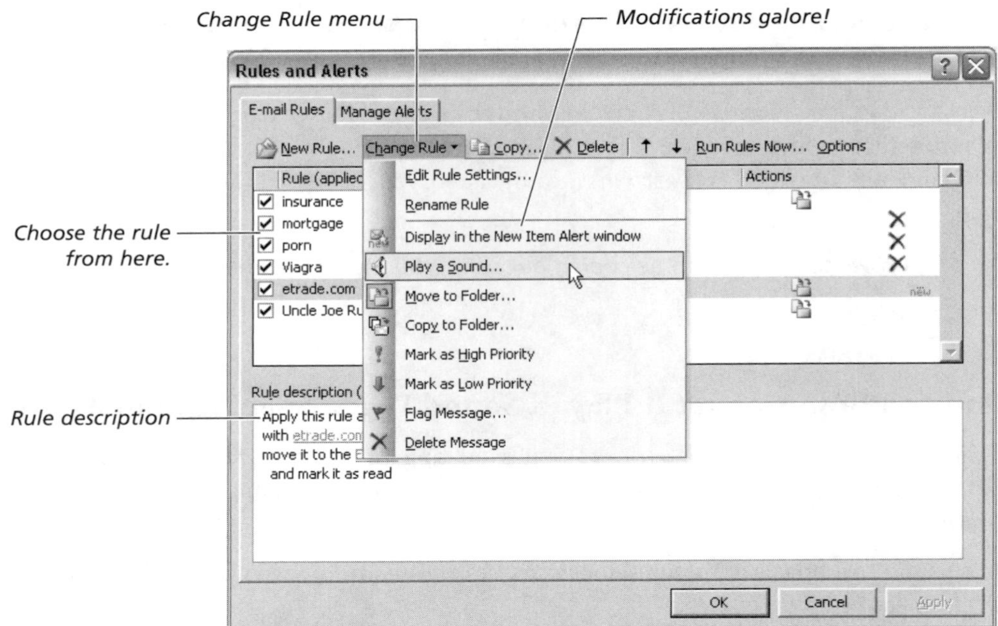

Figure 18.5 Easily modifying a rule in Outlook 2003

You Must Know This: Places to Find Sounds on Your Computer

The number one repository of sound on most Windows computers is in the Media folder, which is found right off the main Windows folder (`C:\Windows` *or* `C:\WinNT`*). This folder may not exist if you haven't added the Windows Plus! Package to your computer.*

The second location is in the My Documents folder, My Music subfolder, which may store some sounds.

Note that non-Microsoft programs tend to store files in their own folders, so you may also want to check the `C:\Program Files` *folders for specific sound applications. But the main place to check is the main Media folder in the Windows folder.*

*To use the Find Files or Find command to locate sound files, search for files ending in WAV. For example, searching for all files *.WAV will find all the sound files on your computer.*

Modifying a Rule in Outlook XP/2000

Modifying a rule in Outlook 2000 basically requires that you rerun the Rules Wizard and add the new aspect to the rule there. Here's how it's done, specifically to add a sound file that plays when the rule executes:

1. Choose Tools ➤ Rules Wizard.
2. Click to select the rule you want to add a sound to.
3. Click the Modify button.

   There's old Mr. Wizard again.

4. Click the Next button twice.

   You want to end up on the screen that starts "What Do You Want to Do with the Message?"

5. Scroll through the list and put a checkmark by "Play a Sound."
6. Ensure that no other items are checked.

   Outlook may check another item in the list for you; just do a quick scroll up and down to ensure that only the "Play a Sound" item is checked.

7. Click the underlined text "Sound" in the bottom part of the dialog box.
8. Use the Select a Sound to Play dialog box to choose a sound.

   It works like the Open dialog box, though only sound files are displayed. See the sidebar, "You Must Know This: Places to Find Sounds on Your Computer" for additional information.

To preview a sound, right-click its icon and choose Play from the pop-up menu.

9. Click Open to select the highlighted sound file.
10. Click the Finish button.

    No need to further work through the wizard; your job is done.

11. Close the Rules Wizard dialog box.

How Can I Construct a Rule That Filters Out Any E-mail Not to Me?

This is a tricky rule to create because a great volume of e-mail does arrive in your Inbox that may not be directed to you. For example, e-mail from a mailing list or subscription service or even e-mail where you're listed in the Bcc field. In those examples, you're getting legitimate e-mail but your name may not be shown.

The solution to this problem is to create multiple rules for e-mail and then order them properly.

For example, you can create a rule that reads as shown in Figure 18.6 (which also tells how to create the rule). I call this the "Not to me" rule. It's a vital rule, but it can't be the only rule because, as I mentioned above, not all my legitimate e-mail has my name on it.

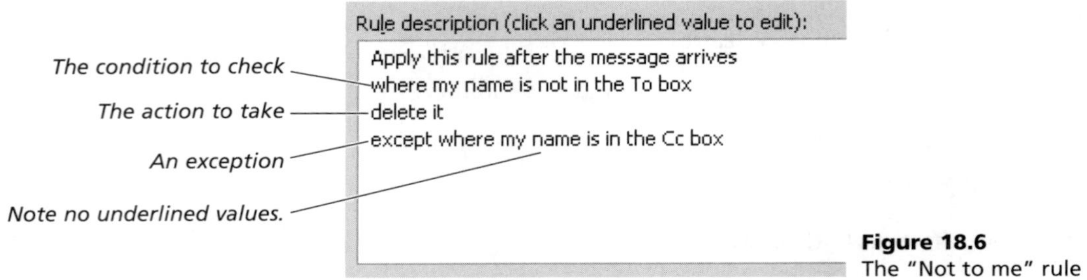

Figure 18.6
The "Not to me" rule

E-mail messages I get from the Mailman mailing list group do not have my name in them. Even so, I don't want them deleted. So what I do is create a special rule for those messages. It's shown in Figure 18.7, and I call it the "Mailman" rule.

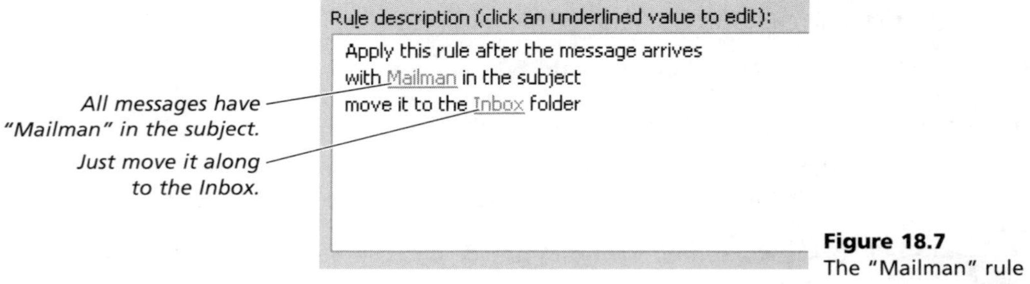

Figure 18.7
The "Mailman" rule

As a third example, my pal Jerry routinely sends his friends jokes and other e-mail but puts all of us in the Bcc field. A similar rule to the "Mailman" rule (Figure 18.7) exists for his e-mail; it's the "Stuff from Jerry" rule.

To make these three rules work, I've modified their order in the Rules and Alerts dialog box, as shown in Figure 18.8 for Outlook 2003. The rules on top are executed first when a message is received. So the message is tested against each rule, starting with "Uncle Joe Rule" in the figure and going down the list one at a time. When a rule matches, the message is dealt with.

Figure 18.9 shows the similar setup for Outlook XP/2000 in the Rules Wizard window. Things are basically the same, though the arrangement of the items in the window is different from Figure 18.8.

This does require a lot of trial and error to get it right. Remember that your "deleted" e-mail does show up in the Deleted Items folder, so do check it often for anything these rules may have missed. If you find another exception, then create a new rule and properly position it in the list, as shown in Figures 18.8 and 18.9.

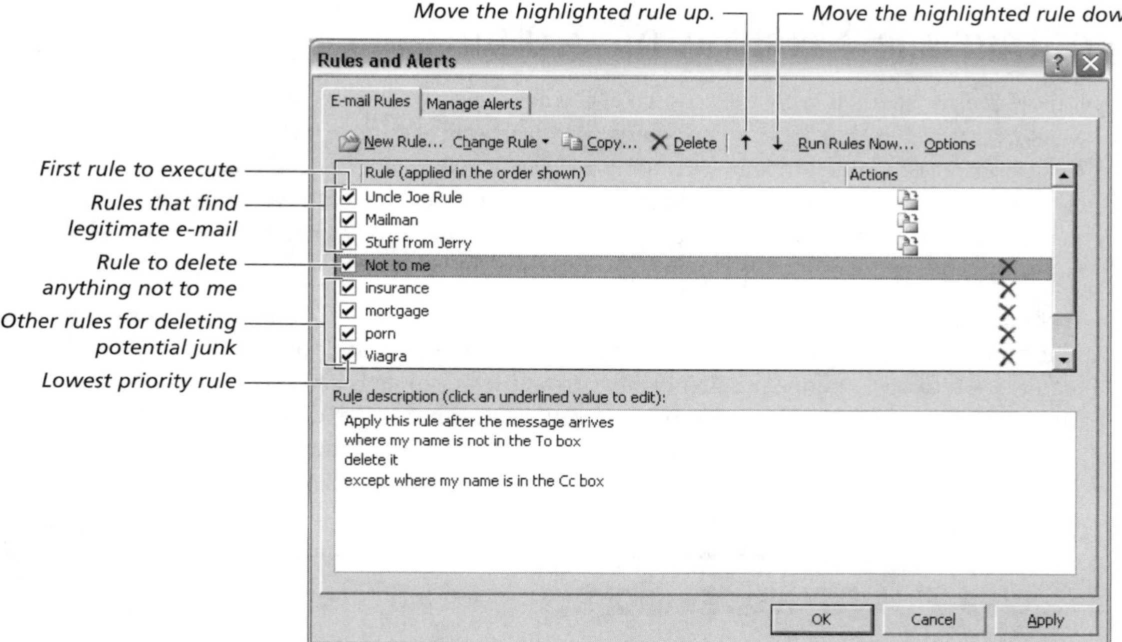

Figure 18.8 Setting the rule order (Outlook 2003)

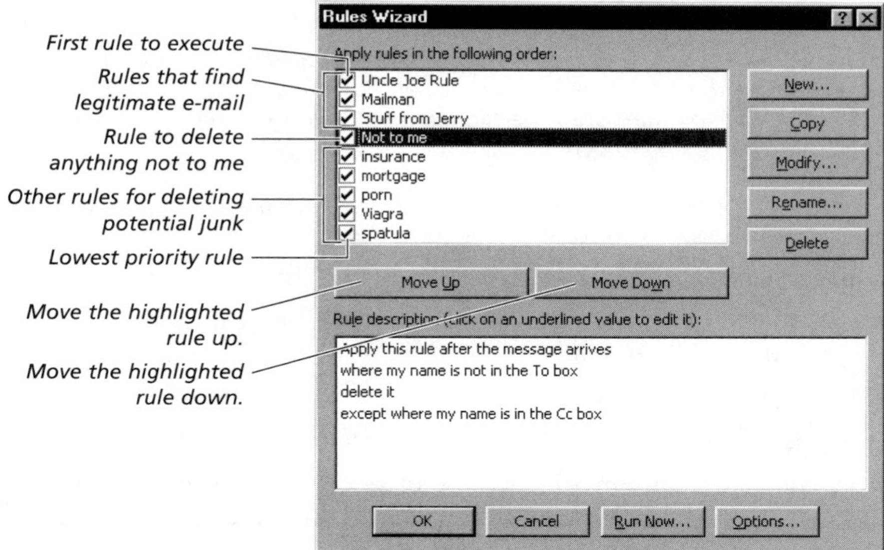

Figure 18.9 Setting the rule order (Outlook XP/2000)

Fighting the Scourge of Spam

Junk e-mail, or spam, is truly the scourge of the new century. The statistics are mind-boggling: Millions of unwanted e-mails are sent every day, advertising legitimate businesses as well as pornography and get-rich-quick schemes. For only pennies, a spammer can send out millions of e-mails, clogging up inboxes around the world and costing computer users time and money to get rid of them. Yet it takes only one dork to reply to a spam message or buy a product sold through spam, and the spammers continue to hammer us with their junk.

Technologically the cure to spam is to legitimize the source. Presently, e-mail can be *spoofed*, or sent from an unverified location. In fact, if you bother to read spam, you'll find that most of it requires you to dial a phone number or reply to a different e-mail than the sending address. Therein lies the problem: If the return address were legitimate, then it would be simple to block spam. However this isn't yet possible, so we must battle spam in other ways.

NERD'S CORNER

Cocktail Party Trivia, Part X

TED: Everyone loves SPAM!

MARY: I don't. I spend hours trudging through it every morning. It must waste half a cup of coffee opening new messages and deleting them because they want me to have a larger this or a smaller that or get rich or—Oh! I'm so sick of it!

TED: Not that, SPAM the lunchmeat. I love a SPAM and mayonnaise sandwich. I had my mother teach my third wife, Glenda, how to make them exactly as I had them in boyhood. In fact, Mother has moved in with Glenda and me just so she can oversee the lunch-making operation.

BILL: That's swell, Ted.

MARY: But then you mean SPAM and not spam? Because SPAM is the lunchmeat product from the good folks at the Hormel Company. Lowercase "spam" refers to junk e-mail.

TED: Right. Everyone knows that. Even Mother.

BILL: I suppose you're going to tell us how "spam" came about. You know? That old Monty Python sketch with the Vikings and all? Don't you?

TED: No.

MARY: Really, Ted, your mother lives with you and she oversees your third wife making you lunch?

TED: Uh-huh! And I'm darn proud of that! Hmm. I feel like another cocktail weenie!

What's the Easiest Way to Block Spam?

Simple: Don't use e-mail. But if you must do e-mail, and I assume it's serious e-mail because you're using Outlook and not Outlook Express or Hotmail, then you have not only a spam-blocking command but a whole dang-doodle spam-blocking menu at your disposal.

When you receive spam, simply choose the proper blocking command, depending on your version of Outlook.

Blocking Spam in Outlook 2003

Outlook 2003 is already configured to battle junk e-mail. When you receive a junk e-mail message, simply choose Actions ➤ Junk E-mail ➤ Add to Junk Senders list. That shoves the message's vital information into a list that Outlook uses to continually examine your incoming message.

To further adjust spam-fighting options, choose Actions ➤ Junk E-mail ➤ Junk E-mail Options. This displays the Junk E-mail Options dialog box, shown in Figure 18.10. There you can make additional adjustments to Outlook's behavior toward what it suspects to be junk e-mail.

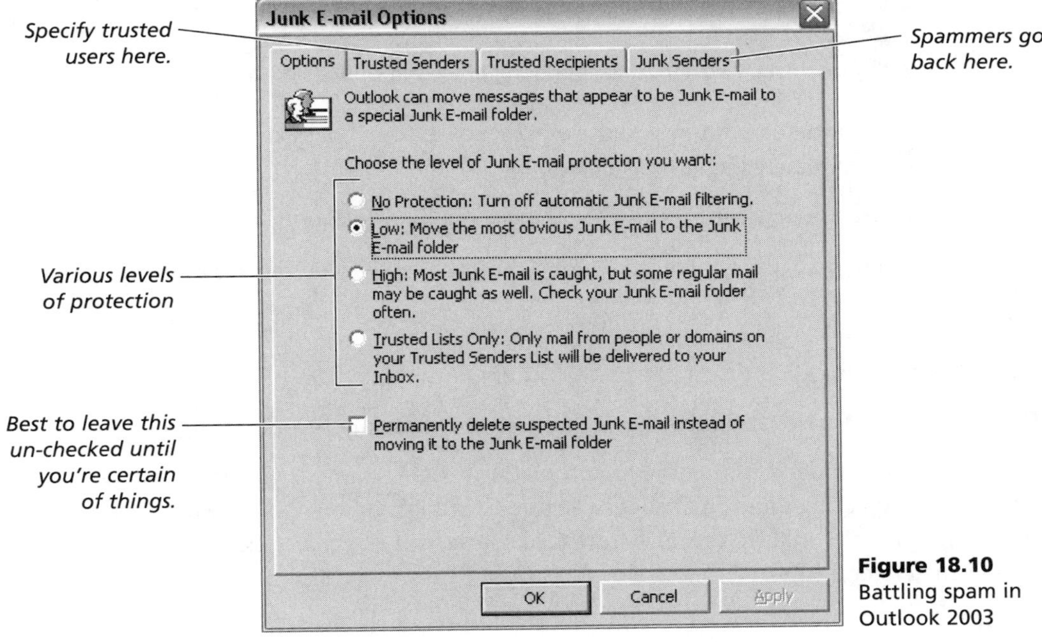

Figure 18.10
Battling spam in Outlook 2003

If you click the Trusted Senders tab, you'll see a check box for "Also Trust E-mail from My Contacts." Keep this item checked; it tells Outlook to cross-reference addresses of suspected spam with your e-mail contacts. That way, as long as the e-mail comes from someone in your contact list, it won't be trashed as spam.

Blocking Spam in Outlook XP/2000

In Outlook 2000, you need to first switch on the Junk E-mail feature:

1. To go your Inbox.
2. Choose Tools ➤ Organize.
3. Click the "Junk E-mail" item.

   It's on the left end of the "Ways to Organize Inbox" area. Clicking that item displays a few of Outlook's anti-spam options, as shown in Figure 18.11. Refer to the figure for the exciting options.

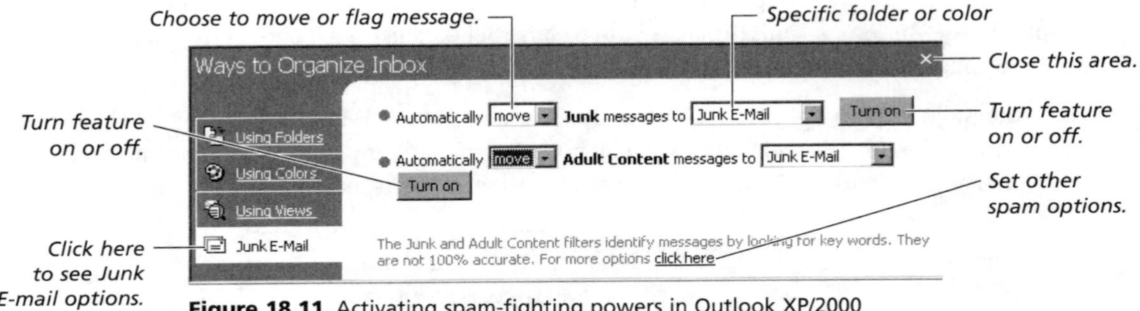

Figure 18.11 Activating spam-fighting powers in Outlook XP/2000

4. To activate anti-spam filters, choose whether to automatically move junk or adult e-mail to a folder or to merely flag it with a color.

   If you're unsure how this works, then choose the Flag option instead of Move.

Outlook may prompt you to create the Junk E-mail folder at this time; do so.

5. Click the Turn On buttons to activate the spam-fighting powers.
6. Close the "Ways to Organize Inbox" area, as shown in Figure 18.11.

Outlook is now properly configured to automatically fight spam for you. If a message slips by the automatic suspecting filters, just choose Actions ➤ Junk E-mail ➤ Add to Junk Senders List from the menu. Any new mail you receive from that source will automatically be shuffled off into the Junk E-mail folder.

I Accidentally Added Aunt Debra to the Spammer List!

Providing that she's not a spammer and you want to get back on her good side, the following sections tell how to remove her:

Editing the Junk Senders List in Outlook 2003

To repeal an addition to the Junk Senders list, follow these steps:

1. Choose Actions ➤ Junk E-mail ➤ Junk E-mail Options.
2. Click the Junk Senders tab.
3. Locate the hapless victim in the list.

Typing the first letter of a name instantly scrolls to that position in the list.

4. Click the said hapless victim.
5. Click the Remove button.
6. Click OK.

   Their mortality has been restored!

Editing the Spammer List in Outlook 2000

To undo an addition to the spammer list, obey these steps:

1. Click to select the Junk E-mail folder in the folder list.
2. Choose Tools ➤ Organize.
3. Click the Junk E-mail item on the left of the "Ways to Organize Inbox" panel.

   Refer to Figure 18.11.

4. Click the underlined text that says, "Click Here."
5. Click the underlined text that says, "Edit Junk Senders."

   The Edit Junk Senders dialog box appears (Figure 18.12), which lists all the bad folks who've been sending you spam—including, accidentally, Aunt Debra.

6. Locate the misplaced name in the list.
7. Click to select the name.

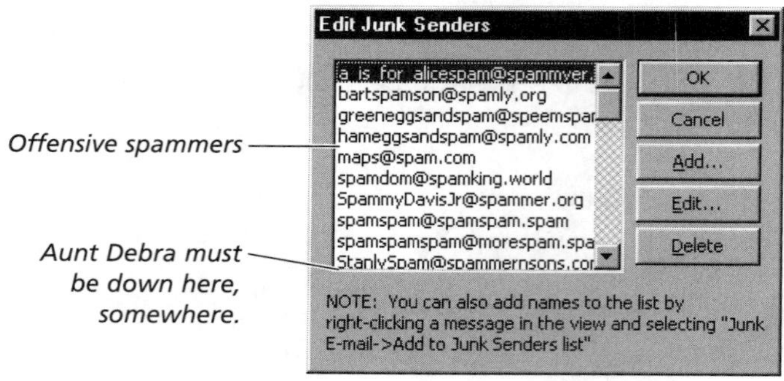

Figure 18.12 The Edit Junk Senders dialog box

8. Click the Delete button.
9. Click OK.

   You can also close the "Ways to Organize Inbox" thing by clicking the X in its upper-right corner, shown in Figure 18.11.

What Do I Do with the Crap in the Junk E-mail Folder?

Review it occasionally to ensure that legitimate mail doesn't sneak in. After that, just delete it.

Can I Use a Mail Rule to Block Spam?

Certainly, you should create one any time you notice the automatic spam filters seem to be failing you.

The most successful anti-spam filters are based on message *subject*, not by who sends them. (The names spammers use are fake, often not real e-mail addresses, and only used once.) Use your filter-creating powers to build an anti-spam filter based on common subject words most spammers use. Here's a sampling:

Approval	Debt	Life Insurance	Pharmacy
Approved	Diet	Loan	Porn
Cable descrambler	Free	Mortgage	Septic tank
Credit card	Ink cartridges	Payment	Viagra

Eventually you'll be able to build your own list as you get more and more spam. Yes, it's not stopping, so you might as well brace yourself for it now!

More Automation Tricks

Oh, I could go on with Mail Rules all day. They can really get fancy and do all sorts of amazing things with your e-mail and how you keep stuff organized in Outlook.

Beyond Mail Rules there are still a few automation tricks up Outlook's sleeves. These are covered in the remaining sections of this chapter, along with some things you might believe Outlook is capable of, but sadly it's still lacking.

How Can I Set Up an Automatic Response to All My E-mail?

You might be intrigued by one of the Mail Rule options that states, "Reply Using a Specific Template." This feature does not work unless you are using Outlook on a network that runs the Microsoft Exchange Server. If so, then you'll need to ask the network administrator how to set up the Out of Office Assistant for use with your e-mail.

By the way, I do not recommend configuring an "out of office" reply or any automatic reply to any e-mail. The reason is that e-mail servers can get into what are called "autoresponder wars," which is where an automatic response from one person bounces to another person who also uses an automatic response and so on. Over a few hours of this, with the e-mail traffic increasing back and forth at a geometric rate, eventually the e-mail servers stop working and, well, then you've got problems. So don't bother.

Can I Set Up an Automatic Response to Only Some E-mail?

Only when using the Exchange Server, described in the previous section.

Can My E-mail Be Forwarded to Another Location?

To be honest, the easiest way to do this is to have your ISP forward your e-mail. They're set up to do it cleanly and directly; you'll get all your e-mail at the new location. Otherwise, you can create a Mail Rule to do the same thing.

The Mail Rule reads as shown in Figure 18.13. Note that in the Rules Wizard's first step you must *not* choose any option. The wizard will warn you that the rule applies to *all* of your e-mail. Great. That's what you want.

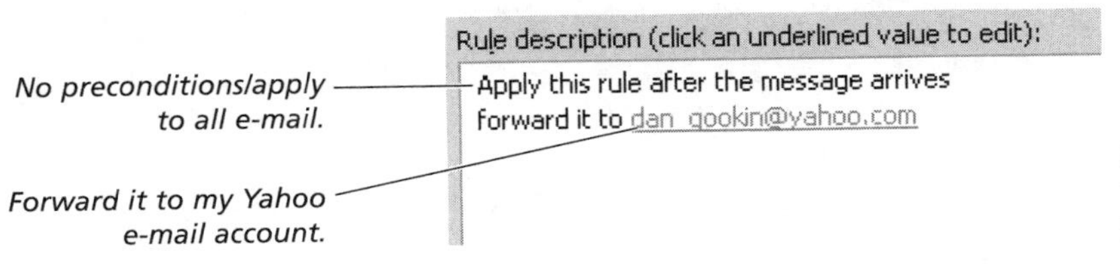
Rule description (click an underlined value to edit):
Apply this rule after the message arrives
forward it to dan_gookin@yahoo.com
No preconditions/apply to all e-mail.
Forward it to my Yahoo e-mail account.

Figure 18.13
The "Forwarding all your e-mail" rule

This should be the first rule in the list. Or, you can have it be the last rule and simply un-check the remaining rules so that they don't operate.

Or, if you want to take another approach, you can have this be the *last* rule and keep your anti-spam and other filter rules above it, which means only selected e-mail would be forwarded.

The next step requires that you configure Outlook to automatically pick up your e-mail. The idea is to leave the computer on with Outlook running and have it check in every so often to get mail and then automatically send it out to you. (This means leaving the computer on all the time.)

The final step requires that you either have your computer be online all the time, such as it would be with a broadband (cable, DSL, and so on) connection, or have the computer dial in to the Internet at given intervals to pick up the mail.

I've found that to best handle the last two steps, simply combine them to have the computer check for e-mail four times a day. The following sections tell how to configure Outlook to do that, depending on your version of Outlook.

Automatic E-mail Pickup in Outlook 2003/XP

To direct Outlook to automatically pick up your e-mail at a given interval, follow these steps:

1. Choose Tools ➤ Options.
2. Click the Mail Setup tab in the Options dialog box.
3. Click the Send/Receive button.

   There are two settings in the Send/Receive Groups dialog box that control how often Outlook picks up your e-mail, as shown in Figure 18.14. My advice is to set them both just to be certain.
4. Checkmark both automatic pickup items, as shown in Figure 18.14.
5. Enter **360** minutes for the time interval, which is six hours.
6. Click the Close button; then click OK to close the Options dialog box.

If you have a dial-up connection, then Outlook will order a connection to be made when it comes time to pick up the mail. To be sure that Outlook disconnects when it's done, you need to configure your dial-up Internet connection to hang up after one minute of idle time. This is an operating system function, and the method differs depending on your version of Windows. (For example, it's in Chapter 21 of my *Dan Gookin's Naked Windows XP* book.)

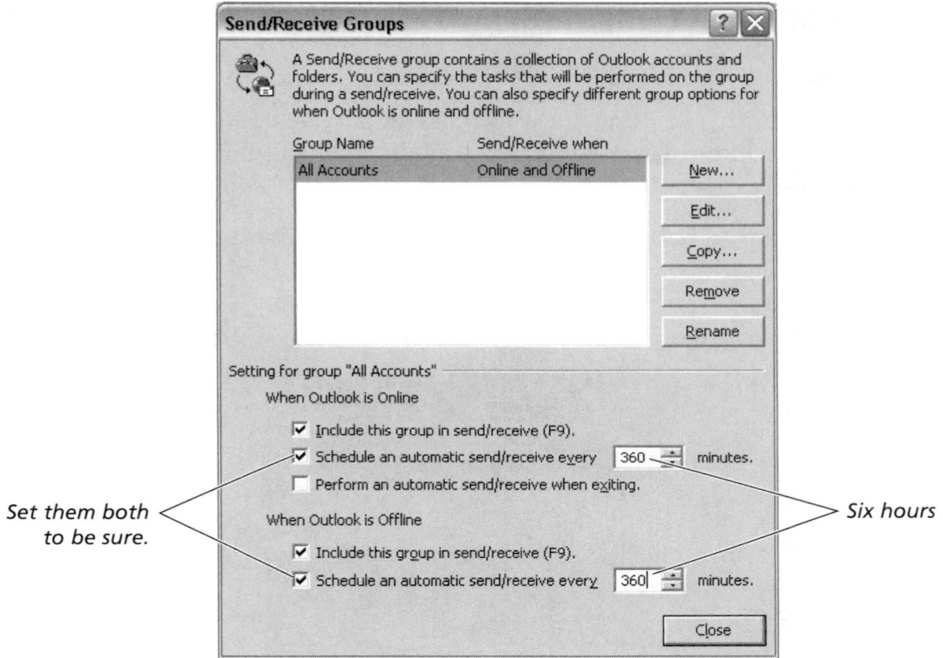

Figure 18.14 Setting the automatic mail picker-upper timer

Automatic E-mail Pickup in Outlook 2000

Here are the steps required in Outlook 2000 to have it automatically pick up your e-mail at a given interval:

1. Choose Tools ➢ Options.
2. Click the Mail Delivery tab in the Options dialog box.
3. Click to put a checkmark by "Check for New Messages Every … Minutes."
4. Enter **360** into the Minutes box.

   That tells Outlook to go out and pick up e-mail every six hours.
5. Also put a checkmark by the "Send Messages Immediately When Connected" option.

   That's it!
6. Click OK.

How Can I Find Old Mail from the Same Person?

The easiest way is to sort the messages in the mailbox.

In Outlook 2003, sort by right-clicking the header, as shown in Figure 18.15. Then choose how you want to sort from the pop-up menu. In this case, you sort by From, and all e-mail from a specific person will be grouped together.

In Outlook 2000, simply click the heading you want to sort by. In this case, click the From heading, as shown in Figure 18.16.

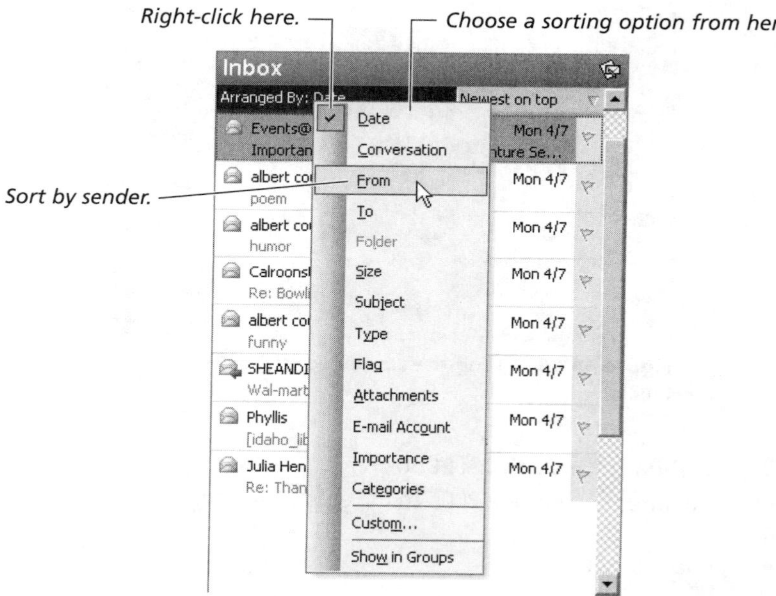

Figure 18.15 Sorting a mailbox in Outlook 2003

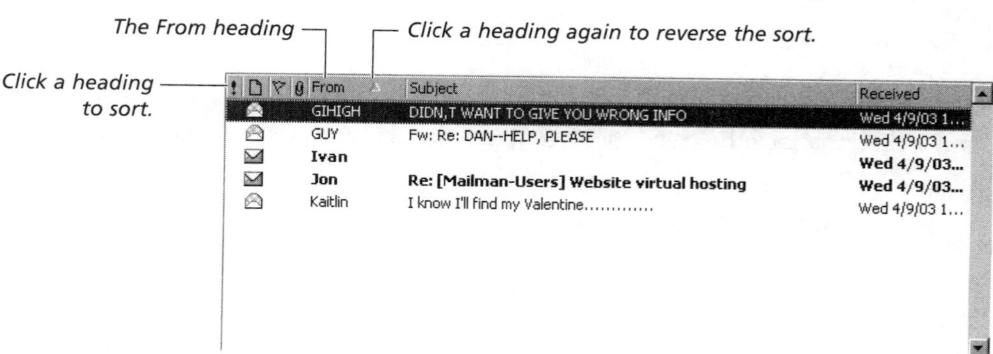

Figure 18.16 Sorting a mailbox in Outlook XP/2000

Any Way to Search the Entire Clutch of Folders for a Specific E-mail?

This can be done by using Outlook's Find command. As you probably suspect, there are different versions of Find depending on your version of Outlook.

Finding an E-mail in Outlook 2003/XP

To find all e-mail from a specific user in Outlook 2003, heed these steps:

1. Click the Find button on the toolbar.

This opens the Find strip thing, shown in Figure 18.17.

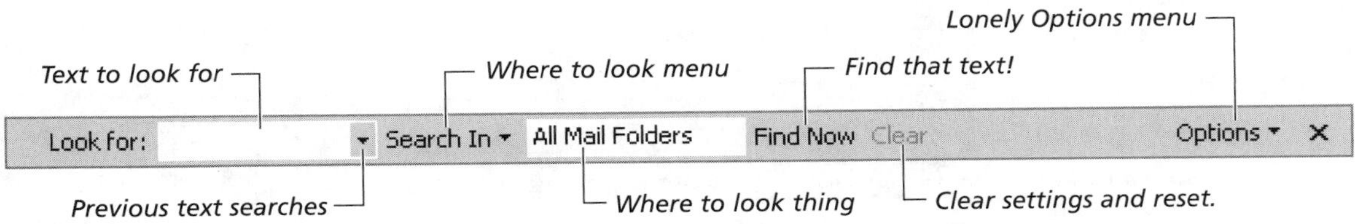

Figure 18.17 The Find strip thing

2. Enter the person's e-mail address into the "Look For" box.

3. From the "Search In" drop-down list choose "All Mail Folders."

4. Click the Find Now button.

The results are displayed below the Find toolbar strip thing. But you may notice that they're nonspecific; if the user's e-mail address appears in the body of a message, then it too is listed. Must be more specific!

5. Click the lonely Options menu and choose "Advanced Find."

The Advanced Find dialog box appears in Figure 18.18. This is where you can tell Outlook precisely where to find the person you're looking for.

6. In the "Look For" drop-down list, choose Messages.

7. Click the From button.

The Select Names dialog box appears, which lists everyone in your Contacts list.

8. Scroll to find and click to select a name from the list.

9. Click the From button to select that name; then click OK.

The name is placed into the From text box in the Advanced Find dialog box (Figure 18.18).

10. Click the Find Now button.

Any matching messages appear in the bottom of the Advanced Find dialog box. Refer to Figure 18.19, which shows the results for Outlook 2000, but it looks pretty much the same.

You can click the Find button again to hide the Find strip bar thing.

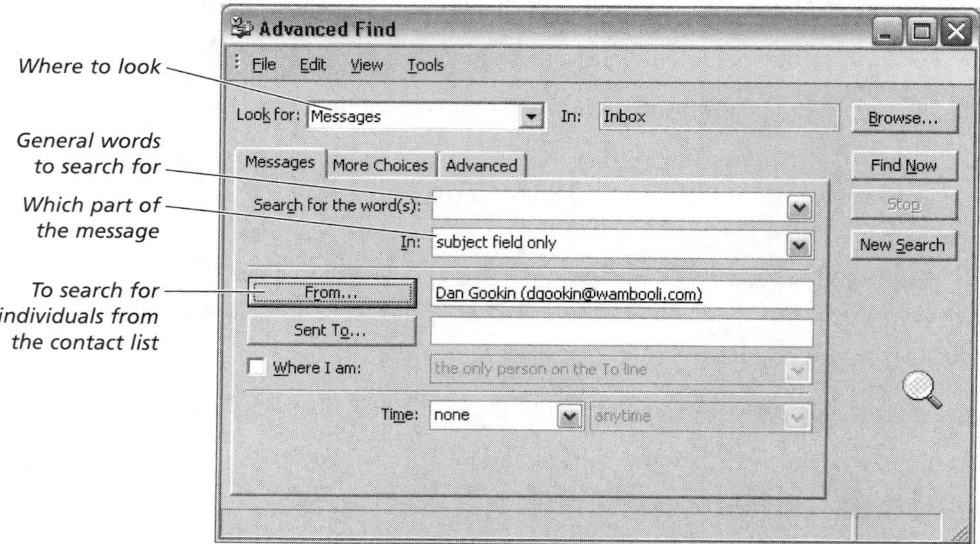

Figure 18.18 The Advanced Find dialog box in all its loveliness

Finding an E-mail in Outlook 2000

Outlook 2000 lacks some of the quick finding features of Outlook 2003/XP, but the operation can still be done.

Rather than mess with the Find button on the toolbar, which displays a nice, roomy Find area, you should just cut to the chase:

1. Choose Tools ➢ Advanced Find.

This displays the Advanced Find dialog box, similar to what's shown in Figure 18.18.

2. Choose Messages from the "Look For" drop-down list.

3. Click the From button.

The Select Names dialog box appears, and there you can see all your contacts displayed in a scrolling list.

4. Find the person you're looking for in the list; then click to select the name.
5. Click the From button.

   This places the person's name into the "Message Recipients" list.
6. Click OK.

   Back in the Advanced Find dialog box, the person's name appears by the From button. Perfect.
7. Click the Find Now button.

   The results appear in the bottom of the dialog box, as shown in Figure 18.19. Refer to the figure for more information.

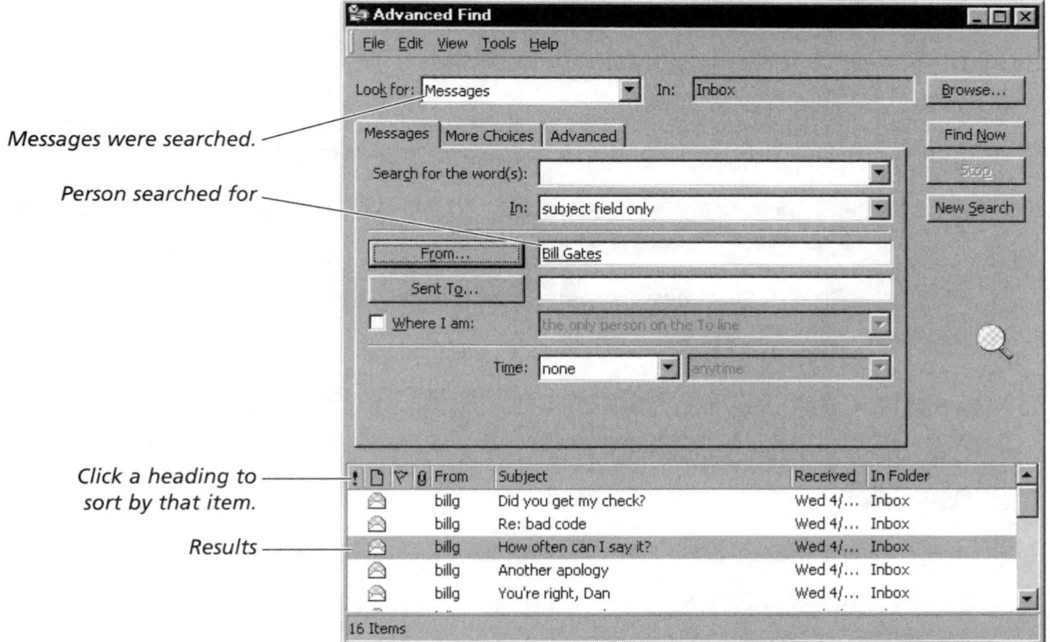

Figure 18.19 The results of finding e-mail from a specific human

Can I Apply Color to Specific Messages?

Yes, and this can be a fun and useful tool for tracking down e-mail from special people. (Well, that and creating a Mail Rule that plays "Stars and Stripes Forever" whenever their e-mail shows up.) Follow these handy steps:

1. Select the mailbox you want to organize, such as the Inbox.
2. If you can, click to select e-mail from that special person.

   If you can find a message from them, click to select it. This saves a step later.
3. Choose Tools ➤ Organize.

   The "Ways to Organize Inbox" pane (is it a pane?) thing shows up.
4. Click the "Using Colors" link.

   Refer to Figure 18.20.

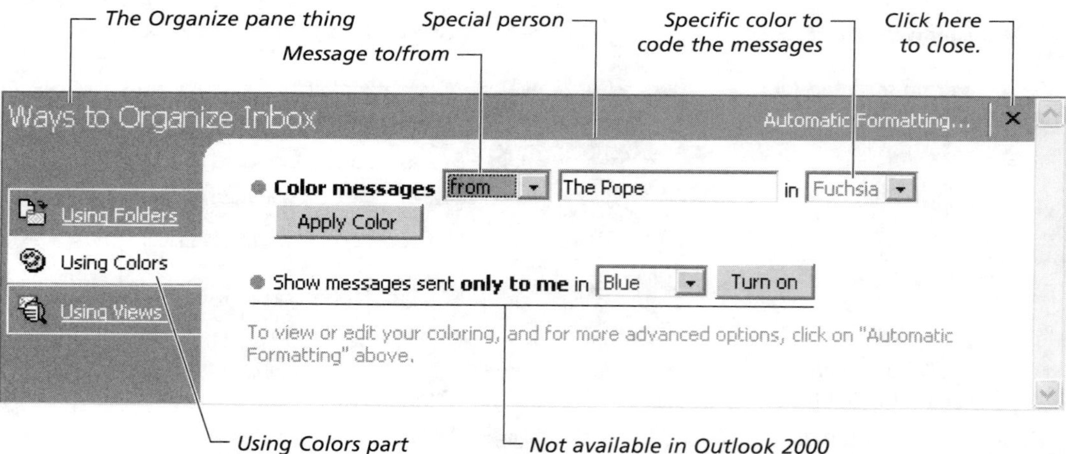

Figure 18.20 Applying color to specific messages

5. To highlight messages from a specific person, from the drop-down list choose From (Figure 18.20).

6. Type in the person's e-mail address if you need to.

   This is unnecessary if you were able to select a message from them in Step 2.

7. Choose a color from the drop-down list.

   Now any e-mail coming into the Inbox from that person will be flagged in the specific color you selected.

In Outlook 2003/XP you can also choose to have mail that was sent only to your own account displayed in a given color, also shown in Figure 18.20. Click the Turn On button to activate this feature.

Click the X button on the Organize panel pane task thing to close it when you're all done.

19 Making the Best of Your Contacts

I'm sorry, but when I see "contacts" I think of those tiny, on-the-eyeball replacements for eyeglasses. Those are contacts. Or they're tiny metal doodads in electronics that need to be touched by something else in order for electricity to flow. But contacts as people? Now that will take some time.

In Outlook parlance, *contacts* means people. But they're more than just names and e-mail addresses. Outlook is a powerful database system designed to help you manage even the most miniscule aspect of information about the people you know or, well, come into *contact* with. (I suppose that's how the word fits.)

So consider yourself lucky. If it were up to me, I'd call them *folks* just because I love that word. But they're contacts and they're about more than just doing e-mail. This is the chapter that explains the second tier, or "intermediate," information you need to know about creating and managing your contacts.

Smoke Cleared and Tempests Quelled:

- Discovering how to come by new contacts
- Importing contacts from elsewhere
- Using the contacts to send e-mail
- Taking advantage of a nickname
- Sending and receiving vCards
- Learning all about distribution lists
- Getting Outlook and Word to communicate

Making Up New Contacts

Obviously you want contacts, even if it's just a basic list of e-mail addresses and the names associated with them. That makes sending e-mail so much easier. Outlook offers more than that, but don't feel pressured into filling in every silly field for all your contacts. As with any computer program, feel free to use as much or as little of it as you need.

> **Don't Be Dumb: Basic Outlook Contacts 101**
>
> *Contacts are one of the basic parts of the Outlook program. To view the contacts, you select Contacts from the list on the left side of Outlook's window. This displays the list of contacts on the right side of Outlook's window.*
>
> *To adjust the view, or how the contacts are displayed, use the My Contacts area in Outlook 2003; choose a view from the options displayed on the left end of the window. In Outlook XP/2000, choose the view from the menu, View ➤ Current View, and then pick an option from the submenu.*

What's a Good Way to Fill Up My Contacts List?

Just steal the addresses from your old e-mail program.

How Can I Steal the Addresses from My Old E-mail Program?

If you already have an e-mail program that you've been using, you can order Outlook to peer into it and steal, or rather, *copy* the information from it and import the vital stuff into Outlook. Here's how:

1. Choose File ➤ Import and Export.

   It's the Import and Export Wizard. You may have already seen this used earlier in this book. That was for exporting. Now you're importing (and you don't even have to live near the coast).

2. Choose "Import Internet Mail and Addresses."

3. Click the Next button.

   The next screen displays a list of e-mail programs, some of which may already be installed on your computer, as shown in Figure 19.1.

4. Choose your former e-mail program from the list.

   If it's not listed, then refer to the section "How Can I Import My Contacts When My Program Isn't Listed in the Wizard?"

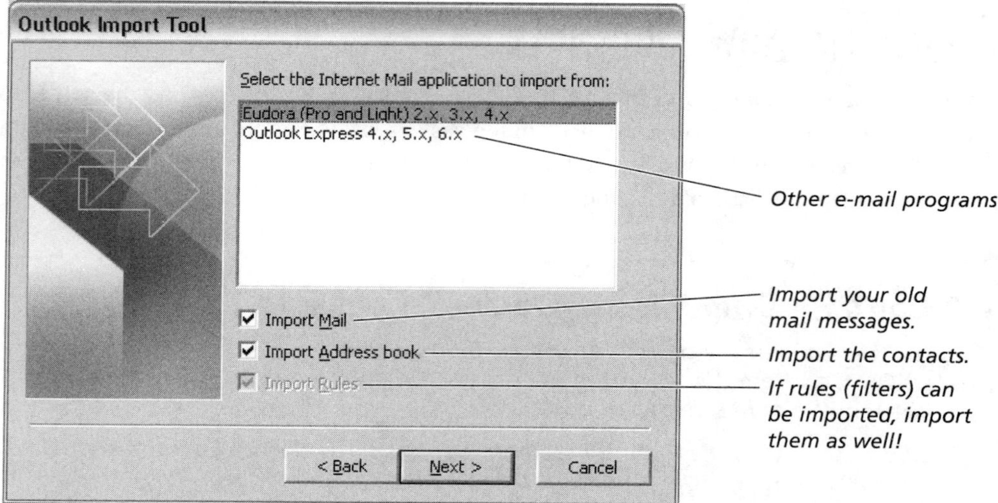

Figure 19.1 Importing your e-mail and address contacts

5. Review the checkmarks at the bottom of the dialog box and un-check what you do not want imported.

For example, I typically leave e-mail in the old program, so I would un-check the "Import Mail" box.

6. Click the Next button.

The next screen may be confusing because the word "duplicates" is undefined. What it means is e-mail addresses or records that are the same in both programs. For example, you've been using Outlook for a while and have already added Ed to your list of contacts. If so, importing Ed from your old e-mail program would create a duplicate situation. The dialog box is asking which record you want to keep:

Replace Duplicates with Items Imported: Use the contact information from the old e-mail program and discard the contact you created in the new program.

Allow Duplicates to Be Created: Keep both records; you can clean up later.

Do Not Import Duplicate Items: Keep the copy in Outlook but don't import the duplicate.

7. Choose how to deal with any duplicate records.

In some cases other options may be shown on this screen, such as whether to place the addresses into the Contacts folder or the Address Book. I'd choose the Contacts folder option for now.

8. Click the Finish button.

Outlook churns and chugs and attempts to import any records it finds. These are placed into the Contacts area. An Import Summary appears, letting you know things are done.

9. Click the OK button.

Importing the names, or even e-mail, from the old program does not remove that information from the old program. This is not theft! In fact, you can go back and use the old program if you like. But note that new mail messages appear only in whichever program you're using to pick up and read your e-mail.

What About Theft from Other Contact Management Programs?

Not every program that keeps a list of contacts is an e-mail program. Some are pure contact management, tickler, or even just personal database programs. If so, you can pull the information from those programs by using Outlook's Import command.

My personal experience with this has been less than successful, so if you don't succeed the first time, try again or refer to the following section, "How Can I Import My Contacts When My Program Isn't Listed in the Wizard?" for another approach.

1. Choose File ➤ Import and Export.
2. Choose "Import from Another Program or File."
3. Click the Next button.

   The next screen lists a jillion different contact management and e-mail programs, one of which you may have been using in the past, as shown in Figure 19.2.

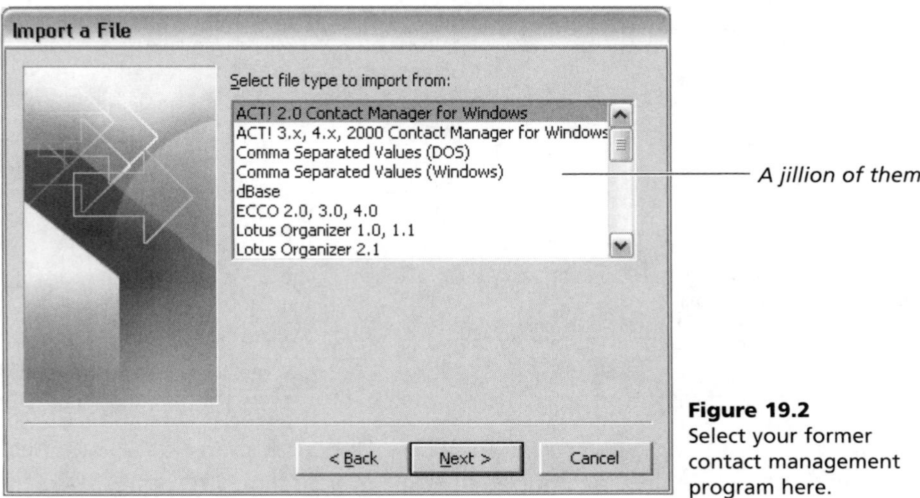

Figure 19.2
Select your former contact management program here.

4. Choose your program from the list.
5. You may be asked to install a translator; click the Yes button if so.

   Another screen appears.

6. Use the Browse button to locate the file.

   This opens a Browse (Open) dialog box, which you can use to navigate the surly waters of your sea of files to locate the long-lost data island. Click OK when you've found the file.

7. Refer to the previous section, Step 6, for information on the importing duplicate items options.

8. Click the Next button.

9. Select your Contacts folder from the list.

10. Click the Next button.

11. I recommend clicking the Map Custom Fields button here.

    You want to ensure that the data from the other program is properly read into Outlook. To make certain it's done properly—or at least as close as possible—click the Map Custom Fields button and then use the Map Custom Fields dialog box, as shown in Figure 19.3, to help you associate the proper fields. The figure explains more about how this works.

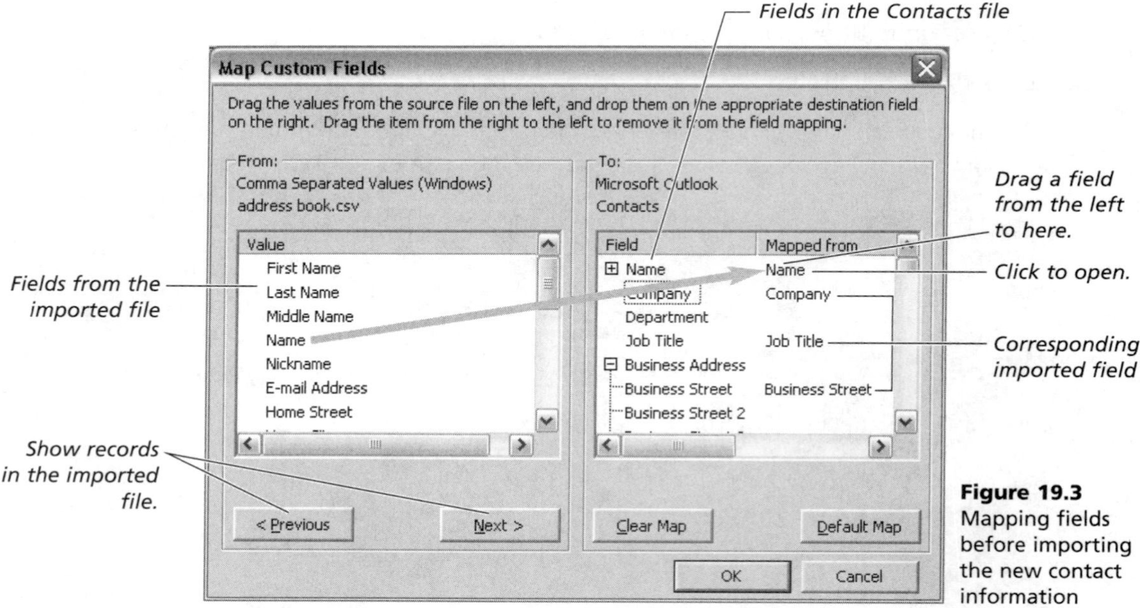

Figure 19.3 Mapping fields before importing the new contact information

Normally you won't have to do anything else here; Outlook is pretty smart at matching up fields. But say, for example, the imported field for "Middle Name" reads as "Middle Initial." If so, you would drag the "Middle Initial" field on the left over to the "Middle Name" field on the right. That's how the fields are "mapped" between the two programs.

12. Click OK when you're done matching files and reviewing records of the imported file.

13. Click the Finish button.

How Can I Import My Contacts When My Program Isn't Listed in the Wizard?

In my travels, I've rarely seen a contact management or Address Book program that lacked an export feature or some other way of getting the information out of the program and into some type of common data file format. That's the trick you need to use to start the export-import journey.

Note that these steps are general in nature; your program will no doubt have specific commands to do this job:

1. Open the original program, the one from which you want to get the contact information.

2. Use the File ➤ Export or a similar command to get the information out of this program.

   Sometimes there is a File ➤ Export command, as with the Palm Desktop organizer. Otherwise, you can try File ➤ Save As and then choose an exporting format from the "Save As Type" drop-down list.

   The most common shared file type for database-like information is the delimited file. Outlook can read two types: comma-separated values (CSV) or tab-separated values (which has no specific filename extension). Either type of file is a simple text file, with each "record" appearing on a line by itself, items within the record separated by either commas or tabs, such as:

   Washington,George,1600 Pennsylvania Ave.,DC,etc, and so on.

   If the other program can export directly into an Outlook format, then choose it. Obviously that would be the best option.

3. Give the file a memorable name and save it in a logical location.

4. Quit the original program.

   This is important; you don't want to have Outlook tell you that the exported file is "busy," which may happen if the other program is still open.

5. Start Outlook.

   Continue with the instructions, starting at Step 1, from the previous section, "What About Theft from Other Contact Management Programs?"

The operation at this point follows the steps from the previous section, importing the values and mapping them to their Outlook counterparts.

Don't be surprised if it takes a few tries at different formats to get this thing to run right. Don't get overly frustrated. Especially if you have a lot of contacts, experimenting with different import formats still saves time over having to retype all that information.

I Don't Have a Previous Contact Management Program, so What Am I Supposed to Do?

The best way to get contacts is to accumulate them as you use Outlook. You may want to start collecting a few names and entering them manually, but I believe you'll find that as you use Outlook you can add the names as they come across your desk. This also helps to keep your list of names up to date since most people move or change information every few years or so.

What's the Quickest Way to Move a Human's Information into the Contacts List?

Read their e-mail! After you're done, or whenever you remember this trick, right-click their name (in the From field) in the message header. Choose "Add to Outlook Contacts" or "Add to Contacts" from the pop-up menu. This displays a new Contact information sheet dialog box for that person, as shown in Figure 19.4. Note that the dialog box looks different between the versions of Outlook, though all the parts are still there.

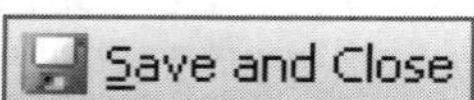

Click the Save and Close button to return to your e-mail.

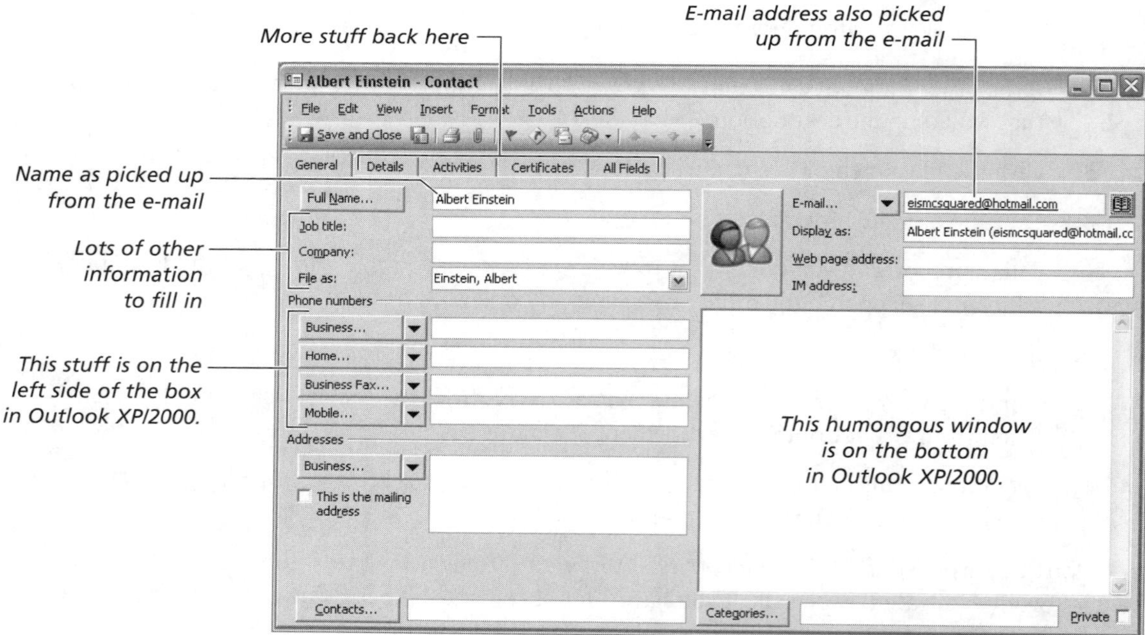

Figure 19.4 A contact sheet for a guy who sends me e-mail all the time

You Must Know This: Adding Yourself to the Contact List

Have you added a contact for yourself yet? It may seem silly, but it's actually tremendously handy. One of the first entries into an Address Book or Contacts list I always make is for myself, whether I'm using a new e-mail program or starting up another personal database.

Another trick to pull is to give yourself a nickname. I use "me" for my own account. That way, if I want to include myself in a Bcc list or e-mail myself something—and as silly as that sounds it does happen—I just type `me` *into the field and, well, there I am!*

How Much Information Do I Need to Put into a Contact?

There is no minimum required, other than their name and e-mail address. Any other information you add is up to you. Obviously, the more information you add, the more you can do with the contact.

What's So Important About an E-mail Nickname?

When you start a new e-mail message you may click the To button to display the Select Names dialog box, from which you choose the name of the person or persons to whom you're sending the message. By having a nickname, however, you can avoid those steps and just type in the nickname(s) instead.

For example, I usually create nicknames for all the folks I regularly send mail to. My mother's e-mail address? I don't know it! But I know her nickname is "mom" so I just type `mom` into the To field, and eventually Outlook expands it into the proper address.

To set a nickname for a person, follow these steps:

1. Click to choose Contacts from the list on the left side of Outlook's window.
2. Double-click the contact entry you want to nickname.

   For example, my literary agent, Matt Wagner.
3. In the Contacts dialog box, click the Details tab.
4. Type the nickname into the Nickname text box.

   This is where you need to be clever. For most folks I send e-mail to, I simply use their first name as the nickname. But for people I often send e-mail to, I use only the first letter of their name as the nickname. So agent Matt is just `m` in my book. That saves typing time.

Outlook does not warn you if you enter a duplicate nickname. The only way you'll know this is that when you go to send the e-mail, only the first contact using that nickname appears in the From field.

'Nuther warning: Nicknames are case sensitive! Just try to use lowercase all the time, and it shouldn't be a problem.

5. Save and Close — Click the Save and Close button to cement your changes.

Any Way to Automatically Add People I Respond to in the List of Contacts?

Not that I can see.

What's that VCF E-mail Attachment I Keep on Seeing?

The VCF is a virtual business card or vCard. It's a way to send your contact information over e-mail so that other folks don't have to manually type in all that stuff. Here's how it works:

1. You receive an e-mail with a vCard attachment.

   Figure 19.5 shows how the vCard looks in the message header. The key is that little business card icon. Also note that the file has the extension `.vcf`.

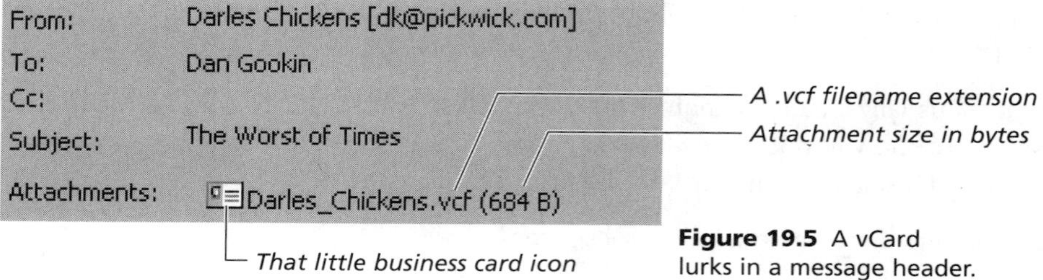

Figure 19.5 A vCard lurks in a message header.

2. Double-click the business card icon.

   You'll see a healthy warning about opening file attachments. Be careful here! Some viruses do attach themselves to e-mail and disguise themselves as vCards.

You're a fool if you aren't running antivirus software along with Outlook.

3. Click the Open button.

   The vCard information is read and placed into a contact sheet.

4. Save and Close — Click the Save and Close button.

If there is already a card in Outlook with the same name, you'll be asked how to deal with the duplicate. Generally speaking, the option already selected, "Update New Information..." is the best one, so just click OK if you see that in the dialog box.

5. Continue reading the e-mail.

As a shortcut, you can also drag the vCard icon from the e-mail message onto the Contacts thing on the left end of Outlook's window. Either way, you're adding the contact information via the vCard, which is a heck of lot easier than typing all that information.

How Can I Create My Own vCard?

Oh, yeah! I tell you and then *everyone* will be creating a vCard and this nonsense will never stop!

First you have to create a contact for yourself. Fill in all the information you want to share in the Contact dialog box.

Second, you modify your signature so that the vCard is included. Refer back to Chapter 16, "Just Your Intermediate E-mail," the section titled "The Signature Overview." In Step 7 you use the Edit Signature dialog box to create a signature. If you look at the bottom part of that dialog box (Figure 16.13), you'll see the vCard options. Just add these steps to those already listed in that chapter:

7a. Click the New vCard from Contact button.

7b. Double-click your name in the list of contacts.

7c. Click OK.

That does it; continue on with saving your signature as covered in Chapter 16.

Having Fun with Your Contacts

Having fun depends on your definition of fun. Obviously some people won't see the rollicking humor in sending out an electronic epistle to everyone telling them that you've contracted leprosy and are moving to a remote South American village to try "that cannibalism thing."

No, when I think of fun, I think of doing the more outrageous yet useful things with a program. These are things that you wouldn't normally think of off the top of your head, yet interesting or unusual features of Outlook that have a real purpose—if you know about them. I call them fun. You may end up calling them handy and necessary.

Whoa! There's a Map Feature in the Contacts List?

You don't need to draw the map to a contact's location; the Internet will do that for you. But to get there from here, follow these steps:

1. Double-click the name of the contact you want to locate in the physical world.

This displays their Contact sheet or the dialog box with all their information in it (Figure 19.4). Note that the Address information must be entered for this trick to work. This information is found near the lower-left corner of the Contact dialog box.

2. Click the Display Map of Address button.

Or you can choose Actions ➤ Display Map of Address. (Isn't "Map of Address" stilted? Sounds like it was translated from some Eurasian tongue.)

Instantly your web browser opens and you're dialing in to the Internet, specifically to an MSN map page, shown in Figure 19.6. You can then use the link to get directions on the web page to print out how to get there. And when you get close, just look for the huge pushpin stuck into the ground and, well, there you are!

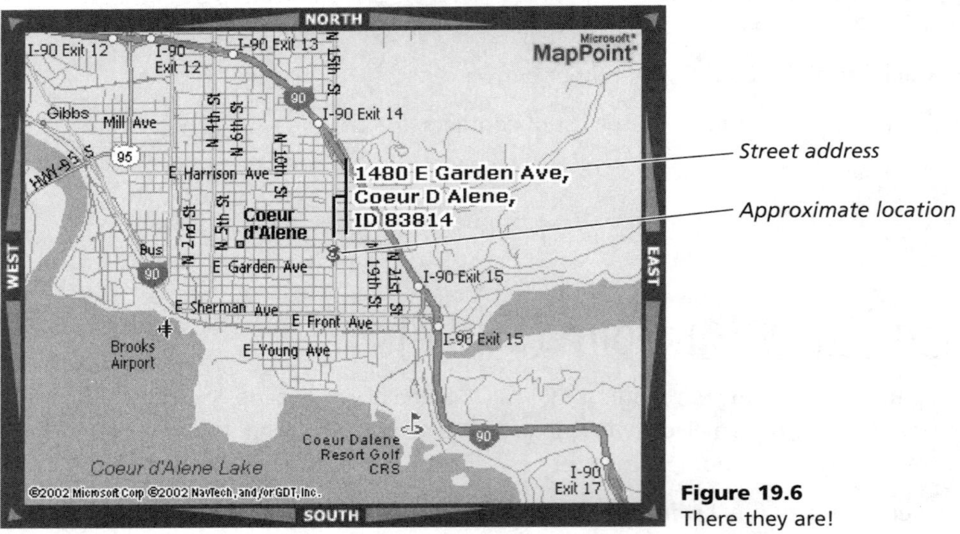

Figure 19.6
There they are!

Here's a Total Non-Office Trick

If you know the phone number of someone, and that phone number is not unlisted, then go to Google (`www.google.com`*) and type in their phone number, complete with the area code. Clicking the Search button displays contact information about that person. A link to Yahoo Maps displays a map to that location.*

How Can I E-mail All My Contacts?

It's time for you to move on and things are changing, so you want to let all your e-mail gang know about it. First, a few words of etiquette before you commit to gang-mail:

- Please do put all the names in the Bcc field. If you don't, your e-mail will look sloppy and unprofessional and will probably be interpreted as junk e-mail.
- Check with your ISP to determine if you can e-mail a bunch of people at once. Some ISPs put a limit on the number of folks you can e-mail at once. The number can be as low as 50, though my ISP limits the number to 144. (This limit is designed to help prevent spamming.)
- Avoid the temptation to "be a hero" and e-mail all your contacts to warn them about viruses, send them e-mail in hopes of winning a contest, or fall prey to any of the many Internet e-mail hoaxes out there. Before you're tempted to send out such an e-mail to *everyone*, use the Internet to search for verification of what it is you're sending out.

Second, follow these steps to broadcast an e-mail to everyone:

1. Start a new message as you normally would.
2. Type your own e-mail address into the To field.

   This is optional, but I do it anyway. Leaving this item blank often causes the recipient's e-mail program to put "undisclosed recipient" into the e-mail header, which is a flag for junk e-mail. By putting your own name into the To field you may avoid that trap.
3. Bcc... Click the Bcc button.

   If you don't see this button, choose View ➤ Bcc Field from the menu.
4. In the Select Names dialog box, click to select the first name in the list.
5. Scroll down to the end of the list.
6. Press and hold the Shift key and click the last name in the list.

   All the names are selected.
7. Click OK.

   And the huge stack of names goes into the Bcc field.
8. Enter a subject.

   As another anti-spam tip, try using your name in the Subject field. So instead of writing "I'm moving" or "Here's my new address"—both of which are common junk e-mail subjects—I would say, "Dan Gookin is moving" or "Here is Dan Gookin's new e-mail address."
9. Type the contents of the message.

   Be short. Be brief. You may even want to add that if people want more information, simply to respond and you'll let them know.

Again, be professional here. Avoid fancy fonts and formatted text. Doing so makes your e-mail look less like spam and it also keeps the message size smaller, which means busy people are more apt to read it on first glance as opposed to passing it over for later review.

10. Send the message.

Again, there is a possibility that your ISP may reject the message for having too many recipients. If so, phone them and ask tech support what the limit is on e-mail messages. Then you'll have to resend the message and divide up the contacts into groups of certain sizes. Keep reading this chapter for more information on dividing your contacts into groups.

What Are Groups?

Some e-mail programs may refer to a gang of people you can e-mail at once as a group. In Outlook such a thing is called a *distribution list.*

Why Would I Want to Create a Distribution List?

The best reason is to instantly send e-mail to a group of similar folk.

For example, you can have a distribution list of people in your family or a list of folks you routinely send jokes to. Maybe there's a need to have a distribution list of people in your department at work, or you need a list of the parents of your kids' friends. Any and all of these could be a distribution list.

Here is how you build such a thing in Outlook:

1. Choose File ➤ New ➤ Distribution List.

The Distribution List dialog box shows up, depicted graphically in Figure 19.7, though the one you see will be empty at this time.

2. Enter a descriptive name for the distribution list.

Family. Friends. Jokes. The Gang at Work. Neighborhood. And so on.

3. Click the Select Members button to add contacts to the list.

The Select Members dialog box appears.

4. Double-click the names you want to add to the list.

Keep on doing this until the list contains all the members you desire.

5. Click OK when you're done.

The names then appear in the Distribution List dialog box, as shown in Figure 19.7.

6. Save and Close Click the Save and Close button in the Distribution List dialog box.

You're done.

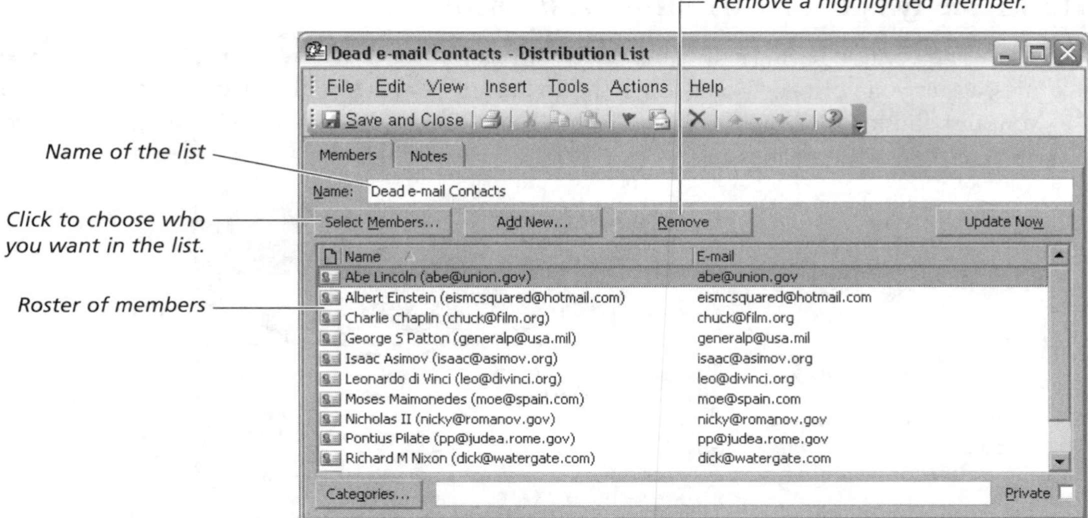

Figure 19.7 A distribution list

The distribution list now appears in your list of contacts. If you choose the Address Cards or Detailed Address Cards view, you'll see the list shown with a double-headed icon on the top, as shown in Figure 19.8. Now you're ready to use the list.

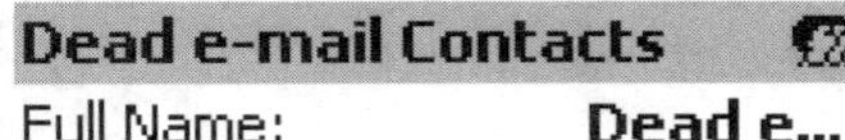

Figure 19.8 The distribution list as it looks in the Address Cards view of the Contacts part of Outlook

Hey! How About Creating a Distribution List with Everyone on It!

Sounds like a good idea. On my system, it's called the "All" list. Using that list is how I send e-mail out to everyone, an alternative to the method described in the section, "How Can I E-mail All My Contacts?" earlier in this chapter.

How Can I Add Someone to the List?

Double-click the distribution list to open it, and then click the Select Members button as you did to create the list. Add whatever members you want (refer to the section "Why Would I Want to Create a Distribution List?"). Click OK. They're in there.

I Need to Remove Someone from a Distribution List.

To remove someone from the list, open the list: Find the distribution list in the list of contacts and double-click to open it. Then locate the person's name in the dialog box, click to highlight it, and then click the Remove button.

Note that removing someone from a list does not delete them from your overall list of contacts.

How Exactly Is the Distribution List Used?

There's no point in having a distribution list unless you use it. This is cinchy: Just start a new e-mail message as you normally would. Click the To button—or better still, the Bcc button—then select your distribution list from the Select Names dialog box, as described in Figure 19.9. Then click OK and continue with the message.

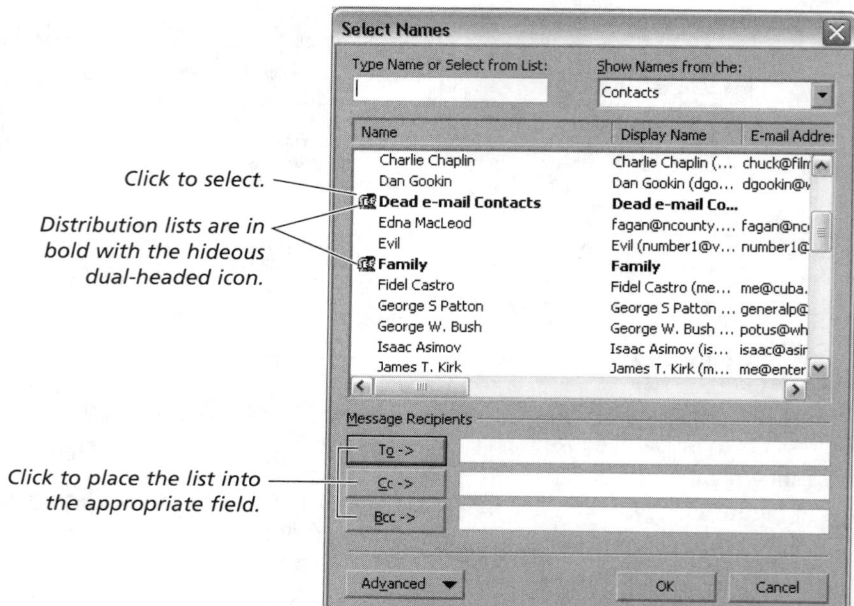

Figure 19.9
Selecting a distribution list for a new e-mail

The distribution list appears in the message in bold text, which tells you that you're working with a distribution list and not a normal nickname or contact.

In Outlook 2003, there is a + (plus sign) before the distribution list name. You can click the + to expand the list into individual names. Note that if you do this, it cannot be undone.

By the way, Outlook does expand the distribution list to individual names when you send the message.

Any Quicker Way to Use a Distribution List?

Of course: Right-click the list in the Contacts area. Choose "New Message to Contact" from the pop-up menu.

Can I Print Out a List of Labels for My Contacts?

This acrobatic act requires the coordination of both Outlook and Word. Outlook provides the source for the labels and Word the method by which they are printed. But there are problems.

Combining Word and Outlook works great in Office 2000. It works horribly in Office XP (2002) and even worse in Office 2003. In fact, the best way to accomplish such a task is to forgo Word entirely and use the Access database program instead. You can export contacts to the Access database file format and then use Access to quickly and easily create sheets of labels. This is really the best way to go about things.

You Mean I'm Screwed?

Not entirely. The operation can be done, it just cannot be done well or as smoothly as you would think given that these applications are all from the same developer and were supposedly designed to work well together.

What Can I Do between Outlook and Word?

There is one operation that does work well between Outlook and Word. So rather than dwell on what doesn't work well, here are some things you can do in Word that involve Outlook.

- In Word 2003/XP, choose Tools ➤ Letters and Mailings ➤ Envelopes and Labels.
- In Word 2000, choose Tools ➤ Envelopes and Labels.

The Envelopes and Labels dialog box appears. This is where you can print an individual envelope or a sheet of identical labels, as shown in Figure 19.10.

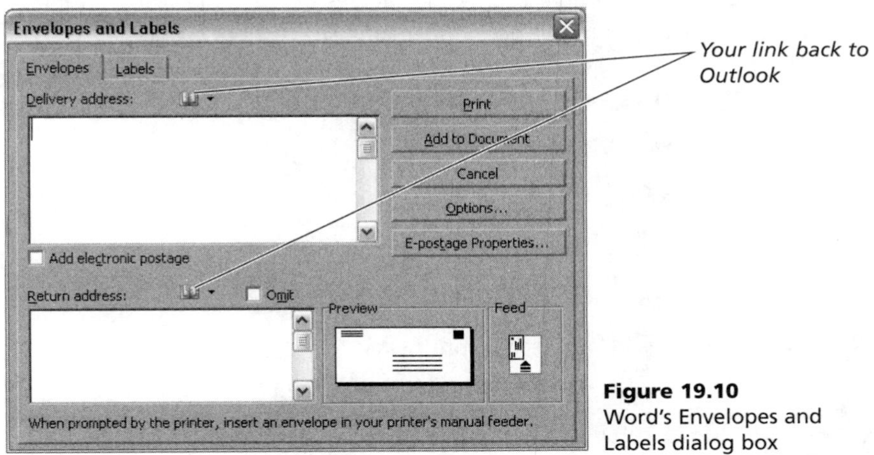

Figure 19.10
Word's Envelopes and Labels dialog box

The connection to Outlook? Why, it's that teeny Address Book button found above the Address area in both the Envelopes and Labels tabs in this dialog box. When you click that button, you'll see the now-famous Select Name dialog box. To insert a contact's address, simply select them from the list and click the OK button.

That's the best way that information transfers from between Outlook and Word. I really wish the full list of contacts was as easy to import for doing a mail merge or creating a sheet of labels, but it just isn't so.

20 Organizing the Rest of Your Life

Don't you ever find yourself saying, "I really need to use my computer to get my life organized"? Worse, don't you find yourself typing that message in an e-mail?

Despite the promise of the personal computer, we all still have pocket calculators, notepads, wall calendars, and digital clocks on or around our desks. I honestly don't know anyone who is fully, completely, absolutely reliant on a computer or handheld gizmo to organize their life. At least I haven't yet met anyone *organized* who lives such a life.

Outlook's organizational and task-related activities are fairly easy to understand, thanks to a clever interface. Anyone familiar with poking around Windows will probably understand how to set dates, break appointments, screw up schedules, and then get on with their life. To supplement that, I present this brief chapter that covers a few of the handier tricks you might play while using the rest of Outlook.

Dice Cast and Fates Foretold:

- Viewing life through Outlook's Calendar
- Changing an appointment
- Scheduling a recurring appointment
- Modifying and messing with tasks in the Tasks list
- Completing your tasks

Taking, Making, and Breaking Appointments

Appointments are made (or broken) in the Calendar part of Outlook. So put on your touring hat, and let's go take some time to play in the Calendar.

The Cheap-Ass Tour of the Calendar

The Outlook Calendar is broached by clicking the Calendar icon or button on the left end of Outlook's window. This displays the Calendar on the right side of the window, either a single day, week, or entire month as shown in Figure 20.1.

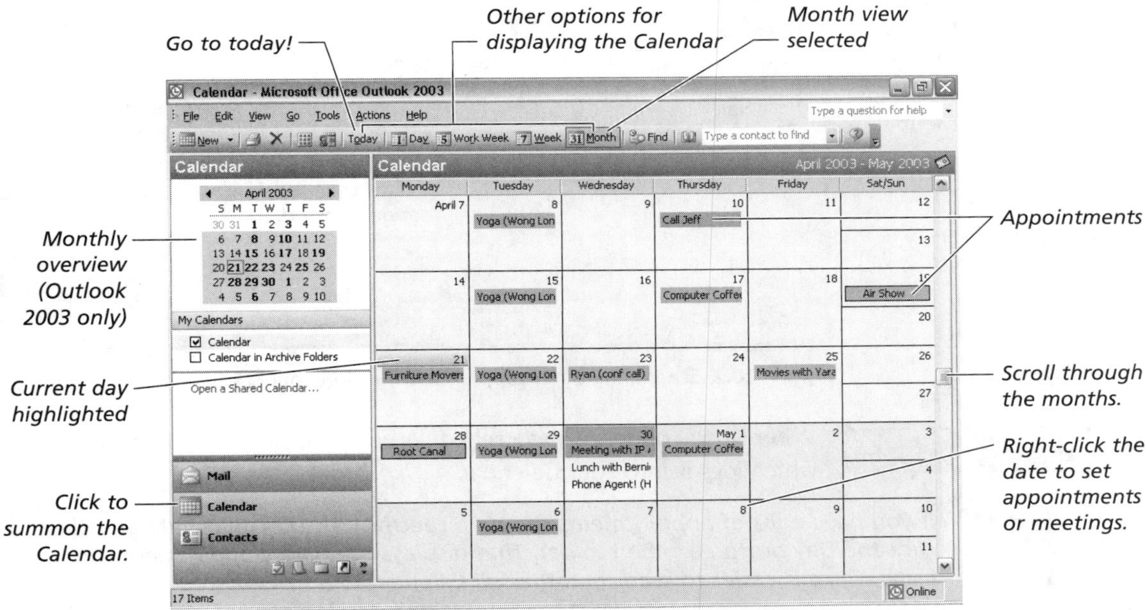

Figure 20.1 Calendar in the merry, merry month of April

To schedule an appointment, click to select the date on the Calendar and then click the New button. This displays the Appointment dialog box, shown in Figure 20.2, where you tell Outlook about the appointment.

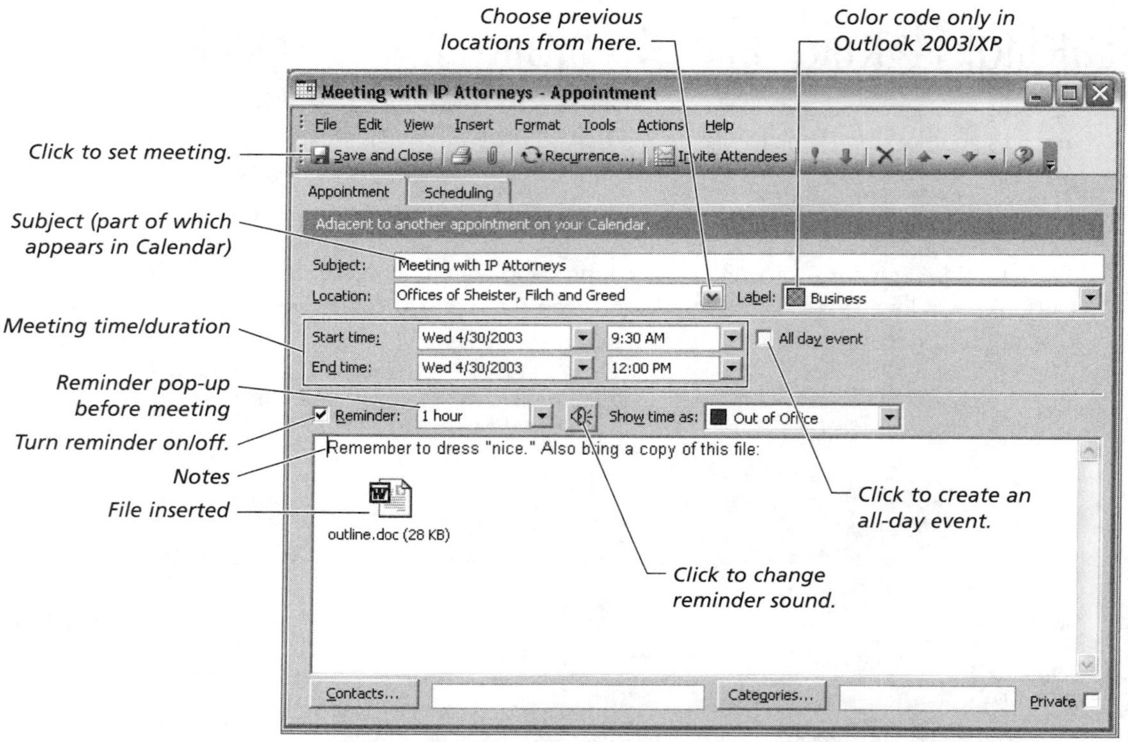

Figure 20.2 Scheduling a new appointment is done here.

When you're done setting a schedule, click the Save and Close button, which logs it into your Calendar.

If you have a lot of appointments during a specific day, click that date and then click the Day button on the toolbar. That displays the day's appointments graphically, which is easier to read than the full Calendar window.

To schedule an all-day event, double-click the date of the event. This also displays the Appointment dialog box, but with the "All Day Event" check box preselected.

Note that the easiest way to schedule time for an event is to click the Scheduling tab in the Appointment dialog box, shown in Figure 20.3. (It's called the Attendee Availability tab in Outlook 2000.) You can use the gizmos in this part of the dialog box to move events, plus it also shows the schedule for the day.

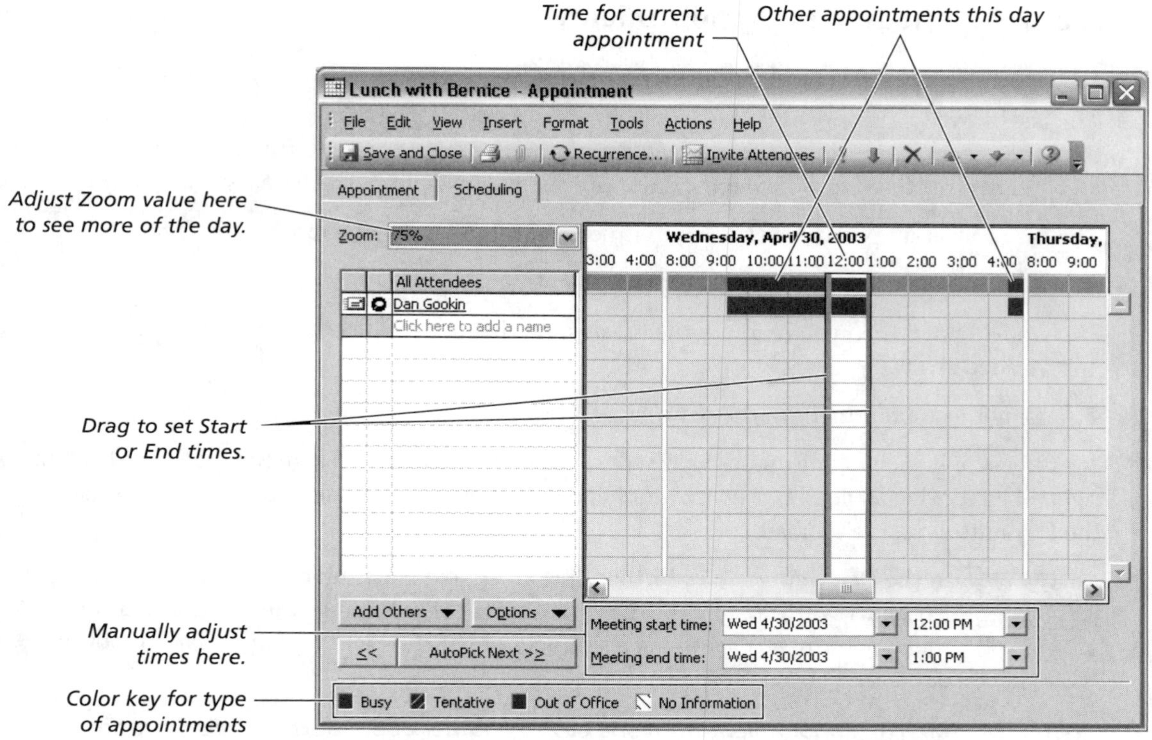

Time for current appointment

Other appointments this day

Adjust Zoom value here to see more of the day.

Drag to set Start or End times.

Manually adjust times here.

Color key for type of appointments

Figure 20.3 Setting time for an appointment in the Scheduling tab

What's the Difference between an Appointment, an Event, and a Meeting?

Appointments are personal, you-only things.

Events are all-day appointments.

Meetings are appointments involving too many other people. One feature of setting a meeting is that you can e-mail other folks in your Contacts list to invite them to attend, as well as manage the list of folks who are supposed to attend the meeting.

A meeting is a device that allows uninformed management to prevent the staff from completing the task the meeting is about.

I Need to Reschedule an Appointment.

There's the easy way and the hard way.

The hard way involves opening the appointment and entering a new date and time. Actually, that's necessary if you plan on moving an appointment more than a month away. But for hopping an appointment forward a few hours, days, or even a couple of weeks, there's the easy way.

The easy way is simply to drag the appointment around by using the mouse. Here's how:

1. Point the mouse at the left end of the appointment.

   You'll know when you've found the sweet spot; the mouse pointer changes to a four-headed arrow.

2. Drag the appointment to the new day.

Now if you're just changing an appointment on the same day, or to assure that you have the time right when moving an appointment to another day, switch over Outlook to the Day view by clicking the Day button on the toolbar.

In the Day view you can further drag an appointment up or down, again by using the left end. (Don't drag by the top or bottom or you'll change the Start or End times for the appointment.) Set the appointment down at whichever particular hour of the day that it's been moved to.

Dragging an appointment from one day to another does not change its Start time.

Can I E-mail Myself an Appointment Reminder?

The only thing you can't e-mail yourself is a reminder to pick up your e-mail, because that would constitute a time paradox and the universe would implode. But it's silly to e-mail yourself an appointment reminder when Outlook can automatically remind you before any appointment.

Setting a reminder is done in the Appointment dialog box, shown in Figure 20.2. Here are the baby steps you take to set the reminder:

1. Click to put a checkmark by Reminder (if one isn't already there).

2. Use the drop-down list to set the reminder time.

   That's the number of minutes, hours, seconds, or weeks beforehand that Outlook will pop up a Reminder window. For example, to be reminded five minutes before a meeting, choose "5 minutes" from the drop-down list, shown in Figure 20.4.

Time before the appointment to pop up the reminder

Set the reminder. Reminder: 5 minutes Choose a sound to play.

Figure 20.4 Setting a reminder time

3. Click the speaker button to set a tone to play when the reminder pops up.

4. Continue setting options in the Appointment dialog box.

5. Save and Close Click the Save and Close button when you're done.

Note that you're not limited to the time allotments shown in the drop-down list. You can type in your own time values there, providing you understand Outlook's AutoDate abbreviations. Refer to the sidebar, "You Must Know This: AutoDate Time Period Abbreviations."

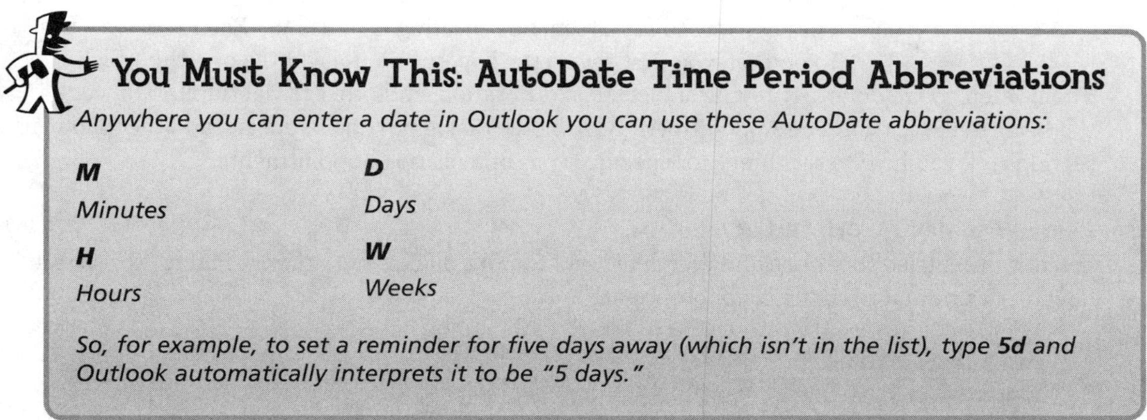

You Must Know This: AutoDate Time Period Abbreviations

Anywhere you can enter a date in Outlook you can use these AutoDate abbreviations:

M	***D***
Minutes	*Days*
H	***W***
Hours	*Weeks*

*So, for example, to set a reminder for five days away (which isn't in the list), type **5d** and Outlook automatically interprets it to be "5 days."*

I Like the Pop-up Reminder but Detest the Sound!

You can change the sound to anything or turn it off. To do so, click the speaker button (Figure 20.4) and you'll see the dialog box shown in Figure 20.5. Follow the instructions in the figure for how to fix the sound.

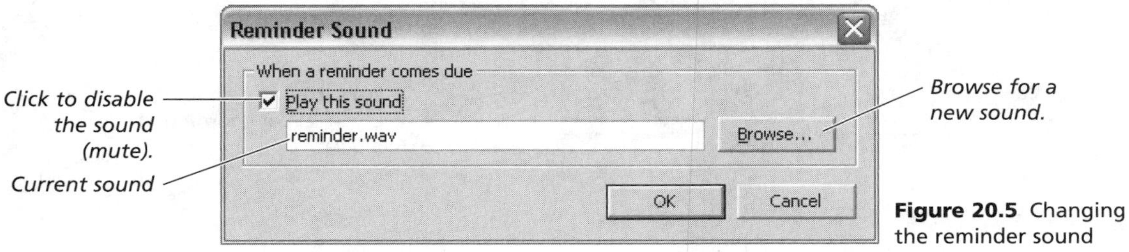

Figure 20.5 Changing the reminder sound

Can I Color My Appointments and Events to Differentiate Them?

This trick is possible only in Outlook 2003/XP. You use the Label drop-down list in the Appointment dialog box (Figure 20.2).

If the appointment has already been set, then right-click it in the Calendar and choose a new label color from the Label menu.

You can change the label meanings by clicking the "Edit Labels" menu item from the pop-up menu. Right-click an appointment and choose Labels ➤ Edit Labels. You can then rename any label Outlook uses. (You cannot, sadly, change the colors.)

How Can I Get an Appointment to Repeat Automatically?

The secret to setting a repeating meeting is *not* to keep entering it into the Calendar over and over. No, that's being silly and wasteful.

The easy way to set a recurring meeting is to use the Recurrence button. To do that, you first set up the appointment as if it's a one-time deal. Then, when you're done setting the subject, place, duration, and other trivial tidbits, you click the Recurrence button. The Appointment Recurrence dialog box then appears, and the following sections tell you how to set things for specific types of recurring appointments.

Every Weekday I Work Out at 6:00 A.M.

You're a nut. I tried that once and I felt like I had to puke all day. But anyway, Figure 20.6 shows how to set up such a recurring appointment.

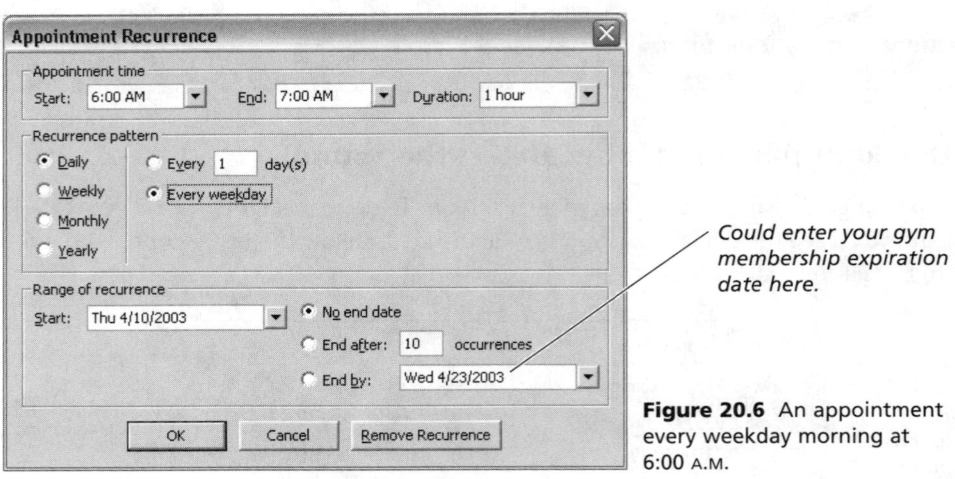

Figure 20.6 An appointment every weekday morning at 6:00 A.M.

I Work Out Every Other Day after Work.

I did this for a few years and found it was much better on my stomach than working out before my body was awake, as shown in Figure 20.7.

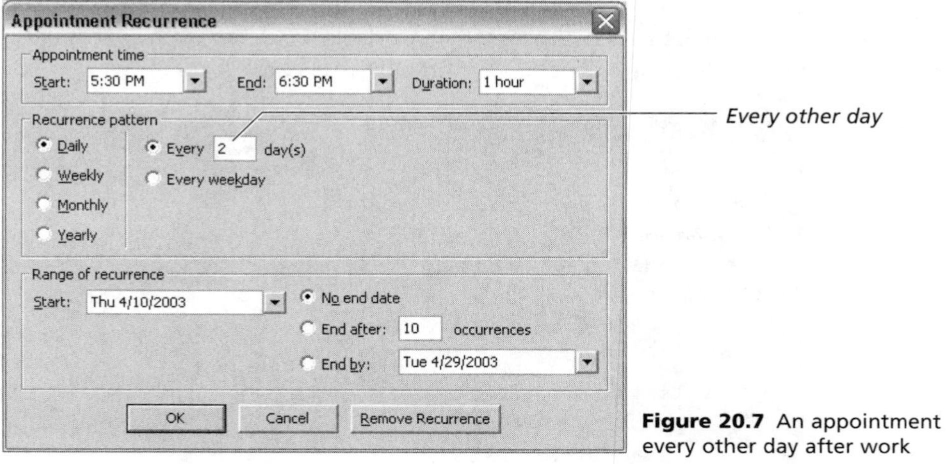

Figure 20.7 An appointment every other day after work

My Meeting Is Every Tuesday at Breakfast.

Weekly meetings are set by clicking the Weekly option in the Appointment Recurrence dialog box, as shown in Figure 20.8.

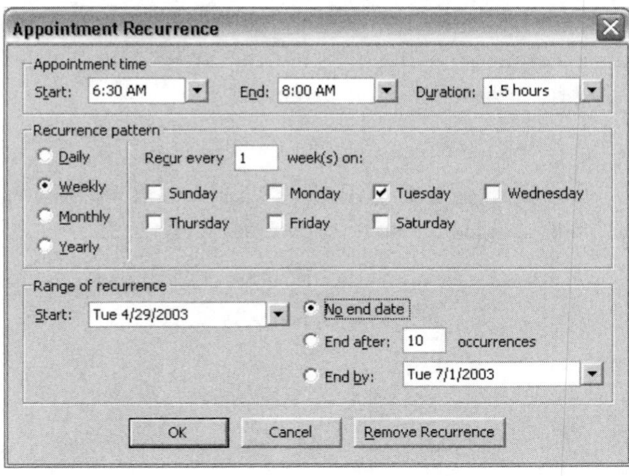

Figure 20.8 Setting up a weekly meeting

For the Next Six Weeks I Have a Class on Tuesdays and Thursdays at 7:00 P.M.

It's a class on how to pretend you're in management. Required for all executive officers.

This is one of those recurring schedule monsters that takes a bit of explaining. First, the "Recur Every '1' Week(s) On" item is set to 1 because these appointments are still weekly, one week after the other. But the key to making them repeat for six weeks is to set the Occurrences option (Figure 20.9) to 12 for the total number of appointments (or classes).

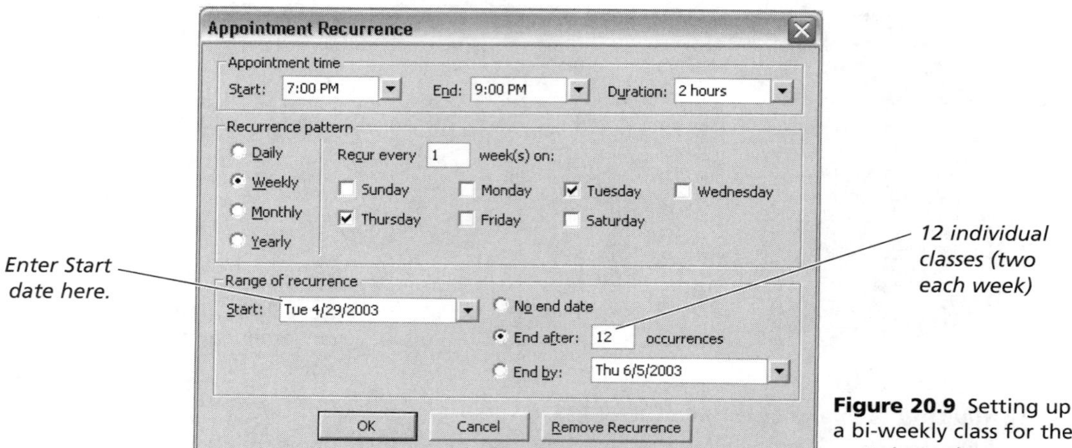

Figure 20.9 Setting up a bi-weekly class for the next six weeks

Another thing you should check is that you properly entered the Start date. If you didn't do this when you first set up the appointment, then do it here in the Appointment Recurrence dialog box, as shown in Figure 20.9. You can also confirm the End date, but that value doesn't need to be specifically set if you've entered the proper number of occurrences.

My Meeting Is Every Other Week.

For some folks this is the hardest type of meeting to remember. Thank goodness there are computer programs such as Outlook to help. Set things up as shown in Figure 20.10.

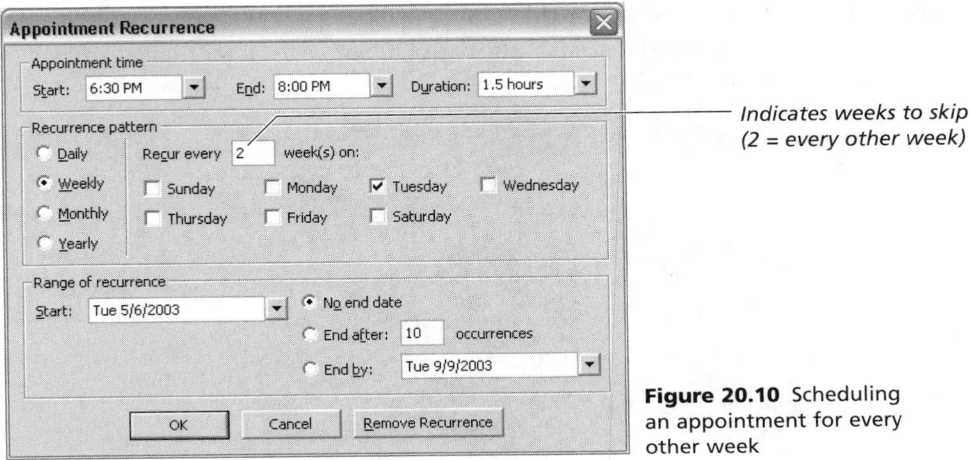

Figure 20.10 Scheduling an appointment for every other week

My Meeting Is Always the Third Thursday of the Month.

The third Thursday is always going to happen every month. Which date is it? Who cares! Just set up the recurring schedule as shown in Figure 20.11.

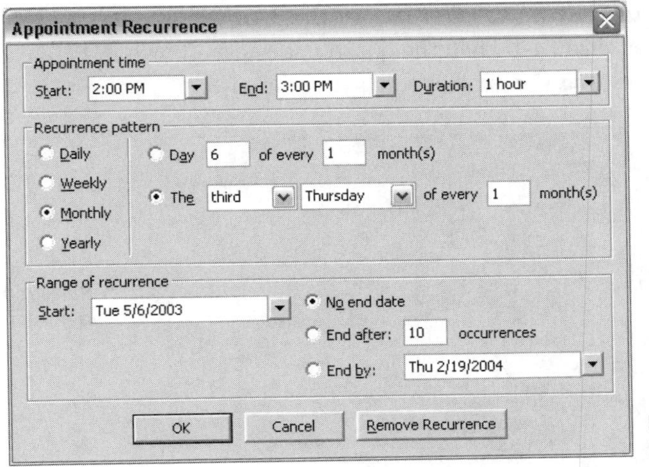

Figure 20.11 Every third Thursday

My Meeting Is on the First and Third Wednesdays of the Month.

You can set this up so that you actually have two recurring appointments, one for the first Wednesday and another for the third Wednesday. Use the example from the previous section and simply create two appointments.

Payday Is the 15th Day of the Month!

This is a monthly appointment based on the day of the month, rather than any specific day of the week, as shown in Figure 20.12.

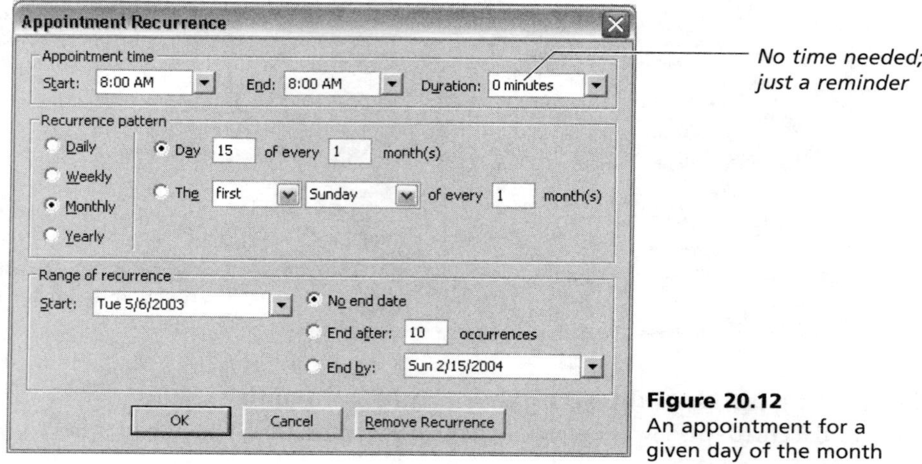

Figure 20.12
An appointment for a given day of the month

We Hold Meetings Every Quarter on the First Day of the Month.

With this type of meeting, be sure you set when the quarter starts, as shown in Figure 20.13. Otherwise, Outlook just assumes that the quarter starts "next month."

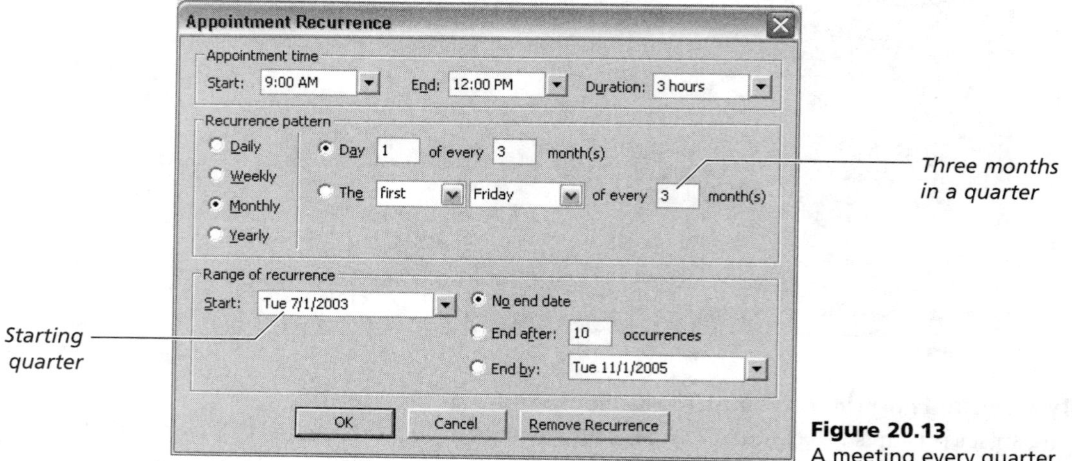

Figure 20.13
A meeting every quarter

Election Day Is the First Tuesday in November.

Figure 20.14 shows how the Founding Fathers would have set their Outlook 1776 calendars to remind them of Election Day.

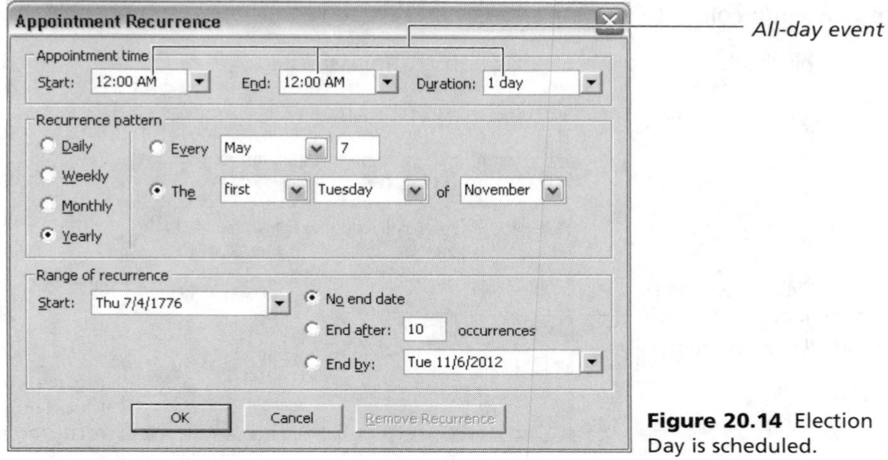

Figure 20.14 Election Day is scheduled.

I'd Like to Be Reminded of My Mother-in-Law's Birthday.

Birthdays are annual events that occur on the same date every year, not the same day or time of the month. Figure 20.15 illustrates such a thing.

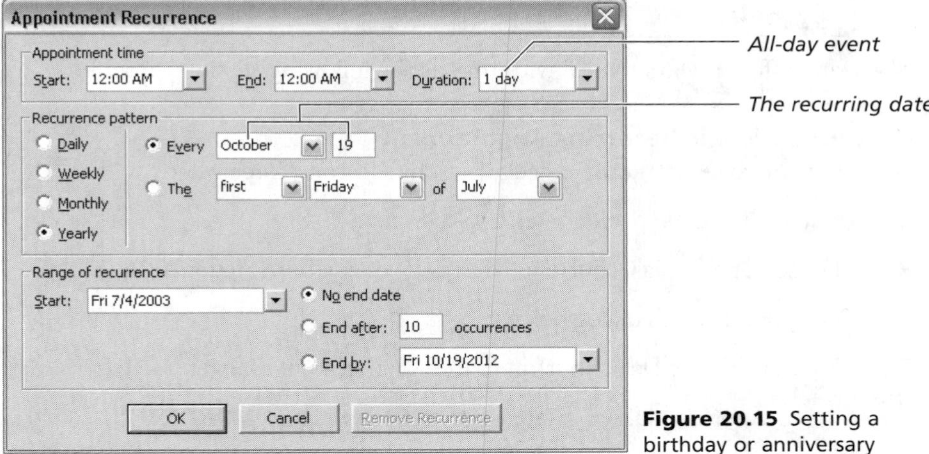

Figure 20.15 Setting a birthday or anniversary

I Need to Change a Recurring Appointment.

There are two ways to change an appointment that's been scheduled to recur globally, that is to change all the appointments, or specifically, to change one single appointment. Outlook is most helpful when it comes to accomplishing this. Regard these steps:

1. Double-click any of the recurring appointments.

   A dialog box is displayed, shown in Figure 20.16.

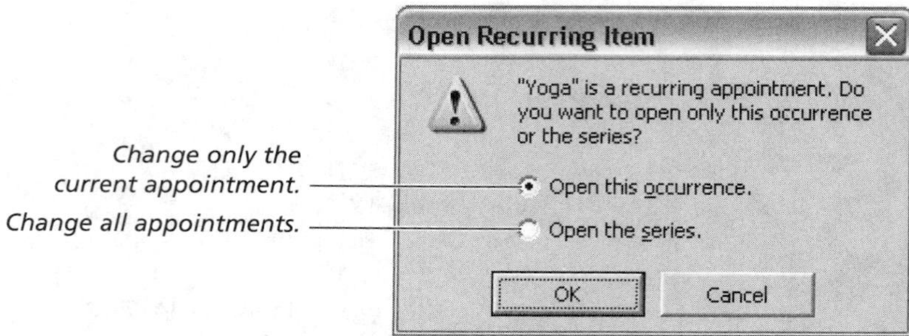

Figure 20.16 Modifying a recurring item

2. Select an option, per the descriptions given in Figure 20.16.
3. Click OK.
4. Make the changes in the appointment's dialog box.
5. Save and Close Click the Save and Close button when you're done.

There are different ways to deal with this, as the following sections describe.

Canceling a Single Recurring Appointment

Suppose your yoga instructor cancels Tuesday's lesson. Here's what you do:

1. Double-click that specific Tuesday's lesson.
2. Choose "Open This Occurrence" from the dialog box (Figure 20.16).

   The appointment's dialog box appears.

3. Click the Delete button in the Appointment dialog box.

   Another dialog box appears, similar to Figure 20.16.

4. Choose "Delete This Occurrence" and click OK.

That one appointment is then gone, but the rest of them remain.

Changing a Single Recurring Appointment to Another Day

Every music student knows that piano teachers don't die and they don't get sick. An axiom to that law is that piano teachers never cancel appointments; they merely move them. So to move Wednesday morning's regular lesson to Saturday, do this:

1. Double-click to open the Wednesday night lesson that's moving.
2. Choose "Open This Occurrence" in the dialog box and click OK (Figure 20.16).
3. Enter the new Start date and time.

   Figure 20.17 shows an example of changing the date and time.

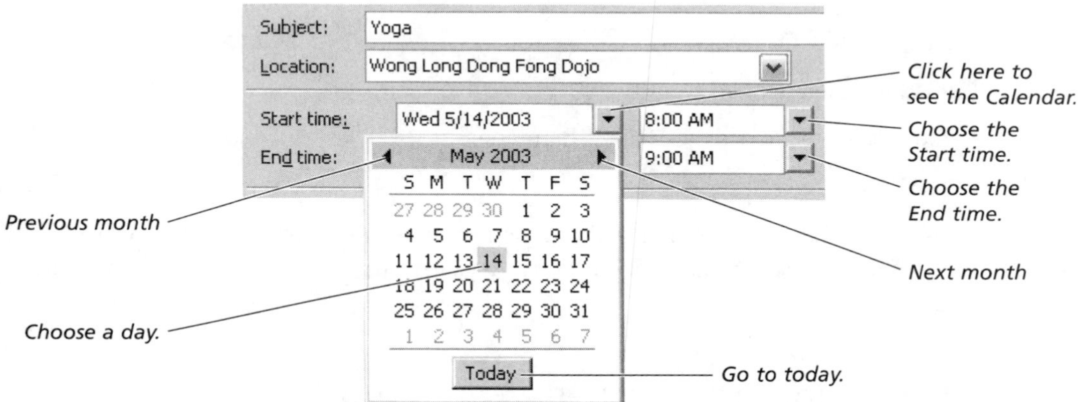

Figure 20.17 An example of changing the date and time

4. Set the End time.
5. [Save and Close] Click the Save and Close button.

   Outlook confirms that you're changing only one of a series of recurring appointments.
6. Click the Yes button.

Moving All Recurring Appointments to a New Date or Time

Enough people finally have conflicts so the third Thursday board meetings have been changed to the third Wednesday instead. Here's how to change that:

1. Double-click one of the recurring appointments.
2. Choose "Open the Series" and click OK (Figure 20.16).
3. [Recurrence...] Click the Recurrence button.

4. Edit the Appointment Recurrence dialog box to change Thursday to Wednesday.
5. Click OK.
6. [Save and Close] Click the Save and Close button.

All the appointments are shifted to the next date.

Any Way to Automatically Disable the Alarm for My Appointments?

If you find yourself routinely shutting off the alarm warning, then why not just disable it entirely? Here's how:

1. Choose Tools ➢ Options.
2. Click the Preference tab.
3. Remove the checkmark by "Default Reminder."
4. Click OK.

From now on, the Reminder option in the Appointment dialog box (Figure 20.2) will be unchecked by default. You can manually reassert the alarm simply by adding the checkmark to any appointment you make.

Scheduling Tasks and To-Do Lists

The difference between an Outlook appointment and an Outlook task is that the appointment happens at a specific time and date and the task is a project-oriented thing—such as a to-do list.

Between the two, I spend more time scheduling appointments than I do making tasks. For some reason, keeping tasks in my brain seems to work for me. I do, however, understand that other people live by their Tasks lists. Outlook is, once again, fairly straightforward in how it presents the Tasks lists and what you can do with them. The following sections highlight some of the lesser known but yet still useful tricks.

Why Use a Task When I Can Just Schedule Something?

The best way I've heard it put is as follows Create a task for those things that you want a reminder for, but that you wouldn't notice on your calendar.

For example, every month you need to clean the filters in the furnace. That's a recurring task, but something you probably don't need on your appointment calendar. Ditto for cleaning the gutters or working on some garage project. Yeah—like a "Honey Do" list.

Why Are the Tasks in My Calendar TaskPad Different from the Tasks in My Tasks Folder?

This is merely a perception problem; there are most likely different "views" selected for the Calendar TaskPad than for the Tasks folder itself.

To change the view for the Calendar window, first ensure that you've chosen a view other than Monthly. (The TaskPad doesn't show up in Monthly view.) Then choose View ➤ TaskPad View and select another view from the submenu.

I Want a Task to Repeat Itself Two Weeks After I Finish It, Not Every Two Weeks on the Calendar.

This is officially known as a *regenerating* task, not a recurring task. When you regenerate a task, it automatically resets itself when the task is completed, starting you back over again. For example, painting the Golden Gate Bridge is a regenerating task; once they finish, it's time to start over again on the other side.

To make a task regenerating, click the Recurrence button when you create the task in the Task dialog box, shown in Figure 20.18. This summons the Task Recurrence dialog box, shown in Figure 20.19. There you select the "Regenerate New Task" option to make a new task start as soon as the current one is completed.

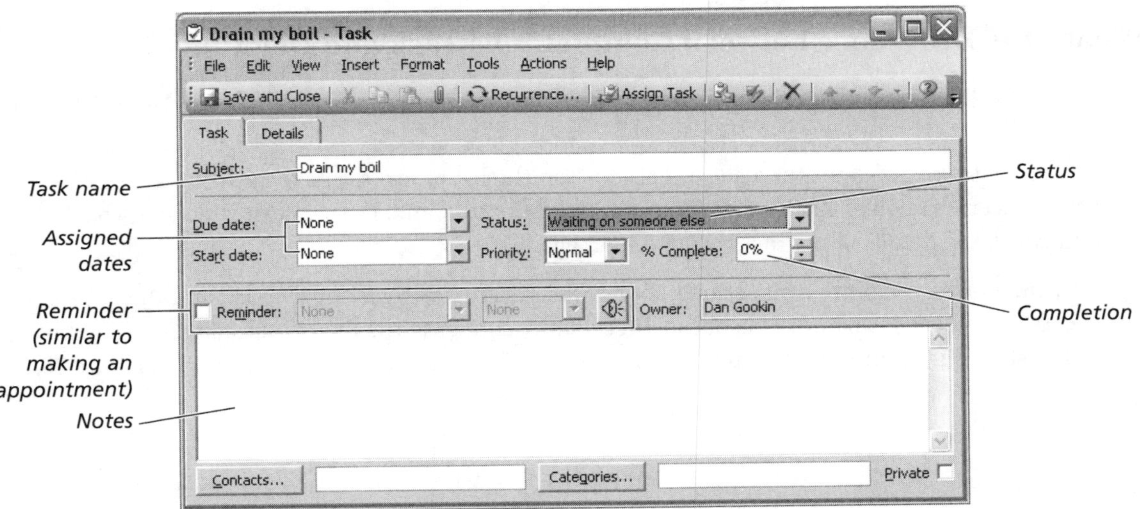

Figure 20.18 Creating a new task

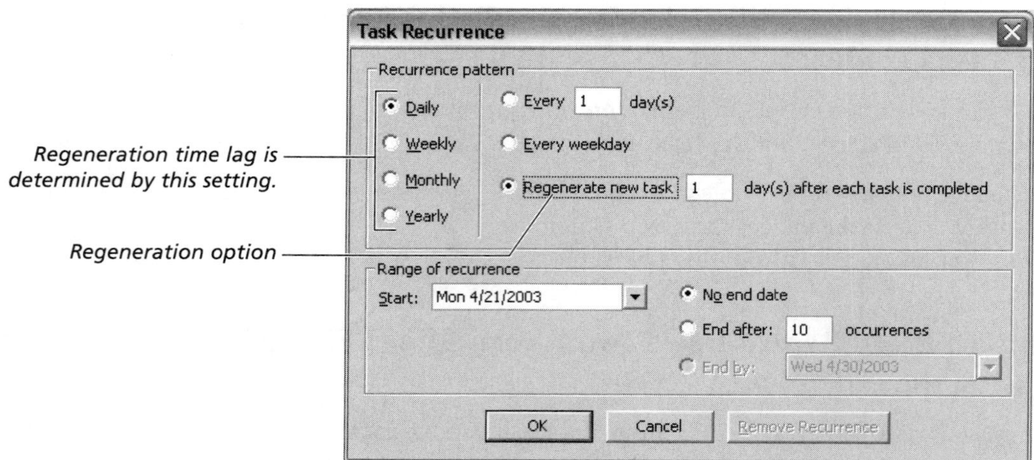

Figure 20.19 Making a task recur

Note that the space of time Outlook waits before regenerating a task is set by the Daily, Weekly, Monthly, and Yearly options, as shown in Figure 20.19. So if you want a task to regenerate as soon as it's completed, choose Daily, then "Regenerate New Task Every 1 Day(s) After Each Task Is Completed." To have the new task kick off a week after you're done—allowing some resting time—choose Weekly and then set the number of weeks at 1.

What's the Difference between Completing a Task and Deleting a Task?

I suppose that one is more satisfying than the other, but that really depends on the person and the task!

To mark a task complete, put a checkmark by it in the list of tasks. The task then stays on the list but is crossed out. That way, you know you did the task and, if necessary, you can go back and check the details of the task by opening it again.

To send a task straight to everlasting hell (e.g., delete it), click to select the task and then press the Delete key on the keyboard. This doesn't necessarily condemn the file to eternal damnation but rather shoves it off into the Deleted Items folder. Yes, it can be recovered, as shown in Figure 20.20.

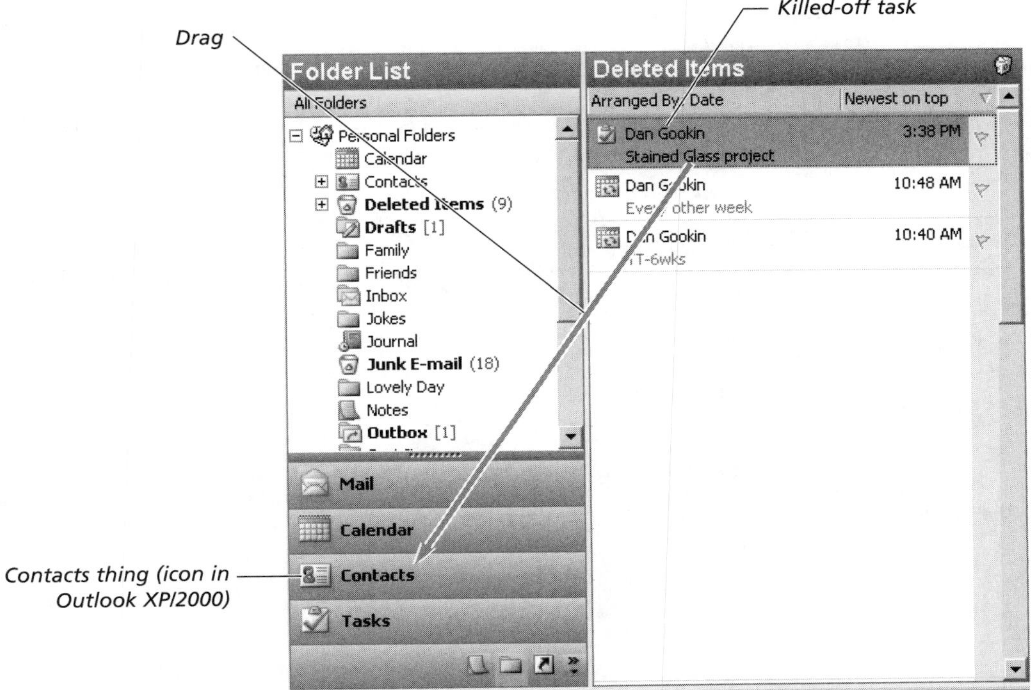

Figure 20.20 Recovering a task from the Deleted Items folder

Be sure to click the Save and Close button in Outlook 2000 after rescuing a deleted task from the Deleted Items folder.

How Can I Tell When a Task Was Completed?

Yup, sometimes those tasks do sneak up on you and, well, there they are all done! Or finished. Completed?

No, I understand. The problem here is that the Tasks list doesn't really show when a task was completed or whether it was completed. The problem is the view, which can be fixed by following these steps:

1. Right-click the column heading in the list of tasks.

For example, right-click just to the right of the word "Subject" (see Figure 20.21).

2. From the pop-up menu, select the "Field Chooser" command.

A scrolling list of fields—the Field Chooser—appears.

3. Locate "Date Completed" in the list.
4. Drag that heading up into the heading row in the Tasks list, shown in Figure 20.21.

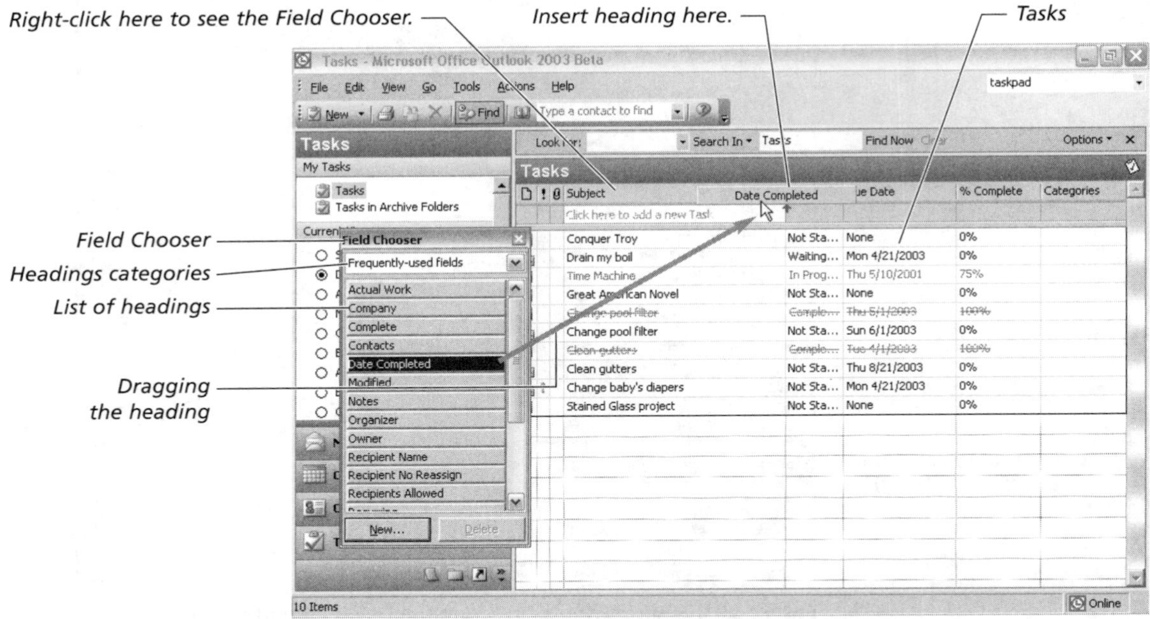

Figure 20.21 Adding a new heading to the list of tasks

5. Close the Field Chooser window.

Now it's easier to check on the task's progress and see what's completed and what's not.

To remove any field, just grab it with the mouse and drag that field down. A big black X appears on the field, indicating that you've dragged far enough; release the mouse button and the field is gone.

You can use these techniques to add or delete the headers in any table-like view in any Outlook folder.

PART 4

PowerPoint

21 Beyond Your Basic Slide Show

Nothing beats good old-fashioned presentations. I relish them. I am alone in a big room, weary and head-heavy after staying up in the bar 'till closing. It's warm. The lights dim. Then come hushed voices; they can't get the projector to work. Connections are checked. Some nerds volunteer their services from the audience. But wait—the laptop has gone to sleep. No big deal. Ching! It wakes up, and there is the presentation. Fortunately, no loud sounds are played during the transitions and the speaker natters in a banal monotone. I'm quickly nodding off to sleep in an upright position, giveaway pen poised on the free pad of paper, my head bobbing forward like every other schmo in the audience. It's PowerPoint time!

If you can work Word or Excel, then PowerPoint is a snap. In fact, it's been proven that young schoolkids can slap together a PowerPoint presentation in no time. It's really no big deal. Well, unless you want to do something special or avoid some of the main pitfalls that besmirch even the best intentions of beginning PowerPoint users. It's those kinds of tips and tricks you'll find presented in this chapter.

Darkness Illuminated and Fun Unleashed:

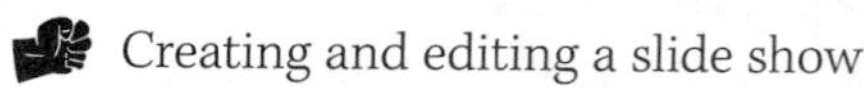

- Creating and editing a slide show

- Deciding what to put first (and last)

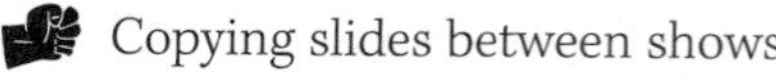

- Copying slides between shows
- Using outlines and speaker notes
- Adding a fancy background
- Improving the presentation with animation
- Adding sound
- Properly formatting your images

Working a Simple Presentation

Before we march down the merry lane of helpful hints and tricks, the following sections provide an overview of how to work the basic presentation thing in PowerPoint. Consider this a healthy review. Or if you're new to PowerPoint, this is the $1.98 tour.

From Itch to Scratch to Slide Show

Building a slide show is easy—providing that you know four things:

- Your subject
- Your audience
- Where you're going to start
- How you're going to get to where you end

Unless your slide show is going to run automatically, you're most likely going to be talking through the thing. So one key element to remember is that you don't have to put *everything* into the slide show—only the major notes or points, plus necessary illustrations.

A presentation is not a novel.

To create the slide show, first configure PowerPoint to look something like Figure 21.1. This isn't a requirement, but it's perhaps the best way to work with a slide show you're creating.

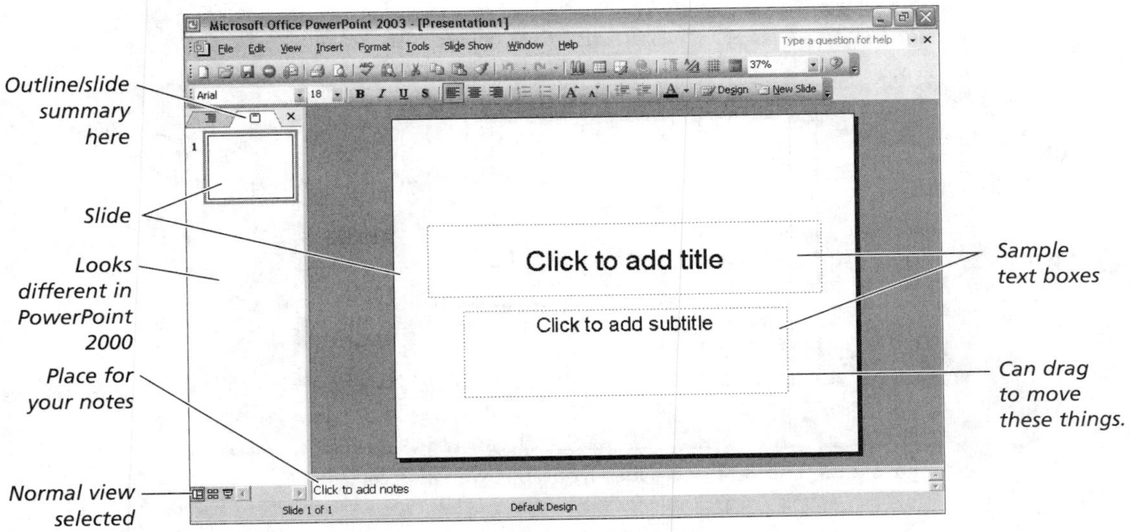

Figure 21.1 A happy way to set up the slide show

Click the New or New Slide button to begin creating your presentation. (In PowerPoint 2000, the button has just the icon.) You'll see a list of slide layout options, as shown in Figure 21.2 or 21.3, depending on your version of PowerPoint.

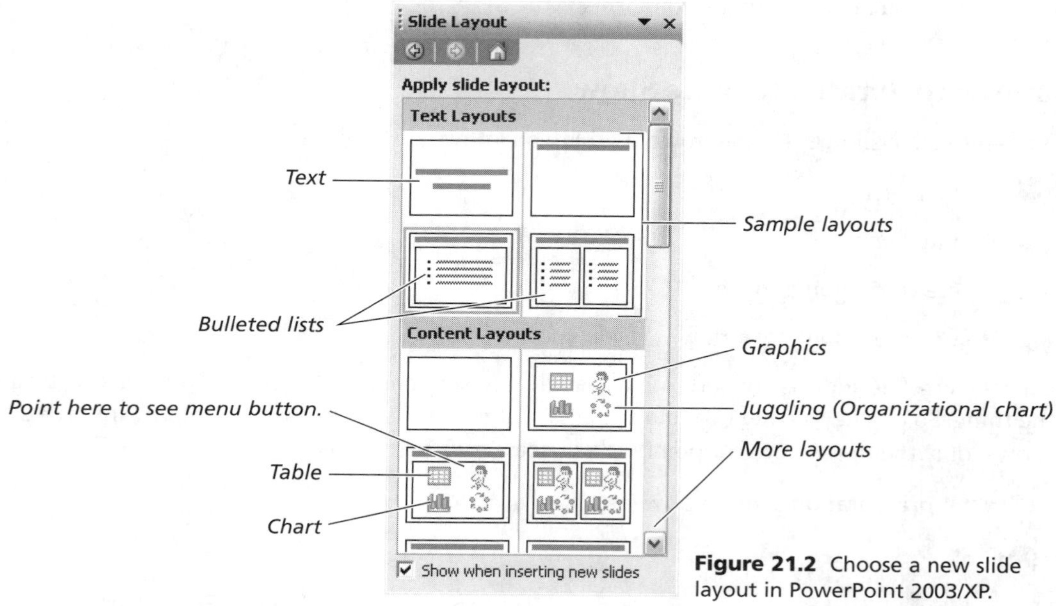

Figure 21.2 Choose a new slide layout in PowerPoint 2003/XP.

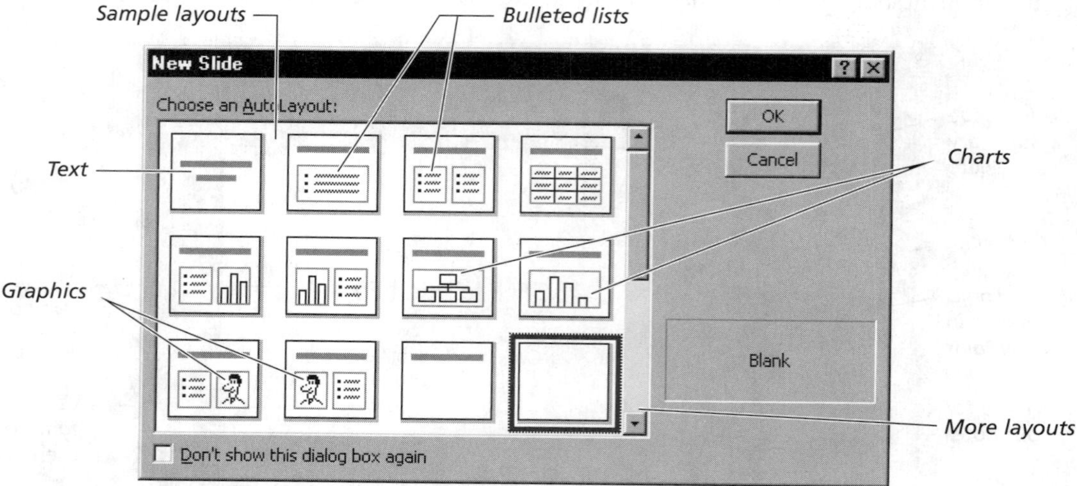

Figure 21.3 Choose a new slide layout in PowerPoint 2000.

Your job is to pick a preset slide layout from the list. Chances are one of the layouts matches what you need exactly.

After you choose a layout, the slide template appears, as shown in Figure 21.1. Your task is to fill in the blanks with your own information, creating the slide.

As you work on your slide show, be sure to save it to disk every so often!

As you work, you can add other elements to the slide: a background, color text, and objects. Use the Drawing toolbar as you would in Word or Excel to help spice up a dull slide; choose View ➤ Toolbars ➤ Drawing if you must, and the old, familiar Drawing toolbar shows up on the bottom of the window.

To preview your slide show, choose Slide Show ➤ View Show or press the F5 key. Use the mouse or whack the keyboard's spacebar to advance from one slide to another.

Along the way you can add color, sounds, animation effects, and other interesting things to your presentation. The remainder of this chapter offers the details for many of those and other exciting slide show features.

When everything is to your liking, save to disk one last time and then you're done. Well, actually, if you have more time, you'll probably continue to mess with the slide show. I do so all the time until I actually present the thing.

Don't Be Dumb: Be Logical in How You Save Your Presentations to Disk

Rather than just save your slide shows in the My Documents folder, do this:

First, create a subfolder in the My Documents folder. Call it `Slideshows` *or something similar, something that reminds you of the contents.*

Second, into that subfolder, create more subfolders, one for each slide show. This is optional, of course; but as your slide shows grow more advanced and may require their own set of illustrations or other information, keeping all that stuff in separate folders is part of being very organized.

Of course, if your slide show just stands by itself and doesn't require any extra files, then you can keep it in the main Slideshows folder.

What's the Importance of Using the Page Setup Box Before I Design a Show?

The Page Setup dialog box is used to format the basic type of slide you're using, setting its size. The problem comes when changing the size. For example, if you have your show set up as a standard "On-screen Show" but then convert the format to "35mm Slides," things are going to change. On a slide with a lot of information, stuff will need to be reset and adjusted. So it's better to set up your slide show as you want it *before* you start as opposed to *after* it's done.

To set the slide show format, choose File ➤ Page Setup. The Page Setup dialog box appears, as shown in Figure 21.4. Be sure to set things up properly as you want the show to be displayed. Do it now, before you create a show.

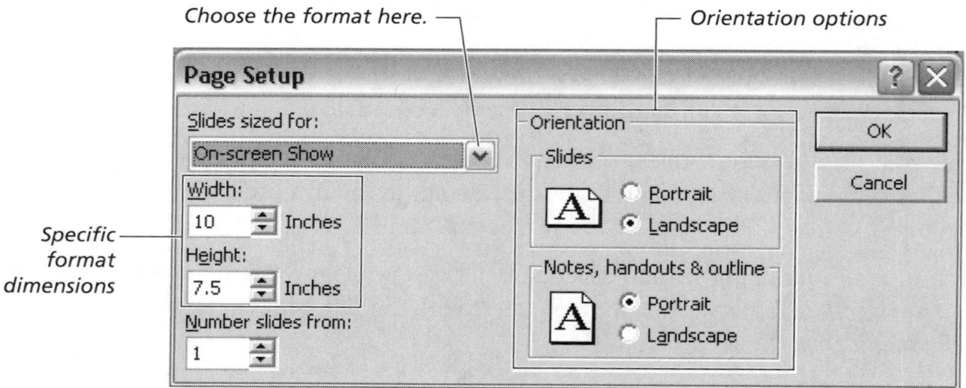

Figure 21.4 Choosing a slide show presentation format

The worst situation is going from the 35mm format to the "On-screen Show" format, which is narrower.

Why Should I Care About Which Fonts I Use?

Not every computer has the same cast of fonts. If you use something unique on your computer, you may discover that the same font doesn't exist on the computer you're presenting with or when you take the presentation disk to the printer for a hard copy.

The best solution is to stick with standard fonts: Times, Arial, Courier, plus a few others that tend to exist on every Windows computer.

Bullets also may present a problem; if you use unique bullets to mark a bulleted list, they may not be available on other Windows machines.

A potential solution in PowerPoint 2003/XP is to save the text as a picture and use the picture instead. For example, suppose you have a fancy font all formatted and created as your document's title. If so, follow these steps to convert it to a picture:

1. Click to select the fancy title.
2. Right-click the title and choose "Save As Picture" from the menu.

   This is shown in Figure 21.5.

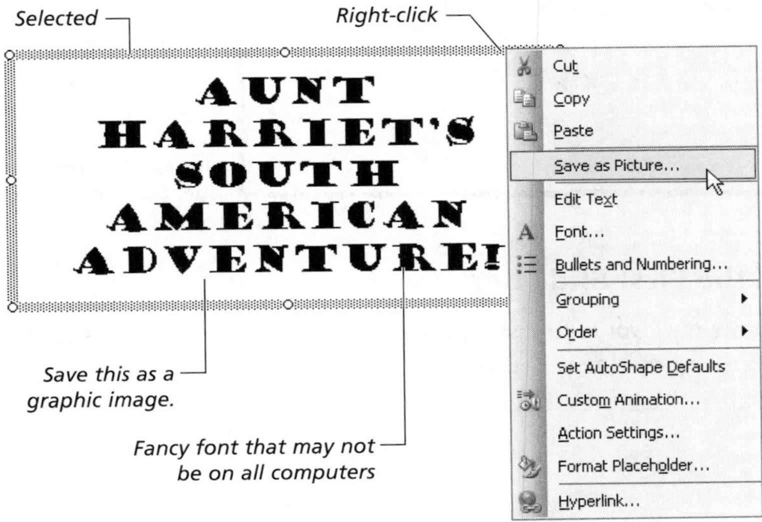

Figure 21.5 Saving text as a picture image

3. Use the Save As Picture dialog box to save the text to disk as an image; click the Save button after giving the file a location and a name.

   If you have a specific folder for the presentation, be sure to save the image into that one folder.
4. Back on the slide, press the Delete button on your keyboard to delete the current slide title.
5. Choose Insert ➢ Picture ➢ From File.
6. Use the Insert Picture dialog box to browse to the location where you saved the title picture; locate the picture and click the Insert button.

   And the title appears on the slide just as it did before, but it's a picture now (Figure 21.6); no need to worry about missing fonts.

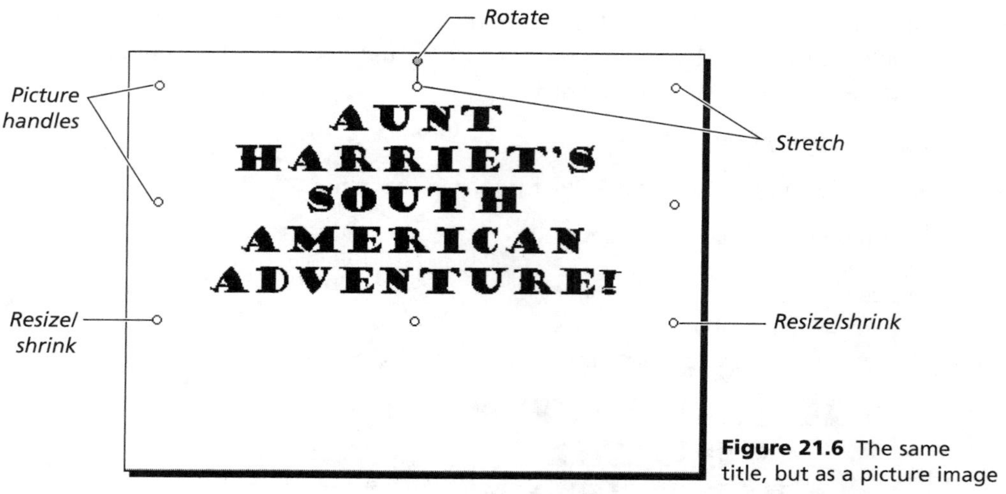

Figure 21.6 The same title, but as a picture image

What Should the First Slide Be?

Figure 21.7 shows my favorite first slide. Odd that in the years I've been using it, no one has really been fooled. Perhaps rotating it 90 degrees...?

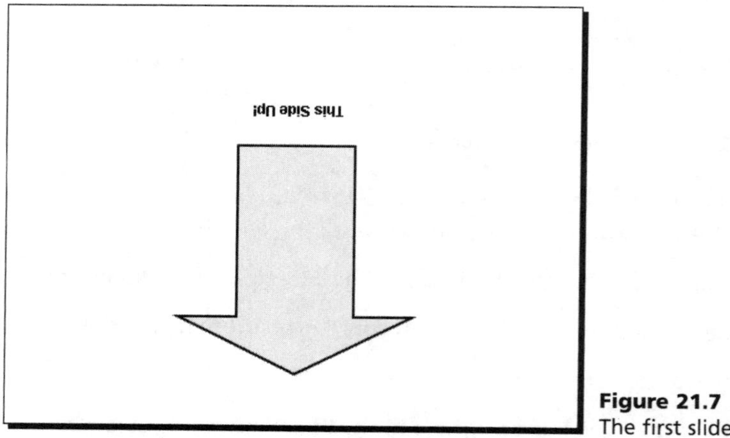

Figure 21.7 The first slide

Here are the steps to create such a slide:

1. Start with a blank slide.
2. Ensure that the Drawing toolbar is visible; choose View ➤ Toolbars ➤ Drawing if it's not.
3. Choose the up arrow from the Drawing toolbar's AutoShapes menu.

   This is shown in Figure 21.8.

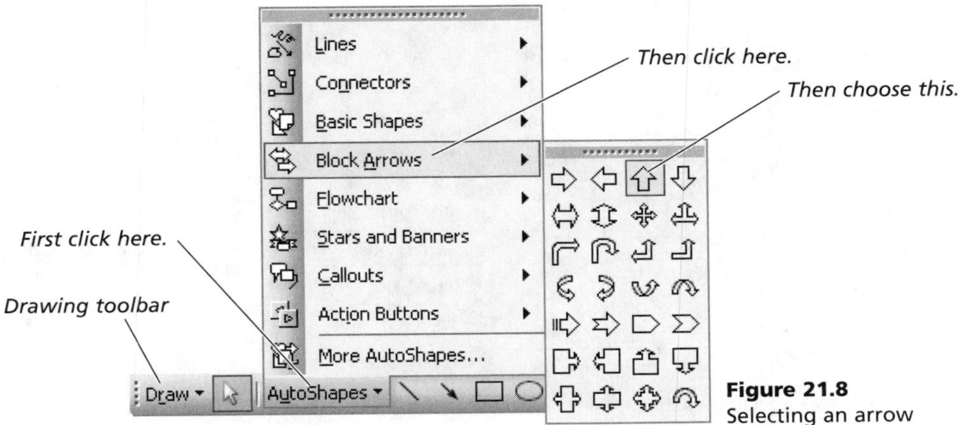

Figure 21.8
Selecting an arrow

4. Draw the arrow in the slide.

Drag the mouse from the upper left to the lower right, creating and sizing the arrow as you go.

5. Click the Fill icon and change the fill color to yellow.

You may need to choose the "More Fill Colors" item from the menu to select a bolder yellow than what appears in the menu.

6. Make the outline thicker by choosing a thicker line style from the Line Style button.

I chose 3 pts in my example.

7. Click the text box button to create the "This Side Up" text box.

Drag the mouse in the slide to create the text box.

8. Type `This Side Up!` inside the text box

9. Press Ctrl+E to center the text.

That's the old Word Justify Center keyboard command.

10. Select the text and press Ctrl+B to make it bold.

11. Select both the arrow shape and the text box.

You can drag the mouse around both or press and hold the Ctrl key as you click both objects.

12. On the Drawing toolbar choose Draw ➤ Align or Distribute ➤ Align Center.

Figure 21.9 can be of some help here; after you choose this command the two objects are aligned according to their vertical centers.

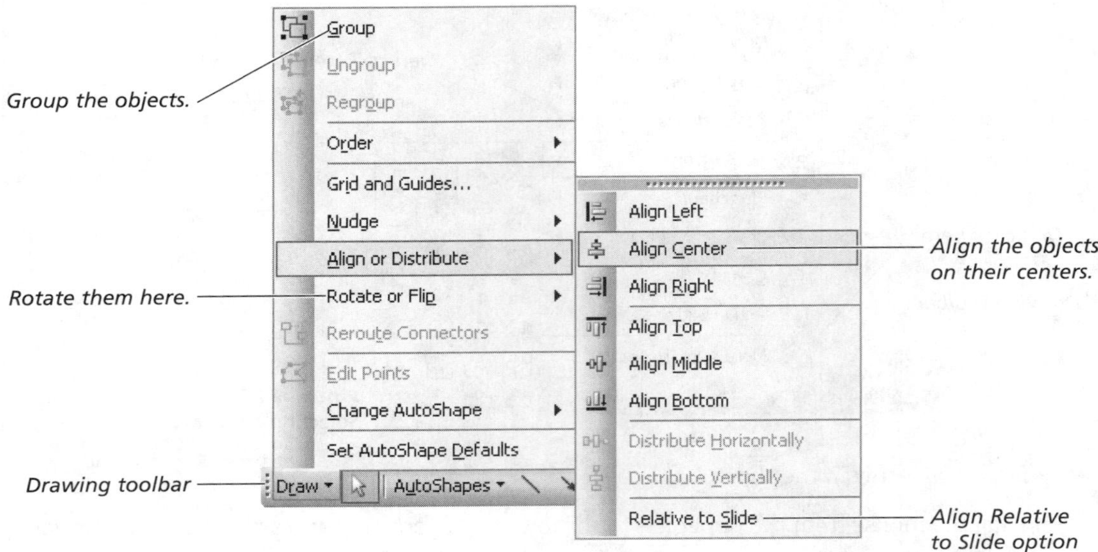

Figure 21.9 Finishing the slide with some Draw menu tricks

13. From the Drawing toolbar choose Draw ➤ Group.

This glues the two items together so that they're treated as one for the next operation.

14. From the Drawing toolbar choose Draw ➤ Rotate or Flip ➤ Rotate Left 90º.

This rotates the grouped items so that the arrow is pointing to the left.

15. Press Ctrl+Y.

The Repeat command, Ctrl+Y, rotates the image another 90 degrees, rendering it just like Figure 24.7.

With this image as your first slide, you're bound to set off your audience on the right foot. And while it may not fool people (as has been my experience), if you rotate the *second* slide the same way, then it really will cause people to wonder if something isn't wrong with the projector!

No, Serious: What Should the First Slide Be?

I prefer the first slide to be something to kick off the presentation, such as a title slide. Figure 21.10 shows an example of such a slide. You can introduce the talk, introduce yourself, present your company, or show a personal graphic.

Remember: Everyone will look at the first slide. It sets the tone for your presentation. And it may also be displayed for a few minutes while the crowd gets settled, so you can afford to be informative.

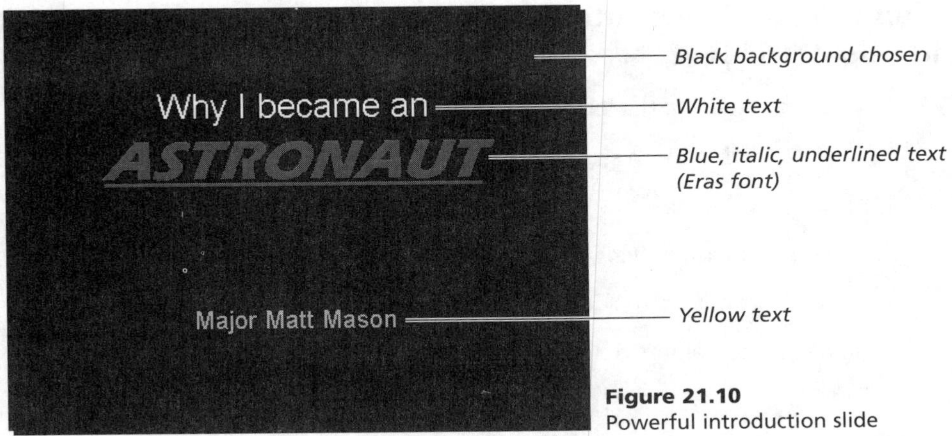

Figure 21.10
Powerful introduction slide

I Want to Change My Slide Design to Add My Picture to the Title!

Then you need to remember to select the proper format, such as the one shown in Figure 21.11. Here's how to change your slide's layout should you be inclined to do so:

Figure 21.11
A different layout for your title slide

1. View the slide you want to change.

2. Choose Format ➤ Slide Layout from the menu.

3. Choose a new layout option from the list.

4a. In PowerPoint 2003/XP, point the mouse at the right side of the layout, click the triangle button that appears, and then choose "Apply to Selected Slides" from the pop-up menu.

4b. In PowerPoint 2000, click the Apply button.

The new design is applied to your slide. If there are similar elements (titles, bulleted lists) in both the previous and new layout, they are shifted to reflect the new layout.

Continue building your slide.

You can close the task pane in PowerPoint 2003/XP when you're done with it.

How Can I Get a Picture into the Slide and Not Have to Mess with the Stupid Clip Art Thing?

Even if there is the Silly Clip Art Guy in the image, do this:

1. Click once to select the region the Clip Art Guy lives in.
2. Choose Insert ➤ Picture ➤ From File.
3. Use the Insert Picture dialog box to locate the image you want to insert.
4. Click the Insert button to add that image to your slide.

   The image is then plopped down into the slide, available for further manipulation, as shown in Figure 21.12.

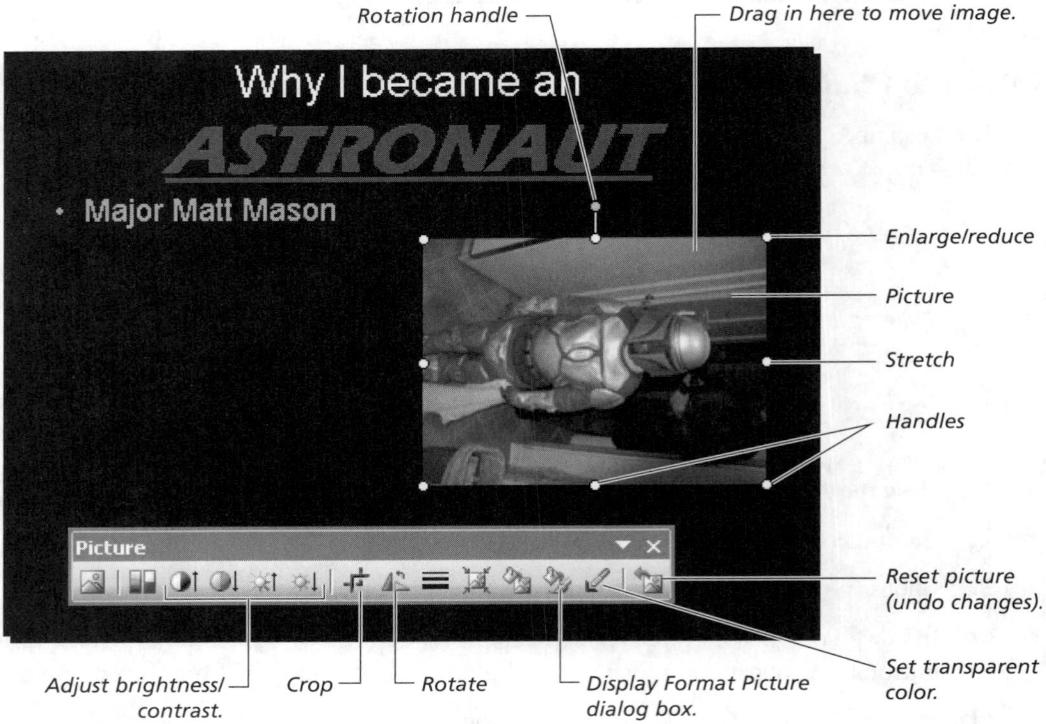

Figure 21.12 Editing an image in a slide

If the Picture toolbar doesn't automatically appear, right-click the image and choose "Show Picture Toolbar" from the pop-up menu.

Can I Change Bullets into Regular Text or Vice-Versa?

My editors tell me that you shouldn't bullet only one item, as shown in Figure 21.12. In that case, you should remove the bullet, unless you want all the editors in the audience to sit and silently squirm as they wish they could whip out a giant red marker to correct the slide. Heh, heh.

To un-bullet a single line of text, click to select that line and then click the Bullets button on PowerPoint's Formatting toolbar. Likewise, you can add bullets this way by selecting the text and clicking the Bullets button to add bullets. Bang! Bang! Bang!

You Must Know This: Changing the Type of Bullet

You turn the bullets on and off by using the Bullets button, but to change the type of bullet used, you must employ the Format ➤ Bullets and Numbering command, which is instant déjà vu if you're used to working with Bullets and Numbering in Microsoft Word.

The Bullets and Numbering dialog box displays a wealth of bullet (and numbering) options for your text. Plus you can choose new bullets by clicking the Customize button or even select a picture to be used as a bullet by clicking the Picture button. Oh what fun.

My Text Is Too Large for Its Area.

Two things you can do: First, make the area larger; grab one of the eight "handles" on the area and drag it with the mouse to make the area larger.

Second, you can change the size of your text: Select all of the text, and then use the Decrease Font Size button to make the text smaller than it is.

Any Way to Exactly Center This Text?

To center any text on a slide, use the Draw menu on the Drawing toolbar. Follow these steps:

1. Summon the Drawing toolbar: View ➤ Toolbars ➤ Drawing.
2. Click the Draw button, and from the menu choose Align or Distribute ➤ Relative to Slide.

   This command changes the menu so that the alignment options in the menu are relative to the slide itself and not to other objects on the slide. (See Figure 21.9.)
3. Click to select the box containing the title or other object you want centered.
4. Click the Draw button and choose Align or Distribute ➤ Align Center.

   The object will be perfectly centered on the slide.

The top of the "Align or Distribute" submenu indicates that it can be "torn off" and floated like a toolbar. If you plan on doing a lot of aligning on your slides, just tear that menu off and use it like a toolbar.

My Text Won't Appear in the Outline!

Why are you using the Outline? No one uses the Outline. Outlines are boring and they're an indication that you have a boring slide show, meaning that it's mostly text, which is just the most unforgivable sin you could ever commit against a willing audience.

All-text slides are BORING!

I would suppose that one way to use the Outline thing in PowerPoint would be to start with the Outline and then build a show around it. But I don't know anyone who does that either. So this problem is a moot one. Regardless:

The biggest reason for not seeing your text in the useless Outline window is that you're not using the predefined slide layouts. Only by using those layouts will your text be displayed in the Outline view. Otherwise, if you just create a text box for the text, nothing appears in the Outline, as shown in Figure 21.13.

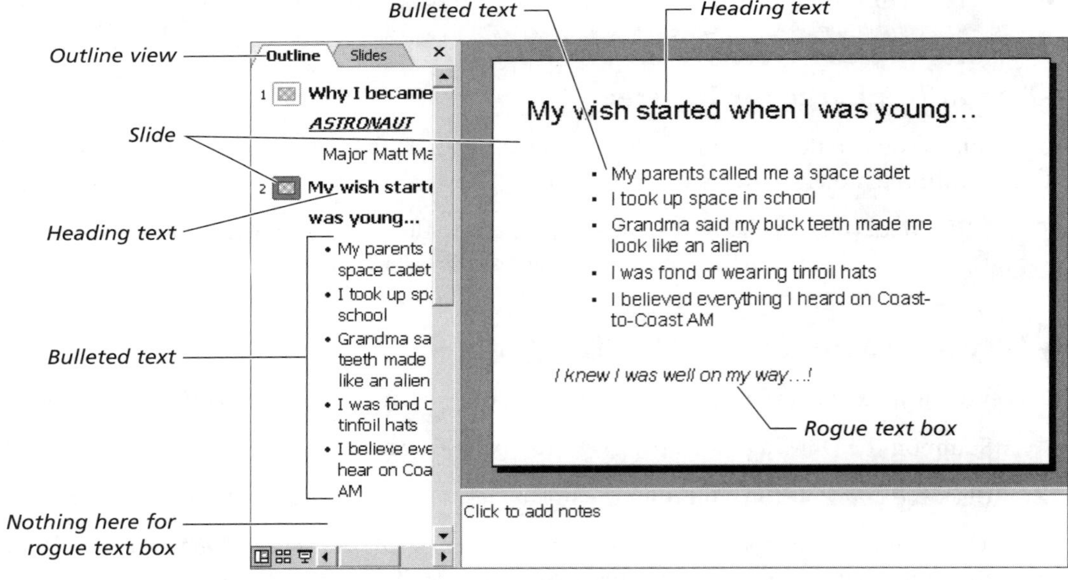

Figure 21.13 Text on the slide and in the outline

Unlike other Office applications, you cannot assign an Outline-level style to any random shape or text box you create and throw text into. It's just not done, nor is it needed because, well, *no one uses the Outline.*

One way to get at the styles is to use the View ➤ Master ➤ Slide Master command. You can edit the Master slide style in that window (Figure 21.14), but it's really a waste of time.

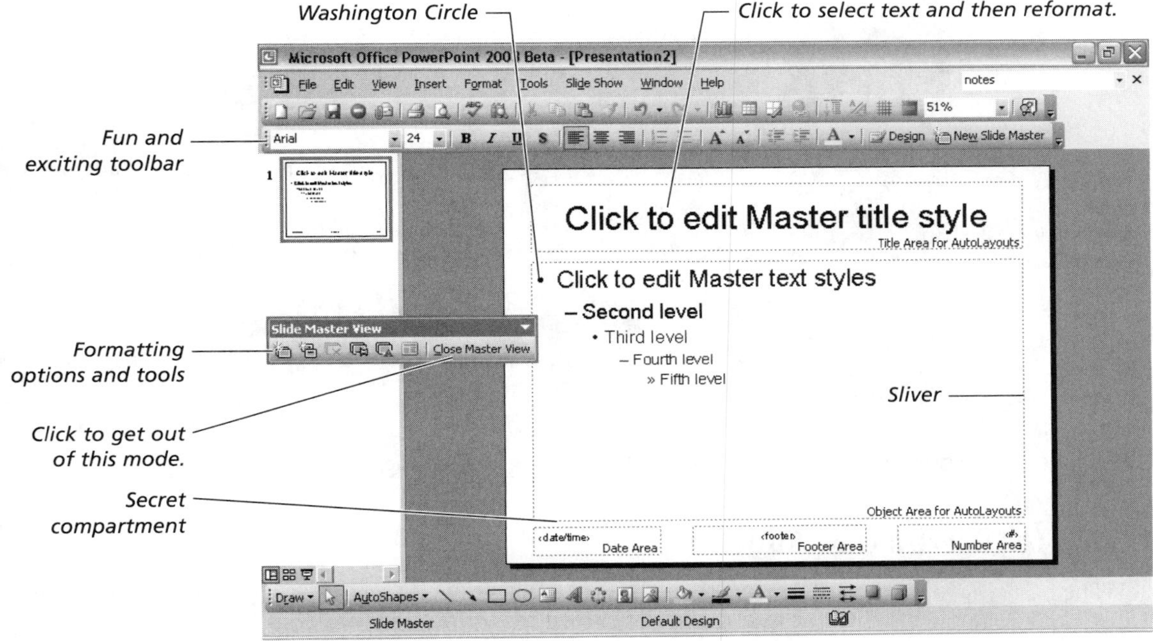

Figure 21.14 Wasting time editing the Master slide

What's the Easiest Way to Change the Order of My Slides?

Dragging the slides around with the mouse sufficiently rearranges them, almost like a deck of cards.

First, select the Slide Sorter view from the lower-left corner of the window. This allows you to see your slide show all splayed out like an open drawer full of 35mm slides, as shown in Figure 21.15.

Second, to move a slide, drag it with the mouse. Release the mouse button when the mouse pointer is between two other slides, or before the first or after the last slide. You'll see a vertical bar appear, showing you where the slide will be moved. Release the mouse button to complete the move. This shuffles all the slides and changes the order of that particular slide to where you dropped it.

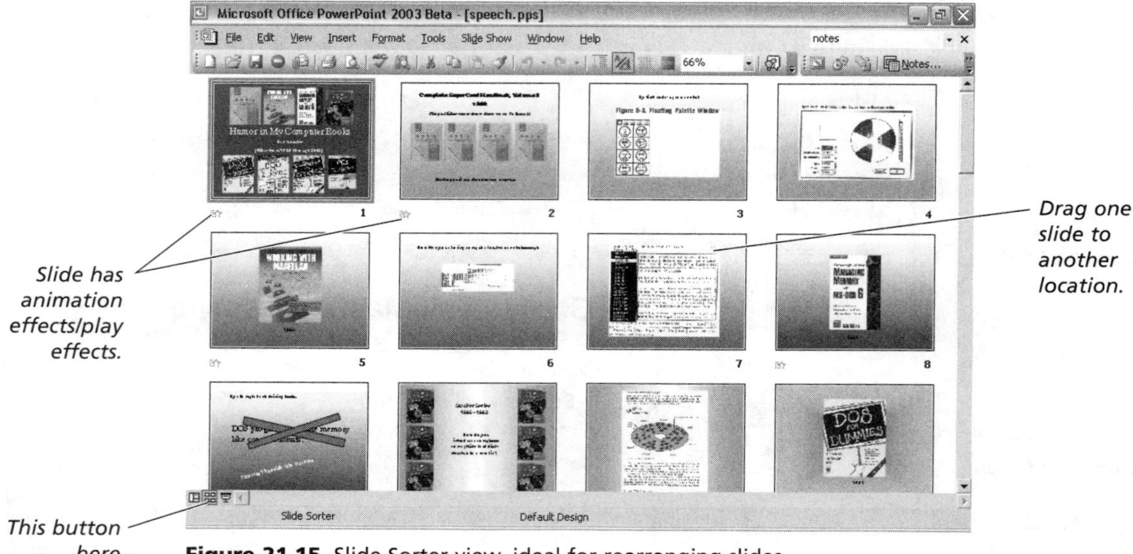

Figure 21.15 Slide Sorter view, ideal for rearranging slides

I Need to Insert a New Slide!

The best way to do this is from Normal view with the Slide panel selected for PowerPoint 2003/XP, as shown in Figure 21.16. Or from Slide view in PowerPoint 2000.

First, click to select the slide *before* the insert. Then click the New Slide button to insert the new blank slide *after* the selected slide.

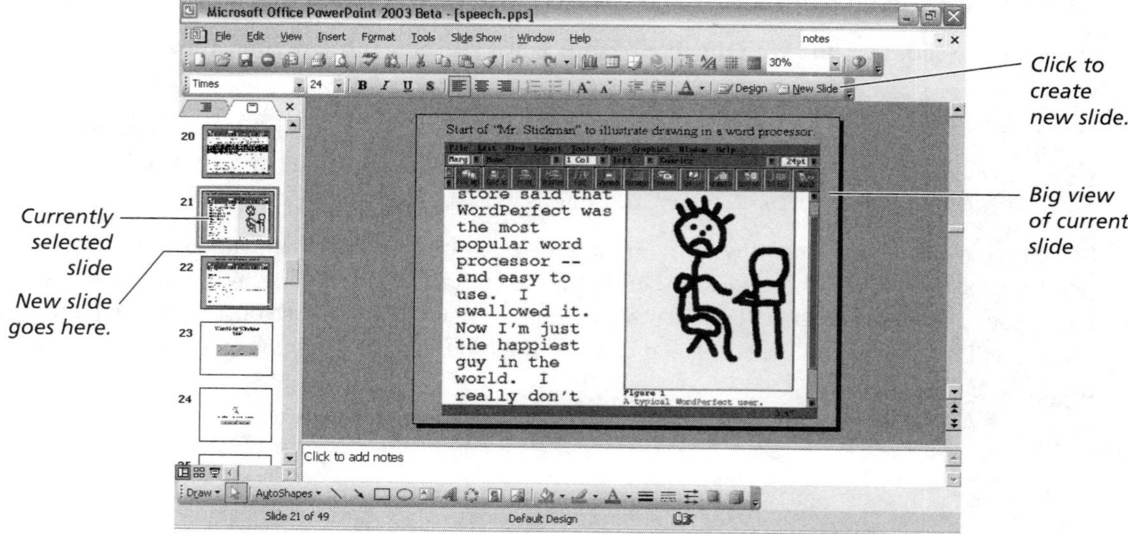

Figure 21.16 Inserting a new slide

I Need to Copy a Slide from One Show to Another Show!

This is a lot easier than it sounds, providing that you follow these steps:

1. Open both slide shows.
2. Use the Window menu to choose the first slide show, the one containing the original slide.
3. Display the slide you want to copy.
4. Right-click the slide's icon on the left side of the window and choose Edit ➤ Copy from the pop-up menu.

   You can use just about any view here; locate the slide's "mini icon" on the left side of the window. Refer to Figure 21.17.

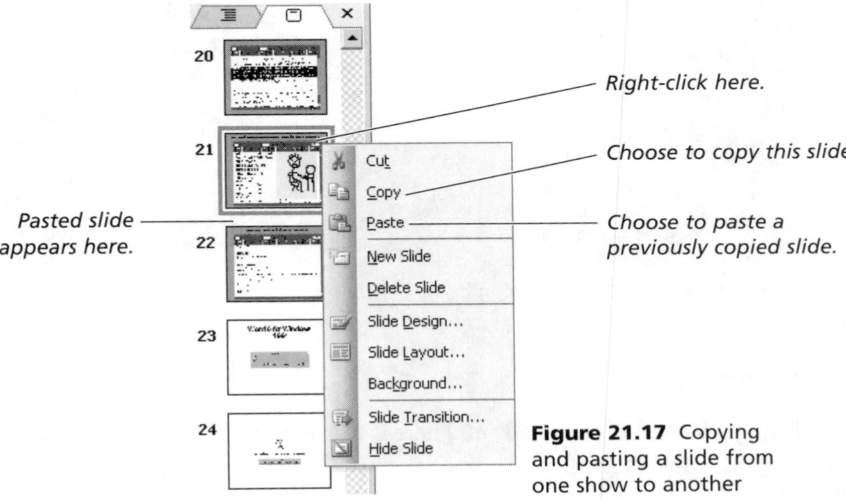

Figure 21.17 Copying and pasting a slide from one show to another

5. Use the Window menu to choose the second slide show.
6. On the left side of the window, right-click the slide before the spot where you want to paste.

   So the pasted slide appears *after* the selected slide.
7. Choose Edit ➤ Paste.

   You can close whichever slide show you want and continue working on the other one.

What's the Point of Speaker Notes?

Please don't read your slides! Use the slides to remind you of what to say, but not verbatim. If you need help, then take advantage of the speaker notes. These you can type in as you create the slide show, as shown in Figure 21.1.

To have your notes displayed for you when you deliver the speech, right-click the slide show and choose Screen ➤ Speaker Notes from the pop-up menu. The Speaker Notes dialog box then appears, from which you can read the notes.

My advice is to have your notes prepared separately from the screen. To print out a copy, choose File ➤ Print. In the Print dialog box, choose "Notes Pages" from the "Print What" drop-down list.

I Need to Do a Search and Replace through My Entire Slide Show.

This is easy to do—for text: Just choose Edit ➤ Replace or press the Ctrl+H keyboard shortcut, which is the same keyboard shortcut used by Word for its Replace command. Even the dialog box looks similar, though much simpler (shown in Figure 21.18).

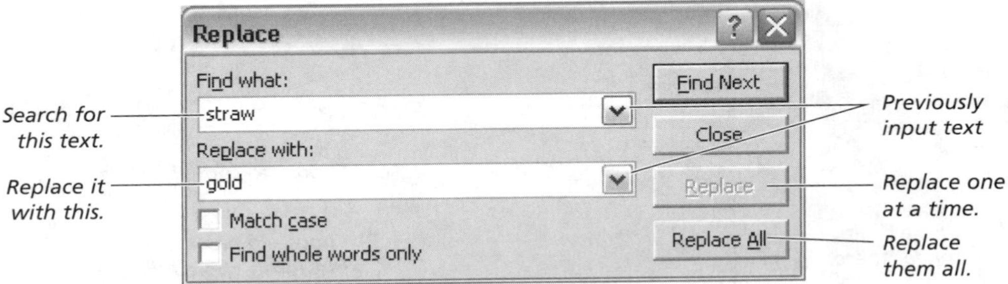

Figure 21.18 Replace dialog box

Do I Really Need a Summary?

This depends entirely on your style of presentation. There is a school that says: Tell them what you're going to tell them, tell them, and then tell them what you told them. Or, put another way; tell them three times in order to drive the message home. If the third time is in a summary, then so be it.

NERD'S CORNER

Cocktail Party Trivia Part XI

MIKE: I never need notes. I've given the same old talk over and over so many times I can do it with my eyes closed.

MARY: Like your audience?

BRUCE: Well, you should brush up on the new sales figures; it's embarrassing when you don't read the slides to see what the new figures are.

MARY: Or when the audience corrects you.

BRUCE: And it's the chairman of the board.

What Should the Last Slide Be?

There is no official preference for a last slide, though because this slide is often projected longer than others, such as during an after-show Q&A session, you might consider putting your name and contact information on the last slide. That way, people can copy it down without having to ask you or come up and get your business card later.

As comic relief, your last card could look like the one I designed in Figure 21.19. It also helps if you assign the Windows error "bleep" sound to play when the slide is displayed.

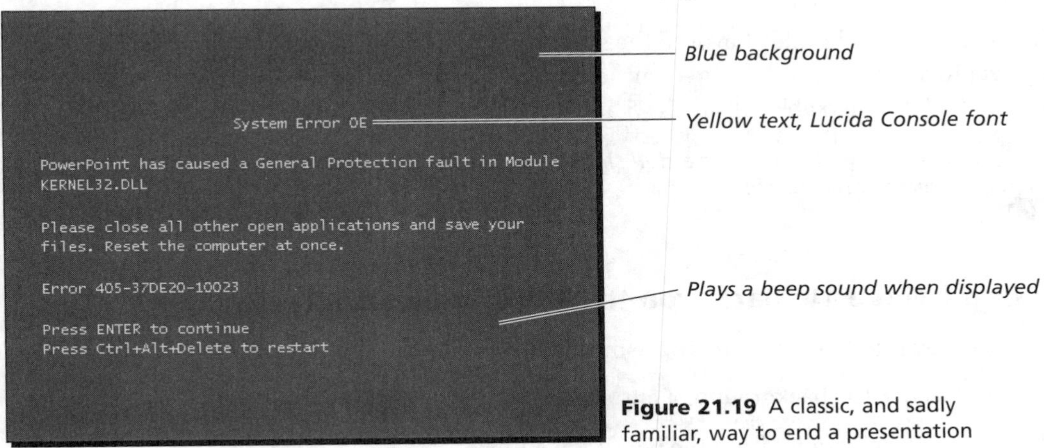

Figure 21.19 A classic, and sadly familiar, way to end a presentation

KEYBOARD MASTER

Slide Presentation Keys to Save Your Butt

I don't click the mouse to advance slides. Instead, I rely on having memorized the following keyboard shortcuts, valuable when giving a presentation:

Space, Enter, N, Down arrow, Right arrow
Display the next slide or next animation on a slide.

Up arrow, Left arrow, P, Backspace
Display the previous slide or back up through a slide's animation.

A, =
Show or hide the pointer and navigation box.

B, . (period)
Quickly display a blank black slide.

W, , (comma)
Quickly display a blank white slide.

Ctrl+S
Display a summary of slides/Go to Slide dialog box.

Esc, - (hyphen)
Cancel show, stop.

Spicing Up Your Slide Show

The most abhorrent slide show sin you can commit is the all-text presentation. Don't be wimpy and counter that you just don't have any graphics or charts to help you. That's nonsense. It is your duty to avoid the all-text slide show at all cost.

What you want to strive for is the lively presentation. Your audience craves excitement like a dry sponge yearns for water. Fortunately, there are many simple tricks to make even the dullest of slide shows shine with wild creativity.

As the clove of garlic adds flavor to the salad, as insanity adds genius to the art, the sections that follow provide the essential ingredient to add *oo-la-la* to your slide shows. Call it zest. Call it punch. Call it remarkable relish. It's what will make your slide shows stand out from the crowd.

The one-word cure for a dull slide show: animation. As my PowerPoint guru tells me: Animation is bitchin'.

How Can I Make My Backgrounds More Interesting?

The first key is to know that there are more background possibilities than meet the eye. Observe:

1. Right-click the background of any slide.
2. Choose Background from the pop-up menu.

   The small and timid Background dialog box appears, innocently concealing its power. The secret to this dialog box lies in its unnamed drop-down list, as shown in Figure 21.20.

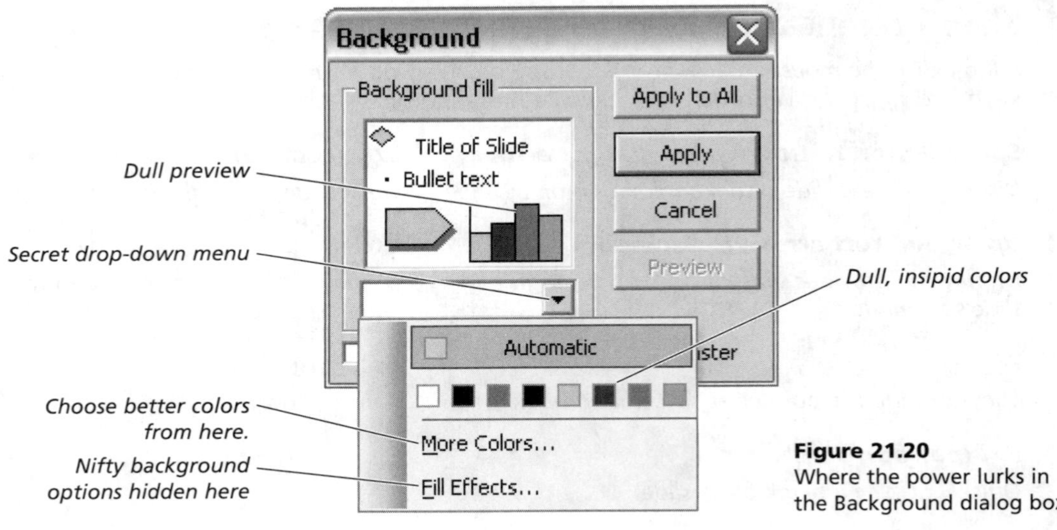

Figure 21.20
Where the power lurks in the Background dialog box

3. From the secret drop-down list, choose "Fill Effects."

   Refer to Figure 21.20. This displays the Fill Effects dialog box, shown in Figure 21.21. Now you can bless your background with something better than a solid color or boring old white.

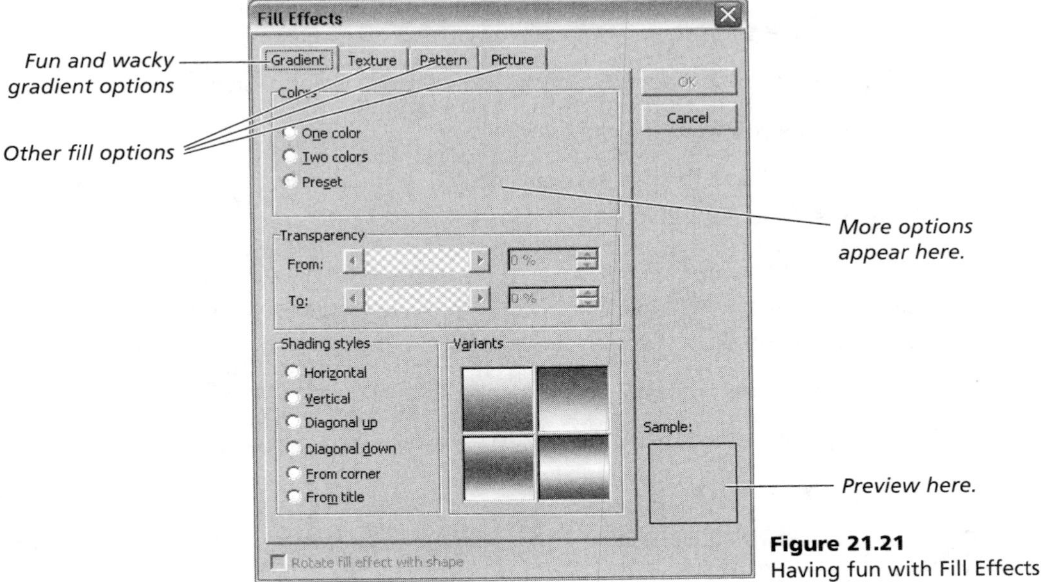

Figure 21.21
Having fun with Fill Effects

4. Select a background.

   I like the Gradient tab myself. It's a great place to play. To get a hint at what it can do, choose the Preset option from the Colors area. Then click to select any of the preset colors from the drop-down list that appears.

   The Texture tab contains predefined backgrounds that can give your slides that "marbled" or "woven" look, but if you want to insert an image from the hard drive and use it as the background, then you would use the Picture tab. Click the Select Picture button there to browse for any image on the hard drive.

   The Pattern tab is my least favorite. I just find the patterns rather silly.

5. Click OK to select your background and close the Fill Effects dialog box.

6. To apply the background to a single slide, click the Apply button; otherwise click the Apply to All button to apply the background effect to all your slides.

Can I Animate the Backgrounds?

No, and you wouldn't want to: It would be distracting. Even subtle animation, such as twinkling starts, will pull focus from the meat of your slides.

How Can I Make the Slide Changes More Interesting?

Slide changes are called *transitions*. Normally, one slide merely disappears and the next slide appears. But you can set it up so that each slide appears in a new and interesting way or that each slide appears in the same way. It's all about transitions. Here's how to make it happen:

1. Choose View ➤ Slide Sorter.

This displays your slides so you see an overview of the entire show.

2. Click the slide you want to transition into.

Any slide other than the first slide will do. What you're selecting is how this slide will appear on the screen.

3. Choose Slide Show ➤ Slide Transition.

The Slide Transition task pane appears in PowerPoint 2003/XP; in PowerPoint 2000 you get a Slide Transition dialog box. Both work the same way.

4. Choose a transition from the drop-down or scrollable list.

For example, choose "Box In" and observe the preview to see what happens.

Don't be shy! Try a few.

In PowerPoint 2003/XP, ensure that there is a checkmark by AutoPreview in the bottom of the task pane.

5a. In PowerPoint 2003/XP, you're done.

5b. In PowerPoint 2000, click the Apply button to apply that transition to the slide.

6. Choose another slide and repeat these steps to apply a new transition into it.

In PowerPoint 2003/XP, you can just click a slide in the Slide Sorter view and then choose a transition from the scrollable list. In PowerPoint 2000, you must click to select a slide and then choose Slide Show ➤ Slide Transition to set its transition options.

The transition speed is set just below the box where you choose the transition. Not all the transitions need to be fast.

Any Way to Improve the Basic Bulleted List?

I like to use what I call "check-off lists" instead of bulleted lists. These are lists where the items appear one after the other as opposed to all at once. This effect is accomplished through simple animation. Follow these steps:

1. Start with a blank slide.

   You don't need nor do you want any predefined boxes.

2. Select the Text Box tool from the Drawing toolbar and drag to create the first bulleted item in the list.

   To summon the Drawing toolbar, choose View ➢ Toolbars ➢ Drawing.

   Place the text box high on the slide; it is the first of many, as shown in Figure 21.22.

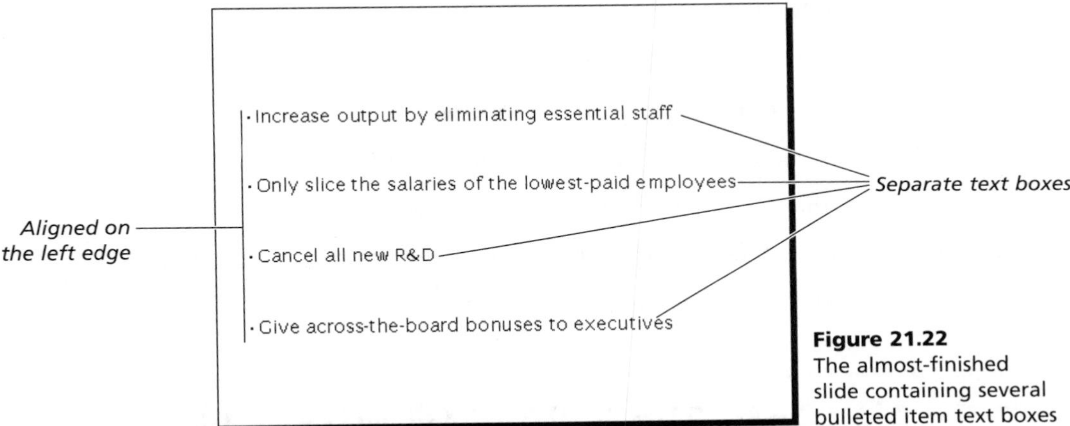

• Increase output by eliminating essential staff
• Only slice the salaries of the lowest-paid employees
• Cancel all new R&D
• Give across-the-board bonuses to executives
Separate text boxes
Aligned on the left edge

Figure 21.22
The almost-finished slide containing several bulleted item text boxes

3. Type in the bulleted list text.
4. Format the text, if you like.
5. Click the Bullets button to make the line of text a bullet.
6. Duplicate the text box to create the next item.

   You're not creating a block of bullets but actually separate text boxes, each containing a bulleted item. Here is a quick way to duplicate the text box:

   a. Click to select the existing text box.
   b. Press the Ctrl and Shift keys.
   c. Point the mouse at the "fuzzy border" around the text.
   d. Drag the text box down a wee bit.
   e. Release the mouse button and the Ctrl and Shift keys.

      By holding the Ctrl key you create a copy of the box; holding the Shift key ensures that the copy is dragged parallel to the first box.

Don't worry about spacing yet or even alignment. We'll fix that in a few steps.

7. Continue creating and duplicating the text boxes until you have something similar to what's shown in Figure 21.22.

   Fill in each text box with its proper text and formatting. Don't forget to add the bullets!

When you're done, you may want to double-check the alignment of the objects. This is done from the Draw menu on the Drawing toolbar:

8. Select all the text boxes on the slide.

   I use the Ctrl+click method to select each box with the mouse.

9. From the Drawing toolbar choose Draw ➤ Align or Distribute ➤ Align Left.

   That ensures that each item is lined up on its left edge.

10. From the Drawing toolbar choose Draw ➤ Align or Distribute ➤ Distribute Vertically.

    That ensures that the items are all evenly spaced.

You Must Know This: Bulleted Lists Can Be Displayed One at a Time Anyway

The steps in the section "Any Way to Improve the Basic Bulleted List?" do tell you how to make elements on a slide appear one after the other, but the ugly truth is that PowerPoint can be coerced into displaying items in a bulleted list one after the other anyway. It's rather automatic:

First, create the bulleted list, or format any text as a bulleted list by clicking the Bullets button on the Formatting toolbar. Second, choose an animation for the chunk of text: Right-click it and select "Custom Animation" from the pop-up menu.

In PowerPoint 2003/XP, set things up as described in the text nearby. After creating the effect, click the down-pointing triangle on the right end of the effect in the Custom Animation task pane. Choose "Effect Options" from the menu. In the Effect Options dialog box, choose the Text Animation tab. Choose "By 1st Level Paragraphs" from the "Group Text" drop-down list. Click OK.

In PowerPoint 2000, in the Custom Animation dialog box, Effects tab, choose "All At Once" from the "Introduce Text" drop-down list. Then put a checkmark by "Grouped" and keep "1st" in the "Level Paragraphs" drop-down list.

By making these changes, you're directing PowerPoint to reveal the text in a text box one paragraph at a time. This is yet another way to animate an otherwise boring bulleted list.

Now you add the animation. This is done by setting how each element appears when the slide shows up on the screen. Sadly, this is done differently between PowerPoint 2003/XP and PowerPoint 2000.

11. Right-click to select the first item in the list, the item you want to appear first.

In this case, it's the first bulleted item.

12. Choose "Custom Animation" from the pop-up menu.

13a. In PowerPoint 2003/XP, click the Add Effect button/menu in the Custom Animation task pane.

13b. In PowerPoint 2000, click the Effects tab in the Custom Animation dialog box.

14a. Choose Entrance ➤ Appear from the Add Effect button's menu.

If you don't see "Appear," choose Entrance ➤ More Effects and then find and choose the Appear effect from the list in the dialog box displayed; click OK.

14b. Choose Appear from the drop-down list in the "Entry Animation and Sound" area, and then click OK.

Now you've set the animation for how the first item is going to appear on the slide. In this case, it just appears when you click the mouse.

15. Repeat Steps 11 through 14 for the rest of the items on the list.

When you're done, it's time to preview how the slide appears and how each item in the list animates. Press the F5 key to preview your slide show. (In PowerPoint 2003/XP you can press Shift+F5 to preview a single slide.) Press the spacebar or click the mouse to see how the items appear. And, voilá, you have a check-off list.

Note that these appearance effects can be added to any objects on the slide, not just bulleted items or text. Simply set the animation to have the element "appear," and you can control when it shows up on the slide.

How Can I Really Fancy Things Up with Objects That Appear Automatically?

Have fun with your presentations! If you can imagine it appearing on the slide, chances are that PowerPoint can do it.

Shown in Figure 21.23 is a slide that has five animations on it, three of which work on the mouse click and the last two of which roll out automatically. The figure describes what happens. The following steps show how the animation was done.

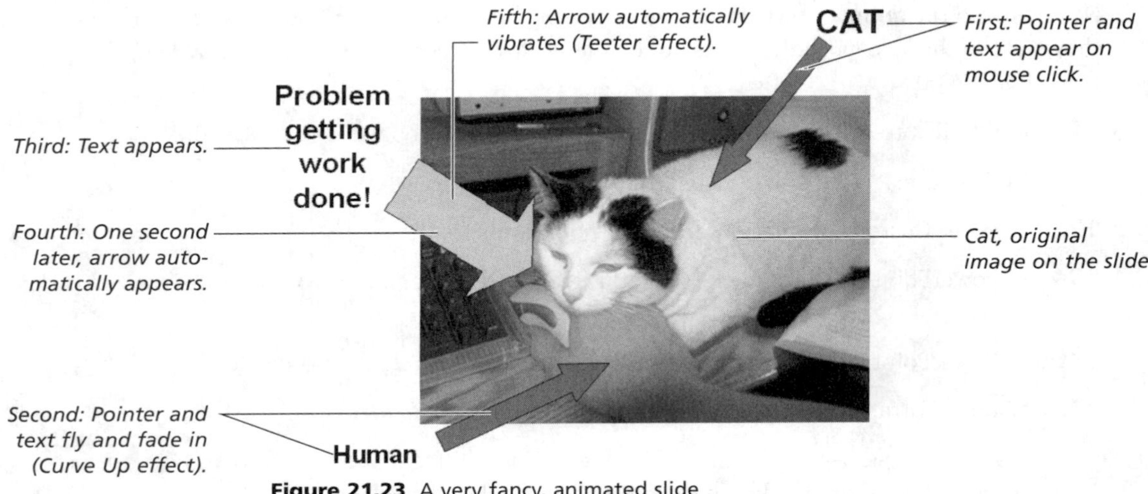

Figure 21.23 A very fancy, animated slide

The slide starts out with the image of the cat. Next, I created the arrow and the word "Cat" and grouped them together to form a single object.

To group two items, select both items and then from the Draw button on the Drawing toolbar, choose Group.

I also grouped the text "Human" with the arrow pointing to the hand. Then I created the text "Problem getting work done" in a text box. Finally, I created, rotated, colored, and placed the last arrow.

All told, the slide has five objects:

- The cat picture
- The grouped AutoShape arrow and "Cat" text box
- The grouped AutoShape arrow and "Human" text box
- The "Problem getting work done" text box
- The big AutoShape arrow

To animate the first object, I clicked the Cat-arrow group and set it simply to "Appear" on a mouse click.

The second object, the arrow and "Human" text box, also merely appears on the mouse click, but I chose the animation style "Curve Up" effect instead of just appearing. (This is similar to the "Peek" effect in PowerPoint 2000.)

The third object, the text box "Problem getting work done" also merely appears, just as the first object did.

I wanted the last object, the big arrow, to appear after a delay of one second. The following sections tell how I carried this out.

Nifty Animation in PowerPoint 2003/XP

To animate the large arrow so that it automatically appears and then automatically teeters, follow these steps:

1. Right-click to select the object, choosing "Custom Animation" from the pop-up menu.

   The Custom Animation task pane appears, if it's not there already.

2. From the Add Effect button, choose Entrance ➢ Appear.

   The object will appear...*but* after a time delay. Still, you have to choose what it does first and then set the timer.

3. From the Start drop-down list, choose "After Previous."

   It's not a mouse click or keyboard tap that displays the big arrow but a timer.

4. From the effect's menu in the task pane, choose Timing.

   Refer to Figure 21.24 to see where to click. This displays the Appear dialog box, Timing tab.

5. Into the Delay box enter 1 second.

   So the effect starts one second after the previous item appears.

6. Click OK.

   Now after the big arrow appears (after the delay), I'd like it to wiggle. To do this, you need to add a *second* effect to that object:

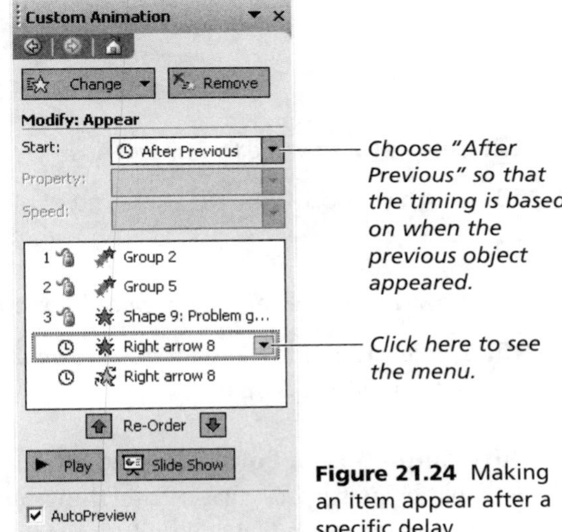

Figure 21.24 Making an item appear after a specific delay

7. Right-click the object again and choose "Custom Animation" from the pop-up menu.

8. In the task pane, choose Emphasis ➢ Teeter from the Add Effect button's menu.

   If you don't see "Teeter" there, then choose Emphasis ➢ More Effects and locate the Teeter effect in the dialog box that appears.

   Note that a new entry for the object appears in the list of effects.

9. From the Start drop-down list, choose "After Previous."

   Again, this is an automatically timed effect.

10. If you don't want the object to blink in another color, choose its original color from the Color drop-down list.

11. Click the down arrow by the effect (Figure 21.24) and choose the Timing option from the pop-up menu.

    This displays the Timing dialog box, as shown in Figure 21.25. Here you can adjust the timing for when the image starts to animate as well as timing for the animation itself.

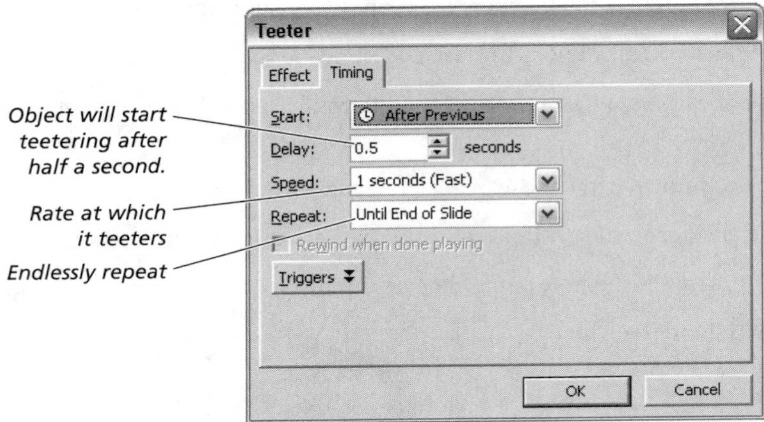

Figure 21.25
Setting the Teeter effect to endlessly repeat

12. Set the Delay value to `0.5` seconds.
13. Set the Repeat value to "Until End of Slide."
14. Click OK.

    Now the arrow eternally wiggles (or teeters).

15. Preview the slide show to see if it's what you want; press Shift+F5 or click the Slide Show button in the task pane.

Nifty Animation in PowerPoint 2000

It should be no surprise that setting things up in PowerPoint 2000 is actually easier than in PowerPoint 2003/XP. The main difference is the lack of advanced animation options, but personally I prefer the dialog box approach to Microsoft's horrid task pane design. The Custom Animation dialog box is shown in Figure 21.26.

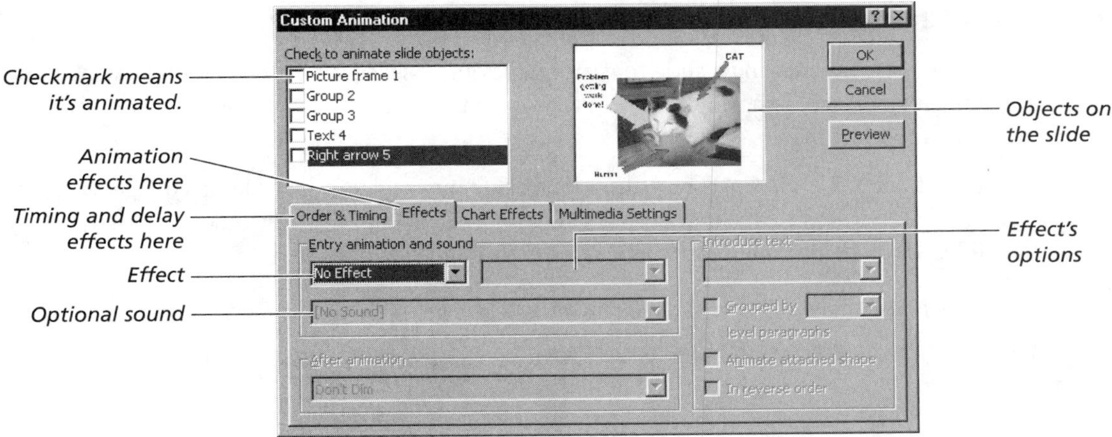

Figure 21.26 Animating the slide in PowerPoint 2000

Follow these steps to animate the slide:

1. Click to select "Group 2" from the list of slide objects.
2. Choose Appear as the effect.

   Choose this from the drop-down list.

   There is no need to set this effect based on a mouse click; that's done automatically.
3. Click to select the second group, "Group 3," from the list.
4. Also choose Appear as the effect.
5. Click to select the text box and have it appear as well.

   Finally you come to the big arrow, which you want to appear automatically after the last object ("Text 4" in Figure 21.26).
6. Click to put a checkmark by the last object.
7. Choose Appear as the effect.
8. Click the Order & Timing tab.
9. Click to select the Automatically option.
10. Input 1 second into the box.

    And that object appears after the previous object shows up, plus the one-second delay.

Alas, you cannot add a second animation option to the object, as you can in other versions of PowerPoint.

How Can I Change the Order of What Gets Animated?

The best way to avoid creating a slide that animates out of sequence is to keep previewing and playing the slides. Double-check to confirm that everything runs right. If not, then you can change the order of things.

In PowerPoint 2003/XP, the Custom Animation task pane is where the order is changed. The animations are listed in the task pane, shown in Figure 21.27. Note how they link up to their objects on the slide, which helps you identify which animation goes where.

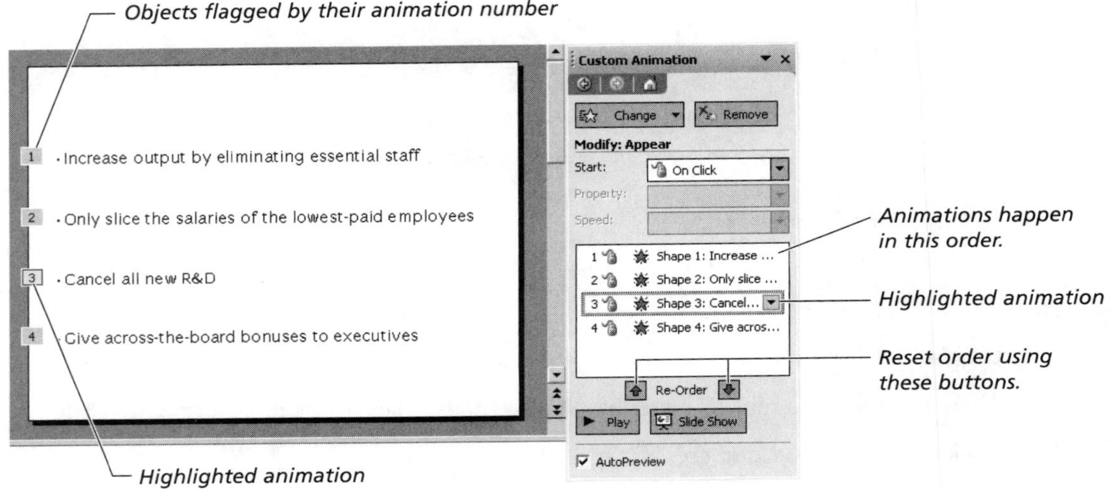

Figure 21.27 Re-ordering animations in PowerPoint 2003/XP.

To change the order, use the up arrow and down arrow buttons by Re-Order, as shown in Figure 21.27. Then be sure to click the Slide Show button to preview what you have, making certain it's what you want.

Be aware that any slides triggered by an activity (as opposed to a mouse click) are also affected when you move things around. Check your timing!

In PowerPoint 2000, the Order & Timing tab in the Custom Animation dialog box is used to change the order of your animations, as shown in Figure 21.28. Note that you can see which objects in the slide are selected by clicking them, as shown in the figure. Use the up or down arrow to change the order of a highlighted object.

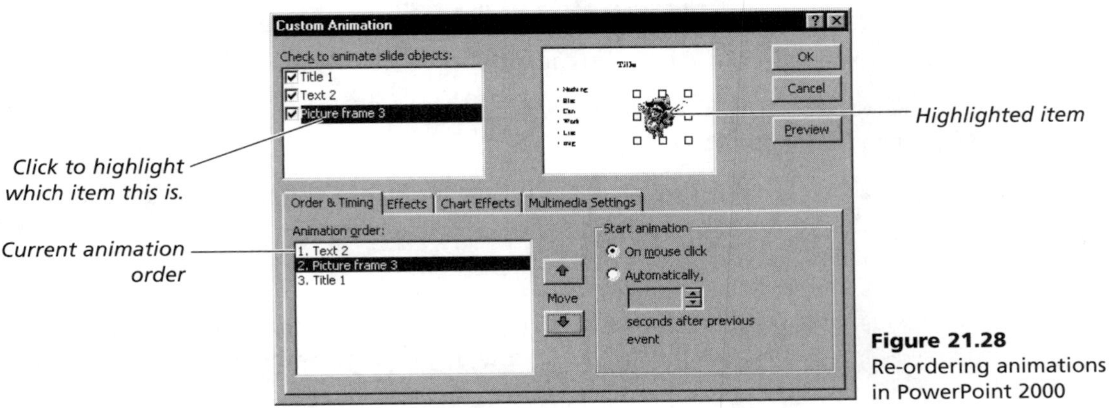

Figure 21.28 Re-ordering animations in PowerPoint 2000

How Can I Use Animation to Subtly Underline a Point in My Presentation?

Animation doesn't need to be complex or obnoxious to be effective. Consider Figure 21.29. That's a simple quote, but to emphasize what's important an animation appears that "circles" the vital text, which is shown in Figure 21.30. To make such a thing, follow these steps:

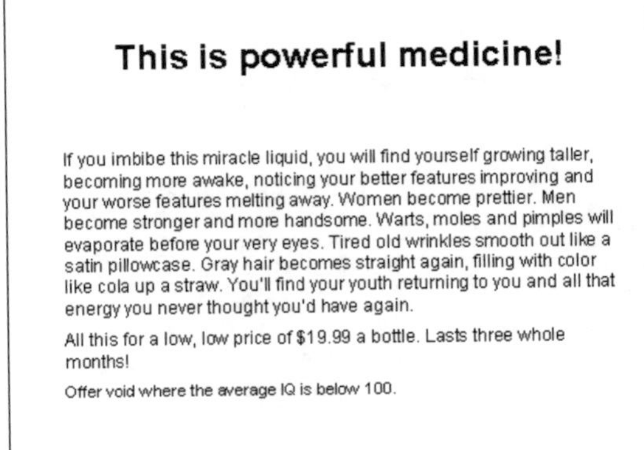

Figure 21.29 The original slide

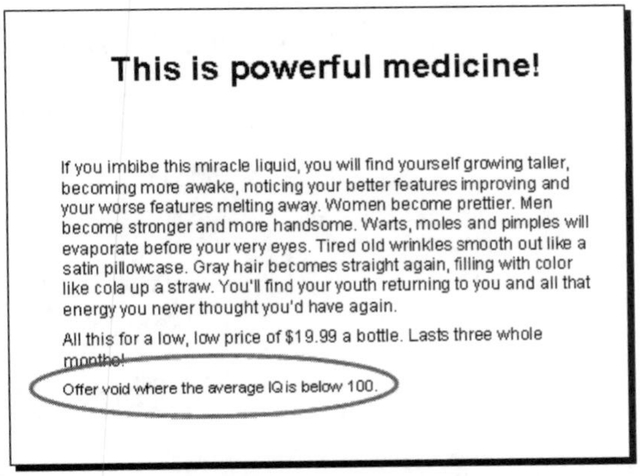

This is powerful medicine!

If you imbibe this miracle liquid, you will find yourself growing taller, becoming more awake, noticing your better features improving and your worse features melting away. Women become prettier. Men become stronger and more handsome. Warts, moles and pimples will evaporate before your very eyes. Tired old wrinkles smooth out like a satin pillowcase. Gray hair becomes straight again, filling with color like cola up a straw. You'll find your youth returning to you and all that energy you never thought you'd have again.

All this for a low, low price of $19.99 a bottle. Lasts three whole months!

Offer void where the average IQ is below 100.

Figure 21.30 Animation that emphasizes some text

1. Create the slide with the text on it.
2. Add the red oval.

   Use the Drawing toolbar for this: Select the Oval tool to draw the oval. Then choose "No Fill" as the fill color. Set the line width to something very thick and the line color to red.
3. Right-click the oval and choose "Custom Animation" from the pop-up menu.

4a. In PowerPoint 2003/XP, click the Add Effect button/menu in the Custom Animation task pane, and choose Entrance ➢ Wipe from the list of effects.

If the Wipe effect isn't in the list, choose Entrance ➢ More Effects and locate the Wipe effect in the dialog box that appears; click OK.

4b. In PowerPoint 2000, click the Effects tab in the Custom Animation dialog box and choose Wipe from the drop-down list; click OK.

5. To test the animation, click Preview.

After the text appears, click the mouse button or press the spacebar and the important text is circled in red—a very powerful way to draw attention to what may otherwise be a boring slide.

Can I Add Sounds to the Effects?

Of course, but as you would expect, this is done differently for each version of PowerPoint. The good news is that PowerPoint comes with an array of sounds, and you can always add more from the Internet.

In PowerPoint 2003/XP, you add sounds after creating the effect and it appears in the list in the Custom Animation task pane. Click the effect's menu button (Figure 21.24) and choose "Effect Options" from the menu. This displays effect's dialog box, shown in Figure 21.31.

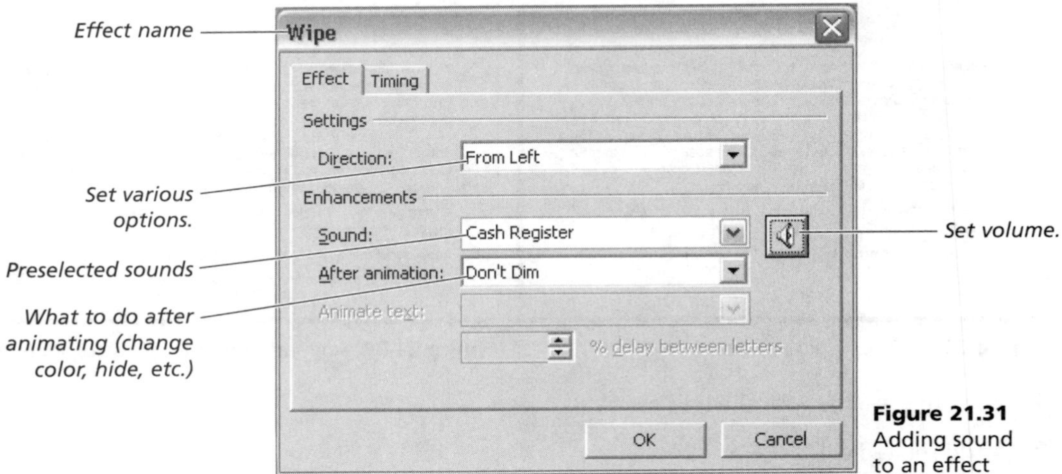

Figure 21.31
Adding sound to an effect

Choose a sound from the Sound drop-down list. There is a whole slate of them, or you can choose the "Other Sound" item to browse for a sound file on disk to play.

In PowerPoint 2000, sounds are added in the Custom Animation dialog box, just below where the effect is selected (see Figure 21.26). To select a sound other than what you see on the list, choose "Other Sound" and use the dialog box to browse for a sound file to play.

How Can the "Stop Previous Sound" Option Be Used?

Just as sound can be used effectively, blessed silence can also drive home a point.

Say that a slide opens with a sound playing. To do that, simply assign the Appear effect to any element in the slide and give it a sound to play. When the slide is displayed, the sound plays. (Have the animation play "With Previous" or "Automatically" so that it begins at once, not waiting for a mouse click.)

To stop the sound, reselect the same object in PowerPoint 2003/XP, or select a new object in PowerPoint 2000, and assign to it the Appear effect but with the "[Stop Previous Sound]" option selected.

As an example, suppose you're giving a slide show on brake repair. To stop the ugly squealing brake noise, the presenter merely clicks the Brake Shop logo.

How Can I Add a Soundtrack to My Entire Show?

Applying a soundtrack to a slide show implies that the slide show is running automatically. If not, then the sound will stop as you change slides. So you have to set up what is, basically, the traditional vacation slide show, or a series of images and perhaps some text, but all of which un-spools as the audience watches, mesmerized by the images and soundtrack.

Oh, and the soundtrack must be in the form of a WAV file. MIDI won't do. MP3 is way out. And any other sound file format is basically verboten. So you must get whatever it is you plan on playing into the standard Windows WAV file format for this to work.

After you have your sound file and your collection of slide images, follow these steps to create the show, automatically playing with a soundtrack:

1. Click to select the Slide Sorter view.
2. Click the very first slide in your presentation.
3. Choose Slide Show ➢ Slide Transition.

   In PowerPoint 2003/XP, the Slide Transition task pane appears; a Slide Transition dialog box shows up in PowerPoint 2000. Both have the same features, illustrated in Figure 21.32.
4. Select a transition.

   "No Transition" simply displays each slide one after the other, or you can choose to fade in each slide—or if you can't make up your mind, do a "Random Transition."
5. From the Sound drop-down list, choose "No Sound."

   Work with me here.

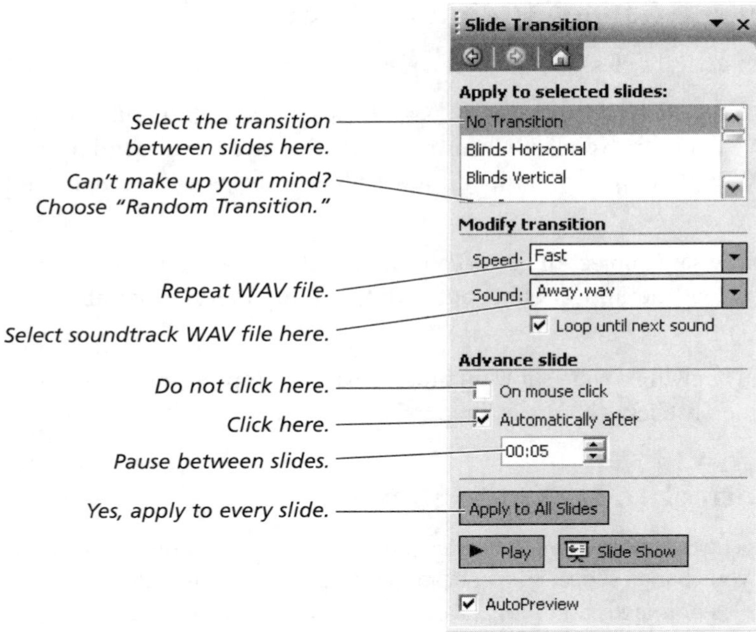

Figure 21.32
Setting options for an automatically playing soundtrack slide show

6. Remove the checkmark by "On Mouse Click"; you want the slides to progress automatically.
7. Put a checkmark by "Automatically After," and enter the time interval into the box.

   I like 5 seconds myself, though you should avoid anything too long that makes people think the slide show is over (or broken).
8. Click the Apply to All Slides (or Apply to All) button.

   Now you can preview your slide show.
9. Press the F5 key to preview.

   There will be no sound, but preview it anyway to check the transitions.

   Now you're ready to add sound: Click the mouse to end the sample slide show preview.
10. Select the first slide.
11. Choose Slide Show ➤ Slide Transition.
12. From the Sound drop-down list, choose "Other Sound."
13. Use the Add Sound dialog box to locate the background WAV file you want to play; click OK.
14. Put a checkmark by "Loop Until Next Sound."

15. Click the Apply button.

    This is important! Apply the soundtrack only to the first slide. It will continue to play over all the other slides. Otherwise, if you choose "Apply to All," then the soundtrack restarts with each new slide, which is probably not what you want.

16. Press the F5 key to preview your slide show.

    And it should be just what you want.

There are better ways than PowerPoint for displaying your vacation slides as a slide show. Searching the Internet yields many fine slide show programs for displaying your digital pictures, much easier than what PowerPoint offers.

What About the Insert ➢ Movies and Sounds Submenu?

That option works okay, and you can insert a variety of sound formats or even computer videos—but only for one slide at a time. Most people want soundtracks, which that submenu doesn't provide; see the previous section.

What's This Damn Red X For?

The infamous red X means that you've inserted an image that has overloaded PowerPoint's circuitry. Basically, the computer is using too much overhead to display that image, which means the image was saved in the wrong format. Too many such images will literally "explode" PowerPoint and make it behave in unpredictable ways.

If you start seeing Red Xs, save immediately! Then remove some of the higher resolution images and attempt to replace them with lower resolution copies.

How Can I Format My Images so I Don't Explode the Slide Show?

PowerPoint isn't really a graphics program. Because of that, inserting high-quality TIFF images is not a must. In fact, the simple JPEG and GIF images that populate a web page are good enough for a PowerPoint presentation.

If you're scanning images, keep the resolution to about 150 dpi. That's high enough to avoid an overly pixilated image but not high enough to overburden the computer's memory. Sizewise, keep your images at between 300 and 400 pixels wide or tall. That's a good "average" size for any image, such as what you would send through e-mail to grandma or the kids.

22 Giving a Show without Breaking a Leg

It's bad luck to wish a performer "good luck." That's one of many strange and interesting theatrical traditions. So instead of saying "good luck," you should wish an actor to "break a leg." Saying "good luck" would tempt the gods, so the phrase "break a leg" is used. It's based on the happy German (or could be Yiddish) expression *Hals und Beinbruch*, which means to break your leg *and* your neck. (I won't get into what the French say for "good luck" in the theater.)

Whether you admit it or not, giving a slide show presentation in PowerPoint plants you squarely into show business. You may not boast the same salary as the latest screen idol, but you're doing pretty much the same thing: presenting a show for others to watch. In fact, with animations, sounds, and a sparkling personality, your slide show may rival many of Hollywood's feeble efforts.

To assist you with giving the best show possible, I've crafted this chapter with a slew of helpful show presentation tips, tricks, and techniques. These are pulled from many sources and various kind folk who really know how to give a great talk and are eager to share that information with you. So go ahead: Break a leg.

Bones Fractured and Audiences Mesmerized:

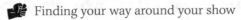

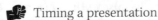

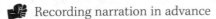

- Finding your way around your show
- Timing a presentation
- Recording narration in advance
- Keeping your audience awake
- Controlling how the audience views a slide
- Using various tricks to help get your point across

The Show Must Go On

More than death, more than spiders, even more than snakes, most people's biggest fear is speaking in public. I just don't understand this, but I can accept it. As a born ham and amateur actor, I enjoy any chance I can get to be in front of an audience. But I accept that for many people, such an experience can be sheer, solid, cold terror.

One source I read explained that people are afraid to speak in public because they might utter the truth. Or it could be years of obedience training as a child with your parents and grandparents hounding you to "be quiet"—especially when there was company.

> *"Speak the truth, but keep a fast horse by the door."*
> *—Old Indian saying*

What's the Fastest Way to End a Show?

Yell "Fire!" at the top of your lungs.

But the fastest *legal* way to end a show is to press the Esc key. Or you can right-click any slide and choose "End Show" from the pop-up menu.

Oops! I'm Lost! How Do I Get Back to My Slide!

If you know the slide number, then type that number and press the Enter key. For example, to return to slide 5—which you know starts the introduction to the current section, type 5 and press Enter on the keyboard. (Granted, this method relies a lot upon knowing your slide numbers.)

As an alternative, you can press the Ctrl+S key combination to see the All Slides dialog box, as shown in Figure 22.1. Choose a slide from the list and click the Go To button to return to that slide.

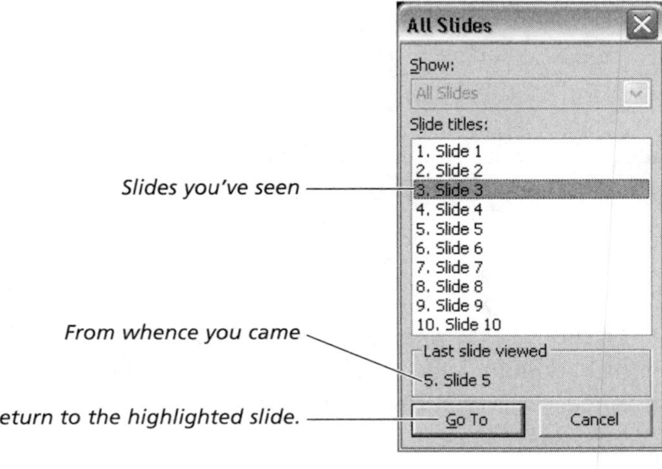

Figure 22.1
Desperately seeking a slide!

Any Way to Display the Slide Numbers in a Show?

This can easily be done by adding a footer to each of your slides. Here's how:

1. Switch to the Slide Sorter view.

   Choose View ➤ Slide Sorter or click the Slide Sorter View button in the lower-left corner of PowerPoint's window.

2. Click to select the first slide in your show.

3. Choose View ➤ Header and Footer.

   The Header and Footer dialog box appears, as wonderfully illustrated in Figure 22.2.

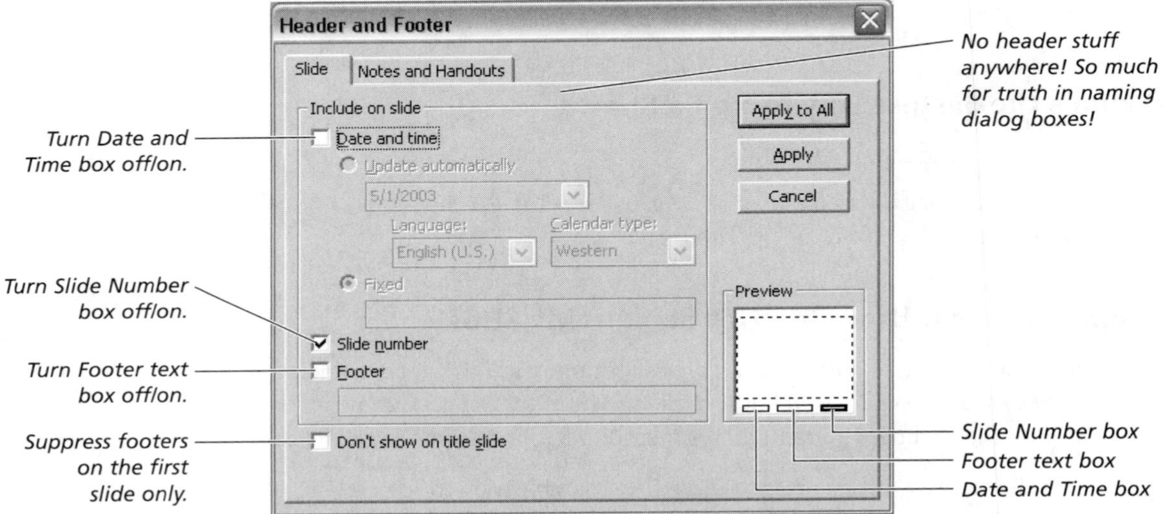

Figure 22.2 That wonderful illustration of the Header and Footer dialog box

4. Click to put a check mark by "Slide Number."

   Refer to Figure 22.2

   Optionally you can remove the check marks by "Date and Time" and "Footer," as shown in the figure.

5. Click the Apply to All button.

   All the slides grow numbers.

Alas, you cannot change the style or position of the number. In fact, it might end up being hidden behind elements of a slide or even the background. If so, you'll need to move things around on the slide or even choose another background so that you can see the number.

How Can I Name the Slides So That the All Slides Dialog Box Makes More Sense?

In Figure 22.1 the slides are all shown with dull, insipid names that would make plucking out a specific slide in the show pure guesswork. That's because those slides lack title text; when the slide design was chosen, the title text box was either deleted or simply not filled in.

To give the slide a title, you must select a new design for the slide, one that has a title, as shown in Figure 22.3. This can be applied to any slide, even one that already has text on it. Simply fill in the title box with the slide title you want, and that title appears in the All Slides dialog box. Here's how to do that:

Figure 22.3 How to spot a title in a slide's layout

1. Switch to Normal view.

   Choose View ➤ Normal from the menu or click the Normal button in the lower-left corner of PowerPoint's window.

2. Bring up the slide you want to title.

   You don't need to title all the slides. In fact, what I would do is title only key slides in the presentation. After all, if your only reason is so that something more interesting shows up in the All Slides dialog box (Figure 22.1), then just title key slides that you would most likely be hopping to.

3. Choose Format ➤ Slide Layout.

4. Choose the "Title Only" layout for the slide.

   This is shown in Figure 22.4.

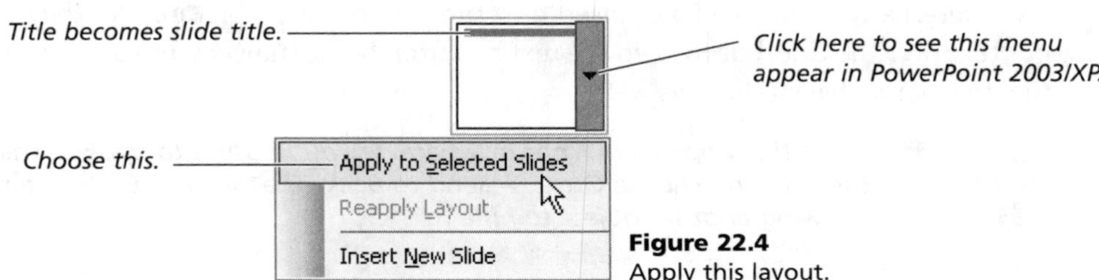

Figure 22.4 Apply this layout.

5a. In PowerPoint 2003/XP, click to display the menu and choose "Apply to Selected Slides."

You can optionally close the task pane at this point.

5b. In PowerPoint 2000, click the Apply button in the Slide Layout dialog box.

6. Select the subtitle box and delete it (if you want).

7. Type the slide's title into the title box.

   That title then becomes the slide's title and appears in the "All Slides" list for when you get lost.

Now there may be times when you don't really want the title to appear on the slide. For example, I put titles on slides that contain graphics and then cover the title up with the graphics. Or maybe the title is "just for me" and I don't want the audience to see it. If so, here are the techniques for hiding the title text:

1. Select all the text in the title box.
2. Use the Font Color button on the Formatting toolbar to set the text color the same as the background color.

   For example, if you have a black background, color the text black. This effectively washes out the title, rendering it invisible—though the text is still there as far as PowerPoint is concerned.

Obviously you can't color the text if the background uses a gradient, texture, pattern, or picture. But in that case it's possible to add a block of color and simply cover the title. Or you can cover the title with something already on your slide, such as a picture or other text.

To create a simple block to cover the title text, follow these steps:

1. Choose View ➤ Toolbars ➤ Drawing to summon the Drawing toolbar if it's not already visible.
2. Click to select the Rectangle tool.
3. Draw the rectangle over your title text.
4. Color the rectangle with the Fill tool.

   Try to color the rectangle as close to the background as possible, or just be creative and use whatever color you like.

As an alternative, you could also insert a picture and place the picture over the title. Or you can put text over the title, but to keep the text box from being transparent you'll have to use the Fill tool to color its background as well.

If the title appears in front of whatever you're using to mask it, then right-click the title and choose Order ➤ Send to Back. That shoves it into the background, allowing another object to hide it.

Is the Pointer a Necessity or Just Plain Annoying?

The necessity of the pointer depends on the skills of the person giving the show. Nothing can be more annoying that a nervous presenter and a shaky pointer. Such a thing will draw attention directly to the pointer and away from everything else in a highly negative manner—not what you want.

To see the pointer, just wiggle the mouse while you're giving the presentation. The mouse pointer shows up as well as control box in the lower-left corner of the presentation, shown in Figure 22.5 and Figure 22.6.

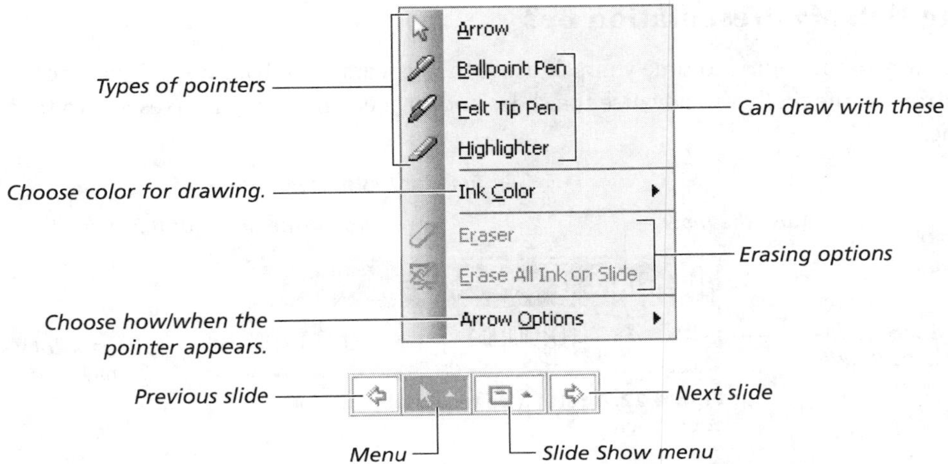

Figure 22.5 Pointer options for PowerPoint 2003/XP

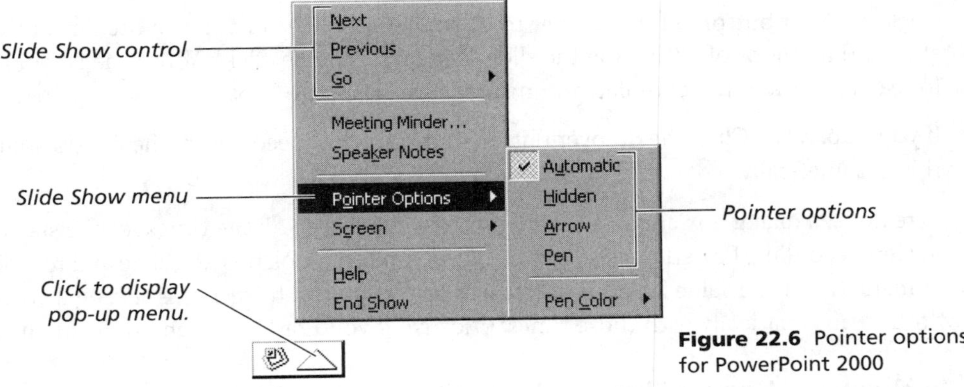

Figure 22.6 Pointer options for PowerPoint 2000

You can also get to these and other slide show options by right-clicking a slide during a presentation.

What? I Can Annotate a Slide?

Yes, you can do so by using the Pen options (shown in Figure 22.5). However, drawing or writing text with a mouse pointer is not something most people do well. Instead, I recommend using text boxes or AutoShapes to help annotate your text and bring them into the slide via animation, which was covered in Chapter 21, "Beyond Your Basic Slide Show."

How Long Will My Presentation Be?

The best way to find out is to time yourself using the Rehearsal toolbar, shown in Figure 22.7. Use the controls on the toolbar to advance the slides and to check how long it takes you to talk about each one.

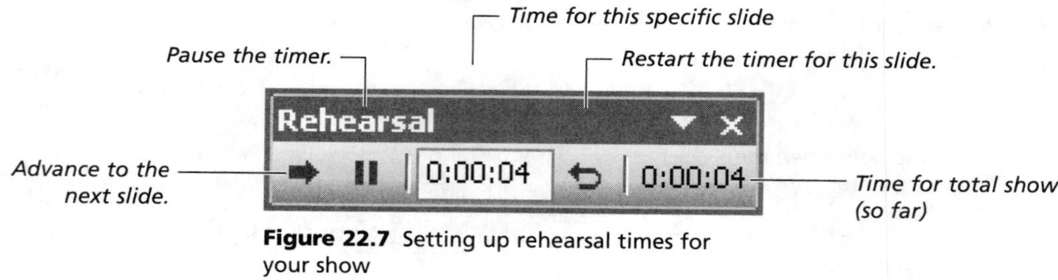

Figure 22.7 Setting up rehearsal times for your show

To summon the Rehearsal toolbar, choose Slide Show ➤ Rehearse Timings. Then carefully recite your speech as you review each slide. Speak slowly; you don't want to rush.

Click the Next button on the toolbar to go to the next slide, or you can use any of the standard methods of advancing the slide (key press, mouse click). Your time is recorded for each slide, and the cumulative time for the show is also kept.

If you flub, relax. Click the do-over button and start the speech over. The timers adjust for this automatically.

When you're done, a dialog box appears asking if you want to keep all the times for the slides. You see, as you were recording, PowerPoint kept track of the time you took on each slide and recorded it as the automatic transition value for each slide. Click the Yes button to keep this setting if you want the show to run automatically with those times. Click No if you'd rather run the show manually.

I Have 15 Minutes to Give the Show but My Timings Are for 12 Minutes.
This is fine; it's better to go under the time limit. If you have time left over, you can always ask for questions.

I Have 15 Minutes to Give the Show but My Timings Are for 18 Minutes.
Something needs to be cut. If you're allotted only a given amount of time, do not go over. People get restless and annoyed when you overshoot a preset time limit.

I'm Too Nervous to Give the Presentation in Person. How Can I Record My Voice Ahead of Time?

This is really easy to do, plus it can be more relaxing because you don't have 500 people in their underwear sitting and staring at you and waiting for you to make a mistake.

To record your own audio track with a slide show, follow these steps:

1. Create the slide show first.

   Build all the slides. Apply animation. Work on the transitions.

   Be sure all the slides advance on the mouse click, not on preset times. To change this:

   a. Choose View ➤ Slide Sorter.
   b. Click to select the first slide in the show.
   c. Choose Slide Show ➤ Slide Transition.
   d. Remove the check mark by "Automatically After."
   e. Apply a check mark by "On Mouse Click."
   f. Click the Apply to All Slides or Apply to All button.

2. Click to select the first slide.
3. Choose Slide Show ➤ Record Narration.
4. Click the Set Microphone Level button.

   Speak into the microphone connected to your computer. Ensure that the levels are as high as indicated in Figure 22.8.

Figure 22.8 Setting the microphone levels

5. Click OK to set the microphone levels.

   Get ready to record. Once you start, you need to run the entire show; there is no pause option. If you goof, you'll have to restart. Prepare!

6. Click OK to begin recording the show.

If you're not on the first slide, a dialog box prompts you to switch to the first slide or start recording at the current slide.

7. Talk your talk for each slide.

8. Pause.

   You need to allow some time here before you advance to the next slide. If you advance too quickly, the last part of your speech will be cut off.

9. Click the mouse to advance to the next slide.

10. Repeat Steps 7 through 9.

11. When you're done, if you're happy, click the Save button.

    Otherwise, click the Don't Save button and start all over.

In PowerPoint 2000 you may be asked if you want to save the slide timings as well; click the Yes button.

Now review the slide show; press the F5 key to watch the replay. You'll notice that the slides now automatically advance along with your narration—which means you don't even need to be there to click the mouse when you show the thing!

Double-check that it all works and makes sense.

You Must Know This: Setting Up a Microphone on Your PC

Nearly all PCs have a connection for a microphone. Laptops may as well, though I often see laptops with built-in tiny microphone "holes" instead of official microphone plugs or jacks.

Any old microphone will do for a computer. If you want, you can spend money, but you should do so only if creating audio productions is your thing. (And if so, then you'll want to click the Change Quality button in the Record Narration dialog box to choose something better than 10Kb/second for your soundtrack.) I personally use a cheap-ass microphone I stole from Radio Shack because the lad was too busy flirting with a girl who wanted to buy a cell phone.

Plug the microphone into the MIC IN jack on the back of your PC.

If you have a newer computer, the MIC IN jack is color-coded pink.

If you have a DVD player in your PC, plug the microphone into the MIC IN jack on the DVD expansion card.

I Want to Change the Narration for Just One Slide.

To change the narration of just one slide, heed these steps:

1. Click to select the slide.

2. Choose Slide Show ➤ Record Narration.

3. Click OK.
4. Click the Current Slide button.

   The current slide is displayed.
5. Speak!
6. Press the Esc key when you're done recording for that one slide.
7. Click the Save button.

   The new sound is saved only for the current slide. Any other narration for the other slides is unchanged by this.

I Want to Remove the Narration from Just One Slide.

This is easy: The narration recorded for each slide appears as a speaker icon somewhere on the slide. To remove the narration for the slide, find the icon on the slide, click to select it, and then press the Delete key on your keyboard. The slide is silenced.

A Slew of Slide Show Suggestions

Here are some handy suggestions you may want to heed the next time you're out there in presentation land giving it your all. Some of these are presentation tips; some are tips on how to make the slide show that much better.

How Can I Drive the Point Home?

The key is to tell them three times, which I mentioned back in Chapter 21, in the section "Do I Really Need a Summary?" It works like this:

- Tell them what you're going to tell them.
- Tell them.
- Tell them what you've told them.

You can be subtle with this, or you can be overt. Humor helps. Animation is a blessing.

Obviously, if you have some sort of introduction to your talk, either verbally or on a slide, then that fulfills the first step. You're saying, "Here is what I'm going to cover: How most folks spend their vacation dollar."

The next step is easy: Cover it. Give examples. Provide illustrations. Use something real and substantial. Don't say, "This is how a median-income white-collar worker would spend their vacation dollar." Do say, "Oscar is 34 and manages a pharmacy, and here is where he would like to go on holiday this year."

Finally, summarize. This can be an official summary, which merely restates the introduction or overview, or it can be a mere confirmation of the facts: "So when you have money, you can take a nicer vacation."

Also refer to the final section of this chapter on how to effectively use propaganda techniques in your slide show.

How Does One Keep the Audience from Falling Asleep During a Presentation?

The key is to infuse personality into your presentation. Don't just sell them the facts on the slides, *sell yourself!* Despite the fact that charisma isn't sold from vending machines, personal anecdotes and humor go a long way in livening up a dull presentation.

Yes, animation helps. Rather than using the pen to highlight something, make an AutoShape appear or import a graphic image. Make a sound play when the image appears. This is a powerful tool, and it keeps people's attention because they don't know when to expect something new to pop up.

Another key to keeping an audience's rapt attention is *interactivity*—that is, a moderate yet highly controlled level of audience participation. It keeps them awake and makes them feel involved, all while maintaining your control of the presentation.

The simplest way to keep the presentation interactive is with handouts, specifically fill-in-the-blanks handouts. Yep, it's busywork, but people love it.

How Can I Easily Create a Handout for My Show?

"Easily" is the operative word here. Good handouts aren't easy to make.

Providing that you used the predefined layouts, you can save your outline to disk: Choose File ➤ Save As, but from the "Save As Type" drop-down list choose "Outline/RTF" as the format. This saves the outline text to an RTF document on disk.

RTF is a common word processor file format. It stands for Rich Text Format.

You can use Word to open up the RTF file and then craft it into an outline. Even then, you'll have to do some work—especially if you want the valued fill-in-the-blanks part of the outline.

Also note that the RTF format does not save slide numbers. You can, however, put Word in one window and PowerPoint in another, and then switch back and forth to properly create a handout that refers to each slide in the show.

If you merely want to create a handout illustrating the slides in your show, then choose File ➤ Print. In the Print dialog box, use the Handouts area to set up how many slides are printed on a sheet of paper and in what order. Figure 22.9 shows what's up with that part of the Print dialog box.

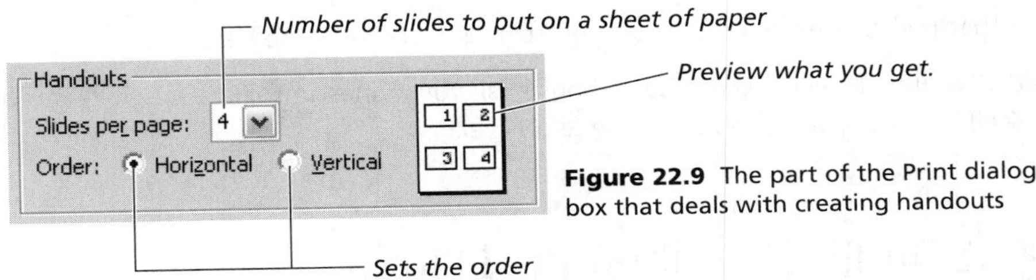

Figure 22.9 The part of the Print dialog box that deals with creating handouts

My Boss Is Too Cheap to Let Me Print Out Handouts.

This happens. And it may not be due to a parsimonious boss either; giving a handout to several hundred people requires hundreds of sheets of paper. While I personally think the price is worth it (because people are more apt to keep handouts that have their own notes on them), there are alternatives for keeping your audience interested.

Stingy boss? Then really spend money printing up the slides on thick stock in four colors nicely bound. Charge $4 each for them.

The first alternative is to give up a wee bit of control and pose an open question to the audience. The first time you do this, someone will invariably shout out the answer, and it will most likely be someone from the middle or back of the audience (where such misfits typically sit).

Better than turning over the floor to the mob, make pointed connections to people in the first several rows. For example, find someone up front and ask them their name. Try to find someone who looks like a good sleeping candidate—someone tired or even someone already dozing. Ask their first name and maybe what city they're from. You don't want to get into their company name because their competition is most likely sitting in the audience and you're not there to embarrass a company. An individual, certainly, but not their company.

Ask the victim the question. If they have the right answer, praise them. If they have the wrong answer, explain that it's good and why it's good, but then describe why the real answer is better.

As you work your slide show, find two or three more victims to interact with. Then go back and refer to them as you need more interactivity. You may even try pitting them against one another in harmless and fun ways. For example:

- "Bill, I'm sorry, but that's not right. You know June was giving me great answers a while back. June? I hear that Bill's company is hiring!"
- "I'm sorry, Dave, but you're going to have to stay here during lunch."
- "Bob that makes four in a row. Have you seen this presentation before?"
- "Kathy? Still no answer? Okay, how about I ask you a question? How much longer until the break? There's one you should be able to answer."

Sneaky Human Psychology Tricks

"I love humanity, it's people I can't stand."
—Charlie Brown

It's harder to manipulate a person than it is to manipulate a group. Even so, there are common tricks you can play on people to get them to do things. The following sections illustrate some common tricks for manipulating people. They aren't secrets but rather psychological tricks you can use to help craft better slide shows that can really control your audience.

Which Colors Go Well Together?

Some would argue that all colors go together "well"; beauty is in the eye of the beholder. Modern artists love to push this point, but your audience wants to be informed and not subjected to modern art. (Well, maybe.) Still, there is a reason for everything.

This book has black text on white paper. There is a reason for that: It reads well. White text on black paper may seem like it would read just as well, but it doesn't. The eye doesn't pick up the text as well, so reading slows. If that's what you want, great! But most of the time you want your reader to enjoy reading, not struggle with it.

Follow these steps:

1. Create a new slide.
2. Create a text box if one doesn't already exist.
3. Into the text box, type `Wonderful view in here!`
4. Select all the text.

5.  Use the Fill tool on the Drawing toolbar to color the background purple.

   You'll need to open the Fill tool's menu and then choose "More Fill Colors" from the menu. Choose a nice purple from the Colors dialog box that appears.

6. Use the Font color tool to set the text color to bright Red.

   Again, you may have to choose the "More Colors" item from the Font color tool's menu to get a nice red.

   Ugly! Red on purple is just awful to see. Those colors *do not* go together well.

7. Change the background to a cheery bright yellow and the text color to black.

   In this case, black on yellow picks up very well. This is why warnings are often written using these colors.

8. Change the text color to green and the background color to blue.

   Awful! The green text is very difficult to read on the blue background. But:

9. Change the text color to yellow.

   That's better, but still not as good as black on yellow.

10. Change the background to green and the text color to red.

    Physiologically this is the worst combination for humans to behold. The text is truly irritating. Even the opposite, which is green text on a red background, is still irritating to watch.

11. Change the text color to bright red and the background to a deep blue.

    This combination isn't as annoying as green-red, but you'll notice that mixing red and blue often creates an illusion of depth. Red text appears to float before a blue background. If you can get the colors right, the red may even shimmer a tad. This can be very dramatic.

    Finally, the obviously dumb combinations:

12. Change the text color to blue and the background color to the same shade of blue.

    No text! Or worse, you can use subtly different shades of the same colors and people will have a heck of a time reading the text.

Continue to experiment with colors on your own. Remember that the idea is to present text that's easy to read. Big, brief chunks of text. And presented in colors that work well on the eye—if that's what you want.

You Mean I Can Control Where They Move Their Eyeballs?

Quick! Look at Figure 22.10.

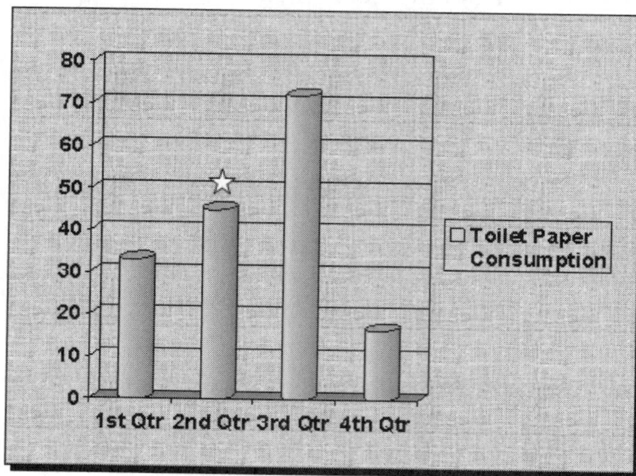

Figure 22.10
A chart on a slide

Why did you look at the 2nd Quarter results first or notice them more than the other results? Of course! It's the silly star (AutoShape) above that column. You see, simply by inserting that star, I was able to draw more attention to the part of the slide I wanted you to look at. It seems dumb, but it certainly worked. In fact, if your eyeball were to draw a laser line on the chart, you'd probably see it wandering all over the chart but constantly returning back to that star.

Now look at Figure 22.11.

Figure 22.11
Nine apes

Yep, it's that one white ape that draws your eye, right? The other apes are different colors (trust me), but it's the white object that draws the attention of the human eye more than anything else.

In Figure 22.12 you see a similar effect, but in this case it's the "lighting" of the slide that draws focus to the giraffe instead of the dog or tiger. Obviously, of the three, the giraffe must be most important—at least that's the way the human brain will perceive things.

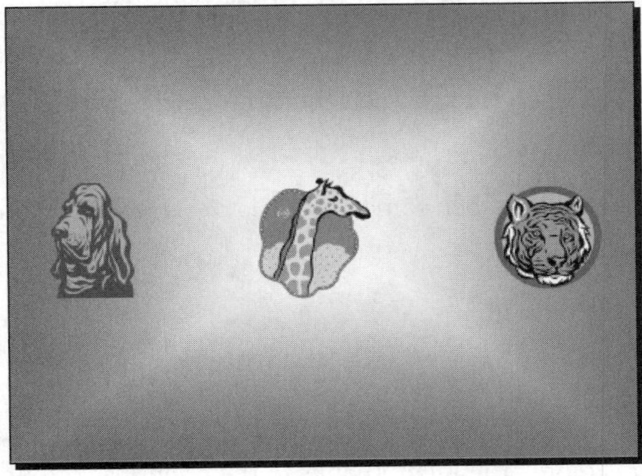

Figure 22.12
Three animals

Finally, although you can't see the animation in this book, Figure 22.13 shows a slide with important points off to the right and an animated bee on the left. Because the bee is moving, everyone watching the slide will be looking at the bee—not at the "important" text. That's yet another trait of how humans view things.

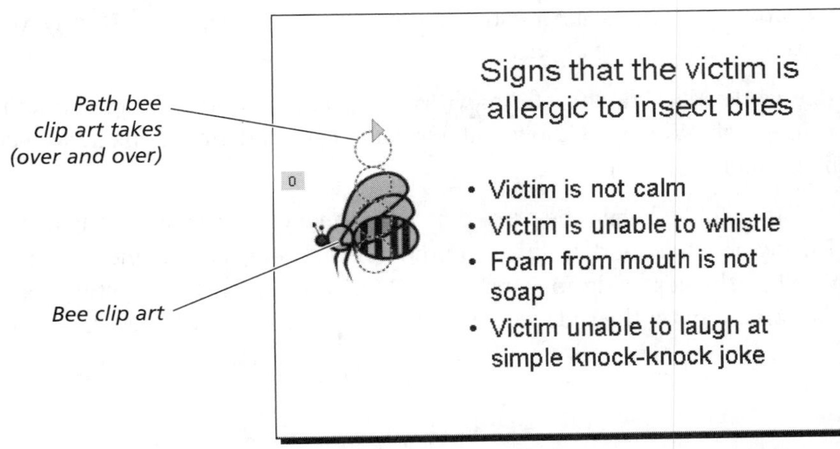

Path bee clip art takes (over and over)
Bee clip art
0
Signs that the victim is allergic to insect bites
• Victim is not calm
• Victim is unable to whistle
• Foam from mouth is not soap
• Victim unable to laugh at simple knock-knock joke

Figure 22.13
Animated distraction

If you still need help visualizing how all of this works, then imagine that your slide is a theatrical production. The most important actor on the stage is the one who is talking. That's the part of the slide you want your audience to see, just as the actor in a play should be the center of attention while he is talking. Here's why people will not look at your main actor:

 There is something more interesting on stage.

A half glass of wine is teetering on the table, left there by an actor from an earlier scene.

There is a tiny star on your chart.

 The actor is wearing dark clothing when someone else is wearing white clothing.

People look at the white objects first.

The white ape draws more attention.

 The actor is in the dark.

He's not properly lit, or other things around him are brighter.

The animal in the center is more prominent, thanks to the bright background.

Another actor on stage is moving about or there is snow falling outside a window.

People prefer to watch moving objects rather than static ones.

The bee draws attention, preventing the rest of the slide from being read.

All of these traits can work for you or against you. Use them wisely and you can instantly focus your audience's attention on any part of a slide.

A final trick—one that works in a slide show (or movies and TV) but not on the stage—is knowing where you've left their eyeball. When you know that, you can position them to look at a specific spot on the next slide, guaranteed every time.

Consider the slide in Figure 22.14. When the presenter clicks the mouse to move to the next slide, the text dissolves, leaving only the hot dog clip art on the screen. Perhaps the sound of a dog barking is added for fun. When the next slide appears, Figure 22.15, the audience's collective eyeballs are still staring at the same spot on the slide where the hotdog was. See how Figure 22.15 takes advantage of that?

- Auto Dealerships
- Convenience Stores
- Furniture Stores
- Lumber Yards
- Pawn Shops
- Hot Dog Stands

Figure 22.14 The hot dog is the last thing to disappear.

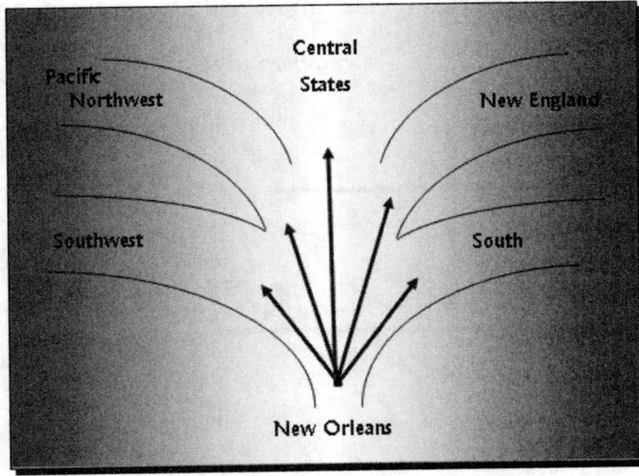

Figure 22.15 The eye is already focused at the base of the distribution tree.

Oh, Come On. You Mean Arrows Really Do Work?

Yes. The most powerful indicator you can use on a chart is a simple AutoShape arrow. Figure 22.16 illustrates a slide with a simple, yet powerful arrow. It draws attention to the specific part of the map in question. No one in the audience will be confused by this.

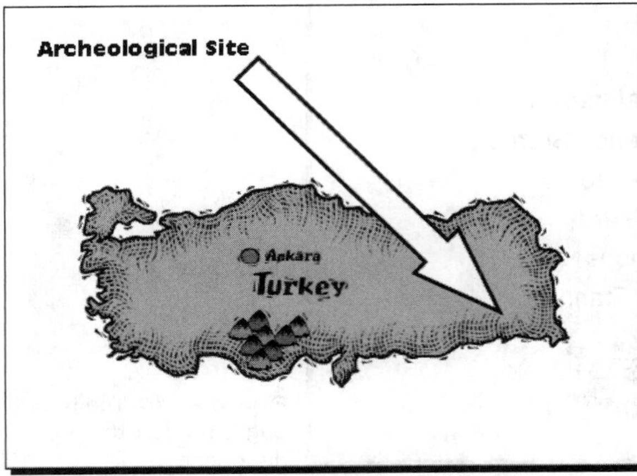
Archeological Site
Ankara
Turkey

Figure 22.16
Getting to the point

Figure 22.17 tells a little bit more about how to manipulate an AutoShape arrow in PowerPoint.

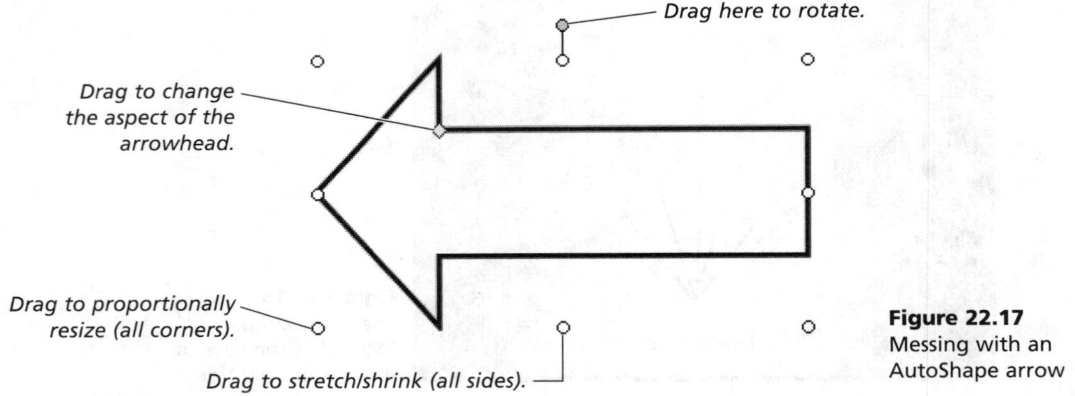
Drag here to rotate.
Drag to change the aspect of the arrowhead.
Drag to proportionally resize (all corners).
Drag to stretch/shrink (all sides).

Figure 22.17
Messing with an AutoShape arrow

What the Heck Is a Logarithmic Scale?

Producing a chart in a logarithmic scale can either exaggerate or dampen the effects of a chart. For example, consider Figure 22.18. Pretty dismal results, huh? The numbers keep going down and down, which makes you wonder if whatever comes next will be zero or negative. Contrast that with Figure 22.19.

In Figure 22.19, the results don't seem that bad—despite the fact that both charts display the same values! Note the vertical axis in Figure 22.18. It shows regular intervals of 10, but in Figure 22.19 logarithmic intervals of powers of 10 are used, which skews the way the data appears. Unwitting audiences may not be able to spot the differences; all they see is a more gradual decline with a logarithmic scale shown in Figure 22.19, as opposed to the dramatic drop of a normal chart, Figure 22.18.

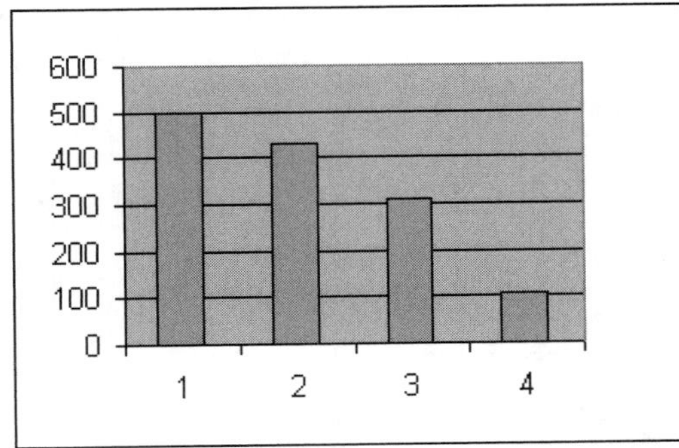

Figure 22.18
A normal chart

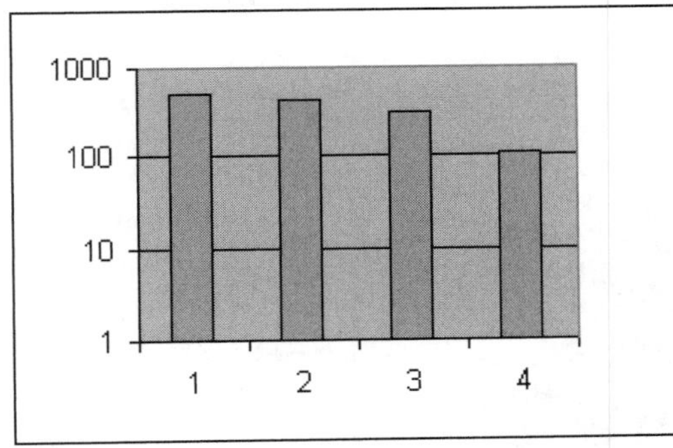

Figure 22.19
A logarithmic chart

To create a logarithmic chart you'll have to use Excel. After creating the chart, double-click the vertical axis. In the Format Axis dialog box, click the Scale tab and put a check mark by "Logarithmic Scale." Click OK to change the chart to a Logarithmic one, and then copy and paste the chart into PowerPoint.

How Can I Make a Majority Exist Where None Existed Before?

This is a statistical trick. Like all statistical tricks, it really depends on the question you're asking as opposed to what people really think. The result can easily be manipulated by using the Chart function in PowerPoint (or even Excel).

To properly gauge public opinion on a topic, you must ask several questions on the same subject, rephrasing the question every time. That's because people don't always understand the questions and, well, people lie. But if you hit them with the same theme enough times, you'll get a good grasp of what they're really thinking.

If the people are thinking one thing and you're thinking another, however, then it's a simple matter of finding the right question to use and then applying some sneaky graphics to get the result you want.

For example, suppose you want to prove that people have a favorable opinion of Evil Corp. So you ask the following question:

Q: What's your opinion of Evil Corp.?
A. Strongly oppose
B. Mildly oppose
C. In favor
D. Strongly in favor
E. Don't care

The results of this survey are mapped into the graph shown in Figure 22.20. Now as I would read the chart, I would see that the opposition ranks at 62 percent, which is visibly a very large chunk of the pie. But sadly that doesn't express the desires of Evil Corp., which commissioned you to do the slide show.

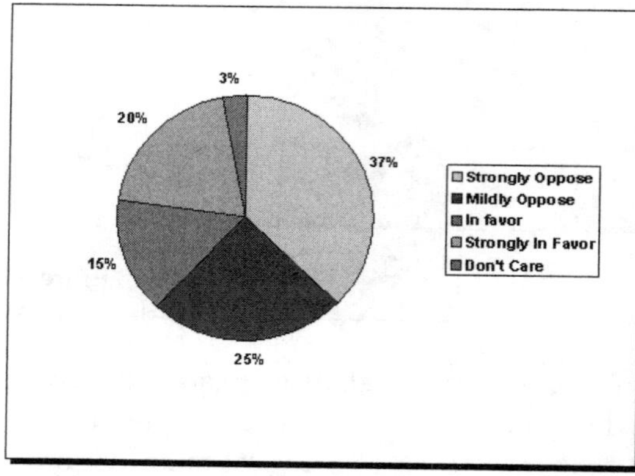

Figure 22.20
A typical, and informative, pie chart

Observe the pie chart in Figure 22.21. Same data, but check out the loaded phrasing. Looks a lot better, eh? Now is the chart a lie? No. It tells the truth, but it doesn't represent all the data collected. That's okay; your job is to present the graphic to display the data that helps sell your point. This is simply one way to do it.

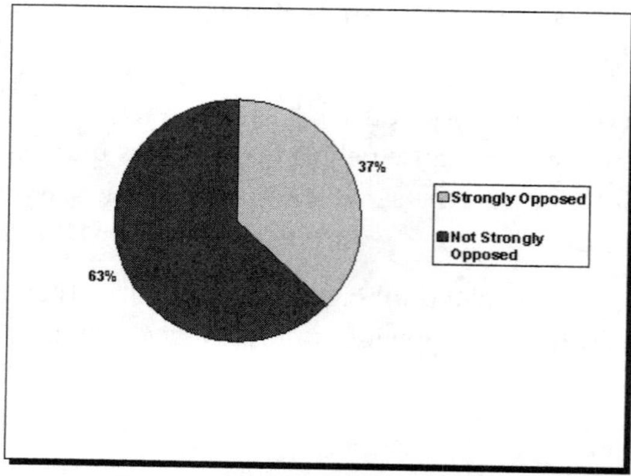

Figure 22.21
The same data, sneaky graphics

What Will Really Help Sell My Presentation?

In a word: *propaganda*. Of course, that's a loaded term (see below). I'll say *finely honed sales techniques used by some of the best*. Yeah. That's it!

Finely honed sales techniques (or the "P" word) constitute that basic science of persuading people to support your cause or to discredit your competition. Despite any negative connotations, these techniques are used by just about everyone, from folks on a personal level to big companies, advertising agencies, schools, religion, and government. Why? Because the techniques work. PowerPoint is the perfect vehicle for using such techniques to their fullest advantage.

Of course, you're not going to begin your slide show with a rousing fanfare announcement that the show is riddled with common propaganda techniques, many of which were honed in various Evil Empires real, imagined, or intergalactic. No, you're just going to give a show and yet keep in mind that the following propaganda techniques are proven to be effective:

 Testimonials

 Get on the bandwagon

 Plain folks

 Card stacking

 Loaded language

Some of these can be woven quite well into your PowerPoint presentation with effective results. The following sections explain more.

Propaganda is typically viewed as bad or evil, but it's used effectively by everyone from advertisers to teachers to the clergy to drive home good messages every day.

The Value of the Testimonial

Having a famous person, celebrity, or anyone influential lend their voice to your stuff is a clear bonus.

For example, if your product has an athlete or Hollywood star vouching for whatever it is you're trying to sell, then include some quotes from them or their photograph in your presentation.

Even better than a quote or image, consider something subtle in your slide show. For example, include a few images of the current teen idol wearing a specific brand of sneakers. There is no specific message there; everyone will recognize the teen idol, but subconsciously the shoes come into play. The teen idol's imitators around the globe will suddenly want those sneakers.

Another valuable testimonial trick is what I call the Man in the White Lab Coat. You don't even have to claim that he's a scientist, but just by having a slide of people who look "official" lends official backing to whatever you're presenting on the slide. It's subtle and powerful.

Get on the Bandwagon

The bandwagon is the unstoppable crowd, pulling at our tribe-based ancestry. Imagine a presentation that starts with a few sayings, each on its own slide: "Hey! Everyone is doing it! Don't be left out! Don't be the last one on your block!" It takes a lot of willpower to stand up against the sordid mob, and your audience will be eager to hear about what it is they need to join. (Now they may not join, but you have their attention simply by manipulating humanity's common desire to be part of a group.)

The key to making the bandwagon effect work is to use the words "everyone" or "everybody" and to do it over and over. For example, "Everyone agrees that watermelon is a fun snack!" Or the milk producers' old ad slogan, "Milk has something for every body." Adding a few reinforcing slides with such slogans cannot hurt.

To make this technique most effective, repeat the "everyone" phrase over and over. In the slide shown in Figure 22.21, you could narrate it as, "Most people are not strongly opposed to Evil Corp."

We're Just Plain Folks

They may not believe the Man in the White Lab Coat, and they may distrust the professional athlete who hawks everything from shoes to credit cards to fast food, but they'll believe sweet old Mildred Smith, sitting in her rocking chair with a hand-crocheted afghan over her shoulders. When she talks about how good the folks are over at the Cancer Center, well, we just have to believe her, right? Good old Mildred wouldn't lie? Right?

Wrong! Whether it's our love of the old-fashioned "simple" days or that these people look like you and me, plain folks can sell a product or idea. So if they won't believe a Hollywood star, they'll believe a slide of your Average Joe with back pain who's just finished mowing his lawn with the caption, "It works because it's good" (which is a glittering generality).

So if you need people in your slide show, consider the three types mentioned so far: officials in uniform (white lab coats); heroes, sports stars, or celebrities; and finally good-old plain folk. Choosing one over the other depends on whom you're giving your presentation to.

Card Stacking

I love this trick. Sadly, because I know it too well I tend to laugh at it rather than be duped by its effectiveness.

Say that you want to promote one product while persuading the audience to avoid another. Easy: Show your product in the best light—literally. Use big, friendly colors. Easy-to-read slides. Show images of people happy, smiling, friendly. That all makes sense. Now switch to the slide of your competition. It's dark. It's hard to read. The lettering is a similar color to the background. People in the slide look sad or bewildered. Now that has great comic potential—but when played on a subtle level it can be very effective.

Loaded Language

This is my favorite propaganda tool and one that the media loves more than anything. Certain words carry meaning with the public. The meanings can be positive or negative. And while they're descriptive, it's the nature of the words that shade the person or institution being described.

For example, you could say you were a "back to nature" type. But if they don't like you, they can use the loaded term *environmentalist* instead. Go to church? Then you're a member of the *religious right*. You could be a senator from Idaho, but the media labels you *arch conservative*. The lady at the DMV could be a civil servant, but on a bad day she's a *bureaucrat*. Your friend Phil may work in the state capitol as a public interest advocate, but to his enemies he's a *lobbyist*, or maybe even a *special-interest lobbyist*. And are those guys in the masks *freedom fighters*, *revolutionaries*, or *terrorists*?

These are all descriptive terms, but the words carry meaning beyond the simple description. In other words, the descriptions are not neutral and are used specifically to color a person or persons in a specific, typically negative light. Remember that when you construct your slide show. Choose your words carefully. But also choose words to describe your competition with equal consideration.

Two More Effective Items That Can Help Sell Your Slide Show

In addition to the seven finely honed propaganda techniques presented in the previous section, I'd like to add two more tricks:

 Cute kids and animals

 Sex

Nothing sells as well as tossing in a few babies or cute toddlers, kittens, puppies, or even a mixture of them. Remember Mikey? He sold Life cereal. If you lived on the West Coast in the 1970s, you may remember a commercial featuring four-year-old Rodney Allen Rippey, who told the narrator that his hamburger was "too big a eat."

Then there was the chilling political ad for Lyndon Johnson during the 1964 presidential election campaign. It showed a little girl picking the petals from a daisy only to be interrupted after a few moments by a nuclear explosion. It was very effective (but it didn't stop kids from picking daisies).

Sex also sells. Want to wake up a presentation to a bunch of salesmen? Toss in some cheesecake. Note that sex is not pornography. You don't want to shock your audience, but nothing says a girl in a bikini won't wake them up. Just keep it in context.

For example, every summer we ran a "bikini photo" on the cover of the magazine I edited. It was a computer magazine, so we showed the girls using laptop computers by a pool (which is a ridiculous thing to attempt), but yet that issue moved off the newsstands faster than any other issue—even though the bikini-clad girls were only on the cover.

Be aware that using sex to sell may backfire on you. Of course, if you make that mistake, then you probably don't know your audience well enough to persuade them anyway.

INDEX

Note to the Reader: Page numbers in **bold** indicate the principle discussion of a topic or the definition of a term. Page numbers in *italic* indicate illustrations.

NUMBERS

A

B

C

D

E

G

H

I

J

K

L

M

P

U

V

W

Z